my BusinessCourse

FREE WITH NEW COPIES OF THIS TEXTBOOK*

Scratch here for access code

Scratch here for access code

Start using *my* BusinessCourse Today: **www.mybusinesscourse.com**

my BusinessCourse is a web-based learning and assessment program intended to complement your textbook and faculty instruction.

Student Benefits

- **eLectures**: These videos review the key concepts of each Learning Objective in each chapter.
- **Guided examples**: These videos provide step-by-step solutions for select problems in each chapter.
- **Auto-graded assignments**: Provide students with immediate feedback on select assignments. **(with Instructor-Led course ONLY)**.
- **Quiz and Exam preparation**: myBusinessCourse provides students with additional practice and exam preparation materials to help students achieve better grades and content mastery.

You can access *my* BusinessCourse 24/7 from any web-enabled device, including iPads, smartphones, laptops, and tablets.

Interactive content that runs on any device.

Built for PCs, iPads, Laptops, Tablets, Smartphones

Third Edition

Skills for Accounting Research

FASB Codification *and* eIFRS
Text and Cases

Shelby Collins
University at Buffalo

With Tax Research Chapter By
Martha L. Salzman
University at Buffalo

Cambridge
BUSINESS PUBLISHERS

Cambridge Business Publishers, LLC

ISBN: 978-1-61853-177-3

Printed in the United States.
10 9 8 7 6 5 4

Foreword

For 16 years, I taught the graduate accounting policy and research class at the University of Georgia's J. M. Tull School of Accounting. And then, I worked closely with my successor to help him develop materials to teach the course. These experiences have taught me firsthand what a challenging, albeit rewarding, topic accounting research is for students, and what a challenging course it can be to develop. Prior to this position, my 26 years with Ernst & Young and 10 years as Chairman of the Financial Accounting Standards Board (FASB) have shown me that despite this challenge, research and communication skills are what set graduates apart in practice.

My class required students to prepare reports on real-world case studies and to participate actively in class discussions of research and current events. However, these research and communication skills did not always come naturally to students. I'll never forget the time when, after assigning students a case involving revenue recognition at CBS Sports, a student approached me and said that he could not find "NFL Football" anywhere in the accounting literature. I hinted to him that terms such as "revenue recognition" or "licensing fees" were more likely to result in relevant information for this particular case. Frequently, even identifying the right keywords to search can involve practice and finesse.

While the introduction of the FASB Codification has done a lot to facilitate guidance searches, accounting research remains a daunting challenge for many students. In part that's simply because of the sheer volume of guidance included within U.S. GAAP, and in part it is because accounting policy issues often don't have black or white answers.

It's therefore imperative that students are well trained in the resources that can help them make informed judgments. These include not only the authoritative literature, but also guidance for similar issues that may be relevant "by analogy" and nonauthoritative sources, such as examples from practice and interpretive guidance.

Shelby Collins is one of my former students, and a standout whom I had the privilege of nominating for a position at the FASB. When she approached me with the idea for this book, I was immediately supportive. After all, throughout my 16 years of teaching, I was unable to find a resource that met the challenge of teaching accounting students the skills necessary to perform great research, let alone prepare instructors for the challenge of teaching this course.

This book does just that. Shelby and I worked closely on the initial draft of this book, and this edition builds upon that strong foundation to incorporate even more feedback from the community of accounting research instructors. I am pleased to say that the result is a useful, and necessary resource that will enhance the quality of accounting research education—for students, instructors, and professional users alike.

With the help of this book, we can make this challenging, yet important, skill more attainable for students.

Dennis R. Beresford

Executive in Residence, University of Georgia

Former Chairman of the Financial Accounting Standards Board

About the Authors

Shelby Collins has taught the accounting and auditing research course at the University at Buffalo since 2011. Prior to this position, Shelby's career focused on technical accounting research, first at the Financial Accounting Standards Board (FASB)—as a postgraduate technical assistant—then in KPMG's Accounting Advisory Services group, then in the accounting policy and research group at Exelon Corporation in Chicago. In each of these roles, Shelby focused on the application of technical accounting guidance to complex and judgmental transactions.

When Shelby began her current teaching position, she searched for a textbook that offered a hands-on, active learning approach to accounting research, and which teaches students to research the way professionals do. Finding none, she chose to create her own course materials including handouts, lecture slides, and case studies. Many of these materials have been incorporated into this book and its supplements. It's her hope that this book, and the exercises herein, will prepare students to shine when they encounter accounting research opportunities as professionals.

Martha L. Salzman authored the tax research chapter of this book. Martha is a clinical assistant professor at the University at Buffalo School of Management, where she teaches the Masters-level professional tax research course and business law courses. Martha is a graduate of the University of Rochester (B.A., Political Science) and the University of Pennsylvania Law School (J.D.), and is licensed to practice law in the State of New York. Martha spent 18 years at the law firm of Phillips Lytle LLP, where her practice focused primarily on taxation, including advising clients regarding tax planning, compliance, audits and disputes. Martha enjoys using her real-world tax experience to better prepare students for their futures as tax and accounting professionals.

Preface

Increasingly, accounting research and communication skills are being regarded as fundamental to success in our profession. Professionals who excel in these areas will likely experience a *distinct competitive advantage* relative to their peers. At the same time, in today's highly regulated business climate, the consequences of inadequately researching and documenting accounting judgments can be severe (e.g., PCAOB or SEC enforcement actions). Recognizing the importance of research skills, research simulations are now a key component of the national CPA exam. What's been missing, until now, is a high-quality, hands-on textbook that can teach students these important skills.

In this book, students will learn to confidently address and communicate accounting research issues, from start to finish. Students will not only take away the ability to identify the accounting problem (the "researchable question"), but will gain experience locating and applying guidance within key research tools (including the FASB Codification and eIFRS), in a variety of accounting environments. In learning to use these research tools, students will have the opportunity to apply guidance to a variety of actual accounting topics.

Recognizing that students cannot learn to research simply by reading about research, the textbook offers students numerous opportunities to actively apply chapter lessons, throughout each chapter. Students will come away from this book armed with the research and critical thinking skills necessary for success as accounting professionals.

TARGET AUDIENCE

This book is intended to serve as the primary teaching materials for graduate and undergraduate courses in accounting research. The book may also be used to supplement materials used in an intermediate or advanced accounting course, given the many opportunities provided within the text to apply Codification guidance to related accounting topics (including, for example, leases, investment accounting, revenue recognition, and fair value measurements). Practitioners and staff training programs can also benefit from the research and communication strategies covered in this book, while gaining exposure to actual excerpts and topics covered in the Codification and other research databases.

Colleges and universities are increasingly including accounting research as a curriculum requirement for undergraduate and/or graduate-level accounting students. Often, students reaching this stage of their accounting program will have just completed their first accounting internship. Interns, as with new staff accountants, will quickly discover that they are expected to learn on the job (accounting can be a sink-or-swim environment). These students will likely have had just enough exposure to the challenges of research that they will crave more formal instruction on this critical skill. This book will offer that to students, in a format that is understandable and engaging.

Prerequisites for Users of this Book

To get the most value from this textbook, students studying this material should have already taken introductory-level accounting courses and—to the extent that the chapters on tax and auditing research will be covered—introductory tax and introductory auditing courses.

Users of this book will need access to the FASB Codification research tool. The American Accounting Association (AAA) provides academic access to the FASB *Accounting Standards Codification* and the Governmental Accounting Standards Board's *GARS Online* database for a low annual fee of $250 per year, per institution.

Instructors may also choose to require students to obtain a $20 annual subscription to eIFRS through the IAAER; alternatively, students can register on www.ifrs.org to obtain free access to individual standards.

To complete the exercises and case studies within the tax chapter of this book, it is suggested that users have access to an online tax research service, such as Thomson Reuters Checkpoint or CCH IntelliConnect. Access to these services is often available at reduced rates (or free-of-charge) for students enrolled in a tax or tax research course. Information on Thomson Reuters Checkpoint is available at: https://tax.thomsonreuters.com/products/brands/checkpoint. For information on CCH IntelliConnect, go to www.cchgroup.com, then "Select a Solution" > Accounting Firms – Tax, then click on IntelliConnect.

OUTSTANDING FEATURES OF THIS BOOK

This book unites research techniques with actual technical accounting issues. Students will move their understanding of accounting issues and research techniques forward along the knowledge continuum, from simply *understanding* to having the ability to *critically think* about and *apply* accounting issues. The practical examples and exercises in this book will challenge students to actively learn while they read.

Instructors will value that this book allows students to independently read and practice the baseline skills necessary to become accounting researchers, leaving instructors free to expand lectures into discussions of accounting judgments, student presentations, current events, and classroom discussions of (or hands-on group practice with) case studies. In short, instructors will be able to actively engage students in classroom debates and discussions, because they can spend less of their valuable classroom time lecturing on basic research and communication skills.

Overview of the Book

Chapters 1–5 of this book provide baseline knowledge that is necessary for understanding the rest of the book; the remaining chapters are written independently of one other, allowing instructors to choose to utilize only those chapters that fit their individual course needs.

Chapter 1 offers an overview of accounting research, including discussion of who performs accounting research and in what circumstances, and introducing key standard setters.

Chapter 2 provides an in-depth introduction to the FASB Codification, and emphasizes that students should perform *Browse* (as opposed to keyword searches) when possible.

Chapter 3 introduces the research process, and Chapter 4 introduces the fundamentals of effective technical writing, including the format of an accounting issues memorandum, techniques for effective email communication of research, and appropriate style for technical accounting writing.

Chapter 5 teaches students how to properly use *nonauthoritative* resources (e.g., Concepts Statements, firm resources, benchmarking), an essential but often overlooked skill for professionals learning to perform research.

Chapters 6–8 give students the opportunity to apply guidance to accounting issues following the order of *sections* in the Codification: first, issues involving scope and recognition (Ch. 6), followed by accounting measurement (Ch. 7), and specifically fair value measurement (Ch. 8). The revised revenue standard is emphasized in this edition, within Chapter 6.

Chapters 9–12 introduce skills specific to performing research in other environments, including auditing and professional services research (Ch. 9), governmental research (Ch. 10), tax research (Ch. 11), and international research (Ch. 12). Each of these chapters stands on its own, so instructors can choose to cover only the chapters relevant to their own courses.

Finally, **Chapters 13 and 14** focus on softer skills. Chapter 13 teaches students how to prepare and deliver effective presentations. Chapter 14 emphasizes the need for professionals to *stay current* as accounting requirements change and introduces the standard setters' *due process* for issuing new guidance. This chapter is a must-read and encourages students to sign up for accounting news alerts.

Engaging Pedagogy

Research is a skill that you learn by doing; accordingly, the pedagogy in this book is designed to foster active learning.

Chapter Opening Vignettes, Learning Objectives, and "Organization of This Chapter" Diagrams

Each chapter opens with a brief vignette placing students in the shoes of a beginning researcher. This opening vignette is followed by a list of the learning objectives for the chapter, and then by a diagram illustrating the organization of content within the chapter. These chapter-opening elements are intended to generate reader enthusiasm for chapter content, as well as provide students with an overview of the information to come.

Example Chapter Opening Vignette (from Chapter 6, Scope)

Printout in hand, Julie taps on her boss's door. She is feeling pretty good; she just found a paragraph in the guidance that appears to speak directly to the tax accrual issue her boss asked her to research. As she shows him the guidance, he taps his pen thoughtfully on the desk.

"Are you sure this guidance applies to our type of transaction?" he asks.

He continues, "I think the guidance for gross receipts taxes (which are based on revenue measures) may differ from guidance for taxes based on income. You've brought me guidance specific to income taxes."

Julie shakes her head; she realizes that she forgot to review the scope section of the guidance that she had printed. "Let me double check the scope section for this guidance," she says. "I'll stop by again later to let you know what I've found."

Confirming that a transaction is within the scope of a Codification topic may seem like an extra step, but much of the guidance within the Codification includes specific instructions for its use. Don't get caught like Julie, forgetting to do the appropriate diligence work on guidance that may otherwise appear to be on point. A proper review of the scope section is critical to identifying appropriate recognition, and then measurement, guidance for a transaction.

Example Learning Objectives (from Chapter 2, regarding the FASB Codification)

After reading this chapter and performing the exercises herein, you will be able to

1. **Describe** the purpose of the Codification, and the meaning of *authoritative*.

2. **Identify** standard setters that have contributed to the current body of authoritative guidance.

3. **Understand** the organization of guidance within the Codification.

4. **Perform** effective Browse searches within the Codification, reviewing all areas of *required reading*.

5. **Search** the Codification using other methods, including the keyword search feature, the Master Glossary, and the Cross Reference feature.

6. **Differentiate** between existing versus pending content, and understand how to interpret transition date guidance.

7. **Recognize** accounting alternative guidance available for private companies.

Example "Organization of This Chapter" Diagram (from Chapter 3, regarding the research process)

Each chapter includes a graphic showing the organization of topics within the chapter, along with narrative discussion of what the reader can expect key chapter themes to include. Following is one such chapter organization graphic:

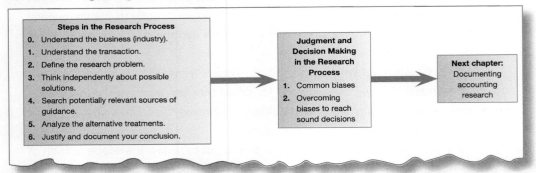

Chapter Features

Chapters are written in concise, easy to understand language, with boldfaced key terms to call students' attention to certain topics. In addition, chapters include extensive screenshots (from research tools, particularly the Codification) and diagrams illustrating key chapter concepts, intended to both engage students and improve their familiarity with research tools.

Chapters also include the following features, intended to engage students in active learning:

Now You Try

Throughout each chapter, students are challenged to practice and apply key skills as they are taught (**Now YOU Try** questions). These exercises might involve, for example, a student being asked to "draw a picture" of a transaction, to "draft an email" describing an issue, to "show the search path you would use," or to "identify the journal entries" for a scenario, using guidance from the Codification as a guide for the appropriate accounting. Instructors can use these questions as a lead-in to active in-class discussions.

For example, following is a **Now YOU Try** from Chapter 3, on identifying the accounting problem (the "researchable question"), a key step in the accounting research process.

Now
[YOU]
Try
3.4

Identifying the Researchable Question

Take a moment to practice identifying a single, researchable question for the following issues.

1. A company ships its widgets to a customer on December 31 but has not yet collected payment from the customer. The customer has promised to pay within 30 days but has never purchased goods from the company before.

   Researchable question? _____

2. A customer is suing the local grocery store for a slip-and-fall incident. The grocery store believes the lawsuit will likely be considered frivolous and rejected by the court. The grocery store must decide whether to record or disclose this matter.

   Researchable question? _____

3. An investor is suing a corporation that has just absorbed another entity in a merger. The investor is alleging that the corporation overstated on its balance sheet the values of certain equity investments that were acquired during the merger. The investor's attorney needs to understand how the equity investments should have been valued.

   Researchable question? _____

Tips from the Trenches

Periodically throughout the text, students will find **TIPS from the Trenches**, which offer additional insight on chapter content. These tips are designed to be like the insights you might hear an audit senior offer an audit staffer from across the table.

Your ultimate goal with the issues memo is to create a "one-stop shop" for knowledge about this transaction and its accounting. A reader, after picking up your memo, should not have to do additional digging to fully understand the background or the support for the accounting conclusion. After reading your memo, if a reader finds it necessary to get additional key facts from the contract, or to read additional guidance from the Codification, then you have failed to make your memo a one-stop shop.

[TIP] from the Trenches

End of Chapter Questions and Case Studies

At the conclusion of each chapter, review questions and exercises are provided, which instructors may choose to assign as homework.

- The **review questions** encourage students to recall and apply key points from the reading. Instructors may choose to use these as a basis for quiz questions.

- The **exercises** provide students with an opportunity to practice their research skills using external resources, such as the FASB Codification, AICPA literature, eIFRS, or Thomson Reuters Checkpoint.

In addition, **case study questions** are included at the end of each chapter, providing students with the opportunity to apply the research process to more involved accounting issues. Students are frequently asked to respond to these questions in the form of an email or by drafting an accounting issues memo. Cases of varying degrees of complexity are provided; accordingly, instructors may choose to assign case study questions as individual homework or as group research assignments.

Example Case Study Question (from Chapter 4, regarding effective communication)

> **Writing a Brief Issues Memo, Inventory** You are a plant accountant for Kelly Corp. You have been asked to draft a brief (1- to 1.5-page) issues memo ("to the files") documenting the accounting for the following issue.   4.5
>
> Kelly Corp has leased a mine from which it recently extracted 1,000 kilograms of bauxite (a mineral that can be used to make aluminum). Kelly Corp plans to sell the bauxite to aluminum manufacturers. Kelly Corp is analyzing whether its bauxite inventory can be carried at its selling price per ASC 330-10-35-16(b). Assume that quoted market prices are generally available for bauxite, and that the market for bauxite is active.
>
> Using the standard memo format, analyze whether all necessary conditions are met for the accounting treatment proposed. If assumptions are needed to fully evaluate the guidance, identify those assumptions in your analysis. For this particular memo, you are not required to present alternative treatments; assume for this issue that you have solely been asked to document whether the conditions in ASC 330-10-35-16(b) are met.

NEW TO THIS EDITION

- Separate chapters now devoted to the research process (Chapter 3) and effective writing (Chapter 4)
- Coverage of judgment and decision making in the research process
- A detailed research example running through Chapters 3 and 4, including a full sample accounting issues memo at the end of Chapter 4
- Full chapter on delivering effective presentations
- Consolidation of (previously separate) chapters on Scope and Recognition
- In-depth coverage of *how to navigate* existing versus revised revenue guidance, and key principles
- Coverage of the AICPA's revised Code of Conduct
- More hands-on Now YOU Try exercises throughout each chapter
- Cases, cases, cases! More cases, of varying degrees of difficulty, in every chapter

SUPPLEMENTS

All supplements for this book have been created by the book's authors.

Instructors Manual—Includes resources for instructors of this course, including sample course schedules and grading considerations, teaching tips for each chapter, and links to external resources.

PowerPoint Slides—Available for each chapter, PowerPoint lecture slides highlight key matter from each chapter.

Solutions Manual—Includes solutions to all end-of-chapter review questions, exercises, and case studies.

Now YOU Try Responses—Available to instructors, solutions to the **Now YOU Try** exercises are intended to assist instructors in leading class discussions.

ACKNOWLEDGEMENTS

I would like to first thank Denny Beresford, for providing his support at every stage of this project, and whose ideas have helped to make this a great book.

Additionally, my sincere appreciation to Nicholas Stell for his contributions to the Energy Works memo.

Martha and I would also like to thank our colleagues at SUNY-Buffalo for their comments on select chapters, and for their support of this project. In particular, thanks to Ron Huefner, Ann Cohen, Arlene Hibschweiler, and Susan Hamlen.

We were fortunate to receive review comments on this book from accounting research faculty from across the country, and we are sincerely grateful to these individuals for their time and important contributions to this book. These individuals are

Sheila Ammons, *Austin Community College*
Salem Boumediene, *Montana State University*
Megan Burke, *Texas A&M University—Commerce*
Kimberly Charland, *Kansas State University*
Yu Chen, *Texas A&M International University*
Mary Christ, *University of Northern Iowa*
Ann Cohen, *SUNY-Buffalo*
Amanda Cromartie, *University of North Carolina—Greensboro*
John DeJoy, *Union Graduate College*
Victoria Dickinson, *University of Mississippi*
Lynn Dikolli, *University of North Carolina at Chapel Hill*
Emily Doyle, *University of South Carolina*
Robert Elya, *Golden Gate University*
Patricia Fairfield, *Georgetown University*
Tim Firch, *California State University—Stanislaus*
Caroline Ford, *Baylor University*
James Fornaro, *SUNY at Old Westbury*
Jim Fuehrmeyer, *University of Notre Dame*
Carl Gabrini, *College of Coastal Georgia*
Patricia Galletta, *CUNY—College of Staten Island*
Alan Glazer, *Franklin & Marshall College*
Hubert Glover, *Drexel University*
Rita Grant, *Grand Valley State University*
Mahendra Gujarathi, *Bentley University*
Leslie Hodder, *Indiana University*
Patrick Hopkins, *Indiana University*
Ron Huefner, *SUNY-Buffalo*
Venkataraman Iyer, *University of North Carolina—Greensboro*
Mark Jackson, *University of Nevada—Reno*
Carol Jessup, *University of Illinois—Springfield*
Vicki Jobst, *Benedictine University*
Jeff Jones, *Auburn University*
Sara Kern, *Gonzaga University*
Katherine Krawczyk, *North Carolina State University*
Sudha Krishnan, *California State University—Long Beach*
Benjamin Lansford, *Penn State University*
Siyi Li, *University of Illinois—Chicago*
Linda Lovata, *Southern Illinois University—Edwardsville*
Jason MacGregor, *Baylor University*
Dawn McKinley, *Harper College*
Janet Mosebach, *University of Toledo*

Kelly Noe, *Stephen F. Austin State University*
Elizabeth Oliver, *Washington & Lee University*
Kevin Packard, *Brigham Young University—Idaho*
Susan Parker, *Santa Clara University*
Laurel Parrilli, *St. John Fisher College*
Terry Patton, *Midwestern State University*
Marlene Plumlee, *University of Utah*
Richard Price, *Utah State University*
K.K. Raman, *University of Texas, San Antonio*
Paul Recupero, *Newbury College*
Phil Rohrbach, *University of Richmond*
John Rossi, *Moravian College*
Beverly Rowe, *University of Houston Downtown*
Lee Schiffel, *Valparaiso University*
Debra Sinclair, *University of South Florida*
Randall Stone, *East Central University*
Walter Teets, *Gonzaga University*
Thomas Vogel, *Canisius College*
Changjiang Wang, *Florida International University*
Jeannie Welsh, *LaSalle University*
Jeff Wilks, *Brigham Young University*
John Williams, *Missouri State University*
Philip Woodlief, *Vanderbilt University*

In particular, a big thanks to Sheila Ammons, Lynn Dikolli, Tim Firch, Jim Fornaro, Jim Fuehrmeyer, Carol Jessup, Sara Kern, Debbie Sinclair, Jeff Wilks, and Phil Woodlief, for their valuable feedback and counsel on the development of this text.

For their support and encouragement, thanks to my husband Mathew and our daughters Claire, Paige, and Lily.

A sincere thanks to the many institutions and corporations that permitted the use of their material in this book, especially the generosity of the Financial Accounting Foundation, PCAOB, and AICPA.

I would also like to thank George Werthman, Marnee Fieldman, and Jocelyn Mousel at Cambridge Business Publishers for their dedication to this book.

Finally, thank you to the instructors, students, and firms using this book. I look forward to your comments and suggestions.

Shelby Collins

Brief Table of Contents

Contents

Chapter 9
Audit and Professional Services Research 250

Chapter 10
Governmental and Industry Accounting Research 290

Chapter 11
Fundamentals of Tax Research 330

Chapter 1

Overview of Accounting Research

Each chapter in this book begins with an opening scenario, involving a beginning research-er who has been challenged to perform research. The opening scenario for this chapter is about *you*.

You are a senior or graduate-level accounting student, or you are an associate in an accounting firm. Your coursework and experiences to date have given you a strong accounting foundation; however, now you are being asked to perform accounting research. As an accounting student, you are told that you'll need research skills for your upper-level coursework and for the CPA exam. Or, as a professional, your supervisor is already asking for your help researching client issues.

To perform this research, you will need the following:

- ■ An understanding of which research tools apply in each research environment,
- ■ Confidence applying a step-by-step research process to open-ended questions, and
- ■ Strong written communication skills, to effectively communicate your research results.

Continued

Continued

Learning Objectives

After reading this chapter and performing the exercises herein, you will be able to

1. **Identify** parties who perform accounting research, and circumstances in which accounting research is required.

2. **Describe** the ideal *timing* for performing accounting research, and understand cir-cumstances in which this timing may not be feasible.

3. **Understand** that different standards apply to different research environments (e.g., financial, governmental, audit, tax, and international research).

4. **Identify** key standard setters involved in establishing U.S. accounting guidance.

You've come to the right place to obtain these skills. By actively participating in the lessons in this book, and by practicing your skills through research exercises and case studies, you can become an effective researcher. Get ready to roll up your sleeves—the ability to perform accounting research can pay dividends for your career, but mastering this skill requires practice.

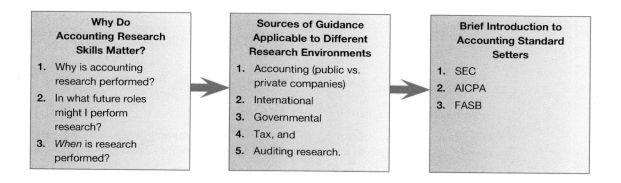

Organization of This Chapter

This chapter provides essential background information for researchers about to engage in their first experiences with the FASB Codification (in Chapter 2). In particular, the chapter emphasizes the importance of research skills—critical even for entry-level accountants—and then describes circumstances in which these skills may be required. Additionally, the chapter emphasizes the benefits of researching transactions before they take place.

Next, the chapter highlights that accounting research doesn't just come from one source; rather, each accounting environment (U.S., international, tax, governmental, and auditing) is governed by its own unique standards. Finally, the chapter offers brief, but essential, background on the key standard setters responsible for establishing U.S. generally accepted accounting principles (GAAP).

The preceding graphic illustrates the organization of this chapter.

Following the introduction to accounting research presented in this chapter, Chapters 2-8 of this book focus on various aspects of financial accounting research, primarily related to U.S. public and nonpublic companies. Discussion of other research environments, including guidance on auditing, governmental, tax, and international research, is provided in Chapters 9–12. Chapter 13 offers techniques for delivering effective research presentations. Finally, Chapter 14 teaches readers the importance of staying current as accounting standards continually change.

WHY ACCOUNTING RESEARCH SKILLS MATTER

LO1 **Identify** parties who perform accounting research, and circumstances in which accounting research is required.

Ever heard the one, where you tell someone you're an accounting major, and they say: "Oh, you must be good at math!"?

Numbers certainly have a place in our profession. But I'll let you in on a little secret . . . *research* and *communication* will also be a key part of your career as an accountant. In fact, excelling in these areas can have a profound effect on your advancement. Consider this very rough sketch of research and your career:

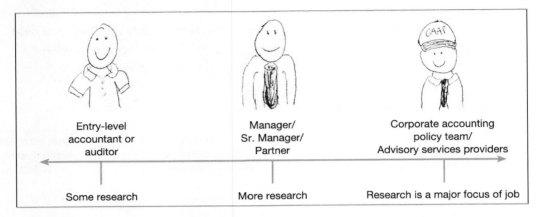

From this illustration, here are three takeaways:

- One, there's no way around it. You'll need at least a minimum level of competency in research to do your job as an entry-level accountant or auditor. This book will help.

- Two, the more you advance in your career, the more research you will likely perform. But the inverse is also true; do research well, and you'll be asked to do more of it. Soon, you'll start being viewed as a higher-level professional, and you'll have the ultimate learning experience as you are invited to participate in increasingly important projects.

- Three, if you find that research is something you love, you can actually make a career of it. Most major corporations have accounting policy teams, which focus on reviewing accounting judgments and implementing new standards. Accounting firms also have teams devoted to assisting clients with accounting policy judgments, like KPMG's Accounting Advisory Services and EY's Financial Accounting Advisory Services.

You'll learn the most about accounting research by actually doing it. So the next chapter jumps right into the FASB Codification. But before we get there, this chapter offers a little background on *who* performs research in our profession, *when*, and in *what environments*. Finally, the *standard setters* responsible for establishing accounting guidance are also briefly introduced.

What Is *Accounting Research*, and Why Is It Performed?

The term **accounting research** is used to describe two very different types of research:

- Research done in practice, by accountants and other interested parties, often in conjunction with the preparation or review of financial statements or tax returns; and

- Academic research, primarily done by candidates pursuing—or academics who have obtained—a PhD in accounting.

This book focuses solely on the accounting research that is done in practice, also known as *technical accounting* research.

The objectives of performing this type of accounting research are generally twofold:

1. To account for transactions or items in a manner that is *appropriate* and *supportable* based on authoritative guidance, and

2. To create *documentation* describing the research performed and supporting the conclusion reached.

That is, accountants often need to consult guidance requirements in order to determine the appropriate accounting treatment for a transaction or event, or to locate guidelines for the preparation of financial statements. In particular, accounting research may be necessary for transactions that are new or infrequent for a company, highly material, or for which a company does not have an established accounting practice. Ultimately, this accounting research can be necessary to ensure that a company's accounting complies with authoritative guidance, thus allowing the company to receive an unmodified (aka, unqualified) audit opinion.

Additionally, a key objective of accounting research is to create robust *documentation* supporting the conclusions reached. Proper accounting research documentation summarizes—in one place—all relevant background on an issue, the guidance considered, and the basis for the selected accounting position. Documenting the basis for accounting positions is especially critical in circumstances where the accounting for a transaction involves judgment (for example, if two or more alternatives are present). Chapter 4 offers additional discussion of *why* and *how* to create robust documentation.

As noted earlier, accounting research is generally only performed for transactions and events that are considered *material* to an entity and that are therefore relevant to users of an entity's financial statements. Recall that:

> "Information is **material** [emphasis added] if omitting it or misstating it could influence decisions that users make on the basis of the financial information of a specific reporting entity."[1]

Materiality can be evaluated based on an item's quantitative or qualitative significance. More resources are generally devoted to researching an entity's most material business issues, and less resources are generally devoted to less material issues.

> Recognizing the importance of research skills, the uniform CPA exam tests candidates' research and other critical thinking skills through *task-based simulations*. Task-based simulations can account for between 40% and 50% of candidates' exam scores on each of the regulation (REG), auditing (AUD), and financial accounting (FAR) sections of the exam.[2]

[**TIP**] from the Trenches

Next, let's look at *who* typically performs accounting research.

In What Future Roles Might I Perform Accounting Research?

No matter what accounting career path you pursue, you can expect to perform accounting research. In fact, you will likely be asked to research basic issues during your very first internship, or during your first year in the profession.

As illustrated in Figure 1-1, here are some circumstances in which the following parties typically perform accounting research:

- ▪ *Corporate accountants:* Also referred to as preparers of financial statements or tax returns, accountants working for a company may perform accounting research in conjunction with the preparation of the company's financial statements or tax returns, or for purposes of tax planning.

---

[1] FASB Concepts Statement No. 8, *Conceptual Framework for Financial Reporting,* Chapter 1 (September 2010). Paragraph QC11.

[2] AICPA, *Content and Skill Specifications for the Uniform CPA Examination.* Approved by the Board of Examiners May 15, 2009 (with updates approved on October 3, 2013). Effective January 1, 2015. Page 35.

Particularly for small companies, accounting firm personnel are sometimes engaged to help companies prepare their accounting records or financial statements. This can involve performing accounting research on behalf of the company.

■ *Auditors:* Auditors often must research whether a company's accounting positions are supportable based on authoritative guidance, in order to conclude that the company's financial statements are presented fairly in conformity with GAAP.

■ *Regulators*: Regulatory agencies (either governmental or independent) are responsible for overseeing certain corporations and industries. Certain regulators, such as the SEC, routinely review the financial statements of companies they oversee. Regulators may need to perform research to understand positions taken in companies' financial statements.

■ *Investors*: Often referred to as *users* of financial statements, professional investors monitor accounting positions taken by companies and, in some cases, may raise concerns (or make adjustments to models they maintain) when a company's accounting positions are inconsistent with those of other companies in the same industry.

Figure 1-1

Parties performing accounting research

Parties Performing Accounting Research

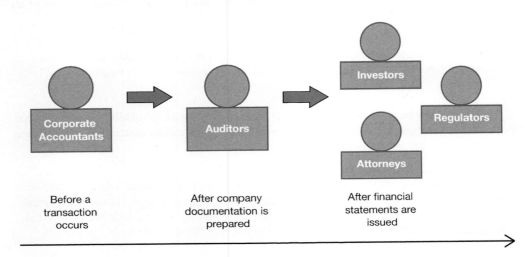

Regardless of the career path you choose, during the early stages of your career, your research will generally be reviewed by a supervisor before it is relied upon or shared with a client. That said, a well-documented and supportable initial recommendation and research from you can open doors to higher-level projects.

Now
[YOU]
Try
1.1

Your Role as a Researcher

Based on the preceding descriptions of parties who perform accounting research, in what role(s) do you imagine that you might perform research?

_____

_____

WHEN IS ACCOUNTING RESEARCH PERFORMED?

Accounting research can occur at different stages in the financial reporting process. Ideally, companies with sufficient resources (often, public companies) will research the accounting for a transaction before the transaction takes place. However, the accounting research process may differ for small or nonpublic companies, which may be subject to more resource constraints and which generally have less user demand for financial statements. In these environments, research may only occur as financial statements are being prepared, or it may occur at the request of an auditor seeking further support for a company's accounting methods.

LO2 **Describe** the ideal *timing* for performing accounting research, and understand circumstances in which this timing may not be feasible.

Let's take a closer look at each of these circumstances now.

Researching a Proposed Transaction

Performing accounting research before a transaction occurs is beneficial for a few reasons. This research allows

- Company management to evaluate whether the *expected financial statement impacts* of the transaction, as drafted, are acceptable.
- Management to *adjust forecasted earnings* to reflect the expected impacts of the transaction.
- The accounting team to *prepare timely documentation* of the expected accounting position.
- The *audit team to review* the proposed accounting treatment before the transaction is recorded.

Corporate management teams are frequently on the lookout for business opportunities that are profitable and aligned with their companies' strategic objectives. While management evaluates the merits of a potential transaction, the company's accounting team should be engaged concurrently to evaluate the accounting implications of the transaction. Management will take the expected financial statement impacts of the transaction into consideration when assessing whether the transaction is worth pursuing.

EXAMPLE ——

> For example, assume that a company is closely monitoring its debt-to-equity ratio to remain compliant with its current debt covenants (promises to lenders). Said another way, assume the company has very little remaining *debt capacity* (ability to issue more debt under its current debt covenants).
>
> If the company needs to raise additional capital, it would likely evaluate potential instruments to confirm that they would be accounted for as equity, not debt, before executing a final agreement with a bank. The company's accounting department would be responsible for researching the details of the capital issuance to determine whether the issuance would indeed be accounted for as equity instead of debt.

In addition to being responsible for reporting *past* transactions and events, corporate managers are often held equally accountable for providing accurate short- and long-term earnings *forecasts*. Investors rely on corporate earnings forecasts in setting a reasonable share price for a company's stock, and lenders review forecasts to monitor compliance with debt covenants. Accordingly, once management determines that a proposed transaction is worth pursuing, the company must adjust its future earnings expectations to reflect the anticipated financial statement impacts of the transaction. The following Now YOU Try depicts an example in which management asks the accounting team to evaluate the financial statement impacts of a proposed transaction.

Figure 1-2

Reviewing the financial
statement impacts of a
proposed transaction

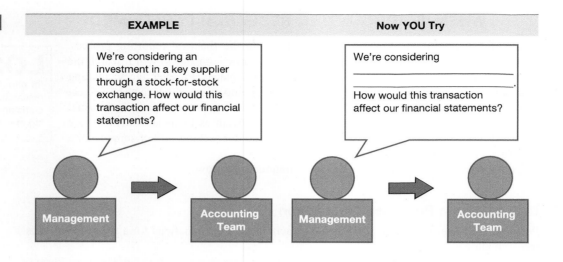

EXAMPLE

We're considering an
investment in a key supplier
through a stock-for-stock
exchange. How would this
transaction affect our financial
statements?

Management   Accounting
                    Team

Now YOU Try

We're considering
_____
_____.
How would this transaction
affect our financial statements?

Management   Accounting
                    Team

Now
[YOU]
Try
1.2

Fill in the box above by describing a transaction that management might need the accounting
team to review in advance, to evaluate potential financial statement impacts.

For their part, the accounting team must not only communicate the financial statement impacts of a transaction to management, but they must also document the research supporting their accounting conclusions. This documentation serves as support for the proposed accounting treatment shared with management and is the preliminary support for the accounting position to be reflected in the financial statements. This research should be saved in company files for future reference and updated with final contracts if the transaction is executed.

> Certain accounting elections *must* be documented at the time a transaction is executed. For example, so-called **contemporaneous** documentation requirements apply to entities electing hedge accounting for their derivative positions (this election typically reduces income statement volatility).[3] To comply with this requirement, companies usually review draft transaction documents to evaluate whether the proposed instrument will meet all required criteria for hedge accounting, then prepare draft documentation based on this review.

Finally, researching and documenting the planned accounting for a transaction allows a company's *auditors* to offer their tentative concurrence with the proposed treatment before a transaction is recorded. While the accounting remains the responsibility of management (and auditors must take care to maintain their independence from management), it is often helpful for auditors to review draft agreements—as well as management's documentation of an accounting issue—in order to perform their own independent research and offer a preliminary view of management's position. Seeking this auditor "buy in" early in the process can minimize last-minute differences of opinion that could arise at quarter- or year-end, when financial statements are being finalized.

Researching a Past Transaction

When it is not possible to research a transaction before its execution, accounting research may be necessary at the time, or after, a transaction occurs. The purpose of this research is simply to determine how to record the event in the financial statements, and to document this determination. Figure 1-3 illustrates a sample situation in which accountants must perform research related to a past transaction.

---

[3] FASB Accounting Standards Codification 815-20-25-3 (Derivatives and Hedging - Hedging).

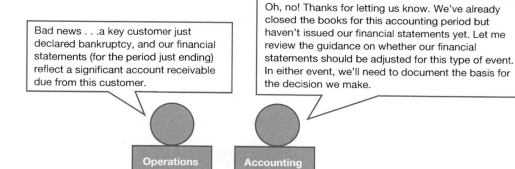

Figure 1-3

Researching a past transaction

Following are examples of circumstances in which research may be required at the time, or after, a transaction is executed:

- The transaction was *time-sensitive*; therefore, there was not sufficient lead time to research its accounting treatment.
- The transaction was *highly confidential*; therefore, details of the transaction were only released to the accounting team after the transaction was executed.
- The transaction or event *could not have been anticipated*; for example, the company suffered from a building fire or natural disaster.
- *Communication broke down* between the dealmakers in the organization and the accounting team; consequently, the accounting team was only informed of the transaction after it was executed.
- The preparer has *limited resources* and therefore only performs research at the time financial statements are being prepared. For example, the company is a small or nonpublic company, and management is not required to prepare earnings forecasts.
- Finally, *documentation* (and—as necessary—research) prepared previously, for proposed transactions, should be updated to reflect final contract terms.

Take particular note of the fourth bullet above; a communications failure between a company's operations teams and accounting team should be reviewed to determine what went wrong. To avoid a recurrence of the communications failure, a formal process in which material or unusual contracts are reviewed by the accounting team may need to be established.

As with the process for researching proposed transactions, accounting research performed for past transactions should be documented and shared with the company's audit team. This documentation and review process will support the accounting positions reflected in the financial statements.

Imagine this scenario. You are an accounting manager at ABC Corp, a nonpublic company that prepares GAAP financial statements in order to receive financing from banks.

The operations team at ABC is moving forward quickly on a deal to invest in a key supplier, but has not yet informed the accounting team of this possible deal.

Make your best case: Convince the operations team that the accounting department should be involved in reviewing the deal before it is executed.

Now
YOU
Try
1.3

_____

_____

_____

_____

Research Performed After Financial Statement Issuance

After financial statements have been issued, accounting research may be performed by various parties, as follows:

- Investors may research a company's choice of accounting methods and may seek to understand alternatives available in the literature. Using this information, investors may choose to adjust their internal models to improve consistency across companies they are evaluating.

- Regulators, such as the SEC or other industry-specific regulatory agencies, periodically review the amounts and disclosures presented in the financial statements of companies they oversee (see example in Figure 1-4). To assess whether companies' accounting judgments and disclosures are appropriate, regulators may perform research to familiarize themselves with accounting requirements.

- Attorneys may perform accounting research in order to argue (or to defend against claims) that a company's financial reporting has harmed an investor or other interested party. The attorney must support such arguments with citations from accounting guidance.

Questions from these parties may require corporate accountants to perform further research to explain or defend their accounting positions taken. Robust, timely documentation of accounting positions (ideally, prepared before financial statement issuance) can assist corporate accountants in responding to such inquiries.

Figure 1-4

SEC inquiry regarding valuation disclosures presented in company financial statements

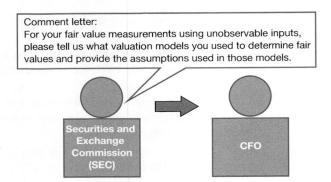

Comment letter:
For your fair value measurements using unobservable inputs, please tell us what valuation models you used to determine fair values and provide the assumptions used in those models.

Securities and Exchange Commission (SEC)

CFO

Research for the Purpose of Shaping Future Accounting Standards

Accounting standards are dynamic; that is, the current body of accounting guidance is continually being reviewed and revised. Many of the parties who perform accounting research also participate in shaping future accounting standards. For example, the preparer who encounters gray areas in GAAP may request clarification from the Financial Accounting Standards Board (FASB). The investor who observes inconsistent disclosures may lobby the FASB for more transparent disclosures in a given area.

For their part, accounting and auditing standard setters follow a *due process* that depends heavily on input from their constituents. Chapter 14 introduces readers to the standard-setting process and describes steps researchers can take to stay current.

IN WHAT ENVIRONMENTS IS ACCOUNTING RESEARCH PERFORMED?

LO3 Understand that different standards apply to different research environments.

Accounting research is performed in a variety of environments, including in public and nonpublic companies (domestic and international), governments, and for purposes of researching tax requirements.

Public companies (e.g., companies that issue publicly traded debt or equity securities) are generally required to file financial statements with the SEC (Securities and Exchange Commission). By contrast, **nonpublic**, or **private**, **companies** are generally not required to file financial statements with the SEC; however, financial statements may be necessary to satisfy lenders, venture capitalists, or other stakeholders. In both cases, research is frequently necessary to ensure that the financial statements have been prepared in accordance with all applicable accounting standards.

Outside of the United States, accounting research is performed by public and nonpublic companies, as required by their national laws to issue financial statements. Many non-U.S. countries prepare their financial statements in accordance with IFRS (International Financial Reporting Standards); other countries continue to follow country-specific financial reporting guidance.

Governmental entities, including state, local, and federal governments and agencies, are frequently required to prepare financial statements to demonstrate how they have used the funds allocated to them. Accountants involved in the preparation of governmental financial statements must be able to research and understand requirements for their preparation.

Tax research is performed by (and for) corporations and other entities that consider the tax consequences in planning transactions and that are required to report their activities to a government body (federal, state, and/or local). To understand tax reporting requirements, and to take advantage of all available tax incentive programs, researchers must become familiar with tax research sources ranging from the Internal Revenue Code to court decisions.

Different Guidance for Each Research Environment

Each research environment is subject to a different set of standards. Figure 1-5 identifies the rule makers (or "standard setters") for each research environment.

Preparer Type	Accounting Standard Setter	Audit Type	Auditing Standard Setter
Public companies	FASB and SEC	Audits of public companies	PCAOB
Private companies	FASB*	Audits of private companies	AICPA
Governmental entities—state and local	GASB (Governmental Accounting Standards Board)	Audits of state and local government entities	GAO (Government Accountability Office)
Governmental entities—federal	FASAB (Federal Accounting Standards Advisory Board)	Audits of federal government entities	GAO
International companies	IASB (International Accounting Standards Board), or other local standard setter	Audits of international companies	IAASB (International Auditing and Assurance Standards Board), or other local standard setter

Figure 1-5

Sources of accounting and auditing guidance

*The Private Company Council advisory body advises the FASB on standard-setting activities affecting private companies.

Tax research, by contrast, requires researchers to consult multiple sources including the Internal Revenue Code, tax regulations, IRS rulings and other guidance, and judicial rulings. Sources of tax research guidance are listed in Figure 1-6; note that this list is not all-inclusive. See Chapter 11 for a more complete discussion of tax sources.

Sources for Tax Research	
Statutory Sources	• Internal Revenue Code • Other statutes with tax-related provisions (e.g., the Bankruptcy Code)
Administrative Sources	• Treasury regulations • IRS Revenue Rulings • Written administrative agency determinations
Judicial Sources	• U.S. Supreme Court • U.S. Court of Appeals • U.S. District Court • U.S. Court of Federal Claims • U.S. Tax Court

Figure 1-6

Sources of tax research guidance

[TIP] from the Trenches

This book will introduce you to each of the preceding research environments and standard setters. However, in practice, you will likely specialize in only one or two of these areas. For example, public company accountants and auditors will primarily perform research using FASB guidance for accounting, and PCAOB guidance for auditing.

[Now YOU Try 1.4]

In Figures 1-5 and 1-6, put a check mark next to any standard setters whose guidance you have researched, such as in previous accounting or auditing coursework. Then put an open circle next to other standard setters you expect to learn about in this course.

Following is an introduction to key U.S. accounting standard setters, which will set the stage for the accounting research topics discussed in Chapters 2–8. The standard setters responsible for creating auditing, governmental, tax, and international accounting guidance are introduced in Chapters 9–12.

ACCOUNTING STANDARD-SETTING BODIES

LO4 Identify key standard setters involved in establishing U.S. accounting guidance.

The next several chapters of this book (Chapters 2–8) provide in-depth coverage of the guidance and research process involved in performing U.S. accounting research. In preparation for these chapters, following is a brief history of—and introduction to—the standard-setting bodies primarily responsible for establishing U.S. accounting guidance. Having a basic familiarity with these standard setters provides context for understanding the accounting guidance applicable today.

This history follows a chronological order, beginning with the SEC—the first entity given formal authority to establish U.S. accounting standards. Figure 1-7 illustrates a timeline of key U.S. accounting standard setters.

Figure 1-7

Brief timeline of key U.S. accounting standard setters

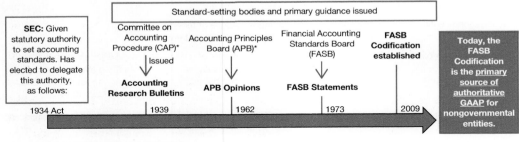

* A committee formed by the AICPA

The Securities and Exchange Commission

Following a crisis in investor confidence resulting from the stock market crash of 1929 and subsequent Great Depression, the **Securities Exchange Act of 1934** (the "1934 Act") created the SEC with the objective of providing investors with reliable financial information about public companies. First and foremost, the SEC's role is to act as a *law enforcement* agency, tasked with the authority to enforce securities laws in order to protect the investing public. The SEC describes the work of its Division of Enforcement, in part, as follows:

> *Each year the SEC brings hundreds of civil enforcement actions against individuals and companies for violation of the securities laws. Typical infractions include insider trading, accounting fraud, and providing false or misleading information about securities and the companies that issue them.*[4]

---

[4] www.sec.gov, "About" - "What We Do." Accessed April 22, 2015.

A second authority granted to the SEC in the 1934 Act was the authority to establish accounting standards. The SEC elected to delegate this responsibility—first to the AICPA (American Institute of Certified Public Accountants) and later to the FASB. (Notably, the **Sarbanes-Oxley Act of 2002** established criteria—such as funding and independence requirements—related to the SEC's choice of standard setter.) The FASB website describes its relationship to the SEC as follows:

> *The SEC has statutory authority to establish financial accounting and reporting standards for publicly held companies under the Securities Exchange Act of 1934. Throughout its history, however, the Commission's policy has been to rely on the private sector for this function to the extent that the private sector demonstrates ability to fulfill the responsibility in the public interest.*[5]

As noted, the SEC relies on the private sector to establish accounting guidance, on condition that the private sector demonstrates its "ability to fulfill" this responsibility. Accordingly, the SEC closely monitors the FASB's agenda and routinely provides input on tentative decisions reached by the FASB.

That said, the SEC does periodically issue accounting guidance applicable primarily to public companies. For example, the SEC establishes public company financial statement and disclosure requirements through its **Regulations S-X and S-K**. The SEC also periodically issues interpretive guidance on topics of key interest to the SEC, in the form of **Staff Accounting Bulletins** (SABs) and **Financial Reporting Releases** (FRRs).

Finally, it is worth noting that the SEC's Division of Corporation Finance reviews, at least every three years, the financial statements and disclosures of all companies with publicly traded securities.[6] These reviews can result in **comment letters** to corporations requesting additional explanation of a company's financial reporting. In some cases, unsatisfactory responses to comment letters, for material matters, can result in the SEC requesting that a company restate previously issued financial statements. Chapter 5, on nonauthoritative sources, describes how researchers can use the SEC website to search for company filings and SEC correspondence.

The SEC is headed by five commissioners, each appointed by the President of the United States, and each serving a five-year term. The President designates one of the commissioners to serve as Chairman of the SEC. Current SEC Chairman, Mary Jo White, is shown in Figure 1-8.

Figure 1-8

SEC Chairman, Mary Jo White

Mary Jo White, Chairman since 2013 (former prosecutor)

The SEC chairman is appointed by the President, with the advice and consent of the senate.

1. Which of the SEC's roles—as enforcement agency or as accounting standard setter—are you more familiar with? Give an example of prior exposure you've had to the SEC in one or both of these capacities.

_____

_____

2. In your own words, explain the SEC's relationship to the FASB.

_____

_____

_____

_____

Now **YOU** Try **1.5**

---

[5] www.fasb.org, "Facts about FASB." Accessed April 22, 2015.

[6] Sarbanes-Oxley Act of 2002, Sec. 408(c). Also known as Public Law 107-204. July 30, 2002.

The American Institute of Certified Public Accountants

As noted, the SEC first delegated its accounting standard-setting authority to the AICPA.[7] In 1936, the AICPA formed the **Committee on Accounting Procedure (CAP)** which, at the urging of the SEC, began actively issuing guidance in 1939. In 1959, facing criticism of the CAP's ad hoc approach to setting standards and the tendency for its standards to allow preparers to choose between two acceptable accounting treatments, the AICPA replaced this committee with the **Accounting Principles Board (APB)**.

The membership of both the CAP and APB consisted of volunteers who also maintained full-time positions with other employers. These early standard setters were criticized for their lack of independence, their slow response time to emerging issues, and for their failure to develop a conceptual framework to guide their decisions. The APB was dissolved in 1973 and was replaced by the FASB. Still today, a portion of the guidance issued by the CAP and the APB continues to be in effect within the FASB's *Accounting Standards Codification.*

Upon the dissolution of the APB, the AICPA formed an accounting standards committee to continue its participation in, and influence over, standard setting. In the years that followed, this committee issued guidance including AICPA Statements of Position (SOPs), industry-specific Audit and Accounting Guides (A&A Guides), and Practice Bulletins, some of which is still part of the body of GAAP today.

While the AICPA no longer issues standards that are considered GAAP, the AICPA has recently worked to create guidance for entities that are not required to issue GAAP financial statements. In 2013, the AICPA introduced the *Financial Reporting Framework for Small- and Medium-Sized Entities (FRF for SMEs)*, a non-GAAP reporting framework intended to simplify financial statement preparation for smaller entities.

Additionally, today the AICPA remains a key authority in establishing standards for *professional services* (such as auditing) and for accountants' *professional conduct*. These standards are discussed further in Chapter 9.

Now YOU Try 1.6

One criticism raised regarding the AICPA's two standard-setting committees is that they were not independent. Based on the preceding discussion, explain the characteristics of these Boards that might have caused this criticism. Why should we care whether an accounting standard setter is independent?

_____

_____

_____

_____

The Financial Accounting Standards Board

Note to Instructors:

You may choose to cover the standard-setters' *due process* at this point (see Chapter 14).

The **FASB** was created in 1973, following the dissolution of the APB. The FASB is an independent organization focused on developing standards that result in decision-useful information for investors and other financial statement users. Both the SEC and the AICPA recognize the FASB as the entity with authority to set accounting standards for nongovernmental entities. To that end, the FASB developed and maintains the FASB *Accounting Standards Codification*, described in detail in the next chapter.

The FASB's seven full-time board members are required to represent a diversity of backgrounds. Specifically, board members must "collectively have knowledge and experience in investing, accounting, finance, business, accounting education, and research."[8] These

---

[7] Founded in 1887, the AICPA is the professional association for CPAs in the United States.

[8] FASB Rules of Procedure, amended and restated through December 11, 2013. Page 8.

board members are appointed by the FASB's parent organization, the **Financial Accounting Foundation (FAF)**. The FAF oversees the operations of the FASB; its objective, in part, is to protect the independence and integrity of the standard-setting process.[9] Figure 1-9 depicts the current Chairman of the FASB, Russell G. Golden, who was appointed in 2013.

Russell G. Golden,
FASB Chairman since 2013
(former partner, Deloitte & Touche LLP)

The FASB Chairman is appointed to a five-year term by the trustees of the Financial Accounting Foundation.

Image used with permission of the Financial Accounting Foundation.

Figure 1-9

FASB Chairman, Russell Golden

The FASB's board typically includes representation from the preparer, academic, investor, and auditor communities. That is, board members typically come from a mix of these backgrounds. What perspectives might each of these parties bring to the standard-setting process?

Preparer: _____

Academic: _____

Investor: _____

Auditor: _____

Now YOU Try 1.7

As required by the Sarbanes-Oxley Act, the FASB's annual operating costs are primarily funded by **accounting support fees** assessed to public companies. Companies pay a share of this fee based on the size of their market capitalization (that is, the market value of a company's outstanding shares). This funding mechanism is designed to maintain the FASB's independence; that is, rather than rely on donations that could impair the Board's objectivity, public companies are required to participate in supporting the FASB's operations.

In response to criticism that compliance with GAAP is too burdensome for nonpublic companies, in 2012 the FAF created the **Private Company Council** (PCC). This Council identifies areas within existing and proposed GAAP that can be simplified for private companies, and these efforts have given rise to simplified **accounting alternatives** being made available to private companies.

The standard setters responsible for establishing auditing, tax, international, and governmental accounting standards will be introduced in Chapters 9–12 of this book. For now, understanding the roles of these three U.S. accounting standard setters will provide the foundation for your next challenge: learning to perform *great* accounting research.

---

1. Explain how levying the accounting support fee, as opposed (for example) to relying upon individual corporate donations, helps maintain the FASB's independence.

_____

_____

_____

Now YOU Try 1.8

2. Considering the preceding introduction to accounting standard setters, which entity would you expect to have authority to adopt IFRS as the applicable reporting standards in the United States? Explain.

_____

_____

_____

---

[9] FASB Rules of Procedure, amended and restated through December 11, 2013. Page 6.

3. Contrast the role of the AICPA's FRF for SMEs with the role of the FASB's Private Company Council.

_____

_____

CHAPTER SUMMARY

This chapter emphasized that research and communication will play a role in your career as an accountant. Indeed, accounting research is integral to the work of many corporate accountants, auditors, investors, and regulators, as this chapter discussed.

Accounting research is ideally performed *before* transactions take place; however, this is not always feasible given resource constraints. Sources of research vary based on the diverse research environments (accounting, governmental, audit, tax, and international); it's important for practitioners to understand which standard setter has authority before beginning research.

Finally, this chapter introduced the organizations historically responsible for setting U.S. GAAP, and which contributed to the expansive population of accounting guidance available today. In the next chapter, we'll discuss the FASB Codification, which brings together these many diverse sources of guidance.

REVIEW QUESTIONS

1. What are two key objectives of performing technical accounting research?

2. Identify four parties who typically perform accounting research and explain why they perform research.

3. Name three reasons for which accounting research should ideally be performed before a transaction is executed.

4. Name three circumstances in which it might not be possible to research the accounting for a transaction until *after* it has occurred.

5. What is the meaning of the term *contemporaneous*? Explain.

6. Differentiate between the requirements for public (versus nonpublic) companies to prepare financial statements, and state why—in both cases—accounting research is frequently necessary.

7. To what research environment do the following standards apply?
   a. Standards of the GASB
   b. Standards of the FASB
   c. Standards of the AICPA
   d. Standards of the IASB
   e. Standards of the FASAB

8. List the organizations, in chronological order, that have historically been responsible for setting accounting standards.

9. What legislation gave the SEC the authority to set accounting standards? What was happening at the time that led to this need for accounting standards?

10. What two committees did the AICPA form, which were at one point responsible for setting accounting standards? *And*, what were some of the criticisms raised regarding these first two standard-setting bodies?

11. Define *accounting support fees* and explain why these fees help the FASB maintain its independence.

12. Fill in the blanks: The SEC has _____ authority to establish accounting standards but has historically delegated this authority to the _____ sector. Then, explain this statement.

13. What does the SEC view as its most important role? Explain.

14. What is an SEC comment letter? Explain.

15. Why was the PCC formed, and what impact has it had on accounting standards?

EXERCISES

1. Go to marketwatch.com, a Dow Jones & Co. site. Look for the magnifying glass symbol (at top right of blue banner at top of page), click it, then type the stock symbol "AAPL" into the search bar that appears. Next, click on the tab for "Analyst Estimates."
   a. What is the *mean* earnings per share estimate for this quarter? (Indicate what date your information is "as of"—i.e., the date on which you performed this search.)
   b. What is the mean EPS estimate for the next fiscal year? (Indicate what date your information is "as of.")
   c. Explain why performing accounting research before a transaction occurs might be important to Apple's management.

2. Go to wsj.com and type "Accounting Method" into the search bar. (Again, look for the magnifying glass at top right of the page to access the search bar.) Summarize one of the headlines and issues discussed in the search results. Brainstorm (and explain) why readers of the *Wall Street Journal* might have an interest in this article.

3. Go to fasb.org and locate (under *Latest News* on the bottom left side of the homepage) a recent news release. Describe the subject matter of the news release then identify *two parties* (such as parties depicted in Figure 1-1) who would be interested in this issue. Be as specific as possible, describing why the parties might be monitoring this issue.

4. Go to fasb.org and look up pre-Codification standards (located under the tab *Reference Library*, then *Superseded Standards*). Identify and summarize the subject of one standard issued by the CAP and one issued by the APB. What is the current status of these standards?

5. Look up the website for EY's Financial Accounting Advisory Services (FAAS) practice. Explain how experience performing accounting research could prepare you for a career in this practice.

6. Brainstorm an example of: 1) a financial accounting issue that would be researched before a transaction is finalized, 2) an accounting issue that would be researched after a transaction has been executed, and 3) an accounting issue that would be researched following financial statement issuance.

7. The chapter states that a communications failure between a company's accounting team and operations teams could result in company accountants evaluating the accounting for a transaction after it has occurred. Brainstorm a process that companies could put in place to encourage the timely communication of proposed transactions.

8. The SEC has five divisions. Using www.sec.gov as a starting point, name these five divisions. Which division would you expect to issue guidance to companies for complying with SEC reporting requirements?

9. Using sec.gov, go to *Regulations* then *Staff Interpretations*. Locate Staff Accounting Bulletin No. 99 ("SAB 99") and summarize the issue addressed by this guidance.

10. Using www.sec.gov, go to Divisions, then Division of Corporate Finance. Under Statutes, Rules, and Forms, go to Rules then to "Regulation S-K." Under Item 303 (Management's Discussion and Analysis) of Regulation S-K, list the five items (items 303(a)(1-5)) that must be included in a public company's MD&A disclosures.

11. Refer to the previous question. Describe two parties who might perform research to understand the MD&A requirements in Regulation S-K, and the circumstances that might drive them to perform this research.

12. Go to sec.gov, then *Divisions*, then *Division of Enforcement*. Under Federal Court Actions, locate the June 18, 2015, enforcement action brought against Norstra Energy. Summarize the charges brought by the SEC against Norstra. Describe how this enforcement action fits with the SEC's mission.

13. Search for information from the AICPA about its new *FRF for SMEs*. State again what the purpose of this framework is, and how it compares to the FASB's authoritative Codification. What entities are expected to benefit from application of this framework?

CASE STUDY QUESTIONS

1.1   **Purposeful reading: The 3-2-1 Assignment**[10] Complete the following steps intended to enhance your understanding of the chapter reading, and document your responses.

     3:   Read the chapter, then describe what you feel are the three most important concepts or facts from the reading.

     2:   Describe two aspects of the reading that you don't fully understand, or which are somewhat confusing.

     1:   Pose one question to the author (this should differ from the areas of confusion described in (2) above), which goes beyond the reading content, such as inquiring about implications or applications of the reading.

1.2   **Relationship Between the FASB and SEC** The relationship between the FASB and the SEC has been dynamic over time. Given that the SEC is a government agency, and that it has delegated its standard-setting power to the FASB, the SEC has periodically been lobbied by both lawmakers and corporations who have disagreed with FASB decisions. Using an Internet search engine such as Google, locate one article involving both the FASB and SEC; the article does not have to be current. In approximately one page summarize the issue raised in the article and the interplay you observe between these two organizations in the article.

     Variation, Case 1.2(Alt.): See the instructions to Case 1.2 above; rather than documenting your observations about the interplay between these organizations, come to class prepared to describe your article and to discuss your observations to your fellow classmates. In this Case 1.2(Alt), you are *not* being asked to submit any documentation of your findings.

1.3   **Researching Original FASB Standards** Using the FASB website, locate the original (superseded) standard FASB Statement No. 5, *Accounting for Contingencies* (as amended). In approximately one paragraph, describe when accrual of a loss contingency is required by this standard, and cite the FASB standard and paragraph number that provides this guidance. State also which disclosures must accompany loss contingency accruals. Finally, considering the background of this project described in Appendix B, was there uniform guidance for contingency accounting available prior to this standard? What committees or agencies, at that time, participated in establishing accounting guidance? Explain.

1.4   **Parties Performing Accounting Research (FASB Comment Letters)** In May 2013, the FASB issued a proposed Accounting Standards Update on Leases (Topic 842) and solicited constituent feedback. The proposed guidance would require most leases to be recorded on the balance sheet, with estimates of certain variable lease payments to be updated each period. In this case study, you are being asked to review two comment letters related to this proposal and to consider the perspective of each commenter.

     To begin, go to fasb.org then navigate to Projects, then Comment Letters. Click on the link for Leases (Topic 842)– May 2013, then locate Comment Letter No. 42, from Johnson & Johnson (J&J). Read this comment letter, then respond to the following:

1. What would you describe as J&J's primary concern related to the proposed guidance? From what perspective are they raising this concern (e.g., financial statement user, preparer, etc.)?
2. What steps does it appear J&J has already taken to evaluate or prepare for the proposed standard? Explain.
3. Describe one of J&J's recommendations to the FASB, regarding ways to reduce the cost/effort involved in complying with revised guidance. Explain J&J's rationale for this specific recommendation.

     Next, locate Comment Letter No. 44, from the American Bankers Association (ABA), then respond to the following:

4. From what perspective(s) is the ABA writing this letter? To respond, refer to page 1 of the letter.
5. Flip to pages 5-6 of the letter. What are some of the concerns the ABA raises from a user perspective, related to the proposed standard?
6. Flip to page 9 of the comment letter...what recommendation does the ABA make to the FASB?
7. Finally, contrast the perspectives that these particular users and preparers brought to this issue, and describe how you might expect the FASB to respond to the concerns raised by these letters.

1.5   **Understanding How FAS 168 Established the Codification as GAAP** Using the FASB website, locate the original *(superseded standard)* FASB Statement No. 168, *The FASB Accounting Standards Codification and the Hierarchy of Generally Accepted Accounting Principles* (as amended) then respond to the following. Include paragraph numbers to support your responses.

---

[10] Geraldine Van Gyn, PhD. *It's The Little Assignment with the Big Impact: Reading, Writing, Critical Reflection, and Meaningful Discussion.* Faculty Focus.com, May 6, 2013.

1. Read the Summary of this standard, which begins on page FAS168-1. Based on this Summary, describe the purpose of this standard and the key changes effected by this standard.

2. Summarize par. 3, Objective. In doing so, also comment on the role of SEC guidance in the Codification (this is also described in par. 3).

3. Describe the "GAAP hierarchy" introduced by Statement 168. Use information within the standard to respond.

4. What are some examples, provided in Statement 168, of nonauthoritative sources of guidance? Use information within the standard to respond.

5. In Appendix A (Background Information and Basis for Conclusions) of this standard, locate the discussion of *why* the FASB Codification was introduced. That is, what was the issue the Codification attempts to resolve?

6. Using Appendix B (Amendments to the FASB Codification) of this standard, describe where in the Codification a user can find the principles established by FAS 168. That is, in which topic will the principles of FAS 168 be described?

Networking with a Professional, and Understanding the Role of Research in His or Her Work Contact a professional in your planned or chosen field (auditing, tax, systems, internal audit, etc.). While you might set up the meeting via email, make every effort to have this conversation *live* (in person, or on the phone). Ask for just 10 minutes of their time, and be mindful to not exceed this time limit.   1.6

Ask the professional what role research plays in their current job responsibilities, and ask what resources they refer to most often in order to perform this research (e.g., the Codification? Firm audit program? Tax research database? Daily news updates?). Finally, ask what advice they would offer a beginning researcher.

Once you've asked your questions, let the professional do most of the talking; practice your listening skills during the conversation. Summarize the professional's responses—including his or her name and organization, and the setting for your conversation—in 1–3 paragraphs (less than one page). Be prepared to discuss your findings during class.

Chapter **2**

The FASB Codification: Introduction and Search Strategies

Jeremy has just been asked to research an issue related to his company's "volatility" assumption, one of the variables used to estimate the fair value of his company's outstanding stock compensation awards. Jeremy is a staff accountant, with only a limited understanding of stock compensation accounting. He doesn't feel very competent in this area.

Nevertheless, Jeremy gets right to work. First, he asks his supervisor for more background on the issue then reviews a memo describing how the company has estimated this assumption in the past. Next, Jeremy logs on to the FASB *Accounting Standards Codification* (the "Codification") and begins reading more about this assumption within the stock compensation topic. Before long, he has a basic understanding of the requirements for estimating volatility, and he is pleased to have learned something new in the process of researching this issue.

Continued

After reading this chapter and performing the exercises herein, you will be able to

1. **Describe** the purpose of the Codification, and the meaning of *authoritative*.

2. **Identify** standard setters that have contributed to the current body of authoritative guidance.

3. **Understand** the organization of guidance within the Codification.

4. **Perform** effective Browse searches within the Codification, reviewing all areas of *required reading*.

5. **Search** the Codification using other methods, including the keyword search feature, the Master Glossary, and the Cross Reference feature.

6. **Differentiate** between existing versus pending content, and understand how to interpret transition date guidance.

7. **Recognize** accounting alternative guidance available for private companies.

Learning Objectives

As you begin working with the Codification, your experience may be similar. You may be asked to research topics that you know very little about, and this may initially be uncomfortable; however, users of the Codification quickly learn that research is a skill you learn by doing.

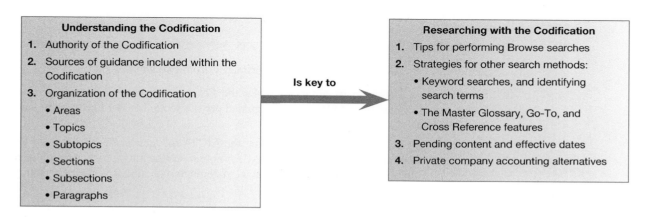

Understanding the Codification
1. Authority of the Codification
2. Sources of guidance included within the Codification
3. Organization of the Codification
   • Areas
   • Topics
   • Subtopics
   • Sections
   • Subsections
   • Paragraphs

Is key to

Researching with the Codification
1. Tips for performing Browse searches
2. Strategies for other search methods:
   • Keyword searches, and identifying search terms
   • The Master Glossary, Go-To, and Cross Reference features
3. Pending content and effective dates
4. Private company accounting alternatives

Organization of This Chapter

This chapter introduces the FASB Codification, including (1) the meaning of the term *authoritative*, (2) what sources of guidance were used to populate the Codification, and (3) how guidance is organized within the Codification. Examples abound in this chapter, as it is critical for beginning researchers to develop a hands-on feel for this important research tool.

Following this introduction, the chapter describes several methods for searching the Codification, including techniques for efficiently performing those searches. The chapter emphasizes that researchers should *Browse* to applicable research topics whenever possible, as this is the method used by research professionals. In our discussion of Browse searches, readers will learn not only how to find information, but also what other sources of *required reading* should be consulted to ensure that a research effort is thorough.

However, there are certainly times when keyword searches are valuable. The chapter describes how to perform such searches and offers readers the opportunity to practice identifying possible search terms. The chapter is rich in information, also covering other search strategies (e.g., the Master Glossary and Cross Reference feature), the role of pending content, and private company alternatives.

As illustrated in the preceding graphic, this chapter emphasizes that understanding how the Codification is organized is key to performing effective research.

WHAT IS THE FASB CODIFICATION?

LO1 Describe the purpose of the Codification, and the meaning of *authoritative*.

The FASB *Accounting Standards Codification* ("ASC" or the "Codification") is considered the primary source of **authoritative**, generally accepted accounting principles (GAAP) for nongovernmental entities. (Guidance from the SEC is also authoritative for public companies.) The Codification became effective in 2009, with the objective of simplifying research. Prior to the issuance of the Codification, accounting guidance in the form of individual standards had piled up for nearly a century. Accounting practitioners often had to search several different standards to find guidance on a single topic. This created the risk that practitioners could miss important sources when searching for guidance. The Codification reduces that risk by organizing accounting guidance by topic, within a single research source.

> What does it mean for the Codification's guidance to be *authoritative*? It means that the Codification establishes GAAP. In order to receive an unmodified (aka, unqualified) audit opinion, U.S. nongovernmental entities must prepare their financial statements in accordance with Codification guidance.

The FASB gets its authority to set GAAP primarily from two sources.

■ First, the SEC, acting in its authority under the Securities Exchange Act and Sarbanes-Oxley, has identified the FASB as the designated private sector standard setter with authority to establish GAAP.[1]

■ Second, in its Code of Professional Conduct, the AICPA recognizes the FASB as the organization with the authority to establish GAAP for nongovernmental entities. An auditor may not issue an unmodified opinion for financial statements containing a material departure from GAAP.[2,3]

Using this authority, the FASB has designated the Codification as the sole source of its authoritative guidance.

The term **nongovernmental entities** encompasses both public and nonpublic (private) entities, as well as not-for-profit entities. However, these entities are not always treated as equals within the Codification. That is, due to resource constraints and often lesser demand for nonpublic entity financial statements, nonpublic entities are exempt from some requirements (such as segment reporting requirements) and are frequently given longer transition periods for adopting new guidance. As noted in Chapter 1, the Private Company Council (PCC) was created in 2012 and advocates for simplified reporting options for private companies. The PCC's work has already led to a handful of private company alternatives available within the Codification.

Accounting guidance for *industries*, including *not-for-profit entities*, also falls within the Codification's authority. As industries often have unique activities and transactions, industry-specific content must be followed *in addition to* the other general requirements of the Codification. That said, in limited cases, industry-specific content may indicate that it should be applied in lieu of a specified topic or paragraphs from the Codification's general requirements. Industries addressed in the Codification include airlines, financial services, not-for-profit entities, real estate, and software.

---

[1] SEC Release No. 33-8221, *Policy Statement: Reaffirming the Status of the FASB as a Designated Private-Sector Standard Setter*. April 25, 2003.

[2] AICPA Code of Professional Conduct, ET 1.320.001 (*Accounting Principles Rule*), par. 01: "A *member* shall not (1) express an opinion or state affirmatively that the *financial statements* or other financial data of any entity are presented in conformity with [GAAP] or (2) state that he or she is not aware of any material modifications that should be made to such statements or data in order for them to be in conformity with [GAAP], if such statements or data contain any departure from an accounting principle promulgated by bodies designated by *Council* to establish such principles that has a material effect on the statements or data taken as a whole...."

[3] AICPA Code of Professional Conduct, Appendix A: "...the FASB...hereby is, designated by this *Council* as the body to establish accounting principles pursuant to the "Accounting Principles Rule...."

Describe what types of entities the Codification applies to. Does it apply equally to these entities? Explain.

_____

_____

[Now YOU Try 2.1]

What Sources of Guidance Were Used to Populate the Codification?

The Codification is an aggregation of many, many accounting standards issued over the course of the past century. These include, for example,[4]

LO2 Identify standard setters that have contributed to the current body of authoritative guidance.

- FASB Statements and Interpretations,
- Emerging Issues Task Force (EITF) Abstracts, and
- AICPA Statements of Position.

Additionally, the Codification includes all still-effective guidance from the two standard-setting bodies that preceded the FASB, namely,

- The Committee on Accounting Procedure (CAP), which issued Accounting Research Bulletins (ARBs) and
- The Accounting Principles Board (APB), which issued APB Opinions.

In 2009, when the guidance from these original standards was moved into the Codification, the original standards were superseded and became *nonauthoritative*. Today, these so-called *pre-Codification standards* still serve a limited role in research. This role is discussed further in Chapter 5, which describes the use of nonauthoritative guidance.

Figure 2-1 depicts the many sources of guidance used to populate the Codification. All guidance in the Codification today has equal authority.

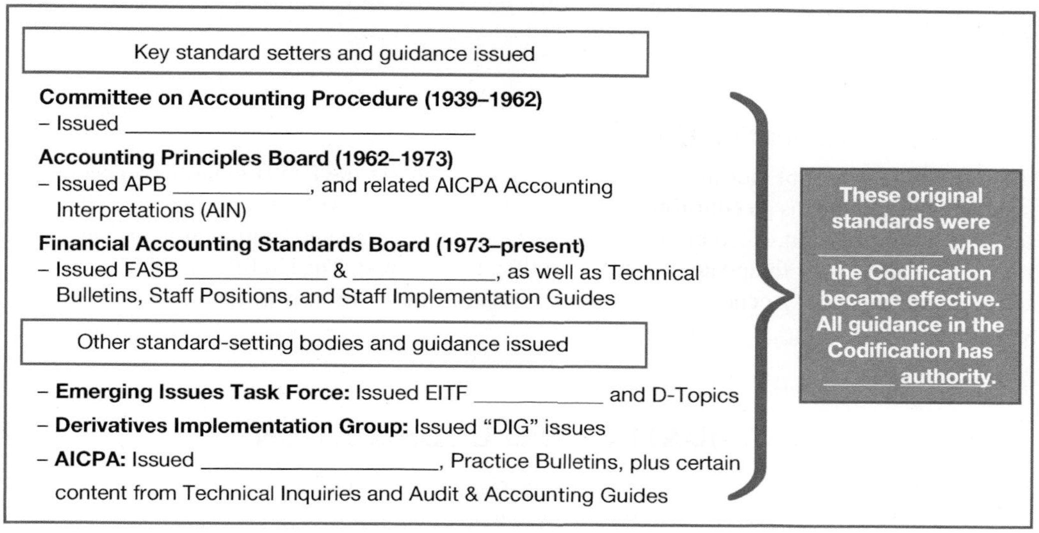

Figure 2-1

Sources of guidance used to populate the Codification

| Key standard setters and guidance issued |

Committee on Accounting Procedure (1939–1962)
– Issued _____

Accounting Principles Board (1962–1973)
– Issued APB _____, and related AICPA Accounting Interpretations (AIN)

Financial Accounting Standards Board (1973–present)
– Issued FASB _____ & _____, as well as Technical Bulletins, Staff Positions, and Staff Implementation Guides

| Other standard-setting bodies and guidance issued |

– **Emerging Issues Task Force:** Issued EITF _____ and D-Topics
– **Derivatives Implementation Group:** Issued "DIG" issues
– **AICPA:** Issued _____, Practice Bulletins, plus certain content from Technical Inquiries and Audit & Accounting Guides

These original standards were _____ when the Codification became effective. All guidance in the Codification has _____ authority.

[4] To view the complete list of guidance used to populate the Codification as of its adoption in 2009, consult the FASB notice *About the Codification,* accessible from the homepage of the Codification.

Now
YOU
Try
2.2

1. Considering the discussion preceding Figure 2-1, fill in the blanks in Figure 2-1 with the types of guidance that were used to populate the Codification.

2. Then, in the blue box in Figure 2-1, fill in the blanks regarding the effects of these standards being moved into the Codification.

Additionally, the Codification includes certain content issued by the Securities and Exchange Commission (SEC), which is authoritative for public companies. Portions of the following SEC guidance have been included within the Codification:

- Regulation S-X (SX)
- Financial Reporting Releases (FRRs)/Accounting Series Releases (ASRs)
- Interpretive Releases (IRs)
- SEC Staff guidance in
  - Staff Accounting Bulletins (SABs)
  - EITF Topic D and SEC Staff Observer comments

However, it's important to understand that not all SEC content has been incorporated within the Codification. Some SEC rules and requirements, such as management's discussion and analysis (MD&A) disclosure requirements, are also authoritative for public companies but are only available at www.sec.gov, and in related accounting research databases.

The role of SEC guidance is further described in the following TIP from the Trenches.

TIP from the Trenches

Students are often confused by the role of SEC guidance in the Codification. Here's what you need to know:

- Guidance from the SEC *is authoritative for public companies*.

- Portions—but not all—of the SEC's guidance have been included in the Codification. Companies can access the full population of SEC guidance at www.sec.gov.

- Nonpublic companies may find it helpful, but are not required, to follow SEC guidance in the Codification.

How is the Codification Updated?

The FASB is responsible for maintaining the Codification. As the FASB issues new accounting standards (referred to as **Accounting Standards Updates**), the FASB amends or adds to the content in the Codification. Accounting Standards Updates are not authoritative in their own right; rather, they serve only to update or amend Codification content. The Codification includes links to proposed and final Accounting Standards Updates; these are also available on the FASB's website (www.fasb.org).

NAVIGATING THE CODIFICATION

LO3 Understand the organization of guidance within the Codification.

In my time as an accounting research instructor, I've noticed a disconnect between how students are *inclined* to research versus the method that *professionals* use to research.

As a beginning researcher who has grown up on Google searches, your tendency may be to perform *keyword searches* in the Codification. By contrast, professional researchers tend to perform *Browse* searches, where the researcher directs the search by navigating to topics that might apply. In fact, the FASB actually *recommends* that researchers should primarily perform Browse searches, as well.[5]

Browse searches are a *user-directed* search. This means that you—as the researcher— would navigate to content in the Codification that you believe might apply. In doing so, you'll have *context* as you perform the search, and will better understand *relationships* between topics in the Codification. You'll also learn more about which paths *don't* work, often an equally important lesson. By contrast, **keyword searches** may dump you off into the middle of guidance that you may not understand, and that may not be relevant. These searches can result in some off-the-wall answers, trust me!

Figure 2-2 illustrates the difference between a Browse and keyword search for guidance on accounts receivable.

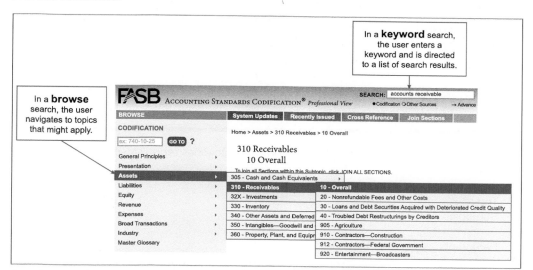

Figure 2-2

Browse versus keyword searches of the Codification

A *key goal* of this chapter is to improve your confidence in performing Browse searches. In order to do this, though, you must first understand how the Codification is organized. To get the most out of this discussion, please log into the Codification and follow along while you read.

How is Information Organized Within the Codification?

The Codification is organized into areas, topics, subtopics, sections, subsections, and paragraphs. These categories are relevant not only to users browsing within the Codification, but also are used in *referencing* the Codification (such as in a memo). References to the Codification are generally presented using the following format:

Topic (XXX) – Subtopic (YY) – Section (ZZ) – Paragraph (PP)[6]

For example, ASC 840-20-30-1 refers to Topic 840 (Leases), Subtopic 20 (Operating Leases), Section 30 (Initial Measurement), Paragraph 1.

Figure 2-3 illustrates the location and purpose of these various categories within the Codification.

---

[5] FASB Accounting Standards Codification, *About the Codification (v4.10)*. December 2014. Page 6.

[6] Notice that areas and subsections aren't included in numerical Codification references.

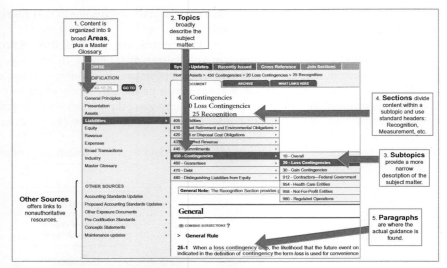

Reproduced with permission of the Financial Accounting Foundation.

**Now
YOU
Try
2.3**

1. Refer to Figure 2-3, then describe the following categories represented in this Codification
    search.
    Area: _____
    Topic: _____
    Subtopic: _____
    Section: _____
    Paragraph: _____

2. What is the ASC reference for this search? Use the format: ASC XXX-YY-ZZ-PP.
    _____

3. Now, notice the nonauthoritative "Other Sources" shown in Figure 2-3 . Name two of these
    resources.
    _____

Let's now take a closer look at each of these categories in the Codification.

Areas and Topics

The Codification includes nine broad **areas**, listed on the left-hand side, from which researchers
can begin a Browse search. Within these areas, guidance is further organized by **topic**. Topics are
generally titled in a way that indicates the subject matter they cover. For example, if you have a
question related to inventory valuation, begin by locating the topic "Inventory."

Certain topics are organized into areas based on their balance sheet category. For example,

- The topic "Inventory" is available under the **Assets** area.
- The topic "Debt" is available under the **Liabilities** area.
- The subtopic "Treasury Stock" is available under the **Equity** area.

Straightforward, yes? However, where would you start a search for guidance on Leases?
This topic is found under **Broad Transactions**. When you think about the different types of leases (e.g., capital, operating), you may notice that leases don't fit neatly into either area—Assets
or Expenses—because they could be classified as either. Therefore, lease guidance is organized
under a transaction-specific topic located in the Broad Transactions area of the Codification.

Where would you find guidance on employee pensions? This topic is found under **Expenses**.
Costs related to paying employees are considered compensation expenses. Therefore, you would

navigate to the Expenses area, then Compensation, to find the topic entitled "Compensation-Retirement Benefits." You'll find that locating the right starting point in the Codification requires a certain amount of trial and error. But after a fairly short period of experience, these starting points will become much more intuitive.

Here is a brief description of other Browse areas:

- The **General Principles** area includes information on broad conceptual matters.
  Example topic: Generally Accepted Accounting Principles
- The **Presentation** area includes topics related to how information is "presented" on the financial statements.
  Example topics: Balance Sheet, Income Statement, and Statement of Cash Flows
- The **Broad Transactions** area includes topics relating to specific transactions, or topics involving multiple financial statement accounts.
  Example topics: Business Combinations, Fair Value Measurement, and Derivatives
- The **Industry** area includes topics where the accounting is unique for an industry or type of activity.
  Example topics: Airlines, Software, and Real Estate
- Finally, the **Revenue** area includes the existing and revised models for revenue recognition, namely, Revenue Recognition (ASC 605) and Revenue from Contracts with Customers (ASC 606).

In particular, familiarize yourself with the list of topics located in the Broad Transactions area (see Figure 2-4). Topics listed under Broad Transactions are subject to specialized, transaction-specific guidance. It is inappropriate to apply general revenue recognition guidance, for example, to a transaction subject to transaction-specific accounting guidance.

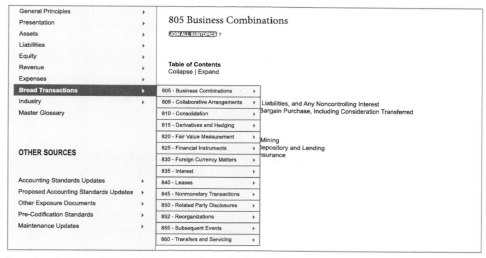

Figure 2-4

Topics available under the Broad Transactions area

Reproduced with permission of the Financial Accounting Foundation.

Consider the list of Broad Transactions topics shown in Figure 2-4 . Which of these topics, if any, have you had experience with, in your previous coursework or work experience? Put a check mark next to any such topics.

Now
YOU
Try
2.4

Finally, notice the link to access the "Master Glossary," shown on the left-hand side of Figure 2-4, immediately following the nine areas of the Codification. The Master Glossary is discussed later in this chapter.

Subtopics

Each topic is broken down into one or several **subtopics**. For example, the Leases topic (**ASC 840**) is broken down into subtopics including Overall ("**10**"), Operating Leases ("**20**"), Capital Leases ("**30**"), Sale-Leaseback Transactions ("**40**"), and so on. It is important to understand how these subtopics interact.

Each topic contains an "Overall" subtopic ("**10**"), which often contains guidance that is pervasive to the topic. When researching accounting issues, take a moment to review guidance contained within the Overall subtopic. For example, even if you know with certainty that you are dealing with an operating lease (addressed in the "Operating Leases" subtopic), you're still responsible for complying with any guidance available under the Overall subtopic as well.

On the other hand, assume you are evaluating an arrangement and need to determine whether it qualifies for operating lease accounting. Since you have not yet determined which subtopic applies to your transaction (capital leases or operating leases), you would begin your search at "Overall." In this case, the Overall subtopic contains guidance for distinguishing between operating and capital leases.

In addition to transaction-specific subtopics, several industry-specific subtopics are available under Leases. Industry-specific content should be followed in addition to the other general content (unless stated otherwise). Assume that a not-for-profit entity is evaluating an operating lease. In this case, the researcher should check not only the "Not-For-Profit" subtopic, but also "Operating Leases" and, of course, "Overall" for guidance related to that transaction.

Now
[YOU]
Try
2.5

Identifying Subtopics to Review

Assume that you are accounting for the sale of a product that has a right of return. You are trying to determine when it is appropriate to recognize revenue from the sale using existing revenue guidance (ASC 605).[7]

Following is an excerpt of subtopics available under the Revenue Recognition topic.

10 - Overall
15 - Products
20 - Services
25 - Multiple-Element Arrangements
28 - Milestone Method
30 - Rights to Use

1. Which two subtopics should you review in order to find potentially applicable guidance? For each response, explain why.

   _____

   _____

2. How would you write the numerical **ASC references** to these two subtopics (for example, ASC XXX-YY)?

   _____

A final note: The subtopics listed in this example may describe accounting treatments that are unfamiliar to you (for example, "Rights to Use"). If a subtopic appears to be potentially relevant based on its title, read the Overview and Background of the subtopic to learn about common arrangements accounted for using this model.

---

[7] Note that the FASB's new revenue guidance (ASC 606, Revenue from Contracts with Customers) will become effective in 2018. This new model is discussed in more detail in Chapter 6.

Sections

Good news—guidance within the Codification is organized very logically, once you become familiar with the **sections**. Sections are used to organize guidance within each subtopic; each subtopic uses the same section titles, to the extent they apply.

Figure 2-5 illustrates a list of sections available under the subtopic Investments—Equity Method and Joint Ventures—Overall. Notice that each section includes a + sign, indicating that a user must click on the section title to be directed to content. Finally, notice that a user's search path is shown at the top of the screenshot. In this case, the search for the Investments topic began in the "Assets" area.

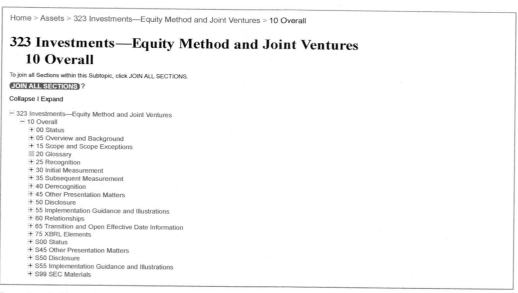

Reproduced with permission of the Financial Accounting Foundation.

Figure 2-5

List of sections available under the Equity Method Investments topic

So, how do you know which section is relevant to your search? Take a moment to understand what information is located within each section, as described below.

Section Number (xxx-yy-00)	Section Name	Description
00	Status	Provides references and links to Accounting Standards Updates that have changed the content of the subtopic.
05	Overview and Background	Provides general overview and background information for subtopics. Describes in general terms what transactions the subtopic is intended to address.
10	Objectives	States the high-level objectives of the subtopic.
15	Scope and Scope Exceptions	Answers the question: Does this guidance *apply* to my transaction? It is assumed that all transactions and entities are subject to guidance unless granted a scope exception.
20	Glossary	Defines all glossary terms used in a subtopic. The Codification also includes a Master Glossary, which includes all glossary terms used within the Codification.
25	Recognition	Describes *what* items can be recorded in the financial statements, *when* an item can be recorded, and *how* an item should be recorded.
30*	Initial Measurement	Describes at what value (i.e., how much?) a financial statement item should be initially recognized. Also known as "day 1" measurement.

Continued

Section Number (xxx-yy-00)	Section Name	Description
35*	Subsequent Measurement	Provides guidance on how to change the value of an item after it is initially recorded. Also known as "day 2" measurement.
40	Derecognition	Describes when and how a recorded item should be removed from the financial statements.
45	Other Presentation Matters	Provides additional guidance on how the transaction should be presented in the financial statements.
50	Disclosure	Provides disclosure requirements for a particular transaction or financial statement item.
55	Implementation Guidance and Illustrations	Includes (1) interpretive guidance describing how the guidance should be applied to specific scenarios and (2) illustrative examples.
60	Relationships	Provides references to other subtopics containing related guidance.
65	Transition and Open Effective Date Information	Provides transition guidance for content that has not yet become fully effective.
70	Grandfathered Guidance	Not generally relevant, but applies to practices that are no longer acceptable for new transactions but that some practitioners continue to apply to transactions that occurred prior to 2009 (when the Codification became effective).
75	XBRL Elements	Contains the XBRL-related elements for this subtopic. XBRL is a reporting format, for the benefit of financial statement users, in which companies "tag" certain financial statement data and information, allowing users to easily compile and compare information across companies.
S-00	"S" sections	Provides select SEC guidance, generally organized into sections similar to those described above. S-sections do not contain the full population of SEC guidance; limited guidance is provided for the convenience of Codification users.

* Note that the revised revenue topic (ASC 606) combines the Initial Measurement and Subsequent Measurement sections and refers to this combined section as *Section 32: Measurement.*

Certain of these sections warrant additional discussion. Following is additional background and tips for reviewing these key sections.

Overview and Background (-05)

The **Overview and Background** section provides users with general knowledge about a Codification topic and highlights types of transactions covered by the guidance. Read this section to obtain a basic understanding of guidance that is new to you.

Try to avoid citing the Overview as a source. For example, this section may say: "This topic introduces the requirement that . . ." Beware: Quoting this sentence is not as impactful as quoting the requirement itself. You would be better off finding the actual requirement in the guidance, for example under a Recognition or Measurement section.

Objectives (-10)

The **Objectives** section answers the question: What were the standard setters hoping to achieve when they created these requirements? Like the Overview section, "Objectives" should not be read as actual requirements; rather, this section provides users with overarching principles to consider when applying guidance requirements.

Scope (-15)

The **Scope** section is one of the most critical sections of an accounting topic. It indicates which transactions or entities are subject to the guidance within the topic. However, beginning researchers often overlook this section, choosing instead to focus on the more "useful" guidance they expect to find under Recognition or Measurement. Pages and pages of professional literature have been devoted to analyzing nuances of the scope guidance contained within the Codification, as recognizing when you are within the scope of a standard is critical to properly applying the guidance.

Scope guidance is commonly presented in one of two ways:

- The guidance may list transactions that are *not* within scope. For example, scope guidance in **ASC 350-10** (Intangibles—Goodwill and Other) states

> **15-3** The guidance in the Intangibles—Goodwill and Other Topic does not apply to the following transactions and activities: a. The accounting at acquisition for goodwill acquired in a business combination. . .

- Alternatively, some scope guidance contains tests to determine what transactions should be included within the scope of the topic. For example, scope guidance in **ASC 840-10** (Leases) states

> **15-6** An arrangement [qualifies as a lease] . . . if any of the following conditions [are] met . . .

Therefore, before you evaluate what type of lease you have (capital or operating), you should first ensure that you pass the test for the arrangement to fall within the scope of lease guidance.

Recognition (-25)

Guidance in the **Recognition** section describes what, when, and how an item should be recorded in the financial statements. Following are examples of each issue:

- *What* should be recorded? Asset retirement obligation (ARO) guidance tells you that the obligation to pay money upon retirement of an asset must be recognized in the financial statements (**ASC 410-20-25**).
- *When* should items be recorded? Revenue recognition guidance tells you whether revenue can be recognized at the time of sale, for a product with a right of return attached (**ASC 605-15-25**).
- *How* should items be recorded? Derivatives guidance states that derivatives should be recognized as assets or liabilities in the balance sheet (**ASC 815-10-25**).

Initial Measurement (-30)

Guidance in the **Initial Measurement** section describes at what value (or for how much?) a financial statement item should be recognized. This value is also known as an item's "day 1" measurement.

For example, in general,

- Inventory is initially measured at cost (**ASC 330-10-30**).
- Guarantee liabilities are initially measured at fair value (**ASC 460-10-30**).
- Property, plant, and equipment is initially measured at historical cost, including interest (**ASC 360-10-30**).

Subsequent Measurement (-35)

Guidance in the **Subsequent Measurement** section describes how to change the value of an item after it is initially recorded. This value is also known as an item's "day 2" measurement.

For example,

- Inventory obsolescence would be considered in determining its "day 2" value (**ASC 330-10-35**).

- Collectibility of an account receivable (for risk of uncollectible accounts) would be considered in determining its "day 2" value (**ASC 310-10-35**).

- Depreciation of property, plant, and equipment is considered in determining its "day 2" value (**ASC 360-10-35**).

Other Presentation Matters (-45)

The **Other Presentation Matters** section provides additional guidance on how a transaction should be presented in the financial statements. This goes beyond the presentation guidance provided under the Recognition section.

For example,

- Treasury Stock—Other Presentation Matters addresses where within the Equity section of the balance sheet to classify repurchased shares, when the repurchased shares may not be retired (**ASC 505-30-45**).

Disclosure (-50)

The **Disclosure** section sets forth required and recommended disclosures for a particular transaction or financial statement item. This section provides disclosures related only to the specific subtopic being addressed; other general disclosure requirements are addressed in Topic **235**, (Notes to Financial Statements).

For example,

- The Inventory topic requires disclosure of "substantial and unusual losses" resulting from application of the *lower of cost or market* rule (**ASC 330-10-50**).

Implementation Guidance and Illustrations (-55)

The **Implementation Guidance and Illustrations** section includes the following, as applicable to each topic:

- Interpretive guidance describing how the guidance should be applied to specific scenarios.
- Examples illustrating application of the guidance.

For example, according to the Recognition guidance in the topic "Loss Contingencies," an estimated loss from a loss contingency must be accrued if the loss is probable and reasonably estimable (**ASC 450-20-25**). The Implementation Guidance section for loss contingencies:

- Identifies additional factors that should be considered in determining whether the "probable" threshold has been met (**ASC 450-20-55**).
- Illustrates appropriate accruals and disclosures for sample loss contingency cases.

SEC Sections (S-00)

SEC sections are identified in the Codification by an "S" that precedes the section reference number. These sections include accounting and reporting guidance that is authoritative for public companies. Often, SEC guidance offers further interpretation of general Codification requirements; for this reason, although the guidance is only required for public companies, public and nonpublic companies alike can benefit from the SEC's interpretations of GAAP.

SEC guidance is generally organized into the same sections as other Codification content. For example, **S-25** offers SEC recognition guidance. However, beware: Creators of the Codification did not want to change content issued by the SEC; therefore, any content not fitting neatly within separate sections (e.g., **S-25** for recognition) is available under **S-99**. Therefore, researchers searching for recognition guidance should check both sections: **S-25** and **S-99**.

The following Now YOU Try is intended to improve your familiarity with *sections* in the Codification.

Understanding Sections

For this example, we'll use a sample of the guidance from possibly one of the most daunting topics in the Codification—Derivatives (**ASC 815**). Your challenge will be to label each excerpt from the Derivatives topic with the **section** in which the excerpt is located. Then, identify the likely **paragraph number** for this excerpt (presented as Section XX – Paragraph YY).

As you'll notice in this example, the guidance within a topic becomes much more approachable once you understand how it is organized.

Sections to select from: Scope, Recognition, Initial Measurement, Subsequent Measurement, Other Presentation Matters, Disclosure, or Implementation Guidance.

Paragraphs to select from (from ASC 815-10): par. **15-83**, **25-1**, **30-1**, **35-1** and **35-2**, **45-4**, **50-1**, **55-1**.

		Section?	Likely Para. Number?
1	An entity shall recognize all of its derivative instruments in its statement of financial position as either assets or liabilities depending on the rights or obligations under the contracts.		
2	Definition of a derivative instrument A derivative instrument is a financial instrument or other contract with all of the following characteristics. . . .		
3	An entity with derivative instruments . . . shall disclose information to enable users of the financial statements to understand all of the following: a. How and why an entity uses derivative instruments (or such nonderivative instruments) b. How derivative instruments (or such nonderivative instruments) and related hedged items are accounted for under Topic 815 . . .		
4	This section provides guidance on the following implementation matters: a. Determining whether a contract is within the scope of this Subtopic b. Unit of accounting—a transferrable option is considered freestanding, not embedded c. Definition of derivative instrument d. Instruments not within scope		
5	All derivative instruments shall be measured initially at fair value.		
6	1. All derivative instruments shall be measured subsequently at fair value. 2. . . . . Except as noted in the following paragraph, the gain or loss on a derivative instrument not designated as a hedging instrument shall be recognized currently in earnings.		
7	Unless the conditions in paragraph 210-20-45-1 [Balance Sheet > Offsetting] are met, the fair value of derivative instruments in a loss position shall not be offset against the fair value of derivative instruments in a gain position.		

Chapters 6, 7, and 8 of this book provide additional discussion and examples of applying section guidance in the Codification, in particular, scope, recognition, and measurement guidance.

Subsections and Paragraphs

Paragraphs are where the actual guidance is found within the Codification. Paragraphs are sometimes organized into groups, called **subsections**. For example, within the Leases topic, under the Recognition section, you'll find a subsection containing guidance for Lessees, and a separate subsection containing guidance for Lessors. Whenever you find a paragraph with content that appears relevant to your search, be certain that you understand the context. That is, be sure you are reading guidance within a subsection that is relevant to your issue.

For example, assume you word search (ctrl + f) within the Leases topic for "contingent rent" and land in section "c" below.

Broad Transactions > Leases > Overall > Recognition
Lessees
a. Lessee application of lease classification criteria
b. Indemnifications
c. **Contingent rentals**
d. Lessee classification of a lease involving real estate
Lessors
a. Lessor application of lease classification criteria
b. Transfer-of-ownership criterion—lease involving integral equipment
c. . . .

Before you share this paragraph with your supervisor, wait! Consider the context. What if your company is actually the lessor in this arrangement? To avoid errors, be sure to scroll up and down on the page to understand all related section and subsection headers when you find guidance that appears to be on point.

In addition to understanding what subsection you are in within the guidance, you must also pay attention to *paragraph groups*, indicated by a header and **>>** notations. For example, paragraphs could be organized as follows:

Issue header
>Issue 1
>>Subissue A
>>Subissue B
>Issue 2

Assume that you encounter paragraphs organized in this fashion, and the guidance in Subissue B is relevant to your research. Since Subissues A and B are extensions of the guidance in Issue 1, it would not be appropriate to follow the guidance in Subissue B without also reading Issue 1. You would not be required to read Subissue A if it does not appear to be applicable.

Now
YOU
Try
2.7

Subsections and Paragraphs

Following is an example from **ASC 820** (Fair Value Measurement), showing the organization of paragraphs within the Subsequent Measurement section.
> Definition of Fair Value

>>   The Asset or Liability
>>   The Transaction
>>   The Principal (or Most Advantageous) Market
>>   Market Participants
>>   The Price
>>   Application to Nonfinancial Assets

>>>   **Highest and Best Use for Nonfinancial Assets**
>>>   Valuation Premise for Nonfinancial Assets

>>   Application to Liabilities and Instruments Classified in a Reporting Entity's Shareholders' Equity

Questions:

1. If you find guidance you are looking for under the header "Highest and Best Use for Nonfinancial Assets," what two other issues should you also read?

_____

_____

2. Explain.

_____

_____

If you lose track of where you are in the Codification, you can hover your mouse over the paragraph number to be reminded of the subtopic and section number for your current location.

For example, by hovering your mouse over par. 15-6 (circled in the illustration), you'll see the "Currently Viewing" screen, which describes your location.

$\begin{bmatrix} \text{TIP} \end{bmatrix}$ from the Trenches

> **Other Considerations**

>> **Significant Influence**

15-6)Ability to exercise significant influence over including the following:

Currently Viewing:

323 Investments—Equity Method and Joint Ventures
  10 Overall
    15 Scope and Scope Exceptions
    General
      > Other Considerations
        >> Significant Influence

Reproduced with permission of the Financial Accounting Foundation (circle and cursor image added).

Let's look now at some tips for performing effective, and efficient, Browse searches.

TIPS FOR PERFORMING BROWSE SEARCHES

Now that you have a basic understanding of how the Codification is organized, you are capable of performing basic searches using the **Browse** feature.

As noted previously, the Browse feature is essentially a user-directed search. You, as the user, will click through a series of topics and subtopics that will, with a little experience, take you right to the appropriate guidance for a given transaction. As your understanding of the Codification increases, your efficiency in performing these searches will improve.

The starting point in a Browse search is to locate the specific topic and subtopic that you are searching for. See Figure 2-6, illustrating a researcher browsing to the revised Revenue from Contracts with Customers—Overall subtopic in the Codification.

LO4 Perform effective Browse searches within the Codification, reviewing all areas of *required reading*.

Join All Sections

Once you're in the appropriate subtopic, I suggest that you click on the **Join All Sections** button. This button displays all subtopic content on one page and allows you to navigate more easily through the subtopic.

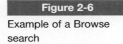

Figure 2-6

Example of a Browse search

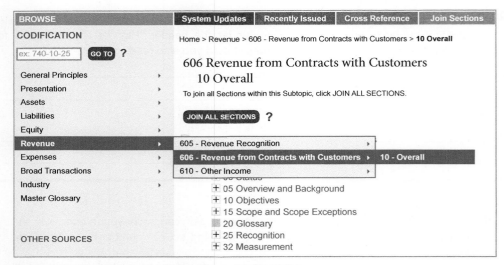

Reproduced with permission of the Financial Accounting Foundation.

For example, assume you are looking for the term *collectibility*, and you know the term is somewhere within this revenue subtopic (ASC 606-10). Selecting "Join All Sections" puts the full content of the subtopic on one page, allowing you to search the full subtopic for this term using "ctrl + F" (find).

Now
YOU
Try
2.8

Circle the "Join All Sections" button that appears in Figure 2-6. Remember, this is the button you'll click on once you navigate to a subtopic.

Navigating a Subtopic, Considering All Areas of "Required Reading"

You are now ready to begin reviewing the subtopic for relevant guidance. As discussed earlier in this chapter, the first section you should read, if you are unfamiliar with a subtopic, is the Overview section (05). Next, consult the Scope section (15) to confirm that your specific transaction is within the scope of this guidance. Then, think about what question you are asking: Is it about Recognition? Initial Measurement?

Go to the appropriate section, and find guidance applicable to your search question. Let's assume that relevant guidance was available in par. 1 under Recognition. You've found your answer; you're done, right? Not so fast.

There are several important additional steps that you should "check off" before you can be confident that your research effort was thorough. In particular, treat any relevant Implementation Guidance and SEC content (particularly for public companies) as required reading. Often, the interpretive guidance located in these sections can confirm or change your view of how the guidance should be applied. Also, remember that these sections are equally as authoritative as other sections within the topic.

Figure 2-7 illustrates the following steps:

1. First, confirm that your transaction (or entity) is within the scope of the guidance you are searching.

2. Next, find guidance that appears to respond to your search question by navigating to the section that you anticipate is most relevant. For example, after confirming that your transaction is within the scope of a topic, head straight to "Recognition" for questions about recognizing an asset.

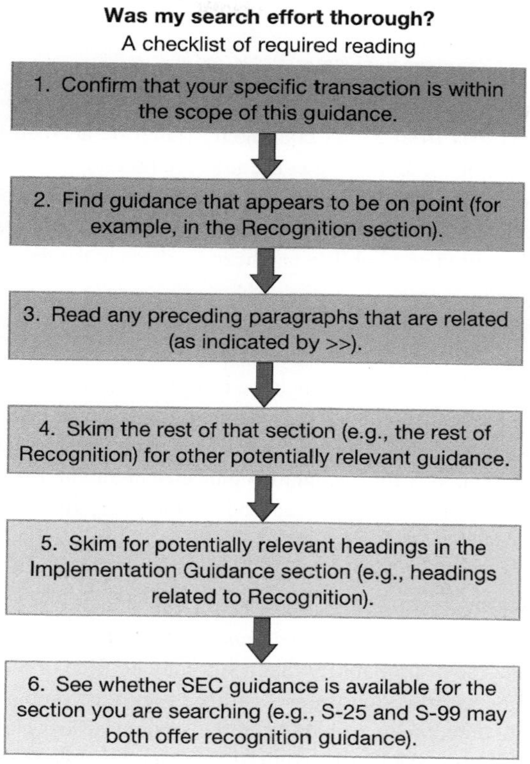

Was my search effort thorough?
A checklist of required reading

> 1. Confirm that your specific transaction is within the scope of this guidance.
>
> ↓
>
> 2. Find guidance that appears to be on point (for example, in the Recognition section).
>
> ↓
>
> 3. Read any preceding paragraphs that are related (as indicated by >>).
>
> ↓
>
> 4. Skim the rest of that section (e.g., the rest of Recognition) for other potentially relevant guidance.
>
> ↓
>
> 5. Skim for potentially relevant headings in the Implementation Guidance section (e.g., headings related to Recognition).
>
> ↓
>
> 6. See whether SEC guidance is available for the section you are searching (e.g., S-25 and S-99 may both offer recognition guidance).

Figure 2-7

A checklist of required reading

3. Ensure that you have read any preceding paragraphs that are related. In doing so, pay attention to the hierarchy of paragraphs, indicated by > >, as discussed earlier in this chapter.

4. Fully skim the rest of the section you are searching (for example, the Recognition section), to ensure that you have considered all relevant guidance. Subsequent paragraphs within that section may offer additional detail or situation-specific guidance that you should consider. Pay particular attention to boldfaced headings used to organize paragraphs, as they can assist you in quickly determining whether groups of paragraphs are potentially relevant.

5. Next, review the list of topics included within the Implementation Guidance section (55). In some cases, the first paragraph of the Implementation Guidance section includes a list of the topics it addresses; in other cases, you may have to skim through the guidance, reviewing for potentially relevant headings. For example, look for headings related to recognition.

6. Finally, particularly for public companies, scan the S-sections to check for relevant SEC guidance.

Be patient; it may initially be frustrating to use the Browse feature as your primary means for searching the Codification. However, it is essential that you learn how the guidance is organized. You will become more efficient with practice.

The following example illustrates how Implementation Guidance can assist in interpreting content within the Codification.

EXAMPLE

Understanding Why Implementation Guidance (Section 55) Is Integral to Your Browse Search

Assume that a customer slipped and fell in ABC Grocery, but the customer has *not yet filed suit.* Should ABC Grocery record a loss, due to the possibility that the customer will file a lawsuit? If the customer does file suit, the amount of loss is expected to be approximately $100,000.

Continued

Continued from previous page

ASC 450-20 (Loss Contingencies) states:

> **25-2** An estimated loss from a loss contingency shall be accrued by a charge to income if both of the following conditions are met:
> a. Information available before the financial statements are issued or are available to be issued . . . indicates that it is probable that an asset had been impaired or a liability had been incurred at the date of the financial statements . . .
> b. The amount of loss can be reasonably estimated.

The preceding guidance states that a loss should be recorded if it is *probable* that a liability has been incurred; this determination involves judgment. Experienced researchers know that additional guidance, when available, can assist in framing judgmental issues. After finding this guidance under Recognition, look for Recognition guidance in the Implementation Guidance section (55) of the Codification. There, you can find the following guidance even more specific to this issue:

> Assessing Probability of the Incurrence of a Loss (ASC 450-20)
> **55-14** With respect to *unasserted claims and assessments*, an entity must determine the degree of probability that a suit may be filed or a claim or assessment may be asserted and the possibility of an unfavorable outcome. If an unfavorable outcome is probable and the amount of loss can be reasonably estimated, accrual of a loss is required by paragraph **450-20-25-2**. [Italicized emphasis added].

Armed with this guidance, management should consider the probability that a suit will be filed, as well as the probability of an unfavorable outcome. Both guidance references (par. **25-2** and par. **55-14**) should be cited in a memo documenting the position taken. Note: Even if no accrual is made, it is a best practice to document the basis for such a judgment.

Next, let's look at an example illustrating how—particularly for public companies—reviewing SEC content is critical to carefully researching an issue.

EXAMPLE

Understanding Why SEC Content (Section "S") Can Be Integral to Your Browse Search

Consider the following requirements from the Codification's existing revenue guidance regarding when revenue can be recognized.

ASC 605-10-25-1 (Recognition) requires that revenue, in order to be recognized, must be both realized or realizable and earned.

ASC 605-10-S99-1 (SEC guidance) states: "The staff [of the SEC] believes that revenue generally is realized or realizable and earned when all of the following criteria are met: . . ."

The SEC guidance goes on to list the following criteria for revenue recognition:

- Persuasive evidence of an arrangement exists.
- Delivery has occurred or services have been rendered.
- The seller's price to the buyer is fixed or determinable.
- Collectibility is reasonably assured.

If a public company is documenting its policy for recognizing revenue, the documentation would be lacking if it did not include consideration of both sources of literature just shown.

Notice how the preceding SEC guidance came from Section **S-99**? As noted previously, SEC content not clearly fitting within a single section (such as **S-25** for recognition) is available under **S-99**. A researcher in this case should check for SEC recognition guidance in both Sections: **S-25** and **S-99**.

---

1. Describe how, in the preceding contingent liability example, the Implementation Guidance (Section **55**) goes beyond the Recognition guidance (Section **25**).

   _____

   _____

2. What four conditions for revenue recognition are provided in the SEC content, but are not in the FASB content? Explain how this guidance might be relevant to a public company, and to a nonpublic company.

   _____

   _____

   _____

   _____

[Now
YOU
Try
2.9]

OTHER SEARCH METHODS

In addition to Browse searches, several other methods are available for searching the Codification:

LO5 Search the Codification using other methods, including the keyword search feature, the Master Glossary, and the Cross Reference feature.

1. Search by **keyword**, using the Search/Advanced Search feature.
2. Jump directly to guidance using the **ASC reference number** (e.g., type in **ASC 820-10-30-1** to jump directly to fair value measurement guidance).
3. **Cross-reference** by the "historical" GAAP designation (e.g., type in **FAS 157** to be directed to **ASC 820**).
4. Search using the **Master Glossary**, finding a keyword of interest and clicking on that word to be directed to the guidance.

These search methods are discussed further in the sections that follow.

Keyword Searches

A **keyword search** (i.e., a text search) is most useful when you are looking for a specific term in the guidance, or when you are uncertain where you would begin a browse search. For example, assume you want to find guidance on "involuntary conversions." Unless you have experience with this topic, you would likely not know that this term is addressed primarily in revenue recognition guidance. In this case, a keyword search would be appropriate.

When a researcher performs a keyword search, the results of the search are listed by topic and include an excerpt from the guidance containing the term. As this type of search allows researchers to see a term in multiple contexts, keyword searches can be a useful brainstorming tool. Researchers can choose to pursue one or several search results, or the results can be used to generate ideas for other search terms that might be effective.

Figure 2-8 illustrates a simple search for the term "involuntary conversion" (see search bar at top right). Notice that seven search results were found, in areas including Revenue Recognition, Liabilities, and Broad Transactions. Researchers seeking to narrow instances of this term to a single area (or multiple areas)—or by related term—can use the "Narrow" option shown on the right-hand side of Figure 2-8.

Figure 2-8

Search results for the term "involuntary conversion"

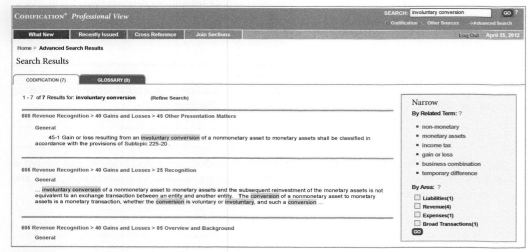

Reproduced with permission of the Financial Accounting Foundation.

Users can choose to conduct either simple or advanced searches. A simple search involves a simple empty search bar, similar to Google. This is the type of search illustrated in Figure 2-8. Note the following about the simple keyword search:[8]

- Multiple terms: Entering **troubled debt** is equivalent to searching for **troubled** and **debt**.
- Phrases: To search for an exact phrase, use quotes. For example, entering **"development stage"** returns results about **Development Stage Entities**.
- Singular/plural: A search for either **intangible** or **intangibles** will yield the same results.

An advanced search offers additional search options. For example, users can enter a phrase, such as **involuntary conversion** and can elect to search for

- "any" words (results will display any guidance containing the word **involuntary** OR **conversion**),
- "all" (results will display any guidance containing both **involuntary** AND **conversion**),
- "exact phrase," or
- words that occur within "n" words of each other (for example, users can specify that **involuntary** and **conversion** must be within five words of each other).

The advanced search feature also allows users to choose a specific area to search; for example, a user could specify upfront that search results for **involuntary conversion** must be from the Revenue area. Figure 2-9 illustrates an advanced search for the exact phrase **involuntary conversion**, limited by area.

---

[8] Source: FASB Codification, Search Help. Accessed April 2015.

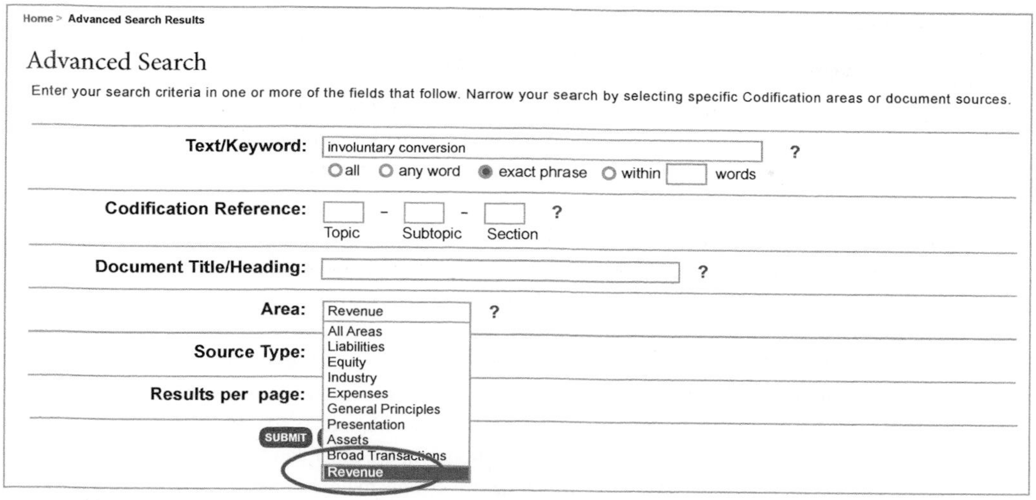

Figure 2-9

Advanced search for an exact phrase, limited by area

Reproduced with permission of the Financial Accounting Foundation.

Identifying Search Terms

Keyword searches are based on specific language. Therefore, you must use proper **search terms** (terms that are actually found in the guidance), or you will not find the appropriate guidance.

Identifying search terms can be a sort of brainstorming exercise. Write down all possible terms that you think might be useful, including words that may be synonymous with other search terms you have identified. With time, you'll learn the terms used most commonly in the accounting literature.

After entering a search term, a researcher will be directed to a search results page. At this point, a researcher can choose to pursue one or several search results, or the researcher could use the results to generate ideas for other search terms that might be effective.

Following are steps a researcher can take to determine whether a result he or she has pursued is relevant (and if not, what to do):

1. If you see a paragraph in the search results that appears to be directly on point, follow your instinct! Read that paragraph and determine whether it is responsive to your question.

2. If, however, the search results just lead you to a topic but no perfect paragraph, begin by reviewing the Overview and Background section of that topic. See whether the guidance appears to be on the right track for your search.

3. Next, review the scope section for the topic. Is your issue within the scope of this guidance?

4. As you perform the preceding steps, take note of other useful terms, or links to other related guidance. Perhaps these clues will lead to more relevant guidance, if what you're reading is not already on point.

5. Finally, if you have hit a "dead-end" (the guidance doesn't appear to apply, and you have not successfully identified alternate search terms), scroll down to Section **60** of that topic (Relationships). This section includes links to other related topics; reviewing this list might trigger ideas, as well.

Following are two examples illustrating the brainstorming exercise involved in identifying search terms. Note that a "researchable question" has been identified for each situation below. Researchable questions are discussed further in Chapter 3.

EXAMPLE ———————————————————————————————————————

Situation 1:

Company A (your company) has acquired 51% of the common stock of Company B.

- Researchable question: How should Company A account for its investment in Company B?
- Possible search terms: equity investment, acquisition, investment, equity method, consolidation, consolidate, majority owner

Commentary—Situation 1:

Very little information is given about this situation; additional facts would be needed before an accounting position could be selected. That said, we have sufficient information to brainstorm some possible initial searches.

Unfortunately, beginning researchers often have to learn through trial and error which search paths are most effective for a given situation. For example, guidance on *whether* to consolidate an investee is located under the topic "Consolidation" (under the "Broad Transactions" area). A search for the term "acquisition," on the other hand, will generally land you in business combinations guidance, which describes *how* to consolidate a majority-owned subsidiary. In this case, therefore, a search for "consolidation" would be more effective than guidance on "acquisitions," since you need to decide whether consolidation is required.

A search for the terms "majority" or "majority owner" is likely to lead a researcher to click on the Consolidation topic, so these terms would be effective. However, a search for the term "equity investment" or "equity method" will land researchers in guidance that does not apply, given that this situation involves a purchase of greater than 50% of the outstanding common shares of an entity. Reviewing the Overview or the Scope guidance in these topics will indicate to the researcher that another search term should be tried.

With a little experience, you will learn to browse right to the "Consolidation" topic for this issue. This is appropriate because a purchase of greater than 50% of an entity's common stock generally results in consolidation (assuming the investee's capital structure is fairly simple). The Consolidation topic also addresses the accounting for an investor's involvement in more complex "variable interest entities."

EXAMPLE ———————————————————————————————————————

Situation 2:

Company A (original debtor) has paid $10 million to Company B to assume its liability to pay off a 10-year loan obligation, payable to Bank. Bank agrees to release Company A from its payment obligation, but only on the condition that Company B assumes the obligation and that Company A will still pay if Company B defaults.

- Researchable question: Can Company A remove the loan obligation to Bank from its financial statements?
- Possible search terms: debt extinguishment, liability extinguishment, liability derecognition, secondary liability, guarantee, primary obligor, secondarily liable

Commentary—Situation 2:

Ultimately, the most relevant guidance for this research question would be found by keying "secondarily liable" into the search bar. Researchers would be directed to the derecognition section of the Liability Extinguishments topic (**ASC 405-20-40**), which indicates that the original debtor becomes a guarantor and must recognize a guarantee obligation.

Researchers entering "debt extinguishment" into the search bar will be led to guidance that includes links to the liability extinguishments topic; however, researchers unfortunately might overlook those links and get stuck reading a lot of guidance that does not apply.

A search of the term "guarantee" would result in guidance indicating how to value a guarantee, but such guidance doesn't indicate whether this arrangement should be recorded as a guarantee. A link to liability extinguishment guidance is available in the Relationships section of the guarantee topic.

The lesson: Often, even using the wrong search term initially will lead you to the right answer eventually. Just keep following all "leads" that appear to be potentially relevant.

Do not try to fit a round peg into a square hole; if it seems like the guidance page you are reading isn't clear in responding to your question, look for links to related content or try another search term. This is all part of the process; you will become more efficient with time.

Identifying Search Terms

Now
YOU
Try
2.10

Read the following practice scenarios, then brainstorm search terms you would use to look for relevant guidance. Identify at least two possible search terms.

1. A company ships its widgets to a customer on December 31 but has not yet collected payment from the customer. The customer has promised to pay within 30 days but has never purchased goods from the company before.

   Possible search terms to use in researching the company's accounting for the sales?

   a. _____

   b. _____

2. A customer is suing the local grocery store for a slip-and-fall incident. The grocery store believes the lawsuit will likely be considered frivolous and rejected by the court.

   Possible search terms to use in determining whether the grocery store should record or disclose the matter?

   a. _____

   b. _____

3. An investor is suing a corporation that has just absorbed another entity in a merger. The investor is alleging that the corporation overstated the values of certain equity investments on its balance sheet, which were acquired during the merger.

   Possible search terms to use in determining how the corporation should have valued the acquired investments?

   a. _____

   b. _____

TIP from the Trenches

Search terms are obviously necessary for performing keyword searches, but they have other uses, as well. For example, search terms can be used to quickly find key guidance on a page during a Browse search (using the "find word on page" shortcut, or "ctrl + f"). Search terms also can help a researcher maintain focus during Codification searches, as beginning researchers can occasionally start reading guidance and lose sight of what they were looking for. Keep your search terms at top of mind to maintain efficiency and focus during a search for guidance.

Caution: In some circumstances, keyword searches are inefficient (which is why, when possible, browse searches are preferable). Assume you need guidance on accounts receivable. A simple search for this term returns 47 search results, as shown in Figure 2-10. Notice how these search results would have a researcher running every which way, trying to identify the most relevant guidance. Of course, a researcher could "Narrow" the search by area or related term, but wouldn't a browse search for this topic be much simpler?

Figure 2-10

First four search results
for the term "accounts
receivable"

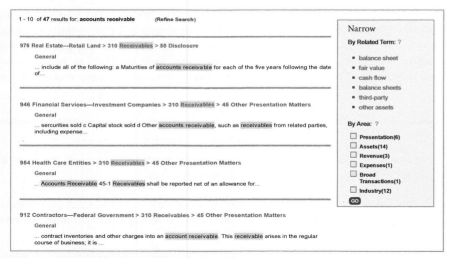

Reproduced with permission of the Financial Accounting Foundation.

Now YOU Try 2.11

1. When is it most appropriate to use the keyword search feature?

_____

_____

2. If you're working with a search term that leads you to inapplicable guidance, what strategies might you use to identify other possible search terms?

_____

_____

Next, let's look at another search option.

Search by ASC Reference Number

Researchers can use the "Go To" feature to jump directly to specific content, by typing in the content's ASC reference number. This feature can be useful to a researcher who wants to verify a particular reference in the guidance, or for experienced researchers who have certain search paths memorized (e.g., many researchers now instinctively know that entering ASC 606-10 will take them to the revised guidance for revenue recognition)!

Figure 2-11 illustrates the use of this feature. In this example, entering **606-10-25-1** in the box at top left takes the researcher directly to revised revenue guidance.

Figure 2-11

Using the Go-To box

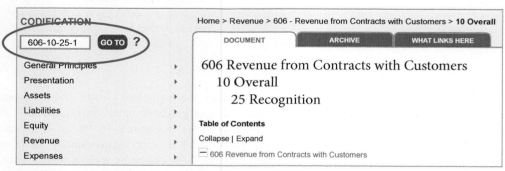

Reproduced with permission of the Financial Accounting Foundation.

Cross Reference Tab

The **Cross Reference** feature allows users to link Codification topics with the original standards that were used to populate the Codification. Users can either key in a Codification topic to find the original standard number, or they can key in the number of an original standard and be directed to the corresponding Codification topic. For example, entering ASC Topic No. 820-10 (Fair Value Measurement) into a cross-reference search directs the user to FASB Statement No. 157, *Fair Value Measurements* (**FAS 157**), as illustrated in Figure 2-12.

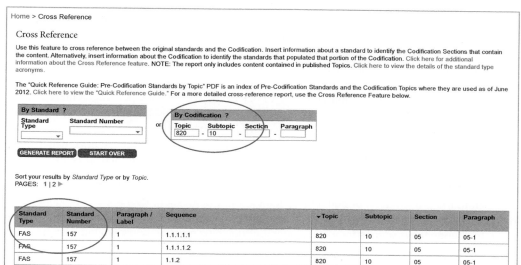

Figure 2-12

Using the Cross Reference feature to find the original standard corresponding to ASC 820-10

The FASB continues to make its original pronouncements available on its website, as well as through a link included in the Codification (to "Pre-Codification Standards"). The abbreviations used in referring to original pronouncements are listed under the **acronyms** link within the Cross Reference page. Chapter 5 discusses circumstances in which it can be valuable to reference pre-Codification standards.

Master Glossary

The **Master Glossary** is another useful starting point for researchers seeking further information about a specific term. Click on any term in the Master Glossary, and you will be directed to where that term is used within the Codification. Beware that some terms listed in the Glossary are listed more than once, and the definitions may differ slightly depending on what topic they are used in. Review all duplicate terms before deciding which context best fits the topic you are searching. Individual topics also include Glossaries (Section **20**), which define terms specific to that topic.

> Including a defined term in your research paper? If so, it is generally best to reference the definition in the context of the appropriate Codification topic. For example, if you are performing research on a probable loss, cite **ASC 450-20-20** (Loss Contingencies—Glossary) as your source for the definition of *probable*, rather than citing the Master Glossary as your source.

$$\begin{bmatrix} \text{TIP} \end{bmatrix}$$ from the Trenches

Now, let's take a moment to discuss another area that can cause confusion for beginning researchers: pending content in the Codification.

PENDING CONTENT AND EFFECTIVE DATES

LO6 Differentiate between existing versus pending content, and understand how to interpret transition date guidance.

What is "Pending Content"?

When new guidance (that is, an "Accounting Standards Update") is issued by the FASB, it is added to the Codification as **pending content**.

Pending content shows up in a box, immediately following existing paragraphs in the Codification. Often, pending content has the same paragraph number as the content just above it, meaning that it will replace that guidance once it becomes fully effective.

This process can take up to several years, given that companies can have different fiscal year-ends, and given that small or nonpublic entities are occasionally granted delayed effective dates. Once the pending content becomes fully effective, the previous (nonboxed) guidance will be removed from the Codification and the revised content will remain.[9]

If you see pending content directly under a paragraph that appears to be relevant to your research, click on the "Transition Guidance" link provided next to the pending content paragraph. Carefully read the transition guidance to determine whether the pending content will be effective for the transaction you are accounting for. If so, you should read the pending content in lieu of the identical paragraph number that precedes it. If pending content is in addition to existing content (for example, if there is existing content labeled par. 1-2, and pending content begins at par. 3), then consider whether this guidance should be followed in addition to existing content.

Now YOU Try 2.12

To illustrate the presentation of pending content in the Codification, take a look at Figure 2-13, featuring guidance from ASC 810-10 (Consolidation). This topic was recently amended, in particular to change the guidance for when limited partnerships must be consolidated. Using Figure 2-13, respond to the following questions.

Figure 2-13

Pending content from ASC 810-10

General

⊕ COMBINE SUBSECTIONS **?** ✚ RELATED EXPOSURE DRAFTS **?**

25-1   Consolidation is appropriate if a reporting entity has a controlling financial interest in another entity and a specific scope exception does not apply (see Section 810-10-15). The usual condition for a controlling financial interest is ownership of a majority voting interest, but in some circumstances control does not rest with the majority owner.

Pending Content: ?
Transition Date: *(P) December 16, 2015; (N) December 16, 2016* | **Transition Guidance:** 810-10-65-7
For legal entities other than limited partnerships, consolidation is appropriate if a reporting entity has a controlling financial interest in another entity and a specific scope exception does not apply (see Section 810-10-15). The usual condition for a controlling financial interest is ownership of a majority voting interest, but in some circumstances control does not rest with the majority owner.

25-1A

Pending Content: ?
Transition Date: *(P) December 16, 2015; (N) December 16, 2016* | **Transition Guidance:** 810-10-65-7
Given the purpose and design of limited partnerships, kick-out rights through voting interests are analogous to voting rights held by shareholders of a corporation. Consolidation is appropriate if a reporting entity has a controlling financial interest in a limited partnership and a specific scope exception does not apply (see Section 810-10-15). The usual condition for a controlling financial interest in a limited partnership is ownership of a majority of the limited partnership's kick-out rights through voting interests, but, in some circumstances, control does not rest with the majority owner.

Reproduced with permission of the Financial Accounting Foundation.

Questions:

1. Which pending content guidance, paragraph 25-1 or 25-1A, will *replace* (aka, supersede) existing requirements? Which is *adding* new guidance? Explain.

_____

_____

2. Where in this screenshot would a researcher click to find out when the boxed content will become effective?

_____

---

[9] FASB *Accounting Standards Codification, About the Codification* (v4.10). December 2014. Page 30.

Understanding Effective Dates

As the FASB issues new guidance, it is common for that guidance to have a delay between its issuance date and its **effective date**. This gives companies time to review and implement the new guidance. Here are three examples of how effective dates are commonly worded:

a. For fiscal years ending after December 15, 20x1

b. For fiscal years beginning after December 15, 20x1

c. For fiscal quarters beginning after December 15, 20x1

Each implies quite a different time frame. For example, assume it is the year 20x1.

■ A company with a calendar year-end would have to immediately apply any new guidance with the effective date described in (*a*) above (i.e., to its 12/31/20x1 financial statements).

■ On the other hand, if new guidance was issued with the effective date described in (*b*), the company would first reflect the new guidance in its 12/31/20x2 financial statements.

To check your understanding of the effective date in (*c*) above, see the **Now YOU Try** that follows.

Now
YOU
Try
2.13

1. Now assume that guidance has been issued with the effective date described in point *c* above. When would a company with a calendar year-end first have to reflect the new guidance in its financial statements?

Let's look now at the transition guidance provided for ASC 810-10, shown in Figure 2-14.

> **Transition Related to Accounting Standards Update No. 2015-02, *Consolidation (Topic 810): Amendments to the Consolidation Analysis***
>
> 65-7   The following represents the transition and effective date information related to Accounting Standards Update No. 2015-02, *Consolidation (Topic 810): Amend*
>
> a.   The pending content that links to this paragraph shall be effective as follows:
>
>   1. For public business entities, for fiscal years, and for interim periods within those fiscal years, beginning after December 15, 2015.
>
>   2. For all other entities, for fiscal years beginning after December 15, 2016, and for interim periods within fiscal years beginning after December 15, 2017.

Reproduced with permission of the Financial Accounting Foundation.

Figure 2-14

Transition guidance for recent changes to ASC 810-10

2. First, what *section* was this screenshot taken from (for example, Section 25—Recognition)?

3. Assume your client is a public company with a calendar year-end. In what period must the company begin applying the pending content for ASC 810-10? Explain.

PRIVATE COMPANY ACCOUNTING ALTERNATIVES IN THE CODIFICATION

Finally, recall that the Private Company Council (PCC) has been advising the FASB on areas within existing U.S. GAAP, and in the FASB's current projects, that could be simplified for private companies. The work of this council has led to an increasing number of **private company alternatives** becoming available within the Codification. Figure 2-15 illustrates scope guidance for one such alternative; this particular alternative allows private companies to *amortize goodwill*, as opposed to performing costly annual impairment tests (ASC 350-20).

LO7 Recognize accounting alternative guidance available for private companies.

Figure 2-15

Private company accounting alternative from ASC 350-20 (Goodwill)

Accounting Alternative

○ COMBINE SUBSECTIONS **?**

15-4

Pending Content: ?

Transition Date: *(P) December 16, 2014; (N) December 16, 2014* | **Transition Guidance: 350-20-65-2**
A private company may make an accounting policy election to apply the accounting alternative in this Subtopic. The g[...]
following transactions or activities:

    a. Goodwill that an entity recognizes in a business combination in accordance with Subtopic 805-30 after it has [...]

    b. Amounts recognized as goodwill in applying the equity method of accounting in accordance with Topic 323 or in[...]
    recognized by entities that adopt fresh-start reporting in accordance with Topic 852 on reorganizations.

Reproduced with permission of the Financial Accounting Foundation.

As with other standards, unique transition guidance applies to each newly issued private company alternative. Private companies can elect to apply one, all, or none of the available alternatives.

Now
[YOU]
Try
2.14

Brainstorm: What is one potential downside of a private company electing an accounting alternative? One potential upside?

_____

_____

CHAPTER SUMMARY

The FASB Codification is the essential source of authoritative accounting guidance for nongovernmental entities. SEC content is also authoritative for public companies. The Codification brings together many individual standards issued over the years in a single research database where all content has equal authority. The FASB continues to update the Codification today, through the issuance of *Accounting Standards Updates*.

    Content within the Codification is organized by topic, and then further segregated into subtopics and sections. For a research effort to be thorough, certain of these sections must be included in every search. Although several methods are available for searching the Codification, users will likely find that user-directed "Browse" searches are most efficient. With practice, you will become increasingly comfortable searching the Codification.

REVIEW QUESTIONS

1. Explain what it means for the Codification's guidance to be "authoritative."
2. Explain why the Codification was developed.
3. Aside from the FASB, name three other standard-setting bodies whose guidance is included in the Codification.
4. What two organizations give the FASB the authority to establish "authoritative" accounting guidance? Explain.
5. Explain the role of industry-specific guidance in the Codification. Does it apply instead of other general Codification guidance?
6. Which search method does the FASB suggest that researchers use as a starting point when conducting research? Explain.
7. In the following template for a Codification reference, what does each group of letters represent?

   XXX–YY–ZZ–PP

8. What entities does guidance in the Codification apply to?

9. Is all SEC guidance contained within the Codification, and is SEC guidance considered authoritative for all entities?

10. In which area of the Codification would a researcher begin a Browse search for the Leases topic?

11. In which area of the Codification would a researcher begin a Browse search for the Inventory topic?

12. Considering the *section* descriptions provided in the chapter, identify the section that you'd consult to determine:
    a. Whether lease guidance applies to natural resources, such as land with mineral deposits
    b. How entities should present basic EPS for continuing operations on the income statement
    c. What disclosures are required for companies preparing consolidated financial statements
    d. How to measure the effects of inventory obsolescence.

13. Which *section* might you read first if you are unfamiliar with a topic and need general information? *But*, what caution was provided regarding this section? Explain.

14. Which section, within the Revenue Recognition topic, tells you whether revenue can be recorded at the time of sale for a product with a right of return attached?

15. What are some possible benefits to a researcher reviewing the Implementation Guidance section (55) when conducting research?

16. Explain the numbering for S-sections from the SEC. Why does the chapter recommend that researchers consult S-99 in addition to other S-sections that might apply?

17. When including a defined term in your research paper, is it better to cite the source for this term as the Master Glossary, or the glossary located within an individual Codification topic? Explain.

18. Following is an example from ASC 350-20 (Intangibles—Goodwill), showing the organization of select paragraphs within the **Subsequent Measurement** section.

    If you find guidance you are looking for under the header "Deferred Income Tax Considerations," which other two headers should you read (at a minimum)? (For convenience, the following headers are numbered.)
    1. > Overall Accounting for Goodwill
    2. > Recognition and Measurement of an Impairment Loss
    3. >> Qualitative Assessment
    4. >> Step 1
    5. >> Step 2
    6. >> Determining the Implied Fair Value of Goodwill
    7. >>> **Deferred Income Tax Considerations**
    8. > Determining the Fair Value of a Reporting Unit

19. Which additional areas in the guidance are considered "required reading" for a researcher who has found general guidance in the Initial Measurement section, but who needs to be sure his or her search was thorough? (Name three other areas the researcher should consider.)

20. What is the name of the guidance currently issued by the FASB to update the Codification? Is this guidance considered "authoritative" in its own right?

21. When should a researcher rely on guidance shown under "Pending Content" instead of existing content?

22. What is the purpose of the cross-reference feature in the Codification? When might this feature be useful to a researcher?

23. What type of entity is permitted to apply accounting alternatives in the Codification? If a company elects to apply a given accounting alternative, does it mean the company must apply all of the available accounting alternatives? Explain.

EXERCISES

Use the FASB Codification to answer the following questions. There is a specific, correct answer to each of the following questions. Keep looking in the Codification until you find the reference that directly responds to these questions.

1. Suppose you wanted to understand whether prepaid expenses should be classified (presented) on the balance sheet as "current assets."
    a. Show how you would navigate to the appropriate guidance using the "browse topics" feature on the left side of the screen. (example: liabilities-contingencies-loss contingencies-initial measurement)
    b. Now provide the numerical ASC reference for the relevant guidance, *down to the paragraph*.

      c. What search term(s) might I enter, if I wanted to perform a keyword search to locate this guidance?

      d. What is the Codification reference (ASC xxx-xxx) if I were looking specifically for guidance on healthcare entities' prepaid expenses? *Hint:* This is an industry-specific topic.

2. Describe how you would navigate to the Stock Compensation topic within the Codification.

3. In the following reference, label the Topic, Subtopic, Section, and Paragraph. Also, provide the description from the Codification for each of these (e.g., the description for Topic 840 is Leases). Here's the reference: ASC 715-30-25-1.

4. Name four of the topics listed within the Broad Transactions area.

5.   *a.* Go to the tab entitled "cross reference" on the Codification homepage. What is the FASB Statement No. that corresponds to Topic 480-10 (Distinguishing Liabilities from Equity)?

      b. Using the "Other Sources" list on the left side of the Codification, go to pre-Codification standards. What is the full name of this FASB Statement that you identified in (a) above?

      c. Next, go to the Basis for Conclusions of the standard (as amended) that you identified in step (b). (To find this, you might start in the standard's Contents list on page 4.) Considering the introduction to the Basis for Conclusions, describe two reasons for which this standard was issued.

      d. Finally, did any FASB Board members dissent to the issuance of this FASB statement? Explain.

6. Use the "advanced search" feature (search by exact phrase) to answer part (a).

      a. Find the ASC reference (ASC xxx-xx-xx-x) for the following guidance excerpt:

      "The acquirer shall recognize separately from goodwill the identifiable intangible assets acquired in a business combination."

      b. Does this guidance (that is, in the ASC subtopic just identified) apply to private companies? Explain why or why not. Cite your sources.

For the next set of questions, identify the ASC reference—*down to the paragraph level of detail***—that you would look to for guidance on each issue.**

7. Criteria for determining whether information about an operating segment should be reported separately (i.e., as a *reportable segment*) in the notes to a company's financial statements.

8. Guidance on whether Treasury share transaction guidance in the Codification applies to nonpublic entities.

9. Criteria for determining whether a lease should be classified as capital versus operating.

10. Guidance indicating which assets are generally classified on the balance sheet as "current assets."

11. The requirement that entities shall disclose all significant accounting policies in the financial statement footnotes.

12. For number (9) above, describe the browse path you used (or would use) to locate this guidance.

For the next set of questions, answer each question using the FASB Codification and cite your source down to the paragraph[s]. Respond using complete sentences.

13.   *a.* Is SEC guidance considered authoritative GAAP? And,

      b. Is all SEC guidance housed within the Codification?

14. Provide two examples from the Codification of "nonauthoritative" sources of GAAP.

15. Name a circumstance (using existing revenue guidance) in which a company selling a product subject to a customer right to return cannot recognize revenue at the time of sale.

16. In determining whether the equity method should be applied to an investment in common stock, an investor should consider whether it can exercise significant influence. Significant influence is characterized by certain quantitative factors (20% ownership) and qualitative factors. What are two of the qualitative factors an investor should consider?

17. Are investments in life insurance within the scope of derivative accounting guidance?

18. What is the initial measurement objective when recording guarantees?

19. When should an entity record the effects of changes in tax laws and rates in recording its income taxes?

20. Should the cash surrender value of life insurance policies be classified within current assets on the balance sheet?

21. Within the Codification, navigate to the revised revenue standard (Revenue from Contracts with Customers).

      a. What paragraph within that topic provides transition guidance for this new topic? Also, in what period would this guidance first apply to a public company with a calendar year end?

      b. Why does all of the content within this topic appear in boxes, as pending content? Explain.

22. Navigate to the *About the Codification* document, shown in the middle of the Codification's homepage. Using this document, describe/name:
    a. The authoritative status of the Codification.
    b. Two pronouncements of the AICPA that were considered part of the population of codified standards as of July 1, 2009 (and which are now superseded by the Codification).
    c. What content is considered *essential* versus *nonessential*. Explain.

23. Locate an example in the Codification of implementation guidance that might clarify or enhance your understanding of other requirements in that subtopic.

24. Within the stock compensation topic (ASC 718), you can find the following two headers (among others). Describe the relationship between the content that you would find within these headers.

    \> Fair-Value-Based

    \>> Terms of the Award Affect Fair Value

25. Explain the need for a researcher to consider all sections of *required reading* when performing Codification research.

26. Identify search terms that you might use to research the following issues. Then, identify the browse path (down to the section) you would likely use to navigate to guidance for these issues (example of a browse path: Assets-Inventory-Overall-Initial Measurement).
    a. A company's auditor is questioning the appropriateness of the company's discount rate assumption, which it uses to measure its defined benefit pension obligation.
    b. Needing to raise capital, a company has just issued convertible debt, which converts into shares of common stock upon certain defined events, such as a sustained increase in the company's share price. The company must determine how to record this issuance.
    c. A company's existing defined benefit pension portfolio holds certain investments in private companies, and these investments must be measured at fair value. The company must determine an appropriate fair value measurement for the private equity investments.
    d. An airline has incurred significant cost to update the interior of its aircraft, changing the configuration of seats and overhead storage space (these parts are considered part of the airframe). The airline must determine whether these costs shall be charged to expense or capitalized.
    e. A popular website primarily generates revenue through ad sales. Ad buyers must pay a specified cost per click, and this cost is based on agreed-upon terms between the website and ad buyer. The typical term of an advertising arrangement is approximately 30 days with billing generally occurring after the delivery of the advertisement. The website must estimate the revenues it has earned but not yet collected as of the end of the period.

27. Consider the search terms you identified in the preceding question. In addition to using search terms to perform keyword searches of the Codification, what are some of the other benefits and uses for search terms? Explain.

CASE STUDY QUESTIONS

IT, or not to IT?   2.1

Issue: You work in the accounting policy group for a consumer products company. The company has set aside funds in its budget for a complete overhaul of its computer information systems this year. The CFO is aware that the FASB and IASB are making steady progress on a project to overhaul lease accounting, which would put most (if not all) leases on balance sheet, and has asked your team to work with IT to identify needed systems changes based on the FASB's proposal. The CFO suggested that the company should adopt the FASB's proposals (and begin accounting for leases under the proposed model) once the updated computer systems are in place at the end of this year.

You have been closely monitoring the FASB Board's recent meetings and proposed standard, so you have a good sense as to what the Boards *want* companies' accounting to look like. Your company has given you the greenlight to early-adopt the changes being contemplated by the FASB, and to incorporate these proposals into the new IT system. But the question is—is it the right thing for your company to do, to adopt this guidance so soon? Based on your close monitoring of the FASB's recent meetings, you know this is the way the boards believe leases *should* be accounted for.

Required: Draft a half-page to one-page response to the CFO's suggestion.

2.2 **Locating and Understanding Private Company Accounting Alternatives** Locate an example of a private company *accounting alternative* in the Codification. Cite the ASC reference for this alternative, and explain the nature of the alternative. Additionally, describe the transition guidance applicable to the alternative.

For cases 2.3–2.5, please respond in a brief paragraph (for part 1 of each case study). Start a new paragraph to respond to part 2. In your responses, remember that you are being asked not only to locate the appropriate guidance, but also to *apply* it to the case facts presented.

2.3 **Current or Non-Current?** Harper and Associates purchased U.S. Treasury notes five years ago, which are now three months away from maturity. Harper and Associates has asked you whether it is appropriate to reclassify these notes into the current assets category of its balance sheet, as cash equivalents.

Required:
1. Citing guidance from the Codification, respond to Harper and Associates.
2. Explain how you located the relevant guidance, including the search method used, and which section you searched within the appropriate topic.

2.4 **Heiring on the Side of Caution** Walker Corp has a $1 million note payable due to its founder, Jim Walker. Mr. Walker is recently deceased and has no heirs that Walker Corp's executive team is aware of. Walker Corp has asked for your help to determine whether it is appropriate to derecognize the liability from its financial statements.

Required:
1. Citing guidance from the Codification, respond to Walker Corp. Your response should discuss the guidance and its applicability to this situation, and should include excerpts from the guidance as helpful in supporting your response.
2. Explain how you located the relevant guidance, including the search method used, and which section you searched within the appropriate topic.

2.5 **Customer Discounts** Schwartz Glass ("Schwartz") is a public company and offers its customers payment terms of 1/10, n/30, where purchasers making payment within 10 days of product receipt will receive a discount of 1% off the purchase price, or must pay the full balance due within 30 days. Schwartz has just received payment from a new customer who paid within the 10-day window and is thus entitled to the 1% discount. This discount will not result in a loss to Schwartz on the sale of the product. Schwartz needs your help to determine when the 1% sales incentive should be recognized, and how it should be recorded—as a reduction in revenue, or as a cost of sales?

Required:
1. Citing guidance from the Codification, explain *when* and *how* Schwartz should account for the sales incentive. Use only currently-effective guidance (do not use pending content). Your response should discuss the guidance and its applicability to this situation, and can include excerpts from the guidance as helpful in supporting your response.
2. Explain how you located the relevant guidance, including the search method used, and which section you searched within the appropriate topic.

2.6 **Applying Transition/Effective Date Guidance and Going Concern Guidance** Go-Go & Co. is preparing its financial statements for the year ended 12/31/2015. As of 12/31, the company's current assets are less than its current liabilities. The company is evaluating whether it must comply with the Codification's going concern disclosure requirements, established in ASU 2014-15. Locate the Codification topic that addresses this issue. Explain whether disclosure of going concern issues is *currently required* for Go-Go & Co, considering the transition guidance provided for this topic. Next, explain whether such disclosure will be required for the company once this guidance becomes effective. Your response should require approximately one page.

2.7 **Website Development Costs—Applying the Codification, plus Consideration of Original Standards** Jenny and Jim have created a new website that they think will help families share photos more easily, create calendars and photo books, and share and edit family videos. Hoping their new site will go viral, Jenny and Jim named their new company PhotoShare, Inc. and are preparing their first financial statements as required by their investors. Jenny and Jim have incurred the following costs to develop their website:

- $1 million to create the web platform capable of storing photos and allowing multiple users to view and edit photos
- $100,000 for website design, including the photo that appears on the homepage and the placement of each tab and link
- $50,000 to content writers, who wrote the Welcome screen message, plus who wrote instructions for users on how to use the site

1. Using only the Codification, research whether Jenny and Jim should treat each cost as an asset or expense on the company's financial statements. Include excerpts as helpful in supporting your responses.
2. Next, locate the source document (the FASB Statement, EITF Issue, or ASU, for example) that gave rise to the Codification guidance you located. How does the information in this source document confirm, revise, or change your interpretation of the Codification? Explain.

Using the Codification as a Learning Tool, Understanding Industry Guidance You've just been assigned to the audit of an agriculture company, and you notice that the company has a written capitalization policy that differentiates between the accounting for permanent land development costs, versus limited-life land development costs. You are unfamiliar with these terms.

2.8

In approximately one page, and using the Codification as your only source, explain what is meant by these two terms (permanent and limited-life land development costs), and contrast how costs meeting these definitions are recognized and subsequently measured. Craft your response clearly, as if you were educating someone who is facing this issue for the first time.

Next, (1) describe one other accounting requirement of interest from this same Codification subtopic. Then, (2) discuss: Was agriculture accounting a topic you understood prior to performing research? Did this Codification research improve your familiarity with the industry?

Wally's Calls—Revenue Recognition Wally's Calls is a public company that makes duck calls. On June 1, Wally's received a purchase order and payment from a customer (Matt Smith) for the purchase of 500 custom duck calls. The calls will be used as a wedding favor and engraved "Matt and Jennifer, 2015."

2.9

On June 28, Wally's shipped the completed order to Mr. Smith, and Mr. Smith received the duck calls to his door via UPS on June 30. Company policy allows customers to test the duck calls and to return the calls within 90 days for a full refund if they are not to the customer's satisfaction. Historically, Wally's has experienced very low product defect rates and thus few customers exercise this option.

Wally's must now determine whether it can recognize the revenue from the sale of the duck calls or whether it must wait until the 90-day customer acceptance window lapses.

Using existing revenue recognition guidance (not pending content), evaluate whether Wally's meets the criteria to recognize revenue.

Chapter 3

The Research Process

Richard has just joined the accounting policy team at Energy Works, Inc., a nonpublic oil and gas company, and has been asked to take the first shot at addressing the following issue.

Energy Works is forming a joint venture (JV) with Big Oil, Inc. for the extraction of proved oil reserves in the arctic. Both venturers wish to share in the risks and rewards of this venture, while benefiting from each other's technical expertise and sharing of key assets. Energy Works will contribute a floating production storage and offloading facility (FPSO), valued at $100 million, along with $20 million in cash, to the venture in exchange for a 50% equity interest. Energy Works is not in the business of marketing its production facilities and equipment for sale; rather, it uses these facilities in its own oil and gas producing activities.

Big Oil will contribute its arctic drilling permit, also valued at $100 million, along with $20 million in cash, to the venture in exchange for a 50% equity interest. Assume that the cost basis of the contributed assets is the same as the fair values of these assets. Profits and losses of the venture will be shared based upon the equity interest held by each investor.

Operations of the joint venture will be overseen by its Board of Directors. Each venturer will receive two seats on the Board, for a total of four seats, and all significant decisions of the JV require the unanimous consent of the Board, with any disputes to be settled by an independent arbitrator (binding arbitration). The Board has appointed Energy Works to manage the day-to-day operations of the FPSO facility. Additionally, both venturers will provide employees and managerial personnel with technical expertise to perform day-to-day operations for the JV. Energy Works will not receive separate compensation for its role as manager. The joint venture will be legally organized as an LLC.

Continued

Learning Objectives

After reading this chapter and performing the exercises herein, you will be able to

1. **List** the six steps of the research process.

2. **Identify** sources for learning about an industry, and for gathering transaction facts.

3. **Define** the research problem, through the identification of "researchable questions."

4. **Search** broadly for potentially relevant guidance.

5. **Examine** alternative viewpoints in an accounting research analysis.

6. **Justify** and document your conclusion.

7. **Identify** common decision traps and judgment biases.

Energy Works needs to determine how it will record its investment in this proposed joint venture. Richard has had plenty of experience researching limited scope issues in the past, but this issue seems more complex. He wonders—should he go right to the Codification for guidance, or are there other steps he should take first?

In this chapter, you'll be introduced to the accounting research process, which will arm you with an approach you can apply when faced with complex research issues. As we walk through this process, we'll consider the steps that Richard can take in order to thoughtfully, and efficiently, evaluate his company's proposed transaction. Notably, this Energy Works example continues into the next chapter, which covers writing techniques.

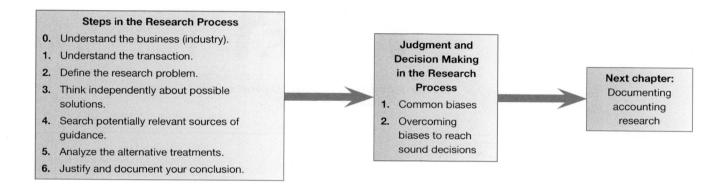

Organization of This Chapter

This chapter introduces the accounting research process, which is the step-by-step process that researchers can apply to a wide range of business and accounting issues. As illustrated in the preceding graphic, this process involves—first—fully understanding a transaction (within the context of a given industry), then identifying the issues, thinking through these issues, locating applicable research, considering alternatives, and—finally—reaching a thoughtful and defensible conclusion.

In applying the research process, it helps to understand some of the decision traps and biases that you may be prone to as a researcher and decision maker. For this reason, an introduction to judgment and decision making concepts follows our discussion of the research process.

Documentation skills, also integral to accounting research, are addressed in the next chapter of this book.

The challenge for beginning researchers is not in reading and understanding the research process described in this chapter. It's in actually applying it, when faced with challenging issues. Overcoming the tendency to reach for the first potentially applicable source of guidance takes time and practice. My hope is that the lessons and exercises in this chapter will get researchers closer to the place where using a thoughtful process becomes automatic.

WHY USE A RESEARCH PROCESS?

As a beginning researcher, your tendency might be to dive right into authoritative guidance when faced with a research question. But your professor—and professionals—would tell you there's a better way to research. The goal of this chapter is to teach you a more thoughtful approach.

Consider the research approaches illustrated in Figures 3-1 and 3-2. Which research approach would you trust more?

Figure 3-1

Approach 1

Beginning researchers often go straight to the guidance when they receive a research question, often necessitating return trips to their supervisor for additional facts.

Figure 3-2

Approach 2

| Take time to fully understand the issue. Don't be afraid to ask questions. | Define the research question, then think through possible alternatives. | Perform research, then use this guidance to analyze alternatives. | Justify and document your conclusions. |

The research process introduced in this chapter involves broadly understanding the issues, and their context, plus thinking through the issue yourself, all *before* looking for guidance in the Codification. This chapter may sound like a lot of theory. But it's not. In practice, accounting researchers *actually* apply a similar process.

THE ACCOUNTING RESEARCH PROCESS

LO1 List the six steps of the research process.

The **accounting research process** is the step-by-step process that researchers can apply to a wide range of open-ended accounting issues encountered in practice.

The research process described in this book consists of the following steps:

Pre-Step: Understand the Business (Industry).

| 1. Understand the facts. | 2. Define the problem. | 3. Stop and think. | 4. Search for guidance. | 5. Analyze and document alternatives. | 6. Justify and document conclusion. |

Note that multiple variations of this process exist (for example, in other textbooks, in accounting firm literature, etc.); this book describes just one of many possible approaches. The approach described here is particularly geared to the beginning researcher, who may require a few extra steps in order to fully analyze an issue. Generally speaking, the similarities among the various research approaches tend to outnumber their differences.

To best understand this process, 1) first, read about it; 2) second, practice applying it to case studies. In time, the steps in this process will become second nature to you. Professionals with a mastery of this process may find themselves being asked to participate on increasingly higher-level projects—offering valuable opportunities to grow in knowledge and skills.

Pre-Step: Understand the Business (Industry)

Perform this step upon being assigned to a new client, or before starting work in a new industry.

Your first task in the research process, before you even begin understanding a specific research question, is to get to know your company's—or your client's—business. Understanding the business (or industry) gives you the appropriate context for considering company-specific accounting issues. **In other words, you first need to understand the business before you can understand the transaction.** Without preliminary research on the client's business, you risk asking questions about a transaction that are not informed.

> **LO2** Identify sources for learning about an industry, and for gathering transaction facts.

Consider this comment from a fellow accounting research instructor:

> "When I created this course I met with several Partners at Big 4 firms. One thing I heard more than once was they thought new hires lacked the ability to research and understand their client's business. Therefore, I try to teach that prior to performing accounting research we should research and understand the business itself."

The business environment, supply chain, sources of revenues and expenses, and timing of cash flows can vary greatly for different industries. Just imagine how different the accounting issues faced by an Agriculture company, versus an Airline, might be.

To address these unique accounting issues, the Codification includes an Industry area with industry-specific accounting guidance. Figure 3-3 illustrates the topics included in the Industry area, and provides examples of companies.

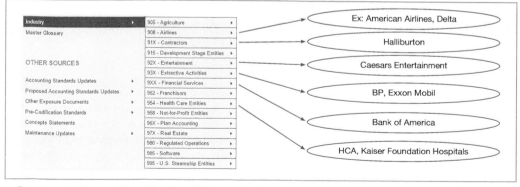

Reproduced with permission of the Financial Accounting Foundation.

Figure 3-3

Industry-specific topics in the Codification, plus examples of companies in select industries

To become more informed about an industry, your goal during this pre-step is to understand:

- What are the primary business activities of companies in this industry?
- What are key revenue sources, and costs, for companies in this industry?
- What accounting practices are unique to this industry?
- What are some of the peer group companies in this industry?

How Do I Learn About a New Industry?

AICPA Audit and Accounting Guides (**A&A Guides**) are arguably the best resource for getting to know a new industry. See Figure 3-4. These guides contain general background on the industry, including typical operations and ownership structures, guidance on auditing techniques for the industry, and accounting guidance for transactions specific to the industry.

For example, by consulting the A&A guide for his industry, Richard would learn that joint ventures are a quite common arrangement used by oil and gas-producing entities to share risks and rewards related to exploration and/or production. He would also gain insight into some accounting considerations for these structures.

Figure 3-4

Snapshot from the A&A Guide, *Entities with Oil and Gas Producing Activities*

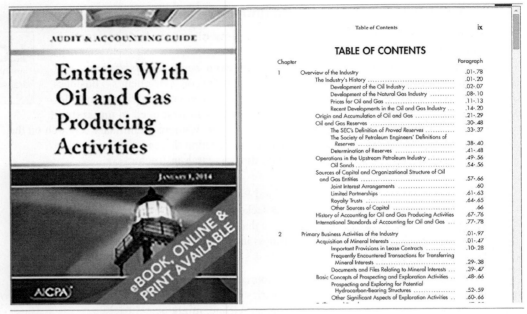

A&A Guides can be purchased directly from the AICPA, or can be accessed through certain research databases, such as the AICPA's online research system and Deloitte's *Technical Library*.

> [**TIP**] from the Trenches
>
> While the *auditing* guidance in A&A Guides is authoritative, the *accounting* guidance in A&A Guides is nonauthoritative. See Chapters 5 and 9 of this book for more on authoritative versus nonauthoritative accounting and auditing sources.

Suppose that you do not have access to A&A Guides. What then?

Your next best option is to consider other sources that can provide you with an overview of the industry. Your university's online library may provide you access to the **Hoovers** or **IBIS** databases, which offer a great introduction to specific industries, including their operations, supply chain, major companies, and more. If these resources are not available, try a Google search for: "Overview of Oil Industry" for example, and look for reputable industry trade organization websites designed to teach about the industry.

Additionally, you can find the names of other companies in the industry with the **Mergent Online** database, by inputting a company name then clicking on Competitors.

Finally, another excellent way to learn about an industry is to review the annual report (Form 10-K) of your client, or of another company that is a key player in the industry. To locate a company's 10-K, simply Google search "10K Halliburton", for example. Or go to the company's website, then look for their Investor Relations page.

Focus on the following sections of the 10-K to broadly learn about the company and its unique accounting issues:

■ Business (Item 1)

■ Critical Accounting Policies and Estimates (a component of Item 7, MD&A)

■ Significant Accounting Policies (generally Note 1 or 2 of the financial statement footnotes)

You'll quickly realize that it would be impossible to adequately perform research without first broadly understanding the business and specific company strategy.

Now YOU Try 3.1

Recall from the opening scenario of this chapter that Richard recently joined the accounting policy team at Energy Works, Inc. Imagine that Richard has come to you for advice about how to quickly get up to speed on his new industry. What resources would you recommend that he read, and specifically what sections of these resources?

_____

_____

_____

_____

Why is *understanding the business* a pre-step?

Don't wait until you're given your first research assignment to start understanding a company's business model and peer group. By then, the expectation will be that you're ready to go on Step 1 of the research process.

The time to complete this step 0 is when you first get assigned to a client in a new industry, or during the transition period before you start as an employee of a new company. You may need to do this reading off the clock—think of it as doing your homework on the company.

Step 1: Understand the Facts/Background of the Transaction

Let's assume that your involvement in this whole transaction review process began when your supervisor dropped a contract on your desk and said: "Read this and tell me what you think the accounting should be." What would you do first?

Your first challenge in any accounting research assignment is to *fully understand* the transaction and *why* it is being entered into. Obtaining this understanding often starts with

■ Reading transaction documents, including draft or final contracts, and

■ Talking to parties within your organization who have knowledge of the transaction. This can help you understand the purpose of the transaction, plus clarify any unique terms of the transaction.

After considering the two preceding resources, think about whether you understand the big picture for this transaction. Do you have a clear understanding of *who* the parties are to this transaction, and *why* they are entering into it? Do you clearly understand the *economics (financial costs and benefits)* and *cash flows* of the arrangement? Without realizing it, beginning researchers may go through several rounds of research with incomplete information, gathering additional facts each time they stop to ask ("frequent fliers" to the boss's office). Save yourself time and effort by trying to form a complete picture during this first step of the research process.

It might help at this point for you to sketch out—for your own benefit—a picture of the transaction. Instructions for doing this are provided in the next chapter.

As discussed in Chapter 1, researching the accounting for a transaction should ideally occur before the transaction takes place (and before contracts are finalized). Be careful, however. An accounting position documented based on *draft* agreements could change as contracts are edited and finalized. Changes to contracts and final drafts should be reviewed to ensure that they do not change the accounting analysis.

Once you have a working understanding of a transaction, consider whether the following resources would shed additional light on the transaction:

- Has my company undertaken any transactions similar to this in the past? If so, try to get your hands on any memos documenting the background and accounting positions taken for those transactions. This will not only save you time and effort in researching the issues, but it may also provide additional context as to the company's business purpose in entering this transaction.

- Have peers in my industry completed similar transactions? If so, look for discussion of these transactions in
  - Peer companies' public filings (Form 10-Ks), press releases, or responses to SEC comment letters (where the company may describe to the SEC its rationale for accounting positions taken).
  - Industry-specific publications, such as whitepapers or accounting guides.

  Take note of the accounting elections or judgments addressed by your peers that may be relevant to your transaction; be aware, however, that differences in terms may exist between the transactions.

  See Chapter 5 for further discussion of SEC comment letters and accounting firm resources.

- Should specialists be involved? Certain transactions can be highly nuanced and may require the involvement of individuals with specialized knowledge. Examples of such nuanced transactions include business combinations, securitizations, so-called hybrid debt offerings, or transactions related to a company's pension obligations, to name a few. If such specialized knowledge is not available within your own company, your auditors may be a good resource. Types of specialists include
  - Technical accounting specialists
  - Actuaries
  - Valuation specialists, and
  - Legal counsel.

Any steps that you are able to take to fully understand the purpose and economics of a transaction should be taken.

In some cases, however, you might be given only limited background on an issue (verbally, or in writing) and told what to research. This may be especially true early in your career. For example, your supervisor may not want to divulge all relevant transaction facts to you, and may only be asking for your help with one aspect of the research. Even in such cases, it is helpful to go through the preceding list of steps as a sort of checklist; ask yourself: "Can I still perform this step for my limited-scope research question?" Often, even without access to contracts, many of the listed steps will still apply, such as consideration of company past practices and comparison to peer transactions.

Recall the joint venture arrangement described in the opening scenario of this chapter. In your opinion, what are some of the most critical resources that Richard should consider—and key questions he should ask—in his effort to understand this proposed transaction?

_____

_____

_____

_____

_____

A Final Note: Listening Skills during Step 1

Listen up! In this step of the research process, _listening skills_ are key. Being assigned to this research project gives you the opportunity to reach out and learn from others in your organization (or your client's). Your supervisor, and your operations contacts, have a perspective about the company and this transaction that you do not have. This research project is your opportunity to learn from them.

In a 2014 survey of employers, listening skills were ranked as the second most important skill (out of 25) for new graduate business school hires. (Oral communication was ranked as the most important skill, with written communication ranked as the third)[i].

How can you be a better listener? It's simple: Give the person your full attention, and just listen. Be patient if the speaker communicates differently from you; focus on what is being said, not how. Don't plan your next comment or question, and don't interrupt. Take notes as necessary. Try to walk away from the conversation having learned from, and understood, what was said.

[i] Based on the 2014 Corporate Recruiters survey by the Graduate Management Admission Council.

Step 2: Define the Problem. That Is, Identify the "Researchable Question."

The next step of your research process is to define the problem; that is, identify the **researchable question(s)**. Doing so will help to focus your research efforts. Avoid long or complex questions; if your question has multiple parts, break that issue into two or more questions.

> **LO3** Define the research problem, through the identification of "researchable questions."

Following are examples of researchable questions that might come to mind during your initial review of a contract:

- _If my company will receive money under the contract_: Will we recognize revenue for this? Will receiving these funds cause us to incur a liability? Have we received any capital contributions? Have we entered into a lease arrangement?

- _If my company will pay money under the contract_: Have we created or purchased an asset? Have we incurred an expense? Have we entered into a lease arrangement?

- _If my company purchased an ownership interest in another entity:_ Will my company have to consolidate the entity? Alternatively, should my company record an investment in the entity?

- _If the contract involves the purchase or sale of a commodity (e.g., oil, gas, gold) or currency:_ Does this contract contain a derivative that requires mark-to-market accounting?

Notice that each of these question includes a topic that you could navigate to in the Codification, as a starting point for your research. For example,

■   To respond to the question: "Will we recognize revenue for this?", an appropriate starting point for a browse search would be

Revenue Recognition (**Topic 605** or **606**) > Overall (**10**) > Recognition (**25**)

■   An appropriate starting point for the question: "Have we entered into a lease arrangement?" would be

Broad Transactions > Leases (**Topic 840**) > Overall (**10**) > Scope (**15**)

■   An appropriate starting point for the question: "Does this contract contain a derivative?" would be

Broad Transactions > Derivatives and Hedging (**Topic 815**) > Overall (**10**) > Scope (**15**)

Look again at the questions above. Notice that, in some cases, the research question and related browse path focus on the application of general accounting methods (such as revenue recognition).

In other cases, the research questions focus on the *type of transaction* being evaluated, and therefore the browse path focuses on whether the arrangement is within the scope of transaction-specific guidance. This search focus is most effective in the case of structured, or complex transactions for which the accounting is unique to that class of transaction (such as topics listed in the Broad Transactions area of the Codification).

Now
YOU
Try
3.3

Assume that you have been asked to review a contract related to a securitization of accounts receivable (i.e., the sale of investments in a portfolio of accounts receivable). In this case, knowing that this is a unique type of transaction that may be governed by its own set of rules, you should begin by searching for guidance specific to this type of transaction.

Your first researchable question for this contract might be: "Should this transaction be accounted for as a securitization?"

What browse path might be an appropriate starting point for this question?

_____

The questions just illustrated are provided with the intent of helping beginning researchers draw connections between contract terms and research questions. As such, these questions have been intentionally kept broad. In practice, however, it is often appropriate for questions to be more specific. For example, the question: "Is Energy Works required to consolidate the joint venture?" would likely be more effective than the broader wording: "How will Energy Works record its investment in the joint venture?" As you work through the research process, you will find that you can become more specific with your questions.

Identifying the Researchable Question

Now
YOU
Try
3.4

Take a moment to practice identifying a single, researchable question for the following issues.

1.   A company ships its widgets to a customer on December 31 but has not yet collected payment from the customer. The customer has promised to pay within 30 days but has never purchased goods from the company before.

Researchable question? _____

2.   A customer is suing the local grocery store for a slip-and-fall incident. The grocery store believes the lawsuit will likely be considered frivolous and rejected by the court. The grocery store must decide whether to record or disclose this matter.

Researchable question? _____

3. An investor is suing a corporation that has just absorbed another entity in a merger. The investor is alleging that the corporation overstated on its balance sheet the values of certain equity investments that were acquired during the merger. The investor's attorney needs to understand how the equity investments should have been valued.

   Researchable question? _____

Finally, additional researchable questions will often become apparent as you work through the research process. For example, assume that Richard has determined the variable interest model is not required to be applied in evaluating the joint venture for consolidation (a scope issue). Next, Richard might identify the following additional questions:

- Is Energy Works required to consolidate the joint venture based on the *voting model* for consolidation?

- If consolidation is not required, what accounting method (cost, fair value, or equity) should Energy Works use to record its investment?

Once an accounting method has been selected, additional researchable questions might focus on *how to apply* the method selected. To illustrate this point, consider the following **Now YOU Try**.

Assume that Richard and his team have determined that Energy Works should record its investment in the joint venture using the equity method. Brainstorm some additional research questions that could arise as a result of this conclusion, regarding *how to apply* the equity method and comply with related disclosure requirements.

_____

_____

_____

Now
YOU
Try
3.5

Again, word your research questions as specifically as possible, as this provides a good framework for conducting research.

The remaining steps in the research process should be performed for each research question identified.

Step 3: Stop and Think: What Accounting Treatment Will Likely Be Appropriate?

The third step of the research process requires researchers to "stop and think." That is, before you turn to the Codification for guidance, stop and think on your own: What accounting treatment do *you* think would be most appropriate for this transaction or event? Coming up with your own, independent idea of how a transaction should be accounted for will help you to stay objective as you look for guidance in the Codification and can help you avoid anchoring to the first possible solution you find.

This is not your first accounting course—you have the knowledge to think through accounting issues independently. Use that knowledge now. Think through one or two accounting alternatives for this transaction that make logical sense to you, and jot down these alternatives.

Finally, it can be helpful at this point to jot down possible *search terms* (see Chapter 2) related to your researchable question and the possible accounting treatments you just identified. Doing so will help you avoid getting bogged down in Codification guidance once you start your search. Keep your research question, and your list of search terms, at top of mind in order to maintain efficiency and focus as you move to the next step of the research process.

> To illustrate the importance of this step, consider the following. I once assigned two teams of students to research a lease case (operating versus capital?), to write an issues memo on the case, then to work in teams to present the case to their peers.
>
> The students' peers (assigned to present different cases) were asked to read the lease case then to provide their "gut instinct" as to how they would conclude, without consulting professional literature. Believe it or not, the non-presenting students concluded more correctly on the case than those assigned to present. The presenting students anchored so quickly to the guidance that they failed to stop and think through the issues.
>
> Bottom line: Think through the accounting, and ask your gut what the answer should be, before diving into the guidance.

Step 4: Search Potentially Relevant Sources of Guidance, Copying Any Relevant Guidance into a Word Document

LO4 Search broadly for potentially relevant guidance.

Now that you have given some thought to your research question, you are ready to search the Codification (or other authority) for applicable guidance.

If you have a sense as to which topic might be most applicable to your research question, begin by browsing to that topic in the Codification.

To save yourself time, always start your research by locating the topic that you expect to be most relevant. If you don't know which topic is appropriate for your search, use the Codification's keyword search feature instead. Follow all leads (search results) that appear to be relevant, as the keyword may lead you to several useful sources of guidance. Bear in mind that sometimes, researching a single accounting issue can involve consideration of multiple Codification topics.

[Now]
YOU
[Try]
3.6

Let's return to our Energy Works example, but let's back up for a moment. Assume that Richard's very first researchable question is: *Is Energy Works required to consolidate the joint venture?* What Codification topic (or, if you're unsure, what keywords) would you expect to be most relevant to this issue?

Accordingly, Richard should begin his research by navigating to this topic first.

As a beginning researcher, you may end up exploring a lot of places in the Codification before you find guidance that is directly on point. Keep track of potentially relevant guidance that you find by copying sections of the guidance into a Word document. Finding potentially relevant guidance can still be, essentially, a brainstorming exercise. Look for guidance that is either directly on point or, if not available, guidance that may be relevant by analogy (for example, guidance that is on point, but for a similar transaction that differs from your transaction). Be exhaustive in your search; attempt to find all possible relevant guidance that can be used to answer your research question. Consult all sources of *required reading*, as defined in Chapter 2. In this stage of the research process, you may also choose to consult nonauthoritative sources of guidance, which are discussed further in Chapter 5.

At the end of this step, review the guidance you have collected. Ideally, you will have found some guidance that is relevant to your research question, and which you will analyze in the next step. Other sources, upon further review, may appear to be less relevant and can now be weeded out (deleted from your Word document). This locating, then weeding out, step is particularly geared toward beginning researchers. As you gain experience with research, you may find it easier to identify—as you go—whether or not a source is relevant, and whether it's worth pursuing. Eventually, you will be able to determine in real time which sources are most responsive to your research question.

Now
YOU
Try
3.7

Let's assume that, as Richard begins his search, he comes across guidance in ASC 810-10 (Consolidation) describing two models for evaluating consolidation: the variable interest (VIE) model and the voting interest model. According to the Codification, arrangements should first be evaluated to determine whether they fall within the scope of the VIE model and, if not, shall apply the voting model.

Richard has found scope guidance indicating that some *businesses*, which are *operating joint ventures*, may be outside the scope of the VIE model, as follows:

> 15-17(d). A legal entity that is deemed to be a business need not be evaluated by a reporting entity to determine if the legal entity is a VIE under the requirements of the Variable Interest Entities Subsections unless any of the following conditions exist . . .:
>
> 1. The reporting entity . . . participated significantly in the design or redesign of the legal entity. However, this condition does not apply if the legal entity is an operating joint venture under joint control of the reporting entity and one or more independent parties or a franchisee.
> 2-4. [For simplicity of this example, conditions 2-4 will not be evaluated at this time, however in practice entities are required to evaluate these conditions.][1]

While these terms may be used loosely in practice, GAAP offers specific definitions for the terms *business* and *joint venture*.[2] For example, the Codification defines a **corporate joint venture** as:

> A corporation owned and operated by a small group of entities (the joint venturers) as a separate and specific business or project for the mutual benefit of the members of the group . . . .The purpose of a corporate joint venture frequently is to share risks and rewards in developing a new market, product or technology; to combine complementary technological knowledge; or to pool resources in developing production or other facilities. A corporate joint venture also usually provides an arrangement under which each joint venturer may participate, directly or indirectly, in the overall management of the joint venture. Joint venturers thus have an interest or relationship other than as passive investors . . . The ownership of a corporate joint venture seldom changes, and its stock is usually not traded publicly . . . (Source: ASC 323-10-20)

Walk Richard through this step 4 for this issue. He wants to evaluate whether his company qualifies for the so-called business scope exception to the VIE model.

What other guidance (authoritative or not)—or other *sections* (e.g., Recognition, Measurement, or other sources of *required reading*) in his current Codification topic—might he review for more information about this definition, or about this scope exception? What guidance

---

[1] Other exceptions to the business scope exception—omitted for simplicity of this example—include that substantially all of the JV's activities cannot be performed on behalf of one investor, and that the reporting entity cannot have contributed over half of the fair value of the JV's equity. We will assume for simplicity that neither of these exceptions applies to this case.

[2] The definition of *joint venture* is meaningful because—as noted—certain joint ventures are exempt from the variable interest model of consolidation (**ASC 810**). Additionally, *joint ventures* are exempt from aspects of the nonmonetary transactions topic (**ASC 845**), and formations of *joint ventures* are outside the scope of the business combinations topic (**ASC 805**). All of these topics could possibly be relevant to the arrangement that Richard is evaluating.

should he copy into his Word document as he looks for additional sources? Remember at this point that Richard should search broadly for any guidance that might apply.

> **A Final Note: Avoiding Distractions during Step 4**
>
> Caution: This step 4 is the part of the research process where you may be most at risk for distractions.
>
> Reading authoritative literature, such as the Codification, is mentally strenuous. You're going to need a quiet setting, free of distractions.
>
> *Consider this: A study by UC-Irvine professor Gloria Mark showed that each time an office worker was interrupted on a task (such as by responding to an email), it took on average 25 minutes to return to that task. Researchers in other studies have found that 40% of the time, delayed tasks are not resumed right after the interruption.*[3, 4]
>
> In other words, not only will interruptions slow you down, but they may derail you from the research project altogether. Wouldn't you rather just get this research done now?
>
> Your best bet: Find a quiet place to sit (the upper floors of the library are great). Turn your phone on airplane mode to avoid beeps and alerts, and close your email browser. Set aside at least a full hour or two; you'll need at least this amount of time to conduct really thoughtful, thorough research.
>
> If you do stop research to respond to an email, 1) keep your research windows open, and 2) jot down on a Post-it where you left off: *Next: Search ASC 810 for "joint venture."* Stick the Post-it right in front of your keyboard. These two small actions will improve your chances of resuming research after an interruption, and will minimize your mental recovery time.
>
> (In the field of "interruption science"—yes, it's a thing!—this is described as helping to jog your prospective memory. That is, before dealing with an interruption, remind yourself of the step you plan to tackle next.)

Step 5: Analyze Alternatives, Documenting Your Consideration of Each

LO5 Examine alternative viewpoints in an accounting research analysis.

Now that you have found guidance that appears to be relevant to your issue, the next step is to **analyze** that guidance, or to evaluate how the guidance applies to your research question. This process can involve judgment; that is, guidance in the Codification may not offer specific answers to the researcher's precise issue, or the Codification may allow for alternative accounting treatments. In such circumstances, it is essential for a researcher to clearly identify and analyze the relative merits of the alternative treatments available.

Sometimes, "weighing alternatives" can also mean thinking critically about whether a certain treatment is, or is not, met. In other words, don't just assume that an accounting treatment you find in the Codification is applicable. You must fully investigate the guidance before concluding that its use is acceptable.

---

[3] Mark, G., Gonzalez, V. M., and Harris, J. *No task left behind? Examining the nature of fragmented work.* In CHI '05: Proceedings of the SIGCHI Conference on Human Factors in Computing Systems, pages 321–330, (New York: ACM Press, 2005).

[4] O'Connail, B. and Frohlich, D. *Timespace in the workplace: Dealing with interruptions.* CHI '95 Conference on Human Factors in Computing Systems, Extended Abstracts, pages 262–263 (New York: ACM Press, 1995).

For example, if a defined term is included within a paragraph you're evaluating, stop to evaluate whether your arrangement meets the definition provided for that term. Or, go back to re-check the scope of the guidance you're reading. Be open to the possibility that the treatment you're considering might not apply.

To illustrate this point, complete the following **Now YOU Try** exercise, considering the facts presented in the opening scenario of this chapter.

Recall that Richard is evaluating whether Energy Works' arrangement meets the GAAP definition of a joint venture. Richard understands that there may be more to understanding this definition than just applying the words given in the Codification's glossary. Use of this scope exception is *judgmental*.

To that end, Richard has also sought interpretive guidance from nonauthoritative sources. The following excerpt, from EY's Financial Reporting Developments publication, *Consolidation and the Variable Interest Model* (2014), offers further discussion of the definition of *joint venture*.

> The actual term [joint venture] is narrowly defined for accounting purposes in ASC 323-10-20. The fundamental criteria for an entity to be a joint venture are (1) joint control over all key decisions, with (2) control through the owners' equity interest. [Explanation added.] (Page 53).

Using the facts from this chapter's opening scenario, help Richard analyze how this guidance applies to Energy Works' arrangement.

Energy Works has evaluated EY's two fundamental criteria for an entity to be a joint venture, as follows:

1. *The venturers must have joint control over all key decisions.*

   Analysis: This criterion is <u>met/not met</u>, because _____
   _____

2. *The venturers must be able to control the entity through their equity investments.*[5]

   Analysis: This criterion is <u>met/not met</u>, because _____
   _____

Now **YOU** Try **3.8**

To bring this all together, let me briefly walk you through some key points of the Energy Works analysis that Richard would have performed. The full memo documenting this issue—and pointing out many of the critical judgments involved along the way—is presented in the Appendix to Chapter 4. Additional discussion of this example is also provided throughout Chapter 4.

- First, Richard evaluated the JV for potential consolidation. Per the requirements of ASC 810, he first had to determine whether the variable interest model applies.
- While in practice it's very difficult to qualify for the business scope exception, Richard carefully evaluated the guidance and determined that this is an *operating joint venture under joint control*, which meets the definition of a *business*. Therefore, this arrangement is outside the scope of the VIE model.
- Next, Richard applied the voting model of consolidation and determined that neither venturer has a *controlling financial interest* and thus is required to consolidate the JV.

Richard's next step would be to determine what accounting method Energy Works should use to record its investment, as we'll discuss shortly, in our next **Now You Try.**

[5] EY's Financial Reporting Developments (June 2014). *Joint Ventures*. Chapter 2, page 4.

In some cases, two acceptable alternatives may appear to be available, and it may not be clear from the authoritative guidance which should be used. In such cases, you must weigh the relative merits of each alternative, considering the following:

- If authoritative guidance (i.e., the Codification) does not express a preference as to which alternative should be used, do sources of nonauthoritative guidance (e.g., accounting firm publications) address this issue?

- Does one alternative appear to better reflect the economics of the transaction (to users of the financial statements)?

- Which alternative is most consistent with the company's prior practices, if the company has entered into similar transactions in the past?

- Is this position consistent with the positions elected by peers in my company's industry?

- Have I vetted this accounting position with the appropriate levels of management?

- Finally, do our auditors agree with this treatment?

Document all factors considered in your analysis of the alternative treatments. Start with the guidance you collected from your search of the Codification, providing discussion (in your own words) of how you considered that guidance relative to your company's fact pattern. After you have presented the authoritative guidance, next you should document all "other" factors considered in your analysis (including any meaningful consideration you gave to the bulleted items just listed).

Now YOU Try 3.9

Having concluded that consolidation of the joint venture is not required, Richard must now consider how to record the investment on Energy Works' financial statements. He considers the following guidance from ASC 325-20 (Investments—Cost Method):

> 05-2 Investments are sometimes held in stock of entities other than subsidiaries, namely corporate joint ventures and other noncontrolled entities. These investments are accounted for by one of three methods—the cost method (addressed in this Subtopic), the fair value method (addressed in Topic 320), and the equity method (addressed in Topic 323).

Help Richard think through the alternatives presented in this guidance.

1. Considering par. 05-2, what three accounting methods might possibly apply to this investment?

_____

2. How would you recommend that Richard evaluate which method is most appropriate?

_____

_____

3. Would it be appropriate for Richard to document only the alternative selected? Explain.

_____

_____

As we'll discuss further in the next chapter, any reasonable alternative or indicator that you weigh (positively or negatively) in evaluating an issue should be documented. In this case, Richard's documentation should highlight any alternatives that he considered as possible accounting methods.

Finally, be wary of selecting an alternative that represents a departure from a past practice of your company, or of companies in your peer group. Such a departure should be addressed in your analysis, as well as discussed with management and your auditors. Your company may risk being questioned by investors or by the SEC if you elect a position (on a material transaction) that is inconsistent with past practices or unique among those in your industry.

The next chapter describes how the researcher should document key factors considered—both from authoritative and nonauthoritative sources—in his or her written analysis of an accounting issue.

Step 6: Justify and Document Your Conclusion

The final step of the research process is to reach a conclusion—that is, determine which accounting treatment is most appropriate given the authoritative guidance and, if applicable, other key factors you have analyzed. Next, clearly document this conclusion, summarizing salient points from your analysis as justification for your position.

> **LO6** Justify and document your conclusion.

Guidance for documenting your conclusion is provided in the next chapter of this book.

In addition to fully analyzing the literature and considering alternatives, the SEC's staff have suggested that preparers should support accounting judgments by considering *how the selected treatment reflects the economic substance and business purpose* of the transaction.[6] At this point of the research process, pause to reflect upon whether your accounting conclusion appropriately reflects the substance of the transaction.

However if, when you reach this step, you have inadequate information to reach a conclusion, consider whether you obtained sufficient information in the previous steps. Once a robust analysis has been performed, and sufficient sources have been considered, you should be able to point to key factors from the analysis as support for the conclusion reached.

> In our Energy Works example, Richard concluded that use of the equity method is appropriate. However, recall that Richard's research was based on draft contracts between Energy Works and Big Oil. Richard will need to monitor any changes that are made to these draft contracts, then should carefully review all final, executed agreements to ensure that they are consistent with his previous research.

> [**TIP**] from the Trenches

You now understand how to apply the research process. But one more thing. Every step of this process—every decision you make—could be subject to your own behind-the-scenes decision prejudices. Let's take a look now at a topic that is catching the interest of industries from law, to medicine, to investing, to our own profession.

JUDGMENT AND DECISION-MAKING—A BRIEF INTRODUCTION

You may not even be aware of it, but in each step of the research process, your judgments may be prone to silent prejudices, or **biases**.[7]

> **LO7** Identify common decision traps and judgment biases.

These biases are part of our human nature. Each day, we are faced with large volumes of information, and it's normal for our minds to apply mental shortcuts in order to filter and process this information. These shortcuts can greatly influence how we make decisions. Yes—we are talking about how *psychology* actually influences the judgments we make as accountants!

Today, accounting firms and professional organizations alike are realizing that—in order to make sound professional judgments—it's critical that we apply a consistent research process, *and* we must be aware of common decision traps. This focus is not surprising. A 2008 report from the SEC indicated that our profession needs more guidance in the area of professional

---

[6] Final Report of the Advisory Committee on Improvements to Financial Reporting to the United States Securities and Exchange Commission, page 95. August 1, 2008.

[7] Select resources that were consulted in developing this discussion are listed at the end of this chapter, under Additional References.

judgment, in light of increases in principles-based accounting guidance, subjectivity in measurements, and regulatory oversight of the profession.[8]

It won't be enough, if a regulator asks your company about a material, highly judgmental position, for you to argue that you applied the guidance that seemed the most on point. Rather, you'll have to be able to demonstrate the *quality* of your judgment—that your *process* for evaluating the issue was robust, and that you considered an appropriate mix of factors in reaching your ultimate conclusion. To do this, it helps to be aware of some common biases that can impact your professional judgment.

Common Biases

- **Confirmation bias**: Our inclination to seek (or weight more heavily) information supporting our existing viewpoint, and to downplay (or minimize) information supporting different options.
  - Example: After the client offers up his initial thoughts on an accounting judgment, his auditor inadvertently looks for more guidance that confirms the client view, as opposed to guidance that could oppose the client's position.
  - Investors who have a positive feeling about a company tend to focus on information about the company that confirms their prior beliefs.

- **Availability bias:** The tendency to weight more heavily that information which is readily available (or mentally accessible), and to overlook information which takes more time or effort to gather. Examples:
  - You generally feel as though the U.S. economy is improving, based in part on the fact that you recently received a raise.
  - Asked to come up with reasons for budget variances, managers tend to think of examples from recent experiences they've had.

Also related is **recency bias**, or tending to give more weight to information that you received most recently.

- **Anchoring and Adjustment:** The tendency to fixate on initial information received, and failing to adjust adequately for subsequent information. Such as fixating on a number we observe early on, then later comparing this to every other number we consider.
  - Example: If I asked you whether you thought today's temperature would be hotter or colder than 65 degrees, your responses might be closer to this number than if I had not provided this initial anchor point.
  - Asked in 1983 (when the prime interest rate was 11%) if the prime interest rate in 6 months would be above or below 8%, respondents in a study provided responses closer to this anchor point (10.5%) than respondents who were given an initial estimate of 14% (they guessed 11.2%), or given no initial estimate (they guessed 10.9%).[9]

- **Group think:** Prioritizing the views of the most vocal, most respected, or most senior, member of a group. Or agreeing too readily to a path in the interest of group harmony, without independently thinking through an issue or challenging the group's initial path.
  - Example: An accounting professor assigned a group of students to perform a gross vs. net revenue analysis. The group came back having analyzed just one weak reporting indicator (credit risk) out of 11 possible indicators that could have been evaluated. How could this have happened, if all individuals were independently thinking through this case, or challenging each other's views? (The group, by the way, reportedly got along very well.)

- **Hindsight bias:** Thinking—after the fact, once the outcome is known—that you would have made the right decision, or that you knew the right answer all along. Or viewing an event as more foreseeable after the fact than prior to the event.

---

[8] Final Report of the Advisory Committee on Improvements to Financial Reporting to the United States Securities and Exchange Commission, August 1, 2008.
[9] Edward Russo, J. and Paul Schoemaker, J.H. *Winning Decisions*, page 95 (Currency Doubleday, 2002).

- Example: An auditor who exhibits professional skepticism when evaluating an inconsistency may tend to be rewarded (by the client and his own manager) if a misstatement is found, but penalized for exhibiting skeptical behavior if no misstatement is found.[10]

■ **Escalation of commitment:** Staying with a decision even when you suspect or have evidence that the decision is wrong. That is, not "cutting your losses" once it's clear a decision is not working.

- Example: Internal auditors involved in an initial decision related to budgeting were more inclined to stay the course, making final decisions consistent with their initial decisions but which differed from internal auditors who made only a final decision on the same budget issue.[11]
- An investor buys a stock expecting its price to rise. Instead, the price falls and the investor ends up pouring more money into the failing stock than initially planned, in an attempt to justify and recoup the initial investment losses.

Notably, these are just a few of the many possible biases that can influence your decision making. Just imagine how these biases could impact each step of the research process, from deciding which facts to gather, to identifying alternatives, to reaching a conclusion.

Identifying Biases in Your Own Decision Making

Think of a recent decision you've made, either in a personal or professional context. What is one bias that may have affected your decision-making approach? Describe.

_____

_____

_____

Describe one step of the research process that could be impacted by decision biases. Explain.

_____

_____

Now
YOU
Try
3.10

How Do You Overcome These Biases? (To Reach a Sound Decision?)

To overcome judgment biases, first be aware that such biases exist. Next, obtain information and viewpoints from a variety of sources. Seek information that will challenge your existing views, or which offers a different perspective. Listen and understand when someone disagrees with you. And finally, applying a systematic research process will help you evaluate issues carefully and methodically. Your best evidence of this systematic process is high-quality documentation, as we'll discuss in the next chapter.

Challenge your existing views by asking _disconfirming questions_, or questions that explore opposing views. Consider this example, from the book _Winning Decisions_:

If [an investment analyst] thinks the disposable diaper business is becoming less price competitive, for example, he will ask executives a question that implies the opposite, such as "Is it true that price competition is getting tougher in disposable diapers?" This kind of question makes him more likely than competing analysts to get the real story.[12]

---

[10] Brazel, Jackson, Schaefer, and Stewart. Hindsight Bias and Professional Skepticism: Does the End Justify the Means?, (Abstract). A working paper. November 2013. Retrieved from http://www3.nd.edu/~carecob/Workshops/13-14Workshops/Brazel%20Paper.pdf

[11] Brody, R. and Kaplan, S. "Escalation of Commitment Among Internal Auditors," _Auditing: A Journal of Practice & Theory_, 1996, pages 1–15.

[12] Russo and Schoemaker, page 87.

When it comes time to reach a decision, focus on the issues that are most material. What matters most in this decision, and therefore what information is most important to consider? In many cases, reaching a decision will require the team to discuss and debate reasonable alternatives. Some decision researchers favor systematic techniques, such as importance-weighted decision matrices, where numerical values are assigned to the importance of each decision criterion. Increasingly, accounting firms are issuing decision frameworks which outline their firm policies for applying proper professional judgment (such as the KPMG *Professional Judgment Framework*).

In short, make sure that you gather sufficient, diverse information to make a high-quality decision. A recent *Journal of Accountancy* article suggested that accountants should have an attitude of *professional skepticism* toward even their own judgments.[13] While this chapter encourages you to "stop and think" about possible accounting before performing research, be careful to apply these principles even to your own instincts—remember to seek information that could confirm or disconfirm your initial views.

Learn from Your Mistakes (and Successes!)

Finally, much of our ability to make quality professional judgments comes from experience. Let's face it—you won't get every issue right the first time, especially early on in your career. Becoming a great accounting researcher involves a steep learning curve. To fast-track your learning, take the time to reflect—after the fact—on your mistakes and successes.

For example, if you recommend an accounting position that is later rejected or disproven, perform a *root cause analysis* of sorts, and review your process for coming to this conclusion. Was it flawed in some way? Did you fail to consider enough alternatives, or did you anchor too quickly to a solution?

You can also learn from projects that were successful. What process steps did you take that resulted in a favorable outcome? What lessons can you apply to future projects?

Writing your learnings down can be so simple—I'm a fan of Post-it notes. Simply jot down the key lesson learned and stick it on the wall ("Remember to check Section 55 Implementation Guidance"), until you feel like you've committed the lesson to memory. You might consider maintaining a brief Word document log of successes, as this list can be valuable at performance evaluation time.

Now
[YOU]
Try
3.11

Brainstorm, then briefly describe, a "lesson learned" that you've experienced already, in your brief career-to-date as an accounting researcher.

_____

_____

CHAPTER SUMMARY

This chapter introduced you to a step-by-step approach that you can apply to a range of research challenges. Your mission now is to practice using this approach, so that you'll be ready to shine when you have the opportunity to perform research professionally.

As you apply the research process described in this chapter, keep in the back of your mind some of the common judgment biases we discussed, as these can impact the choices you make in applying the research process. As discussed, your best defense against judgment biases is, first, awareness that these biases exist and next, application of a consistent, high-quality research process. As you gain experience as a researcher, take the time to identify lessons learned.

---

[13] Fay, Rebecca and Montague, Norma R. "I'm not biased, am I?" *Journal of Accountancy*, February 1, 2015.

REVIEW QUESTIONS

1. What is the accounting research process? What steps are involved in this process?
2. Why use a research process?
3. Why is it important to know a company's business before performing research on a given transaction?
4. What information should you try to understand, during the pre-step of understanding the business?
5. Name three of the resources recommended for getting to know a company's business or industry.
6. In what sections of a 10-K should a researcher look for background on a company's business and industry accounting issues?
7. What's the ideal timing for completing "step 0" of the research process?
8. Identify three resources a researcher might consult when gathering facts and background necessary to understand a transaction.
9. Why are listening skills highlighted as important for success during step 1 of the research process?
10. Why is it important to identify the "researchable question(s)" early in the research process?
11. Explain some of the ways that a researcher may revise or refine his or her research questions as he or she works through the research process.
12. What is a benefit of performing step 3 of the research process: *stop and think*?
13. Describe the process recommended in step 4 (search for guidance), for collecting then narrowing down guidance.
14. Complete the following sentence from the chapter's description of step 4. "Bear in mind that sometimes, researching a single accounting issue can involve consideration of _____."
15. What strategies does the chapter offer for avoiding distractions when performing research?
16. Name four resources (or questions) a researcher might consider when weighing alternative accounting treatments.
17. Explain the final step of the research process. Should additional evidence be gathered at this stage?
18. What caution does the chapter offer about accounting conclusions reached based on draft contracts?
19. What is a bias, and how might biases affect how you apply the research process?
20. Name the six biases described in this chapter, and briefly describe each.
21. Name three strategies for overcoming biases.

EXERCISES

1. You have just been assigned to provide client services to the following entities. For each, identify three resources you could consult in order to better understand the company's business model and industry.
   a. Ascension Health
   b. General Motors
   c. Time Warner Cable
2. For the first company in the preceding question, Ascension Health, use a library database to:
   a. Identify two competitors (aka, major companies in the industry).
   b. Next, look for an industry description page. Quoting verbatim from the database, name one interesting fact about this industry.
3. Look up the AICPA Audit & Accounting Guide, *Depository and Lending Institutions*, then look for the table of contents to this guide. Imagine that you've just been assigned to the audit of a bank. Name two chapters from this book that you might read (or skim) in advance of the engagement, and explain why you chose these.
4. Understanding the facts/background of a transaction: Certain businesses may choose to invest in projects that provide them with tax credits (such as a developer who builds low-income housing developments). In some cases, these tax credits can be sold or traded, when these investor businesses have more credits than they can use. Assume that your company has entered into a contract for the purchase of tax credits from a developer and has asked you to evaluate the accounting implications. You are in the first step of the research process (understanding the facts/background of the transaction). Identify three resources you could consult to gather additional background/precedent for this issue.

5. You are once again in the first step of the research process (understanding the facts). Now, your company is looking to repurchase some of its outstanding stock. You are about to attend a meeting between representatives of your company's Treasury department and a bank. Identify three resources you could consult, or questions you might ask of others on your team or in the organization, to gather additional background/precedent for this issue before you attend the meeting.

Identify at least one researchable question for each of the following issues (in questions 6–12).

6. A cable network has just entered into an agreement granting it the right to show reruns of a hit TV series. In exchange for this right, the network must pay the TV show's creators a fee each time the show airs.

7. An online travel agency sells a $400 airline ticket to a customer; of this amount, the travel agency must remit $370 to the airline, and the travel agency will retain a $30 commission related to the sale of the ticket.

8. A popular website primarily generates revenue through ad sales. Ad buyers must pay a specified cost per click, and this cost is based on agreed-upon terms between the website and ad buyer. The typical term of an advertising arrangement is approximately 30 days with billing generally occurring after the delivery of the advertisement.

9. Tar, Inc. (i.e., "the original polluter") has paid $8 million to a waste disposal company to clean a contaminated site, and to assume its environmental liability (currently recorded as an $8 million liability on Tar's financial statements). State regulators have signed off on the liability transfer and now look to the waste disposal company as the responsible party for the cleanup.

10. Acknowledging publicly that its Pie Division is its most unprofitable business unit, Bakeries, Inc. has announced the sale of the Pie Division's four baking facilities, along with planned layoffs of Pie Division's employees. Bakeries, Inc. is hoping to segregate the results of the Pie Division's operations in its financial statements. (Identify at least two possible research questions.)

11. Your company is planning to issue convertible bonds, also known as hybrid debt, which are bonds that can convert into shares of common stock upon the occurrence of certain triggering events.

12. For the following researchable question, identify two additional questions that might arise as the researcher digs deeper into the research topic. Assume that a company has just sold a portfolio of its accounts receivable, in exchange for cash and certain retained interests in the receivables. The initial question: Can the company record the transfer as a sale?

13. Stop and think. In this example, you'll be asked to stop and think about an issue, then to search the Codification for applicable guidance.
    a. Stop and think. Your company has just paid in advance for 12 months of billboard advertising. The company must determine how to record the cost of this advertising. What does your instinct tell you?
    b. Now, perform research within the Codification to find guidance on this issue. List two Codification subtopics that you think are most relevant to this issue and provide a one-sentence summary for each. Assume this is not a *direct response advertising cost*. Also, assume that ASC 340-20 does not apply.
    c. Consider: How might your response to this research question have differed if you had not stopped to think about the issue before performing research?

14. Identifying alternative accounting treatments: A joint venture was just formed, and one of the venturers (companies that invested in the JV) contributed a drug patent with a basis of $10 million but an estimated fair value of $20 million. List two accounting measurement alternatives available for the joint venture to recognize the contributed patent. Explain. (Notably, the Codification does not directly provide guidance for this issue, so your goal during this exercise is just to brainstorm.)

15. What are two types of "Accounting Changes" described in the Codification? Identify these "alternative" types of accounting changes, and cite where you found these listed in the Codification.

For each of the following sample scenarios (in questions 16–19), identify one or more biases that could be at play, then explain.

16. Following the discovery of fraudulent financial reporting by a company, a group of the company's investors sued the auditors. In court, the judge reviewed the auditors' workpapers and found that they were insufficient. What bias may have been at play for the judge?

17. The company's stock price was dropping fast. A task force was convened that consisted of senior vice presidents from across the company, plus one executive vice president (the CFO). The CFO came to the meeting prepared to offer a solution. When she did, the group agreed it was the appropriate path forward and set in motion a plan to implement her recommendation.

18. A member of the company's accounting policy team was asked to weigh in on whether a cost should be classified as an asset or as an expense. The operator who requested the review is responsible for managing her division's budget and is hopeful that the cost will be recorded as an asset. She points out similarities between this cost and other items historically recorded by the company as assets.

19. The auditors of XYZ Company are evaluating XYZ's estimate of the fair value of a hard-to-value private equity investment. The auditors submitted XYZ's estimate to their valuation team to ask whether the value appears reasonable.

20. The six decision traps and biases are not an all-inclusive list. Perform an Internet search for one other bias that you believe could be applicable to accounting or auditing, and which was not named in this chapter. In two or three sentences, explain this bias and its potential application to our profession.

CASE STUDY QUESTIONS

Understanding the Importance of Using a Research Process You are the manager on the audit of James & Sons Insurance. You have just assigned a new staff member to a limited-scope research assignment, asking her to research whether commissions to sales staff, incurred for the purpose of acquiring new customers, can be capitalized. You told her you weren't in a hurry, so she could take her time in responding. Nevertheless, the staff member quickly got to work and responded to you within a half hour with an email including an excerpt from ASC 340-40-25-1 and saying that in her opinion based on this guidance, the costs can likely be capitalized.   **3.1**

It looks like this staff person needs some coaching. In approximately one page, tactfully but clearly walk this staff person through the steps in the research process, including "step 0," that she could have approached more thoughtfully. Include in your response references to (but not necessarily excerpts from) guidance that would have been more responsive to this question.

Researching Energy Works' Industry Recall Energy Works, the (fictitious) oil and gas exploration and production company introduced in this chapter. Assume that you have just been assigned to work on the Energy Works audit team, but you do not have prior experience in the oil and gas industry. You need to do a little homework before the engagement begins.   **3.2**

Using an online library database that is available to you (such as Hoovers or IBISWorld), research and respond to the following:

- Key companies (competitors) in this industry
- Key sources of revenue for companies in this industry, products and operations
- Information about this industry's supply chain
- Industry growth trends and forecasts
- Plus, one other industry-specific fact you learned (e.g., industry jargon, analyst call preparation questions, and so on)

Summarize your research in approximately one page. Please do not cut and paste directly from the database; rather, summarize your research using your own words. Finally, describe one other source you might consult for additional background on this industry, prior to beginning the audit.

Researching an Industry of Your Choice Using an online library database that is available to you (such as Hoovers or IBISWorld), choose a company of interest, and identify its related industry. In approximately one page, describe: **3.3**

- Whether the company you've identified is public or private
- Key sources of revenue for companies in this industry
- Key competitors for this company
- Information about this industry's supply chain
- Industry growth trends and forecasts
- Plus, one other industry-specific fact you learned (e.g., industry jargon, analyst call preparation questions, and so on)

Please do not cut and paste directly from the database; rather, summarize your research using your own words. Finally, describe a circumstance in which you can envision performing similar industry research as a professional.

Identifying Researchable Questions *Facts:* Importer Corp. is a public company with a calendar year-end. Importer purchases auto parts from China and sells them to used car dealerships around the U.S. On November 1, 20X1, Importer received shipment on account of $500,000 worth of wheel bearings from its Chinese supplier. Unfortunately, these bearings were defective. Faced with commitments to deliver working parts to its own customers, Importer paid $200,000 on 11/15/X1 to a domestic third party to fix the defective parts. However, even after the repair effort, the bearings remained defective.   **3.4**

Importer has not yet paid the Chinese company for the parts purchased.

In early December, Importer requested repayment from the bearings manufacturer for its costs of repair ($200,000). However, when the manufacturer refused to pay, Importer sued the manufacturer on 12/15/X1 for its amount invested ($200,000) plus an additional $100,000 for lost revenues.

On February 2, 20X2, a court ruled in favor of Importer, awarding Importer $300,000 payable ratably in three monthly installments to begin on 2/15/X2.

Required:

1. Identify Importer's researchable questions as of 12/31/X1 related to this series of issues.
2. Identify Importer's researchable questions as of 2/2/X2 related to this series of issues.

3.5   **Identifying Alternative Accounting Treatments** Upon the initial adoption of fair value measurement guidance, companies debated whether cash and cash equivalents should be presented in their fair value tables (a disclosure issue). Although likely not a significant area of concern to investors, companies wanted to apply the guidance appropriately and had to therefore think through this issue.

Review applicable Codification topics (your search might include, for example, guidance for cash, fair value, or financial instruments, and so on). Identify any paragraphs that would support a) disclosure, or b) non-disclosure of this item in a company's fair value tables. Summarize these alternatives, your research, and your recommendation in approximately one page.

3.6   **Practice Your Listening Skills** The chapter mentioned that an important part of the research process is learning to *listen* to others, so that you can learn from them. Conduct a two-minute interview with a peer or friend who is studying a different field. Ask that person to teach you something that they find interesting about their field. For two minutes, work very hard to listen attentively. Document the conversation, describing what you learned. Finally, describe a circumstance in which you think these listening skills could benefit you as an accounting professional.

3.7   **Weighing Alternatives—Change in Estimate versus Error Correction** *Facts:* You are the owner of a lawn service company (LawnCo) which provides grounds and maintenance services to a range of corporate customers. Customers are expected to pay on the first of each month, in advance of receiving services. One of your corporate customers is an eldercare facility whose grounds you have maintained for many years. The customer has not paid for the last three months of services (from Oct.–Dec. 20X1); nevertheless, to maintain a positive relationship, your company continued to provide mowing and weed control services to the eldercare facility during that time. Your company ceased providing services in January 20X2 and found out in that same month that the eldercare facility filed for bankruptcy in September. Your company now believes that collection of the missed payments is extremely unlikely.

Your company has already issued financial statements to lenders (for the period ending 12/31/X1) which reflected revenue and a corresponding account receivable related to this customer of $10,000 per month for services provided to this customer. Those financial statements also reflected the company's standard allowance (reserve) amount on receivables, of 4% of sales. In total, your company's average monthly sales amount to $500,000.

Required:

1. Evaluate whether receipt of this information indicates you have a *change in accounting estimate* or whether the customer's bankruptcy should result in this event being considered *an error in previously issued financial statements*.
2. Next, describe the accounting treatment (as required by the Codification) for each alternative, then support your explanations with draft journal entries.
3. Finally, briefly state which treatment appears to be more appropriate given the circumstances. If you must make any assumptions in reaching this conclusion, state these.

3.8   **Determining Whether to Adopt the Goodwill Accounting Alternative Available to Private Companies** *Facts:* Smith Brothers, Inc. is a privately-owned corporation that manufactures and sells exterior window shutters. Opened and privately-owned by two brothers in 2000, Smith Brothers began with a single retail outlet and has since expanded to be the #1 seller and manufacturer of shutters in the entire southern United States. This success has been fueled not only by adding new stores, but also through targeted acquisitions of competing small businesses in key states across the south. As consideration for certain of these acquisitions, in addition to cash payments, the brothers privately sold shares of the company, for an external ownership stake amounting to 15%. In recent years, to reward select company executives for strong performance, the company has also given select key executives a combined 5% ownership in the company. As of 2015, the brothers each owned 40% of the company, and the aforementioned external owners own 20% of the company. Shares are subject to restrictions on transfer, as they must first be offered to the brothers, then to other existing shareholders. The brothers must approve any sales of shares to outside parties.

Given its rapid expansion, Smith Brothers has not ruled out the possibility of one day taking their company public through an IPO. Doing this would give the company the cash to grow at a more rapid pace, through additional targeted acquisitions. However, for now, the company is privately-held and prepares GAAP financial statements as required by three of its bank lenders. Its existing bank loans were solicited through a competitive bidding process, in which a third-party broker matched Smith Brothers with the bank willing to offer it the lowest interest rates on borrowed funds. Smith Brothers does not currently file financial statements with the SEC or other regulators.

As a result of its past acquisitions, Smith Brothers has a considerable amount of recorded goodwill on its financial statements. Smith Brothers is aware that the FASB, working with the recently created Private Company Council (PCC), recently released an alternative allowing private companies to amortize their goodwill, and Smith Brothers is considering whether to adopt this alternative. Amortizing, rather than impairment testing, its goodwill is expected to save the company approximately $20,000 in fees paid annually to valuation specialists.

Required: You are an associate in the accounting advisory practice of a public accounting firm. Smith Brothers periodically engages your team to assist in accounting for the company's acquisitions. Today, Smith Brothers has asked for your team's assistance in evaluating the appropriateness, and possible ramifications, of employing this private company alternative. In doing so, you must address the following questions:

1. First, locate this recently-issued standard from the FASB. What is the name of this standard? Where is this guidance codified in the FASB Codification? What entities are eligible to apply the guidance in this standard?
2. Is Smith Brothers, specifically, eligible to apply this standard?
3. What is the transition/effective date for applying this alternative? Also, is there a certain date by which Smith Brothers must make this election?
4. If Smith Brothers were to elect this accounting alternative, describe how the company would account for and present its goodwill.
5. Would such a change be considered a change in accounting principle, and what are the implications of this? To respond, you will need to consult a separate topic within the Codification.
6. What other counsel would you give Smith Brothers, related to application of this accounting alternative? Said another way, what other considerations might be useful for Smith Brothers related to this or other private company alternatives? (There is no single, correct answer. Just think about other implications of this decision, or other considerations you might pass along to management.)

Evaluate each of the above-listed issues for Smith Brothers management, citing excerpts from the relevant ASU (or from the Codification) as applicable.

You Create the Case (Applying the Accounting Research Process) On your own, create a fictitious fact pattern (accounting problem/business issue) to which you can apply the accounting research process. If you are able, use a fact pattern based on a real situation that you've encountered professionally (such as from a work experience or an internship). That is, think back to an accounting question that required some thought or discussion.

3.9

Alternatively, consider the following sources to generate ideas for fact patterns: (1) The Codification: browse for ideas of topics or examples that you can use to "back into" a fact pattern; (2) Recent business news articles, such as from the *Wall Street Journal*; (3) A situation a parent or small-business owner you know has encountered; or (4) Corporate annual reports, for ideas of transactions/events.

For this fact pattern, create four PowerPoint slides to share with your class:

1. The first should show only the fact pattern you created, including discussion of all relevant facts necessary to understand the issue. Next, describe any industry-specific guidance you might consult for background on the company's business.
2. The second should include a researchable question for this fact pattern (identify at least one). On the same slide, brainstorm the likely answer to the question.
3. The third slide should provide the applicable Codification reference (identify just one or two key paragraph(s)), alternatives considered (if any), and discussion of the process you used to research this issue using the Codification. Consider this step a journal of your research actions, including a description of the method you used to find this guidance (search or browse path), dead ends you found, etc.
4. The fourth slide should include a brief statement of your conclusion.

Alternatively, your instructor may ask you to respond to this case study in the form of a one- or two-page written document.

ADDITIONAL REFERENCES

1. Kahneman, Daniel. *Thinking, Fast and Slow.* Farrar, Straus and Giroux, 2013.
2. Russo, J. Edward and Schoemaker, Paul J.H. *Winning Decisions: Getting It Right the First Time.* Crown Business, 2001.
3. Fay, Rebecca. "I'm not biased, am I?" *Journal of Accountancy*, February 1, 2015.
4. *Elevating Professional Judgment in Auditing and Accounting: The KPMG Professional Judgment Framework.* 2011, KPMG.

Chapter 4

Creating Effective Documentation

Recall Richard, the accounting policy analyst at Energy Works who was introduced in the opening scenario of the previous chapter. Now that Richard has learned a step-by-step research process to apply to Energy Works' joint venture, his next challenge is to prepare thoughtful documentation of the accounting issues identified.

Richard's supervisor has asked him to prepare an accounting issues memo that walks through each step of his accounting analysis related to the joint venture. Accordingly, Richard plans to document the path he took to concluding on Energy Works' accounting—from how he determined the arrangement was outside the scope of the variable interest model (including his evaluation of the terms *business* and *joint venture*), to how he evaluated the arrangement for consolidation under the voting interest model, to how he concluded that use of the equity method (as opposed to fair value or cost method) is appropriate.

In practice, *documenting* accounting research is integral to the process of *performing* research. So Richard would have prepared much of this documentation while performing his research. However, this chapter specifically focuses on writing. This chapter covers writing conventions, style, and tips that are particular to technical accounting research. Read on, and find out what tips we can offer Richard on preparing a memo that professionally addresses his company's proposed transaction.

After reading this chapter and performing the exercises herein, you will be able to

1. **Explain** the importance of documentation.

2. **Draft** effective emails to communicate the results of limited-scope research.

3. **Formulate** an effective background section and issues list in an accounting research memo.

4. **Prepare** an effective research analysis, including consideration of alternative viewpoints, and a well-supported conclusion.

5. Properly **reference** passages from the Codification.

6. **Communicate** using professional style.

Learning Objectives

Organization of This Chapter

This chapter begins by discussing the key role that documentation plays in the performance—and preservation—of accounting research. Next, the chapter describes how to (1) draft effective emails and (2) prepare technical accounting research memoranda. The chapter concludes with writing strategies, including how to effectively reference authoritative guidance, and style tips for professional communication. To bring all of these ideas together, the chapter appendix includes a sample issues memo.

It's quite common for beginning researchers to view documentation style as an area of personal preference, or as an area where instructors nitpick needlessly. "This isn't an English class!" is a comment that accounting research instructors have come to dread. I urge you to approach this chapter with an open mind. The more effectively you can communicate your research, the more you'll be seen as an effective researcher. The tips outlined in this chapter are intended to help you communicate in the style used by technical accountants in our field, from junior staff to national offices.

DOCUMENTATION IS INTEGRAL TO ACCOUNTING RESEARCH

LO1 **Explain** the importance of documentation.

Recall from previous chapters that the objectives of accounting research are generally two-fold:

1. To account for transactions or items in a manner that is appropriate and **supportable** based on authoritative guidance, and
2. To create **documentation** describing the research performed and supporting the conclusion reached.

In other words, *performing* accounting research is only half the battle. You must also clearly *document* your research.

Documentation is critical to accounting research because

- The exercise itself of creating documentation can cause you to think through accounting issues more critically than if you simply discuss the issues.

- Creating documentation of the basis for accounting positions creates an audit trail. Not only will the files be useful for historical reference, but current documentation can be shared with the company's auditors, helping the auditors understand and review the company's accounting judgments in real time.

- This transaction sets precedent for future transactions. Without proper documentation, company accountants could risk reaching a different conclusion if this type of transaction is later repeated. This could result in inconsistent accounting or, worse, restatement if company accountants conclude that the prior transaction's accounting is improper and the transaction is material.

- If your company's accounting position on a transaction is ever questioned (for example, through an SEC comment letter, in the event of a lawsuit, or by regulators), ideally, your company's rationale for the accounting would already be neatly summarized into a memo. In theory, that memo could be forwarded straight over to the SEC in response to their inquiry, for example.

- Auditors must also maintain documentation evidencing their reviews of judgmental client accounting positions. This documentation shows that the auditor was diligent in researching and evaluating whether client positions are appropriate.

Furthermore, know that when you create robust documentation, you protect yourself—in a sense—from the sort of "hindsight bias" that we read about in Chapter 3. The following comments from the SEC staff, which emphasize the importance of robust, timely documentation to support judgments, further illustrate this point:

> "The alternatives considered and the conclusions reached should be documented contemporaneously. This will ensure that the evaluation of the judgment is based on the same facts that were reasonably available at the time the judgment was made . . ."[1]

By walking your reader through your analysis, in real time as you make accounting judgments, you demonstrate to the reader that your process for evaluating the issue was robust and appropriate in light of facts known at the time.

Remember that it's often your end product—your research report—which determines whether your research is seen as high-quality. Understanding the importance of writing skills, this chapter walks you through not only the form and content of professional accounting docu-

---

[1] Final Report of the Advisory Committee on Improvements to Financial Reporting to the United States Securities and Exchange Commission, August 1, 2008. Page 96.

mentation, but also some of the finer points to writing in a style that will impress even the most technical of accountants.

COMMUNICATING ACCOUNTING RESEARCH

Let's take a closer look at how to communicate the results of your research. We will explore two common methods for communicating accounting research:

- Emails
- Accounting issues memoranda

Notably, client letters are another form of communicating accounting research, but are not a focus of this chapter. See Chapter 11 for a sample client letter and guidance for preparing client letters.

One overarching tip, as we move into our discussion of writing: *Know your audience.* Start out any writing assignment by considering who will read your work, then write at a level that your reader will understand.

For example, the level of detail you provide in your Codification references (**ASC 840**, versus "the Leases topic") may depend upon whether you are writing to a technical accountant, versus a member of the Finance team at your company.

In his Preface to the SEC's Plain English Handbook, Warren Buffett offers the following suggestion:

> One unoriginal but useful tip: Write with a specific person in mind. When writing Berkshire Hathaway's annual report, I pretend that I'm talking to my sisters. I have no trouble picturing them: Though highly intelligent, they are not experts in accounting or finance. They will understand plain English, but jargon may puzzle them. My goal is simply to give them the information I would wish them to supply me if our positions were reversed. To succeed, I don't need to be Shakespeare; I must, though, have a sincere desire to inform.[2]

In many cases, your audience for accounting research communications will be your supervisor, your auditors, and—possibly—regulators who might later scrutinize a transaction. Accordingly, much of the accounting research communication that we will cover in this chapter will be written to an audience of fellow accountants. However, it's important in all cases to consider your audience before you begin writing.

Let's look now at how to write professional emails.

EMAILING THE RESULTS OF RESEARCH QUESTIONS

Email is often useful for communicating the results of limited-scope research questions. This is often the case when you are not the "owner" of the issue (i.e., the party responsible for documenting or concluding on the complete issue), but rather are helping provide relevant guidance to some aspect of an issue that a colleague is managing.

LO2 **Draft** effective emails to communicate the results of limited-scope research.

Here is an example of a professional email responding to a limited-scope research question. In this example, John, a staff member at Energy Works, has been asked to help Richard research whether the new joint venture meets the definition of a *business*. As you may recall, understanding whether the JV is a business is critical to understanding whether Energy Works can apply the so-called "business scope exception" to the variable interest model. John's response is as follows:

---

[2] Office of Investor Education and Assistance, of the U.S. Securities and Exchange Commission. *A Plain English Handbook: How to create clear SEC disclosure documents.* 1998. Preface.

Re: Whether the joint venture meets the definition of a business

Richard,

You asked me to research whether Energy Works' proposed joint venture would meet the definition of a business for purposes of applying **ASC 810-10** (Consolidation). Given my understanding of this arrangement, I am assuming that one or both of the venturers will share their technological know-how for operating the FPSO facility that Energy Works is contributing. However, let me know if that's not the case.

ASC 810-10-20 defines a **business** as:

> An integrated set of activities and assets that is capable of being conducted and managed for the purpose of providing a return in the form of dividends, lower costs, or other economic benefits directly to investors or other owners, members, or participants. Additional guidance on what a business consists of is presented in paragraphs 805-10-55-4 through 55-9.

Implementation guidance in par. 55-4 (of **ASC 805-10**, Business Combinations) elaborates on this definition, stating: "A **business** consists of inputs and processes applied to those inputs that have the ability to create outputs." Inputs are described as including long-lived assets (including intangible assets), and processes are described as including operational processes, documented or known by a skilled workforce.

In this case, the JV appears to meet this definition, given that it has both inputs (an FPSO and drilling permit) and processes (the venturers have agreed to provide employees with technical expertise and presumably their technological know-how for operating the facility) that are capable of generating returns (outputs) for the venturers. Furthermore, it's my understanding that the purpose of this JV is for the venturers to pool their resources to conduct operations, thus generating returns. Therefore, this arrangement does appear to meet the definition of a business.

It's worth noting that meeting this definition would be a higher hurdle if the venture was formed for the purpose of *exploring* for oil resources, where the ability to provide a return would be much less certain.

Let me know if you need anything further. Thanks for letting me assist with this question.

John

The sample email above exhibits qualities that you should generally try to include in your professional email communications. Here are some of the lessons learned from this email:

- Keep it brief. The sample email above is concise, yet complete in its response to the question raised.

- Include a subject line that briefly describes the accounting issue you've researched, and the client name.

- Re-state the question: "You asked me to research . . ."

- Include an excerpt from authoritative guidance to support your response.

- Use complete sentences.

- If you made any assumptions in researching the issue, state what you assumed. It's likely that you will have to make assumptions if you have only limited background on an issue.

- Reread, possibly print, the email before you send it. This will help you identify confusing or weak language, as well as grammatical errors.

- Do not say "I think/feel"; this isn't about you. It's about what guidance is on point. If you are unsure about how guidance should be read, you can say: "It appears . . ."

- Avoid exclamation points, in order to keep your tone as professional as possible.

- Include an offer to be of further assistance.

One of my former **accounting research** colleagues made it a habit to print and reread *every* substantive email to a client or supervisor before sending it. She wanted to always put her most professional self forward. Her thoughtful approach to research—combined with her attention to detail—has paid dividends for her career; she went on to work in the national office of a major firm, and currently works in the SEC's Office of the Chief Accountant.

TIP from the Trenches

Drafting a Professional Email

Now **YOU** Try 4.1

You are a staff auditor reviewing the Statement of Cash Flows for Auto Corp (the client). The senior on your audit team (Matt) has asked you to research whether the client has appropriately classified the proceeds from the sale of its manufacturing facility as cash flows from investing activities.

Draft an email response to Matt's question. Use the Codification guidance in Figure 4-1 to support your response.

> **Classification**

45-10 A statement of cash flows shall classify cash receipts and cash payments as resulting from investing, financing, or operating activities.

> > **Cash Flows from Investing Activities**

45-11 Cash flows from purchases, sales, and maturities of available-for-sale securities shall be classified as cash flows from **investing activities** and reported gross in the statement of cash flows.

45-12 All of the following are cash inflows from investing activities:

a. Receipts from collections or sales of loans made by the entity and of other entities' debt instruments (other than cash equivalents and certain debt instruments that are acquired specifically for resale as discussed in paragraph **230-10-45-21**) that were purchased by the entity

b. Receipts from sales of equity instruments of other entities (other than certain equity instruments carried in a trading account as described in paragraph **230-10-45-19**) and from returns of investment in those instruments

c. Receipts from sales of property, plant, and equipment and other productive assets . . .

Reproduced with permission of the Financial Accounting Foundation.

Figure 4-1

Codification excerpt for email exercise (ASC 230-10, Statement of Cash Flows)

Your response here _____

_____

_____

_____

_____

_____

_____

_____

_____

_____

_____

_____

_____

_____

[TIP] from the Trenches

A final tip, on the subject of emails . . . Ever wonder if sending a higher-ranking colleague a quick "thank you" email, after they have assisted you, will bother them? As a young professional, I recall wondering the same thing.

But trust me, a quick "Thanks for your help!" note is never a bother to receive. These emails are a win-win: You're showing that you're a grateful, appreciative person, and the note will make your colleague or instructor smile (and can be easily deleted—it's really not a nuisance).

As a general rule of thumb, if someone assists you, don't second guess it. Send a quick thanks.

DRAFTING AN ACCOUNTING ISSUES MEMORANDUM

Documentation in the form of an accounting issues memorandum is generally warranted when a transaction is complex, judgmental, or highly material. Each company should have policies in place for when such documentation is required, and at what point in the transaction review process. It is considered a best practice to evaluate and document the accounting for a transaction at or before the time the transaction is executed. In certain cases, such "contemporaneous" documentation is *required*, as discussed further in Chapter 1.

Accounting issues memos are often organized into sections similar to those presented in Figure 4-2. Of course, this format is subject to some variation by company; for example, some companies prefer to locate the Conclusion section at the beginning of the issues memo. Nevertheless, we'll refer to the layout presented in Figure 4-2 as the **standard memo format**.

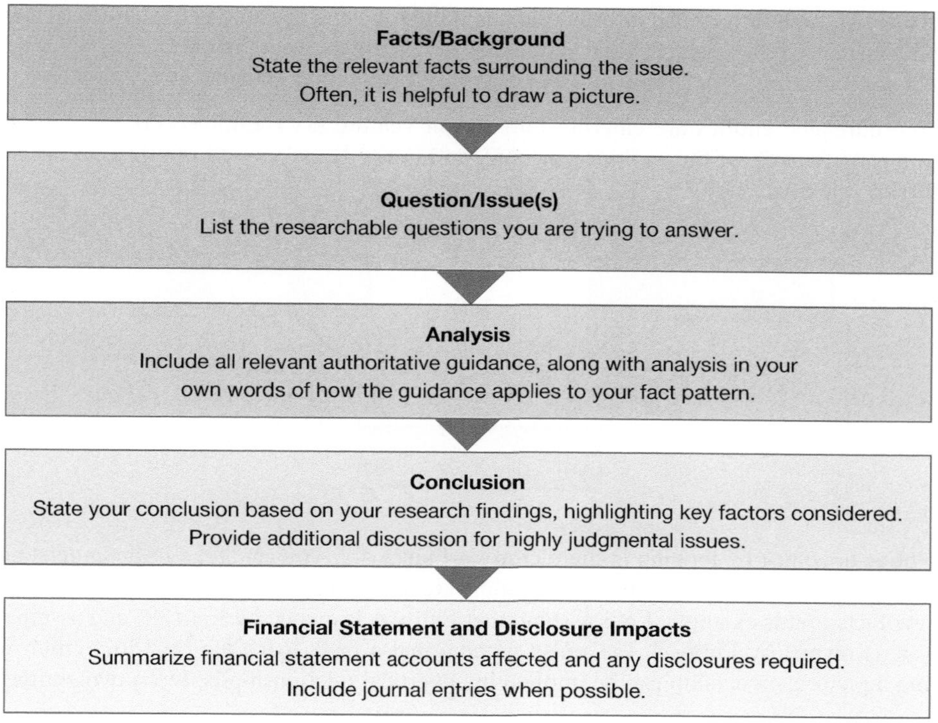

Figure 4-2
Standard memo format

```
┌─────────────────────────────────────────────────────────┐
│                    Facts/Background                       │
│         State the relevant facts surrounding the issue.   │
│           Often, it is helpful to draw a picture.         │
└─────────────────────────────────────────────────────────┘
                            ▼
┌─────────────────────────────────────────────────────────┐
│                    Question/Issue(s)                      │
│      List the researchable questions you are trying to    │
│                          answer.                          │
└─────────────────────────────────────────────────────────┘
                            ▼
┌─────────────────────────────────────────────────────────┐
│                       Analysis                            │
│   Include all relevant authoritative guidance, along with │
│   analysis in your own words of how the guidance applies  │
│                   to your fact pattern.                   │
└─────────────────────────────────────────────────────────┘
                            ▼
┌─────────────────────────────────────────────────────────┐
│                      Conclusion                           │
│   State your conclusion based on your research findings,  │
│       highlighting key factors considered. Provide        │
│       additional discussion for highly judgmental issues. │
└─────────────────────────────────────────────────────────┘
                            ▼
┌─────────────────────────────────────────────────────────┐
│          Financial Statement and Disclosure Impacts       │
│   Summarize financial statement accounts affected and any │
│   disclosures required. Include journal entries when      │
│                        possible.                          │
└─────────────────────────────────────────────────────────┘
```

The issues memorandum should include all of the sections shown in Figure 4-2. Present these section headers in bold to improve the readability of your memo. A sample accounting issues memo, which addresses the Energy Works scenario introduced earlier in this chapter, is included in an Appendix at the end of this chapter.

> Your ultimate goal with the issues memo is to create a "one-stop shop" for knowledge about this transaction and its accounting. A reader, after picking up your memo, should not have to do additional digging to fully understand the background or the support for the accounting conclusion. After reading your memo, if a reader finds it necessary to get additional key facts from the contract, or to read additional guidance from the Codification, then you have failed to make your memo a one-stop shop.

[**TIP**] from the Trenches

Facts/Background

The Background section of an issues memo should include *all relevant background* necessary for understanding the transaction and its accounting. This section should be concise, but not sparse. Aim to provide enough detail about the issue that a party uninvolved with the matter could pick up the memo—even years later—and understand the issue well enough to form an opinion as to whether or not the accounting treatment is appropriate.

LO3 Formulate an effective background section and issues list in an accounting research memo.

Step 1 of the research process, described in the preceding chapter, outlines the **process** necessary to understand the facts and background of a transaction. Relevant information obtained from this step 1 should be included in the Background section of an issues memo.

Transactions are often complex. A *picture of a transaction*, included within the Background section of a memo, can greatly enhance a reader's understanding of the relationships and parties involved in the issue. These can be fairly easy to create using the "shapes" feature in Word. In the picture, try to show as much information about the relationships among the parties as you can (parent/subsidiary relationships, what each party gives or gets from the other, etc.).

For example, here is a simple picture for the following arrangement:

■ Two unrelated entities are entering into a joint venture (JV). Entity A contributes $1,000 to the JV for 50% of the equity ownership, and Entity B makes a $2,000 loan to the JV for 50% of the ownership.

Figure 4-3

Picture of joint venture arrangement

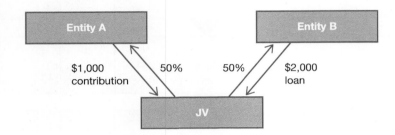

Notice how, just by looking at the picture in Figure 4-3, you can get a basic understanding of the relationships between the parties. To illustrate a slightly more complex arrangement, let's add new facts to this example. Let's assume that Entity A is owned by Entity 1, and assume that Entity B is owned by Entity 2. Let's also assume that a bank loans the JV $500. Often when drawing a picture, ownership can be implied by a vertical relationship between two entities.

Figure 4-4

Picture of joint venture with ownership by Entities 1 and 2

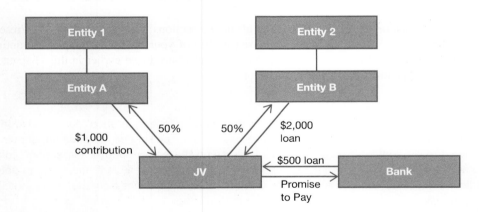

Notice a few things about the picture in Figure 4-4. First, even without "100%" written next to the line connecting Entity 1 and Entity A, the vertical relationship implies full ownership. Second, as the bank is not involved as an owner, it is not drawn in a vertical relationship; it is shown to the side of the JV to indicate that it is an outside, third party.

There is no magic to drawing a picture for inclusion in a memo. The idea is just to portray relationships in a way that readers can easily understand.

Now

[YOU]

Try

4.2

Drawing a Picture

Draw a picture for the following arrangement:

■ Entity A owns Entity B and Entity C. Entities B and C enter into a joint venture ("the JV"). Entity B contributes $20,000 for 99% of the equity ownership. Entity C contributes $500 for 1% of the equity and will serve as manager of the JV. Bank lends the JV $1 million.

■ Hint: Beside the line representing Entity C's contribution of $500, you can also write "manager," as this is a type of service that Entity C is contributing to the JV.

Your picture here

> The approach for drawing pictures outlined in this chapter came from what I learned in the field, informally. My colleagues at the FASB used to sketch out transaction structure pictures on whiteboards—just to facilitate conversations we had amongst ourselves, and that practice continued in my roles in advisory and corporate accounting. More formal diagramming methods exist but are not covered in this book.[3]

[**TIP**] from the Trenches

A picture depicting the Energy Works scenario introduced earlier in this chapter has been included in the sample issues memo in the Appendix to this chapter.

Finally, it is often helpful at the end of the Facts section to very briefly (1–2 sentences) set up the overall issue to be addressed. That is, you're not listing out your research questions yet, but you can set the stage for the overall themes that you plan to address in the memo.

For example: Energy Works must determine how to record its investment in the JV.

Beginning researchers often struggle with wording when setting the stage. Avoid statements such as:

- Energy Works *must choose* how to record its investment. Or,
- Energy Works *has the option* to consolidate the JV or record its investment as an asset.

Rather than describing an accounting policy determination as a *choice* or an *option*, think of Energy Works' objective as to *determine* which accounting method is *most appropriate*. Or, to determine *whether it should* consolidate, versus record its investment as an asset.

Question/Issue(s)

The Question/Issue(s) section of the memo should follow immediately after the background. Under the header "Issue(s)," list your researchable question(s). Often, there may be multiple questions to address. For example, the following research questions are listed in Richard's memo documenting Energy Works' joint venture arrangement:

Issues:

1. Is Energy Works required to consolidate the joint venture?
2. If consolidation is not required, what accounting method should Energy Works use to account for its investment in the JV?
3. How will Energy Works record the transfer of the FPSO facility to the JV?

---

[3] E.g., Resources, Events, and Agents (REA) Modeling.

Notice that each issue is phrased in the form of a question, and these research questions should be listed together at the beginning of the memo (in the Issues section). It's often the case with complex issues (as is the case here) that each research question builds on the previous question. Had this been a simpler topic, a single issue ("Issue 1") might suffice to determine the accounting, and a second issue ("Issue 2") might address required disclosures.

There is no magic to picking the perfect research questions. In fact, in the Energy Works scenario, Richard could have broken Issue 1 down into several issues, such as:

1.   Is the joint venture within the scope of the VIE model?

2.   If not, how should Energy Works apply the voting model to this arrangement?

Or, more detailed still: *Does Energy Works have a variable interest in the joint venture? Does the joint venture meet the definition of a business?*, and so on.

In short, the goal in selecting issues is to organize your accounting analysis in a logical way, which clearly walks your reader through the issues you faced and the research you performed. Use your judgment as to how best to organize your issues.

[**TIP**]   from the Trenches

As an accounting research instructor, I often assign case studies that have questions intended to guide the students in addressing all key issues. A common mistake students make is to organize their memo entirely based on these discussion questions, exactly as provided.

But the thing is, *you*—as writer—are responsible for deciding how to organize your memo in a manner that most clearly introduces the topic and walks readers through the relevant issues. This all starts with how you organize the issues list. Of course, you need to address all required points. But the discussion questions as provided shouldn't become the de facto outline or issues list for your memo.

Analysis

LO4 Prepare an effective research analysis, including consideration of alternative viewpoints, and a well-supported conclusion.

The Analysis section is arguably the most critical component of a well-written issues memo. In this section, you will address each issue listed, one at a time. Title the first Analysis section, for example, **Analysis of Issue 1:** *Is Energy Works required to consolidate the joint venture?*

Tying Together the Guidance and Case Facts

The Analysis section is aptly named because in it you will include *excerpts* from authoritative guidance, along with *commentary* in your own words about how the guidance applies to your transaction. Nonauthoritative guidance may also be included in this section of your memo, as a supplement to authoritative guidance.

A leading professor in accounting research described a common student struggle with the analysis section, as follows:

The Analysis section is really the key and what I often find most lacking in students' reports.
     That's because they don't do a good job of reasoning from the facts of the case, using the literature they found, to reach the appropriate conclusion. Rather, their process is more like: here are the facts, here is research, here is a conclusion.

In other words, the analysis section is your chance to bring together the facts of the case, the literature, and your evaluation of judgments or alternatives in the guidance. You must take the time to really *relate the guidance to your specific fact pattern*. Pull in actual words from your summary of the facts, and describe how they relate to actual words from the guidance.

As an example, consider the following excerpt from Richard's analysis of Energy Works' joint venture arrangement. In this excerpt, Richard is reviewing **ASC 810-10** (Consolidation) to see whether this transaction qualifies for a scope exception to application of the variable interest model. Notice how Richard's analysis brings together authoritative guidance and the facts of this arrangement.

EXAMPLE

Energy Works believes that this arrangement may qualify for the so-called "business scope exception" in par. 15-17(d) of **ASC 810-10**, as follows:

> 15-17(d). A legal entity that is deemed to be a **business** need not be evaluated by a reporting entity to determine if the legal entity is a VIE under the requirements of the Variable Interest Entities Subsections unless any of the following conditions exist . . .:
> 1. The reporting entity . . . participated significantly in the design or redesign of the legal entity. However, this condition does not apply if the legal entity is an operating joint venture under joint control of the reporting entity and one or more independent parties or a franchisee.
> 2-4. [For the simplicity of this example, conditions 2-4 will not be evaluated at this time, however in practice entities are required to evaluate these conditions.][4]

According to this guidance, a business is not required to be evaluated under the VIE model *unless* the reporting entity "participated significantly in the design" of the entity; however, this "design" exception does not apply to *operating joint ventures* under *joint control* of the venturers. As Energy Works participated in the design of the JV, the JV must meet the GAAP definition of a joint venture, under joint control, to qualify for this scope exception.

Therefore, Energy Works must evaluate whether the JV: 1) is a *legal entity*; 2) is considered a *business*; and 3) is an *operating joint venture* under *joint control*. If all of these conditions are met, Energy Works may apply the business scope exception to use of the variable interest model.

Did you notice in Richard's analysis that he discussed how the guidance relates specifically to Energy Works' fact pattern? See how he says: "As Energy Works participated in the design of the JV . . ." He is walking us through his *reasoning*, as opposed to simply stating: *This scope exception applies.*

Present Available Alternatives

Recall that the analysis section should clearly describe any alternatives available in accounting for a given transaction, weighing their relative merits. Remember that accounting research isn't always just about the destination; *how you get* to a particular accounting treatment matters too. I don't accept the argument from students that the only goal is to get to the right answer. Rather, the analysis section is your opportunity to walk the reader through your thought process. What guidance did you consider? What alternatives were present? Was application of the guidance judgmental? Could other guidance have applied?

In Richard's case, for example, it would not have been enough for him to assume the VIE model does not apply, and to go straight to the evaluation of the voting model. Even though the end result may be the same, Richard must walk his readers through his evaluation, showing us how he determined that the VIE model does not apply.

---

[4] Other exceptions to the business scope exception—omitted for simplicity of this example—include that substantially all of the JV's activities cannot be performed on behalf of one investor, and that the reporting entity cannot have contributed over half of the fair value of the JV's equity. We will assume for simplicity that neither of these exceptions applies to this case.

By presenting available alternatives in your memo, you are being upfront with your reader. You are showing the reader that your conclusion involved judgment. This is a good thing. To illustrate this point, consider the following TIP from the Trenches.

The only way someone reading your documentation will trust your conclusion is if you have clearly identified the available alternatives in your analysis.

In the past, I have asked students to document the accounting required for a certain transaction, knowing that when they began to explore the guidance, they would be presented with two alternatives.

- The "A" papers are the ones where students say: "Two alternatives exist (method A and method B). Method A appears to be more appropriate for this situation because . . ."

- The "B" or "C" papers are the ones where students say: "Method A should be followed because . . ." without mentioning that an alternative treatment is available.

As an employer, I would place more trust in the work of the "A" students. Even if I disagree with their choice of accounting method, at least I have been made aware that two choices exist. In contrast, the "B" or "C" papers did not give me the full story. When reviewing future submissions from these "employees," I would likely perform the extra step of rechecking the guidance they cite for completeness.

In our Energy Works example, once Richard determined that consolidation is not required, he next considered whether use of the cost, equity, or fair value method is most appropriate. Take a look at Issue 2 of the memo (in the Appendix of this chapter) to see how Richard analyzed and weighed these alternatives.

Tips for Incorporating Guidance—the Guidance Sandwich

Recall the "one-stop shop" concept described earlier. Your Analysis section should include enough excerpts from the authoritative guidance that a reader will not have to go back to the Codification (or other applicable authority) in order to understand the support for your analysis. Don't just refer generally to the guidance, or paraphrase the guidance into your own words. Rather, include enough actual excerpts to clearly make your case, then analyze this guidance in your own words.

As a general rule of thumb, your own commentary should *precede and follow* all guidance excerpts.

Ever heard of the interpersonal communication concept of a "compliment sandwich"? It goes something like this: If you're going to criticize someone, say something nice before and after the criticism. For example, "Joe, I like your tie today. I really wish you would do something about your bad breath. By the way, nice job on that report."

Think of your analysis section as a series of *guidance sandwiches*, with your own words introducing, and then analyzing each guidance excerpt.

EXAMPLE

Following is a simple guidance sandwich that illustrates Richard's analysis of whether the JV meets the definition of a legal entity. Recall that this is one of the criteria for use of the business scope exception.

> *Legal Entity*
>
> ASC 810-10-20 defines a **legal entity** as:
>
> > Any legal structure used to conduct activities or to hold assets. Some examples of such structures are corporations, partnerships, limited liability companies, grantor trusts, and other trusts.
>
> As the joint venture will be legally organized as an LLC, it is considered a legal entity. Therefore, this condition for use of the business scope exception is met.

Notice how the example provides commentary in Richard's own words before and after the guidance excerpt. The first sentence of the example introduces the guidance and states why it is being considered. The quote from the guidance is inserted next. Finally, the last sentence applies the guidance to the company's own set of facts.

Nonauthoritative sources that you consider would be presented in a similar manner, following the authoritative sources you present. See Chapter 5 for more on citing nonauthoritative sources.

In the commentary that follows guidance excerpts, incorporate key words considered from the guidance. Don't be creative in re-stating guidance requirements. Rather, use the words that were just provided to you, so as to avoid inadvertently changing the meaning of the guidance.

Take a moment now to identify the guidance sandwich you used in the email example earlier in this chapter.

Guidance Sandwiches

Remember the email you drafted to your audit senior (Matt) regarding the Statement of Cash Flows for Auto Corp? Take a moment now to identify the guidance sandwich you used in that email (or, take a moment to create one now). Recall that you are responding to Matt's question about whether the client has appropriately classified the proceeds from the sale of its manufacturing facility as cash flows from investing activities.

Hint: Your guidance sandwich could start with, for example:

- ■ **ASC xxx** states that cash flows from investing activities include . . . "(x)."

Your response here _____

_____

_____

_____

_____

_____

> Now
> [**YOU**]
> Try
> **4.3**

Next, let's focus on how to organize your analysis.

Organizing Your Analysis

Use additional *subheaders* throughout your analysis, as needed to help guide your reader. For example, in Richard's memo evaluating Energy Works' joint venture, he uses the following subheaders, among others, to help guide readers through his evaluation of Issue 1.

> **Analysis—Issue 1: Is Energy Works required to consolidate the joint venture?**
> ***Consideration of Whether the VIE Model Applies***
> > *Legal Entity*
> > *Business*
> > *Operating Joint Venture under Joint Control*
> ***Application of the Voting Model***

Notice how Richard uses subheaders to clearly organize his analysis of the VIE scope exception requirements (namely, *legal entity*, *business*, and *operating joint venture under joint control*). Use of subheaders can be valuable for organizing your analysis of guidance with multiple conditions. Of course, you might choose to break this single "Issue 1" down into multiple issues, or researchable questions. Refer to the Appendix to see how Richard used these subheaders to organize his Issue 1 analysis.

In some cases, you will encounter guidance with multiple conditions, often shown as "and" or "or" conditions. Generally speaking, "and" conditions must all be met in order for a certain accounting treatment to apply. With "or" conditions, only one condition must be met.

In such cases (both for "and" or "or"), it is a best practice to evaluate each condition provided. Take, for example, the definition of a derivative. For a contract to meet the definition of a derivative, it must: 1) have a notional and an underlying (e.g., a quantity and a price); *and* 2) require little/no initial net investment; *and* 3) be capable of net settlement. A researcher in this case might organize his or her analysis as follows:

ASC 815-10 (Derivatives) defines derivative instruments as follows:

[Guidance Excerpt]—Par. 15-83 (Definition of a derivative instrument)

The company has analyzed each characteristic, as follows.

Characteristic 1 - The contract has both an underlying and a notional amount.
Analysis:

Characteristic 2 - The contract requires no initial net investment.
Analysis:

Characteristic 3 - The contract can be settled net.
Analysis:

In this example, the full guidance excerpt is presented, followed by analysis of each required characteristic. Notice how the use of these subheaders improves the readability of the analysis.

Now
[YOU]
Try
4.4

Assume you are preparing a memo to evaluate whether a lease should receive operating or capital treatment. Four conditions are provided; if any one condition is met, the lease should be classified as capital. Assume the first condition (transfer of ownership) is met. Should you still evaluate the remaining three conditions? Explain.

_____

_____

Could subheaders be used to organize your analysis of the lease criteria? Explain.

_____

Consider Including Journal Entries for Each Alternative

To the extent you are weighing alternative accounting treatments, consider including (in your Analysis section) the journal entries that would apply to each alternative. Identifying the impact each alternative will have on the financial statements can help you recognize a client's motivation for a particular accounting treatment (e.g., income manipulation). Also, seeing how alternative treatments would play out on the financial statements can help researchers visually connect the substance of a transaction to its possible financial statement impacts.

You won't always find journal entry guidance in the Codification, so you'll often need to think through this part of the analysis on your own, or by considering other sources.

Document Other Factors Considered

Finally, in addition to analyzing the requirements of accounting guidance (both from authoritative and nonauthoritative sources), the Analysis section of an issues memo is also the appropriate place for discussion of other key factors considered in determining an appropriate accounting treatment. For example:

- How are peer companies accounting for this type of transaction?
- How has our company handled this type of transaction historically?
- Did we consult with subject-matter experts in analyzing this issue?

Present your consideration of these other factors, as applicable, following your review of authoritative literature.

Now
YOU
Try
4.5

Flip back to the par. 15-17(d) example presented earlier, and respond to the following.

1. First, label the guidance sandwich shown in that example. Use the following labels: 1. Introduction in the author's own words. 2. Guidance excerpt. 3. Commentary in author's own words.

2. Next, in the author's commentary (which follows the guidance excerpt), underline any words that the author repeated from the guidance.

3. What might be a benefit of restating parts of the guidance when performing your analysis?

_____

_____

4. Circle places where the author discusses the case facts, and how they relate to the guidance.

5. Why is it important to discuss case facts in your analysis of guidance excerpts?

_____

_____

Conclusion

Complete your discussion of each separate issue with a clearly written **conclusion**. This section should briefly summarize key points from your analysis that were considered in arriving at the conclusion reached.

Once you reach the point of documenting your conclusion, in many cases it may already be fairly obvious from your analysis which treatment is most appropriate. In such cases, your conclusion can be fairly brief. For example, following is Richard's conclusion section documenting his determination that Energy Works should record its investment in the joint venture using the equity method.

> Having determined (in the previous Issue) that it is not required to consolidate the JV, Energy Works considered whether its investment should be accounted for under the cost, equity, or fair value methods. Energy Works has concluded that the fair value method should not be applied, given that the joint venture will not have a readily determinable fair value. Use of the cost method is generally most appropriate for investments where the investor does not have significant influence.
>
> In this case, based on its 50% equity ownership (which well exceeds the 20% rebuttable presumption that equity method applies), and its substantial participation in all aspects of the joint venture (from policy-making, to governance, to day-to-day management, to technology sharing), Energy Works has the ability to exercise significant influence over the joint venture. Accordingly, Energy Works has concluded that use of the equity method is most appropriate.

What are some of the factors that Richard pointed to when describing how he reached the conclusion that equity method should be applied?

_____

_____

_____

Notice that, even in this example of a brief conclusion, the author summarized the most compelling points in the analysis as support for the conclusion. It is not sufficient to say:

> In conclusion, this investment will be accounted for using the equity method.

Rather, the following underlined text should be added to such a conclusion, restating the rationale for the conclusion:

> In conclusion, <u>because of factors x, y, and z,</u> this investment will be accounted for using the equity method.

[TIP] from the Trenches

Don't "jump to" conclusions. Make sure your conclusion includes your rationale (for example, "because of factors x, y, and z"), rather than simply naming the alternative selected.

In cases where the choice between two or more alternatives is highly judgmental, the conclusion should be longer and more detailed. The conclusion should clearly explain which requirements from the guidance, along with other factors considered, were compelling in selecting an alternative. The researcher might comment on why the alternative selected best reflects the substance and business purpose of the transaction. The rationale articulated in the conclusion could later become a critical part of the audit trail if the accounting for the transaction is ever called into question. That said, do not introduce new arguments in your conclusion. Rather, all relevant factors should be introduced in your Analysis, and then the most key factors should be discussed and referred back to in the conclusion.

[TIP] from the Trenches

Should you use one Conclusion section, or several, in a memo with multiple issues?
   It depends on the complexity of the issues you've analyzed. If the issues are straightforward, and your analysis is fairly brief, having one Conclusion section in your memo may be sufficient. However, when addressing issues that are more complex, include a clear conclusion for each issue, before moving on to the next issue.

Financial Statement and Disclosure Impacts

When applicable, conclude your memo with a summary of **financial statement and disclosure impacts**. Journal entries can be useful in describing anticipated financial statement impacts.
   Continue to use the same writing process and format, such as citing authoritative guidance as support, in writing this section. In other words, show the journal entries that will be required

based on your conclusion. If you are able to find authoritative excerpts that support either side of the entry (debits or credits), then include that guidance as support for the entry. As noted previously, journal entry guidance is often not provided in the Codification; to the extent you refer to other sources for journal entry guidance, you should include a reference to those sources.

For disclosures, include authoritative excerpts describing disclosure requirements, followed by discussion of how the company will comply with these requirements, specifically to address this issue.

Re-read Your Work Before Submitting (and what to look for)

By now, you've prepared a thoughtful, complete accounting analysis. But is it ready to send to your supervisor?

Always re-read your work before submitting. Check for:

- Commas, spelling, and proper grammar (more on this in a moment)
- Consistent font (generally, go with 12 point, Times, single spaced but double space between paragraphs)
- Concise, clear sentences
- Active voice

In other words, this re-read process is your chance to fine-tune your writing. Doing so will give your paper extra polish, and will add that "wow" factor (what a professional, strong writer!).

> In writing this book, the goal of my first draft is to get my rough draft thoughts down, and to get the technical details in place. I then re-read my work, adjusting the ordering of sentences and paragraphs as necessary to organize my thoughts in a more logical manner. On my final pass, I look carefully at whether my wording could be clearer or more direct.

[**TIP**] from the Trenches

Concise, Clear Sentences

Recognizing that technical accounting is challenging to communicate, the SEC released a *Plain English Handbook* in 1998. In it, the SEC encourages companies to prepare disclosure documents that investors can easily understand, and offers strategies to that effect (Write in active voice! Use clear section headings! Know your audience! Be concise!). The handbook states: "A plain English document uses words economically and at a level the audience can understand. Its sentence structure is tight."[5]

In reviewing your own work for clear and concise wording, ask yourself: Can I rephrase any of my sentences to be more concise? Can I eliminate unnecessary words?

Active Voice

Your writing will generally be clearer, and more direct, if you write in active voice. Consider the following examples of active vs. passive voice.

The girl was bit by the dog.   (Passive voice)

The dog bit the girl.   (Active Voice)

In active voice, the subject performs the action described by the verb. For clarity, keep the subject and verb close together.

---

[5] Office of Investor Education and Assistance, of the U.S. Securities and Exchange Commission. *A Plain English Handbook: How to create clear SEC disclosure documents.* 1998. Page 5.

Now
YOU
Try
4.7

Change the following sentence to active voice, and see if you can word it more concisely.

The documentation put together by you should be carefully subjected to an editing process.

_____

_____

TIP from the Trenches

While the research you submit should always be your own effort, you might consider having a reviewer proofread your writing. Especially if you struggle in this area, a trusted peer, or the school's writing center, can offer comments on your grammar and spelling. Have your reviewers hand-write their comments, so you can input and learn from their edits.

PROPERLY REFERENCING ACCOUNTING GUIDANCE

How Do I Reference a Passage from the Codification?

LO5 Properly **reference** passages from the Codification.

Excerpts from authoritative guidance are critical to effective accounting research communications. Paraphrasing guidance (that is, summarizing it into your own words) is not enough; authoritative guidance is far more impactful in a memo than a summary of guidance in your own words. Additionally, quoting "Codification excerpts" from articles or textbooks is inappropriate; always get authoritative guidance directly from the Codification. This discussion focuses on how to properly cite guidance excerpts from the Codification.

The first time you refer to the Codification in a memo, give its full title ("FASB Accounting Standards Codification"). Include the numerical reference for the topic you are citing, as well as a parenthetical description of the topic name. For example:

■ Per FASB Accounting Standards Codification (**ASC**) topic **840-10-20-1** (Leases), . . .

Remember that not everyone reading your memo was an accounting major and understands the acronym **ASC**. Therefore, it is important initially to provide the full name of the Codification, then to use the parenthetical (**ASC**) to show that you will abbreviate this term in future references within the memo.

After your initial reference to the Codification, it is acceptable to refer to the topic using the abbreviation "**ASC**," and omitting the parenthetical topic name (Leases). For example,

■ Per **ASC 840-10-20-2**: . . .

Note how these sample numerical references go all the way down to the paragraph level. Always provide as much detail as possible. Your reference would be lacking if you sent readers to Topic **840-10**, as that leaves them with pages of guidance to sort through to find what you are trying to reference. Do your readers the favor of getting them directly to the appropriate paragraph within the guidance.

In citing guidance, don't get creative with sentence structure. Following are examples of both strong and weak references. Stick to the strong references, and your memos will have a more professional tone.

■ Strong references:
- According to **ASC xxx**, "Quote"
- **ASC xxx** states or **ASC xxx** requires: "Quote"
- Per **ASC xxx**: "Quote"
- **ASC xxx** provides the following guidance: "Quote"
- The rate of return shall be based on: "Quote" (**ASC xxx**).

- The rate of return shall be based on: "Quote" [fn 1]
  (at end of page) Footnote 1: **ASC xxx**

■ Weak references:
  - **ASC xxx** asks readers to . . . "Quote"
  - **ASC xxx** believes . . . "Quote"
  - The Codification writes . . . "Quote" (**ASC xxx**)
  - The FASB says . . . "Quote" (**ASC xxx**)
  - I found the following guidance . . . "Quote" (**ASC xxx**)

Take careful note of the language and punctuation used in the preceding examples. "Per **ASC xxx**" is followed by a colon (:). "According to **ASC xxx**" is followed by a comma (,). All of the lead-ins just listed should be followed by excerpts from the guidance. Additionally, each excerpt includes a reference to the source of the guidance (**ASC xxx**). Note that these numerical references should get down to the paragraph-level of detail, since each provides a quotation directly from a paragraph of the guidance.

Referencing the Codification

Fill in the blanks using strong reference words.

1. _____ ASC 840-20-50-1, "For all **operating leases**, the lessee shall disclose . . ."

2. ASC 840-20-50-1 _____: "For all **operating leases**, the lessee shall disclose . . ."

3. _____ ASC 840-20-50-1: "For all **operating leases**, the lessee shall disclose . . ."

4. Show two ways that the underlined words in this reference could be stated more clearly.

<u>According to</u> <u>ASC 840-20-50-1</u> <u>it states</u>: "For all **operating leases**, the lessee shall disclose . . ."

_____ or _____

[Now
YOU
Try
4.8]

Should I Ever Use Footnotes in Professional Memos?

The use of footnotes and endnotes (that is, numerical references leading readers to a "works cited" source at the end of a page or document) should be fairly rare in accounting research memos. That is, you should primarily expect to cite the Codification or other authoritative sources of guidance, and these source references can be included in the body of your memos.

Footnotes or endnotes are appropriate, however, if you are referencing a less-common source of guidance, which requires a lengthier source citation. For example, if you find guidance in an academic paper or in a professional journal, a footnote or endnote citation is appropriate, as the reference must include not only the author's name, but the article name, date published, title of journal, edition number, and page number. Including all of this detail in the body of a memo would bog down your reader.

When Should I Use Quotation Marks?

Any guidance copied directly from the Codification must be enclosed in double quotation marks, *and* you must cite the source of the guidance down to the paragraph-level of detail (e.g., Per ASC xxx-xx-xx-xx . . .).

For example, ASC 715-30-35-47 (Compensation—Pension) states: "The expected long-term rate of return on plan assets shall reflect the average rate of earnings expected on the funds invested or to be invested to provide for the benefits included in the projected benefit obligation."

Notice the use of double quotation marks to enclose the quote, and notice the full reference to the Codification source.

There is one (and only one) instance in which quotation marks are not required: If you are including a long excerpt—roughly three lines or more—from the Codification, and you *indent the guidance*. Indenting long excerpts (as opposed to integrating the quotation within other text) can also improve the readability of your memo.

EXAMPLE

When indenting guidance, it's nice to split the Codification reference. The full reference for this paragraph is ASC 715-30-35-47, but we have split this reference between the introduction (715-30) and the excerpt (35-47).

> ASC 715-30 (Compensation—Pension) requires that companies consider future expected returns on investments in selecting an expected return on assets assumption:
>
> **35-47** The expected long-term rate of return on plan assets shall reflect the average rate of earnings expected on the funds invested or to be invested to provide for the benefits included in the projected benefit obligation. In estimating that rate, appropriate consideration shall be given to the returns being earned by the plan assets in the fund and the rates of return expected to be available for reinvestment . . .
>
> Therefore, an asset return assumption is appropriate if management believes this rate is achievable in the future.

Notice how this example includes both: (1) a reference (**ASC xxx**) down to the paragraph level of detail and (2) guidance that is indented, indicating that it is a direct quote.

When Is It Appropriate to Alter an Excerpt from the Guidance?

It is only appropriate to alter an excerpt from the guidance if (1) in doing so, you do not change the meaning of the guidance, and (2) you clearly tell the reader what you have altered. Use brackets [ ] to identify any words you have changed, or to acknowledge that you have added emphasis to part of a quote.

For example, note the following altered excerpt from **ASC 840-10** (Leases—Overall):

15-6. ". . . The right to control the use of the underlying [PP&E] is conveyed if **any** of the following conditions is met . . ." [Emphasis added]

In the preceding example, the author omitted the words "property, plant, or equipment" in favor of using the bracketed term [PP&E]. Additionally, the author added boldface type to the term "any," and acknowledged this change by stating "[Emphasis added]." As neither change alters the meaning of the guidance, and as both changes were identified with brackets, these changes are appropriate.

When Is It Appropriate to Use Ellipses?

Ellipses, or those three dots in a row (. . .) are used when a writer *omits* some text in a quote or *doesn't quote the full sentence or paragraph*. As you begin writing technical emails and memos, you may find that ellipses are useful in trimming fat; that is, eliminating irrelevant sections from a paragraph may improve the readability of your analysis. While sufficient guidance is critical to a strong issues memo, too much guidance can be burdensome.

EXAMPLE ——————————————————————————————————

> Here is original guidance from **ASC 405-20** (Extinguishments of Liabilities) describing how a debtor's secondary liability should be recorded as a guarantee.
>
> **40-2** If a creditor releases a debtor from primary obligation on the condition that a third party assumes the obligation and that the original debtor becomes secondarily liable, that release extinguishes the original debtor's liability. However, in those circumstances, whether or not explicit consideration was paid for that guarantee, the original debtor becomes a guarantor. As a guarantor, it shall recognize a guarantee obligation in the same manner as would a guarantor that had never been primarily liable to that creditor, with due regard for the likelihood that the third party will carry out its obligations. The guarantee obligation shall be initially measured at fair value, and that amount reduces the gain or increases the loss recognized on extinguishment. See Topic **460** for accounting guidance related to guarantees.

Here's an example of the proper use of an ellipsis to abbreviate a sentence from the preceding text.

> 40-2 "However . . . , ~~in those circumstances,~~ whether or not explicit consideration was paid for that guarantee, the original debtor becomes a guarantor."

Here's an example illustrating the proper use of an ellipsis when the full paragraph is not being quoted. Here, the ellipsis shows that the paragraph continues on, even beyond this excerpted text.

> 40-2 "If a creditor releases a debtor from primary obligation on the condition that a third party assumes the obligation and that the original debtor becomes secondarily liable, that release extinguishes the original debtor's liability. However, in those circumstances, whether or not explicit consideration was paid for that guarantee, the original debtor becomes a guarantor . . ."

While ellipses may become a great tool in your toolbox, you must always *check and double check* that the text you are skipping over is not critical to the understanding of a passage, and that using the ellipsis does not change the meaning of the original guidance.

Here's an improper use of an ellipsis. Notice how pertinent guidance has been omitted.

> 40-2 "If a creditor releases a debtor from primary obligation on the condition that a third party assumes the obligation . . . ~~and that the original debtor becomes secondarily liable,~~ that release extinguishes the original debtor's liability."

STYLE TIPS FOR PROFESSIONAL COMMUNICATION

We'll conclude our chapter on communication by discussing a few points on style. Attention to style will improve the professionalism of your work products.

LO6 Communicate using professional style.

Use Proper Voice in Your Memos

Avoid saying "I" or "we" or "you" in accounting research communications. Technical accounting memos are not about you; they should not be written in the first person.

- For example, do not say: "We found the guidance in **ASC 605**."
- Do not say: "I think" or "We have concluded" in a memo.
- Do not say: "You have asked us for the appropriate accounting treatment . . ." in a memo.

When referring to a company, do not say "they" or "their." Rather, call the company by its name initially, and identify (in parenthesis) any abbreviations you plan to use for the company name thereafter.

- For example, Flyaway.com ("Flyaway" or "the Company") shall recognize revenue on a net basis. This is appropriate given the Company's role as agent.

Notice how this example initially introduces Flyaway.com using its full name, and then uses the parenthetical ("Flyaway" or "the Company") to show how the company will be described in future references within the memo. Finally, note the following additional examples of proper and improper voice:

- Do say: The Company has evaluated its accounting.
- Do not say: The Company has evaluated their accounting.

Keep Your Language Neutral (Avoid Strong Words)

To improve the professionalism of your writing, keep your language neutral. I once asked students to review a company's accounting election and to comment on whether it was supportable based on guidance from the Codification. A few students described the company's position as "wrong," and one may have even called the company's accounting "ridiculous."

The lesson here: Try to leave your emotions out of technical writing. Keep your language neutral. Here are examples of more appropriate ways to comment on an accounting position. The accounting is

- "Appropriate/not appropriate."
- "Consistent/not consistent with" the guidance.
- "Supported/not supported by" the guidance.

Also, try to avoid "absolutes" in your technical writing. It's better to play it safe and use qualifying words.

- Use the word "generally" rather than "always."
  - Analysts "generally" (not "always") listen to companies' earnings calls for the purpose of understanding more of the qualitative factors behind a company's performance.
- Use the word "could" rather than "will."
  - The company "could" (not "will") have to restate later if it chooses an accounting position that is not supported by the guidance.
- Use the word "specialist" rather than "expert."

[**TIP**] from the Trenches   One of the writing conventions that I picked up during my time at the FASB is use of the verbs *states*, *stated*, or *said* in technical writing. The guidance *states*. The Board members *stated*. My project manager's red pen frequently came out when my draft board minutes included more creative terms such as "argued," "pointed out," or "asserted." In each case, he suggested that I change the word to "stated" or "said." (Board minutes have since changed to focus on decisions reached, as opposed to discussions held.)

Get the Grammar Right

Grammatical errors in your writing can undermine the quality of your whole research effort. Before submitting a memo to your supervisor or to a client, carefully reread it for proper grammar, spelling, and clarity. Even an offense as seemingly minor as a misplaced comma can tarnish the polish on an otherwise great paper.

Commas

Following is a brief refresher on commas. If this is a trouble area for you, please review this section carefully.

- Use commas between "independent clauses"—each with a *subject* and a *verb*:
  - *I went* to the store, and *you went* home.
  - Comparative *income statements must* be presented for three years, but comparative *balance sheets must* be presented for two years.
  - Note: Each of these clauses could be a sentence all by itself, so a comma is needed between them.
- Use commas after an *introductory phrase*:
  - *Although the company's earnings were below expectations,* the company's stock price did not change.
  - *If two alternatives are available,* both should be analyzed in your memo.
  - Note: Note that each phrase has its own subject and verb; the introductory phrase also includes a transition (if, although, after, before, etc.). Separate these two phrases with a comma.
- Use commas when you insert a phrase into a sentence that isn't necessary for understanding the sentence.
  - He said, *with an encouraging nod,* that I should read more.
  - Nonauthoritative guidance, *which is available from a number of different sources,* can be useful in supporting authoritative references.
  - Note: If the phrases "with an encouraging nod" or "which is available from a number of different sources" were stricken from these sentences, the sentences would still read just as clearly. As these phrases are purely descriptive, and not necessary for understanding the sentence, they are set off in commas.

Criteria versus Criterion

Students are frequently uncertain how to form the singular, verus plural, form of the word *criteria*. Here's the deal:

- *Criteria* is plural. There are *four criteria* for evaluating lease classification.
- *Criterion* is singular. The *first criterion* involves whether the lease transfers ownership by the end of the lease term.

Getting Feedback On Your Writing

I still, to this day, cringe when I get feedback on my work. This may be a natural thing to do. But I've also learned to tell myself: "Wait. I can learn from this." And just like that, I go from dreading the feedback to appreciating the learning opportunity it presents.

If your instructor or supervisor takes the time to provide feedback on your writing, understand that they do this because they *believe in your potential to improve.* I can attest that providing detailed feedback to each student takes a ton of time. Take the time to read and learn from any comments you are given.

Consider taking the following steps when getting feedback:

1. Don't panic when it's given to you. Think: *I can learn from this.*
2. Read it closely, and with an open mind.
3. Consider how the feedback might help you improve next time. If you don't understand the feedback, or if you disagree, talk to the person who gave you the feedback.
4. Appreciate the feedback—either silently, or by thanking the person who provided it.

As you advance in your career, there may be increasing circumstances where you consider, but then reject, feedback you are given. In many cases, however, you aren't there yet! Be open to learning from others.

Common Instructor Notations

For reference, here are some notations that I commonly use in providing handwritten feedback to my students. Your instructor may (or may not) use similar notations.

¶	Start a new paragraph.
S/, C/, W/	Should, could, or would
S/b, C/b, W/b	Should be, could be, would be
^	Insert
= dbl underline	The first letters should be uppercase.
Strikethrough	The first letter should be lowercase.
sp	Spelling error
stet	Means: "What you had is fine. Disregard my comment."
ℯ	Delete
w/r/t	with respect to
K	contract

CHAPTER 4 APPENDIX

Sample Accounting Issues Memo

The following accounting issues memo illustrates Energy Works' evaluation of its joint venture arrangement.

Draft—For Discussion Purposes Only ◄————————

<u>**Memorandum**</u>

To: Energy Works, Inc. Accounting Files

From: Richard Smith, Accounting Policy team

Date: 12/1/20X1

Re: Accounting for proposed joint venture with Big Oil, Inc. ◄————————

Facts

Energy Works, Inc. is a nonpublic oil and gas company that is forming a joint venture (JV) with Big Oil, Inc. for the extraction of proved oil reserves in the arctic. Both venturers wish to share in the risks and rewards of this venture, while benefiting from each other's technical expertise and sharing of key assets. Energy Works will contribute a floating production storage and offloading facility (FPSO), valued at $100 million, along with $20 million in cash, to the venture in exchange for a 50% equity interest. Energy Works is not in the business of marketing its production facilities and equipment for sale; rather, it uses these facilities in its own oil and gas producing activities.

Big Oil will contribute its arctic drilling permit, also valued at $100 million, along with $20 million in cash, to the venture in exchange for a 50% equity interest. Assume that the cost basis of the contributed assets is the same as the fair values of these assets. Profits and losses of the venture will be shared based upon the equity interest held by each investor.

Operations of the joint venture will be overseen by its Board of Directors. Each venturer will receive two seats on the Board, for a total of four seats, and all significant decisions of the JV require the unanimous consent of the Board, with any disputes to be settled by an independent arbitrator (binding arbitration). The Board has appointed Energy Works to manage the day-to-day operations of the FPSO facility. Additionally, both venturers will provide employees and managerial personnel with technical expertise to perform day-to-day operations for the JV. Energy Works will not receive separate compensation for its role as manager. The joint venture will be legally organized as an LLC.

The following picture illustrates the relationships between the parties in this arrangement.

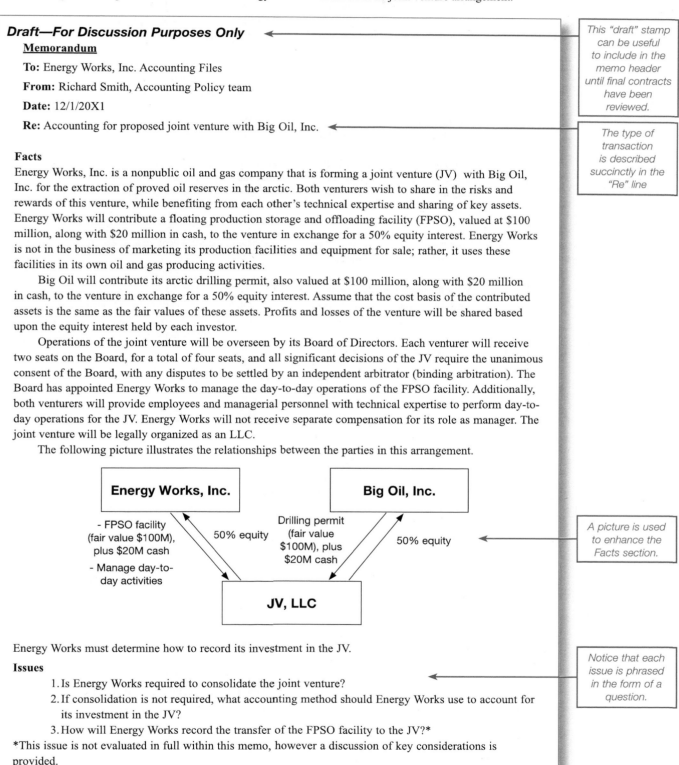

Energy Works must determine how to record its investment in the JV.

Issues

1. Is Energy Works required to consolidate the joint venture? ◄————————
2. If consolidation is not required, what accounting method should Energy Works use to account for its investment in the JV?
3. How will Energy Works record the transfer of the FPSO facility to the JV?*

*This issue is not evaluated in full within this memo, however a discussion of key considerations is provided.

Side annotations:

This "draft" stamp can be useful to include in the memo header until final contracts have been reviewed.

The type of transaction is described succinctly in the "Re" line

A picture is used to enhance the Facts section.

Notice that each issue is phrased in the form of a question.

Analysis—Issue 1: Is Energy Works required to consolidate the joint venture?

FASB Accounting Standards Codification (ASC) 810-10 (Consolidation) provides guidance for determining when consolidation of another entity is required. Two consolidation models are provided: the variable interest entity (VIE) model and the voting interest model. Arrangements should first be evaluated to determine whether they fall within the scope of the VIE model and, if not, shall apply the voting model. This requirement is described in par. 15-3 of ASC 810-10, as follows:

> **15-3** All reporting entities shall apply the guidance in the Consolidation Topic to determine whether and how to consolidate another entity and apply the applicable Subsection as follows:
> a.   If the reporting entity has an interest in an entity, it must determine whether that entity is within the scope of the Variable Interest Entities Subsections in accordance with paragraph 810-10-15-14. If that entity is within the scope of the Variable Interest Entities Subsections, the reporting entity should first apply the guidance in those Subsections. Paragraph 810-10-15-17 provides specific exceptions to applying the guidance in the Variable Interest Entities Subsections.
> b.   If the reporting entity has an interest in an entity that is not within the scope of the Variable Interest Entities Subsections and is not within the scope of the Subsections mentioned in paragraph 810-10-15-3(c), the reporting entity should use only the guidance in the General Subsections to determine whether that interest constitutes a controlling financial interest.

Energy Works has an interest (an equity ownership share) in the joint venture and, accordingly, will begin by evaluating whether the VIE model applies.

Sidebar: Energy Works has not made an accounting policy election to apply *proportionate consolidation* to its investments in legal entities. (This is an accounting election available to companies in the extractive and construction industries, where an entity records its share of each asset, liability, revenue, and expense of the investee.) Rather, Energy Works will apply the consolidation accounting framework set forth in ASC 810, honoring the legal form of the transaction.

Consideration of Whether the VIE Model Applies

As noted in par. 15-3 above, the VIE model applies to entities that meet the definition of a VIE (par. 15-14) and which do not qualify for the scope exceptions provided in par. 15-17.

Energy Works believes that this arrangement may qualify for the so-called "business scope exception" in par. 15-17 of ASC 810-10, as follows:

Notice how guidance excerpts are indented.

> **15-17(d).** A legal entity that is deemed to be a **business** need not be evaluated by a reporting entity to determine if the legal entity is a VIE under the requirements of the Variable Interest Entities Subsections unless any of the following conditions exist . . . :
> 1.   The reporting entity . . . participated significantly in the design or redesign of the legal entity. However, this condition does not apply if the legal entity is an operating joint venture under joint control of the reporting entity and one or more independent parties or a franchisee.
> 2-4.   [For the simplicity of this example, conditions 2-4 will not be evaluated in this memo, however in practice entities are required to evaluate these conditions.]

According to this guidance, a business is not required to be evaluated under the VIE model *unless* the reporting entity participated significantly in the design of the entity; however, this "design" exception does not apply to *operating joint ventures* under *joint control* of the venturers. As Energy Works participated in the design of the JV, the JV must meet the GAAP definition of a joint venture, under joint control, to qualify for this scope exception.

Therefore, Energy Works must evaluate whether the JV: 1) is a *legal entity*; 2) is considered a *business*; and 3) is an *operating joint venture* under *joint control*. If all of these conditions are met, Energy Works may apply the business scope exception.

Legal Entity

First, we note that the JV is a legal entity. **Legal entities** are defined in ASC 810-10-20 as:

> Any legal structure used to conduct activities or to hold assets. Some examples of such structures are corporations, partnerships, limited liability companies, grantor trusts, and other trusts.

As the joint venture will be organized as an LLC, it is considered a legal entity.

Business

Next, ASC 810-10-20 defines a **business** as:

> An integrated set of activities and assets that is capable of being conducted and managed for the purpose of providing a return in the form of dividends, lower costs, or other economic benefits directly to investors or other owners, members, or participants . . .

Implementation guidance in par. 55-4 (of ASC 805-10, Business Combinations) elaborates on this definition, stating: "A **business** consists of inputs and processes applied to those inputs that have the ability to create outputs." Inputs are described as including long-lived assets (including intangible assets), and processes are described as including operational processes, documented or known by a skilled workforce.

In this case, the JV meets this definition, given that it has both inputs (an FPSO and drilling permit) and processes (the venturers have agreed to share their technological know-how for operating the facility as well as employees with technical expertise) that are capable of generating returns (outputs) for the venturers. Furthermore, the purpose of this JV is for the venturers to pool their resources to conduct operations, thus generating returns.

Sidebar: It's worth noting that describing the JV as a business would be a higher hurdle if the JV were involved in the exploration, as opposed to the production, of oil. In this case, the Codification (as well as industry-specific nonauthoritative resources) makes it clear that the JV meets the definition of a business. In fact, it could be argued that the assets being contributed by Big Oil alone (the permit and technical know-how embodied in its employees (i.e., processes)) would represent a business when viewed in isolation.

Notably, the FASB is currently revisiting the definition of business, in particular as it relates to groups of nonfinancial assets.

Operating Joint Venture under Joint Control

Finally, Energy Works must consider whether the JV meets the GAAP definition of a joint venture. The term **corporate joint venture** is defined in ASC 323-10-20 (Investments—Equity Method and Joint Ventures) as:

> A corporation owned and operated by a small group of entities (the joint venturers) as a separate and specific business or project for the mutual benefit of the members of the group . . .The purpose of a corporate joint venture frequently is to share risks and rewards in developing a new market, product or technology; to combine complementary technological knowledge; or to pool resources in developing production or other facilities. A corporate joint venture also usually provides an arrangement under which each joint venturer may participate, directly or indirectly, in the overall management of the joint venture. Joint venturers thus have an interest or relationship other than as passive investors. An entity that is a subsidiary of one of the joint venturers is not a corporate joint venture. The ownership of a corporate joint venture seldom changes, and its stock is usually not traded publicly. A noncontrolling interest held by public ownership, however, does not preclude a corporation from being a corporate joint venture.

In this case, the JV will be owned by a small group of (in this case, two) entities for the benefit of the group. The purpose of the JV is indeed to share risks and rewards, as well as technology and key assets related to this project. Both venturers will participate actively in management of the venture through their required approval on all significant decisions. Therefore, this definition appears to be met.

In its Financial Reporting Developments publication, *Consolidation and the Variable Interest Model* (2014), p.53, EY provides additional interpretive guidance related to this scope exception, as follows:

> The actual term [joint venture] is narrowly defined for accounting purposes in ASC 323-10-20. The fundamental criteria for an entity to be a joint venture are (1) joint control over all key decisions, with (2) control through the owners' equity interest. [Explanation added]

Therefore, Energy Works will also consider these fundamental criteria described by EY.

> Sidebar: Sometimes, guidance in the Codification may seem straightforward, but interpretive guidance may point out additional factors that need to be considered to correctly apply the Codification. In this case, consideration of EY guidance offers two additional hurdles that we must clear in order to determine that the JV qualifies for this scope exception.

Joint control over key decisions

Regarding "joint control," EY's publication *Joint Ventures* (2014) states:

> We believe joint control exists when all of the venturers have, at a minimum, substantive veto or approval rights allowing them to effectively participate in all of the significant decisions of an entity. (For this reason, a joint venture would not be a consolidated subsidiary of any of the equity holders).
> ...decisions are significant when they relate to the significant financing, operating and investing activities expected to be undertaken by an entity in the normal course of business... To be jointly controlled, we believe each significant decision of the entity must require the consent of each of the venturers.[7]

As stated in the Facts of this memo, the venturers will share control of all significant decisions related to the entity, with no one venturer having more weight than the other. Regarding Energy Works' day-to-day management of the JV, EY's publication states:

> The existence of a contract or other agreement with one of the venturers . . . to perform the day-to-day management of the entity does not automatically prevent the entity from meeting the definition of a joint venture . . .As long as the contract does not convey decision-making authority over significant decisions to the venturer or the third-party, the entity could meet the definition of a joint venture . . .[8]

While this decision requires significant judgment, we will assume in this case that the manager does not have authority to make significant decisions for the JV without the other venturer's consent. A thorough reading of all contracts related to joint venture formation and management is needed to confirm this.

> Sidebar: Establishing joint control is a key judgment. You must be able to argue—all the way down to the last detail—that the entities have equal voting power. For example, in the event the parties cannot agree on a matter, a common feature in a joint control arrangement is that the parties agree to seek a third-party arbitrator.

Control through owners' equity interest

Finally, the venturers must be able to exercise this joint control as a right of their equity ownership. By contrast, per EY:

> If a venturer exercises its decision-making authority through a means other than an equity interest (e.g., through a management services contract) or if an interest holder other than one of the venturers has voting or substantive veto rights (e.g., via a debt instrument), we do not believe the entity is a joint venture.

In this case, the venturers (as equity holders) will each have two seats on the Board as a right of their equity ownership, and these Board seats give them the authority to approve key decisions of the joint venture and to oversee the management of the venture. Energy Works was appointed by the Board to manage the FPSO facility but: 1) must act as directed by the Board, in a manner that serves the Board's interests; 2) is not operating under a separate management services contract; and 3) is not receiving separate compensation for this service.

As the equity holders have both: 1) joint control, and 2) control through their equity interests, the JV meets the GAAP definition of an *operating joint venture under joint control*. Therefore, the business scope exception applies. Next, Energy Works will evaluate the JV under the voting interest model.

Application of the Voting Model

The voting model in ASC 810-10 applies differently to limited partnerships (and similar entities), versus other legal entity structures (such as corporations). ASC 810-10 indicates that LLCs can fall within either model, depending on how they are structured. Based on a careful review of contract terms, Energy Works has determined that this particular LLC functions more like a corporation than a partnership.

ASC 810-10 provides the following consolidation guidance for entities other than limited partnerships:

As a style point, notice how nonauthoritative sources are also presented in guidance sandwiches, following consideration of authoritative guidance.

---

[7] EY, Financial Reporting Developments: *Joint Ventures*. June 2014. Page 10.
[8] EY (Joint Ventures). Page 19.

25-1 For **legal entities** other than limited partnerships, consolidation is appropriate if a reporting entity has a controlling financial interest in another entity and a specific scope exception does not apply (see Section 810-10-15). The usual condition for a controlling financial interest is ownership of a majority voting interest, but in some circumstances control does not rest with the majority owner.[8]

Said another way, equity holders with greater than 50% equity are presumed to consolidate, but in certain cases would not consolidate if partners with a lesser ownership percentage have rights that block the majority owner's control.

In this case, neither of the venturers has a controlling financial interest in the JV because neither venturer owns a majority (of greater than 50%) of the JV's equity. Additionally, both parties have equal *participating rights* to establish key decisions for the JV—that is, neither venturer controls the decision making of the entity.

Accordingly, neither venturer will consolidate the JV.

> Sidebar: The determination of applying the voting model using the "limited partnership" approach versus "other entity" approach involves judgment. Entities should consider, for example, whether the LLC maintains a specific ownership account for each investor (as in a partnership), and whether the venturers' roles are akin to a general partner/limited partner relationship (as in a partnership).

Conclusion—Issue 1

Energy Works has evaluated its investment in the JV for potential consolidation, and has concluded that it is not required to consolidate the JV. Under ASC 810, companies must first consider whether an investment is within the scope of the VIE model then, if not, apply the voting model. Energy Works determined that this arrangement qualifies for the so-called business scope exception to the VIE model. That is, the JV meets the GAAP definition of a *business*, as well as the definition of a *corporate joint venture*, where the owners have joint control. A key judgment in applying these definitions is that the venturers share control, with no one partner having unilateral decision-making authority, as a right of their equity interests. Next, Energy Works applied the voting model and concluded that consolidation is not required because it does not have a *controlling interest* in the JV.

> Sidebar: In practice, it's a high hurdle to qualify for the business scope exception and, once applied, a reporting entity must continually evaluate (e.g., each reporting period) whether the entity continues to be eligible for this exception.

Analysis—Issue 2: If consolidation is not required, what accounting method should Energy Works use to account for its investment in the JV?

Energy Works considered whether the fair value, equity, or cost method is most appropriate for accounting for its investment. First, Energy Works considered whether the fair value method (ASC 320-10) applies, but concluded that it does not, as this investment does not have a *readily-determinable fair value*. The company has also not historically elected to apply the fair value option to its investments.

> Sidebar: Investments in the stock of entities—other than subsidiaries—can be accounted for using one of three methods: the fair value, cost, or equity method.

Regarding the cost method, very little scope guidance is available. Per ASC 325-20 (Cost Method Investments):

> **05-3** While practice varies to some extent, the cost method is generally followed for most investments in noncontrolled corporations, in some corporate joint ventures, and to a lesser extent in unconsolidated subsidiaries, particularly foreign.

While this investment appears to fall within the scope of this guidance, it's important to consider whether the equity method is more appropriate. Instruments within the scope of ASC 323-10 (Investments—Equity Method and Joint Ventures) are described as follows:

> **15-3** The guidance in the Investments—Equity Method and Joint Ventures Topic applies to investments in **common stock** or **in-substance common stock** . . . including investments in common stock of **corporate joint ventures** . . . Subsequent references in this Subtopic to common stock refer to both common stock and in-substance common stock that give the **investor** the ability to exercise **significant influence** (see paragraph 323-10-15-6) over operating and financial policies of an **investee** even though the investor holds 50% or less of the common stock or in-substance common stock (or both common stock and in-substance common stock).

In other words, investments in common stock that give an investor *significant influence* are within the scope of this topic. ASC 323-10 includes a rebuttable presumption that investments of greater than 20% indicate significant influence:

> **15-8** An investment (direct or indirect) of 20 percent or more of the voting stock of an investee shall lead to a presumption that in the absence of predominant evidence to the contrary an investor has the ability to exercise significant influence over an investee.

Based on this par. 8 guidance, it appears that Energy Works would be presumed—based on its 50% ownership—to have significant influence, and that application of ASC 323 (Equity Method) is appropriate. Additionally, par. 15-6 offers the following indicators of significant influence:

> **15-6** Ability to exercise significant influence over operating and financial policies of an investee may be indicated in several ways, including the following:
> a. Representation on the board of directors
> b. Participation in policy-making processes
> c. Material intra-entity transactions
> d. Interchange of managerial personnel
> e. Technological dependency
> f. Extent of ownership by an investor in relation to the concentration of other shareholdings (but substantial or majority ownership of the voting stock of an investee by another investor does not necessarily preclude the ability to exercise significant influence by the investor).

Energy Works has representation on the board, will participate in policy-making related to the entity, will provide employees and managerial personnel to the JV, and the JV will rely upon technological expertise of Energy Works. As several indicators of significant influence are present, and given Energy Works' 50% equity ownership interest, Energy Works has concluded that it has significant influence over the JV. Accordingly, application of the equity method is appropriate.

Conclusion—Issue 2

Having determined that it is not required to consolidate the JV, Energy Works considered whether its investment should be accounted for under the fair value, cost, or equity method. Energy Works has concluded that the fair value method should not be applied, given that the joint venture will not have a readily determinable fair value. Use of the cost method is generally most appropriate for investments where the investor does not have significant influence.

In this case, based on its 50% equity ownership (which well exceeds the 20% rebuttable presumption that equity method applies), and its substantial participation in all aspects of the joint venture (from policy-making, to governance, to day-to-day management, to technology sharing), Energy Works has the ability to exercise significant influence over the joint venture. Accordingly, Energy Works has concluded that use of the equity method is appropriate.

Analysis—Issue 3: How will Energy Works record the transfer of the FPSO facility to the JV?

Next, Energy Works would need to consider how to record the transfer of its FPSO facility to the JV, in exchange for an equity method interest in the JV. This is a complex issue and is not evaluated in detail in this memo. Instead, rather than perform the complex scope evaluations involved in this issue, let's briefly walk through *how* you'd go about this analysis. Energy Works would consider (and document):

■   First, whether industry-specific guidance from ASC 932 (Oil and Gas Activities) applies.

■   Next, whether the FPSO being transferred is *integral equipment* (i.e., *in-substance real estate*), which should be evaluated under ASC 360 (Property, Plant, and Equipment).

■ If the above two topics do not apply, next Energy Works would consider whether the assets it is transferring (the FPSO facility and related employees and processes) are considered a *business*. If Energy Works *is* contributing a business, it should apply *deconsolidation accounting* guidance (ASC 810, Consolidation).

■ If the assets contributed are *not* a business, Energy Works would evaluate whether this transaction is considered a nonmonetary exchange (of nonfinancial assets for an equity method investment) under ASC 845 (Nonmonetary Transactions).

■ If the transfer is not subject to nonmonetary transactions guidance, Energy Works would apply standard equity method investment guidance (ASC 323).

The case studies included at the end of this chapter will give you the opportunity to consider and document these alternatives.

Sidebar: In practice, it's common to have "basis differences" between the carrying amount of assets contributed and their fair values. These basis differences can give rise to some highly complex accounting judgments, both at the venturer and JV level. These judgments are particularly complex when considering equity investments issued in exchange for nonmonetary assets (as is the case here). Note that the FASB has recently proposed changes intended to simplify the equity method of accounting by removing the requirement that entities track and account for basis differences.

Financial Statement and Disclosure Impacts

Energy Works will record its investment in the joint venture, and its contribution to the JV of the FPSO facility, as follows:

Dr. Investment in JV	$120M	
Cr. FPSO facility		$100M
Cr. Cash		$20M

ASC 323-10-50-3 sets forth required disclosures for equity method investments. As stated in par. 50-2, the extent of these disclosures shall depend on the significance of the investment to the investor. ◄—

It can be helpful to support this disclosure section with excerpts from the guidance. However, in the interest of brevity, this example does not include such excerpts. Also, had Energy Works been a publicly-traded company, the company would need to consider whether incremental SEC disclosure requirements apply.

Energy Works must disclose the following in the notes to its financial statements, related to this investment:

1. The name of the investee and percentage of ownership of common stock.
2. Energy Works' accounting policies with respect to investments in common stock.
3. Any differences between the carrying amount of its investment and the amount of underlying equity in net assets, and how such differences are accounted for.

Also, for equity method investments in corporate joint ventures that are material to the investor, summarized financial information about the investee (assets, liabilities, and results of operations) "may be necessary." Energy Works will therefore monitor the significance of this investment and will provide such disclosure in accordance with its existing accounting policies.

My heartfelt thanks to Nicholas Stell for his contributions to this memo.

CHAPTER SUMMARY

Effective documentation serves several functions for the company and its auditor. Not only does the process of creating documentation allow the accountant to think critically about the issues at hand, but a complete set of documentation serves as support for key judgments, a valuable historical reference, and—in the case of auditors—evidence of a robust evaluation of client positions.

This chapter introduced a standard format for preparing accounting issues memoranda and draft professional emails. The chapter also provided guidance on style tips for professional communication, including how to cite from the FASB Codification, use neutral language, and use professional voice. Commit these tips to memory, as they will serve you well in your professional career.

REVIEW QUESTIONS

1. Cite two reasons why documentation is a critical part of performing accounting research.
2. Explain how creating clear documentation might provide some protection against hindsight bias.
3. Contrast the circumstances in which an email should be used to communicate research, versus circumstances in which a memo may be warranted.
4. Name three of the tips provided for drafting effective emails.
5. The chapter notes that email communications should be kept fairly brief. In light of this, is it appropriate to include guidance excerpts in an email? Explain.
6. Name the sections included in the standard memo format introduced in this chapter.
7. Explain what is meant by the statement that a memo should be a one-stop shop.
8. How much detail should be included in the Background section of an issues memo?
9. Should your issues list always be organized around the case study questions, as given to you? Explain.
10. Complete the following sentence. Issues should be phrased in the form of _____.
11. What is the goal of the Analysis section of the memo? Explain.
12. When alternative accounting methods are available, why is it essential for a researcher to identify these possible alternatives in his or her documentation?
13. In what circumstances might subheaders be useful to help organize your analysis?
14. Explain why researchers should include actual excerpts from the guidance in accounting memoranda, rather than paraphrases of guidance (in the researcher's own words).
15. Which section of an accounting issues memorandum is often enhanced by a picture (or diagram) of the transaction?
16. Is it acceptable to document other sources considered, such as nonauthoritative sources, in a memo? Explain.
17. What is meant by the advice: Don't *jump* to conclusions!
18. What does the term "guidance sandwiches" mean? Where would you find these in an accounting issues memorandum?
19. Should new arguments or guidance references be introduced in the Conclusion section of a memo? Explain.
20. Why is a Conclusion section necessary in an issues memo?
21. What is the role of journal entries in an accounting issues memo? Where should these be discussed?
22. What are three things you should check for when reviewing your writing?
23. How should a researcher refer to guidance from the Codification, the first time it is cited in a memo?
24. Which of the following Codification references is stronger? Explain.
    - *Per* ASC xxx: "Quote"
    - ASC xxx *asks readers to . . .* "Quote"
25. Describe what "voice" should be used in accounting research communications. (Feel free to respond by describing what voices "should not" be used.)
26. Explain what it means for the language in an accounting memorandum to be "neutral."

EXERCISES

1. For each of the following pieces of information, state whether it should be included in, or excluded from, the Facts section of an issues memo, assuming that the objective of the issues memo is to evaluate whether a new issue of preferred stock should be classified as a liability or as equity. Briefly explain your reasoning.
    a. The fact that the issuer is a public company.
    b. The key terms of the preferred stock, including its par value and any conversion or redemption features.
    c. The anticipated size of the issuance, in dollars.
    d. The date on which the issuance is expected to occur.
    e. Background on the company and its primary sources of revenue.
    f. The fact that the company entered into a similar transaction several years ago.
    g. Detail about the counterparty (investor) who is expected to purchase a large share of the preferred stock issuance.

2. As the Energy Works memo in this chapter illustrates, accounting issues are not always straightforward. The following questions are intended to highlight some of the many judgments and alternatives present in that memo. Considering that memo, respond to the following. Use the Energy Works memo, and your own thinking, to respond. (Codification research is not necessary for this exercise.)

   a. Why is it important for Energy Works to determine which consolidation model applies (variable or voting)? What difference does it make which model applies, if the company might come to the same conclusion (to not consolidate) either way?

   b. Describe the judgments involved in determining whether the JV is considered a *business*.

   c. What would have happened if Energy Works had not qualified for use of the business scope exception? What analysis would have been performed next?

   d. The facts state that Energy Works will manage the day-to-day operations of the JV. In what circumstances might this day-to-day management have caused the venturers to not be considered an *operating joint venture under joint control*?

   e. What three possible alternative treatments are considered or described in Issue 2 of the memo? Very briefly, explain each.

   f. The evaluation of Energy Works' transfer of equipment to the joint venture is not straightforward; many possible Codification topics could apply. Sketch out a simple flowchart of the decisions an accounting researcher would have to make in evaluating Issue 3.

3. Draw a picture illustrating the following fact pattern:

   Company A is exchanging its patent for a building in Michigan, plus $750,000 cash, from Company B. Company B has taken out a loan for $750,000 from Sub Bank in anticipation of the exchange. Sub Bank is a wholly owned subsidiary of Parent Bank.

4. Draw a picture illustrating the following fact pattern involving an *interest rate swap:*

   Company A has issued bonds that pay LIBOR (a floating rate) to investors (in exchange for cash). Company B has issued bonds with a fixed 5% rate to investors (in exchange for cash), with interest payable semiannually. Company A and Company B enter into an interest rate swap. In this swap, Company A will pay a fixed 5% rate to Bank (a financial intermediary); in turn, Bank passes this payment on to Company B. Company B will pay LIBOR to Bank, which in turn passes this payment on to Company A. (Through this derivative transaction, Company A has essentially converted its payment obligation from a floating to a fixed rate; Company B has converted its obligation from fixed to floating).

   (*Hint:* To begin this picture, draw four boxes in a row horizontally, to depict, respectively, Investors, Company A, Company B, Investors. There should be lines between each company and its investors depicting the consideration they exchange. Above this horizontal row, draw one box for Bank.)

5. a. Draw a picture illustrating the following fact pattern involving *trust-preferred securities*:
      Bank Z sets up a trust (a subsidiary entity) and owns 100% of the common stock in the trust. That trust issues preferred securities to investors (in exchange for cash), and the investors earn periodic fixed dividend payments on their preferred shares. Using the funds from the sale of preferred stock, the trust purchases junior subordinated debt from Bank Z, and this debt pays periodic fixed interest payments equal to the dividend payments made by the trust. The trust has a call option, allowing it to call back the preferred shares from investors at its option. Additionally, Bank Z has a call option, allowing it to call back its debt from the trust at its option. Bank Z guarantees to the trust's investors that the trust will use its available cash to make interest payments.

   b. Next, imagine that you are writing an issues memo documenting this arrangement from Bank Z's perspective. What are four researchable questions that you might list in the Issues section of the memo?

6. a. Briefly, describe whether your base-level understanding of interest rate swaps and trust-preferred securities has improved after completing exercises 4-5 above. Explain.

   b. Now, describe one other circumstance in which drawing a picture could be useful in performing or communicating accounting research.

7. Savvy Sisters, a high-end furniture production company, has purchased a new plant and has asked you: *Over what period* should our new plant be depreciated? The plant's estimated useful life is 40 years. Using a guidance sandwich, respond to this question. That is, introduce the issue, quote relevant guidance, then summarize how the guidance applies to the issue in your own words.

8. Savvy Sisters has also asked you at what point the company should record a liability for employee vacation time that has been earned by employees but not yet taken. Using a guidance sandwich, respond to this question. If assumptions are required to respond, describe any assumptions you made.

9. Read the following issue. Next, add an ellipsis to par. 25-10, to reflect the removal of any guidance not considered relevant to this issue.

Issue: A company is executing a business combination in stages. Assume that the acquirer has not recognized any business combination–related amounts in other comprehensive income in prior reporting periods.

ASC 805-10 (Business Combinations, Recognition)

25-10 In a business combination achieved in stages, the acquirer shall remeasure its previously held equity interest in the acquiree at its acquisition-date **fair value** and recognize the resulting gain or loss, if any, in earnings. In prior reporting periods, the acquirer may have recognized changes in the value of its equity interest in the acquiree in other comprehensive income (for example, because the investment was classified as available for sale). If so, the amount that was recognized in other comprehensive income shall be reclassified and included in the calculation of gain or loss as of the acquisition date.

10. Starting with the *second sentence* of the following, correct any errors in the paragraph, or fix any areas where the professionalism of the writing could be improved. Consider proper voice, language, and punctuation. You do not need to use the Codification to complete this exercise.

> You indicated that Zeta Corp ("the Company") is planning to close a plant and therefore plans to lay off a number of its employees. They are planning to apply the guidance in 715-30 (Compensation, Defined Benefit Pensions) to this event. You asked me to determine whether the guidance they've chosen is right or wrong. Their conclusion is wrong because I found guidance in Code section 712-10-05 (Compensation—Nonretirement Postemployment Benefits) saying that severance is covered by that guidance so they will need to follow that guidance.

11. Change the following sentences to active voice.
    a. The incorrect accounting applied by the company resulted in a restatement.
    b. New guidance was issued by the PCAOB that will result in changes to the audit report.

12. Add commas to the following sentences, and for each sentence briefly justify why the commas were needed.
    a. Although Greece is a small country its financial woes have widespread impact.
    b. James Company which is based in the UK is privately-held.
    c. We need to evaluate the company's balance sheet income statement and cash flow statement.
    d. Energy Works contributed an FPSO and Big Oil contributed cash and a permit.

13. Replace the following weak Codification references with stronger language.
    a. In the Codification, ASC 405-20-40-1 says that "A debtor shall derecognize a liability if and only if it has been extinguished."
    b. I found the following guidance in ASC 330-10-30-1, "The primary basis of accounting for inventories is cost…"
    c. Per GASB Statement No. 51, "…all intangible assets not specifically excluded by its scope provisions be classified as capital assets." (Summary page).

    [Hint: This letter (c) example starts with a *strong* reference, but the reference doesn't flow with the rest of the quote. Find a way to fix this.]

14. Introduce the following guidance using a strong reference, then indent the guidance following your introduction. Split the guidance reference (topic-subtopic), (section-paragraph) in a manner similar to the example shown on p. 98.

> ASC 210-10-45-13 **(Balance Sheet)**
>
> Asset valuation allowances for losses such as those on receivables and investments shall be deducted from the assets or groups of assets to which the allowances relate.

15. In the following excerpt, explain why *brackets* [ ] are present (e.g., what are the two functions of the brackets in this example?). Also, explain why it's necessary for the researcher to show any changes to quoted text in brackets.

> Per ASC 840-10-15-6, ". . . The right to control the use of the underlying [PP&E] is conveyed if any of the following conditions is met . . ." [Emphasis added]

CASE STUDY QUESTIONS

4.1 **Understanding the Importance of Documentation** A company is evaluating a lease to determine whether it should receive capital or operating treatment and concludes that it should be capitalized. However, company accountants realize that a similar lease contract, executed just two years ago, has been receiving operating lease treatment. The company is unable to locate documentation explaining the rationale for the earlier lease's operating classification. Think through this issue. What should the company do? What lessons can the company learn from this?

Drafting an Email, Industry Revenue Recognition Your audit firm has a new client in the cable television industry. The audit partner, Dan, has asked you to find out whether the client can recognize revenue (under currently effective revenue guidance) immediately for hookup services provided to new customers. Assume that the client's hookup revenues generally approximate $75 per customer, and related direct selling costs generally amount to approximately $10 per customer. Draft an email to Dan, responding to this question.

4.2

Drafting an Email, Earnings per Share Your audit team is reviewing the second quarter financial statements of Sparks, Inc., a publicly traded company. The audit senior, Will, thinks the client may have omitted an important item and has asked you to research whether interim financial statements are required to include earnings per share amounts. Prepare an email responding to Will's question. Comment on any other potential ramifications of Sparks, Inc.'s omission that come to mind, which you can offer to research.

4.3

Writing an Analysis, Derivatives Definition Facts: You are a corporate accountant for Omega, Inc. Today's date is 12/31/20x6. You've been asked to review a contract in which Omega agrees to purchase 500 shares of GE stock from Zeta (seller) in 1 year (on 12/31/20x7), for $30 per share. Said another way, Omega has entered into a forward contract for the purchase of stock.

4.4

Required: Act as though you are writing just the Analysis section of an issues memo, and research the following question: Does Omega's contract with Zeta meet the definition of a derivative? In your response, include applicable excerpts and guidance sandwiches that relate the guidance to this fact pattern.

In your research, you need only consider the following paragraphs from the guidance:

> ASC 815-10-05-4
> ASC 815-10-10-1
> ASC 815-10-15-83, 15-88, 15-92, 15-96
> ASC 815-10-15-119 and 120

Please do not include all of these paragraphs in your analysis; choose only those paragraphs that are most compelling and relevant to this issue. Assume that no scope exceptions apply.

Writing a Brief Issues Memo, Inventory You are a plant accountant for Kelly Corp. You have been asked to draft a brief (1- to 1.5-page) issues memo ("to the files") documenting the accounting for the following issue.

4.5

> Kelly Corp has leased a mine from which it recently extracted 1,000 kilograms of bauxite (a mineral that can be used to make aluminum). Kelly Corp plans to sell the bauxite to aluminum manufacturers. Kelly Corp is analyzing whether its bauxite inventory can be carried at its selling price per ASC 330-10-35-16(b). Assume that quoted market prices are generally available for bauxite, and that the market for bauxite is active.

Using the standard memo format, analyze whether all necessary conditions are met for the accounting treatment proposed. If assumptions are needed to fully evaluate the guidance, identify those assumptions in your analysis. For this particular memo, you are not required to present alternative treatments; assume for this issue that you have solely been asked to document whether the conditions in ASC 330-10-35-16(b) are met.

ENERGY WORKS CASES

Analyzing Guidance, Relating Guidance to the Fact Pattern The chapter notes that a key feature of an effective analysis is that it *relates* the guidance to the specific fact pattern. Consider the Energy Works fact pattern provided in this chapter. Assume for a moment that the JV was determined to be a variable interest entity (VIE), and assume that you must now analyze *whether Energy Works has a variable interest in the JV*. Analyze the definition of *variable interests* in ASC 810, taking care to explain how the authoritative guidance relates to this particular fact pattern.

4.6

To be clear, the question is not whether the JV is a VIE; rather, focus on whether Energy Works has a variable interest.

Drafting an Email, Evaluation of ASC 845 (Nonmonetary Transactions) In the Energy Works memo, the company considers whether the transfer of nonfinancial assets to the joint venture should be accounted for under ASC 845. Considering guidance from the Codification, draft an email to assist Richard in evaluating this possible accounting treatment.

4.7

(Alt.) Preparing an Issues Memo, Evaluation of Energy Works Issue 3 Prepare an accounting issues memo documenting Energy Works' analysis of Issue 3. For the Facts section, you can simply write: "See Facts in text." Your focus in preparing this memo should be on *"What guidance applies* to Energy Works contribution of assets to the JV?" Do not go into the next step, of documenting the implications of the chosen accounting treatment.

4.7 ALT

Chapter 5

Using Nonauthoritative Sources to Supplement Codification Research

Occasionally, guidance in the Codification may require further explanation, even for the most seasoned of researchers. Just ask Lisa, a senior corporate accountant. She has been asked to evaluate her company's recent purchase of a 5% equity ownership stake in EquityElite, a privately-held investment company.

Lisa has carefully reviewed the terms of the investment and has spoken to her manager for additional background. While EquityElite's shares will trade among only a handful of investors, the company's only business activity will be to invest in large, publicly traded companies. Lisa wonders whether her company should account for the investment using the cost method (Topic 325-20) or using the fair value method, as an available for sale security (Topic 320). She consults the scope section of each topic to understand which is more appropriate.

Continued

After reading this chapter and performing the exercises herein, you will be able to

Learning Objectives

1. **Understand** what nonauthoritative guidance is, and understand its potential benefits.

2. **Become** familiar with the FASB's Conceptual Framework, and gain experience applying this guidance.

3. **Locate** the FASB's basis for conclusions in pre-Codification standards and Accounting Standards Updates.

4. **Locate** useful guidance within accounting firm publications and AICPA publications.

5. **Understand** when peer benchmarking is appropriate and how it is performed.

6. **Describe** circumstances in which references to IFRS may be appropriate.

7. **Utilize** nonauthoritative sources the *right* way (as a supplement to authoritative guidance), and understand how to properly reference these sources.

Key to this scope question is establishing whether the investment in EquityElite has a *readily determinable fair value*. This is a condition for application of the guidance in Topic 320. Seeing limited interpretive guidance for this definition in the Codification, Lisa sets out to locate additional examples. She finds a copy of EY's Financial Reporting Developments publication, *Certain Investments in Debt and Equity Securities*[1] and locates scope guidance using the table of contents. Lisa soon learns that companies should not "look through" an investee to its underlying holdings in determining whether the investee has a readily determinable fair value. Accordingly, the investment is not within the scope of Topic 320; Lisa will now consider whether the cost method applies.

By supplementing Codification research with a nonauthoritative source, Lisa found plain-English guidance that improved her understanding of the Codification's requirements. She can now document both sources considered in her issues memo.

Using Nonauthoritative Sources of Guidance

1. What is nonauthoritative guidance, and how is it used?

2. What are some useful sources of nonauthoritative guidance?

   - FASB's Conceptual Framework
   - Accounting Standards Updates (ASUs) and pre-Codification standards
   - Accounting firm resources
   - AICPA resources
   - Peer benchmarking
   - International Financial Reporting Standards (IFRS) as a nonauthoritative source

3. How to properly use—and cite— nonauthoritative sources

Organization of This Chapter

Nonauthoritative sources can add a great deal of value to a researcher's understanding of the Codification, and can provide guidance when the Codification falls short. Understanding how to use these sources is critical to your skill set as a researcher.

This chapter begins by describing when it is appropriate to utilize nonauthoritative sources, citing guidance from the Codification that permits the use of these sources in certain circumstances.

Next, the chapter introduces several important sources of nonauthoritative guidance, indicating when each source may be used and providing examples demonstrating the use of each source. The chapter concludes with guidance on how to properly use, and cite, nonauthoritative sources.

The preceding graphic illustrates the organization of material in this chapter.

---

[1] EY, Financial Reporting Developments: *Certain Investments in Debt and Equity Securities.* July 2013. Page i.

NONAUTHORITATIVE GUIDANCE: WHAT IS IT, AND HOW IS IT USED?

LO1   **Understand** what nonauthoritative guidance is, and understand its potential benefits.

Nonauthoritative guidance is any source of accounting guidance or practice not included within the FASB Codification. (An exception is SEC guidance, which is also authoritative for public companies.) Because nonauthoritative sources are not included within the Codification, they are not considered part of GAAP and cannot be relied upon exclusively to support an unmodified (aka, unqualified) audit opinion.

Codification Topic **105** (Generally Accepted Accounting Principles) explains the relationship between authoritative and nonauthoritative accounting guidance. Figure 5-1 illustrates the browse path for accessing Topic 105.

Figure 5-1

Browse path for accessing ASC 105, Generally Accepted Accounting Principles

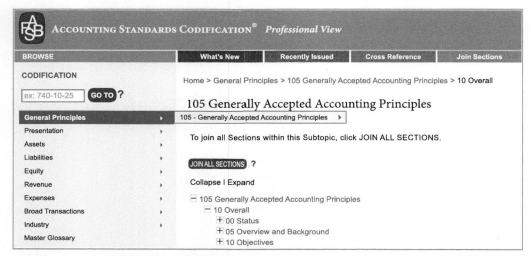

Reproduced with permission of the Financial Accounting Foundation.

Because this topic is foundational to understanding the *authority* of the Codification, you should take a moment to read the following key paragraphs from ASC 105-10.

> **05-1**   This Topic establishes the *Financial Accounting Standards Board (FASB) Accounting Standards Codification®* (Codification) as the source of authoritative generally accepted accounting principles (GAAP) recognized by the FASB to be applied by nongovernmental entities. Rules and interpretive releases of the Securities and Exchange Commission (SEC) under authority of federal securities laws are also sources of authoritative GAAP for SEC registrants. . . .
>
> **05-2**   If the guidance for a transaction or event is not specified within a source of authoritative GAAP for that entity, an entity shall first consider accounting principles for similar transactions or events within a source of authoritative GAAP for that entity and then consider nonauthoritative guidance from other sources. An entity shall not follow the accounting treatment specified in accounting guidance for similar transactions or events in cases in which those accounting principles either prohibit the application of the accounting treatment to the particular transaction or event or indicate that the accounting treatment should not be applied by analogy.
>
> **05-3**   Accounting and financial reporting practices not included in the Codification are nonauthoritative. Sources of nonauthoritative accounting guidance and literature include, for example, the following:
>
>   a.   Practices that are widely recognized and prevalent either generally or in the industry
>
>   b.   FASB Concepts Statements

> c. American Institute of Certified Public Accountants (AICPA) Issues Papers
> d. International Financial Reporting Standards of the International Accounting Standards Board
> e. Pronouncements of professional associations or regulatory agencies
> f. Technical Information Service Inquiries and Replies included in AICPA Technical Practice Aids
> g. Accounting textbooks, handbooks, and articles.
>
> The appropriateness of other sources of accounting guidance depends on its relevance to particular circumstances, the specificity of the guidance, the general recognition of the issuer or author as an authority, and the extent of its use in practice.

Considering the preceding excerpts from ASC 105-10, respond to the following.

1. What two sources are described in par. 05-1 as *authoritative*? Explain.

_____

_____

2. ASC 105-10 sets out a sort of decision tree for researchers to follow if authoritative GAAP isn't available for a *specific transaction*. According to this guidance, researchers should:

First, _____

Then, _____

Now
YOU
Try
5.1

Finally, as you can see, par. 05-3 lists many possible sources of nonauthoritative guidance. This chapter introduces just a few of these sources that you may find most useful as a practitioner.

Benefits of Nonauthoritative Guidance

You might be wondering whether it's better to just play it safe, and to steer clear of sources that are not authoritative. However, nonauthoritative guidance can be useful for providing:

■ Guidance for *issues not addressed* by the Codification,

■ *Interpretive guidance* to help researchers understand and apply Codification requirements, and

■ *Additional context* for understanding the intent of Codification guidance.

First, although the guidance included within the Codification is extensive, there are a few reasons that it may not offer guidance on every possible accounting issue:

■ First, the body of guidance making up the Codification was developed over time, in a manner that responded to practitioners' needs as they arose—often, for very specific fact sets. The guidance was never methodically created in such a manner that all possible accounting topics or financial statement line items would be addressed.

■ Second, transactions are often unique, and it would be impossible for guidance to be on point for every unique set of facts.

Nonauthoritative guidance can assist in addressing these items or transactions not covered by the Codification. For example, *assets* and *liabilities* are not defined in the Codification, so researchers must look to the FASB's Conceptual Framework (a nonauthoritative source) for these definitions. Additionally, very little *journal entry* guidance is in the Codification; sometimes, researchers might look to firm guidance or even textbooks (assuming they are not outdated) for guidance in translating Codification requirements into entries.

Second, nonauthoritative sources can offer **interpretive guidance**, or additional explanations and illustrations, for complex accounting topics. Accounting guidance can be highly **nuanced**; that is, while the words in the authoritative literature may seem straightforward, there are often hidden areas of judgment involved in applying the guidance. Interpretive guidance can help users identify and understand the nuances and areas of complexity within the Codification.

Third, nonauthoritative guidance can offer additional context for understanding the intent of authoritative requirements. In particular, reading a standard setter's *basis for conclusions*, located within the original standard, can often be useful in applying guidance requirements in the manner intended by the standard setter.

TIP	from the Trenches

Don't be afraid to use nonauthoritative sources. Experienced researchers would argue that these sources are often *indispensable* to their understanding of complex guidance. You just have to learn to use these sources the right way, as we'll discuss later in this chapter.

Without further ado, let's explore some very important (and useful) nonauthoritative sources.

SOURCES OF NONAUTHORITATIVE GUIDANCE

This section of the chapter introduces the following sources of nonauthoritative guidance:

- FASB's Conceptual Framework,
- Accounting Standards Updates and pre-Codification standards,
- Accounting firm resources,
- AICPA resources,
- Peer benchmarking, and
- IFRS as a nonauthoritative source of U.S. GAAP.

While many other nonauthoritative sources exist, these are the resources that you'll be most likely to use in practice.

FASB's Conceptual Framework

LO2 **Become** familiar with the FASB's Conceptual Framework, and gain experience applying this guidance.

The FASB's **Conceptual Framework** is a set of principles and objectives that are intended to improve the consistency and quality of accounting standards. This Framework is comprised of the **FASB Concepts Statements** (CON), also known as **Statements of Financial Accounting Concepts** (SFAC).

Although issued by the FASB, the Conceptual Framework is not considered authoritative. Rather, the Conceptual Framework can be accessed within the Codification's *Other Sources* links, or on the FASB website (under *Standards*).

Figure 5-2 illustrates the most recently issued Concepts Statement, CON 8.

Figure 5-2

FASB Concepts Statement No. 8

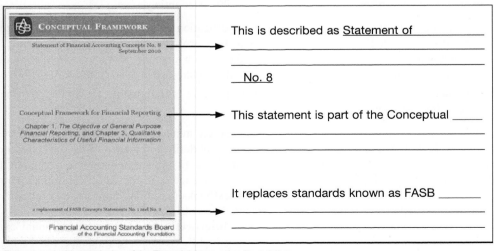

This is described as Statement of _____ _____ _____

____ No. 8

This statement is part of the Conceptual ____ _____ _____

It replaces standards known as FASB _____ _____ _____

Now
YOU
Try
5.2

To familiarize yourself with the terminology used to describe the Conceptual Framework, fill in the blanks shown next to Figure 5-2.

The Conceptual Framework primarily serves two purposes:

■ First, it gives the FASB a common framework, or language, to guide the *development of new standards*.

■ Second, it's intended to provide *practitioners* with key objectives and principles to consider in the preparation of financial statements.

These two purposes are illustrated in the following Now YOU Try.

Now
YOU
Try
5.3

The preamble to CON 8 describes how the Board, and practitioners, might use the Conceptual Framework, as follows:

> The Board itself is likely to be the most direct beneficiary of the guidance provided by Concepts Statements. They will guide the Board in developing accounting and reporting guidance by providing the Board with a common foundation and basic reasoning on which to consider merits of alternatives.
> . . . The objectives and fundamental concepts [of Concepts Statements] also may provide some guidance [to practitioners] in analyzing new or emerging problems of financial accounting and reporting in the absence of applicable authoritative pronouncements.[2] [Explanation added]

Questions:

1. In your own words, and considering the excerpt from CON 8, how is the Conceptual Framework expected to assist the *FASB Board*?

_____

_____

2. In your own words, and considering the excerpt from CON 8, how might *practitioners* benefit from using the Conceptual Framework?

_____

_____

Key Standards in the Conceptual Framework

You may recall that the FASB's predecessors (the CAP and APB) were criticized for their failure to develop a consistent framework that would guide the issuance of new standards. Accordingly, creation of the Conceptual Framework was a key objective of the FASB upon its establishment in 1973.

The Board moved quickly to issue Concepts Statements No. 1–6 between 1978 and 1985; Concepts Statement No. 7, on present value measurement, was issued in 2000. Most recently, Concepts Statement No. 8 was issued in 2010.

Today, the Conceptual Framework comprises the following key standards, among others:

---

[2] FASB Statement of Financial Accounting Concepts No. 8, *Conceptual Framework for Financial Reporting*, preamble. September 2010.

■ CON 8, Ch. 1–2: Objectives of Financial Reporting, and Qualitative Characteristics of Useful Financial Information

■ CON 5: Recognition and Measurement in Financial Statements of Businesses

■ CON 6: Elements of Financial Statements

■ CON 7: Using Cash Flow Information and Present Value in Accounting Measurements

Once you start working with these standards, you'll recognize some of the concepts you've been taught since your very first accounting courses. The following Now YOU Try gives you the chance to match concepts with the standard they come from.

Now YOU Try 5.4

Match each of the following phrases to the Concepts Statement that the phrase likely came from (CON 5, 6, 7, or 8).

Excerpt*	Likely Concepts Statement Number?
1. The primary <u>objective of general purpose financial reporting</u> is to provide information that is <u>useful</u> to users.	_____
2. A <u>full set of financial statements</u> should include: end-of-period financial position, earnings and comprehensive income for the period, periodic cash flows, and changes in ownership.	_____
3. Accounting measurements that reflect the <u>present value</u> of future cash flows are generally more relevant than measures reflecting the sum of undiscounted cash flows.	_____
4. To be recognized, an item must meet four recognition criteria: • An item must meet the definition of an <u>element</u> under CON 6. • An item must be <u>measurable</u>. • Information about the item must be <u>relevant</u> to users. • Information about the item must be <u>reliable</u>.	_____
5. <u>Assets</u> are defined as "probable future economic benefits obtained or controlled by a particular entity as a result of past transactions or events."	_____
6. For information to be useful, it must be <u>relevant</u> and a <u>faithful representation</u>.	_____
7. Present value is most relevant when it is calculated based on <u>observable, market inputs</u>.	_____
8. <u>Expenses</u> are defined as "outflows or other using up of assets or incurrences of liabilities (or a combination of both) from delivering or producing goods, rendering services, or carrying out other activities that constitute the entity's ongoing major or central operations."	_____

*Sources for this exercise (footnotes omitted, and underlined emphasis added):
- Concepts Statement No. 8, Ch. 1 (*The Objective of General Purpose Financial Reporting*), par. OB2, and Ch. 3 (*Qualitative Characteristics of Useful Financial Information*), par. QC4.
- Concepts Statement No. 5, *Recognition and Measurement in Financial Statements of Business Enterprises* (CON 5), par. 13 and 63.
- Concepts Statement No. 6, *Elements of Financial Statements* (CON 6), par. 25 and 80.
- Concepts Statement No. 7, *Using Cash Flow Information and Present Value in Accounting Measurements* (CON 7), "Highlights."

I've seen it in my own students. Their eyes kind of glaze over when we start talking about the Conceptual Framework. But pay attention to this lesson! The concepts in this guidance are *foundational* to our profession. Even today, the FASB is devoting a great deal of resources to reviewing and refreshing these concepts. Plus, there's a *really* good chance you'll need to use the Concepts Statements to perform research in practice.

[TIP] from the Trenches

When Should You Use Guidance from the Concepts Statements?

Before turning to the Concepts Statements for guidance, always first look to the Codification to see whether transaction, or item-specific guidance is available.

That said, the Concepts Statements are, in some circumstances, the only place to find certain guidance that can be critical to accounting research. Please take a few minutes to understand some common circumstances in which the Concepts Statements may be utilized.

- To classify elements of financial statements. The broad meanings of the terms *asset, liability, equity, expenses, gains,* and *losses* are not defined in the Codification. For definitions of these, you will need to consult CON 6. This guidance contains both brief definitions, as well as a detailed discussion of characteristics that are essential to meeting these definitions.

> CON 6 is commonly used to assist in determining whether a cost should be classified *as an asset or as an expense.*

- To understand the computation and objectives of present value. If accounting literature requires that an item be measured at present value, practitioners may choose to consult CON 7. Notably, practitioners are encouraged to consult this guidance only after considering present value guidance within **ASC 820** (Fair Value Measurement), as discussed further in Chapter 8.

> CON 7 can be used to understand how *present value* should be computed.

- To determine whether an event or item should receive financial statement recognition. In the event that the Codification does not address a particular class of transactions or items, it may be necessary to consult CON 5's four *recognition criteria* (illustrated in the previous Now You Try).

> CON 5 establishes *four fundamental recognition criteria*; however, it is not used frequently in practice.

Let's take a moment now to practice performing research using the Concepts Statements. The following questions focus on applying the definitions of financial statement elements.

Researching with the Conceptual Framework

Scenarios 1–2: Asset versus Expense

Use the following excerpts from CON 6 to respond to Scenarios 1 and 2 that follow. Notice that CON 6 presents general principles in the body of the standard (e.g., par. 25–28), while guidance in an appendix to CON 6 (e.g., Appendix B) elaborates on these principles.[3]

Now
[YOU]
Try
5.5

---

[3] Footnotes to CON 6 references incorporated in this chapter have been omitted.

Assets

25. Assets are probable future economic benefits obtained or controlled by a particular entity as a result of past transactions or events.

Characteristics of Assets

26. An asset has three essential characteristics: (a) it embodies a probable future benefit that involves a capacity, singly or in combination with other assets, to contribute directly or indirectly to future net cash inflows, (b) a particular entity can obtain the benefit and control others' access to it, and (c) the transaction or other event giving rise to the entity's right to or control of the benefit has already occurred . . .

...28. The common characteristic possessed by all assets (economic resources) is "service potential" or "future economic benefit," the scarce capacity to provide services or benefits to the entities that use them. In a business enterprise, that service potential or future economic benefit eventually results in net cash inflows to the enterprise . . .

Appendix B: CHARACTERISTICS OF ASSETS, LIABILITIES, AND EQUITY OR NET ASSETS AND OF CHANGES IN THEM

Characteristics of Assets

171. Paragraph 25 defines assets as "probable future economic benefits obtained or controlled by a particular entity as a result of past transactions or events." Paragraphs 26–34 amplify that definition. The following discussion further amplifies it and illustrates its meaning under three headings that correspond to the three essential characteristics of assets described in paragraph 26: future economic benefits, control by a particular entity, and occurrence of a past transaction or event.

Future Economic Benefits

172. Future economic benefit is the essence of an asset (paragraphs 27–31). An asset has the capacity to serve the entity by being exchanged for something else of value to the entity, by being used to produce something of value to the entity, or by being used to settle its liabilities.

173. The most obvious evidence of future economic benefit is a market price. Anything that is commonly bought and sold has future economic benefit, including the individual items that a buyer obtains and is willing to pay for in a "basket purchase" of several items or in a business combination. Similarly, anything that creditors or others commonly accept in settlement of liabilities has future economic benefit, and anything that is commonly used to produce goods or services, whether tangible or intangible and whether or not it has a market price or is otherwise exchangeable, also has future economic benefit. Incurrence of costs may be significant evidence of acquisition or enhancement of future economic benefits (paragraphs 178–180).

174. To assess whether a particular item constitutes an asset of a particular entity at a particular time requires at least two considerations in addition to the general kinds of evidence just described: (a) whether the item obtained by the entity embodied future economic benefit in the first place and (b) whether all or any of the future economic benefit to the entity remains at the time of assessment.

175. Uncertainty about business and economic outcomes often clouds whether or not particular items that might be assets have the capacity to provide future economic benefits to the entity (paragraphs 44–48), sometimes precluding their recognition as assets. The kinds of items that may be recognized as expenses or losses rather than as assets because of uncertainty are some in which management's intent in taking certain steps or initiating certain transactions is clearly to acquire or enhance future economic benefits available to the entity. For example, business enterprises engage in research and development activities, advertise, develop markets, open new branches or divisions, and the like, and spend significant funds to do so. The uncertainty is not about

the intent to increase future economic benefits but about whether and, if so, to what extent they succeeded in doing so. Certain expenditures for research and development, advertising, training, start-up and preoperating activities, development stage enterprises, relocation or rearrangement, and goodwill are examples of the kinds of items for which assessments of future economic benefits may be especially uncertain . . .

Control by a Particular Entity

183. Paragraph 25 defines assets in relation to specific entities. Every asset is an asset of some entity; moreover, no asset can simultaneously be an asset of more than one entity, although a particular physical thing or other agent that provides future economic benefit may provide separate benefits to two or more entities at the same time (paragraph 185). To have an asset, an entity must control future economic benefit to the extent that it can benefit from the asset and generally can deny or regulate access to that benefit by others, for example, by permitting access only at a price.

184. Thus, an asset of an entity is the future economic benefit that the entity can control and thus can, within limits set by the nature of the benefit or the entity's right to it, use as it pleases. The entity having an asset is the one that can exchange it, use it to produce goods or services, exact a price for others' use of it, use it to settle liabilities, hold it, or perhaps distribute it to owners . . .

Occurrence of a Past Transaction or Event

190. The definition of assets in paragraph 25 distinguishes between the future economic benefits of present and future assets of an entity. Only present abilities to obtain future economic benefits are assets under the definition, and they become assets of particular entities as a result of transactions or other events or circumstances affecting the entity. For example, the future economic benefits of a particular building can be an asset of a particular entity only after a transaction or other event—such as a purchase or a lease agreement—has occurred that gives it access to and control of those benefits. Similarly, although an oil deposit may have existed in a certain place for millions of years, it can be an asset of a particular entity only after the entity either has discovered it in circumstances that permit the entity to exploit it or has acquired the rights to exploit it from whoever had them.

191. Since the transaction or event giving rise to the entity's right to the future economic benefit must already have occurred, the definition excludes from assets items that may in the future become an entity's assets but have not yet become its assets. An entity has no asset for a particular future economic benefit if the transactions or events that give it access to and control of the benefit are yet in the future. The corollary is that an entity still has an asset if the transactions or events that use up or destroy a particular future economic benefit or remove the entity's access to and control of it are yet in the future. For example, an entity does not acquire an asset merely by budgeting the purchase of a machine and does not lose an asset from fire until a fire destroys or damages some asset.

Scenario 1: A company purchased 50 hole punchers for its office staff. Each hole puncher cost $5 and should be in service for 5 years or more.

Should the cost of these hole punchers be recorded as an asset or as an expense? Support your answer using references to paragraphs from CON 6.

1.   Analysis—Should the hole punchers be recorded as an asset or expense?

_____

_____

_____

_____

_____

In Scenario 1, note that while you could support your position using *only* the definition of an asset (par. 25), your answer is stronger if you support your conclusion with excerpts from detailed Appendix B implementation guidance, as well. For judgmental issues, reference to this detailed interpretive guidance can be essential.

Scenario 2: Using the definition and characteristics of an asset above, explain why advertising costs are generally recorded as expenses, rather than as assets.

2.   Analysis—Why are advertising costs generally recorded as expenses, rather than as assets?

_____

_____

_____

_____

TIP **from the Trenches**

Be aware that while the Codification does not broadly define *assets and liabilities*, many Codification topics do define specific assets, such as inventory or receivables. A researcher should only turn to the nonauthoritative, Conceptual Framework definition of assets after concluding that more specific guidance is not available within the Codification.

Scenario 3: Revenues, Expenses, and Gains

CON 6 includes the following guidance defining revenues, expenses, and gains.

Revenues

78.   Revenues are inflows or other enhancements of assets of an entity or settlements of its liabilities (or a combination of both) from delivering or producing goods, rendering services, or other activities that constitute the entity's ongoing major or central operations.

Characteristics of Revenues

79.   Revenues represent actual or expected cash inflows (or the equivalent) that have occurred or will eventuate as a result of the entity's ongoing major or central operations. The assets increased by revenues may be of various kinds—for example, cash, claims against customers or clients, other goods or services received, or increased value of a product resulting from production. Similarly, the transactions and events from which revenues arise and the revenues themselves are in many forms and are called by various names—for example, output, deliveries, sales, fees, interest, dividends, royalties, and rent—depending on the kinds of operations involved and the way revenues are recognized.

Expenses

80.   Expenses are outflows or other using up of assets or incurrences of liabilities (or a combination of both) from delivering or producing goods, rendering services, or carrying out other activities that constitute the entity's ongoing major or central operations.

Characteristics of Expenses

81.   Expenses represent actual or expected cash outflows (or the equivalent) that have occurred or will eventuate as a result of the entity's ongoing major or central operations. The assets that flow out or are used or the liabilities that are incurred may be of various kinds—for example, units of product delivered or produced, employees' services used, kilowatt hours of electricity used to light an office building, or taxes on current income. Similarly, the transactions and events from which expenses arise and the expenses themselves are in many forms and are called by various names—for example, cost of goods sold, cost of services provided, depreciation, interest, rent, and salaries and wages—depending on the kinds of operations involved and the way expenses are recognized.

Gains and Losses

82.   Gains are increases in equity (net assets) from peripheral or incidental transactions of an entity and from all other transactions and other events and circumstances affecting the entity except those that result from revenues or investments by owners.

Characteristics of Gains and Losses

84.   Gains and losses result from entities' peripheral or incidental transactions and from other events and circumstances stemming from the environment that may be largely beyond the control of individual entities and their managements. Thus, gains and losses are not all alike. There are several kinds, even in a single entity, and they may be described or classified in a variety of ways that are not necessarily mutually exclusive.

Scenario 3: Assume that a manufacturing company usually pays a waste company (by the pound) to haul away manufacturing waste. Recently, a landfill gas company offered to buy a small portion of the waste for cash, saving the manufacturing facility a portion of its disposal costs and providing it with proceeds from the disposal.

The sale of manufacturing waste is not a primary business activity of the manufacturer; however, it will now result in an inflow of cash.

Which is more appropriate—classifying this transaction as an increase in revenue, a decrease in expense, or as a gain?

3.   Analysis—Record the transaction as increase in revenue or decrease in expense? Alternatively, should the transaction be recorded as a gain?

_____

_____

_____

_____

_____

You're probably well aware that the FASB issued revised revenue recognition guidance in 2014. However, this CON 6 definition of revenue is still current today. In fact, the CON 6 definition served as the basis for the revised definition of revenue that now exists in the Codification. That said, the FASB does plan to revisit its Conceptual Framework discussion of revenue in the future.

TIP | from the Trenches

Scenario 4: Definition of a Liability

CON 6 includes the following guidance defining liabilities.

Liabilities

35.   Liabilities are probable future sacrifices of economic benefits arising from present obligations of a particular entity to transfer assets or provide services to other entities in the future as a result of past transactions or events.

Characteristics of Liabilities

36.   A liability has three essential characteristics: (a) it embodies a present duty or responsibility to one or more other entities that entails settlement by probable future transfer or use of assets at a specified or determinable date, on occurrence of a specified event, or on demand, (b) the duty or responsibility obligates a particular entity, leaving it little or no discretion to avoid the future sacrifice, and (c) the transaction or other event obligating the entity has already happened. Liabilities

Continued

Continued from previous page

commonly have other features that help identify them—for example, most liabilities require the obligated entity to pay cash to one or more identified other entities and are legally enforceable. However, those features are not essential characteristics of liabilities. Their absence, by itself, is not sufficient to preclude an item's qualifying as a liability. That is, liabilities may not require an entity to pay cash but to convey other assets, to provide or stand ready to provide services, or to use assets. And the identity of the recipient need not be known to the obligated entity before the time of settlement. Similarly, although most liabilities rest generally on a foundation of legal rights and duties, existence of a legally enforceable claim is not a prerequisite for an obligation to qualify as a liability if for other reasons the entity has the duty or responsibility to pay cash, to transfer other assets, or to provide services to another entity. [Footnotes omitted]

Scenario 4: Assume you are the occupant of a building for which you have just entered into a 2-year lease agreement. Due to the short-term nature of the arrangement, the lease will likely be classified as an operating lease.

The FASB is currently proposing fundamental changes to lease accounting, based in part on their view that a lessee's obligation to make payments over the lease period meets the definition of a liability. Using language from CON 6, state whether you believe the lessee's obligation meets the definition of a liability.

4. Analysis—Why might a lessee's obligation meet the definition of a liability?

_____

_____

_____

_____

_____

_____

The Conceptual Framework Today

Today, the FASB is taking a fresh look at several areas of the Conceptual Framework, including the possible introduction of a disclosure framework to guide the Board and preparers.

Eventually, the FASB hopes to replace all of its existing Concepts Statements with a single document (CON 8), which is expected to read like a chapter book. So far, as you've seen, Chapters 1 and 3 (*Objectives* and *Qualitative Characteristics*) have been completed.

As part of this project, the Board also expects to reconsider the authoritative status of the Conceptual Framework, and may eventually decide to elevate the Conceptual Framework to authoritative GAAP.

Accounting Standards Updates and Pre-Codification Standards

LO3 Locate the FASB's basis for conclusions in pre-Codification standards and Accounting Standards Updates.

The second nonauthoritative source we will cover is FASB's Accounting Standards Updates and pre-Codification standards.

- The term **Accounting Standards Updates** (ASUs) refers to the guidance periodically issued by the FASB for the purpose of making changes to the Codification. *ASUs are not considered authoritative in their own right.*

- **Pre-Codification standards** refers to all GAAP that predates the Codification. For example, all then-effective FASB Statements, EITF Abstracts, APB Opinions, and Accounting Research Bulletins were used to populate the Codification in 2009, then were superseded when the Codification became effective.

It's worth taking a moment to understand these resources. In some cases, these standards contain content relevant to a topic, but which was deemed "nonessential" and not carried forward by creators of the Codification. Following are three circumstances in which these resources can be useful:

- To read a standard setter's **basis for conclusions**—In most cases, the Board's basis for reaching its conclusions on each standard has been omitted from content moved into the Codification. Understanding the rationale for Board decisions can often be useful in applying guidance requirements in the manner intended by the Board.

- To access **grandfathered content**—This is guidance which is no longer effective for new transactions, but which companies are allowed to continue following if they were already, as of the Codification's effective date in 2009, accounting for a transaction using this guidance.

- To locate **historical guidance**—This is guidance that applied in the past, but that has since been superseded. Practitioners may need to read historical guidance when dealing with restated (historical) financial statements, or in order to understand prior guidance requirements.

Accounting Standards Updates

Let's take a moment to further discuss ASUs. Each ASU begins with a summary of its key provisions and an explanation of why the Codification is being updated. Next, each ASU details the changes it will make to the Codification, then describes the Board's rationale (its basis for conclusions).

Figure 5-3 depicts the cover (at left) and an excerpted page (at right) from a sample ASU.

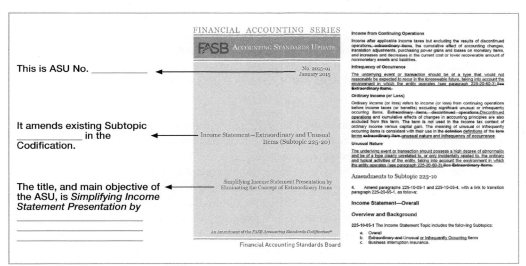

Figure 5-3

Sample ASU cover and excerpts

- On the cover, notice in particular how this guidance is described as "An Amendment of the FASB Accounting Standards Codification."

- On the excerpted page, notice how changes to existing Codification content are marked. Underlined text reflects new Codification requirements; strike-outs reflect deleted content.

To improve your familiarity with ASUs, take a moment to complete the following **Now YOU Try**.

Now
YOU
Try
5.6

1. Fill in the blanks beside the ASU cover in Figure 5-3.

2. Next, what existing concept does this ASU remove from Subtopic 225-20 in the Codification, and what concept does it introduce?

    Concept removed: _____

    Concept introduced: _____

To identify the ASUs that have resulted in changes to a given topic, consult the topic's **Status** section (**-00**) or use the Cross-Reference feature.

Pre-Codification Standards

We will use a Now YOU Try to illustrate the use of a pre-Codification standard.

Now
YOU
Try
5.7

Using Pre-Codification Standards

ASC 730-10 (Expenses—Research and Development) requires that certain elements of research and development costs shall be expensed as incurred. One such element is described as follows:

> **25-2(a).** "... the costs of materials, equipment, or facilities that are acquired or constructed for a particular research and development project and that have no alternative future uses (in other research and development projects or otherwise) and therefore no separate economic values are research and development costs at the time the costs are incurred."

That is, if a physical structure is built as part of a research and development activity, but has no future use, that structure may not be capitalized as an asset.

A researcher wanting more background on this requirement could consult FASB Statement No. 2, *Accounting for Research and Development Costs* (FAS 2). This is the pre-Codification standard that cross references to **ASC 730**. Appendix B (Basis for Conclusions) of FAS 2 states:

> **33.** Consideration was given to the alternative that the costs of materials, equipment, or facilities that are acquired or constructed for a particular research and development project and that have no alternative future uses . . . be apportioned over the life of the project rather than treated as research and development costs when incurred. The Board reasoned, however, that if materials, equipment, or facilities are of such a specialized nature that they have no alternative future uses, even in another research and development project, those materials, equipment, or facilities have no separate economic values to distinguish them from other types of costs such as salaries and wages incurred in a particular project. Accordingly, all costs of those materials, equipment, and facilities should be treated as research and development costs when incurred.

Questions:

1. Explain the Board's rationale for requiring that materials, equipment, and facilities with no alternative future use be expensed as incurred. Did this add value to your understanding of par. 25-2 in the Codification? Explain.

    _____

    _____

    _____

    _____

2. How would a researcher know that **ASC 730** cross references to **FAS 2**? (*Hint:* This search
    method was introduced in Chapter 2.)

Accounting Firm Resources

Within major public accounting firms, a handful of employees often act as *technical
accounting specialists*, who specialize in one or several technical topics and work to
educate other members of the firm on proper application of the topic. These individuals
are often in the firm's national office or may be part of an accounting advisory group. As
illustrated in Figure 5-4, specialists might include, for example, a "securitization specialist" or a "derivatives specialist."

> **LO4** Locate useful guidance within accounting firm publications and AICPA publications.

 In addition to advising peers and clients, technical specialists often write interpretive guidance for their firm and for clients' use in applying complex topics. This guidance frequently
offers additional examples to supplement, as well as plain-English discussion and interpretation
of, guidance found in the Codification. In certain, limited cases, firm specialists may "clear"
any highly judgmental interpretations with the FASB staff before their issuance, to ensure that
Codification requirements are correctly interpreted.

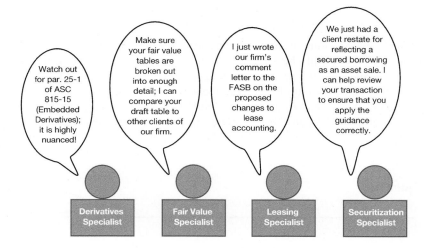

Figure 5-4

Specialists you might
find within public
accounting firms

Resources commonly issued by firm technical specialists include:

- Firm research databases (clients of the firm must log in to view content)
- Firm-published guide books by topic
- Technical accounting alerts and "hot topics" whitepapers

 Additionally, firm auditors may have access to the following useful resources:

- National office consultation databases (where certain audit firms maintain records of inquiries submitted to their national office)
- Auditor's verbal inquiries of his or her peers (how are other clients in this industry handling
  this issue, or interpreting this new guidance?)

 We will discuss each of these resources in turn.

Research Databases

Several large public accounting firms maintain online accounting and auditing research databases for the benefit of their employees, clients, and paid public subscribers. These databases
are generally free of charge to firm employees; all other users are generally charged a subscription fee (but free 30-day trials are often available). These research databases provide users

with access to the FASB Codification, along with auditing guidance, SEC guidance, and firm-generated interpretive guidance.

Firm databases include, for example:	Research databases available from other providers include:
• Deloitte's *Technical Library* • EY's *Global Accounting and Auditing Information Tool* (GAAIT) • KPMG's *Accounting Research Online* (ARO) • PwC's *Inform* database • Grant Thornton's *Client Experience Portal*	• AICPA's *Online Professional Library* • CCH's *Accounting Research Manager*

Many of the research databases just named also contain **accounting manuals** published by the firm sponsoring the database. These manuals often present requirements directly from the Codification, followed by the firm's own interpretive guidance. Accounting manuals are generally organized by topic (similar to the Codification's organization) and can be searched like the Codification (i.e., via keyword or browse searches). Accounting manuals include, for example:

▪ KPMG's *Accounting and Reporting Guide*

▪ EY's *Accounting Manual*

▪ PwC's *Accounting and Reporting Manual* (ARM)

Many users of firm accounting manuals become so comfortable with the plain-English delivery of the content that they consult these manuals even before searching the Codification.

Figure 5-5 includes an image from the homepage of PwC *Inform* and may be helpful in understanding how content within firm research databases may be organized. In this screenshot, notice that researchers can browse (using the left-hand navigation panel) to the FASB Codification, PwC material, AICPA and SEC material, and so on. Using the Search tab (see circle), researchers can search for content within specified materials.

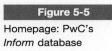

Figure 5-5

Homepage: PwC's *Inform* database

Now YOU Try 5.8

1. Using the homepage of PwC *Inform* (illustrated in Figure 5-5), show how you would search for the phrase *debt extinguishment* within the "FASB Codification" branch.

2. Next, use Figure 5-5 to show how you would search for PwC interpretive guidance related to this phrase (debt extinguishment).

3. Where, within the browse options (at left), would you expect to find the FASB Concepts Statements?

Guide Books

In addition to maintaining research databases, major public accounting firms also frequently write topic-specific guide books. These guide books are intended to provide interpretive guidance and illustrative examples for complex accounting topics (such as those listed under "Broad Transactions" in the Codification).

Firm guide books may be nonauthoritative, but they are incredibly useful. It's very common for technical accountants—both in the Big 4 and in industry—to refer to guide books published by their own firm or auditor, or by other firms, for guidance on complex issues. Put yourself in their shoes—imagine how great it must feel to find an example in a firm guide book that illustrates a transaction just like one that you are reviewing!

Examples of guide book topics include

- Fair value measurement
- Consolidation of variable interest entities
- Revenue from contracts with customers
- Derivatives and hedging
- Stock compensation
- IFRS/U.S. GAAP similarities and differences

Some firms even publish guide books summarizing the recent year's SEC comment letters to public companies, as depicted in Figure 5-6.

At left: EY's derivatives Financial Reporting Developments publication, at 572 pages plus appendices, offers extensive interpretive guidance. At right: Deloitte's SEC Comment Letters guide book is published annually, to summarize comments and questions sent by the SEC to financial statement preparers.

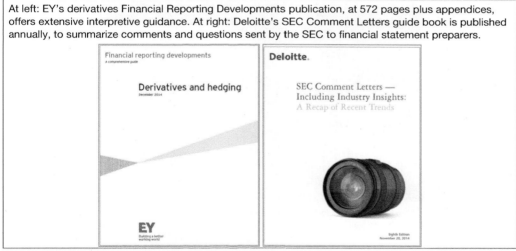

Figure 5-6

Sample accounting firm guide books

© Ernst & Young LLP. Used with permission.
Copyright © 2015 Deloitte Development LLC. All rights reserved.[4]

---

[4] This publication contains general information only and Deloitte is not, by means of this publication, rendering accounting, business, financial, investment, legal, tax, or other professional advice or services. This publication is not a substitute for such professional advice or services, nor should it be used as a basis for any decision or action that may affect your business. Before making any decision or taking any action that may affect your business, you should consult a qualified professional advisor.

• Deloitte shall not be responsible for any loss sustained by any person who relies on this publication.

• As used in this document, "Deloitte" means Deloitte & Touche LLP, a subsidiary of Deloitte LLP. Please see www.deloitte.com/us/about for a detailed description of the legal structure of Deloitte LLP and its subsidiaries. Certain services may not be available to attest clients under the rules and regulations of public accounting.

Firm guide books are often daunting in size. However, they generally include a very detailed table of contents, and are often organized somewhat like the Codification (e.g., scope issues, followed by recognition, and so on). Start with the table of contents when reviewing a guide book; from there, you can often jump to the exact issue you need to research.

One great thing about accounting firm guide books is that they are frequently available for free on the Internet. **Search for them by naming the topic, the word "guide," and the firm name.** For example, a Google search for "Accounting for income taxes guide Deloitte," will direct you to Deloitte's 520-page guide on this topic.

Google	accounting for income taxes guide deloitte	🔍

Google and the Google logo are registered trademarks of Google Inc., used with permission.

In some cases, a no-cost login may be required to view these guides (such as for PwC or EY materials). These guide books are also frequently available within firm research databases.

[TIP] from the Trenches	EY's guides are referred to as *Financial Reporting Developments*, and Deloitte's guides are referred to as the *Roadmap* series. When searching Google for these guides, you might want to substitute these terms ("Financial Reporting Developments," or "Roadmap") for the word *guide*.

Accounting Firm Technical Updates / Whitepapers

Guide books and accounting manuals take time to develop. For issues that are emerging, or that deal with newly issued guidance, practitioners often turn to firm whitepapers and technical alerts.

KPMG's *Issues In-Depth* and PwC's *In Depth* series, illustrated in Figure 5-7, addressed implementation issues raised by clients in the early stages of adopting the revised revenue standard.

Figure 5-7

Example accounting firm whitepapers—KPMG's *Issues In-Depth* and PwC's *In Depth* series

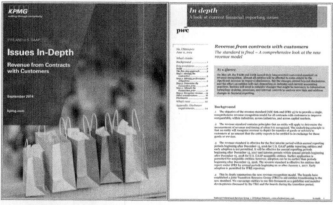

Image at left: Reprinted from KPMG's *Issues In-Depth*, "Revenue from Contracts with Customers," September 2014. Copyright: © 2014 KPMG LLP, a Delaware limited liability partnership and a member firm of the KPMG network of independent member firms affiliated with KPMG International Cooperative ("KPMG International"), a Swiss entity. All rights reserved.[5]

Image at right: © Pricewaterhouse Coopers LLP ("PwC"). Not for further reproduction or use without the prior written consent of PwC.

Firms frequently distribute these emerging issues whitepapers by email; simply sign up for technical accounting alerts on the accounting firm's website, and you will be alerted as the firm issues new interpretive guidance. Chapter 14 provides additional strategies for selecting email subscriptions.

---

[5] All information provided is of a general nature and is not intended to address the circumstances of any particular individual or entity. Although we endeavor to provide accurate and timely information, there can be no guarantee that such information is accurate as of the date it is received or that it will continue to be accurate in the future. No one should act upon such information without appropriate professional advice after a thorough examination of the facts of a particular situation. For additional news and information, please access KPMG's global Website on the Internet at http://www.kpmg.com.

Auditor Inquiry

Auditors are often able to avail themselves of additional sources of interpretive guidance, described next.

■ Some firms maintain a database of inquiries received by their national offices. In some cases, auditors are able to search this database to determine whether a specific client inquiry has been previously addressed by the national office.

■ Auditors are frequently able to make verbal inquiries of their peers, to understand how other clients in an industry are handling a specific issue. For example, if an auditor is addressing a question at Healthcare Company A, he may contact his colleague who performs the audit of Healthcare Company B to ask how the client plans to address the same issue. This practice is generally acceptable as long as the auditors are not sharing confidential or nonpublic information.

When (and How) Should You Use Accounting Firm Resources?

Accounting firm guidance can be used either as a starting point for research or as additional support for your reading of the Codification. As noted previously, some researchers routinely begin their searches with firm manuals. Others may turn to firm guidance only as needed to search for examples of application issues or Q&As.

However you use firm guidance, bear in mind these two notes of caution:

1. Your primary support for accounting positions must still always be authoritative guidance. Nonauthoritative sources can play a supporting role, at best, in your accounting issues memos.

2. There's always a chance that the firm guidance you are reading could be outdated. The FASB continually issues new ASUs that change the content in the Codification, and accounting firm publications may have a lag in reflecting these changes. Therefore, once you find relevant firm guidance, establish a practice of always going back to the Codification to confirm that the guidance you are relying on is still current, then quote from the Codification whenever possible.

That is, researchers who start their searches with firm guidance should establish a practice of going back to the Codification to pull authoritative excerpts for their accounting memos. It is *not okay* to cite firm excerpts where Codification excerpts are available.

> Caution—As with other sources of nonauthoritative guidance, firm guidance is helpful for *interpreting* the Codification, but it should not *replace* your use of authoritative guidance. Guidance citations in accounting memos should primarily come from authoritative sources.

TIP from the Trenches

Imagine that you work for a beverage maker that has just sold its diet soda division, and you are evaluating whether the gain on sale should be reported as related to a *discontinued operation*. Following is guidance from **ASC 205-20** (Presentation of Financial Statements—Discontinued Operations) describing when a disposal shall be reported in discontinued operations:

Now
YOU
Try
5.9

> **45-1B** A disposal of a component of an entity or a group of components of an entity shall be reported in discontinued operations if the disposal represents a strategic shift that has (or will have) a major effect on an entity's operations and financial results when any of the following occur:
>   … b. The component of an entity or group of components of an entity is disposed of by sale. … [6]

You've determined that the division qualifies as a *component of an entity*. Next, you need to evaluate whether the disposal represents a strategic shift that will have (or has had) a major effect on

---

[6] Notably, this excerpt reflects pending content, issued in ASU 2014-08 (Reporting Discontinued Operations).

operations or financial results. You wonder: Can the significance of the gain on sale of the division be used to evaluate whether the disposal had a *major effect* on operations or financial results?

Questions:

1. Use the table of contents from EY's *Discontinued Operations* (November 2014) Financial Reporting Developments publication in Figure 5-8. Where might you start your search for interpretive guidance on this issue? Where else might you look (within this guide book) for potentially relevant guidance? Explain.

_____

_____

Figure 5-8

Excerpted Contents page from EY's *Discontinued Operations* Financial Reporting Developments publication

Contents

2. Describe how you would go about locating this guide book.

_____

3. What cautions would you exercise when relying upon a firm guide book? Explain.

_____

_____

_____

AICPA Resources

The AICPA offers a number of nonauthoritative resources which can be useful to practitioners. These include (1) a non-GAAP reporting framework for small- and medium-sized nonpublic entities and (2) interpretive guidance to assist practitioners in applying U.S. GAAP. We will discuss each of these in turn.

The FRF for SMEs

Issued in 2013, the AICPA's *Financial Reporting Framework for Small- and Medium-Sized Entities* ("FRF for SMEs" or the "Framework") offers an alternative to the use of U.S. GAAP for small- and medium-sized entities and responds to concerns that U.S. GAAP is currently too complex for certain private companies to apply. In fact, prior to the issuance of this Framework, certain private companies even elected to receive qualified opinions from their auditors, rather than complying in full with current U.S. GAAP. For their part, these companies' lenders and creditors would often accept these qualified opinions, understanding the high costs of full U.S. GAAP compliance.

The FRF for SMEs is expected to benefit certain preparers by providing a more concise, simple reporting framework with fewer required disclosures. The Framework is considered an **other comprehensive basis of accounting** (OCBOA), meaning a reporting framework that is not GAAP; use of this framework is entirely optional for preparers.

Notably, this framework does not replace the work of the FASB's Private Company Council, which advocates for including simplified alternatives within *authoritative GAAP* for private companies.

> Unlike other nonauthoritative resources discussed in this chapter, which assist in *interpreting* GAAP, this FRF for SMEs is actually an *alternative* to GAAP, and is expected to be most useful to preparers whose lenders or other creditors will accept non-GAAP financial statements.

[TIP] from the Trenches

Other AICPA Resources

Other nonauthoritative resources from the AICPA include the following:

- AICPA Audit and Accounting Guides ("A&A Guides")—These guides summarize Codification and auditing standards and provide practical guidance to practitioners. A&A Guides are often issued for specific industries (e.g., the *Airlines* A&A Guide) as illustrated in Figure 5-9. The AICPA also issues Audit Guides (e.g., *Audit Sampling*) and Accounting and Valuation Guides, which focus on valuation issues.

- *U.S. GAAP Financial Statements—Best Practices in Presentation and Disclosure* publication—This publication compiles examples from the disclosures of hundreds of public companies, as well as statistical data summarizing disclosure trends. Formerly known as *Accounting Trends and Techniques*, this publication is intended to save corporate accountants and auditors the effort of searching, one by one, for examples within company financial statements of how other preparers are complying with accounting and disclosure requirements.

- Technical Hotline—The AICPA offers this sort of "advice hotline" on matters including the application of accounting and auditing guidance to complex issues. Practitioners can call or email their questions into the Technical Hotline service, but only after doing their own research and involving the highest levels of their own organizations. The AICPA technical staff will provide its views; these views do not represent official positions of the AICPA.

  Small businesses and small or regional CPA firms, which may not have a national office to serve as a resource for such complex questions, may find the AICPA Technical Hotline to be a valuable resource when they have exhausted their internal options.

- AICPA *Technical Questions and Answers*—Developed in large part based on inquiries received through its Technical Hotline service, the AICPA often posts Q&As on its website addressing recent accounting and auditing questions its technical staff has received. Periodically, these Q&As are compiled and issued in the form of a book—the AICPA's *Technical Questions and Answers*.

Figure 5-9

AICPA's Audit and Accounting Guide, *Airlines* (2013)

© 2015, American Institute of CPAs.
Used by permission.

Now
[YOU]
Try
5.10

Utilizing AICPA Resources

Each AICPA resource described above serves a different function. Identify the AICPA resource that might best fit each scenario described next.

Situation	AICPA Resource to Consult?
Amy is new to the audit team of a healthcare entity and is seeking a resource that will assist her in understanding industry-specific accounting and auditing matters. Explain. _____	1. _____
Doug works in the 10-K reporting group at a mid-sized corporation. For years, his team has "rolled forward" the company's pension disclosure, updating numbers but making few changes to content. The company's Controller has asked his team to revisit this disclosure and to see how it can be improved. Doug wants to know how other companies approach this disclosure. Explain. _____	2. _____
After extensive research, the CFO of a small company has hit a dead-end on determining the appropriate accounting treatment for a complex transaction. His accounting firm does not have specialists in this area. He'd like a sounding board for resolving this issue. Explain. _____	3. _____

Peer Benchmarking

LO5 Understand when peer benchmarking is appropriate and how it is performed.

Often, it is not enough to simply apply GAAP correctly; companies and their auditors also want to be sure that what they're reporting is consistent with how other companies are addressing the same issues.

Peer benchmarking is a common practice in which companies (and their auditors) review the reporting and disclosures of others within the company's industry. Benchmarking is particularly relevant for companies interested in seeing how their peers have implemented the latest FASB guidance. It is also useful for companies wanting to identify best practices, or to ensure consistency with their peers' methods for disclosing items or transactions.

Companies must occasionally go outside their peer group for benchmarking compliance with just-issued FASB guidance. That is, companies may be limited to reviewing disclosures of early adopters (i.e., companies who choose to apply new guidance prior to its mandatory effective date).

As discussed earlier in this chapter, the AICPA's *Best Practices* publication summarizes disclosures and trends from hundreds of companies. However, the AICPA's publication is not customized by industry; in some cases, companies themselves want to hand-select the peer group companies that they compare to (e.g., same industry, same size). Additionally, companies may need to access recently issued corporate filings and cannot wait for updates to this publication.

Search for Company Filings

Through its Edgar database, the SEC provides free access to all public filings, including companies' annual (10-K) and quarterly (10-Q) reports. This database is as "real time" as it gets—filings are generally available and searchable to the public immediately upon their receipt by the SEC. Individuals can search for filings by company or by keyword.

Figure 5-10 illustrates two methods for searching the SEC website (www.sec.gov):

■ First, a researcher can search for SEC documents using the keyword search box at top right. However, this may not show all company filing results. For these, click the "Company Filings" link just below the search box.

■ Alternatively, a researcher can navigate to "Filings" then "Company Filings Search" to view additional search options.

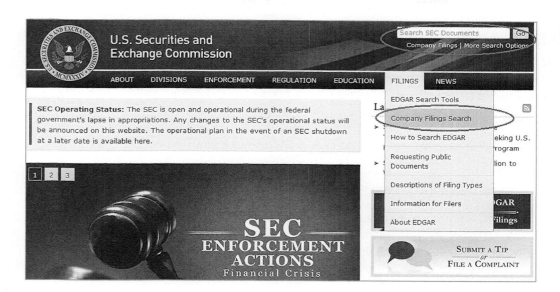

Figure 5-10

Searching company filings on the SEC website

The Edgar database is available free of charge; however it allows for only one search at a time, and only includes public companies. Companies desiring additional functionality can pay a fee to subscribe to professional research databases, such as **Morningstar Document Research**, **SNL Financial**, **LexisNexis**, **Mergent Online**, or **S&P NetAdvantage**. These databases offer advanced search options, including searches by industry, within a predefined peer group, and searches of private company financial statements.

Corporate annual and quarterly reports are also generally available on companies' websites, often through the link "Investors" or "Investor Relations." Figure 5-11 shows the link on GE's website to its public filings.

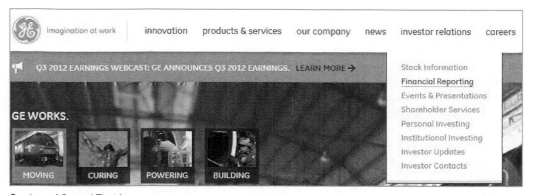

Figure 5-11

Navigating to GE's public filings, through its "Investor Relations" page

Courtesy of General Electric.

Following is an example illustrating one form of peer benchmarking.

EXAMPLE

Imagine your client is in the banking industry and is evaluating whether the fair value hierarchy levels (1, 2, or 3) it has disclosed, in accordance with **ASC 820** (Fair Value Measurements), are consistent with others in its peer group. To provide context to your client's decision, you

Continued

Continued from previous page

prepare a brief summary of fair value hierarchy disclosures from the peer group's annual reports.[7] An excerpt of your analysis is shown next.

Company	Equity Securities	U.S. Treasury and U.S. Agency Securities	Corporate Bonds	Asset-Backed Securities
Bank A	1	1, 2	2	2, 3
Bank B	1	1, 2	2	2
Bank C	1	1, 2	2	2
...				

Using this summary, your client can more clearly determine whether its disclosures are consistent with its peers'.

[TIP] from the Trenches

Form 10-K filings can be lengthy. To skip directly to the financial statements within these filings, (1) look for links within the table of contents (generally located within the first few pages of the filing), or (2) perform a word search (ctrl + f) for "independent registered." These keywords will jump you ahead to the independent auditor's report, which immediately precedes the financial statements.

Review of SEC Comment Letters

In addition to searching company filings, a review of **SEC correspondence**, including company responses to SEC comment letters, is another valuable means for understanding peer companies' rationale in selecting or applying accounting policies.

For example, consider the following response from Apple Inc. to an SEC comment letter, regarding Apple's disclosures of the estimated selling price for iPhone upgrades.

SEC comment: Please tell us if you considered specifying in your disclosures what products you considered to be "similar offerings" in determining the estimated selling price of unspecified upgrades for the iPhone and Apple TV (e.g., specified software upgrades sold for the iPod Touch and AppleCare).

Apple response:
As noted in our previous response letter dated March 4, 2010, in determining estimated selling prices (ESPs) for unspecified software upgrade rights for iPhone and Apple TV the Company considered evidence provided by pricing of actual sales of specified upgrades for iPod touch, iPhone AppleCare (APP) contracts, and upgrades to our iLife and iWork application suites. The Company did consider providing additional specific disclosure regarding selling prices of these products and the relevance of these selling prices to the ESPs…However, the Company concluded such additional disclosure would potentially be misleading. This conclusion was based on the fact the actual selling prices of these products were not considered direct proxies for the ESPs determined for iPhone and Apple TV upgrade rights but instead provided evidence to help define a reasonable range of potential ESPs for those rights. The Company concluded the potential to mislead and confuse its financial statement users by providing the complex and

---

[7] Sample fair value hierarchy comparison table is based on the following source documents. Note that asset category names may not exactly match the annual reports, as in some cases they differ slightly across companies. They are presented in this book with similar names for comparison purposes. Levels shown in summary table indicate predominant levels reflected for these asset categories but may not exhaustively reflect levels actually disclosed in annual reports. This table is presented for illustration only.

- Wells Fargo's 2011 Form 10-K, Exhibit 13, p. 195.
- Citigroup's 2011 Annual Report, p. 171.
- Bank of America's 2011 Annual Report, p. 241.

extensive additional disclosure needed to describe in detail the use of this evidence outweighed the limited benefit such disclosures would provide. The Company believes the disclosure it has provided fully informs investors as to its use and development of ESPs for iPhone and Apple TV software upgrade rights and fulfills the disclosure requirements of ASC Topic 605-25.[8]

Considering the SEC comment, and Apple's response, respond to the following.

Now **YOU** Try **5.11**

1. What is the concern (or question) being raised by the SEC?

    _____

    _____

2. What is Apple's rationale for not providing the disclosure described by the SEC?

    _____

    _____

3. What additional information did you learn about how Apple determines ESP for its products?

    _____

    _____

4. Provide your thoughts: In what circumstances might a fellow financial statement preparer or auditor find this type of correspondence between the SEC and Apple useful?

    _____

    _____

    _____

To locate public company correspondence with the SEC:

1. Go to Company Filings on www.sec.gov, then search for a company. In the field for Filing Type, type in CORRESP.

    Or, if you are searching for a particular term (e.g., "estimated selling price*") within SEC/ company correspondence, try a **full-text**, **advanced search** on the SEC website. Access the *full-text* search by clicking "Search for Company Filings" then "full-text" on the left-hand navigation panel.

    Figure 5-12 illustrates such a search. The asterisk * allows search results to include *price* or *prices*, and the quotation marks indicate a search for the exact phrase: *estimated selling price*.

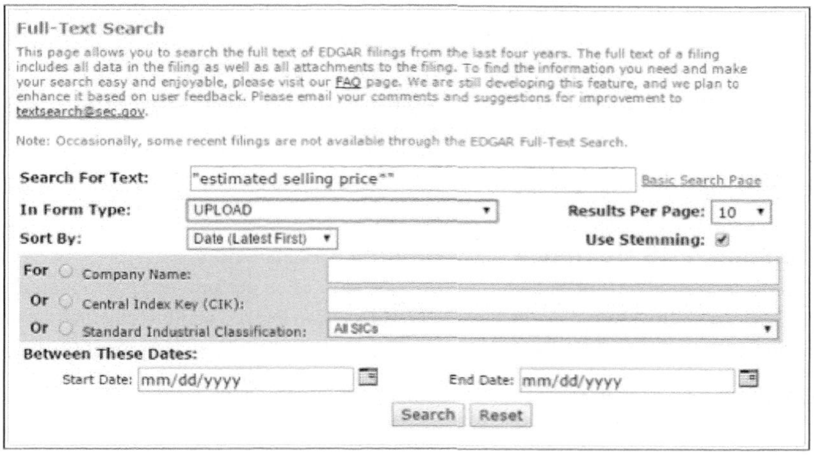

Figure 5-12

Sample full-text search for SEC comment letters

---

[8] Apple Inc. response to SEC comment letter, dated April 1, 2010. Written by Peter Oppenheimer, CFO of Apple Inc.

In the **Form Type** field, you can select **UPLOAD** to view SEC comments, or **CORRESP** to view company responses plus SEC comments.

2. Alternatively, researchers with access to advanced research databases may have even more advanced search options. **Audit Analytics** intelligence service, for example, allows its subscribers to search for SEC correspondence by Codification citation, company name, topic name, date range, and so on. A researcher could therefore type **ASC 605-25** into the database to be directed to this Apple comment letter (and other comment letters on this subtopic). **Westlaw Livedgar** also has comment letter search capabilities.

A Few Final Thoughts on Peer Benchmarking

Remember, of course, when performing peer benchmarking, that companies should always consider their own individual circumstances when determining what level of reporting and disclosures are appropriate and meaningful to investors.

Also, a note of caution: Just because your peers are disclosing an item in a certain way, that doesn't mean that their reporting complies with GAAP. There is always a chance that your peers are misinterpreting GAAP. Keep in mind that your responsibility, first and foremost, is to comply with the authoritative requirements of the Codification. Consistency with your peers should be secondary to that responsibility.

International Financial Reporting Standards (IFRS)

LO6 **Describe** circum-stances in which references to IFRS may be appropriate.

Recall from our earlier discussion of **ASC 105** (Generally Accepted Accounting Principles) that it is acceptable for companies following U.S. GAAP to consult IFRS when authoritative GAAP does not address a particular issue. In such instances, IFRS would be considered a nonauthoritative source of guidance.

When Should You Use IFRS as a Source of Guidance?

References to IFRS should be rare for most U.S. preparers. Given that IFRS guidance strives to be principles-based, it is generally rare for IFRS guidance to offer clarity where U.S. GAAP falls short.

When possible, before turning to IFRS, a researcher should try to resolve his or her issue using U.S. GAAP. For example, if a researcher does not find guidance within the Codification, the researcher might next search for guidance within nonauthoritative U.S. sources, which may offer interpretive guidance on how to analogize other U.S. literature to the issue.

When researchers do utilize IFRS guidance, they should cite it as they would cite other nonauthoritative sources. That is, ideally, the guidance should be used *in addition to* Codification excerpts. This demonstrates to readers of your accounting memo that the IFRS guidance you are relying on is consistent with broad principles presented under U.S. GAAP, when applicable.

Researchers pointing to IFRS requirements, in the absence of directly applicable U.S. GAAP, are often said to be **analogizing to** IFRS guidance. This means that authoritative guidance for the researcher's specific transaction is not available or does not address a particular nuance of the transaction. Therefore, the researcher must rely on specifics within IFRS guidance that is based on similar transactions or principles.

EXAMPLE

Referencing IFRS Guidance "By Analogy"

When companies build new manufacturing facilities, they often perform test production runs to test the facility's ability to produce its intended product. You are researching whether the cost of a test production run can be capitalized as part of the property, plant, and equipment (PP&E).

U.S. GAAP's guidance is vague on the issue of which costs may be capitalized as PP&E:

Continued

. . . the historical cost of acquiring an asset includes the costs necessarily incurred to bring it to the condition and location necessary for its intended use.[9]

Further, test production runs are not addressed in the Codification's implementation guidance.

Capitalization of PP&E under IFRS is based on a similar principle:

The cost of an item of property, plant and equipment comprises . . . (b) any costs directly attributable to bringing the asset to the location and condition necessary for it to be capable of operating in the manner intended by management. . . .[10]

However, IFRS elaborates on this principle, listing "costs of testing whether the asset is functioning properly"[11] as an example of a directly attributable cost that should be capitalized.

In this circumstance, given that IFRS guidance offers more specifics than U.S. GAAP, but is based on the same principle, it may be appropriate to analogize to IFRS guidance, in addition to citing the U.S. GAAP broad principle, as support for the decision to capitalize costs of test production.

Note that there is some weakness inherent in applying guidance by analogy; essentially, you are applying guidance that was not originally intended to apply to your situation. This strategy should be used sparingly.

IFRS

The 2009 economic stimulus bill (American Recovery and Reinvestment Act of 2009) offered federal grant funds to certain qualifying clean energy projects. This left some utility companies engaged in clean energy projects faced with a new accounting issue: How should a for-profit company account for the receipt of federal government funds? U.S. GAAP does not provide guidance directly for this issue, as described in a PwC 2009 whitepaper:

> Now
> **YOU**
> Try
> **5.12**

US generally accepted accounting principles (GAAP) provides limited guidance on the accounting for government grants received by for-profit companies. As such, there may be more than one acceptable alternative for the accounting for government grants. Companies should understand the conditions and restrictions (e.g., repayment conditions) of the government grant and match accounting decisions with the economics and substance of the government grant.

We believe it would be acceptable for companies to apply the guidance in the International Accounting Standard IAS 20, *Accounting for Government Grants and Disclosure of Government Assistance* (IAS 20), by analogy. It should be noted that the AICPA issues paper *Accounting for Grants Received from Governments*, dated October 16, 1979, currently indicates that it has been superseded by IAS 20.[12]

---

[9] ASC 360-10-30-1 (Property, Plant, & Equipment).

[10] International Accounting Standard No. 16, *Property, Plant and Equipment* (IAS 16). Par. 16.

[11] IAS 16, par. 17e.

[12] PwC: *In Pursuit of Government Grants*. Page 10. July 2009. Etheridge, Herman, Hanlon. © PricewaterhouseCoopers LLP ("PwC"). Not for further reproduction or use without the prior written consent of PwC.

For example, assume that a utility company plans to build a solar power production facility, and was awarded a government grant to proceed with the project. The utility might look to the following guidance in IAS 20, given that U.S. GAAP is not available for this issue.

Presentation of grants related to assets

24.   Government grants related to assets, including non-monetary grants at fair value, shall be presented in the statement of financial position either by setting up the grant as deferred income or by deducting the grant in arriving at the carrying amount of the asset.

Questions:

1. What are the two alternative treatments presented in IAS 20, for recording the receipt of grant money?

_____

_____

2. Reread the requirements for citing nonauthoritative sources in **ASC 105-10-05-2** (excerpted earlier in this chapter). State why this analogy to IFRS guidance is permissible.

_____

_____

Notably—acknowledging that U.S. GAAP in this area is not clear—the FASB is currently undertaking a project that would require additional disclosures of government assistance received.

Now that you've seen the great possibilities associated with nonauthoritative guidance, let's talk about how to use this guidance correctly.

USING NONAUTHORITATIVE SOURCES: THERE'S A RIGHT WAY, AND A WRONG WAY

LO7 **Utilize** non-authoritative sources the *right* way (as a supplement to authoritative guidance), and understand how to properly reference these sources.

Ideally, nonauthoritative guidance should be cited *in addition to* Codification references, to support or further clarify Codification guidance. Recall from the documentation guidance in Chapter 4 that a researcher should incorporate key authoritative and—as needed—nonauthoritative guidance considered in the **Analysis** section of an issues memo.

As a general rule of thumb, your documentation should present Codification excerpts first, preceded and followed by commentary in your own words (aka, *guidance sandwiches*), then nonauthoritative guidance can be cited if you considered it in understanding the Codification requirements.

EXAMPLE ———

Recall that our opening scenario focused on Lisa's search for guidance on whether her company's investment in EquityElite has a *readily determinable fair value*. Recall that EquityElite is a private company whose primary business activity is investing in large, public companies. Here is the Analysis section of Lisa's issues memo, where she evaluates whether this investment is within the scope of **ASC 320**.

Issue: Is the Company's investment in EquityElite within the scope of ASC 320-10 (Investments—Debt and Equity Securities)?

ASC 320-10 lists the instruments within the scope of this guidance: ← *Lisa's words*

15-5. The guidance in the Investments—Debt and Equity Securities Topic establishes standards of financial accounting and reporting for both of the following:

   a. Investments in equity securities that have readily determinable fair values

   b. All investments in debt securities, including debt instruments that have been securitized.

← *Guidance excerpt,* **Authoritative**

The glossary of ASC 320-10 defines **readily determinable fair value**, in part, as follows: ← *Lisa's words*

   a. The fair value of an equity security is readily determinable if sales prices or bid-and-asked quotations are currently available on a securities exchange registered with the U.S. Securities and Exchange Commission (SEC) or in the over-the-counter market . . .

. . . c. The fair value of an investment in a mutual fund is readily determinable if the fair value per share (unit) is determined and published and is the basis for current transactions.

← *Guidance excerpt,* **Authoritative**

In this case, the investee (EquityElite) does not have a published per-share value. However, determining the company's per-share value could be accomplished by looking at the value of the company's underlying holdings. The Codification does not discuss whether it is appropriate to "look through" an investment. However, EY's publication, *Certain Investments in Debt and Equity Securities*, provides the following guidance on this issue:[13]

← *Lisa's words, analysis*

When determining whether a security is in the scope of ASC 320, an entity should be careful not to look through the form of its investment to the nature of the securities held by an investee.

← *Excerpt,* **nonauthoritative** *guidance*

Illustration 1-1: Determining whether a security is in scope

Company A holds an interest in an unconsolidated entity and the form of the interest meets the definition of an equity security, but does not have a readily determinable fair value. If substantially all of the investee's assets consist of investments in debt securities and/or equity securities that have readily determinable fair values, it would be not be appropriate for Company A to look through the form of the investment to the nature of the securities held by the investee. The investment would be considered an equity security that does not have a readily determinable fair value and ASC 320 would not apply to that type of investment.

As EquityElite does not itself have a readily determinable fair value, and as companies should not "look through" an investment, we have concluded that ASC 320 (Investments—Debt and Equity Securities) does not apply to this investment. Next, we will explore whether application of **ASC 325-20** (Cost Method) is more appropriate.

← *Lisa's words, analysis*

In the preceding example, even though the Codification offered some guidance for Lisa's question, she included interpretive, nonauthoritative guidance in her memo as a sort of "value add." Readers of her memo will appreciate that Lisa has included guidance specific to the issue her company is facing.

---

[13] EY, Financial Reporting Developments: *Certain Investments in Debt and Equity Securities.* July 2013. Section 1.3.2.1, page 5.

Another thing that Lisa did well is that she only cited the nonauthoritative paragraphs that went *above and beyond* the authoritative guidance available for this issue. This is a common mistake for students when citing from firm guide books. Consider the following example, again related to Lisa's analysis of the EquityElite investment.

EXAMPLE

In this example, consider how Lisa might incorrectly, versus correctly, use firm guidance.

- **Incorrect**: EY defines *readily determinable fair value* as "(definition)."
- **Correct**: ASC **320-10-20** (Investments) defines *readily determinable fair value* as: "(definition)." EY's publication *Certain Investments in Debt and Equity Securities* (2013) offers the following additional, interpretive guidance for situations in which an investor must determine whether to look through to the holdings of an investee:

> …If substantially all of the investee's assets consist of investments in debt securities and/or equity securities that have readily determinable fair values, it would not be appropriate for Company A to look through the form of the investment to the nature of the securities held by the investee. The investment would be considered an equity security that does not have a readily determinable fair value . . .[13]

Notice how in the latter example, Lisa got the definition of *readily determinable fair value* from the Codification, then cited nonauthoritative guidance that went above and beyond Codification requirements.

Is It Wrong to Cite Nonauthoritative Guidance Only?

In rare cases, nonauthoritative guidance may be cited (by itself) as support for accounting positions when Codification guidance is not available. However, this is clearly not ideal, as this guidance is not GAAP.

Only use nonauthoritative guidance by itself after you have conducted an exhaustive search of the Codification. Figure 5-13 illustrates the steps involved in an exhaustive search.

Figure 5-13

Was my search effort exhaustive?

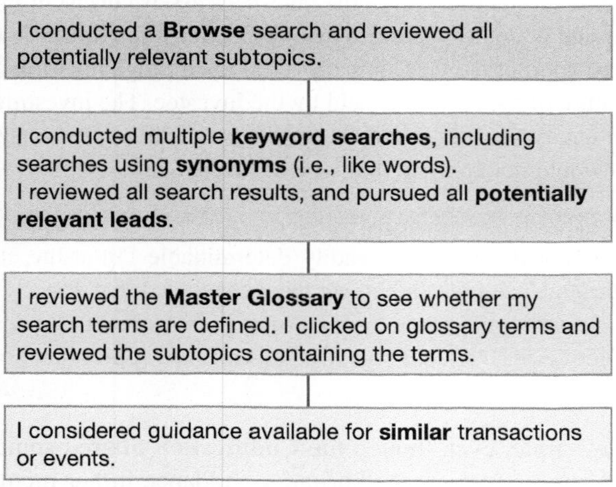

| I conducted a **Browse** search and reviewed all potentially relevant subtopics. |

| I conducted multiple **keyword searches**, including searches using **synonyms** (i.e., like words). I reviewed all search results, and pursued all **potentially relevant leads**. |

| I reviewed the **Master Glossary** to see whether my search terms are defined. I clicked on glossary terms and reviewed the subtopics containing the terms. |

| I considered guidance available for **similar** transactions or events. |

[14] Ibid.

Even after conducting an exhaustive search, nonauthoritative sources can occasionally point you back to the right place within the Codification. Remember, if authoritative guidance can be used, you should use it.

What's the Right Way to Search Nonauthoritative Guidance?

Nonauthoritative sources are commonly organized into chapters, and they often begin with a detailed table of contents. To optimize your efficiency in searching these sources, start your search by consulting the table of contents. From there, you can often advance directly to the content that addresses your issue.

For example, assume you have a question about how to account for a trademark acquired in a business combination. Open an accounting firm guide to business combinations, and scan the table of contents for the topic "Recognition of Intangible Assets." You should generally be able to jump right to the guidance you need.

> Never start a search of nonauthoritative guidance by skimming through the chapters; this search method is inefficient, and you will get lost in detailed guidance!

TIP from the Trenches

How Do I Reference Nonauthoritative Sources?

Citing Concepts Statements

Following is an example of an appropriate reference to a FASB Concepts Statement. The following format is also acceptable for citing pre-Codification standards (such as FASB Statements).

- FASB Concepts Statement No. 6, *Elements of Financial Statements* (CON 6), defines assets as:

> ". . . probable future economic benefits obtained or controlled by a particular entity as a result of past transactions or events" (par. 25).

Note the following required elements included in the preceding citation:

- The type of standard: "FASB Concepts Statement No."
- The title of the standard is fully written out, and italicized
- The paragraph number
- The abbreviation, in parenthesis, that the author intends to use for future references to the standard (i.e., CON 6)

Citing Accounting Firm Guide Books

The objective in citing an accounting firm resource, such as a guide book, is to create a clear trail to exactly where you found the information you're citing. A supervisor or future reader of your memo should have enough information to personally retrace your steps and find the source. For example,

- Deloitte's publication, *A Roadmap to Accounting for Income Taxes* (Second Edition, 2015), Section 6.01, states: "When disclosing gross DTAs and DTLs, an entity should separately disclose deductible and taxable temporary differences" (page 145).

Notice how this reference includes:

- The title of the guide
- Author or firm publishing the guide (Deloitte)

- Year of publication
- The relevant section and page number

As noted in Chapter 4's style tips for professional communication, sources may be cited in the body of an accounting memo or in a footnote attached to any quotes or guidance used from the source.

CHAPTER SUMMARY

Nonauthoritative sources are often indispensable to the research process, both in circumstances where Codification guidance is available and in cases where it is not. The FASB—in Topic 105—permits reference to nonauthoritative sources in cases where U.S. GAAP for a particular transaction, or similar transaction, is not available. Sources of this guidance include FASB Concepts Statements, Accounting Standards Updates, accounting firm resources, AICPA literature, and international accounting standards. Researchers should exercise caution when citing nonauthoritative sources, as they alone would not support an unmodified audit opinion. However, when used properly, nonauthoritative sources can add clarity to a researcher's understanding of complex issues and can add value to accounting issues documentation.

REVIEW QUESTIONS

1. Explain what it means for guidance to be "nonauthoritative."
2. What is the browse path for accessing Topic 105? In other words, in which area would you start?
3. Briefly, summarize the key points made in the first sentence of par. 05-1, and in par. 05-2, of ASC 105-10 (Generally Accepted Accounting Principles).
4. List three sources of nonauthoritative guidance that are named in par. 05-3 of ASC 105-10.
5. Identify two benefits of using nonauthoritative sources.
6. Describe a circumstance in which a researcher might refer to the Conceptual Framework.
7. What is one example of information that a researcher can find in an Accounting Standards Update, but which is not available in the Codification?
8. What are two key purposes of the FASB's Conceptual Framework? What two other names are used to describe this guidance?
9. What future changes is the FASB planning to make to its Conceptual Framework?
10. Considering the guidance from CON 6, what are the three essential characteristics of an asset?
11. Again considering CON 6, what would you say is a key difference between revenues and gains?
12. Describe two circumstances in which reference to a pre-Codification standard may be appropriate.
13. Are Accounting Standards Updates (ASUs) authoritative? Explain.
14. Using the excerpts from the Concepts Statements shown in Now YOU Try 5.4, try to identify the objective of each of FASB Concepts Statements No. 6, 7, and 8. For example: "Concepts Statement No. 5 establishes recognition criteria and describes certain required elements of financial statements."
15. Identify two resources available from the AICPA, and state when each might be useful.
16. What is the AICPA's *FRF for SMEs*? Which entities can apply it, and is it considered GAAP?
17. Name two types of accounting firm resources/publications, and generally describe what each resource offers.
18. On the SEC website, what *form type* is used to describe SEC comment letters and responses?
19. Describe an *incorrect* way to use firm guidance.
20. When is it acceptable to quote from only nonauthoritative sources, as support for an accounting position?
21. What does it mean to *analogize* to IFRS?
22. What are the required elements for a source citation, assuming the researcher is quoting text from a pre-Codification accounting standard?

EXERCISES

Reminder to students: Include the source reference for each response (such as statement and paragraph number). Please do not cite from a standard's *Summary* page if the same information can be found in the standard's requirements. If citing from a guide book, remember to cite your source in accordance with the guidelines presented in this chapter.

1. Go to ASC 105 in the Codification, Generally Accepted Accounting Principles, then Join All Sections. Aside from the paragraphs cited in this chapter, summarize each remaining paragraph presented in section -05 (Overview), -10 (Objectives), and -15 (Scope). Use one bullet point to describe each paragraph from these sections.

Exercises involving the Concepts Statements

2. Describe two ways that a researcher could navigate to the FASB Concepts Statements.

3. Locate FASB Concepts Statement No. 6, *Elements of Financial Statements* (CON 6).

   a. What is the definition of "revenues" in CON 6? Also, cite the paragraph source.
   b. Describe where you would go within CON 6 to find the definition of assets, versus where you would go to find more detailed guidance for applying this definition. How would a beginning researcher know to look for this application guidance? Using CON 6, act as though you are coaching a peer on how to navigate this guidance.

4. Using CON 5, answer the following: What is *recognition*?

5. Also using CON 5, answer the following: What is the purpose of the statement of financial position? Also, does this statement attempt to show the value of a business? Provide the excerpted guidance that responds to these questions, then also summarize the guidance using your own words.

6. Also using CON 5, answer the following: What is the purpose of the statements of earnings and comprehensive income? Provide the excerpted guidance that responds to this question, then also summarize the guidance using your own words.

7. Summarize the four fundamental recognition criteria identified in CON 5. Cite the paragraph source for this information. Following these four recognition criteria are several paragraphs that elaborate upon the criteria. What are the paragraph numbers that elaborate upon these four criteria?

8. Using CON 7, answer the following: What is the objective of present value when used in accounting measurements at initial recognition?

9. Explain: How is CON 8 currently organized? How might this statement change in the future, considering the FASB's plans to revisit its concepts statements described earlier in the chapter?

Exercises involving ASUs and pre-Codification standards

10. Identify the pre-Codification standard that cross-references to ASC 450-20-25-1 (Loss Contingencies). Next, go to par. 59 of that pre-Codification standard. What was the Board intending to prevent by requiring that losses be "reasonably estimable"?

11. Locate EITF 01-6. Why is this EITF presented in grey shading? (Look carefully at the bracketed text at the top of the standard.) Also, would you expect this guidance to have been incorporated in the Codification? Explain.

12. Locate EITF 07-5. This EITF is listed on the FASB website as "superseded" but is not presented in grey shading. Why do you think that is? Where, within the Codification, is this guidance incorporated?

13. Locate ASU 2015-01. What is the title of this standard? What is a key change effected by this standard, and what broader FASB initiative is this guidance reflective of?

14. Now look to the contents page of ASU 2015-01. What are the four sections included within this ASU?

15. Locate ASU 2014-15.

   a. What is the title of this standard, and what are the *main provisions* of this standard? (Use the summary pages at the beginning of the ASU to respond.)
   b. Also using the Summary, describe how the provisions of this ASU differ from existing GAAP.
   c. Now look at the amendments to the Codification that will result from this ASU. What glossary term does this ASU add to the Codification? In what subtopic will this new term be included? Provide the subtopic number and topic description.

Exercises involving firm guidance

16. Locate EY's latest guide book (referred to as the *Financial Reporting Developments* series) on share-based payment. Using the table of contents, identify one topic that is addressed (listed) within the Scope section. State the year of publication for the guide you used.

17. Using PwC's *Guide to Accounting for Income Taxes*,
    a. Identify one potential complexity that can arise in determining the applicable tax rate for recognizing and measuring deferred taxes.
    b. How might PwC's coverage of this issue be useful to a researcher?
    c. Next, briefly summarize one of the examples PwC uses in its guide to illustrate this (or another) potential complexity in determining the applicable tax rate.

AICPA resources

18. Provide the title of two AICPA Audit and Accounting Guides. Please do not use Airlines, which was named already in this chapter. Describe how you located these guides.

19. Using the AICPA website, go to "Research" then "Technical Hotline." Locate a recent Technical Q&A on this site and summarize the issue. Next, describe how a researcher might search for a specific Q&A (e.g., in a publication that compiles these responses?). Specify.

Performing research using company filings

20. Using the SEC website, locate Yahoo's most recent Form 10-K. Describe:
    a. How you went about locating the 10-K. (Describe your search path.)
    b. When was this form filed?
    c. In what footnote can investors read about the company's intangible assets?
    d. Brainstorm: In what circumstances might a peer company (accounting researcher) want to review the company's intangible assets disclosure?

Consideration of IFRS

21. Using ifrs.org (under *IFRS* then *Standards*):
    a. Identify the international accounting standard that corresponds to the FASB's ASC 820, Fair Value Measurement.
    b. Next, compare the definition of fair value used in that standard to the definition of fair value in ASC 820-10-35-2. (You may have to create a no-cost login to view this file.)
    c. Explain, broadly, a circumstance in which a researcher might look to the IASB's fair value guidance.

Properly referencing nonauthoritative guidance

22. Correct the errors in the following source citation. Assume this is the first time this source is being mentioned in an issues memo.

    Concept 6 defines assets as: ". . . probable future economic benefits obtained or controlled by a particular entity as a result of past transactions or events."

23. Circle each of the required elements shown in the following source citations. Then describe each of the required elements that was appropriately included in these references.
    a. Per FASB Statement No. 2, *Accounting for Research and Development Costs* (FAS 2), par. 12: "All research and development costs encompassed by this Statement shall be charged to expense when incurred."
    b. PwC's guide, *Business Combinations and Noncontrolling Interests* (2014), page 1-4 states:

        "Inputs and associated processes used by the seller that were not transferred, but that can be easily obtained, indicate the acquired group is a business."

24. Determine what is improper about the following nonauthoritative reference, then explain why.

    PwC's guide, *Business Combinations and Noncontrolling Interests* (2014), page 1-4 defines a **business** as: "...an integrated set of activities and assets that is capable of being conducted and managed for the purpose of providing a return in the form of dividends, lower costs, or other economic benefits directly to investors or other owners, members, or participants."

CASE STUDY QUESTIONS

Asset or Expense (Email) Jacobs Inc. is a pipeline operator that owns and operates miles of natural gas pipeline across five states. Noticing exterior corrosion in several regions of its pipeline, the company has invested $1 million to purchase and install steel sleeves that will prevent leaks and provide structural reinforcement to the existing pipe section. The installation work involves welding the sleeves to the existing in-service pipeline. By applying these steel sleeves, the company can avoid replacing full sections of the pipeline and temporarily shutting down operations involving the existing pipeline.   **5.1**

Assume that a plant accountant has contacted you to ask whether the steel sleeves (materials and installation) should be recorded as an asset or as an expense. Using guidance from the Conceptual Framework, analyze this issue and prepare an email response to the plant accountant.

Asset or Expense (Email) You are a corporate accountant for a distribution company that provides distribution services to a large online retailer. Your company extensively uses conveyor belts to move shipping boxes and their contents through its warehouse. The seams in the company's conveyor belts have started to jam periodically, at times bringing the belts to a stop. The company has invested $100,000 to apply a special bonding agent to the belts' seams so they won't jam anymore. By applying this bonding agent, the company can avoid replacing the belts to fix this jamming issue. There is a chance that this bonding agent will also result in the belts' useful lives being extended by a few years. Assume that a plant accountant has contacted you to ask whether the bonding agent should be recorded as an asset or as an expense. Using guidance from the Conceptual Framework, analyze this issue and prepare an email response to the plant accountant.   **5.2**

Conceptual Views on Materiality Using CON 8, describe the role of *materiality* in understanding the qualitative characteristics of useful financial information. Specifically, assume you are describing materiality to a small business owner who is trying to determine what information must be reported to his financial statement users. Next, comment on what the Board's basis for conclusions says about the issue of materiality.   **5.3**

Improving Your Familiarity with CON 7 Present Value Techniques As noted within the chapter, CON 7 describes techniques for calculating present value, including the following illustration of the *expected cash flow approach*, reproduced from CON 7. This example illustrates how the expected cash flow approach can be used to assign probability factors to the likelihood of receiving a $1,000 cash flow in any of three possible future years.   **5.4**

Present value of $1,000 in 1 year at 5%	$952.38	
	Probability 10.00%	$ 95.24
Present value of $1,000 in 2 years at 5.25%	$902.73	
	Probability 60.00%	541.64
Present value of $1,000 in 3 years at 5.50%	$851.61	
	Probability 30.00%	255.48
Expected present value		**$892.36**

Source: CON 7, par. 46.

1. Review the guidance in CON 7 and, in your own words, explain in approximately one paragraph the difference between the traditional (best estimate) and expected present value techniques for measuring fair value.
2. Assume that you are a lender determining the present value of this sample receivable illustrated in CON 7. Under the traditional approach, what would the present value of that receivable be?
3. Show the math that would be necessary to add a fourth scenario: collection of the $1,000 in 4 years at 5.75%, with a probability of 10%. (No need for a calculator, just write out how you would compute this scenario).
4. Which approach would you expect users of the lender's financial statements to prefer, and why?

Benchmarking Corporate Disclosures—Intangible Assets Sears and Macy's are both public companies in the retail industry. Review the most recent 10-K for each company and compare their reporting of intangible assets other than goodwill. In particular, consider: **5.5**

- Do the companies have similar items included in this category (Intangible Assets)? That is, what is the nature of each company's recorded intangible assets?
- Have the companies adopted similar policies with respect to categorizing these assets as finite- versus indefinite-lived?

- Do the companies describe their impairment testing policy in detail?
- Within which sections of the companies' annual reports is the above-listed information included? Are the companies consistent in where they report this information?

Finally, brainstorm a circumstance in which you, as a professional, might perform similar benchmarking of a peer company's annual report.

5.6 **Locating and Learning from SEC Correspondence** In 2014, a popular bakery/sandwich chain responded to an SEC comment letter. In the comment letter, the SEC asked the company to clarify its application of ASC 840-20. Locate this comment letter (see comment #2, Rent Expense), and describe:

- What is the SEC's concern?
- What is the company's response? Carefully read, then summarize the company's position and rationale.
- What information can you gather from this correspondence that may go above and beyond the company's annual filing disclosure?

Finally, notice how readily the company was able to refer to SEC staff guidance that supported their accounting position. It's like they already had a thoughtful accounting memo on hand, ready to go!

5.7 **Lease Classification, Considering Firm Guidance (Issues Memo)**
Facts: Tech Startup Inc. ("Lessee") is entering into a contract with Developer Inc. ("Landlord") to rent Landlord's newly constructed office building located at 15 Tech Drive in San Francisco, CA. The lease term is 10 years, and the estimated life of the building is 40 years. Lessee will occupy all 12 floors of the building. At the end of the lease term, Lessee has the option to purchase the property for $16.25 million. The fair value of the building at that time is expected to be $17 million.

Monthly, Lessee will be required to pay $50,000 to occupy the building, *plus* a monthly supplemental rental cost based on Lessee's sales (1% of sales). From experience, Lessee estimates that 1% of its sales should approximate an additional $20,000 per month. For simplicity, please ignore discounting (use of present value calculations, rates implicit in the lease, etc.) for purposes of this example. There are no residual value guarantees present in this example.

Required: You are a corporate accountant for Lessee and have been asked to prepare an accounting issues memo to address the following issue: *Should the lease arrangement be classified as an operating lease or as a capital lease?*

Assume that this arrangement is within the scope of lease accounting guidance. As needed to clarify areas of judgment, support your response with guidance from both the Codification and from EY's most recent Lease accounting guide book.

Case Studies Involving Energy Works (5.8-5.10)

5.8 **Understanding Joint Ventures, using Nonauthoritative Guidance** The term *joint ventures* has a very specific definition and application in U.S. GAAP, as you saw illustrated in the previous chapter's Energy Works example.

1. First, locate Codification guidance defining a corporate joint venture, and explain the requirements for an entity to meet this definition.
2. Next, consult nonauthoritative guidance on joint ventures and provide an example of a situation that would not meet the particulars of this definition.
3. Consider this scenario: Could an entity be considered a joint venture if it has three investors, and votes are decided by majority rule?
4. Finally, considering nonauthoritative guidance, explain the significance of this term—what are the accounting implications of determining that an entity meets this definition?

Prepare a two-page response to these issues.

5.9 **Performing Research Using Pre-Codification Standards, Considering the Joint Venture's Own Accounting** Locate ASU 2014-17, then respond to the following questions considering the Energy Works memo included in the previous chapter.

1. What is the title of this standard?
2. Now, read the summary page of this standard, bearing in mind the Energy Works scenario. How might this guidance possibly affect the joint venture's accounting?
3. Consider the requirements (and no longer the summary page) of this ASU. To what entities does this ASU apply? Would this guidance apply to the joint venture formed by Energy Works and Big Oil?
4. What is *pushdown accounting*? Cite from the ASU to respond. How might pushdown accounting have impacted the FPSO transferred to the JV in the Energy Works scenario, assuming the FPSO had a carrying value of $100 million on Energy Works' books and a fair value of $120 million?
5. Why did the Board issue this guidance?

6. Explain how the guidance in this ASU will be incorporated into the Codification. Broadly speaking, what changes will it make to the Codification?

Performing Research Using Pre-Codification Standards, Understanding *Integral Equipment* Refer again to the Energy Works memo included in the previous chapter. One of the questions raised in Issue 3 (how will Energy Works, the investor, record the transfer of equipment to the JV?) was whether the equipment is considered *integral* and thus within the scope of real estate guidance in the Codification. **5.10**

To research this issue, read EITF 00-13, then respond to the following.

1. Based on this guidance, would you conclude that the FPSO facility is considered *integral* equipment? Explain.
2. Where does the guidance from EITF 00-13 appear in the Codification?
3. Compare the presentation of EITF 00-13 to the Codification's presentation of this guidance. Describe how they compare, and consider: which uses a more *storytelling* tone? In what circumstances might you find it beneficial to refer to original guidance such as this?
4. Citing from the Codification, describe the implications of a conclusion that equipment is considered *integral*.

Chapter 6

Scope and Recognition Guidance: A Brief Introduction

Printout in hand, Julie taps on her boss's door. She is feeling pretty good; she just found a paragraph in the guidance that appears to speak directly to the tax accrual issue her boss asked her to research. As she shows him the guidance, he taps his pen thoughtfully on the desk.

"Are you sure this guidance applies to our type of transaction?" he asks.

He continues, "I think the guidance for gross receipts taxes (which are based on revenue measures) may differ from guidance for taxes based on income. You've brought me guidance specific to income taxes."

Julie shakes her head; she realizes that she forgot to review the scope section of the guidance that she had printed. "Let me double check the scope section for this guidance," she says. "I'll stop by again later to let you know what I've found."

Continued

Learning Objectives

After reading this chapter and performing the exercises herein, you will be able to

1. **Understand** the role that scope guidance plays in professional research.

2. **Apply** basic scope concepts to income taxes, share-based compensation, nonmonetary transactions, and investments.

3. **Perform** simplified scope tests for leases and derivatives.

4. **Understand** the conceptual views underlying recognition guidance.

5. **Contrast** key principles underlying, and techniques for navigating, existing versus revised revenue guidance.

6. **Identify** the recognition threshold applicable to uncertain tax positions and subsequent events.

7. **Apply** derecognition guidance to liabilities.

Confirming that a transaction is within the scope of a Codification topic may seem like an extra step, but much of the guidance within the Codification includes specific instructions for its use. Don't get caught like Julie, forgetting to do the appropriate diligence work on guidance that may otherwise appear to be on point. A proper review of the scope section is critical to identifying appropriate recognition, and then measurement, guidance for a transaction.

Scope Guidance: An Area of Required Reading

1. Role of scope guidance in research
2. Applying scope guidance:
   - Income taxes—Is it a *tax based on income*?
   - Share-based compensation—Is the recipient an *employee*?
   - Nonmonetary transactions—Navigating "subsection" scope guidance
   - Investments—Determining which topic applies
   - Leases—Determining whether an arrangement contains a lease
   - Derivatives—Is the definition of derivative met?

Evaluating scope guidance is key to correctly applying recognition guidance. →

Recognition Guidance: A Brief Introduction

1. Conceptual Framework guidance on recognition
2. Revenue recognition:
   - Concepts behind
   - When to apply ASC 605 versus 606
   - Effectively navigating the two topics
3. Applying different recognition thresholds
   - Uncertain taxes: Recognize if *more likely than not*
   - Subsequent events: Recognize if conditions existed at the balance sheet date
4. Applying derecognition guidance: Liability extinguishments

---

Organization of This Chapter

This chapter introduces two important "sections" in the Codification: Section 15 (Scope) and Section 25 (Recognition). This is the first of several chapters focusing on section guidance from the Codification; Chapter 7 explores Sections 30 and 35 (Initial and Subsequent Measurement), and Chapter 8 continues this coverage with an emphasis on fair value measurement.

As a beginning researcher, scope issues are often not on your radar. You may feel so relieved just to find guidance that seems on point that you fail to ensure that your transaction falls within the scope of the topic. For this reason, I've chosen to emphasize consideration of scope issues in this chapter. The chapter walks through several examples where scope guidance can make or break a researcher's use of a given topic. Having this exposure to areas of scope judgment will help you be equipped to handle scope judgments that you encounter in your own research.

Next, the chapter covers recognition, starting with conceptual views of recognition and then exploring the application of this guidance to revenue, income taxes, and subsequent events. The chapter concludes with a derecognition example related to liabilities. Relative to scope and measurement issues, my intent was for this text to devote slightly less time to covering recognition, as this is one area where I've found students already have some comfort resulting from their intermediate accounting courses. However, in light of the new revenue standard, additional coverage of revenue recognition has been included in this edition.

The topics covered in this chapter are illustrated in the preceding diagram. For the practicing accountant, some of the examples that follow may seem overly simplified. However, to the beginning accounting researcher, these examples will provide a straightforward introduction to some basics of technical guidance. You can use these skills to tackle more complex issues later on.

SCOPE GUIDANCE: AN AREA OF REQUIRED READING

LO1 **Understand** the role that scope guidance plays in professional research.

Recall from previous chapters that scope guidance indicates which transactions, items, or entities are subject to the guidance within a topic. As discussed in Chapter 2, researchers should view the scope section of each topic as *required reading*. Therefore, before relying upon a topic's recognition or measurement guidance, a researcher should first confirm that the guidance applies to his or her transaction.

The scope guidance for most topics is within Section **15** ("Scope"), usually within Subtopic **10** (the "Overall" subtopic). However, scope guidance may also be found within other individual subtopics (e.g., Subtopics 20, 30, and so on) and, in some circumstances, might be provided for individual paragraphs within the guidance.

Information within the scope section is commonly presented in one of two ways:

- The guidance may list specific transactions that *are*, or *are not*, within the scope.
- The guidance may contain tests to determine what transactions *should be* included within the scope of the guidance.

When reviewing the Scope section of a topic, a researcher should read any lists of transactions or entities that are excluded from the guidance's scope. If the guidance contains tests, indicating which transactions are within the topic's scope, a researcher should determine whether his or her transaction meets the tests. For example, a scope test may be presented as three conditions, one or all of which must be met for a transaction to be within the scope of a topic.

Often, it is only the most technical and complex of topics that include tests identifying transactions that *should* be within scope (e.g., derivatives, securitizations, variable interest entities, leases). Notice that many of these topics are within the Broad Transactions area, and therefore are subject to specialized accounting. Given the complexity of some of these topics, bear the following in mind if you find yourself faced with one of these tests:

- Before I perform a detailed scope test, I should read the Overview section of this topic, to make sure that using this topic makes sense.
- If I have to "test into" this guidance, then this guidance may be highly nuanced. I ought to see whether there is implementation guidance (Section **55**) or a nonauthoritative source that can offer additional information on this scope test.

If you find that your transaction is outside the scope of a particular topic, look for references within the Scope section to other topics that might apply. If references are not provided, continue to brainstorm alternative accounting treatments for the transaction you are researching. See Chapter 2 for additional discussion of brainstorming alternate search terms.

[**TIP**] from the Trenches

It's *required reading*, but do I have to read it first?

There is no hard and fast rule about *when*—during your reading of a Codification topic—you must consult the Scope section. My personal tendency is to consult the Scope section first (or, after reading the Overview) for topics listed in the Broad Transactions area. For other topics, I tend to look for recognition or measurement guidance first and then, before relying upon that guidance, I go back to review the Scope section as a final check.

The only "rule" regarding scope evaluations is just that you must consult this guidance at some point in your research.

Let's take a look now at a few topics where application of scope guidance can involve judgment. Our first group of examples involves guidance listing transactions that are or are not within scope. These examples involve income taxes, share-based compensation, nonmonetary transactions, and investments.

Our second set of examples illustrates two scope tests from the Broad Transactions area: leases and derivatives.

Let's begin with our first example, which revisits Julie's gross receipts tax issue from our opening scenario.

APPLYING SCOPE GUIDANCE: A FEW EXAMPLES

Considering Scope, Glossary, and Interpretive Guidance:

Evaluating the Income Taxes Topic

LO2 Apply basic scope concepts to income taxes, share-based compensation, nonmonetary transactions, and investments

Recall from our opening scenario that Julie's boss asked her to revisit whether taxes on gross receipts are within the scope of the Income Taxes topic. We'll explore this issue now.

Located in the Expenses area of the Codification, the Income Taxes topic (**ASC 740**) provides guidance on the recognition of *taxes based on income*. This topic identifies the following primary objectives related to the accounting for income taxes:

a.   To recognize the amount of taxes payable or refundable for the current year
b.   To recognize deferred tax liabilities and assets for the future tax consequences of events that have been recognized in an entity's financial statements or tax returns. (**ASC 740-10-10-1**)

Determining whether a tax is based on income may sound straightforward, but in practice it often requires judgment. Following are two examples illustrating the scope of Topic 740. The first example evaluates whether a "gross receipts tax" (e.g., a tax based on revenue) is within the scope of this topic; the second evaluates a so-called "modified gross receipts tax."

Determining Whether a "Gross Receipts Tax" Is within the Scope of Income Tax Guidance

Facts: Julie's company operates in New Mexico, where businesses are subject to a state "gross-receipts tax." This tax can range in amount from 5.125% to 8.6875%, depending on the business's locale. The tax is imposed on a business's gross receipts, or "the total amount of money or value of other consideration" received from conducting its activities.[1] Julie needs your help determining whether this gross-receipts tax is within the scope of **ASC 740**.

Now **YOU** Try **6.1**

ASC 740-10 includes the following scope guidance:

Transactions

15-3   The guidance in the Income Taxes Topic applies to:
   a.   Domestic federal (national) income taxes (U.S. federal income taxes for U.S. entities) and foreign, state, and local (including franchise) taxes based on income
   b.   An entity's domestic and foreign operations that are consolidated, combined, or accounted for by the equity method.

The Glossary of Topic 740-10 defines **income taxes** and **taxable income** as follows:

Income Taxes

Domestic and foreign federal (national), state, and local (including franchise) taxes based on income.

Continued

---

[1] Source: www.tax.newmexico.gov/Businesses/gross-receipts.aspx.

Continued from previous page

Taxable Income

The excess of taxable revenues over tax deductible expenses and exemptions for the year as defined by the governmental taxing authority.

Net income is defined in the Codification's Master Glossary as follows:

Net Income

A measure of financial performance resulting from the aggregation of revenues, expenses, gains, and losses that are not items of other comprehensive income. A variety of other terms such as net earnings or earnings may be used to describe net income.

Finally, PwC's *Guide to Accounting for Income Taxes* states the following with respect to the evaluation of gross-receipts taxes under the scope of Topic 740.[2]

A gross-receipts tax is generally based upon a jurisdiction's definition of "taxable gross receipts." In devising this tax, many jurisdictions do not take into consideration any expenses or costs incurred to generate such receipts, except for certain stated cash discounts, bad debts, and returns and allowances. Because the starting point of the computation of a gross-receipts tax is not "net" of expenses, we believe that a gross-receipts tax is not a tax based on income for purposes of determining whether ASC 740 applies.

Questions:

1. Contrast the definitions of net income and taxable income, against the method used to calculate New Mexico's gross-receipts tax.

2. Next, consider the interpretive guidance provided by PwC. How does this impact your evaluation?

3. Explain your conclusion: Is this gross-receipts tax considered a tax based on income, and thus within the scope of Topic 740 (Income Taxes)?

Let's change the facts slightly and consider another example now.

[2] PwC, *Guide to Accounting for Income Taxes*. 2013. Chapter 1, page 8. © PricewaterhouseCoopers LLP ("PwC"). Not for further reproduction or use without the prior written consent of PwC.

Evaluating Whether a Modified Gross-Receipts Tax Is within the Scope of Income Tax Guidance

Facts: In Texas, certain businesses must pay an annual franchise tax, also known as a "modified gross-receipts tax," of roughly 0.5%. The tax base (to which the 0.5% tax is applied) is determined as the lowest of the following three amounts: (1) total revenue minus cost of goods sold, (2) total revenue minus compensation, or (3) total revenue times 70%.

You must evaluate whether this is considered a tax based on income and thus within the scope of **ASC 740**.

In addition to the guidance provided for the previous example, consider the following guidance on modified gross-receipts taxes from PwC's *Guide to Accounting for Income Taxes*.[3]

> ... in jurisdictions where the tax is calculated on *modified* gross receipts, consideration should be given as to whether it is a tax based on income. We believe that a modified gross receipts tax constitutes a tax based on income and should therefore be accounted for in accordance with ASC 740 if it is based on gross receipts that are reduced for certain costs (e.g., inventory, depreciable and amortizable assets, materials and supplies, wages, and/or other expenditures).

Questions:

1. Is Texas's franchise tax within the scope of ASC 740? Explain.

    _____

    _____

    _____

    _____

2. Explain the significance (as further described in the text following this example) of a tax being within the scope of ASC 740 versus within the scope of other guidance.

    _____

    _____

As these examples illustrate, the scope of Topic **740** is limited to *taxes based on income*. Other GAAP including, for example, Topic **450** (Contingencies) must be applied for taxes not within the scope of Topic 740. Application of other Codification topics to taxes will not result in deferred taxes, as that concept is unique to income tax accounting.

Evaluating the Scope of Share-Based Compensation Guidance

Companies frequently compensate their employees through a combination of both salary and stock options. The Stock Compensation Topic (Topic **718**), located in the Expenses area of the Codification (under "Compensation"), offers guidance on share-based payments made to employees. Topic 718 requires companies to recognize employee stock awards at their estimated fair value, as determined at the award's grant date. Companies must recognize the award's fair value in compensation expense over the employee's required service period (that is, the period the employee must continue to work before he or she can exercise the option).

The scope of Topic 718 generally extends to all equity awards granted to employees. In some cases, the definition of **employee** comprises certain nonemployee directors of a company. Determining when individuals are subject to this guidance can involve judgment. Following are two **Now YOU Try** exercises demonstrating the scope of Topic 718. As you'll see in these examples, glossary terms and implementation or interpretive guidance can assist a researcher in applying scope guidance.

---

[3] PwC, *Guide to Accounting for Income Taxes*. 2013. Chapter 1, page 8. © PricewaterhouseCoopers LLP ("PwC"). Not for further reproduction or use without the prior written consent of PwC.

Now
YOU
Try
6.3

Stock Award to a Board Member for Board Service

Facts: Charles Draper serves on the Board of Directors of Echo Corp and was elected to this position by Echo shareholders. As compensation for his Board service, Echo Corp pays Mr. Draper a fixed salary plus company stock options. Echo is evaluating whether to account for this compensation under **ASC 718**.

ASC 718-10 includes the following scope guidance.

> **> Transactions**
>
> **15-3** The guidance in the Compensation—Stock Compensation Topic applies to all share-based payment transactions in which an entity acquires employee services by issuing (or offering to issue) its shares, share options, or other equity instruments or by incurring liabilities to an employee that meet either of the following conditions:
>   a. The amounts are based, at least in part, on the price of the entity's shares or other equity instruments. (The phrase *at least in part* is used because an award of share-based compensation may be indexed to both the price of an entity's shares and something else that is neither the price of the entity's shares nor a market, performance, or service condition.)
>   b. The awards require or may require settlement by issuing the entity's equity shares or other equity instruments.
>
> . . . **15-5** The guidance in this Topic does not apply to the following payment transactions:
>   a. Share-based transactions for other than employee services (see Subtopic 505-50 for guidance on those transactions).

Key to applying this scope guidance is understanding the definition of employee. The glossary of Topic 718-10 defines **employee** as follows:

> **Employee**
>
> An individual over whom the grantor of a share-based compensation award exercises or has the right to exercise sufficient control to establish an employer-employee relationship based on common law as illustrated in case law and currently under U.S. Internal Revenue Service (IRS) Revenue Ruling 87-41. . .
>
> . . . A nonemployee director does not satisfy this definition of employee. Nevertheless, nonemployee directors acting in their role as members of a board of directors are treated as employees if those directors were elected by the employer's shareholders or appointed to a board position that will be filled by shareholder election when the existing term expires. However, that requirement applies only to awards granted to nonemployee directors for their services as directors. Awards granted to those individuals for other services shall be accounted for as awards to nonemployees.

Question: Is Echo's award of stock options to Mr. Draper within the scope of Topic 718, Stock Compensation? Explain.

_____

_____

_____

Stock Award to a Board Member, for Professional Services

Facts: Assume the same facts as in the previous example—that is, Charles Draper is an elected Board member of Echo Corp. However, now assume that Mr. Draper also receives stock awards for his work on architectural drawings, which he prepared in order to assist Echo with its plans to build a new facility. Echo is evaluating whether this award is within the scope of **ASC 718**.

Implementation Guidance from Topic 718-10 provides the following example.

Example 2: Definition of Employee

55-91 Nonemployee directors acting in their role as members of an entity's board of directors shall be treated as employees if those directors were elected by the entity's shareholders or appointed to a board position that will be filled by shareholder election when the existing term expires. However, that requirement applies only to awards granted to them for their services as directors. Awards granted to those individuals for other services shall be accounted for as awards to nonemployees in accordance with Section 505-50-25. Additionally, consolidated groups may have multiple boards of directors; this guidance applies only to either of the following:

a. The nonemployee directors acting in their role as members of a parent entity's board of directors

b. Nonemployee members of a consolidated subsidiary's board of directors to the extent that those members are elected by shareholders that are not controlled directly or indirectly by the parent or another member of the consolidated group.

In addition, Echo considers the following guidance from EY's Financial Reporting Developments publication, *Share-Based Payment* (2015):[4]

2.2.3.2 Example—stock options granted to nonemployee directors

Illustration 2-1

Company X has four nonemployee members on its board of directors. Members of the board have several years of business experience and possess specific knowledge and expertise within Company X's industry. The nonemployee directors are elected by Company X's shareholders for a three-year term and meet four times a year. Company X grants each nonemployee director 500 stock options for each meeting he or she attends. Company X would account for the stock options as employee awards because they were granted to elected nonemployee directors for their services as directors.

In addition, one of the nonemployee directors is also an environmental attorney. During the year, Company X is named as a Potentially Responsible Party (PRP) at a Superfund site. Internal counsel has limited experience with environmental remediation and confers numerous times with the nonemployee director. Prior to presenting the motion to dismiss Company X as a PRP, the nonemployee director spends approximately 100 hours consulting with internal counsel. Ultimately, Company X is successful and is dismissed as a PRP. Company X grants the nonemployee director 7,500 options for his consulting services. Company X would account for the 7,500 stock options under ASC 505-50 because the nonemployee director received stock options for services unrelated to his service as a director.

---

[4] EY, Financial Reporting Developments: *Share-Based Payment.* Revised July 2015. Pages 14-15.

Questions:

1. Is the stock award for Mr. Draper's architectural drawings within the scope of Topic 718? Explain.

    _____

    _____

    _____

2. Look back for a moment. Could you have answered this question using scope guidance and glossary definitions alone? Explain what understanding you gained from considering Implementation Guidance (Section 55) and EY's interpretive guidance.

    _____

    _____

    _____

    In certain cases, awards to individuals that are not within the scope of Topic 718 may be subject instead to the guidance in Topic 505 (Equity-Based Payments to Non-Employees).

Evaluating Subsections with Unique Scope Guidance: Nonmonetary Transactions

As a researcher, if you ever come across a transaction in which physical assets are being exchanged, consider exploring whether the transaction is **nonmonetary**. According to ASC 845-10:

> **05-2** Most business transactions involve exchanges of cash or other monetary assets or liabilities [for example, cash or accounts receivable] for goods or services. The amount of monetary assets or liabilities exchanged generally provides an objective basis for measuring the cost of nonmonetary assets or services received by an entity as well as for measuring gain or loss on nonmonetary assets transferred from an entity. Some transactions, however, involve either of the following:
>
> a. An exchange with another entity (reciprocal transfer) that involves principally nonmonetary assets or liabilities . . . [Comments added]

That is, in most transactions, goods or services are exchanged for *cash or other monetary assets*, and the amount of cash generally provides an objective value for the goods being transferred. Nonmonetary transactions therefore present a unique issue, in that they involve assets whose values are not as objectively determinable. Some monetary consideration (boot) may be involved in a nonmonetary exchange, but this amount cannot be significant (as illustrated in **Now YOU Try 6.5**).

The basic principle in Topic 845 is that nonmonetary exchanges should be recognized at the fair values of the assets exchanged.[5] Often, this fair value measurement can give rise to gain recognition (e.g., when the fair value of the exchanged asset exceeds its carrying value). Understandably, the FASB took precautions when developing this guidance to limit this opportunity for gain recognition to circumstances where it was considered most appropriate. Accordingly,

■ Scope guidance within Topic 845 precludes the use of this topic for transactions between entities under common control (e.g., parent-subsidiary relationships).[6]

---

[5] ASC 845-10-30-1 (Nonmonetary Transactions): "In general, the accounting for nonmonetary transactions should be based on the fair values of the assets (or services) involved, which is the same basis as that used in monetary transactions."

[6] ASC 845-10-15-4(b).

■   Measurement guidance within Topic 845 requires that only transactions with *commercial substance* (e.g., a valid business purpose) may be recognized at fair value.

ASC 845 is organized into the following subsections:

■   General

■   Purchases and sales of inventory with the same counterparty

■   Barter transactions

■   Exchanges involving monetary consideration

■   Exchanges of a nonfinancial asset for a noncontrolling ownership interest

Each of these subsections offers not only unique measurement guidance, but also has unique scope guidance. Therefore, determining whether a transaction is within the scope of ASC 845 is a two-step process. Entities must evaluate both (1) "General" Topic 845 scope guidance and (2) subsection scope guidance. Even if a transaction is not precluded from the "general" scope of Topic 845, subsection scope guidance may indicate that the transaction should not be accounted for under Topic 845.

The following example illustrates application of both the General scope guidance as well as subsection scope guidance.

Exchanges Involving Monetary Consideration

Now
[YOU]
Try
6.5

Facts: Company A exchanges printing equipment (fair value: $500,000) for a forklift (fair value: $400,000) and $100,000 cash. Company A must determine whether this transaction is within the scope of **ASC 845**.

ASC 845-10 includes the following scope guidance. Par. 15-12 (below) of this topic is somewhat unusual in that it refers readers to the general subsection guidance in order to evaluate what amount of monetary consideration is considered significant. Accordingly, par. 25-6 has been included, to show how "significant" is defined in Topic 845-10. The definition of *nonmonetary asset* has also been included for reference.

General

>Entities

15-2 The guidance in the Nonmonetary Transactions Topic applies to all entities.

>Transactions

15-3 The guidance in the Nonmonetary Transactions Topic applies to all types of nonmonetary transactions including:
   a. Nonmonetary exchanges involving boot. Some exchanges of nonmonetary assets involve a small monetary consideration, referred to as boot, even though the exchange is essentially nonmonetary. (See the Exchanges Involving Monetary Consideration Subsection of Section 845–10–15 for situations outside the scope of this Subtopic.)

Exchanges Involving Monetary Consideration

>Overall Guidance

15-12 The Exchanges Involving Monetary Consideration Subsections follow the same Scope and Scope Exceptions as outlined in the General Subsection of this Subtopic, see paragraph 845-10-15-1, and address what level of monetary consideration in a nonmonetary exchange causes the transaction to be considered monetary in its entirety and, therefore, outside the scope of the Exchanges Involving Monetary Consideration Subsections and this Topic.

Continued

Continued from previous page

>Transactions

15-13 The guidance in the Exchanges Involving Monetary Consideration Subsections applies to nonmonetary exchanges involving monetary consideration (boot).

25-6 An exchange of nonmonetary assets that would otherwise be based on recorded amounts but that also involves monetary consideration (boot) shall be considered monetary (rather than nonmonetary) if the boot is significant. Significant shall be defined as at least 25 percent of the fair value of the exchange. . .

Definition of **nonmonetary assets and liabilities** (ASC 845-10-20)

Nonmonetary assets and liabilities are assets and liabilities other than monetary ones. Examples are inventories; investments in common stocks; property, plant, and equipment; and liabilities for rent collected in advance.

As you can see from these excerpts, while the General section scope guidance applies to all entities, the subsection scope guidance sets forth even more specific requirements that can result in transactions being deemed outside the scope of this topic. Considering this guidance and the facts presented, respond to the following.

Questions:

1. Does this transaction meet the General scope guidance within Topic 845?

    _____

    _____

2. Does the transaction meet the scope criteria in the subsection "Exchanges Involving Monetary Consideration"? Explain.

    _____

    _____

3. Based on your responses to the above questions, does it appear that use of Topic 845 is appropriate to account for this transaction?

    _____

    _____

4. If you concluded that this transaction is not within the scope of ASC 845-10, where might you go next for guidance? Explain.

    _____

    _____

As this example illustrated, nonmonetary transactions guidance in the Codification (**ASC 845**) can be somewhat challenging for researchers in that they must consult not only *general* scope guidance for the topic, but must also determine whether a transaction is within the scope of *subsection* guidance (i.e., groups of paragraphs) within this topic. In many cases, references to other Codification topics are provided within the Scope section for transactions specifically excluded from the scope of Topic **845**.

Which Topic Applies?: Navigating the Scope of *Investments* Topics

Previous examples in this text, namely the Energy Works example in Chapters 3 and 4, have illustrated how to evaluate an entity for consolidation under Topic **810** (Consolidation). Under Topic 810, companies with a **controlling financial interest** in another entity—based on either the variable or voting model—should consolidate that entity.

The usual condition for a *controlling financial interest* is ownership of greater than 50% of an investee's equity securities or, in the case of limited partnerships, holding greater than 50% of the partnership's kick-out rights. A controlling financial interest can also be achieved through rights and obligations associated with structured "variable interest" entities, such as entities not primarily financed through equity interests.

Once an investor has determined that he or she does not have a controlling financial interest, the next step is to consider other GAAP. The organization of this other GAAP (within various Investments topics) can be a source of confusion to beginning researchers. Figure 6-1 provides a snapshot from the Codification of topics listed under Investments.

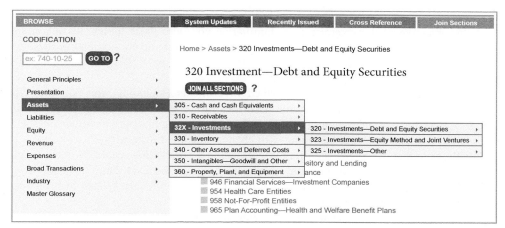

Figure 6-1

Codification topics listed under Investments

Reproduced with permission of the Financial Accounting Foundation.

To improve your comfort in navigating Investments guidance, following is a simplified summary of topics applicable to purchases of **noncontrolling interests**:

- Investments—Equity Method and Joint Ventures (Topic **323**): Applies to purchases of equity securities where an investor has *significant influence*. Significant influence is often characterized by a 20% or greater ownership stake in an investee, but can also be evidenced through qualitative factors.

- Investments—Debt and Equity Securities (Topic **320**): Applies to all investments in debt securities (such as corporate bonds), plus investments in equity securities with *readily determinable fair values*.[7] However, this topic does not apply if the investment is accounted for under the equity method. Topic 320 provides guidance on use of the trading, available-for-sale, and held-to-maturity accounting methods for an investment.

- Investments—Other (Topic **325**): Provides guidance on the cost method of accounting. This method generally applies to purchases of equity securities lacking readily determinable fair values, and where an investor lacks significant influence.

Considering the scope of these topics, and the guidance previously described for controlling financial interests, take a moment to complete the following **Now YOU Try**.

Identify the topic that you might navigate to first for each of the following simple scenarios. Also, briefly justify why you chose this topic.

1. ABC Corp purchases 10% of the voting equity shares in a small, private company.

2. ABC Corp purchases 30% of the voting equity shares in a small, private company.

Now
YOU
Try
6.6

---

[7] ASC 320-10-15-5 (Investments—Debt and Equity Securities).

3. ABC Corp purchases 10% of the voting equity shares in a public company.

_____

4. ABC Corp purchases 55% of the voting equity shares in a public company.

_____

5. ABC Corp forms a limited-purpose joint venture and lends it $2 million, in exchange for a 50% ownership stake.

_____

While the objective of this exercise is to familiarize you with these topics, it's important to understand that these are simplified summaries, and that scope determinations in these areas can involve judgment. For example, in response to questions 1 and 3, did you consider that two possible topics might apply?

Furthermore, certain of the just-described investments (including, for example, equity method investments and available-for-sale securities) are eligible for the *fair value option* in Topic 825-10 (Financial Instruments—Overall). Entities electing this option may report selected categories of financial assets at fair value with changes recorded in earnings.

Finally, note that the FASB is currently working on a project that would overhaul financial instrument accounting; this project could significantly change the accounting for the topics just described and could result in a reorganization of Codification guidance related to Investments. Go to www.fasb.org for updates on this project.

Let's turn now to our two examples involving scope tests.

PERFORMING SCOPE TESTS: LEASES AND DERIVATIVES

Evaluating Whether an Arrangement Contains a Lease

LO3 Perform simplified scope tests for leases and derivatives.

Located in the Broad Transactions area of the Codification, the Leases topic offers guidance on transactions that require specialized lease accounting. Unlike a typical accrual-accounting contract, application of lease accounting, for a lessee, can result in either:

- In the case of an operating lease, straight-line expense recognition of lease costs.
- In the case of a capital lease, the capitalization of a leased asset and recognition of a related lease payment obligation.

Scope guidance for leases is located in Subtopic 10 (Overall) of Topic **840** (Leases) and applies to all subtopics within Topic 840.[8] This guidance is presented in a few ways: first, the scope guidance includes a test for identifying arrangements that qualify as leases. Second, the guidance lists specific arrangements that do not qualify for lease accounting. A researcher with a potential lease would have to review the entire scope section before concluding that application of lease guidance is appropriate for his or her transaction.

The upcoming **Now YOU Try** illustrates how an arrangement conveying the "right to use" property, plant, or equipment can result in lease accounting. Even if a contract is not referred to as a "Lease Agreement," accountants must learn to recognize circumstances in which control over property is being transferred. In the following example, the parties have entered into a power purchase agreement. For accounting purposes, these arrangements can qualify as leases, if certain conditions are met.

In a typical power purchase agreement, a buyer of electricity (often a utility company, which has promised to sell electricity to its own customers) purchases output from a power plant. The buyer could choose to purchase some, or all, of the plant's electricity output. The power plant

---

[8] ASC 840-10-15-1 (Leases): "The Scope Section of the Overall Subtopic establishes the pervasive scope for all Subtopics of the Leases Topic. Unless explicitly addressed within specific Subtopics, the following scope guidance applies to all Subtopics of the Leases Topic."

is typically owned by a third party. Payment for electricity purchased may be fixed per unit of energy purchased (e.g., $0.15 per kilowatt-hour), or in some cases may also include a variable component related to costs of operating the power plant (e.g., plus maintenance costs). See Figure 6-2 for an illustration of this structure.

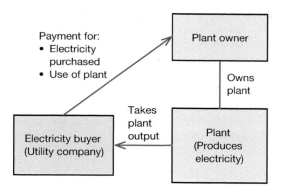

Figure 6-2

Example structure for a power purchase agreement

When evaluating a power purchase agreement, the accountant must determine whether the buyer is just purchasing power, or whether the buyer is really getting the *right to control* the power plant. For example, if the buyer can determine when the plant produces power, and how much, and if the buyer has physical access to the plant, these are indicators that the buyer is leasing the plant. This so-called "power purchase agreement" is not just a simple purchase of power; rather, this activity must be recorded in the financial statements as a lease.

Evaluating Whether an Arrangement Contains a Lease— The Lease Scope "Test"

Now
[**YOU**]
Try
6.7

Facts: An electric utility (buyer) has entered into a power purchase agreement (PPA) for the purchase of electricity from a power plant in Summer, Illinois. The PPA states that the buyer will supply all of the fuel (coal) for the plant, will operate the plant, and will take 100% of the output from the plant. The buyer will pay a fee for the electricity based on:

1. the variable operating costs of the plant (such as utility bills, water usage, etc.), **plus**

2. an amount based on the current market price of electricity.

The buyer must now determine whether this arrangement qualifies as a lease.

ASC 840-10 provides the following Lease scope guidance:

Arrangements that Qualify as Leases

15-6   An arrangement conveys the right to use property, plant, or equipment if the arrangement conveys to the purchaser (lessee) the right to control the use of the underlying property, plant, or equipment. The right to control the use of the underlying property, plant, or equipment is conveyed if <u>any</u> of the following conditions is met:

   a.   The purchaser has the ability or right to operate the property, plant, or equipment or direct others to operate the property, plant, or equipment in a manner it determines <u>while</u> obtaining or controlling more than a minor amount of the output or other utility of the property, plant, or equipment. The purchaser's ability to operate the property, plant, or equipment may be evidenced by (but is not limited to) the purchaser's ability to hire, fire, or replace the property's operator or the purchaser's ability to specify significant operating policies and procedures in the

Continued

Continued from previous page

> arrangement with the owner-seller having no ability to change such policies and procedures . . . .
>
> b. The purchaser has the ability or right to control physical access to the underlying property, plant, or equipment <u>while</u> obtaining or controlling more than a minor amount of the output or other utility of the property, plant, or equipment.
>
> c. Facts and circumstances indicate that it is remote that one or more parties other than the purchaser will take more than a minor amount of the output or other utility that will be produced or generated by the property, plant, or equipment during the term of the arrangement, <u>and</u> the price that the purchaser (lessee) will pay for the output is neither contractually fixed per unit of output nor equal to the current market price per unit of output as of the time of delivery of the output. [Underlined emphasis added]

Questions:

1. Evaluate whether each condition (a, b, and c) for lease accounting is met. For each condition, be sure to address *both parts* of the condition (as indicated by underlined text in par. 15-6). If you have to make any assumptions in evaluating the condition, state what you've assumed.

   Condition (a):

   _____

   _____

   _____

   Condition (b):

   _____

   _____

   _____

   In your evaluation of condition (c), consider also the following interpretive guidance from EY's *Lease Accounting* Financial Reporting Developments publication (2014):[9]

   > Market [price] is intended to address those items for which there is a readily available, actively traded market (e.g., electricity). In addition, market price per unit means the cost is solely a market cost without other pricing factors (e.g., market price per kwh plus percent change in price of natural gas would not be market).

   Condition (c):

   _____

   _____

   _____

2. Having analyzed each condition in par. 15-6, provide an overall conclusion summarizing which conditions for lease accounting were met. Recall from par. 15-6 that an arrangement meeting *any* of the conditions (a, b, or c) meets the definition of a lease.

   _____

   _____

---

[9] EY, Financial Reporting Developments: *Lease Accounting*. November 2014. Section 1.1.3, Page 5.

3. In your own words, try to summarize the concepts illustrated in this example. How could this arrangement possibly be considered a lease when the contract is entitled "Power Purchase Agreement"? Conceptually, how could that be?

_____

_____

_____

Again, after determining that an arrangement qualifies as a lease, the researcher must evaluate (by reading the rest of the Scope section) whether any scope exceptions apply that would preclude use of ASC 840.

Transactions that do not qualify for lease accounting should be reviewed for other specialized accounting treatments, including derivative accounting (for example, if the contract involves commodities) or the presence of variable interests (addressed in the Consolidation topic). Contracts that do not require these specialized accounting treatments are frequently accounted for as accrual contracts, with rights and obligations accounted for as they arise.

Evaluating Whether an Instrument Meets the Definition of a Derivative

Located in the Broad Transactions area of the Codification, Topic 815 (Derivatives) requires that certain instruments must be carried at fair value and marked-to-market (meaning that changes in fair value must be reflected in the asset or liability's recorded value each quarter).

The derivatives topic includes instruments (or contracts) within its scope that "derive" value from changes in some market price or other factor. For example, a contract for the future purchase of oil at a specified price must be carried at fair value. This makes sense because as the value of oil changes, the contract itself will have a positive or negative fair value. The same is true for a contract for the future purchase of a certain stock at a specified price.

In recent years, derivative contracts have become an essential risk-management tool for many companies. Companies frequently turn to derivatives to protect themselves from future commodity price and interest rate changes, in order to improve the predictability of their future cash flows. For example, by early 2012, Southwest Airlines had already entered into contracts locking in prices for 50% of its expected jet fuel purchases for the second half of 2012. (Hedging volumes have since been reduced from this rate.)[10] Given that these contracts have market-based values that can fluctuate, these contracts must be recorded at their current market value.

Investors like the transparency of derivatives, as they are carried at the contract's current value. Companies, however, may find the frequent effort of re-measuring their derivative contracts burdensome.

Derivatives are defined as instruments with all of the following characteristics:

- It has a stated notional (a quantity) and an underlying (a price).
- It requires little or no initial net investment.
- The contract itself, or the asset sold in the contract, is readily marketable.

Determining whether an instrument meets the definition of derivative is a first step in determining whether the instrument is within the scope of ASC 815. Following is an example illustrating the use of derivative scope guidance.

Evaluating Whether an Instrument Meets the Definition of a Derivative

Facts: Albert, Inc. sells office supplies. Albert, Inc. is in the process of signing a contract for the purchase of 10,000 staplers in 1 year from its supplier in China. Albert, Inc. will pay $2 per stapler upon delivery. The contract itself does not allow for net settlement between the parties. Albert, Inc. must determine whether the contract meets the definition of a derivative.

Now
YOU
Try
6.8

_____

[10] Graham, Rachel, "Jet Fuel Hedging Positions for U.S., Canadian Airlines." Bloomberg online. March 26, 2012.

ASC 815-10 (Derivatives and Hedging) includes the following scope guidance.

Definition of Derivative Instrument

15-83 A derivative instrument is a financial instrument or other contract with all of the following characteristics:

a. Underlying, notional amount, payment provision. The contract has both of the following terms, which determine the amount of the settlement or settlements, and, in some cases, whether or not a settlement is required:
   1. One or more underlyings
   2. One or more notional amounts or payment provisions or both.

b. Initial net investment. The contract requires no initial net investment or an initial net investment that is smaller than would be required for other types of contracts that would be expected to have a similar response to changes in market factors.

c. Net settlement. The contract can be settled net by any of the following means:
   1. Its terms implicitly or explicitly require or permit net settlement.
   2. It can readily be settled net by a means outside the contract.
   3. It provides for delivery of an asset that puts the recipient in a position not substantially different from net settlement.

ASC 815-10 goes on to provide additional guidance on the terms included in par. 15-83 definition. Excerpts from that additional guidance follow.

Underlying

15-88 An underlying is a variable that, along with either a notional amount or a payment provision, determines the settlement of a derivative instrument. An underlying usually is one or a combination of the following:
1. A security price or security price index
2. A commodity price or commodity price index . . .

Notional Amount

15-92 A notional amount is a number of currency units, shares, bushels, pounds, or other units specified in the contract. . . .

Net Settlement Under Contract Terms

15-100 In this form of net settlement, neither party is required to deliver an asset that is associated with the underlying and that has a . . . number of shares, or other denomination that is equal to the notional amount . . .

Primary Characteristics of Market Mechanism

15-110 In this form of net settlement, one of the parties is required to deliver an asset of the type described in paragraph 815-10-15-100, but there is an established market mechanism that facilitates net settlement outside the contract. (For example, an exchange that offers a ready opportunity to sell the contract or to enter into an offsetting contract.) . . .

Net Settlement by Delivery of Derivative Instrument or Asset Readily Convertible to Cash

15-119 In this form of net settlement, one of the parties is required to deliver an asset of the type described in paragraph 815-10-15-100, but that asset is readily convertible to cash . . . [Underlined emphasis added]

Continued

15-120 An example of a contract with this form of net settlement is a forward contract that requires delivery of an exchange-traded equity security. Even though the number of shares to be delivered is the same as the notional amount of the contract and the price of the shares is the underlying, an exchange-traded security is readily convertible to cash. . . .

15-121 Examples of assets that are readily convertible to cash include a security or commodity traded in an active market and a unit of foreign currency that is readily convertible into the functional currency of the reporting entity.

Questions:

1. Does this contract meet the definition of a derivative?

   a. Does the contract have a notional amount? An underlying? Explain.

   _____

   _____

   b. Does the contract require an initial net investment? Explain.

   _____

   c. Can the contract be settled net? Explain.

   _____

   _____

   _____

Finally, provide an overall conclusion: Does this contract meet the definition of a derivative? Recall that all three characteristics from par. 15-83 must be met in order for the contract to be a derivative.

2. Overall conclusion: Does this contract meet the definition of a derivative? Explain.

   _____

   _____

   _____

In addition to evaluating the definition of a derivative instrument, researchers must also consider whether the contract is eligible for any scope exceptions to **ASC 815**. Scope exceptions include, for example, insurance contracts and so-called "normal purchases and normal sales" where an entity can assert that it will use the contracted goods for its own operations.

The preceding examples were prepared with the intention of introducing you to some of the complexity associated with scope evaluations. Hopefully, your familiarity with scope issues is now improved as a result of your efforts on these exercises.

Following is one final comment on scope evaluations—to document your evaluation, or not?

To Document, or Not to Document My Scope Review?

A common question that students raise is whether all scope reviews should be documented in accounting issues memos.

In many cases, scope guidance may be boilerplate and may just say: *This guidance applies to all entities.* In those cases, it's usually not necessary to include scope excerpts and analysis in your memo. Just because you reviewed the Scope section doesn't mean this guidance must always be included in your memo.

However, the examples in this chapter involved scope guidance with some complexity. In cases like these, I would expect a student to document his or her consideration of scope guidance. In other words, if there is judgment or specificity in the Scope section that you took time to carefully consider, then this should be described in your memo.

In fact, for certain topics (such as those involving complex scope tests), nearly your entire memo might be devoted to the scope evaluation!

RECOGNITION GUIDANCE: A BRIEF INTRODUCTION

> **LO4** **Understand** the conceptual views underlying recognition guidance.

Accounting recognition broadly describes the "criteria, timing, and location (within the financial statements)" for recording an item.[11] That is, recognition describes *what* should be recorded (e.g., is an item or event required to be recognized?), *when* it should be recorded (e.g., can revenue be recognized at the time of sale?), and *how* (i.e., where within the financial statements) the item should be recorded.

Much of your accounting education to date has likely focused on recognition-type issues (e.g., "What's the journal entry?"), so the issues addressed in this section of the Codification may be more intuitive to you. However, don't mistake this for simplicity. The Codification's recognition criteria vary considerably across transactions and arrangements, as the examples in this chapter illustrate.

Although many individual topics within the Codification separately address recognition, it is also useful to consider the overall objectives of recognition set forth in the FASB's Conceptual Framework. Concepts Statement No. 5, *Recognition and Measurement in Financial Statements of Business Enterprises* (CON 5), describes recognition as follows:

> 6. Recognition is the process of formally recording or incorporating an item into the financial statements of an entity as an asset, liability, revenue, expense, or the like. Recognition includes depiction of an item in both words and numbers, with the amount included in the totals of the financial statements . . .

CON 5 establishes the following four **fundamental recognition criteria**:

> **Fundamental Recognition Criteria**
>
> 63. An item and information about it should meet four fundamental recognition criteria to be recognized and should be recognized when the criteria are met, subject to a cost-benefit constraint and a materiality threshold. Those criteria are:
>
>> *Definitions*—The item meets the definition of an element of financial statements.
>> *Measurability*—It has a relevant attribute measurable with sufficient reliability.
>> *Relevance*—The information about it is capable of making a difference in user decisions.
>> *Reliability*—The information is representationally faithful, verifiable, and neutral.
>
> All four criteria are subject to a pervasive cost-benefit constraint: the expected benefits from recognizing a particular item should justify perceived costs of providing and using the information. Recognition is also subject to a materiality threshold: an item and information about it need not be recognized in a set of financial statements if the item

Continued

---

[11] FASB *Notice to Constituents (v4.6) About the Codification.* January 9, 2012. Page 18.

> is not large enough to be material and the aggregate of individually immaterial items is not large enough to be material to those financial statements. [Footnotes omitted]

That is, items meeting these four fundamental criteria should be recorded in the financial statements, subject to two additional tests:

1.   The benefit of recognizing the item must exceed the cost of doing so.

2.   The item should be considered material to financial statement users.

From time to time, practitioners have historically asserted to the FASB that disclosure is a reasonable substitute for financial statement recognition.[12] However, in CON 5, the FASB emphasizes that recognition is the preferred method of conveying information that is material to financial statement users; the FASB does not view disclosure to be an adequate substitute for recognition.[13] While it is important to be aware of the recognition principles in CON 5, they are rarely utilized in practice by accounting researchers; rather, their primary role is to serve as a foundation for the FASB's standard-setting process.

In most cases, recognition guidance is available within Section 25 of each topic in the Codification. However, the following sources can also provide valuable recognition guidance:

■   Other Presentation Matters (Section 45 in the Codification) also frequently describes *how* items should be recorded in the financial statements.

■   Implementation Guidance (Section 55) and SEC content (Sections S-25 or S-99) may offer additional clarification and examples illustrating recognition guidance.

■   In limited cases, FASB Concepts Statement No. 6, *Elements of Financial Statements* (CON 6), can be useful in determining how items should be recorded (such as asset versus expense determinations).

Derecognition Guidance in the Codification

We'll also briefly touch upon derecognition in this section of the chapter. **Derecognition** guidance describes *when* and *how* an asset, liability, or equity item may be removed from the financial statements, and how to determine related gains and losses (when applicable).

Although organized into a separate category within the Codification, Derecognition guidance (Section "40") is fairly limited. Furthermore, the Conceptual Framework does not currently address the issue of derecognition. Instead, derecognition (or the removal of assets, liabilities, or equity from the balance sheet) often takes place through other means, for example, through amortization or impairments. These other means are generally addressed within the Subsequent Measurement section of a topic (Section "35"). Chapters 7 and 8 of this book address measurement issues.

---

1.   Identify four sources a researcher might consult for recognition-related guidance.

   _____

   _____

2.   Think for a moment: Why might the FASB believe that disclosure is not an adequate substitute for recognition? Explain.

   _____

   _____

   _____

Now
YOU
Try
6.9

---

[12] For example, during the development of FASB Statement No. 123, *Accounting for Stock-Based Compensation* (FAS 123), many constituents urged the Board to require disclosure only, of share-based compensation arrangements, rather than change the accounting recognition of stock awards (see par. 59, FAS 123).

[13] FASB Concepts Statement No. 5, *Recognition and Measurement in Financial Statements of Business Enterprises*, par. 9.

3.   If no Derecognition section (Section 40) is included in a topic you are reviewing, where else might you look for guidance on removing assets, liabilities, or equity items from the balance sheet?

_____

As noted previously, Recognition issues can be somewhat intuitive for students; accordingly, only a limited number of examples are provided in this chapter. These examples involve revenues, uncertain tax positions, and events after the balance sheet date. We'll conclude with a derecognition example related to liability extinguishments.

In the recognition examples we'll explore, notice how different **recognition thresholds** apply to different topics. For example, uncertain taxes may only be recorded if they are *more likely than not*. Subsequent events are recorded only if the c*ondition existed at the balance sheet date*. As another example, liabilities are recorded if they are *probable*.

We'll begin by discussing a very key recognition issue of our day—revenue.

REVENUE RECOGNITION: NAVIGATING THE TRANSITION

LO5 Contrast key principles underlying, and techniques for navigating, existing versus revised revenue guidance.

One area presenting new recognition challenges to students and practitioners alike is revenue recognition.

While the FASB and IASB cheered the issuance of a new, joint revenue standard in 2014, the standard setters have since faced ongoing challenges from practitioners struggling to apply the new model. Expect, therefore, that this new guidance will continue to evolve.

The standard—entitled *Revenue from Contracts with Customers* (ASU 2014-09)—is effective for periods beginning after December 15, 2017, for public companies.[14,15] However, companies must get comfortable with the new model *now*, because transition guidance requires them to select one of two transition options: Companies may present prior periods in accordance with the revised model (the "full retrospective approach") **or** may record a cumulative effect adjustment to opening retained earnings/equity (the "modified retrospective approach"), accompanied by disclosures.[16]

Researchers navigating to revenue guidance in the Codification will now find it presented in two topics: within ASC 605 (we'll call this the "existing" model) and within ASC 606 (we'll call this the "new" or "revised" model), as illustrated in Figure 6-3.

Figure 6-3

Organization of existing (ASC 605) and revised (ASC 606) revenue guidance in the Codification

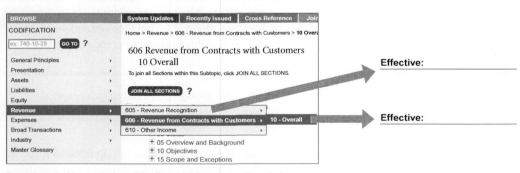

Reproduced with permission of the Financial Accounting Foundation.

_____

[14] Nonpublic companies have an additional year to comply with the standard.

[15] The original effective date of this ASU was for periods beginning after December 15, 2016. In July 2015, the FASB decided to defer this effective date by one year. Entities can, at their option, apply the standard as of the original effective date.

[16] Entities electing the modified retrospective approach must supplement their financial statements with additional disclosures; these include, for example, describing the amount by which each financial statement line item is affected by application of the standard (versus previous revenue guidance).

1. Label the screenshot in Figure 6-3 with the appropriate effective date for each topic (605 and 606).

2. Think: If a public company has a calendar year-end, what is the first date the company should begin applying the new standard?

_____

_____

3. Explain what is meant by "full retrospective" versus "modified retrospective" adoption.

_____

_____

**Now
YOU
Try
6.10**

You are among the lucky generation of students who must learn both models. To that end, let's briefly explore the concepts behind, and research techniques for, each model.

Conceptual Definitions of Revenue

Recall that the Conceptual Framework includes principles that are considered foundational to guidance in the Codification. Revenue guidance is addressed in both CON 5 and CON 6.

CON 6 broadly defines revenues as increases in assets or decreases in liabilities:

> Revenues are inflows or other enhancements of assets of an entity or settlements of its liabilities (or a combination of both) from delivering or producing goods, rendering services, or other activities that constitute the entity's ongoing major or central operations. (par. 78)

By contrast, CON 5 offers a different view, emphasizing that revenue recognition "involves consideration of two factors, (a) being realized or realizable and (b) being earned" (par. 83).

As you can see, the CON 5 approach focuses on the *earnings process*, whereas the CON 6 approach emphasizes that revenue arises from *changes in assets and liabilities*.

Despite issuing a revised revenue standard, the FASB has not yet revisited (or revised) these Conceptual Framework definitions of revenue. That said, the inconsistency between these two descriptions accounts for part of the FASB's motivation to revise revenue guidance.

Let's take a look next at the *existing* Codification model for revenue recognition. You'll notice similarity in this guidance to the CON 5 approach. However, like the conceptual definitions of revenue, our existing GAAP in this area is diverse and at times inconsistent.

Existing Codification Requirements for Revenue Recognition (ASC 605)

Topic 605-10 (Revenue Recognition—Overall) includes the following broad revenue recognition guidance:

> **25-1** The recognition of revenue and gains of an entity during a period involves consideration of the following two factors . . .
>   a. **Being realized or realizable.** Revenue and gains generally are not recognized until realized or realizable. [CON 5] . . . states that revenue and gains are realized when products (goods or services), merchandise, or other assets are exchanged for cash or claims to cash. . . .
>   b. **Being earned.** [CON 5] . . . states that revenue is not recognized until earned. That [guidance] states that an entity's revenue-earning activities involve delivering or producing goods, rendering services, or other activities that constitute its ongoing major or central operations, and revenues are considered to have been earned when the entity has substantially accomplished what it must do to be entitled to the benefits represented by the revenues. . . . [Emphasis and bracketed text added]

As you can see, Topic 605-10 establishes recognition criteria that are consistent with CON 5, emphasizing that revenue must be *realized or realizable* and *earned* in order to be recognized.

In addition to FASB requirements, public companies must also apply the SEC's interpretations of these basic revenue recognition criteria. (Nonpublic companies also often look to this guidance.) Located in the "S99" section of Topic 605-10 are four additional criteria developed by the SEC for interpreting the terms "realized and earned":

> The staff believes that revenue generally is realized or realizable and earned when all of the following criteria are met:
> - Persuasive evidence of an arrangement exists,
> - Delivery has occurred or services have been rendered,
> - The seller's price to the buyer is fixed or determinable, and
> - Collectibility is reasonably assured.[17] [Footnotes omitted]

Notably, these additional SEC criteria are accompanied by extensive interpretive guidance and examples. These are described in section S99 of ASC 605-10, as well as on the SEC website ("SAB 104").

Revised Model: Revenue from Contracts with Customers (ASC 606)

The revised model establishes a new definition of **revenue**:

> Inflows or other enhancements of assets of an entity or settlements of its liabilities (or a combination of both) from delivering or producing goods, rendering services, or other activities that constitute the entity's ongoing major or central operations.[18]

. . . and introduces what's known as a **core principle**:

> . . . an entity recognizes revenue to depict the transfer of promised goods or services to customers in an amount that reflects the consideration to which the entity expects to be entitled in exchange for those goods or services.[19,20]

Also new to the revised model is a five-step process that entities must apply in order to recognize revenue under the core principle. These steps are illustrated in Figure 6-4.

Figure 6-4

The five steps for applying the new revenue model (ASC 606-10)

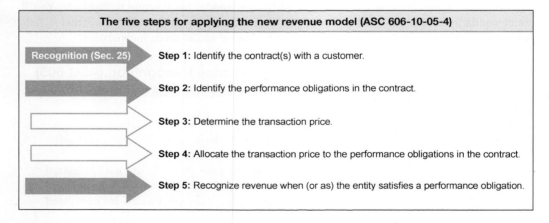

The five steps for applying the new revenue model (ASC 606-10-05-4)

Recognition (Sec. 25)

Step 1: Identify the contract(s) with a customer.

Step 2: Identify the performance obligations in the contract.

Step 3: Determine the transaction price.

Step 4: Allocate the transaction price to the performance obligations in the contract.

Step 5: Recognize revenue when (or as) the entity satisfies a performance obligation.

---

[17] SAB Topic 13.A.1, Revenue Recognition—General, as accessed in ASC 605-10-S99, par. 1.

[18] ASC 606-10-20.

[19] ASC 606-10-05-3.

[20] As you may notice in this principle, and in the definition of revenue, the revised model does away—almost entirely—with the terms *earned* and *realized*. Rather, the concepts try very hard to center around revenue arising due to increases in assets and settlements of liabilities. Nevertheless, many pages of the revised standard are devoted to describing when performance has occurred and revenue may be recognized.

When navigating **ASC 606-10**, you'll find the *core principle* and these *five steps* in the Overview section (**05**). Detailed guidance for applying each step is split between the Recognition (**25**) and Measurement (**32**) sections. Three of the steps depicted in Figure 6-4 are described within the Recognition section, and two steps are discussed under Measurement.

Considering the revised definition of revenue, the new core principle, and the five-step process, take a moment to complete the following **Now YOU Try**.

Now
[**YOU**]
Try
6.11

1. Considering the preceding discussion, take a moment to label the arrows in Figure 6-4 with the section where you'd expect to find guidance for applying each step.

2. Describe how the definition of revenue and the core principle in the new model compare to the existing CON 5 and CON 6 definitions of revenue.

_____

_____

_____

3. What's your best guess: Do you think the FASB will update its Conceptual Framework to reflect issuance of the revenue standard, and if so, how?

_____

_____

Research Techniques for Navigating the Existing versus New Model

Existing Model—A Hodgepodge of Guidance

A key criticism of the existing revenue model is that it is voluminous, at times inconsistent across industries, and can be cumbersome to navigate. Did you know that over 100 individual pieces of revenue recognition guidance were used to populate the existing model in the Codification? Did you also know that **ASC 605** has 36 individual subtopics (e.g., -10 is Overall, -15 is Products, etc.)?

What this means for researchers using the existing model is that they must travel from subtopic to subtopic, first finding the "general principle" in the Overall subtopic (**ASC 605-10**), then navigating to one of the 35 other different subtopics for transaction- or industry-specific guidance. Oh, and don't forget to check all areas of "required reading" for each subtopic you consult.

EXAMPLE ———————————————————————————————

For example, say that you sell a product (which can be returned) that has a rebate offer attached. You would then navigate ASC 605's subtopics as follows:

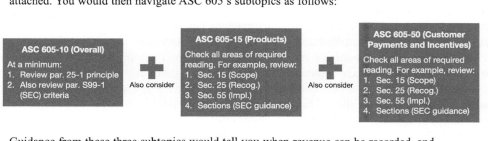

Guidance from these three subtopics would tell you when revenue can be recorded, and whether the rebate should reduce revenue (net presentation) or be recorded separately as a liability (gross presentation).

Revised Model

In contrast, the revised revenue model relies upon a single, consistent principle that can be applied to a range of transactions and industries. The revised model contains just one subtopic (**ASC 606-10**, Overall).

What this means for researchers using the revised model is that they must really get to know this one, supersized subtopic. Explore all aspects of **ASC 606-10**, including the guidance in the Overview, Definitions, Recognition, Measurement, and Implementation Guidance sections. Furthermore, because the guidance is so groundbreaking, double-check any judgments you make against accounting firm interpretations. And keep a constant eye on the FASB (and the activities of its Transition Resource Group, or TRG), which continues to review and interpret aspects of the revised model.

EXAMPLE

For example, you might navigate **ASC 606-10** and additional interpretive guidance as follows.

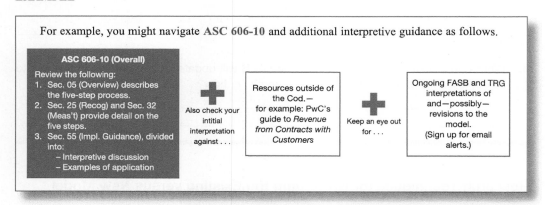

> **[TIP]** from the Trenches
>
> In my opinion, there's one way to get comfortable with the new revenue model: You have to be willing to set aside a few hours and read ASC 606. (Or read a firm guide, alongside ASC 606.) Do it in your free time one evening, before you even enter the workforce. Get to know the five-step model, and then become familiar with how to navigate recognition/measurement issues, related implementation guidance and examples, and related firm guidance. After all, revenue is the most important part of almost any company's income statement, and understanding the proper accounting for it is vital for any practitioner's ongoing professional education.

Let's now walk through an extremely simple example using both the existing and new models. The focus of the example is not to challenge you with complex guidance; rather, it is to show you the process involved in carefully researching and applying revenue guidance.

Facts: Friendly Appliance is a public company (i.e., SEC guidance applies) and is an appliance retailer. Assume that Friendly sells a washing machine and installation services together to a customer for $600. As of 12/31/X1, the washing machine has been delivered, but the delivery crew (also trained to perform installations) was missing a part necessary to perform the installation service. The crew has scheduled a return visit to the customer's home for 1/2/X2, to complete the installation. The purchase contract includes a general right of customer return.

Friendly has a calendar year-end and needs to determine whether these two "deliverables" qualify for separate recognition. This is a question of *what* items can be recorded separately as revenue. For simplicity, this example will focus only on this narrow recognition issue and will not consider measurement, nor will it focus on *when* revenue can be recorded for each item. Again, our focus will be on the process for navigating revenue guidance.

Review Using Existing Guidance

ASC 605-25 (Revenue Recognition—Multiple Element Arrangements) sets forth criteria for separate recognition of elements in a transaction:

> **25-2** The principles applicable to this Subtopic are as follows:
> a. Revenue arrangements with multiple deliverables shall be divided into separate units of accounting if the deliverables in the arrangement meet the criteria in paragraph 605-25-25-5.
> b. Arrangement consideration shall be allocated among the separate units of accounting based on their relative selling prices (or as otherwise provided in paragraph 605-25-30-4) . . . .
> c. Applicable revenue recognition criteria shall be considered separately for separate units of accounting.
>
> **25-4** A vendor shall evaluate all deliverables in an arrangement to determine whether they represent separate units of accounting. . . .
>
> **25-5** In an arrangement with multiple deliverables, the delivered item or items shall be considered a separate unit of accounting if **both** of the following criteria are met:
> a. The delivered item or items have value to the customer on a standalone basis. The item or items have value on a standalone basis if they are sold separately by any vendor or the customer could resell the delivered item(s) on a standalone basis. In the context of a customer's ability to resell the delivered item(s), this criterion does not require the existence of an observable market for the deliverable(s). **[and]**
> b. If the arrangement includes a general right of return relative to the delivered item, delivery or performance of the undelivered item or items is considered probable and substantially in the control of the vendor. [Emphasis and bracketed text added]

Implementation guidance introduces an example similar to ours and concludes:

> **55-35** Based on an evaluation of the circumstances, the first condition for separation is met for Appliance W because it sometimes is sold separately by Entity S. The second condition for separation is also met because, even though a general right of return exists, performance of the appliance installation is probable and within the control of Entity S. Therefore, Appliance W and installation should be accounted for as separate units of accounting.

Existing Revenue Guidance

1. Look closely at par. 25-2. It essentially sets forth three steps for evaluating arrangements with multiple deliverables. Summarize these three steps.

_____

_____

_____

2. Next, considering the guidance in par. 25-5, can the deliverables in this Friendly Appliance example be treated as separate units of accounting? Discuss both criteria.

_____

_____

Now
YOU
Try
6.12a

3. How does Section 55 guidance assist with your understanding of this example?

After concluding upon whether the deliverables are separable, your next step would be to allocate arrangement consideration to each deliverable, using measurement guidance within this same subtopic, **ASC 605-25**. But what subtopic would you go to next, to determine *when* revenue from each unit of accounting may be recognized?

Consider the following graphic, which illustrates the guidance and subtopics that offer recognition or measurement guidance for this single issue.

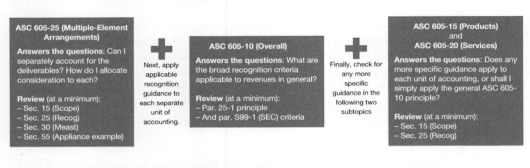

Additional Questions

Now
YOU
Try
6.12b

4. Refer back to the existing ASC 605-10 guidance introduced several pages ago. Describe whether each unit of accounting meets the par. 25-1 and S99-1 recognition criteria.

5. Finally, list the subtopics you'd need to consult in order to fully evaluate this Friendly Appliances example, and describe why consulting each subtopic is necessary.

Notably, the services described in this example are not addressed within **ASC 605-20**; however, **ASC 605-15** does offer guidance applicable to sales of products with rights of return. Friendly management would need to consider this guidance.

As the preceding example illustrates, existing revenue recognition guidance is varied and extends across a number of unique subtopics within **ASC 605** (Revenue Recognition). Each subtopic describes the appropriate approach to revenue recognition for a given situation or set of circumstances; for this reason, it is critical for a researcher to carefully consider which subtopic or group of subtopics is most applicable to his or her situation.

Review Using the New Model—We Must Separate Performance Obligations That Are "Distinct"

Recall the five-step process in the new standard, described in **ASC 606-10**:

05-4 An entity recognizes revenue in accordance with that core principle by applying the following steps:
  a.   Step 1: Identify the contract(s) with a customer . . . .
  b.   Step 2: Identify the performance obligations in the contract . . . .
  c.   Step 3: Determine the transaction price . . . .
  d.   Step 4: Allocate the transaction price to the performance obligations in the contract . . . .
  e.   Step 5: Recognize revenue when (or as) the entity satisfies a performance obligation . . . .

Complexities can arise within each step of this model. This example will focus only on Step 2, which is addressed further within the Recognition section, as follows:

Identifying Performance Obligations

25-14 At *contract* inception, an entity shall assess the goods or services promised in a contract with a *customer* and shall identify as a *performance obligation* each promise to transfer to the customer either:
  a.   **A good or service (or a bundle of goods or services) that is distinct**
  b.   **A series of distinct goods or services that are substantially the same and that have the same pattern of transfer to the customer (see paragraph 606-10-25-15).**
[This paragraph is shown in bold in the Codification because it's considered a "key principle."]

The Glossary of **ASC 606-10** includes the following defined terms related to this par. 25-14 excerpt:[21]

Contract

An agreement between two or more parties that creates enforceable rights and obligations.

Customer

A party that has contracted with an entity to obtain goods or services that are an output of the entity's ordinary activities in exchange for consideration.

The following paragraphs elaborate upon the par. 25-14 principle:

>>   Distinct Goods or Services
25-18 Depending on the *contract*, promised goods or services may include, but are not limited to, the following:
  . . .
  b.   Resale of goods purchased by an entity (for example, merchandise of a retailer)
  . . .
  d.   Performing a contractually agreed-upon task (or tasks) for a *customer* . . . .

Continued

---

[21] Note: The Glossary definition for *performance obligation* is not reproduced here because par. 25-14 actually serves to define this term.

Continued from previous page

25-19 A good or service that is promised to a customer is distinct if both of the following criteria are met:

a. The customer can benefit from the good or service either on its own or together with other resources that are readily available to the customer (that is, the good or service is capable of being distinct).

b. The entity's promise to transfer the good or service to the customer is separately identifiable from other promises in the contract (that is, the good or service is distinct within the context of the contract).

25-20 . . . For some goods or services, a customer may be able to benefit from a good or service on its own. For other goods or services, a customer may be able to benefit from the good or service only in conjunction with other readily available resources. A readily available resource is a good or service that is sold separately (by the entity or another entity) or a resource that the customer has already obtained from the entity (including goods or services that the entity will have already transferred to the customer under the contract) or from other transactions or events.

25-21 Factors that indicate that an entity's promise to transfer a good or service to a customer is separately identifiable (in accordance with paragraph 606-10-25-19(b)) include, but are not limited to, the following:

a. The entity does not provide a significant service of integrating the good or service with other goods or services promised in the contract into a bundle of goods or services that represent the combined output for which the customer has contracted. In other words, the entity is not using the good or service as an input to produce or deliver the combined output specified by the customer.

b. The good or service does not significantly modify or customize another good or service promised in the contract.

c. The good or service is not highly dependent on, or highly interrelated with, other goods or services promised in the contract. For example, the fact that a customer could decide to not purchase the good or service without significantly affecting the other promised goods or services in the contract might indicate that the good or service is not highly dependent on, or highly interrelated with, those other promised goods or services.

Revised Revenue Model

Now **YOU** Try **6.13a**

1. Why is it important to determine whether promises made to the customer are *distinct*? What's the significance of this concept?

_____

_____

2. What are the two criteria for evaluating whether a good or service is *distinct*?

_____

_____

3. Based on this Section 25 (Recognition) guidance, does it appear that the washing machine and installation are *distinct*? Explain.

_____

_____

_____

_____

Recall from our earlier discussion of the revised model that it's important to consult Implementation Guidance (Sec. 55) not only to check for interpretative guidance, but also to look for examples that could be relevant.

Currently, Section 55 interpretive guidance does not further elaborate upon the concept of "distinct" performance obligations. However, Section 55 does include an analogous example.

In this example, software and installation services are provided by an entity, but the software is not customized for the customer, and similar installation services are routinely performed by other entities and do not result in significant modifications to the software. This example concludes:

55-142 The entity assesses the goods and services promised to the customer to determine which goods and services are distinct in accordance with paragraph 606-10-25-19. The entity observes that the software is delivered before the other goods and services and remains functional without the updates and the technical support. Thus, the entity concludes that the customer can benefit from each of the goods and services either on their own or together with the other goods and services that are readily available and the criterion in paragraph 606-10-25-19(a) is met.

55-143 The entity also considers the factors in paragraph 606-10-25-21 and determines that the promise to transfer each good and service to the customer is separately identifiable from each of the other promises (thus, the criterion in paragraph 606-10-25-19(b) is met). In particular, the entity observes that the installation service does not significantly modify or customize the software itself, and, as such, the software and the installation service are separate outputs promised by the entity instead of inputs used to produce a combined output.

Additional Questions

4. Discuss: Did you find the Section 55 example to be analogous to the Friendly Appliance example? Explain what value this example adds to your understanding of the Friendly Appliance example.

Now **YOU** Try **6.13b**

Next, Friendly should consider consulting accounting firm guidance (such as Big 4 guide books) to confirm its views on this issue. Once Friendly determines what separate performance obligations it has to the customer, the company can determine *when* it has satisfied these obligations, and what amount of revenue should be recorded.

Take a moment now to review your process for evaluating this guidance.

5. Explain your process (and sections reviewed) for evaluating the guidance in Topic 606. Contrast this with your process for reviewing the Friendly Appliance example under existing revenue guidance (ASC 605).

6. Which model did you find easier to navigate and apply? Why?

Again, this example focused on *what* can be recorded as separate units of accounting for revenue recognition; remember that this is just one of the five steps in the new revenue model.

Understand that there is so much more to applying the new revenue standard than we've covered in this simple example. For example, make sure your arrangement is within **scope** (Sec. 15). Also, Topic 606 introduces a **collectibility** threshold that must be met before revenue recognition can occur. And, it is important to note that the FASB has already proposed changes to its guidance on the concepts of *distinct* and *collectibility*!

The bottom line: Carefully review the revised revenue topic in full to familiarize yourself with this topic. Then, monitor FASB and TRG deliberations, as ASC 606 continues to evolve.

The next few examples in this chapter explore the recognition thresholds applicable to other Codification topics.

APPLYING DIFFERENT RECOGNITION THRESHOLDS

Uncertain Taxes: Recognize If More Likely Than Not

LO6 **Identify** the recognition threshold applicable to uncertain tax positions and subsequent events.

Differences between an entity's financial reporting amounts and its tax basis in assets and liabilities can give rise to temporary differences. These temporary differences can result in future taxable or deductible amounts and are reflected in the financial statements as deferred tax assets and liabilities.

Reporting deferred tax assets and liabilities in the financial statements can involve judgment. **ASC 740-10** (Income Taxes) establishes a two-step process for the recognition of tax positions.[22] First, entities must determine whether a tax position meets the **more-likely-than-not** threshold for recognition. Next, if this recognition threshold is met, entities must determine the appropriate measurement of the tax position. This chapter discusses only the first step in this process (recognition).

Par. 25-6 and 25-7 introduce the basic recognition principle for income tax accounting:

25-6   An entity shall initially recognize the financial statement effects of a tax position when it is more likely than not, based on the technical merits, that the position will be sustained upon examination. The term *more likely than not* means a likelihood of more than 50 percent; the terms *examined* and *upon examination* also include resolution of the related appeals or litigation processes, if any . . .

25-7   In making the required assessment of the more-likely-than-not criterion:
   a.   It shall be presumed that the tax position will be examined by the relevant taxing authority that has full knowledge of all relevant information.
   b.   Technical merits of a tax position derive from sources of authorities in the tax law (legislation and statutes, legislative intent, regulations, rulings, and case law) and their applicability to the facts and circumstances of the tax position . . .
   c.   Each tax position shall be evaluated without consideration of the possibility of offset or aggregation with other positions.

The following example illustrates application of this *more-likely-than-not* recognition threshold.

Applying the More-Likely-Than-Not Threshold—Uncertain Tax Positions

Facts: A newly formed entity has incurred net operating losses for its first 2 years in operation. However, it has seen a consistent increase in customers and improving gross profit margins

_____
[22] ASC 740-10-25-5 (Income Taxes): "This Subtopic requires the application of a more-likely-than-not recognition criterion to a tax position before and separate from the measurement of a tax position . . . ."

year-over-year. The company believes it can record a deferred tax asset or liability (that is, the net operating losses reported in its first two tax returns can be used to offset future years' taxable income). However, realizing the benefit of its net operating losses depends on having positive future taxable income. The company believes it is probable (or at least 75% likely) that its third and fourth years of operations will result in positive taxable income. Companies have a 20-year period in which net operating losses may be applied against future taxable income. Historically, the company's owners (in previous endeavors) have not let loss carryforwards expire unused. The company must determine whether this carryforward meets the more-likely-than-not threshold for recognition.

The basic principles regarding this issue are outlined in par. 25-6 and 25-7 above. Additionally, consider the following glossary and implementation guidance from **ASC 740-10**:

> **Carryforwards (ASC 740-10-20)**
>
> Deductions or credits that cannot be utilized on the tax return during a year that may be carried forward to reduce taxable income or taxes payable in a future year. An operating loss carryforward is an excess of tax deductions over gross income in a year; . . .
>
> **55-7** Subject to certain specific exceptions . . . a deferred tax liability is recognized for all taxable temporary differences, and a deferred tax asset is recognized for all deductible temporary differences and operating loss and tax credit carryforwards . . .

Questions:

1. Does the company's operating loss carryforward appear to meet the more-likely-than-not threshold for recognition? Explain why this does or doesn't seem appropriate.

   _____

   _____

   _____

2. How shall the loss carryforward be reported (as a deferred tax asset or liability)?

   _____

   _____

   _____

Effective Settlement of a Tax Position

Tax positions that do not initially meet the more-likely-than-not threshold for recognition may be recognized when certain conditions are met. Par. 25-8 of **ASC 740-10** states:

> **25-8** If the more-likely-than-not recognition threshold is not met in the period for which a tax position is taken or expected to be taken, an entity shall recognize the benefit of the tax position in the first interim period that meets any one of the following conditions:
>
> a. The more-likely-than-not recognition threshold is met by the reporting date.
> b. The tax position is effectively settled through examination, negotiation or litigation.
> c. The statute of limitations for the relevant taxing authority to examine and challenge the tax position has expired.

Determining when a tax position has been **effectively settled** (per "b" above) can involve judgment. The following example illustrates guidance on effective settlement.

Now
YOU
Try
6.15

Effective Settlement

Facts: A company claims a research and development (R&D) tax credit on its 2012 tax return. Determining which costs qualified for the R&D credit was judgmental, and the company is concerned that the IRS may question some of the individual costs comprising its amount claimed for the R&D credit. That is, the company is not sure whether, if examined, the IRS would allow the full amount of its R&D credit claimed. Accordingly, the company concluded that only a portion of the credit claimed met the more-likely-than-not threshold for recognition in its 2012 financial statements.

The company filed its 2012 tax return in February 2013, and the return showed a net tax refund due to the company. In April 2013, the company received a tax refund check from the federal government.

See par. 25-8 above. Additionally, **ASC 740-10** offers the following guidance on effective settlement.

25-9   A tax position could be effectively settled upon examination by a taxing authority. Assessing whether a tax position is effectively settled is a matter of judgment because examinations occur in a variety of ways . . .

25-10 As required by paragraph 740-10-25-8(b) an entity shall recognize the benefit of a tax position when it is effectively settled. An entity shall evaluate all of the following conditions when determining effective settlement:

a. The taxing authority has completed its examination procedures including all appeals and administrative reviews that the taxing authority is required and expected to perform for the tax position.

b. The entity does not intend to appeal or litigate any aspect of the tax position included in the completed examination.

c. It is remote that the taxing authority would examine or reexamine any aspect of the tax position. In making this assessment management shall consider the taxing authority's policy on reopening closed examinations and the specific facts and circumstances of the tax position. Management shall presume the relevant taxing authority has full knowledge of all relevant information in making the assessment on whether the taxing authority would reopen a previously closed examination.

Questions:

1. What are the three conditions that would allow for recognition of a tax position that was not previously recognized? (See excerpt from par. 25-8 on the previous page.)

_____

_____

2. Given the company's receipt of a refund check, is it appropriate to conclude that the tax position has been effectively settled (and thus, is the full tax credit eligible for financial statement recognition)?

_____

_____

Additional Facts: Assume the same facts as the previous example, but now assume that tax return has been selected for an IRS audit. The IRS staff member conducting the review has called the company to say that the audit is nearly complete, and the IRS does not have any findings. However, before the staff member can send the IRS's final written clearance of the tax year in question, the audit must be reviewed by the staff member's supervisor. The supervisor's review could result in changes to the staff member's preliminary conclusions. Management believes that, once the final audit report is received, the likelihood of the IRS re-opening this tax year for audit is remote.

3. May the company now consider its tax position to be effectively settled, and thus eligible for recognition? If not, what additional factors should be considered?

_____

_____

_____

Again, once it has been established that a tax position meets the threshold for recognition, a preparer must next evaluate measurement guidance to determine what *amount* of the tax position should be recorded.

Subsequent Events: Recognize If Conditions Existed at the Balance Sheet Date

A **subsequent event** is an event that takes place after the balance sheet date, but before financial statements are issued. Guidance for subsequent event recognition is available in Topic 855 (Subsequent Events), within the Broad Transactions area of the Codification. For public companies, the period by which financial statements must be filed is stipulated by the SEC; for nonpublic companies, the timing depends on the needs of their specific users. For public companies, for example, the SEC requires that annual financial statements be filed within 60 to 90 days of the company's fiscal year end, with the specific timing depending in part on the company's size.[23]

Companies are required to evaluate subsequent events through the date that financial statements are issued or are available to be issued. For public companies, the issue date generally corresponds with the date financial statements are filed with the SEC. Nonpublic companies should generally evaluate subsequent events through the date financial statements are available to be issued (that is, complete and approved by management).[24]

For example, General Electric Co. (GE) has a calendar year-end and generally files with the SEC in late February. For its 2014 annual financial statements, GE's subsequent events period therefore spanned from January 1 to February 27, 2015. This period is illustrated in Figure 6-5.

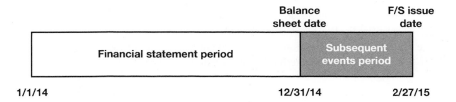

	Balance sheet date	F/S issue date
Financial statement period	Subsequent events period	
1/1/14	12/31/14	2/27/15

Figure 6-5

GE's year-end 2014 subsequent events period, shaded

ASC 855-10 describes two types of subsequent events in par. 25-1 and 25-3:

- **Recognized subsequent events:** Events that provide additional evidence about conditions existing at the balance sheet date, including estimates inherent in preparing the financial statements

- **Unrecognized subsequent events:** Events that provide evidence about conditions that did not exist at the balance sheet date, but which arose after the balance sheet date

---

[23] Per Section 13(a) of the 1934 Securities Exchange Act. Also as described in Section 1330.1 "Exchange Act Report Due Dates" of the SEC Division of Corporate Finance *Financial Reporting Manual.* Updated as of January 12, 2015. Page 38.

[24] ASC 855-10-25-1 through 25-3 (Subsequent Events).

Recognized subsequent events, as the name implies, require adjustment to the financial statements. Unrecognized subsequent events do not require adjustment to the financial statements. However, disclosure of such events may be required to keep the financial statements from being misleading.

Implementation guidance within Topic 855-10 provides examples of events classified as recognized versus unrecognized. The following paragraphs can be used to respond to **Now YOU Try 6.16.**

> > Recognized Subsequent Events

55-1 The following are examples of recognized <u>subsequent events</u> addressed in paragraph <u>855-10-25-1</u>:

   a.   If the events that gave rise to litigation had taken place before the balance sheet date and that litigation is settled after the balance sheet date but before the <u>financial statements are issued</u> or are <u>available to be issued</u>, for an amount different from the liability recorded in the accounts, then the settlement amount should be considered in estimating the amount of liability recognized in the financial statements at the balance sheet date.

   b.   Subsequent events affecting the realization of assets, such as receivables and inventories or the settlement of estimated liabilities, should be recognized in the financial statements when those events represent the culmination of conditions that existed over a relatively long period of time. For example, a loss on an uncollectible trade account receivable as a result of a customer's deteriorating financial condition leading to bankruptcy after the balance sheet date but before the financial statements are issued or are available to be issued ordinarily will be indicative of conditions existing at the balance sheet date. Thus, the effects of the customer's bankruptcy filing shall be considered in determining the amount of uncollectible trade accounts receivable recognized in the financial statements at balance sheet date.

> > Nonrecognized Subsequent Events

55-2 The following are examples of nonrecognized subsequent events addressed in paragraph <u>855-10-25-3</u>:

   a.   Sale of a bond or capital stock issued after the balance sheet date but before financial statements are issued or are available to be issued

   b.   A business combination that occurs after the balance sheet date but before financial statements are issued or are available to be issued (Topic <u>805</u> requires specific disclosures in such cases.)

   c.   Settlement of litigation when the event giving rise to the claim took place after the balance sheet date but before financial statements are issued or are available to be issued

   d.   Loss of plant or inventories as a result of fire or natural disaster that occurred after the balance sheet date but before financial statements are issued or are available to be issued

   e.   Losses on receivables resulting from conditions (such as a customer's major casualty) arising after the balance sheet date but before financial statements are issued or are available to be issued

   f.   Changes in the fair value of assets or liabilities (financial or nonfinancial) or foreign exchange rates after the balance sheet date but before financial statements are issued or are available to be issued

   g.   Entering into significant commitments or contingent liabilities, for example, by issuing significant guarantees after the balance sheet date but before financial statements are issued or are available to be issued.

Subsequent Events

1. Using the guidance in par. 55-1 and 55-2 above, determine whether the following events, occurring on January 15, 20X2, should be classified as recognized or unrecognized by a company whose fiscal year ended on December 31, 20X1. Include specific guidance references (e.g., 55-1a) to support your responses.

Event	Recognized or Unrecognized	Paragraph supporting your response
A customer files for bankruptcy, resulting in the write-down of the customer account receivable.		
A fire damages corporate headquarters, resulting in an impairment of the asset value.		
The company issues bonds (that is, engages in a borrowing).		
Court delivers a ruling on litigation that commenced prior to the balance sheet date.		
Equity securities in the pension fund suffer a significant decline in value.		

2. Explain what the *recognition threshold* is for determining whether a subsequent event must be recorded in current-period financial statements.

_____

_____

3. Would you have been able to evaluate the events described in this example using par. 25-1 and 25-3 guidance alone? (This guidance is shown in bullets preceding the par. 55-1 excerpt.) Explain.

_____

_____

_____

Our final example for this chapter involves the *derecognition* of liabilities. The purpose of this example is to introduce you to Section 40 (Derecognition) guidance and again to emphasize the importance of reviewing implementation guidance (Section 55).

APPLYING DERECOGNITION GUIDANCE: LIABILITY EXTINGUISHMENTS

ASC 405-20 (Extinguishments of Liabilities) provides guidance on when it is appropriate to derecognize a liability (see browse path depicted in Figure 6-6). The guidance acknowledges that entities may choose to settle a liability in a number of ways, including

LO7 Apply derecognition guidance to liabilities.

■ By paying a creditor,

■ By obtaining a release from the creditor (e.g., due to default or nonpayment), or

■ By setting aside assets dedicated to the eventual settlement of a liability.[25]

---
[25] ASC 405-20-05-2 (Extinguishments of Liabilities).

Given that numerous forms of debt settlement may exist, accounting guidance has established its own criteria for determining when it is appropriate to derecognize a recorded liability. ASC 405-20 states:

> **40-1** A debtor shall derecognize a liability if and only if it has been **extinguished**. A liability has been extinguished if either of the following conditions is met:
> a. The debtor pays the creditor and is relieved of its obligation for the liability. Paying the creditor includes the following:
>   1. Delivery of cash
>   2. Delivery of other financial assets
>   3. Delivery of goods or services
>   4. Reacquisition by the debtor of its outstanding debt securities whether the securities are cancelled or held as so-called treasury bonds.
> b. The debtor is legally released from being the primary obligor under the liability, either judicially or by the creditor . . . [Emphasis added]

Following are examples demonstrating application of this guidance.

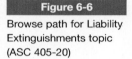
Figure 6-6

Browse path for Liability Extinguishments topic (ASC 405-20)

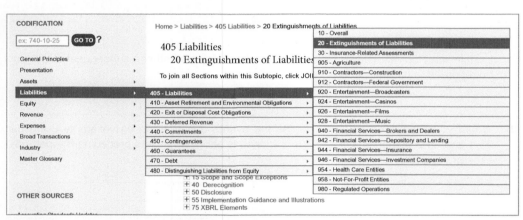

Reproduced with permission of the Financial Accounting Foundation.

In-Substance Defeasance

Now
YOU
Try
6.17

Facts: A private business owner has taken out a loan from a bank, and he has created a separate trust fund with cash equivalents (short-term U.S. treasury bonds and short-term certificates of deposit) sufficient to pay the debt. The business owner is researching whether he must continue to record the loan payable on his financial statements.

The Codification refers to the setting aside of assets, as planned payment of a debt, as an "in-substance defeasance."

The Codification[26] defines **in-substance defeasance** as:

> Placement by the debtor of amounts equal to the principal, interest, and prepayment penalties related to a debt instrument in an irrevocable trust established for the benefit of the creditor.

---

[26] ASC 470-50-20 (Debt—Modifications and Extinguishments).

In addition to applying the general derecognition principle in par. 40-1, researchers should consider the following implementation guidance from **ASC 405-20** specific to in-substance defeasances.

> > > **In-Substance Defeasance Transactions**

55-3 In an in-substance defeasance transaction, a debtor transfers essentially risk-free assets to an irrevocable defeasance trust and the cash flows from those assets approximate the scheduled interest and principal payments of the debt being extinguished.

55-4 Under the financial-components approach, an in-substance defeasance transaction does not meet the derecognition criteria for either the liability or the asset. The transaction lacks the following critical characteristics:

   a. The debtor is not released from the debt by putting assets in the trust; if the assets in the trust prove insufficient, for example, because a default by the debtor accelerates its debt, the debtor must make up the difference.

   b. The lender is not limited to the cash flows from the assets in trust.

   c. The lender does not have the ability to dispose of the assets at will or to terminate the trust.

   d. If the assets in the trust exceed what is necessary to meet scheduled principal and interest payments, the transferor can remove the assets.

   e. Subparagraph superseded by Accounting Standards Update No. 2012-04.

   f. The debtor does not surrender control of the benefits of the assets because those assets are still being used for the debtor's benefit, to extinguish its debt, and because no asset can be an asset of more than one entity, those benefits must still be the debtor's assets.

Question: Does the business owner's so-called "in-substance defeasance" allow him to derecognize the liability? Explain.

_____

_____

_____

Legal Defeasance

Now **YOU** Try 6.18

Facts: Now assume that the private business owner has taken out a loan from a bank but is unable to repay the loan. The business owner files for bankruptcy protection; the court with authority over this matter has not yet approved the terms of a bankruptcy settlement. The business owner is researching whether he can now derecognize the liability.

ASC 405-20 offers the following guidance regarding extinguishments via **legal defeasance**:

55-9 In a legal defeasance, generally the creditor legally releases the debtor from being the primary obligor under the liability. Liabilities are extinguished by legal defeasances if the condition in paragraph 405-20-40-1(b) is satisfied. Whether the debtor has in fact been released and the condition in that paragraph has been met is a matter of law . . .

Recall that the condition from par. 40-1(b) states:

> b.   The debtor is legally released from being the primary obligor under the liability, either judicially or by the creditor . . .

Question: Is it now appropriate for the business owner to derecognize the liability? If not, what additional hurdle must be met for derecognition to occur?

_____

_____

_____

_____

It's worth noting again that not all Codification topics include explicit derecognition guidance. Accordingly, determining when an asset, liability, or equity item may be removed from the balance sheet can involve judgment. In some cases, guidance from the Subsequent Measurement section can assist in this determination (as many assets and liabilities are "removed" from the balance sheet through amortization, impairment, and so on).

CHAPTER SUMMARY

Reviewing scope guidance within the Codification is a critical step in performing accounting research. Scope guidance is presented in various formats; in some cases, only those transactions or entities excluded from the scope of the guidance are listed. In other cases, transactions within the scope of certain guidance may be named, or a scope test may be required. Before performing detailed scope tests for complex guidance, researchers should consult the topic's Overview section to see generally whether the topic is expected to apply. Judgment can be involved in applying scope guidance; in many cases, Codification implementation guidance or accounting firm resources should also be considered.

Recognition guidance describes what, when, and how items should be recorded in the financial statements. Determining whether an item qualifies for financial statement recognition involves consideration of the objectives of recognition (as outlined in the FASB's Conceptual Framework), consideration of cost/benefit constraints, and consideration of topical guidance within the Codification. Although the cases in this chapter were fairly straightforward, judgment is often involved in a researcher's application of recognition guidance. In many cases, the Codification's Implementation Guidance section should be consulted in addition to the Recognition section of a topic.

REVIEW QUESTIONS

Scope

1. What function does scope guidance serve within the Codification?
2. What are two ways that scope guidance is commonly presented within the Codification?
3. At what point during your research should you consult scope guidance?
4. What additional steps should a researcher consider performing, before undertaking a detailed scope test?
5. Briefly explain why you concluded that the New Mexico gross receipts tax is/is not within the scope of ASC 740 (Income Taxes).
6. Briefly explain why you concluded that the Texas modified gross receipts tax is/is not within the scope of ASC 740 (Income Taxes).
7. Can a company's Board member be considered an *employee* under ASC 718 (Stock Compensation)? Explain.
8. Describe what is required for an equity award granted to a nonemployee director to be accounted for under Topic 718, Stock Compensation.
9. Can implementation guidance (Section 55) ever assist in a researcher's understanding of scope guidance (Section 15)?

10. Explain the relationship between *general* and *subsection* scope guidance in ASC 845 (Nonmonetary Transactions).

11. As described in the chapter, what is a unique measurement challenge presented by nonmonetary transactions?

12. What is the threshold for how much boot can be involved in an exchange that is considered nonmonetary?

13. Name two of the indicators used to determine whether an arrangement contains a lease.

14. Name three Codification topics that could apply to a purchase of equity securities that gives the investor a non-controlling interest. Describe the applicability of each.

15. Describe the three characteristics that must be present in order for an instrument to meet the definition of a derivative.

16. In addition to evaluating whether an instrument meets the definition of a derivative, a researcher should also review section 15 to see whether the instrument qualifies for any _____.

17. In what circumstances should your review of scope guidance be included in your documentation?

Recognition

18. In addition to the four fundamental recognition criteria from CON 5, what two additional factors should a financial statement preparer consider before recording an item?

19. What four additional sources (in addition to Section 25) might a researcher consult for recognition-related guidance?

20. The chapter notes that derecognition guidance (Section 40) in the Codification is somewhat limited, but that derecognition can take place through other means, and this type of guidance can be found in other sections of the Codification. Explain this statement.

21. What is a *recognition threshold*?

22. Contrast the effective dates of ASC 605 versus ASC 606.

23. What is meant by the terms *full restrospective* and *modified retrospective* as these terms relate to ASC 606?

24. Contrast the existing CON 5 versus CON 6 approaches to revenue recognition. Which model is more similar to the revised revenue recognition model?

25. What are the two existing criteria for revenue recognition (under ASC 605)? What four additional criteria has the SEC developed for interpreting the FASB's existing model?

26. To locate guidance about the five steps in the revised revenue model, a researcher should consult (at a minimum) the _____ and _____ sections in ASC 606.

27. Contrast the process for reviewing guidance within the existing revenue recognition topic to the process you would apply to navigate the revised topic. Which model (existing or revised) requires consideration of more subtopics? Explain.

28. Why is it important to determine whether promises made to the customer are distinct? What's the significance of this concept?

29. What is the basic threshold for recognition of an uncertain tax position?

30. What does it mean for a tax position to be *effectively settled*?

31. Explain what it means for a subsequent event to be *unrecognized*. Provide one example.

32. How does an in-substance defeasance differ from a legal defeasance? Can both result in the extinguishment of a liability?

EXERCISES

Respond to the following in complete sentences, and cite your source. If you have to make any assumptions in your response, state what you assumed. Responses should primarily come from the Codification, unless otherwise noted.

Scope Exercises

1. Which entities are subject to Earnings Per Share guidance within the Codification?

2. Does the Research and Development—Overall topic within the Codification apply to activities that are unique to entities in the extractive industries, such as exploration? Explain or cite from the relevant paragraph.

3. A company has entered into a forward contract for the purchase of gold, in 2 years, for $1200/oz. Does this arrangement meet the definition of a derivative? Analyze all required parts of the definition. (You may simply refer to the guidance excerpts included within this chapter to respond.)

4. Within the scope section of ASC 815-10 (Derivatives), which guidance comes first—the definition of a derivative, or scope exceptions to this topic? Explain.

5. Guidance within the Overview section (-05) of ASC 810-10 provides a flowchart that entities should follow when evaluating whether to consolidate another entity. The flowchart is entitled "Consolidation Analysis in Subtopic 810-10."
   a. Using a bullet-point list, list the steps shown in this first flowchart.
   b. Next, navigate to the scope section of ASC 810-10. Within which scope section paragraph are *variable interest entities* defined? Name one characteristic of a VIE from this paragraph.
   c. Within which paragraph are scope exceptions to the variable interest model listed? Name one of these scope exceptions.

6. Name two examples of transactions to which the Principal Agent Considerations subtopic (of existing Revenue Recognition guidance, Topic 605) might apply.

7. What is an example of a transaction that does not qualify as a lease (and is thus excluded from the scope of lease accounting)?

8. Are environmental remediation actions undertaken at the discretion of management within the scope of the Codification's Environmental Obligations guidance?

9. Name three examples of organizations that are within the scope of healthcare entities industry guidance.

10. Locate Deloitte's most recent guide to income tax accounting, *A Roadmap to Accounting for Income Taxes*. Does Deloitte believe that refundable tax credits (whose realization does not depend on the generation of future taxable income) are within the scope of Topic 740 (Income Taxes)? Explain.

11. An entity incurs a liability to an employee that must be settled through the issuance of the company's stock, and this liability is unrelated to services provided by the employee. Is this situation within the scope of the Stock Compensation topic? Explain.

12. Does the Nonmonetary Transactions topic apply to transfers of goods from an entity to its customers in exchange for noncash consideration? Explain.

13. Does the Income Taxes topic apply to foreign taxes that are based on income? Explain.

Recognition Exercises

Revenue Recognition Exercises

14. Within ASC 606-10 (the revised revenue model), where can a researcher find:
    a. The *core principle*?
    b. The five steps for applying the core principle?
    c. The objective of the guidance in this topic?
    d. Guidance on the incremental costs of obtaining a contract with a customer?

15. Assume that Schwartz, Inc. is a public company with a calendar year end. Schwartz must determine when and how it will adopt the revised revenue standard.
    a. In what period must Schwartz first apply ASC 606-10?
    b. How must the standard be initially applied (prospectively, retrospectively)? Explain.
    c. Could Schwartz early adopt, if it chose to do so?

16. Contrast the role of *collectibility* in the evaluation of arrangements under existing (ASC 605-10), versus revised (ASC 606-10), revenue guidance.

General Recognition Exercises

17. What is the threshold for recognition of a loss contingency?

18. Are "unconditional promises to give" required to be recognized as liabilities?

19. How does a lessee's recognition of an operating lease differ from the recognition of a capital lease?

20. A retailer distributes $2 off coupons for its product in the Sunday paper. The coupon will not result in a loss to the retailer on the sale of its product. At what point should the retailer recognize the cost of this sales incentive? Respond using existing (not pending) content.

21. You own a company that sells and installs home security systems, and you routinely purchase complete camera systems for installation in customer homes. One camera system manufacturer has offered you $800 cash back after your tenth camera system purchase. So far this year, your company has purchased nine camera systems and expects to place its tenth order next month. Should this probable rebate be recognized, and how? Respond using existing (not pending) content.

22. ASC 350-40 (Intangibles—Internal Use Software) specifically states that capitalization of costs (in an internal use software project) may begin when two criteria are met. What are these two criteria?

23. How is a cost method investment recognized in an investor's financial statements?

24. At the "inception of a guarantee," what must be recognized in the guarantor's statement of financial position? You can limit your response to the one most relevant "recognition" section paragraph.

25. A customer got serious food poisoning from Tasty Feast restaurant on March 30, 20x2, necessitating a trip to the emergency room. On April 5, 20x2, the customer initiated a lawsuit. At December 31, 20x2, Tasty Feast estimated its probable loss to be $50,000. In January, 20x3, before issuance of Tasty Feast's financial statements, a judge ruled in favor of the customer and awarded the customer $80,000 in damages. Must the company recognize the effects of this ruling in its 20x2 financial statements? Explain.

26. An employer offers each of its 50 employees 20 vacation days per year. As of January, no employees have taken vacation; however, each employee has earned 1.5 days. Vacation days that are unused at the end of the year may be carried forward to the following year. The employer encourages employees to use their full vacation allotment and thus does not anticipate forfeitures. Must the employer record a liability for the employees' vacation days earned thus far?

27. When is it appropriate for a not-for-profit entity to recognize the receipt of an unconditional promise to give (a "contribution receivable") from another entity?

CASE STUDY QUESTIONS

Scope Cases

Derivative Accounting—the Normal Purchases and Normal Sales Scope Exception *Facts:* Albert, Inc sells office supplies. Albert, Inc is in the process of signing a contract for the purchase of 10 tons of softwood pulp, a timber product that is used in the production of paper products. Softwood pulp is traded on futures exchanges, such as the Chicago Mercantile Exchange (CME). Albert, Inc will deliver this raw material to its paper producer in China. All paper produced using this raw material will be purchased by Albert, Inc. Delivery will occur in one year, for a price of $900 per ton, plus an adjustment based on the consumer price index (CPI).   6.1

Required: Evaluate 1) whether Albert, Inc's purchase contract meets the definition of a derivative; and 2) whether the contract qualifies for the *normal purchases and normal sales* scope exception to derivative accounting.

Determining Whether an Arrangement Contains a Lease   6.2
Facts: You are in the Controller's Group of Theta Corp. You've been asked to review a contract granting Theta the right to mine a specified parcel of land for gold for a 3-year period from Beta Corp (Lessor). The lease agreement also grants Theta the non-exclusive right to use the existing access road which is privately-owned and currently used by Lessor, and which runs through other property owned and operated by Lessor. Lessor has agreed to maintain the road at a level that would meet standard conditions of safety and functionality. You have been provided with the following sketch of the property.

Required: Your supervisor has asked you to read the lease agreement and to determine whether this agreement should be treated as a lease for accounting purposes. Respond in the form of an issues memo. In doing so, consider first Theta's right to mine the land, and then Theta's right to use Lessor's access road. Clearly explain your conclusion and support your position with authoritative guidance from ASC 840 (Leases).

(Optional) Also, *briefly* brainstorm (but do not perform exhaustive research on) where you would go next, to determine how Theta should account for its contractual lease payments to Beta if this contract is determined not to be a lease for accounting purposes.

6.3   **Variable Interest Entity Scope Exceptions** Several scope exceptions are provided that exclude certain entities from applying the variable interest entity (VIE) model in ASC 810 (Consolidation). Following is an example involving the *not-for-profit entities* scope exception to the VIE model.

Facts: Springfield Modern, an art museum and not-for-profit entity, has purchased an equity investment in David Corp, a for-profit corporation. David Corp has loaned several works from its own private art collection to the museum.

Required: Considering the not-for-profit scope exception, determine whether the art museum is required to evaluate its involvement with David Corp under the VIE model. Next, consider whether David Corp is required to evaluate its loan to the art museum under the VIE model. To assist in your application of Codification guidance, also consult Deloitte's guide book, *Consolidation of Variable Interest Entities.*

6.4   **Asset Exchange (Drafting an Issues Memo)** *Facts:* Paper Paper, Inc. transferred equipment to Achoo, Inc. in exchange for the receipt of $1.5 million cash and a 20% equity ownership stake in Achoo. Paper's book basis in the transferred equipment was $7 million, and the equipment was recently appraised for $7.5 million. The fair value of the investment in Achoo is $6 million, and this fair value was reliably determined. The investment gives Paper significant influence over Achoo but is not a controlling financial interest in Achoo. Achoo is in the business of making and selling tissues (such as Kleenex) and will use the equipment for tissue production.

Prior to transferring the equipment, Paper used the equipment to produce paper plates and napkins. However, significant overseas competition has caused profit margins and demand for the domestic production of paper plates and napkins to fall. Production using the equipment had recently been cut down to only 1 × 8-hr shift per day. Tissues are expected to be a more profitable output, with steady consumer demand. Achoo expects to run the equipment for 3 × 8-hr shifts per day. Paper hopes the investment in Achoo will revive its slowing growth prospects.

Required: You are in the controller's group of Paper and need to prepare an accounting issues memo 1) evaluating the scope of the applicable topic, and 2) documenting the appropriate accounting for this transaction. Include in your memo the journal entries for this transaction, and explain the authoritative basis for all journal entries recorded. Consider including a picture to enhance the Facts section of the memo. Assume that Paper will account for the ownership stake in Achoo using the equity method.

Recognition Cases

6.5   **Understanding the Relationship between ASC 606-10 and ASC 340-40** Describe the relationship between ASC 340-40 and ASC 606-10. These Codification updates were issued together as part of the revised revenue recognition standard.

6.6   **Reporting Customer Discounts under ASC 606-10** Recall Schwartz Glass from Case Study 2.5. Schwartz offers its customers payment terms of 1/10, n/30, where purchasers making payment within 10 days of product receipt will receive a discount of 1% off the purchase price, or must pay the full balance due within 30 days. Schwartz has just received payment from a new customer who paid within the 10-day window and is thus entitled to the 1% discount. This discount will not result in a loss to Schwartz on the sale of the product.

Required:
1. Determine how Schwartz should account for this discount using ASC 606-10.
2. Explain how you located the relevant guidance, including the search method used, and which sections you reviewed within Topic 606.

6.7   **Applying the Definition of *Customer* in ASC 606** Yahoo frequently sells advertising space to companies that advertise on Yahoo websites. Are these ad buyers *customers*? Use ASC 606-10 to respond.

6.8   **Asset Retirement Obligation, Changes in Estimate versus Errors, Writing an Issues Memo** *Facts:* Mega-Corp's corporate headquarters, built in 1970, has asbestos in its insulation. The Company's financial statements reflect a $5 million asset retirement obligation (ARO) for the eventual remediation of the asbestos. This ARO was initially estimated and recorded in 2005 when the company adopted FIN 47, *Accounting for Conditional Asset Retirement Obligations.* (Note: Amounts recorded for AROs are generally estimated, because it is not always possible to know how much remediating asbestos—or other like issues—will ultimately cost.) MegaCorp is a public company with a calendar year-end.

While performing routine maintenance work on the facility, additional sampling identified the presence of asbestos in more places than the Company had documented during its initial estimate. The Company now believes the total cost to remediate the asbestos will be $9 million. The initial estimate ($5 million) was based on sampling around the plant for areas containing asbestos. The newly-discovered areas with asbestos were in a part of the facility that was not sampled.

Required: Assume that you are in the controller's group of MegaCorp and have been asked to prepare an accounting issues memorandum documenting your consideration of the following issues.

1. The Company's controller is questioning whether this liability for asbestos disposal is even necessary at all. He argues that asbestos must only be remediated if it is disturbed (such as through renovations), and points out that the company does not have any immediate plans to renovate the building. Respond to his question using authoritative guidance—is a liability even necessary, if the company's plans for disposal or renovation of this building are uncertain?

2. Determine whether the additional liability for the newly discovered asbestos is considered a change in accounting estimate or an error. Note that this is *not* a change in accounting principle. Support your answer using authoritative guidance.

3. Describe how the company should record this $4 million change (prospectively, or through a retrospective adjustment)? What accounts should be debited/credited? You can disregard use of present value for this example.

Chapter 7

Using the Codification to Research Measurement Issues

Ellen is observing an inventory at her client's warehouse and notices several shelves of boxes marked with the date "20X1." She pauses: that date was nearly 5 years ago! Upon further evaluation, Ellen learns that the inventory is still being sold, but infrequently. Ellen wonders whether the recorded value of this inventory has been (or should be) adjusted to account for possible obsolescence.

Back at her desk, Ellen pulls up **ASC 330** (Inventory) and begins reading about the requirement that inventory should be recorded at the lower of its cost or market value. She pauses: Does this mean that she should also refer to **ASC 820** (Fair Value Measurement)? Is market value the same as fair value?

After some quick research, Ellen understands that inventory is not measured at fair value; rather, the term "market" refers to a measurement defined specifically within **ASC 330**. Furthermore, if the recorded cost of inventory exceeds its *market value*, the recorded value of

Continued

After reading this chapter and performing the exercises herein, you will be able to

1. **Identify** common measurement attributes used within the Conceptual Framework and the Codification.

2. **Locate** sources of measurement guidance within the Codification.

3. **Understand** circumstances in which initial measurements can involve complexity, and apply initial measurement guidance to examples involving inventory, revenue arrangements, and receivables.

4. **Become** familiar with types and timing of subsequent measurements, and apply subsequent measurement guidance to examples involving inventory and receivables.

5. **Understand** the need for robust disclosure to accompany key measurement judgments.

Learning Objectives

the inventory must be adjusted. Armed with this understanding, Ellen goes on to read about how *market value* is determined.

Understanding the many different measurement attributes used in the Codification can be challenging, particularly for beginning researchers. In fact, some measurement issues can require years of experience to master. The next two chapters of this book aim to speed up your journey along this learning curve.

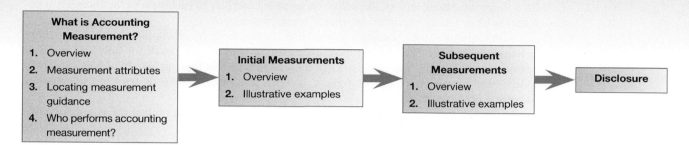

Organization of This Chapter

This chapter is the first of two that focus on accounting measurements. This chapter addresses researching measurement issues in general; Chapter 8 focuses on researching fair value measurements.

This chapter begins with background on accounting measurements, including an overview of key *measurement attributes* found in the Conceptual Framework and the Codification, followed by strategies for locating measurement guidance in the Codification. Next, this chapter highlights differences between initial and subsequent measurements and explains why measurement may be required at different times for different assets and liabilities. Illustrative examples are provided, giving readers the opportunity to apply guidance to various types of measurements. Finally, this chapter emphasizes the need for transparent disclosure to accompany key financial statement measurements.

The preceding graphic illustrates the organization of content in this chapter.

The examples selected for the two measurement chapters in this book are by no means all-inclusive. Admittedly, these chapters will only scratch the surface of the possible measurement issues you could face as a professional. However, it is a surface worth scratching. Without any overview of measurement, you will be faced with a significant learning curve as you learn this information on the job.

The examples within this chapter have been intentionally kept simple; however, in practice measurement can be highly nuanced and may require the involvement of specialists.

Our discussion of measurement primarily focuses on asset and liability measurements because, as described within the Codification's fair value topic, they are generally considered to be a "primary subject of accounting measurement."[1]

---

[1] ASC 820-10-05-1D (Fair Value Measurement).

WHAT IS ACCOUNTING MEASUREMENT?

Overview and Conceptual Background

Accounting measurement describes at what value (i.e., for how much?) a financial statement item should be recognized. Also referred to as **valuation**, measurement determines the value to be assigned to assets and liabilities both:

- initially (when acquired or constructed), and
- subsequently (for all periods after they are initially recorded).

The objective of accounting measurement is to record the economic value of a transaction. To a financial statement user, the *value* management ascribes to each item in the financial statements is often just as important as *what* is being recognized.

Limited conceptual guidance is available on the topic of measurement. That is, neither practitioners nor the FASB itself have access to an overall framework for how and when to perform accounting measurements. Rather, each Codification topic generally provides its own, independent instructions for measurement, with the notable exceptions of items measured at fair value and present value.

That said, two of the FASB's Concepts Statements do provide limited measurement guidance, as follows:

- CON 5 (*Recognition and Measurement*):
  - Lists "measurability" as one of four fundamental recognition criteria:

    Measurability—It has a relevant attribute measurable with sufficient reliability.[2]

  - Identifies and defines various **measurement attributes** (i.e., measurement methods), including historical cost, current cost, current market value, net realizable value, and present value. States that the use of each is fact-dependent.
- CON 7 (*Cash Flow Information and Present Value*):[3]
  - Describes how to measure present value and describes why present value information is relevant in certain cases.

However, these principles are considered to be of limited use in today's environment, in part because they are now somewhat dated. For example, notice how CON 5 (issued in 1984) does not even include *fair value* in its list of key measurement attributes. Also, present value guidance in CON 7 (issued in 2000) has largely been upstaged by present value guidance in **ASC 820** (Fair Value Measurement). And to be clear, the Conceptual Framework is nonauthoritative and therefore should be considered only in limited circumstances.

The FASB is in the early stages of creating a Conceptual Framework chapter focused on measurement, with the objective of establishing overarching measurement principles to guide future decision making by the Board. The new measurement chapter—when issued—is also expected to define key terms, while continuing to support the notion that the use of different measurement attributes is fact-dependent.

LO1 Identify common measurement attributes used within the Conceptual Framework and the Codification.

Measurement Attributes

As noted, each Codification topic generally sets its own rules for measurement. With the exception of *fair value* and *present value*, which are described in detail in **ASC 820**, there is no consistent definition, or framework for applying, most measurement attributes.

---

[2] FASB Concepts Statement No. 5, *Recognition and Measurement in Financial Statements of Business Enterprises* (CON 5), par. 63.

[3] Concepts Statement No. 7, *Using Cash Flow Information and Present Value in Accounting Measurements.*

Nevertheless, it is helpful to consider the broad definitions of measurement attributes that are available. Let's begin by considering CON 5's list of measurement attributes and examples of these attributes, illustrated in the following **Now YOU Try.**

Take a shot at identifying the measurement attribute from CON 5 that corresponds to the definition and example provided.

Choices of measurement attributes for this exercise are: **market value, net realizable value, historical cost, present value,** and **current (replacement) cost.**

Measurement Attribute	Definitions of these attributes	Example of this measurement
	Cash paid to acquire an asset or proceeds from issuance of a liability	Initial measurement of property, plant, and equipment, and most inventories
	The amount of cash that would be paid today to purchase the same asset	Inventory adjustments to market
	Cash that would be received by selling an asset in an orderly liquidation	Subsequent measurements of investments in marketable securities
	The value expected to be received, net of costs, from an asset held, or the net amount expected to be paid to settle a liability	Accounts receivable, after reflecting estimated uncollectible accounts
	The present, or discounted, value of a future cash flow or stream of cash flows	Measurements of long-term notes receivable and notes payable

Source: CON 5, par. 67.

Although use of these CON 5 measurement attributes is required by individual Codification topics, the broad *definitions* of these terms are not included within the Codification. Rather, the Codification defines only a handful of measurement attributes; often, these defined attributes only apply to one or two specified topic(s). For example,

- Two definitions of *net realizable value* are provided, but each definition applies narrowly to a specific topic (Inventory, Agriculture Receivables).
- *Historical cost* is defined, but the definition only applies narrowly to Topic **255** (Changing Prices).
- *Amortized cost* is defined, but the definition only applies narrowly to Topic **320** (Investments—Debt and Equity Securities).

Given this lack of broadly defined measurement attributes (fair value and present value excepted), the Codification instead relies on measurement models that are often topic-specific.

The following **Now YOU Try** illustrates several of these topic-specific measurement models.

For each of the following issues or topics, draw a line matching this issue to its corresponding topic-specific measurement model.

Issue/Topic	Topic-Specific Measurement Model
Uncertain tax positions meeting the more-likely-than-not threshold for recognition	Measure at management's *best estimate* of the possible loss or, if no one amount in a range is a better estimate than other amounts, at the *minimum amount in the range*.
Loss contingencies	Measure initially at *cost*, then adjust each period for the *investor's share of investee earnings or losses*. This measurement model reflects the investor's *proportionate ownership* share in the investee.
Multiple-element arrangements, where individual elements qualify for separate recognition*	Measure at the greatest *amount of benefit* likely to be realized upon settlement with a taxing authority.
Equity method investments	Allocate the total arrangement consideration to individual deliverables based upon the deliverables' relative selling prices.

* This description, and its corresponding measurement, relate to the *existing* revenue recognition guidance in the Codification (**ASC 605**). An example illustrating the use of the *revised* model (**ASC 606**) is presented later in this chapter.

Guidance on applying each of these measurement attributes is available within the related Codification topic. Given the uniqueness of each topic's measurement guidance, individual topics are therefore a researcher's best source for measurement guidance.

Now that you have a general understanding of the *variety* of measurement attributes available in the Codification, we will explore how a researcher can *locate* measurement guidance within the Codification.

Where Can I Find Measurement Guidance?

LO2 Locate sources of measurement guidance within the Codification.

As noted, the first step in locating measurement guidance is to consult individual Codification topics. Specifically, measurement guidance is included within Sections **30** (Initial Measurement) and **35** (Subsequent Measurement) of certain topics. Figure 7-1 illustrates the location of sample topic-specific measurement guidance.

Figure 7-1

Location of topic-specific measurement guidance within the Codification

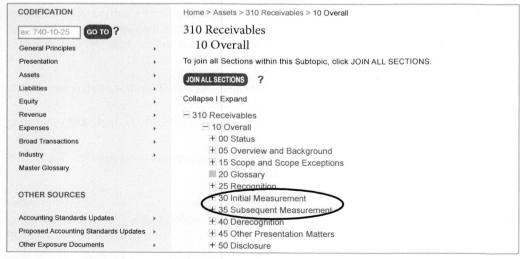

Reproduced with permission of the Financial Accounting Foundation.

For topics requiring *fair value* measurements, researchers should also consult Topic **820** (Fair Value Measurement). Within Topic 820, researchers will find detailed measurement and disclosure requirements for assets and liabilities measured using fair value. This guidance should be used *in addition to* the individual topic requiring the fair value measurement.

Figure 7-2 illustrates the browse path for accessing fair value measurement guidance.

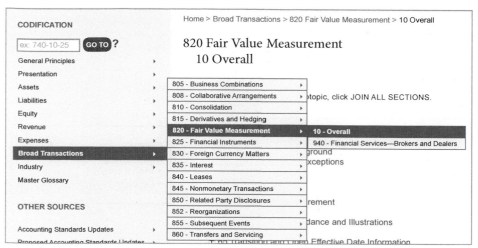

Reproduced with permission of the Financial Accounting Foundation.

Figure 7-2

Browse path for accessing Fair Value Measurement guidance (ASC 820-10)

For topics requiring *present value* measurements, researchers should also consult the "Present Value" section within Topic 820's Implementation Guidance (Section **55**). Additionally, CON 7 may be a useful resource for present value guidance, in rare cases where Topic 820 is not fully responsive to an issue. Again, this guidance should be used *in addition to* the individual topic requiring the present value measurement.

Figure 7-3 illustrates two sources of present value guidance (**ASC 820** and CON 7).

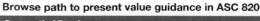

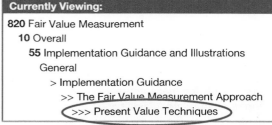

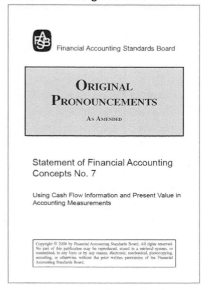

Reproduced with permission of the Financial Accounting Foundation.

Figure 7-3

Two sources of present value guidance: ASC 820 and CON 7

To recap this discussion of locating measurement guidance, complete the following **Now YOU Try** by filling in the blanks provided. This example illustrates an effective approach to researching measurement guidance.

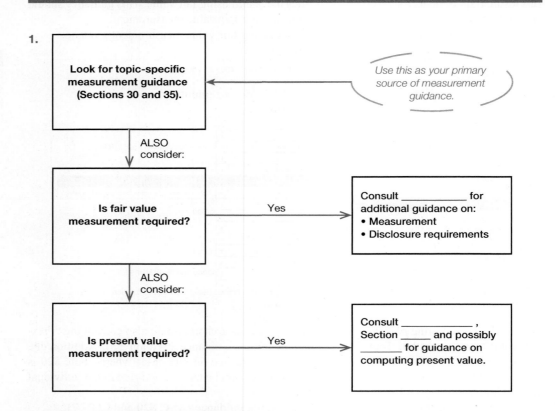

2. When **ASC 820** is consulted, it should be consulted _____ (*in addition to*? Or *instead of*?) any topic-specific measurement guidance.

Chapter 8 of this book provides additional discussion of fair value and present value measurements.

TIP from the Trenches

As with all accounting research efforts, your search for measurement guidance may not be limited to a single topic. Consideration of other related Codification topics, or of nonauthoritative resources (such as firm guide books) may be necessary to enhance your understanding of certain material.

Who Performs Accounting Measurement In Practice?

Accounting measurement has become increasingly complex in recent years, as new structured (complex) transactions have emerged, and as standard setters have placed increasing emphasis on the use of fair value measurements. Corporate accountants and auditors alike are expected to have a basic working knowledge of accounting measurement issues, yet they must also understand when an issue warrants the involvement of a specialist.

More and more, management and auditors are engaging **valuation specialists** to assist them with complex measurements. These individuals include, for example,

■ Accounting firm valuation specialists, who may be engaged to advise management on methods for measuring complex instruments and transactions such as stock compensation, bond issuances, and acquired businesses

- Actuaries, who often assist management in measuring their pension and retiree healthcare costs and obligations
- Independent valuation providers, whom management can engage on a fee-for-service basis to value complex instruments (such as the fair value of a company's bond issuances, the fair value of portfolios of investment securities, etc.)

INITIAL MEASUREMENTS

Overview

Initial measurement occurs when an item is first recorded in the accounting system. That is, assets are initially measured when they are acquired, and liabilities are initially measured when they are incurred. This is also referred to as a "day 1" measurement. For example, generally speaking,

> **LO3** Understand circumstances in which initial measurements can involve complexity, and apply initial measurement guidance to examples involving inventory, revenue arrangements, and receivables.

- Investments in equity securities are initially measured at the transaction date, at an amount equal to their purchase price.
- Many assets and liabilities acquired in business combinations are initially measured at the acquisition date, at their acquisition date fair values (subject to potential adjustments).
- Loss contingencies are initially measured when an entity determines that a loss is probable, and that the amount of loss can be reasonably estimated; loss contingencies are recorded at management's best estimate of the loss amount.

When a single asset is acquired or liability incurred, in an arm's-length transaction, the item received is generally recorded at its transaction price. Transaction price, in arm's-length transactions, is frequently presumed to equal fair value. Assuming cash is exchanged, the asset or liability is recorded for the amount of cash exchanged, and no real "measurement" is required to initially record the item.

Fair value guidance in **ASC 820-10** supports that transaction prices are frequently reflective of fair value:

> **30-3** In many cases, the transaction price will equal the fair value (for example, that might be the case when on the transaction date the transaction to buy an asset takes place in the market in which the asset would be sold).

For this reason, even different measurement attributes (e.g., historical cost, fair value) are often recorded at the same amount initially.

That said, initial measurement can be complicated for certain transactions, such as (to name a few):

- Capital assets or inventories that are self-constructed (rather than acquired), where the entity must determine which costs should be included in the capitalized value of the asset;
- Exchanges where the transaction price must be allocated among multiple acquired assets;
- Transactions where cash flows are long-term in nature and therefore must be discounted;
- Events with uncertain cash flows, such as contingent events; and
- Nonmonetary exchanges, where cash is not an available measure for determining the value of goods exchanged.

Following are illustrative examples of initial measurements. Assume that all examples in this chapter occur at arm's-length.

Applying Initial Measurement Guidance

The following Now YOU Try scenarios demonstrate initial measurement guidance using different measurement attributes:

- Acquired versus self-constructed inventory (historical cost)
- Arrangements with multiple performance obligations (relative standalone selling price method)
- Notes receivable and accounts receivable (present value)

Initial Measurement of Inventory Assets (Historical Cost)

Here's what we know: Inventory is initially measured at cost, and subsequently measured at the lower of cost or market. Simple, yes?

Maybe, maybe not. Assume that you purchase finished goods for resale to your customers. To determine the cost of the goods, you would look to the transaction price you paid to the manufacturer, plus or minus any applicable freight, discounts, and taxes. However, what if you produce the inventory in-house? In that case, judgment will be required to determine which costs should be included in the inventory's cost basis. For example, should direct labor (employee) costs be included in the inventory's cost basis? Can factory overhead costs be included?

The following Now YOU Try illustrates the application of initial measurement guidance for inventory. This example does not cover the determination of which inventory should be charged to expense when sold (e.g., use of the FIFO and LIFO methods); rather, this example focuses solely on the appropriate *cost basis* for capitalized inventory.

Initial Measurement of Inventory

Now YOU Try

7.4

Facts: TireMart operates a retail tire sale and repair shop. TireMart purchases tires from its supplier at a cost of $50 per tire, and incurs freight charges of $5 per tire (payable to a third-party delivery company).

In addition, TireMart runs its own production facility, which is dedicated to producing a line of TireMart's own brand of sporty rims. The materials cost per rim is $25. Direct labor costs for the month, a variable production cost based on hours worked, are $3,000, and the cost of utilities (light and heat) in the factory amounted to $1,000 for the month. The cost of sales personnel amounted to $2,000 for the month, and TireMart incurred $100 in direct-mail advertising expenses. TireMart had a normal production run this month, producing 100 rims.

In this example, you will be asked to determine the following:

- What amount should TireMart include in Inventory related to its tires purchased?
- Which costs should TireMart include in Inventory related to its production of rims?
- Which costs must be charged to expense as incurred?

The following excerpt from **ASC 330-10** (Inventory) provides guidance for the initial measurement of inventory.

> **> Cost Basis**
>
> **30-1** The primary basis of accounting for inventories is cost, which has been defined generally as the price paid or consideration given to acquire an asset. As applied to inventories, cost means in principle the sum of the applicable expenditures and charges directly or indirectly incurred in bringing an article to its existing condition and location. It is understood to mean acquisition and production cost, and its determination involves many considerations.

30-2 Although principles for the determination of <u>inventory</u> costs may be easily stated, their application, particularly to such inventory items as work in process and finished goods, is difficult because of the variety of considerations in the allocation of costs and charges.

30-3 For example, variable production overheads are allocated to each unit of production on the basis of the actual use of the production facilities. However, the allocation of fixed production overheads to the costs of conversion is based on the normal capacity of the production facilities. Normal capacity refers to a range of production levels. Normal capacity is the production expected to be achieved over a number of periods or seasons under normal circumstances, taking into account the loss of capacity resulting from planned maintenance. . . .

30-7 Unallocated overheads shall be recognized as an expense in the period in which they are incurred. Other items such as abnormal freight, handling costs, and amounts of wasted materials (spoilage) require treatment as current period charges rather than as a portion of the inventory cost.

30-8 Also, under most circumstances, general and administrative expenses shall be included as period charges, except for the portion of such expenses that may be clearly related to production and thus constitute a part of inventory costs (product charges). Selling expenses constitute no part of inventory costs. The exclusion of all overheads from inventory costs does not constitute an accepted accounting procedure . . .

Questions:

1. First, brainstorm the "browse path" you would use, to locate guidance for this issue.

   Example: Assets > Receivables (ASC 310) > Overall (-10) > Recognition (-25)

   Assets > _____ (ASC _____) > Overall (-10) > _____ (-____)

2. *Purchased tires*

   What per-tire amount should TireMart include in Inventory for tires purchased? $_____

   Explain the guidance from par. 30-1 supporting this conclusion: _____

   _____

3. *Rims produced by TireMart*

   For each cost listed below, indicate whether it should be included in the capitalized "Rim Inventory" asset account, or whether it must be charged to expense as incurred:

   Materials cost of $25 per rim (Example)
   Per-rim amount to capitalize? <u>$25</u>
   Rationale from guidance?
   <u>Par. 30-1 requires entities to measure inventory based on the sum of applicable expenditures and charges incurred to bring an asset to its existing condition. These materials charges were directly incurred to bring the rims to their existing condition.</u>
   Direct labor cost of $3,000 for the month
   Per-rim amount to capitalize? $_____
   Rationale from guidance? (Hint: Use par. 30-1.)

   _____

   Cost of utilities (light and heat) for the month ($1,000)
   Per-rim amount to capitalize? $_____
   Rationale from guidance?

   _____

Cost of sales personnel for the month ($2,000)
Per-rim amount to capitalize? $_____
Rationale from guidance?

Cost of direct-mail advertising expenses ($100)
Per-rim amount to capitalize? $_____
Rationale from guidance?

Total per-rim amount capitalized in Inventory: $_____
Total period expenses: $_____

Whether acquired or self-constructed, the initial measurement attribute for inventory is "cost." However, as this example demonstrates, determining the historical cost of acquired assets, where there is a third-party transaction that provides an objective basis for the inventory's value, is often more straightforward than determining which costs should be assigned or allocated to self-constructed assets.

Arrangements with Multiple Performance Obligations (Relative Standalone Selling Price)

Topic 606 (Revenue from Contracts with Customers) introduces a relatively new (or at least, amended) measurement attribute—*standalone selling price*—that is used within Topic 606, as well as in a limited number of other Codification topics. Within Topic 606, this measurement attribute is used to allocate the transaction price in arrangements with multiple performance obligations.[4]

Before we explore this measurement attribute, first recall the five-step process in the new standard, described in ASC 606-10:

> **05-4** An entity recognizes revenue . . . by applying the following steps:
> a. Step 1: Identify the contract(s) with a customer . . .
> b. Step 2: Identify the performance obligations in the contract . . .
> c. Step 3: Determine the transaction price . . .
> d. Step 4: Allocate the transaction price to the performance obligations in the contract . . .
> e. Step 5: Recognize revenue when (or as) the entity satisfies a performance obligation . . .

In the previous chapter, we evaluated Step 2 using a simple example that involved multiple performance obligations (Friendly Appliance). The following **Now YOU Try** continues the Friendly Appliance example and focuses on *how to allocate* the transaction price to these performance obligations (Step 4). This allocation issue is a question of measurement. To keep this example simple, we will assume that the transaction price of $600 is given and will not evaluate Step 3.

Now
[YOU]
Try
7.5

Facts: Recall that Friendly is an appliance retailer with two separate performance obligations to its customer; it must deliver: (1) a washing machine and (2) installation services. In exchange for this good and service, the customer will pay Friendly a total of $600.

Following is the guidance from **ASC 606-10** that describes how to allocate a transaction price to multiple performance obligations, and that introduces the *standalone selling price* measurement attribute:

---

[4] A previous version of this example, featuring the existing model's (ASC 605) *relative selling price measurement* attribute, is available on the website that accompanies this text.

32-28   **The objective when allocating the** transaction price **is for an entity to allocate the transaction price to each** performance obligation **(or distinct good or service) in an amount that depicts the amount of consideration to which the entity expects to be entitled in exchange for transferring the promised goods or services to the** customer.

32-29   To meet the allocation objective, an entity shall allocate the transaction price to each performance obligation identified in the contract on a relative standalone selling price basis in accordance with paragraphs 606-10-32-31 through 32-35...

32-31   To allocate the transaction price to each performance obligation on a relative standalone selling price basis, an entity shall determine the standalone selling price at contract inception of the distinct good or service underlying each performance obligation in the contract and allocate the transaction price in proportion to those standalone selling prices.

32-32   The standalone selling price is the price at which an entity would sell a promised good or service separately to a customer. The best evidence of a standalone selling price is the observable price of a good or service when the entity sells that good or service separately in similar circumstances and to similar customers. A contractually stated price or a list price for a good or service may be (but shall not be presumed to be) the standalone selling price of that good or service.

32-33   If a standalone selling price is not directly observable, an entity shall estimate the standalone selling price at an amount that would result in the allocation of the transaction price meeting the allocation objective in paragraph 606-10-32-28. When estimating a standalone selling price, an entity shall consider all information (including market conditions, entity-specific factors, and information about the customer or class of customer) that is reasonably available to the entity. In doing so, an entity shall maximize the use of observable inputs and apply estimation methods consistently in similar circumstances.

32-34   Suitable methods for estimating the standalone selling price of a good or service include, but are not limited to, the following:

　　a.   Adjusted market assessment approach—An entity could evaluate the market in which it sells goods or services and estimate the price that a customer in that market would be willing to pay for those goods or services. That approach also might include referring to prices from the entity's competitors for similar goods or services and adjusting those prices as necessary to reflect the entity's costs and margins.

　　b.   Expected cost plus a margin approach—An entity could forecast its expected costs of satisfying a performance obligation and then add an appropriate margin for that good or service.

　　c.   Residual approach—An entity may estimate the standalone selling price by reference to the total transaction price less the sum of the observable standalone selling prices of other goods or services promised in the contract. However, an entity may use a residual approach to estimate, in accordance with paragraph 606-10-32-33, the standalone selling price of a good or service only if one of the following criteria is met:

　　　　1.   The entity sells the same good or service to different customers (at or near the same time) for a broad range of amounts (that is, the selling price is highly variable because a representative standalone selling price is not discernible from past transactions or other observable evidence).

　　　　2.   The entity has not yet established a price for that good or service, and the good or service has not previously been sold on a standalone basis (that is, the selling price is uncertain).

Continued

> **32-35** A combination of methods may need to be used to estimate the standalone selling prices of the goods or services promised in the contract if two or more of those goods or services have highly variable or uncertain standalone selling prices . . .

Questions:

1. To understand this measurement attribute, it's important to understand the *allocation objective* in par. 32-28. As you read, bear in mind that some entities must consider variable consideration (like rebates, refunds, credits, incentives, and performance bonuses) and discounts when applying this objective. Now, describe this par. 32-28 allocation objective in your own words.

    _____

    _____

    _____

    _____

2. **ASC 606-10** establishes a sort of hierarchy for determining standalone selling price. The best evidence of standalone selling price is:

    _____

    Next, in your own words, describe what an entity should do if this price is not directly observable.

    _____

    _____

    _____

    _____

3. In your opinion, what is a possible explanation for why use of the *residual approach* is limited to only certain circumstances?

    _____

    _____

Now, assume that Friendly's management has gathered the following information about the selling prices of its two deliverables:

i. Friendly Appliance currently offers customers the option to buy (1) just the washing machine, for $500, or (2) the washing machine plus installation service for $600. Friendly Appliance does not sell installation services separately to non-customers.

ii. The price of a washing machine installation service, when performed separately by other venders, is $150.

iii. Friendly Appliance estimates that if it did sell the installation service separately, it would likely charge $150 for this service.

Additional Questions:

4. Considering the guidance from par. 32-32 and 32-34, what type of evidence (or estimation method) corresponds to each numbered piece of information from Friendly's management? Explain.

    i. _____

    _____

    ii. _____

    _____

iii. _____

_____

5. Considering management's information in the list and the "hierarchy" in **ASC 606-10**, which *source of information* provides the best evidence of standalone selling price for:

   ● The washing machine? _____

   ● The installation service? _____

6. According to the guidance, is it acceptable to use two different methods for estimating the standalone selling prices of these two items? Explain.

_____

_____

_____

7. Finally, considering the guidance provided, take a shot at showing how you would allocate the transaction price to the two performance obligations in this arrangement.

_____

_____

_____

_____

Practice, and interpretive guidance around, **ASC 606-10** is still evolving, given that this standard was issued so recently. Accordingly, you should strongly consider consulting interpretive publications (such as firm accounting guides) when faced with measurement issues involving application of the new standard. This interpretive guidance, of course, should only serve to *supplement* your consideration of the authoritative guidance in **ASC 606-10**.

Initial Measurement of Receivable Assets (Present Value)

ASC 310 (Receivables) provides guidance applicable to a range of receivables, including trade receivables, notes receivable, loan syndications (loans involving a group of lenders), and more. Yet within this topic, differences exist in the accounting prescribed for each type of receivable, just as differences exist in the nature of each receivable. For example, the terms of various receivables may differ (trade receivables generally have a short term, while notes receivable—also known in the Codification as "loans"—tend to have longer terms). Also, trade receivables are often satisfied in a single payment, while notes receivable tend to require multiple payments and often include an interest component.

Following is a simple introduction to the initial measurement guidance provided for notes receivable. Initial measurement guidance is not provided for other types of receivables within this topic. This **Now YOU Try** is intended to be a simple introduction and does not touch on all potential complexities, such as discounting, or unit of account issues (e.g., measure the receivables individually, or as a group?), and so on. These topics are, however, addressed in Chapter 8 of this book.

Now YOU Try 7.6

Measuring Receivable Assets

Facts: Assume that an entity has received a note receivable in exchange for providing significant goods and services to a customer. This transaction gives rise to the question: How should the exchange be measured? Recall that when an exchange involves cash, cash sets the "fair value" of the exchange. When a receivable is received instead of cash, an entity must determine an appropriate value for that receivable.

ASC 310-10 provides the following initial measurement guidance for notes receivable.

> > **Notes Exchanged for Cash**

30-2 . . . when a note is received solely for cash and no other right or privilege is exchanged, it is presumed to have a present value at issuance measured by the cash proceeds exchanged . . .

> > **Notes Exchanged for Property, Goods, or Services**

30-4 As indicated in paragraph 835-30-25-2, if determinable, the established exchange price (which, presumably, is the same as the price for a cash sale) of property, goods, or services acquired or sold in consideration for a note may be used to establish the present value of the note. That paragraph explains that, when notes are traded in an open market, the market rate of interest and quoted prices of the notes provide the evidence of the present value. That paragraph notes that these methods are preferable means of establishing the present value of the note.

Questions:

1. Brainstorm the "browse path" you would use, to locate guidance on the initial measurement of notes receivable.

    Assets > _____ (ASC ____) > Overall (-10) > _____(-_____)

2. Per ASC 310, what measurement attribute is used to initially record notes receivable: present value, fair value, or cost?

    _____

3. How is the present value of a note exchanged for cash generally determined?

    _____

4. Par. 30-4 describes two ways in which the present value of a note exchanged for property, goods, or services can be determined. Identify these two options for determining a note's present value.

    i) _____

    ii) _____

In this example, if a cash transaction cannot be used to establish the present value of a note receivable, researchers must look to other information. Although present value measurements are defined generally within **ASC 820** (Fair Value Measurements), researchers should also look to specific guidance within the Receivables topic, for determining the present value of notes receivable.

SUBSEQUENT MEASUREMENTS

Overview

LO4 **Become** familiar with types and timing of subsequent measurements, and apply subsequent measurement guidance to examples involving inventory and receivables.

Subsequent measurements, or "day 2" measurements, are necessary for reporting changes in recorded assets or liabilities. Subsequent measurement guidance provides both (1) information on *what subsequent value* to report for assets and liabilities and (2) information on *how to report* those changes (in which financial statement line item). Changes in recorded assets and liabilities can arise, for example, due to sales of assets or settlements of liabilities, or due to changes in the condition or market value of assets or liabilities. Examples of subsequent measurements include

■ Recording an estimate of uncollectible accounts receivable

■ Recording the effects of inventory obsolescence

■ Adjusting the recorded value of investment securities held to match market prices

■ Testing goodwill for impairment

■ Recording depreciation for fixed assets

■ Determining whether an item of property, plant, or equipment should be impaired

Each topic within the Codification specifies when subsequent measurements must be performed. In some cases, subsequent measurements may be required every period; in other cases, these measurements are only required when events or changes in circumstances (e.g., "triggering events") indicate that the carrying amount of an asset may not be recoverable. Still other cases may require assessment at different periods (such as quarterly or annually).

Following are examples of the required timing for certain subsequent measurements:

■ Investments in equity securities classified as "trading" or "available for sale" must be measured at fair value every period for which financial statements are presented (quarterly or annually).

■ Depreciation of fixed assets must be recorded every period; however, the fixed assets themselves are not generally remeasured each period.

■ Goodwill must be tested for impairment annually (or between annual tests, depending on the circumstances).[5]

■ Property, plant, and equipment held and used is tested for impairment if a triggering event occurs; property, plant, and equipment held for sale is tested for impairment each period.

Following are examples illustrating the appropriate timing and valuation for sample subsequent measurements.

Applying Subsequent Measurement Guidance

The following **Now YOU Try** scenarios continue two of our earlier illustrations: inventory and accounts and notes receivable valuations. However, notice how the measurement attributes have changed from those illustrated in our earlier examples, given that the upcoming examples involve subsequent measurements.

■ Inventory measured using LIFO (lower of cost or market)

■ Notes receivable, accounts receivable (net realizable value)

Additional scenarios illustrating subsequent measurements are included within the fair value measurement chapter of this book (Chapter 8). Those scenarios involve (1) recording unrealized gains on investment securities classified as trading and available-for-sale and (2) fixed asset impairment testing.

Subsequent Measurement of Inventory Assets (Lower of Cost or Market)

Inventory guidance within the Codification (**ASC 330**) requires that, in periods subsequent to initial measurement, inventory measured using last-in, first-out (LIFO) must be recorded at the lower of its cost or market value.[6] In applying this requirement, it is important for researchers to understand that ASC 330's definition of *market* is unique to ASC 330, and it is separate and distinct from the concept of *fair value*. ASC 330 provides detailed guidance necessary for determining the *market* value of inventory assets.

The fair value topic (**ASC 820-10**) further supports this distinction, indicating that inventory measurements are not within the scope of fair value guidance:

---

[5] Notably, an accounting alternative now exists (issued in 2014) that allows private companies to amortize goodwill and to test for impairment only if triggering events occur.

[6] The FASB recently issued guidance (ASU 2015-11) offering a simplified measurement option for inventory that is measured using first-in, first-out (FIFO). This simplified measurement option is referred to as *lower of cost and net realizable value*.

15-2(b)(2) The Fair Value Measurement Topic does not apply . . . To Sections, Subtopics, or Topics that require or permit measurements that are similar to fair value but that are not intended to measure fair value, including . . . **Topic 330**. [Emphasis added]

The glossary of ASC 330-10 defines the term **market** as follows:

As used in the phrase *lower of cost or market*, the term *market* means current replacement cost (by purchase or by reproduction, as the case may be) provided that it meets both of the following conditions:

a. Market shall not exceed the net realizable value [estimated selling price less reasonably predictable costs of completion and disposal]

b. Market shall not be less than net realizable value reduced by an allowance for an approximately normal profit margin. [Emphasis and explanation added]

Par. 35-1 through 35-5 of ASC 330, included next, provide guidance on the subsequent measurement of inventory. This guidance essentially requires a two-step evaluation to determine whether an inventory's market value has fallen below its cost:

1. First, compare the recorded inventory cost to its replacement cost (market value as previously defined).

2. If replacement cost is less (in step 1), recognize a loss if the retailer does not expect to earn normal profits upon sale of the inventory.

The following Now YOU Try continues our earlier TireMart inventory valuation example and illustrates consideration of this subsequent measurement guidance.

Now
[YOU]
Try
7.7

Inventory Subsequent Measurement

Facts: Recall our earlier TireMart example. Due to declines in consumer demand, the per-unit replacement cost for rims similar to those sold by TireMart is now $60. Assume TireMart's rims are carried in inventory at a cost of $65 per rim and that the estimated per-unit sales price, less estimated sales commissions, is $58. Assume that 50 rims remain in inventory. TireMart is considering whether the recorded value of its rims requires adjustment. TireMart's historical practice has been to record inventory obsolescence through Cost of Goods Sold and to measure its inventory using LIFO.

ASC 330-10 offers the following guidance on subsequent measurements of inventory.

> Adjustments to Lower of Cost or Market

35-1 A departure from the cost basis of pricing the <u>inventory</u> is required when the utility of the goods is no longer as great as their cost. Where there is evidence that the utility of goods, in their disposal in the ordinary course of business, will be less than cost, whether due to physical deterioration, obsolescence, changes in price levels, or other causes, the difference shall be recognized as a loss of the current period. This is generally accomplished by stating such goods at a lower level commonly designated as <u>market</u>. . . .

35-4 As a general guide, utility is indicated primarily by the current cost of replacement of the goods as they would be obtained by purchase or reproduction. In applying the rule, however, judgment must always be exercised and no loss shall be recognized unless the evidence indicates clearly that a loss has been sustained. There are therefore exceptions to such a standard. Replacement or reproduction prices would not be appropriate as a measure of utility when the estimated sales value, reduced by the costs of completion and disposal, is lower, in which case the realizable value so determined more appropriately measures utility.

35-5 Furthermore, when the evidence indicates that cost will be recovered with an approximately normal profit upon sale in the ordinary course of business, no loss shall be recognized even though replacement or reproduction costs are lower.

Questions:

1. Brainstorm the "browse path" you would use, to locate guidance on subsequent measurements of inventory.

    Assets > _____ (ASC _____) > Overall (-10) > _____ (-__)

2. Under what circumstances must companies re-evaluate the recorded cost of their inventory? (See par. 35-1)

    _____

3. Considering the guidance above, name three factors that might indicate a decline in the utility of a good.

    _____

    _____

4. What journal entry should TireMart record, to reflect the decline in its inventory value?

    dr. _____ $_____

       cr. _____ $ _____

    Citing from the guidance, explain how you arrived at this journal entry.

    _____

    _____

    _____

5. What measurement attributes did you consider in determining the appropriate subsequent measurement for TireMart's inventory? Explain.

    _____

    _____

    _____

Subsequent Measurement of Receivables (Net Realizable Value)

Subsequent to initial measurement, the value of recorded receivables may require adjustment for several reasons, including:

- To reflect cash collections
- To reflect interest accruals (for interest to be collected from borrowers) and interest income collected
- To reflect losses from uncollectible receivables or impaired loans.

CON 5 states that *net realizable value* is generally the measurement attribute used to measure short-term accounts receivable. CON 5, par. 67(d) describes net realizable value as the undiscounted amount of cash "into which an asset is expected to be converted in due course of business less direct costs. . . ."

Our next **Now YOU Try** focuses on how to measure the net realizable value of receivables; specifically, this example focuses on how to record losses related to estimated uncollectible receivables and impaired loans. This is generally a two-step process:

■ First, if an account is expected to be uncollectible (or a loan is believed to be impaired), an allowance account should be established, with a corresponding charge to income.

■ Next, if an actual loss occurs (that is, if a customer defaults or the account is written off), the allowance account should be adjusted to reflect the loss.

Subsequent measurements of both trade receivables and loans can be complex in that measuring customer credit risk (that is, the likelihood of customer nonpayment) can involve significant judgment. Additionally, the measurement of estimated credit losses can be complicated by variables such as the unit of account being measured (e.g., assess impairment for individual receivables or groups of receivables?) and the use of present value to estimate impairment allowances.

Notably, the FASB is currently revising the accounting for receivables (including, for example, loans, certain debt securities, and trade receivables) and is expected to require companies to recognize their current estimate of expected credit losses at each reporting date through the use of an allowance account, with subsequent changes in expected credit losses (both favorable and unfavorable) recognized in earnings.

The following example illustrates the concept of *net realizable value*, as well as the process for charging off losses from receivables. For simplicity, unit of account and discounting are not covered in this example; however, these topics are addressed in Chapter 8.

Now
YOU
Try
7.8

Receivables—Subsequent Measurement

This **Now YOU Try** illustrates the two-step process involved in recording losses related to estimated uncollectible receivables and impaired loans, and the guidance related to this process.

Step 1: Establish an Allowance Account

The process for establishing an allowance account under **ASC 310-10** depends on what type of receivable is being measured. The first guidance we will review applies to *trade receivables* and to *groups of small-balance loans* where individual loans within the group have not been individually evaluated for impairment. Following that, we will consider guidance on evaluating individual loans for impairment. Considering the excerpts provided, respond to the questions that follow.

> > **Losses from Uncollectible Receivables**

35-7 The conditions under which receivables exist usually involve some degree of uncertainty about their collectibility, in which case a contingency exists.

35-8 Subtopic <u>450-20</u> [Loss Contingencies] requires recognition of a loss when both of the following conditions are met:

    a. Information available before the financial statements are issued or are available to be issued . . . indicates that it is probable that an asset has been impaired at the date of the financial statements.

    b. The amount of the loss can be reasonably estimated.

35-9 Losses from uncollectible receivables shall be accrued when both of the preceding conditions are met. Those conditions may be considered in relation to individual receivables or in relation to groups of similar types of receivables. If the conditions are met, accrual shall be made even though the particular receivables that are uncollectible may not be identifiable.

Questions:

1. Brainstorm the "browse path" you would use, to locate guidance on subsequent measurements of receivables.

   Assets > _____ (ASC ____) > Overall (-10) > _____(-____)

2. In order to record an allowance for uncollectible receivables, what two conditions must be met?

   _____

   _____

3. What other Codification topic is referenced in the preceding ASC 310 excerpt, and how should it be considered?

   _____

Next, let's review the section from ASC 310-10 relating to *individual loans* that are being individually evaluated for impairment. Various factors may indicate that individual evaluation is necessary. For example, a customer's credit risk could become a concern if the customer becomes seriously delinquent in making payments (as indicated in past due reports); alternatively, knowledge that a particular customer is experiencing business interruptions or operating losses could cause an entity to question whether the customer's account is collectible.

The following guidance should be considered in determining whether individual loans, once identified for evaluation, are considered to be impaired. Guidance from this topic permitting the aggregation of similar loans has been omitted for simplicity.

> > **Assessing Whether a Loan Is Impaired**

35-16 A loan is impaired when, based on current information and events, it is probable that a creditor will be unable to collect all amounts due according to the contractual terms of the loan agreement. All amounts due according to the contractual terms means that both the contractual interest payments and the contractual principal payments of a loan will be collected as scheduled in the loan agreement . . .

35-18 The term *probable* is used consistent with its use in Subtopic 450-20 [Loss Contingencies] . . .

> > **Measurement of Impairment**

35-20 Measuring impairment of a loan requires judgment and estimates, and the eventual outcomes may differ from those estimates. Creditors shall have latitude to develop measurement methods that are practical in their circumstances.

35-22 When a loan is impaired (see paragraphs 310-10-35-16 through 35-17), a creditor shall measure impairment based on the present value of expected future cash flows discounted at the loan's effective interest rate, except that as a practical expedient, a creditor may measure impairment based on a loan's observable market price, or the fair value of the collateral if the loan is a **collateral-dependent loan**. If that practical expedient is used, Topic 820 [Fair Value Measurement] shall apply.

35-24 . . . If the present value of expected future cash flows (or, alternatively, the observable market price of the loan or the fair value of the collateral) is less than the **recorded investment** in the loan . . . a creditor shall recognize an impairment by creating a valuation allowance with a corresponding charge to bad-debt expense or by adjusting an existing valuation allowance for the impaired loan with a corresponding charge or credit to bad-debt expense . . .

4. What general principle applies, for determining *whether* a loan is impaired?

    _____

5. What three methods are described in par. 35-22 for *measuring* an impairment loss?

    _____

6. Where might a researcher go to find additional guidance on the expected cash flow method of measuring present value? *Hint:* Locating guidance for present value measurements was discussed earlier in this chapter.

    _____

7. If an impairment must be recognized, what two accounts should the creditor adjust?

    dr. _____

          cr. _____

Step 2: Charge-offs to reflect actual losses

Recall that the second step in recognizing impairment losses, generally after recording an allowance for estimated losses, is to write off accounts deemed uncollectible. The following guidance from ASC 310-10 provides guidance for this entry.

> ### > Credit Losses for Loans and Trade Receivables
>
> **35-41** Credit losses for loans and trade receivables, which may be for all or part of a particular loan or trade receivable, shall be deducted from the allowance. The related loan or trade receivable balance shall be charged off in the period in which the loans or trade receivables are deemed uncollectible. Recoveries of loans and trade receivables previously charged off shall be recorded when received.

8. What journal entry is generally required when a credit loss occurs?

    dr. _____

          cr. _____

9. Was the term *net realizable value* used in any of the literature provided for this example? Explain. If not, explain whether the definition of this term is consistent with the evaluation you performed.

    _____

    _____

    _____

    _____

This example demonstrated the process for performing "day 2" measurements of certain receivables. It's worth noting, however, that this guidance does not apply equally to all industries. Certain industries have specialized accounting practices for receivables; for example, companies in the financial services–mortgage banking industry are required to report certain loans at the lower of cost or fair value.

Through the preceding examples, you have had the opportunity to think critically about, and to apply, several measurement attributes from the Codification. The next section of this chapter briefly describes the relationship between measurement and disclosure.

DISCLOSURE SHOULD ACCOMPANY KEY MEASUREMENT JUDGMENTS

Transparent disclosure should accompany key financial statement measurements, regardless of the measurement attribute used.

Disclosure provides management with the opportunity to explain its choices of measurement methods and the judgments involved in calculating reported amounts. Additionally, disclosure provides financial statement regulators and users with transparency into these methods and judgments.

LO5 **Understand** the need for robust disclosure to accompany key measurement judgments.

The Securities and Exchange Commission (SEC) has historically been a strong proponent of transparent disclosure, emphasizing that companies should clearly explain key financial statement measurements and measurement policies. At times, the SEC has expressed its concerns about disclosure transparency to individual companies (in the form of comment letters), in "Dear CFO" letters issued to public companies in general, and in public speeches. In certain cases, if the SEC determines that corporate disclosures are false or misleading, or otherwise violate securities laws, the agency may bring enforcement actions against individuals or corporations.

Financial statement users also frequently request more transparent disclosures about measurement. During the deliberations of FASB Statement No. 157, *Fair Value Measurements* (later codified as **ASC 820**), for example, investors encouraged the Board to require expanded disclosures of fair value measurements based on unobservable inputs:

> Those users strongly supported the expanded disclosures. They indicated that the expanded disclosures would allow users of financial statements to make more informed judgments and segregate the effects of fair value measurements that are inherently subjective, enhancing their ability to assess the quality of earnings broadly.[7]

Given the importance of accompanying measurements with clear disclosure, challenge yourself as a researcher to always consult Section **50** ("Disclosures") when performing research related to measurement issues.

CHAPTER SUMMARY

Given the lack of broad framework for applying most measurement principles, researchers must consult individual Codification topics for measurement guidance specific to each topic. Within each topic, measurement guidance generally describes when measurement is required, how changes in values should be measured, and how these changes should be reported in the financial statements. Fair value and present value measurements are unique in that a consistent definition of these measurement attributes has been established, as we will discuss further in Chapter 8.

This chapter only scratched the surface of the wide range of measurement issues that researchers may encounter in practice; however, it is only with practice that researchers will become familiar with these issues.

Given that accounting measurement involves judgment and complexity, accountants must take care to provide transparent and thoughtful disclosures about the selection of measurement bases and measurement assumptions. Specialists should be involved, as necessary, in helping to interpret complex measurement guidance.

REVIEW QUESTIONS

1. What is accounting measurement, and what is its objective?
2. What two Concepts Statements address the issue of accounting measurement, and how?
3. What can we expect from the FASB's current project to develop a new Conceptual Framework chapter on measurement?
4. What is a measurement attribute? Are most measurement attributes defined in the Codification?

---

[7] FASB Statement No. 157, *Fair Value Measurements*, par. C98.

5. What measurement attributes are defined in CON 5? What is one measurement attribute that is missing from CON 5?

6. Generally speaking, where should a researcher begin his or her search for measurement guidance?

7. What additional guidance should a researcher consult if the topic requires the use of *fair value*? What if the topic involves *present value*?

8. Inventory costing is a matter of (initial/subsequent?) measurement. Inventory obsolescence is a matter of (initial/subsequent?) measurement.

9. What does it mean, for most of the Codification's measurement guidance to be "topic-specific"? What implications does this have for a researcher, looking for measurement guidance in the Codification?

10. Describe two circumstances in which an initial measurement might involve complexity.

11. Describe two circumstances in which a valuation specialist might be engaged to assist with an accounting measurement.

12. Complete the following sentence: Transaction price, in an arm's-length transaction, is generally presumed to equal _____.

13. What is the initial measurement attribute for inventory? Does this attribute change if inventory is purchased, versus self-constructed? Explain.

14. Describe two ways in which the present value of a note receivable exchanged for property, goods, or services might be determined.

15. What measurement attribute is used to allocate a transaction price to multiple performance obligations?

16. What is the *allocation objective* when allocating a transaction price to multiple performance obligations?

17. Name two examples of subsequent measurements.

18. What measurement attribute applies to the subsequent measurement of receivables?

19. Describe the process for determining whether the value of inventory should be written down, below its cost.

20. Explain why disclosure should accompany key measurement judgments, and provide two examples of parties who lobby for increased transparency in disclosures.

EXERCISES

Respond to the following using guidance in the Codification. Cite your sources for all responses.

Measurement and the Concepts Statements

1. *a.* Go to the Contents page for CON 5. In what paragraphs can a researcher find guidance on *measurement attributes*?
   b. What attribute is generally associated with long-term payables? Explain.

2. Go to the Contents page for CON 7. In what paragraphs can a researcher find guidance on the *traditional* and *expected cash flow* approaches to present value? Next, read par. 20-23. Summarize the key points you believe the FASB is making with this example.

Other Measurement Topics

Respond to the following using guidance in the Codification. Cite your sources for all responses.

3. What basic measurement principle exists for the measurement of nonmonetary transactions? What are two examples in which modifications to the basic principle apply?

4. Perform a keyword search for the term "unit of account" in the Codification. List two of the topics highlighted in your search results, where "unit of account" is a consideration.

5. Is measurement guidance (in Sections 30 or 35 of the applicable topic) available regarding employer obligations for compensated employee absences (such as vacation accruals)? If not, think: Where else might a researcher look for such measurement guidance within this topic?

6. Several assumptions are involved in an employer's measurement of its liability for defined benefit pension benefits. Name three of these assumptions. *Hint:* This is located under the topic related to an *employer's* accounting for pensions; this differs from a pension *plan's* accounting.

7. In periods subsequent to initial measurement, is goodwill amortized? Explain and cite the Codification reference for your response.

8. Generally, how are guarantees initially measured? What are the requirements for day 2 (subsequent) measurements of guarantees?

9. Once an entity has determined that it is probable of having an environmental remediation liability, what costs must the entity initially include in its estimated environmental remediation liability (an "environmental obligation")?

10. What are some of the variables, or assumptions, that enter into the initial measurement of a company's asset retirement obligation? Consider, for example, a wood utility pole, pressure-treated with a chemical preservative and which requires special disposal procedures. What are some factors the company should consider when initially estimating the ultimate disposal cost of this asset? To fully respond, also consider implementation guidance.

11. When should an investor, applying the "equity method" of accounting for an investment, recognize equity method income—in the period the investee reports earnings, or in the period the investee declares a dividend?

12. In periods subsequent to the acquisition date in a business combination, what guidance is available regarding the measurement (by an acquirer) of contingent liabilities assumed? Assume the contingencies were recognized as of the acquisition date.

13. Under Topic 835-20 (Capitalization of Interest), what amount of interest may initially be capitalized as part of the initial investment in an asset, for certain qualifying assets? How should a company determine its "capitalization rate" for capitalizing interest?

14. *a.* What is a *valuation allowance*, as this term relates to income tax accounting?
    b. What guidance within ASC 740-10 requires that entities consider applying a valuation allowance to deferred tax assets?
    c. What are some considerations relevant in determining whether a valuation allowance is required?

15. Refer to the Friendly Appliance example described in this chapter.

    Assume that by the time Friendly completes installation of the washing machine in the year 20X2, its price for selling washing machines (individually, without installation services) has increased to $550. Should this price increase affect Friendly's allocation for this particular arrangement? Explain.

CASE STUDY QUESTIONS

Determining Whether an Impairment Is "Other Than Temporary," Writing an Email Assume you are an auditor, and your client is a public company with a large portfolio of available-for-sale equity securities. The client reports these securities at fair value, with unrealized gains and losses recognized in "other comprehensive income," an equity account, each period.   **7.1**

The client is preparing its quarterly financial statements and is again—for the second consecutive quarter—recording a decline in market value for several of the securities. These securities' fair values are now below their cost. From experience, you know that losses on available-for-sale securities must be recognized in *earnings* if (1) the securities are considered *impaired* (i.e., cost basis in excess of fair value) and (2) if the impairment is considered "other than temporary." Your client has asserted that it has the ability and intent to hold the securities, at least until their value recovers, and believes that the losses need only be recognized in OCI.

Locate the relevant accounting guidance, then draft an email to your audit supervisor (Sean) that

- tells him about this issue,
- explains the general requirement regarding impairment of available-for-sale securities, describes your evaluation of whether the change in security values should be considered an other-than-temporary impairment (and therefore recognized in earnings), and
- suggests next steps.

It may be difficult to reach a definitive conclusion regarding whether impairment is required; however, it is important that you make your supervisor aware of this issue and the relevant guidance. Consider all sources of "required reading" in your response. Try to be succinct, while fully addressing the issue (try not to overwhelm your supervisor with an overly lengthy email).

Accrual for a Lawsuit, Writing an Issues Memo Your company has just been named as defendant in a lawsuit related to a leak of chemicals, from one of your company's plants onto private property. The plaintiff is suing for $5 million in damages; your company's attorneys believe the ultimate amount of loss could range between $1 million   **7.2**

and $3 million, with no amount in the range more likely than other amounts in the range. The lawsuit is expected to be resolved in the middle of next year.

Citing from authoritative literature, prepare a brief accounting issues memo to the files addressing (1) whether a loss should be accrued, and for what amount, and (2) what disclosures should be made in the company's financial statements.

7.3   **Measurement Attributes Used in Public Company Balance Sheets** Working with a group, choose a U.S. public company and locate its most recent year-end balance sheet in the company's 10-K. (Alternatively, your instructor may assign your class to examine a single company.) Your goal is to understand, and describe, how each asset on the balance sheet is measured, citing guidance from the Codification indicating the requirements for the measurement.

The following table and notes show an example of the deliverable you should provide. Follow this format, listing the balance sheet item, amount, and a brief summary of its measurement basis. Use additional notes to show (concisely) the Codification justification for this measurement, as well as to add any discussion that helps a reader's understanding of the item, or to share any facts you find interesting.

Use your own words in your explanations; do not copy directly from the company's financial statements. If you must use the company's words, provide a reference (cite the financial statements, and specific page number, as a source). In particular, when you come across balance sheet items that are industry- or company-specific, provide additional discussion of the items.

Aim for a minimum of seven total items on the balance sheet. You may elect to take a "pass" on one balance sheet item, for example, if you have difficulty locating, understanding, or explaining the item's measurement basis. However, please explain your rationale for any "passes" you elect to take.

Your group's deliverable should be no more than three to four pages (including roughly one page for the table). Feel free to be creative with your explanations/value add in your notes. For example, you can contrast your company's practices to other companies', point out items unique to your company's industry, highlight any recent changes in measurement method, and so on.

Example:

ABC Company, year-end 20X1 balance sheet

Financial Statement Item	Amount	Basis of measurement	Reference (to notes below)
Inventory	100,000	Lower of cost or market	Note 1
Loans receivable, net	200,000	Cost less uncollectible accounts reserve	Note 2

Note 1:

ABC Company has inventory, primarily in the form of purchased fuel, which it carries at cost. This is appropriate in accordance with ASC XXX-XX, which states: " ". One thing that is unique about ABC Company's inventory is that the Company . . .

Note 2:

ABC Company, through its Finance division, routinely makes loans to customers. These loans are carried at cost less a reserve for uncollectible accounts. ASC XXX-XX permits this practice, stating: " ". In 20X1, the auditors for ABC Company found that the Company's uncollectible accounts reserve policy was insufficient and issued a qualified audit opinion.

. . . and so on.

7.4   **Corporate Disclosures of Measurement Uncertainty** In 2014, General Motors Company received a great deal of negative press related to faulty ignition switches. Locate General Motors' most recent Form 10-K and describe how the company describes its methods for estimating its contingent liability associated with ignition switch legal proceedings. Describe how this disclosure supports the accrual for such losses in GM's financial statements, and describe how this disclosure meets the Codification's requirements for loss contingency disclosures.

Next, research the SEC's *Dear CFO Letter* on loss contingency disclosures, released several years ago and aimed at public companies' sparse loss contingency disclosures. Does this disclosure appear to satisfy the SEC guidance in that letter? Explain.

Chapter 8

Fair Value Measurements in the Codification

Jay is a plant accountant for NewTech Corp, a hardware manufacturing company that produces components used in the assembly of cell phones, tablet and desktop computers, and smart watches. Jay is reviewing the recorded value of equipment used to produce hardware components for desktop computers. The equipment has a carrying value of $10 million at 12/31/X1 and represents NewTech's only major investment in its PC hardware line. Recently, the industry has experienced a decline in the demand for personal computers. As a result, Jay is now researching whether the equipment should be tested for impairment.

Jay starts by determining whether a *triggering event* has occurred that will cause the company to perform a PP&E impairment test. From there, he will perform the two-step impairment test applicable to PP&E that is to be held and used. Jay understands that this issue will require him to evaluate at least two Codification topics: **ASC 360** (for PP&E) and **ASC 820** (Fair Value). Follow along with the examples in this chapter, and you too will have a stronger understanding of how to navigate and apply Codification guidance related to fair value.

After reading this chapter and performing the exercises herein, you will be able to

1. Broadly, **understand** the definition of fair value and the approaches for measuring fair value.

2. **Navigate** ASC 820, the Codification topic on fair value measurements.

3. **Understand** circumstances in which fair value measurements are required or permitted.

4. **Explain** the relationship between fair value and present value measurements.

5. **Review** valuation technique disclosures and identify key information about management's measurement approach.

Learning Objectives

Organization of This Chapter

Fair value has become an increasingly important measurement attribute—both within the Codification and in financial statements. And yet, many in our profession struggle to understand and apply fair value concepts. The objective of this chapter is to improve your comfort in applying basic fair value concepts and navigating the Codification's fair value measurement guidance.

The preceding graphic illustrates the organization of concepts in this chapter.

This chapter is not, however, an all-inclusive lesson on fair value accounting. Examples in this chapter have been kept simple for teaching purposes. However, I believe there is much to be gained from having exposure to these important concepts from the Codification, and tips for navigating the guidance, so that you'll be confident in your skills when you (inevitably!) face fair value issues in practice.

FAIR VALUE OVERVIEW

LO1 Broadly, **understand** the definition of fair value and the approaches for measuring fair value.

Unlike other measurement attributes in the Codification (present value excepted), *fair value* is unique in that its definition, and guidance for measuring fair value, is applied consistently across all Codification topics requiring the use of fair value.

Because this measurement attribute is pervasive to many topics in the Codification, this chapter is devoted to improving your comfort in applying certain fair value concepts, navigating Topic 820 (Fair Value Measurement), and understanding the relationship between Topic 820 and other Codification topics.

Let's begin with the definition of fair value. **Fair value** is defined in **ASC 820-10-20** as:

> The price that would be received to sell an asset or paid to transfer a liability in an orderly transaction between market participants at the measurement date.

More on this definition shortly. First, let's discuss some of the items that are required by the Codification to be measured at fair value.

What Is Measured at Fair Value?

The fair value measurement attribute applies to the assets and liabilities depicted in Figure 8-1, among others.

Figure 8-1

Sample assets and liabilities measured at fair value

Asset or Liability	Fair Value Measurement Takes Place on a Recurring/ Nonrecurring Basis?	Explain.
Derivative assets and liabilities		
Measurements of assets and liabilities acquired in a business combination		
Marketable debt and equity securities classified as trading or available-for-sale		
Measurement of exit or disposal activity costs		
Impairments of property, plant, and equipment (PP&E)		
Initial measurements of guarantees (a liability)		

When you look at the preceding list, you may notice that certain of these measurements take place every period, whereas other items are only measured at fair value in certain circumstances. The disclosure requirements in **ASC 820** distinguish between recurring and nonrecurring fair value measurements, as follows:

- **Recurring fair value measurements** of assets or liabilities are those that are required or permitted *each reporting period.*

■ **Nonrecurring fair value measurements** of assets or liabilities are those that are required or permitted *only in particular circumstances*.

Considering these definitions, take a moment to complete the following **Now YOU Try**.

1. Complete Figure 8-1 by indicating whether each item is measured at fair value on a recurring or nonrecurring basis. Provide a very brief explanation for each item.

2. Next, consider the case of goodwill. Public companies and certain private companies must test goodwill for impairment annually by comparing the carrying value of goodwill to its fair value.[1] Would you classify this as a recurring or nonrecurring FV measurement? Explain.

_____

_____

_____

In addition to recurring and nonrecurring fair value measurements, some items—as we'll discuss later in this chapter—are measured at fair value *for disclosure purposes* only or because the *fair value option* has been elected.

Next, let's take a closer look at how fair value is determined.

How Is Fair Value Measured?

Fair value is measured using one or more of the following three **valuation techniques**:

■ A **market approach**, where the valuation is based on market prices for identical or similar assets or liabilities;

■ A **cost approach**, where the valuation is based on the current replacement cost of an asset, as determined from a hypothetical market participant's perspective; or

■ An **income approach**, which uses valuation techniques (such as present value) that convert future cash flow amounts (or future income and expenses) into a single current amount.

These approaches can be used individually or in combination to approximate the fair value of an asset or liability.

In applying these valuation techniques, entities should select measurements that reflect the following:

■ *Market participant perspective*: Entities should focus on how potential buyers and sellers (market participants) would value their asset or liability.

■ *Exit price notion*: Entities should focus on the value they expect to receive or pay when they rid themselves of (i.e., exit) the asset or liability.

■ *Orderly transaction assumption*: Entities should assume that a hypothetical sale would occur between informed, willing market participants.

Considering the three valuation techniques and the definition of fair value, take a moment to complete the following **Now YOU Try**.

---

[1] As noted in the previous chapter, an accounting alternative now exists (issued in 2014) that allows private companies to amortize goodwill and to test for impairment only if triggering events occur. This accounting alternative does not change the annual impairment test requirement for public companies.

Now YOU Try 8.2

1. Match the following sample valuations with the valuation technique used, then explain your response.

> **i. Management estimates the value of its corporate bonds by determining the present value of the bonds using a market-based interest rate.**

> a. Market approach
> b. Income approach
> c. Cost approach

> **ii. Management estimates the value of its specialized machinery by determining the current cost of all inputs necessary to rebuild (and replace) the machine, including construction and installation costs.**

> **iii. Management values its actively traded crude oil futures using quoted prices from the Chicago Mercantile Exchange.**

i. _____

_____

ii. _____

_____

iii. _____

_____

2. Considering the **definition of fair value**, do you think that both of the following measurements are at "fair value"? Explain.

> **i. Investments in trading securities**
> Management values its portfolio of trading securities using quoted stock market prices.

> **ii. Private company investments**
> To value its investment in a nonpublic company, management uses a valuation model that considers:
> • projected future income from the investee, and
> • the trading values of similar publicly-traded companies.

_____

_____

_____

The Fair Value Hierarchy

In the preceding Now YOU Try questions, you may have noticed a difference in the degree of *observability* of certain measurements. For example, the trading securities were valued using quoted trade prices (an observable input), whereas the valuation of the private company investment relied in part upon the company's own projections (an unobservable input).

Observable inputs are inputs that are developed using market data and that reflect market participant assumptions. **Unobservable inputs** are inputs for which market data are not available and that are developed using an entity's best understanding of the assumptions that market participants would use when pricing the asset or liability. Unobservable inputs are inherently subjective.

ASC 820 requires entities to "…maximize the use of relevant observable inputs and minimize the use of unobservable inputs to meet the objective of a fair value measurement . . . ."[2]

_____

[2] ASC 820-10-35-16AA.

Given that fair value measurements can vary in their degree of observability, **ASC 820** introduced a **fair value hierarchy**, which prioritizes the use of observable inputs. For each asset or liability measured at fair value, companies must disclose the hierarchy level of the measurement. The fair value hierarchy is as follows:

■   Level 1: Measurement is observable, price is quoted by market.

■   Level 2: Measurement is mostly observable (e.g., a quoted price is available for similar assets or liabilities).

■   Level 3: Measurement relies heavily on unobservable inputs (such as management assumptions).

Considering this hierarchy, take a shot now at identifying the likely fair value hierarchy level applicable to a few sample fair value measurements.

---

1.   The following chart depicts several of the sample fair value measurements described previously in this chapter. For each asset or liability, identify its likely fair value hierarchy level and explain your rationale.*

Now
[**YOU**]
Try
8.3

Asset or Liability	Likely fair value hierarchy level?	Explain.
Derivative assets and liabilities—a futures contract for the purchase of 5,000 bushels† of corn.		
Marketable debt and equity securities classified as trading or available-for-sale		
Measurement of exit or disposal activity costs		
Impairments of property, plant, and equipment (PP&E)		
Investment in a private company, such as the private company introduced in the previous Now YOU Try.		

† This is a standard quantity for a corn futures contract.

*Note: Clearly, some of the assets or liabilities in this exercise are not specifically defined (as is the case for *exit or disposal activities*). Please think through the assets or liabilities that could be involved in such activities, then take your best shot at identifying the hierarchy level and providing your explanation for this level.

2.   In your own words, explain: What do these fair value hierarchy designations tell financial statement users about these measurements?

Let's consider now how changes in fair value are reported.

The Debits and Credits: How Are Changes in Fair Value Reported?

When an item is periodically remeasured at fair value, the asset or liability value is adjusted. But what is the offsetting debit or credit to that adjustment?

Changes in an asset or liability's value may be recorded:

- In the income statement ("**fair value through earnings**");
- In other comprehensive income ("**fair value through OCI**"); or
- In the case of certain hedged items, changes in fair value may be reported in earnings but largely offset by changes in the fair value of a related asset or liability.

To be clear, all of these measurements are considered fair value measurements, but even fair value measurements can differ in how they are recorded. Subsequent measurement guidance, available within individual Codification topics, indicates how changes in fair value must be recorded. To illustrate this point, complete the following Now YOU Try.

Now
[YOU]
Try
8.4

Assume that an entity has the following two investments:

1. An equity security classified as *trading*, whose quoted market price has increased by $10 this period.

2. An equity security classified as *available-for-sale*, whose quoted market price has increased by $10 this period.

The entity has asked for your help in reporting the changes in these securities' values.

ASC 320-10 (Investments—Debt and Equity Securities) provides the following subsequent measurement guidance for investments in marketable equity securities.

> **35-1** Investments in debt securities and equity securities shall be measured subsequently as follows:
> a. <u>Trading securities</u>. Investments in debt securities that are classified as <u>trading</u> and equity securities that have <u>readily determinable fair values</u> that are classified as trading shall be measured subsequently at <u>fair value</u> in the statement of financial position. Unrealized <u>holding gains and losses</u> for trading securities shall be included in earnings.
> b. <u>Available-for-sale securities</u>. Investments in debt securities that are classified as available for sale and equity securities that have readily determinable fair values that are classified as available for sale shall be measured subsequently at fair value in the statement of financial position. Unrealized holding gains and losses for available-for-sale securities (including those classified as current assets) shall be excluded from earnings and reported in other comprehensive income until realized . . .
> c. <u>Held-to-maturity securities</u>. Investments in debt securities classified as held to maturity shall be measured subsequently at amortized cost in the statement of financial position . . .

Questions:

1. Brainstorm how you would have browsed to the preceding guidance in the Codification.

   Assets > _____ (ASC _____) > Overall (-10) > _____ (-_____)

2. Considering the preceding excerpt, what journal entry is required for the trading security? Provide the paragraph reference from the guidance that supports this journal entry.

   dr. _____ $_____

         cr. _____ $_____   (Par. _____)

3. What journal entry is required for the available-for-sale security? Provide the paragraph reference from the guidance that supports this journal entry.

   dr. _____ $_____

         cr. _____ $_____   (Par. _____)

4. Are both securities required to be measured at fair value? Explain.

   _____

   _____

5. What approach (market, income, or cost) appears to have been used to determine the securities' fair values? Explain.

   _____

   _____

As a reminder, because **ASC 320-10** requires these investments to be recorded at fair value, entities applying this guidance should also look to ASC 820 for fair value measurement and disclosure guidance. The following guidance from ASC 820-10 is relevant to the measurement of these investments:

> 35-36B In all cases, if there is a quoted price in an active market (that is, a Level 1 input) for an asset or a liability, a reporting entity shall use that quoted price without adjustment when measuring fair value . . .

Now consider the following **Now YOU Try.**

Contrast the roles of ASC 320 and ASC 820 in describing how entities should account for investments in marketable equity securities. What function did each topic play in providing guidance for this issue?

_____

_____

_____

> **Now**
> **YOU**
> **Try**
> **8.5**

HOW DO I NAVIGATE FAIR VALUE GUIDANCE?

As illustrated in the preceding **Now YOU Try**, when you encounter a Codification topic that requires the use of fair value, you'll *also* need to consult ASC 820 (Fair Value Measurement). Located under Broad Transactions, ASC 820 is the primary source for fair value measurement and disclosure guidance within the Codification.

> **LO2** Navigate ASC 820, the Codification topic on fair value measurements.

Although ASC 820 provides guidance on *how to measure* fair value, it does not require fair value measurements in addition to those already required by other Codification topics.[3] Entities should consider fair value measurement guidance *in addition to* the individual topic that required the fair value measurement, as illustrated in the following graphic.

---
[3] ASC 820-10-05-1A (Fair Value Measurement)

Organization of ASC 820

ASC 820 (Fair Value Measurement) is organized in a manner similar to other Codification topics; that is, ASC 820 is divided into sections such as Scope, Recognition, Initial Measurement, and so on. Figure 8-2 illustrates the sections included within ASC 820.

Figure 8-2

Organization of ASC 820-10, Fair Value Measurement

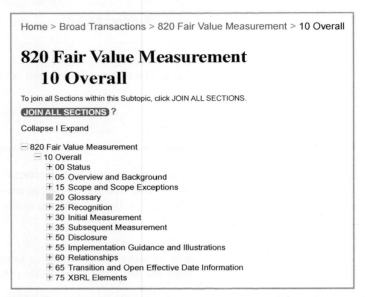

Home > Broad Transactions > 820 Fair Value Measurement > 10 Overall

820 Fair Value Measurement
10 Overall

To join all Sections within this Subtopic, click JOIN ALL SECTIONS.

JOIN ALL SECTIONS ?

Collapse I Expand

– 820 Fair Value Measurement
  – 10 Overall
    + 00 Status
    + 05 Overview and Background
    + 15 Scope and Scope Exceptions
    ▪ 20 Glossary
    + 25 Recognition
    + 30 Initial Measurement
    + 35 Subsequent Measurement
    + 50 Disclosure
    + 55 Implementation Guidance and Illustrations
    + 60 Relationships
    + 65 Transition and Open Effective Date Information
    + 75 XBRL Elements

Reproduced with permission of the Financial Accounting Foundation.

Yet, the subject matter covered by ASC 820 is clearly different from other Codification topics. That is, the objective of ASC 820 is to define the fair value measurement attribute, and to provide guidance necessary to apply that definition. Because the subject matter of ASC 820 is so unique, let's take a moment to discuss how information is organized within this topic.

Arguably, the most important section of ASC 820 is Section 35 (Subsequent Measurement). This section includes the definition of fair value, as well as extensive guidance on how to apply this definition. Section 35 also introduces the three valuation techniques for estimating fair value and discusses the classification of valuation inputs within the fair value hierarchy. Figure 8-3 illustrates the organization of content within Section 35.

Figure 8-3

Organization of ASC 820-10, Section 35 (Subsequent Measurement)

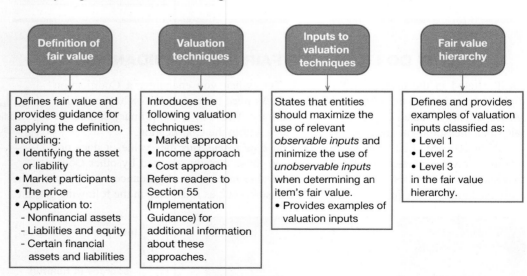

Definition of fair value	Valuation techniques	Inputs to valuation techniques	Fair value hierarchy
Defines fair value and provides guidance for applying the definition, including: • Identifying the asset or liability • Market participants • The price • Application to: - Nonfinancial assets - Liabilities and equity - Certain financial assets and liabilities	Introduces the following valuation techniques: • Market approach • Income approach • Cost approach Refers readers to Section 55 (Implementation Guidance) for additional information about these approaches.	States that entities should maximize the use of relevant *observable inputs* and minimize the use of *unobservable inputs* when determining an item's fair value. • Provides examples of valuation inputs	Defines and provides examples of valuation inputs classified as: • Level 1 • Level 2 • Level 3 in the fair value hierarchy.

Other notable sections within ASC 820, along with a brief (not all inclusive) description of their content, are shown in Figure 8-4.

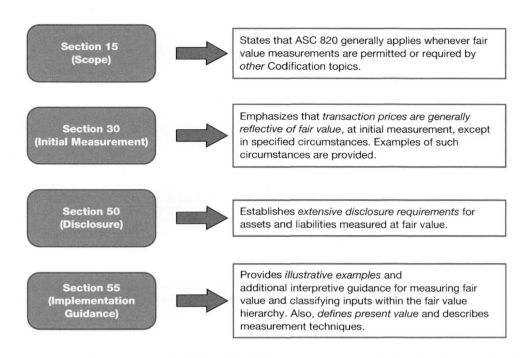

Figure 8-4

Other notable sections from ASC 820, and a brief description of their content

Section 15 (Scope)	States that ASC 820 generally applies whenever fair value measurements are permitted or required by *other* Codification topics.
Section 30 (Initial Measurement)	Emphasizes that *transaction prices are generally reflective of fair value*, at initial measurement, except in specified circumstances. Examples of such circumstances are provided.
Section 50 (Disclosure)	Establishes *extensive disclosure requirements* for assets and liabilities measured at fair value.
Section 55 (Implementation Guidance)	Provides *illustrative examples* and additional interpretive guidance for measuring fair value and classifying inputs within the fair value hierarchy. Also, *defines present value* and describes measurement techniques.

When performing research within ASC 820, remember to consider the list of *required reading* sources introduced in Chapter 2.

Finally, very extensive nonauthoritative resources—such as firm guide books, chapters in firm accounting manuals, and so on—have been devoted to the topic of fair value measurement. As noted in Chapter 5 (regarding nonauthoritative resources), these sources can be useful in *supplementing* authoritative guidance.

> Leave out the word *market* when you search for guidance on fair value. The term *fair market value* is rarely used in the Codification, and it may make you sound funny in conversation. In research and in your communications, simply refer to this measurement attribute as *fair value*.

[**TIP**] from the Trenches

Now that you understand how to navigate fair value guidance, let's take a look at other circumstances in which fair value measurements may be required or permitted.

IN WHAT OTHER CIRCUMSTANCES ARE FAIR VALUE MEASUREMENTS PERMITTED OR REQUIRED?

In addition to the assets and liabilities that are required to be measured at fair value on a recurring or nonrecurring basis, certain items are measured at fair value for disclosure purposes only, or because the fair value option has been elected.

LO3 Understand circumstances in which fair value measurements are required or permitted.

Option to Measure at Fair Value

The **fair value option** may be elected for certain financial instruments not required to be measured at fair value. This option allows entities to measure certain financial assets and liabilities at fair value on a recurring basis.

Although initially issued as a sort of sister standard to FAS 157 (*Fair Value Measurements*), FAS 159 (*The Fair Value Option for Financial Assets and Financial Liabilities*) guidance is included within a separate Codification topic: **ASC 825** (Financial Instruments). See Figure 8-5 for the browse path to this topic.

General Principles ▸
Presentation ▸
Assets ▸
Liabilities ▸
Equity ▸
Revenue ▸
Expenses ▸
Broad Transactions ▸
Industry ▸
Master Glossary

OTHER SOURCES

Accounting Standards Updates ▸
Proposed Accounting Standards Updates ▸
Other Exposure Documents ▸
Pre-Codification Standards ▸
Maintenance Updates ▸

**825 Financial Instruments
10 Overall
25 Recognition**

Table of Contents
Collapse I Expand
─ 825 Financial Instruments

805 - Business Combinations ▸
808 - Collaborative Arrangements ▸
810 - Consolidation ▸
815 - Derivatives and Hedging ▸
820 - Fair Value Measurement ▸
825 - Financial Instruments ▸
830 - Foreign Currency Matters ▸
835 - Interest ▸
840 - Leases ▸
845 - Nonmonetary Transactions ▸
850 - Related Party Disclosures ▸
852 - Reorganizations ▸
855 - Subsequent Events ▸
860 - Transfers and Servicing ▸

uidance on the required criteria,timing,and location (within

10 - Overall
20 - Registration Payment Arrangements
942 - Financial Services—Depository and Lending
944 - Financial Services—Insurance
954 - Health Care Entities

se,at specified election dates,to measure eligible items at

But how would a researcher know to look for "Fair Value Option" guidance within ASC 825? Although the placement of this guidance may seem counter-intuitive, consider this:

> *The fair value option primarily permits the use of fair value for measuring financial assets and financial liabilities.*

For example, scope guidance from ASC 825-10 indicates that entities may elect the fair value option for most financial assets and liabilities, as well as for certain other instruments (such as loan commitments and warranty rights and obligations):

15-4 All entities may elect the fair value option for any of the following eligible items:
- a. A recognized financial asset and financial liability, except any listed in the following paragraph
- b. A firm commitment that would otherwise not be recognized at inception and that involves only financial instruments . . .
- c. A written loan commitment
- d. The rights and obligations under [certain] insurance contracts . . .
- e. The rights and obligations under [certain] warrant[ies] . . .
- f. A host financial instrument resulting from the separation of an embedded nonfinancial derivative from a nonfinancial hybrid instrument . . .

That said, certain financial assets and liabilities are not eligible for the fair value option. For example, the fair value option cannot be elected for employers' pension obligations and for capital lease payment obligations (both financial liabilities). Researchers should carefully consult scope guidance in ASC 825-10 when determining whether the fair value option may be elected.

Understanding the Meaning of "Financial Assets" and "Financial Liabilities"

The FASB and IASB have long emphasized that fair value is a desirable measurement attribute for many financial assets and liabilities and, accordingly, require or permit fair value measurements for many of these.

It is therefore important when discussing the topic of fair value to understand what is meant by the terms *financial asset* and *financial liability*. Following are excerpts from the Codification describing these instruments.

Financial assets are defined as

Cash, evidence of an ownership interest in an entity, or a contract that conveys to one entity a right to do either of the following:

- Receive cash or another financial instrument from a second entity, or
- Exchange other financial instruments on potentially favorable terms with the second entity.*

Financial liabilities are defined as

A contract that imposes on one entity an obligation to do either of the following:

- Deliver cash or another financial instrument to a second entity, or
- Exchange other financial instruments on potentially unfavorable terms with the second entity.*

Together, financial assets and liabilities are referred to as **financial instruments.**

Nonfinancial assets are defined as

An asset that is not a <u>financial asset</u>. Nonfinancial assets include land, buildings, use of facilities or utilities, materials and supplies, intangible assets, or services.*

Nonfinancial liabilities are not defined in the Codification but can generally be viewed as liabilities that are not financial liabilities. Examples include obligations to deliver goods or services.**

*Source: FASB Codification Master Glossary.   **Source: ASC 820-10-35-18.

Financial Assets and Liabilities

Now **YOU** Try **8.6**

1. Using the preceding definitions, complete the following table by indicating what part of the definition of *financial asset* or *financial liability* is met for each item.

Financial Assets/Liabilities	Part of definition met?
Cash	
Accounts receivable	Example: A contract that conveys "the right to receive cash"
Investments in equity securities (shares of stock)	
Stock purchase warrant (a right to buy stock at specified price)	
An in-the-money forward contract to buy shares of IBM (a derivative asset)	
Accounts or notes payable	
Derivative liabilities, such as an out-of-the-money forward contract to buy shares of IBM	

2. What term is used to collectively refer to *financial assets* and *financial liabilities*?

Items Measured at Fair Value for Disclosure Purposes

Also included in **ASC 825** (Financial Instruments) is a requirement that public and large non-public companies must disclose their financial instruments at fair value, whether measured at fair value on the balance sheet or not. Therefore, even an entity's *own debt*, such as bond issuances recorded at amortized cost, must be disclosed at fair value given that an entity's own debt is a financial liability.

Within this disclosure, companies must reflect the instrument's carrying amount, fair value, and the fair value hierarchy level of the measurement. Companies must also describe their valuation techniques for measuring the instruments' fair values.

For example, Figure 8-6 illustrates a disclosure from Wells Fargo's 2014 Annual Report. Wells Fargo's disclosures state that the table presents the fair value of financial instruments not measured at fair value on a recurring basis.

			Estimated fair value		
(in millions)	Carrying amount	Level 1	Level 2	Level 3	Total
December 31, 2014					
Financial assets					
Cash and due from banks (1)	$ 19,571	19,571	—	—	19,571
Federal funds sold, securities purchased under resale agreements and other short-term investments (1)	258,429	8,991	249,438	—	258,429
Held-to-maturity securities	55,483	41,548	9,021	5,790	56,359
Mortgages held for sale (2)	3,971	—	2,875	1,098	3,973
Loans held for sale (2)	721	—	739	—	739
Loans, net (3)	832,671	—	60,052	784,786	844,838
Nonmarketable equity investments (cost method)	7,033	—	—	8,377	8,377
Financial liabilities					
Deposits	1,168,310	—	1,132,845	35,566	1,168,411
Short-term borrowings (1)	63,518	—	63,518	—	63,518
Long-term debt (4)	183,934	—	174,996	10,479	185,475
December 31, 2013					
Financial assets					
Cash and due from banks (1)	$ 19,919	19,919	—	—	19,919
Federal funds sold, securities purchased under resale agreements and other short-term investments (1)	213,793	5,160	208,633	—	213,793
Held to maturity securities	12,346	—	6,205	6,042	12,247
Mortgages held for sale (2)	2,884	—	2,009	893	2,902
Loans held for sale (2)	132	—	136	—	136
Loans, net (3)	789,513	—	58,350	736,214	794,564
Nonmarketable equity investments (cost method)	6,978	—	—	8,635	8,635
Financial liabilities					
Deposits	1,079,177	—	1,037,448	42,079	1,079,527
Short-term borrowings (1)	53,883	—	53,883	—	53,883
Long-term debt (4)	152,987	—	144,984	10,879	155,863

(1) Amounts consist of financial instruments in which carrying value approximates fair value.
(2) Balance reflects MHFS and LHFS, as applicable, other than those MHFS and LHFS for which election of the fair value option was made.
(3) Loans exclude balances for which the fair value option was elected and also exclude lease financing with a carrying amount of $12.3 billion and $12.4 billion at December 31, 2014 and 2013 respectively.
(4) The carrying amount and fair value exclude obligations under capital leases of $9 million and $11 million at December 31, 2014 and 2013, respectively.

Figure 8-6

Wells Fargo disclosure, "Disclosures about Fair Value of Financial Instruments"

This table is preceded by discussion of the valuation techniques used to measure fair value. For example, Wells Fargo states the following regarding the fair value measurement of its own debt:

LONG-TERM DEBT

Long-term debt is generally carried at amortized cost. For disclosure, we are required to estimate the fair value of long-term debt and generally do so using the discounted cash flow method. Contractual cash flows are discounted using rates currently offered for new notes with similar remaining maturities and, as such, these discount rates include our current spread levels.

Items Measured at Fair Value for Disclosure Only

Considering the excerpts from Wells Fargo's annual report, respond to the following questions.

Now
YOU
Try
8.7

1. In its valuation technique disclosure, why does Wells Fargo state that it is required to esti-mate the fair value of its debt?

_____

2. Describe the valuation method used by Wells Fargo to estimate the fair value of its own long-term debt.

_____
_____

3. What level in the fair value hierarchy is predominantly assigned to Wells Fargo's long-term debt? Explain, in light of the valuation technique, why this level is appropriate.

_____
_____
_____

4. Choose two additional assets or liabilities from the preceding table and explain why you think they are included in this disclosure. Also, brainstorm how the company may have arrived at the chosen fair value hierarchy level for these items.

_____
_____
_____
_____

It's worth noting that certain financial assets and liabilities are exempted from these disclosure requirements, such as capital lease payment obligations and employer pension liabilities.

Financial Instrument Accounting: Changes Are Coming

In the very near term, the FASB plans to issue guidance that would change the current model for financial instrument accounting. These changes are expected to do away with the concepts of _trading_ and _available-for-sale_ securities, instead requiring all equity investments not subject to the equity method of accounting to be measured at fair value through net income. However, the proposed changes would allow companies to apply a practicability exception for equity investments without a readily determinable fair value, which may be measured at cost (as adjusted for impairment or observable price changes). Visit the FASB website for updates on this project.

WHAT IS THE RELATIONSHIP BETWEEN FAIR VALUE AND PRESENT VALUE?

Historically, **present value** has been thought of as distinct from _market_ value, and present value was even at one point made the focus of an entire FASB Concepts Statement (CON 7—Present Value Measurements). Today, however, our view of the relationship between these measurement attributes has shifted to the following:

LO4 Explain the relationship between fair value and present value measurements.

> _Present value is a method for measuring fair value._

There are two reasons for which a researcher might use a present value measurement:

■ First, a Codification topic may require the use of present value.

■ Or second, a Codification topic may require the use of fair value, and a researcher may determine that an income approach, using present value, is an appropriate method for measuring fair value.

In either case, researchers looking for present value measurement guidance should consult ASC 820-10, Section 55 (Implementation Guidance), in addition to considering guidance from the individual topic requiring the use of present value. Within Section 55, alternative methods for measuring present value are described: the discount rate adjustment technique and the expected present value technique.

That said, in the unlikely event that present value guidance within ASC 820, Section 55, is not fully responsive to a researcher's questions, CON 7 (Present Value Measurements)—a nonauthoritative source of guidance—may be consulted.

To illustrate, the following Contributions Payable example involves a fair value measurement using an income approach.

Contributions Payable: Measuring Fair Value Using an Income Approach

Per ASC 720-25 (Contributions Made), contributions payable are initially recorded at fair value.

> **30-1** Contributions made shall be measured at the fair values of the assets given or, if made in the form of a settlement or cancellation of a donee's liabilities, at the fair value of the liabilities cancelled.

Contributions payable are considered nonrecurring fair value measurements because they are not required to be remeasured at fair value in periods subsequent to initial measurement.

Section 35 (Subsequent Measurement) of Topic 820 provides certain guidance specific to the fair value measurement of liabilities. In particular, Topic 820-10 provides a hierarchy for measuring the fair value of liabilities, prioritizing methods that result in the most observable valuations.

> **35-16BB** . . . a reporting entity shall measure the fair value of the liability or equity instrument as follows:
>   a. Using the quoted price in an active market for the identical item held by another party as an asset, if that price is available
>   b. If that price is not available, using other observable inputs, such as the quoted price in a market that is not active for the identical item held by another party as an asset
>   c. If the observable prices in (a) and (b) are not available, using another valuation technique, such as:
>   1. An income approach (for example, a present value technique that takes into account the future cash flows that a market participant would expect to receive from holding the liability or equity instrument as an asset; see paragraph 820-10-55-3F)
>   2. A market approach (for example, using quoted prices for similar liabilities or instruments classified in shareholders' equity held by other parties as assets; see paragraph 820-10-55-3A). [Emphasis added]

In other words, the use of present value techniques to determine the fair value of a liability is generally acceptable when quoted market prices for the same, or similar, liabilities are not available.

ASC 820-10 describes different techniques for measuring present value under the income approach:

- The **discount rate adjustment technique**, which measures the present value of future cash flows using an estimated market discount rate.

- An **expected present value technique**, using a combination of expected cash flows (which may/may not be adjusted for risk) and discount rates (which may or may not be adjusted for risk). Two variations of this technique are available.

The first technique is considered to be most appropriate when future cash flows are fixed or contractual in amount, per **ASC 820-10**:

> **55-10** The **discount rate adjustment technique** uses a single set of cash flows from the range of possible estimated amounts, whether contractual or promised (as is the case for a bond) or most likely cash flows . . . The discount rate used in the discount rate adjustment technique is derived from observed rates of return for comparable assets or liabilities that are traded in the market . . . [Emphasis added]

The following example illustrates use of an income approach and, specifically, use of the discount rate adjustment technique, for measuring fair value.

Measuring Fair Value Using an Income Approach

Now **YOU** Try 8.8

Facts: Assume that Herbert Financial, LLC has just announced its commitment to donate $1 million to its local Chamber of Commerce, in 2 years.

Herbert has concluded that:

- This promise to give is not an actively-traded contract. Rather, it is a unique contract between two parties (donor and recipient). Therefore, no quoted price is available in an active (or inactive) market for identical or similar contracts.

- Therefore, use of an income approach (such as a present value technique) is appropriate.

Given that Herbert's future cash flows are fixed in amount, Herbert has determined that use of the discount rate adjustment technique is appropriate for measuring present value. Under this technique, Herbert will use its contractual cash flows, and will discount these cash flows using an observable, market rate for comparable company liabilities.

Herbert observes the interest rates offered on 2-year corporate bonds of companies with a credit rating similar to its own (assume a BB rating), and notes that these rates approximate 10%. Accordingly, Herbert concludes that a 10% discount rate is appropriate for the measurement of its contribution liability.

Herbert computes the present value of its liability as follows:

Year	Contractual Cash Flow	Risk-Adjusted Discount Rate	Present Value
2	$1 million	10%	$826,446*

*Present value = Future value / (1 + interest)^{time}. That is, PV= $1M / (1.1^2)

Questions:

1. What browse path did Herbert follow to identify the measurement requirements for contribution liabilities?

   Expenses > Other Expenses (720) > _____ (-25) > _____ (-30)

2. What *measurement attribute* must Herbert use to measure its contribution liability? Cite the guidance supporting your response.

3. What fair value measurement approach (market or income) did Herbert select for this liability. and how did Herbert conclude that this was appropriate?

_____

_____

_____

4. In your own words, explain: Which present value measurement approach (discount rate adjustment, or expected cash flows) did Herbert select, and why?

_____

_____

5. Explain what it means for a discount rate to be based on "observed" rates of return.

_____

_____

Next, let's turn our attention to a key fair value disclosure requirement: valuation techniques.

VALUATION TECHNIQUE DISCLOSURES: AN INSIGHT INTO HOW FAIR VALUE MEASUREMENTS ARE PERFORMED

LO5 **Review** valuation technique disclosures and identify key information about management's measurement approach.

Fair value measurements—both recurring and nonrecurring—are subject to extensive disclosure requirements. These include disclosure of the fair value hierarchy level (1, 2, or 3), as well as disclosure of the *valuation techniques* used to measure each class of assets and liabilities measured at fair value.

Notably, items measured at fair value on a nonrecurring basis are only subject to these disclosure requirements for fair value measurements that occur *subsequent to an item's initial measurement*. So in the preceding example, Herbert Financial's contribution liability would not be subject to fair value disclosure requirements, because fair value is only required at the initial measurement of this liability.

Valuation technique disclosures can assist financial statement users in understanding how a company arrived at the fair values reported in the balance sheet.

Consider an example. Companies' investment portfolios often include a mix of debt and equity securities. Like investments in marketable equity securities, debt securities classified as *trading* or *available-for-sale* are measured at fair value with changes recorded through income or through OCI.

Following are two common types of securities held by companies with large investment portfolios:

- Investments in "risk-free" U.S. Treasury Notes (i.e., government bonds)
- Investments in corporate bonds (such as IBM bonds, GM bonds, etc.)

Imagine that you have been asked to assign a value to these two types of debt securities (government bonds and corporate bonds). Given that most debt securities' trade prices are not quoted on public exchanges, where would you even begin?

Debt securities are frequently traded through brokers, and recent pricing data for these trades can be used as an observable input to determine the price of the same, or similar, debt securities. Think of valuing debt like obtaining market comps for your home's value, where you would adjust up or down if the comparable homes have more or fewer bathrooms. If recent trade data for a similar debt security are available, adjustments may be required to reflect differences in the specific securities (e.g., adjustments for differences between the issuers' credit standing, or adjustments for the trading volume of different securities). Therefore, valuing debt can involve consideration of multiple inputs, given that quoted prices may not be readily available.

Companies often rely on market pricing services in order to value large investment portfolios, such as by engaging *pricing vendors* to determine the value of each security within the portfolio as of the balance sheet date. Some companies with significant investments may subscribe to services that allow them to perform their own market research. For example, companies that lease Bloomberg terminals can use the terminals to query the real-time values of debt securities using recent trade data.

The following Now YOU Try further illustrates valuation technique disclosures for debt securities.

Valuation Technique Disclosures: Debt Securities

Facts: Following are excerpts from the annual reports of General Electric Company (GE) and Morgan Stanley, which describe each company's valuation techniques related to investments in certain government and corporate debt securities. Using these excerpts, you will be asked to respond to the questions that follow.

GE describes its valuation technique related to government and corporate debt securities as follows:

> Since many fixed income securities do not trade on a daily basis, the methodology of [our] pricing vendor uses available information as applicable such as benchmark curves, benchmarking of like securities, sector groupings, and matrix pricing . . . Thus, certain securities may not be priced using quoted prices, but rather determined from market observable information. These investments are included in Level 2 and primarily comprise our portfolio of corporate fixed income, and government, mortgage and asset-backed securities.[4]

Next, the following excerpt from Morgan Stanley's 2014 Annual Report discusses Morgan Stanley's valuation techniques related to Treasury and corporate debt securities:[5]

> **U.S. Treasury Securities**
>
> U.S. Treasury securities are valued using quoted market prices. Valuation adjustments are not applied. Accordingly, U.S. Treasury securities are generally categorized in Level 1 of the fair value hierarchy.
>
> **Corporate Bonds**
>
> The fair value of corporate bonds is determined using recently executed transactions, market price quotations (where observable), bond spreads, credit default swap spreads [an indicator of credit risk], at the money volatility and/or volatility skew obtained from independent external parties such as vendors and brokers. . . . When position-specific external price data are not observable, fair value is determined based on either benchmarking to similar instruments or cash flow models with yield curves, bond or single name credit default swap spreads and recovery rates as significant inputs. Corporate bonds are generally categorized in Level 2 of the fair value hierarchy; in instances where prices, spreads or any of the other aforementioned key inputs are unobservable, they are categorized in Level 3 of the fair value hierarchy. [Comments added]

Questions:

1. What information does GE's pricing vendor use to measure its debt securities' fair values?

_____

_____

---

[4] GE 2014 Form 10-K, p.145.

[5] Morgan Stanley 2014 10-K. Pages 173–175.

2. What inputs does Morgan Stanley use in valuing corporate debt securities?

    _____

    _____

3. Contrast GE's fair value hierarchy level assigned to government (Treasury) securities to the level assigned by Morgan Stanley. Explain your understanding of why these differ.

    _____

    _____

    _____

As you can see, the valuation of debt securities can be complex and involves consideration of many variables. Additionally, assigning the appropriate fair value hierarchy level to investments can involve judgment; for example in this case, the two companies chose a different fair value hierarchy level for similar instruments (Treasury securities).

Finally, consider the following illustrative example, which walks through impairment testing for an item of property, plant, and equipment.

FIXED ASSETS: TESTING FOR IMPAIRMENT USING FAIR VALUE

Long-lived assets (excluding those acquired in a business combination) are initially measured at historical cost and are subsequently measured at amortized cost (i.e., cost net of depreciation).

However, in certain circumstances, entities must test the cost basis of long-lived assets or asset groups for impairment. The timing of this testing depends upon how the PP&E is classified under **ASC 360** (Property, Plant, & Equipment):

■   If PP&E is classified as *held and used*: The cost basis shall be tested for recovery when events or changes in circumstances (i.e., *triggering events*) indicate that the carrying amount of the asset or asset group may not be recoverable. Triggering events might include, for example, a significant decrease in the market price for an asset or asset group, or current period operating losses related to operation of an asset or asset group.

■   If PP&E is classified as *held for sale*: For every period that an asset is considered "held for sale," entities must compare the asset (or asset group)'s current carrying value to its fair value less costs to sell.

Classification as *held and used* versus *held for sale* depends upon an entity's plans for the asset (e.g., whether the asset is being used in operations, or whether it is available for immediate sale). The model for measuring impairments differs between these two classifications; this discussion will focus only on assets classified as held and used.

The following two-step test is used to determine whether an impairment loss must be recognized for an asset classified as held and used.[6]

---

[6] ASC 360-10-35-17 (Property, Plant, and Equipment): "An impairment loss shall be recognized only if the carrying amount of a long-lived asset (asset group) is not recoverable and exceeds its fair value. The carrying amount of a long-lived asset (asset group) is not recoverable if it exceeds the sum of the undiscounted cash flows expected to result from the use and eventual disposition of the asset . . . An impairment loss shall be measured as the amount by which the carrying amount of a long-lived asset (asset group) exceeds its fair value."

Step 1. Determine whether the asset's carrying value exceeds the sum of the undiscounted cash flows expected to result from the entity's own use and eventual disposal of the asset.

If carrying value exceeds entity's internal cash flow projections, go to Step 2.

Step 2. Measure an impairment loss for the amount by which the asset's carrying amount exceeds its fair value.

That is, if during an impairment evaluation, an entity concludes that the cost basis of an asset held and used is not recoverable (Step 1), the asset's carrying value shall be adjusted to fair value (Step 2). Future depreciation shall be recorded based on this new cost basis.

The following example illustrates an impairment test for PP&E to be held and used.

Testing Property, Plant, and Equipment for Impairment: Step 1

Now **YOU** Try **8.10**

Facts: Recall NewTech Corp, the hardware manufacturing company introduced in our opening scenario to this chapter. Let's revisit the valuation of NewTech's equipment, considering the following facts.

Recall that NewTech owns specialized equipment used to produce a hardware component for desktop computers. This equipment, having a carrying value of $10 million at 12/31/20X1, represents NewTech's only major investment in its PC hardware line, and cash flows from the equipment are largely independent of cash flows from NewTech's other assets. Therefore, NewTech has concluded that the equipment, by itself, is the appropriate unit of accounting for this asset. The equipment's estimated useful life is 3 years, and the equipment is expected to have a residual value of $0.5 million at that time.

As noted previously, changes in the business climate for personal computers have caused NewTech to reassess its future cash flow projections associated with the equipment. Specifically, the increasing market share occupied by the tablet computer market has decreased the demand for NewTech's hardware, and has caused NewTech to lower its earnings projections related to sales of its hardware. Given this change in business climate and projected earnings, plant accountants believe it is necessary to test the equipment for impairment.

Questions:

1. Before we continue further into this example, take a moment to brainstorm the browse path you would use, to locate guidance on impairments of PP&E.

   Assets > _____ (ASC _____) > Overall (-10) > _____ (-_____)

2. Also, identify the "triggering event" that caused NewTech to perform this impairment test.

To perform step 1 of the impairment test, NewTech accountants considered the following guidance from **ASC 360-10**:

35-29 Estimates of future cash flows used to test the recoverability of a long-lived asset (asset group) shall include only the future cash flows (cash inflows less associated cash outflows) that are directly associated with and that are expected to arise as a direct result of the use and eventual disposition of the asset . . .

35-30 Estimates of future cash flows used to test the recoverability of a long-lived asset (asset group) shall incorporate the entity's own assumptions about its use of the asset (asset group) . . .

Notice that the step 1 test does not involve a *fair value* measurement, which would focus on market participant assumptions. Instead, the step 1 test indicates that an entity should use its own, undiscounted assumptions about use of the asset. In this case, NewTech has taken into consideration two alternatives for the asset's use and disposal, and the possible cash flows generated under each alternative.

The following box illustrates "step 1" of NewTech's impairment test.

Step 1 test: Determine whether the asset's carrying value exceeds the undiscounted cash flows expected to arise from use and disposal of the asset.

Carrying value: Expected cash flows (in millions):

$10 million vs.

Scenarios for use/disposal of equipment	Cash flows from use of assets	Cash flows from disposition	Likelihood of realizing these cash flows	Probability- weighted cash flows	Likelihood of selling in 1 year, vs 3 years	Total
Sell in 1 year . . .	3	6	50% × (3 + 6)	4.5		
	4	6	50%	5.0		
Total for scenario				9.5	60%	5.7
Sell in 3 years . .	7.5	0.5	50%	4.0		
	9.5	0.5	50%	5.0		
Total for scenario				9	40%	3.6
Expected cash flows (undiscounted)						9.3

---

3. Does carrying value exceed the entity's own total expected cash flow projections? _____

    Therefore, should NewTech go on to step 2 of the impairment test? _____

4. If NewTech sells the equipment in 1 year, what two possible cash flow amounts might it expect to generate from *use* of the asset? _____ or _____

5. Which scenario (sell in 1 year versus sell in 3 years) results in higher probability-weighted cash flows? Explain.

    _____

6. Does NewTech believe that it is more likely it will sell the equipment in 1 year, or that it will sell the equipment in 3 years? Explain.

    _____

7. Was this "step 1" test intended to determine the fair value of the equipment? Explain.

    _____

8. Explain what is meant by the terms *probability-weighted* versus *undiscounted*, in the context of this example.

    _____

    _____

    _____

Step 2 of the impairment test requires entities to measure an impairment loss for the amount by which the asset's carrying value exceeds its fair value. The following guidance from **ASC 360-10** applies to this test.

> **Measurement of an Impairment Loss**
>
> **35-17** . . . An impairment loss shall be measured as the amount by which the carrying amount of a long-lived asset (asset group) exceeds its fair value.
>
> **Fair Value**
>
> **35-36** For long-lived assets (asset groups) that have uncertainties both in timing and amount, an expected present value technique will often be the appropriate technique with which to estimate fair value.

That is, entities must record an impairment loss for the amount by which an asset's carrying amount exceeds its fair value. The fair value of long-lived assets is frequently measured using an expected present value technique.

ASC 820-10 (Fair Value Measurements) provides the following additional guidance on measuring fair value for nonfinancial assets, which involves consideration of the asset's *highest and best use.*

> **35-10A** "A fair value measurement of a nonfinancial asset takes into account a market participant's ability to generate economic benefits by using the asset in its highest and best use or by selling it to another market participant that would use the asset in its highest and best use." **Highest and best use** is defined as: . . . "the use of an asset by market participants that would maximize the value of the asset . . ."[7]

Finally, **ASC 820-10** provides the following present value measurement guidance which can assist in determining the fair value of long-lived assets.

> **55-5** Present value (that is, an application of the income approach) is a tool used to link future amounts (for example, cash flows or values) to a present amount using a discount rate. A fair value measurement of an asset or a liability using a present value technique captures all of the following elements from the perspective of market participants at the measurement date:
> a. An estimate of future cash flows for the asset or liability being measured.
> b. Expectations about possible variations in the amount and timing of the cash flows representing the uncertainty inherent in the cash flows.
> c. The time value of money, represented by . . . a risk-free interest rate . . .
> d. The price for bearing the uncertainty inherent in the cash flows (that is, a risk premium).
> e. Other factors that market participants would take into account in the circumstances. . . .[Emphasis added]
>
> **55-13** The expected present value technique uses as a starting point a set of cash flows that represents the probability-weighted average of all possible future cash flows (that is, the expected cash flows) . . .
>
> **55-15** Method 1 of the expected present value technique adjusts the expected cash flows of an asset for systematic (that is, market) risk . . .
>
> **55-16** In contrast, Method 2 of the expected present value technique adjusts for systematic (that is, market) risk by applying a risk premium to the risk-free interest rate . . .

---

[7] ASC 820-10-20 (Fair Value Measurement, Glossary)

Recall that expected present value is one possible technique for measuring present value (with another possible approach being the "discount rate adjustment technique"). Under an expected present value technique, cash flow scenarios are assigned probabilities, and then discounted.

Companies using an expected present-value technique can choose to "risk-adjust" their cash flow scenarios (Method 1), or can choose to "risk-adjust" the discount rates used to determine the expected present value (Method 2), as described in the preceding guidance excerpt.

Using this information, let's now perform step 2 of NewTech's impairment test.

Now
[**YOU**]
Try
8.11

Testing Property, Plant, and Equipment for Impairment: Step 2

Facts: NewTech has reviewed the preceding guidance from **ASC 360-10** and **ASC 820-10** regarding approaches to determining fair value, highest and best use of nonfinancial assets, and present value estimation techniques.

Based on consideration of par. 35-36 of **ASC 360-10**, NewTech believes an *expected present value technique* (an income approach) is appropriate for estimating the fair value of its equipment, given that the timing and amount of future cash flows that will be generated by the equipment is uncertain. NewTech believes an income approach is most appropriate given that it does not have reliable inputs available for estimating fair value under the market or cost approaches.

Additionally, NewTech reviewed the par. 35-10 guidance in **ASC 820-10**, regarding highest and best use of nonfinancial assets, and believes the highest and best use of its equipment would be achieved if a market participant uses the equipment to support an existing line of desktop computers. This could increase the possible applications for the equipment and could increase the potential future cash flows from the equipment. Like NewTech, a market participant would likely realize a residual value of $0.5 million upon disposal of the equipment in 3 years.

Finally, in considering how to apply the expected cash flow approach to estimating present value, NewTech has elected to use Method 2, adjusting its assumed discount rates to reflect market risks. NewTech will estimate these discount rates using the assumed rates that a *market participant* would expect to pay to borrow money.

NewTech has performed step 2 of its impairment test, as follows.

Step 2 test: Measure impairment loss as the amount by which carrying value exceeds fair value.

Carrying value: Expected present value technique (in millions):

(**$10 million** vs.)

Year of equipment's life	Possible cash flows from use of equipment	Probability of realizing	Expected cash flows (undiscounted)	Discount rate	Expected present value
Year 1.........	4.0	50%	2.00		
	5.0	50%	2.50		
Total year 1			4.50	10%	4.09
Year 2.........	3.5	50%	1.75		
	4.0	50%	2.00		
Total year 2			3.75	10%	3.10
Year 3.........	3.0*	50%	1.50		
	3.5*	50%	1.75		
Total year 3			3.25	10%	2.44
Total expected present value........					(9.63)

* Includes esimated residual value of $0.5

Questions:

1. An impairment loss _____ (should/ should not) be recognized. The amount of the loss is $_____, which represents the amount by which carrying value exceeds the asset's

   _____.

2. Explain the significance of the second column in the "expected present value" table (possible cash flows from use of equipment). What does this mean?

   _____

   _____

   _____

3. Why are the cash flows in the step 1 test not discounted, but the cash flows in the step 2 test are? As necessary, look back at guidance on both steps of the test to respond.

   _____

   _____

   _____

   _____

4. What is the new carrying value for the equipment, on which depreciation will be calculated?

   _____

Debrief—PP&E Impairment Example

Now that you have performed this simplified PP&E impairment test, you should have a general understanding for the process involved. In practice, performing impairment tests can be very complex and can require the involvement of specialists. Companies must take great care to select appropriate assumptions, such as appropriately estimating future cash flows, evaluating the likelihood of various scenarios and vetting those with management, and identifying market-appropriate discount rates, for example.

One assumption that was kept simple in this example was the "unit of account" determination. Determining whether an individual asset, versus an asset group, should be evaluated for impairment can have significant bearing on the results of the impairment test. In this example, the unit of accounting was determined to be a single asset (the specialized equipment). However, if the cash flows of this asset had been viewed as inseparable from the cash flows of other assets, increases in the fair value of other assets could have offset decreases in the fair value of this asset, avoiding the need for an impairment charge.

Finally, NewTech should be aware that this impairment will give rise to certain disclosure requirements, including disclosure as a "nonrecurring" fair value measurement in NewTech's current period financial statements. Additional disclosures are also required under ASC 360, including discussion of the facts and circumstances giving rise to the impairment, the amount of loss recorded, and methods for determining fair value.

CHAPTER SUMMARY

Fair value measurements are unique in that an authoritative definition of this measurement attribute is available and must be applied consistently across all topics requiring its use. Not only is fair value clearly defined in the Codification, but ASC 820 (Fair Value Measurement) provides extensive guidance for applying this definition to different assets and liabilities.

Accordingly, when a topic requires use of a fair value or present value measurement, researchers must consult not only the original topic, but also ASC 820 for key measurement and disclosure guidance.

Fair value measurements may be required on a recurring basis (e.g., quarterly or annually) or on a nonrecurring basis. Entities may also elect the fair value option for certain financial instruments, essentially choosing to report and disclose items at fair value on a recurring basis. Finally, certain financial assets and liabilities are required to be disclosed at fair value, despite the fact that they are recorded in the financial statements using other measurement attributes. Because of the complexity and potential for judgment involved in fair value measurements, extensive disclosure requirements apply to all assets and liabilities measured at fair value.

Applying fair value measurement guidance can be complex and can involve a specialized skill set; while this chapter attempted to introduce certain fair value principles, this is no substitute for actual experience. Consultation with valuation specialists is often necessary, in practice, to ensure that fair value measurements are performed in accordance with the guidance and with industry standards.

REVIEW QUESTIONS

1. Differentiate between recurring and nonrecurring fair value measurements. Name two examples of each.

2. Describe three *sources of guidance* a researcher might consult, when he or she comes across an individual topic requiring the use of fair value.

3. Identify the three valuation techniques available for measuring fair value, and briefly describe each.

4. What is meant by the term *observable inputs*?

5. What is the fair value hierarchy used for? What information (or, specifically, what characteristic) about a measurement does the hierarchy attempt to convey to financial statement users?

6. What are four major topical areas covered in Section 35 of the Fair Value Measurement topic (ASC 820-10)?

7. What's a key concept described within Section 30 of the Fair Value Measurement topic? Explain.

8. Where, within the Fair Value Measurement topic, would a researcher find present value guidance?

9. Identify two ways that changes in fair value might be recorded. For example, if an asset is debited to reflect an increase in its fair value, what are two possible ways the credit might be recorded?

10. What is the relationship between fair value and present value?

11. Name two alternative techniques for measuring present value. Which technique generally applies when cash flows are fixed or contractual in amount?

12. Identify two assets or liabilities for which the fair value option may be elected.

13. Where would a researcher find guidance regarding the fair value option?

14. Name one example of a financial asset and one example of a financial liability, and describe how these items meet the definition of financial asset or financial liability.

15. What changes are on the horizon for financial instrument measurements?

16. Most debt securities are not quoted on public exchanges. So, how might a financial statement preparer go about valuing a debt security?

17. Explain the difference between step 1 and step 2 of the PP&E impairment test, for assets held and used.

EXERCISES

Recognizing Uses of Fair Value

1. Using content from this chapter and the previous chapter (on measurement), indicate whether you would expect the following accounts (list loosely based on a prior GE balance sheet) to be (1) measured at fair value, (2) tested for impairment at fair value, or (3) measured on some other basis. Explain.

Assets (selected)	Measurement
Cash and equivalents	
Investment securities	
Current receivables	
Inventories	
Property, plant and equipment	
Investment in GECS (assume is an equity-method investee)	
Goodwill	
Other intangible assets	
Assets of businesses held for sale	

Exercises to Improve Your Familiarity with Guidance in ASC 820 Respond to the following, citing your sources for all responses.

2. Refer back to the list of "required reading" areas identified in Chapter 2 of this book. Applying this list to ASC 820, list all areas of "required reading" a researcher should consider when researching fair value measurement questions.

3. Briefly summarize, then explain the significance of, par. 15-1 (scope) of ASC 820-10 (Fair Value Measurement).

4. Briefly summarize par. 30-3 (initial measurement) of ASC 820-10 and provide one example listed in par. 30-3A of an instance when transaction price may not be reflective of fair value.

5. *a.* Briefly summarize par. 35-2B of ASC 820-10.
   b. Next, look for an example of a circumstance in which an asset may have restrictions on its use or sale.
   c. Finally, describe how this restriction should be considered in determining the fair value of the asset.

6. Assume that a wealthy investor owns 15% of a single, publicly traded company. In what level of the fair value hierarchy should this measurement be classified, and should the investor adjust the fair value to reflect the fact that its position would be too large to sell in a single day (without negatively impacting the share price)? Such adjustments may be described as "blockage" factors.

7. Identify one disclosure requirement that is unique to level 3 fair value measurements.

8. Are entities required to disclose valuation techniques for both recurring and nonrecurring fair value measurements? Explain.

9. *a.* Using present value guidance within Topic 820, explain the discount rate adjustment technique in your own words. Support your response with guidance as needed.
   b. Next, contrast this technique with "Method 1" of the expected present value technique.

Other Fair Value Measurement Research Questions (using Other Codification Topics and Sources)

10. Using PwC's *Global Guide to Fair Value Measurements*, look for the discussion of *market participants*, in the context of understanding broad fair value concepts. What is the role of market participants in measuring fair value, and is it necessary for an entity to identify specific market participants when forming fair value assumptions?

11. Broadly speaking, and using only Section 35 (Subsequent Measurement) guidance, how is the fair value of a company's goodwill determined for purposes of impairment testing?

12. How are trading securities measured, in periods subsequent to initial measurement? How does this differ from how available-for-sale securities are subsequently measured?

13. Explain when an impairment loss should be recognized for intangible assets other than goodwill.

14. Name two circumstances in which the carrying amount of property, plant, and equipment (PP&E) may not be recoverable and should be tested for impairment.

15. Can the carrying value of PP&E held for sale ever be "written up" (increased)?

16. How is fair value relevant in evaluating a decline in the value of an equity method investment? Such a decline might also be indicated, for example, by a series of operating losses sustained by the investee.

CASE STUDY QUESTIONS

Corporate Fair Value Disclosures Locate the most recent 10-K filing for a company of your choice. Using this filing, respond to the following, explaining each response: **8.1**

1. What are some of the company's most significant assets and liabilities that are measured at fair value on a recurring basis?
2. For the #1 most significant (by dollar amount) asset or liability, locate the company's "valuation technique" disclosure. Briefly summarize the company's approach to measuring this item.
3. Next, locate the Codification guidance requiring this (most significant) asset or liability to be measured at fair value. Specifically, please include an excerpt from the exact paragraph requiring the asset or liability to be measured at fair value.
4. What, if any, nonrecurring fair value disclosures did the company disclose? Explain.
5. Locate the company's disclosure of financial assets and liabilities disclosed at fair value, but which are not reported at fair value in the financial statements. Describe the most significant of these assets and liabilities; was the difference between carrying value and fair value significant?

8.2   Changes to Financial Instrument Accounting Research the current status of the FASB and IASB's "Financial Instruments" project. Assume you are writing an email to your supervisor, briefing her on this project. What measurement attribute(s) does the project propose (or require) companies to use for financial assets and liabilities, both at initial and subsequent measurement? What is the current status of this project, and when is guidance expected to become effective? How will this project change the current accounting for financial instruments? What might be the reasons for this difference?

8.3   Comparing Corporate Fair Value Disclosures Locate the most recent 10-K filings for two companies of your choice, but which are in the same industry. Compare their fair value disclosures. What are some differences between the categories of assets and liabilities the companies measure at fair value on a recurring basis? What are some differences in the hierarchy levels used by these companies? Explain these differences, using a tabular format with footnotes as necessary to summarize and explain differences noted.

For example,

Assets and liabilities included by Company 1 only	Assets and liabilities included by Company 2 only	Assets and liabilities for which different hierarchy levels were used
-List and describe- . . . and so on	-List and describe-	-List and describe-

8.4   Fair Value Hierarchy Levels Using guidance from the Codification (ASC 820), and the disclosure excerpts included in **Now You Try 8.9**, justify the choice of fair value hierarchy levels for GE and Morgan Stanley's Treasury and corporate debt securities.

8.5   Big Joe's Super Cars, Present Value (Revised Revenue Guidance) Big Joe's Super Cars has just sold a luxury car to customer Tim. The purchase contract establishes a base price of $60,000, plus a contractual interest rate of 4%, payable in 60 monthly installments of $1,105. Control of the car transferred to Tim when Tim signed the contract and drove off the lot. If Tim had obtained separate financing (say, a bank loan) for the purchase of the car, his interest rate would have been 6%.

What amount of revenue should Big Joe's record at the date of sale? What guidance should Big Joe's apply to the subsequent measurement of its receivable?

Next, reflect upon what measurement attribute is being used to record Big Joe's revenues. How does this approach achieve the objective of this measurement attribute?

Hint: This example will require you to perform computations. You might find it useful to use Microsoft Excel's formula options: PMT and PV. Excel walks you through how to input numbers into each formula.

8.6   Reviewing Significant Accounting Policies, Fair Value of Reporting Unit Considering the Significant Accounting Policies footnote disclosure in Nike's most recent 10-K, explain how Nike measures the fair value of a reporting unit for purposes of performing goodwill impairment testing. What value does this disclosure contribute to your understanding of the company's measurement approach? What fair value measurement approach does this reflect?

Chapter 9

Audit and Professional Services Research

You are a new staff member on the audit of Big Box Entertainment, Inc. (Big Box). You have recently befriended a first-year analyst in the controller's group at Big Box, and that individual has invited you to see a movie this weekend. The analyst receives free tickets to Big Box–affiliated theaters and has offered you one of his free tickets. It seems like a silly question, but you start to wonder whether this simple movie invitation could put your professional independence at risk. Erring on the side of caution, you research the audit professional standards and discuss the issue with your supervisor on the engagement.

As a professional, it is important to understand not only *when* auditing or ethics research is required, but also to understand *where to find* relevant research. This chapter explores types of research and sources of professional standards for circumstances where an auditor needs guidance regarding his or her own professional conduct.

Learning Objectives

After reading this chapter and performing the exercises herein, you will be able to

1. **Understand** the role of the AICPA and PCAOB in establishing professional services standards for accountants.
2. **Navigate** and **apply** auditing standards and interpretive guidance of the AICPA, applicable to nonpublic companies.
3. **Navigate** and **apply** auditing standards and staff guidance of the PCAOB, applicable to public companies.
4. **Perform** research using the AICPA's revised Code of Conduct, understanding the Conceptual Framework approach set forth in the Code.
5. **Identify** guidance applicable to other professional services engagements, including attestation, compilation, and review standards.
6. **Understand** the role documentation plays in performing audit and professional services research.

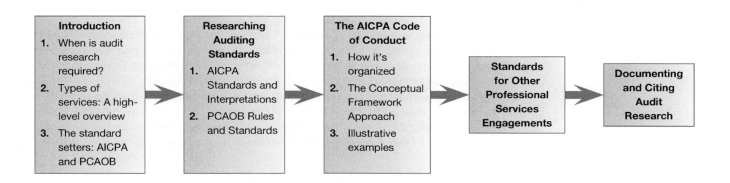

Organization of This Chapter

Previous chapters in this book have focused on accounting research—that is, research supporting an entity's financial reporting. By contrast, this chapter provides guidance on **audit and professional services research**, or research related to an accountant's own professional responsibilities and conduct.

As illustrated in the preceding graphic, this chapter introduces the roles and authority of the AICPA and PCAOB, then explores the body of auditing guidance issued by each standard setter. Next, the chapter walks through how to navigate and apply the AICPA's revised Code of Conduct, which establishes essential ethics guidance applicable to all CPAs.

Next, the chapter identifies the standards applicable to other professional services (e.g., compilations, reviews, and the like), then concludes by discussing the importance of proper documentation in auditing research.

This chapter focuses on services provided to U.S. public and nonpublic companies. Guidance for services provided to governmental and international entities is provided in Chapters 10 and 12 of this book, respectively.

INTRODUCTION TO AUDITING RESEARCH

When Is Audit Research Required?

Both as a CPA exam candidate and as a professional, you will undoubtedly encounter circumstances in which you need guidance regarding your own professional conduct. For example, you could encounter the following issues:

- If I accept gifts from my client, will my independence be impaired?

- If I disagree with my audit supervisor but don't speak up, could I be held accountable?

- What requirements must I consider when performing audit sampling?

- What documentation must be included in my audit files?

Both before and during your participation in any professional services engagement, you should become familiar with professional standards related to that engagement. For example, if you are performing an audit, you should understand the professional standards governing both (1) your own ethical conduct and independence and (2) procedures required to adequately perform the audit. As you perform the audit, you may periodically consult professional standards for guidance on how to comply with evidence, testing, and documentation requirements.

As with accounting research, areas of key risk and judgment may require documentation in the form of a research memo. In professional services research, however, your documentation might focus on whether your audit methodology and approach complied with professional standards for auditors, rather than focusing solely on the application of GAAP.

As a practicing accountant, compliance with professional standards is essential. Consequences for noncompliance can range from PCAOB inspection findings to possible license suspension and/or criminal charges. Take the time now to become familiar with key sources of professional guidance so that you can quickly reference this information when you need it.

We'll begin with a high-level introduction to the types of services provided by accountants, followed by discussion of the standard setters responsible for establishing professional services guidance.

Types of Services—A High-Level Overview

Understanding the type of client service you are providing is the first step in determining what professional guidance applies. Given the extensive education, training, and ethical standards required for CPAs, individuals with this credential are frequently entrusted to provide a diverse range of client service offerings, including reporting on both financial and nonfinancial information.

Let's briefly review a few types of professional services performed by accountants. For simplicity, we'll divide these services into two broad categories: services for which independence is required and services for which independence is not required. These categories are illustrated in Figure 9-1.

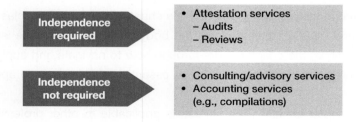

Attestation Services (Independence Required)

An **attestation service** is a type of assurance service in which an accountant *reports* on the reliability of an *assertion* that is the responsibility of a third party. Often, the accountant will issue a report naming the assertion reviewed and the accountant's conclusions on that assertion. Maintaining independence is key to an accountant's ability to objectively provide these services.

Attestation services can be performed for the benefit of an organization internally (for example, when management wishes to have an independent review of its processes) or externally (for example, for the benefit of regulators, financial statement users, etc.).

Attestation engagements include, for example,

- audits of financial statements,
- examinations of prospective financial information prepared by a client,
- financial statement reviews, and
- agreed-upon procedures (i.e., limited-scope procedures as requested by a client).

An **audit** is a specific type of attestation service in which an independent accountant provides an opinion on management's assertions, issued in the form of a report. Two of the most common audit services performed are

- financial statement audits, and
- audits of internal controls over financial reporting.

Notably, the Sarbanes-Oxley Act of 2002 ("Sarbanes-Oxley Act") requires public company auditors to express an opinion *both* on the fairness of management's financial statements and on the effectiveness of a company's internal controls over financial reporting (together referred to as an **integrated audit**).

Consulting Services, Compilations (Independence Not Required)

In **consulting** (or "**advisory**") **services**, an accountant or other service provider performs a value-added service for the benefit of management. In contrast to assurance services, where historical information is reviewed, consulting services are often focused on establishing recommendations for future events or processes.

Two parties are generally involved in consulting engagements: the service provider (accountant) and management. Independence is not required for consulting engagements; rather, the accountant acts as a partner to management, identifying possible strategic improvements and best practices for the client.

CPA firms often market their consulting services as opportunities for clients to strategically grow their businesses. Consulting engagements include, for example,

- Designing a new information system for a client
- Analysis of a potential merger or acquisition
- Litigation support services
- Loaned staff services, for example, where a CPA firm loans one or more members of its staff to a client to perform routine controllership functions

The Sarbanes-Oxley Act prohibits auditors of public companies from providing specified services to audit clients (such as, for example, certain tax consulting services).[1] By contrast, accountants may provide consulting services to nonpublic audit clients in certain circumstances, but are cautioned (by the AICPA) that they should only accept such an engagement if doing so will not impair their objectivity and independence related to the attestation engagement.[2]

Compilation engagements—discussed later in this chapter—also do not require independence; however, a lack of independence must be disclosed.

The Standard Setters: The AICPA and the PCAOB

The AICPA and PCAOB are responsible for establishing **professional standards** for CPAs. This term broadly refers to standards for client service engagements (such as audit and consulting standards), as well as independence and ethics standards.

LO1 Understand the role of the AICPA and PCAOB in establishing professional services standards for accountants.

---

[1] The Sarbanes-Oxley Act of 2002, Title II (Auditor Independence), Sec. 201(g), "Prohibited Activities."

[2] AICPA, Statement on Standards for Consulting Services No. 1, par. 9 and footnote 3.

Applicability of AICPA vs. PCAOB Guidance

Figure 9-2 illustrates the authority of AICPA and PCAOB standards.

Figure 9-2

Areas of PCAOB versus AICPA authority

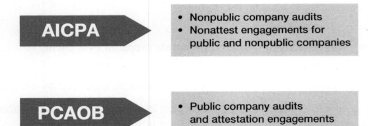

As depicted in Figure 9-2, AICPA standards apply to nonattestation services provided to both public and nonpublic companies, and to audits of nonpublic companies (**nonissuers**). PCAOB standards apply to auditing and attestation services provided to public companies, or **issuers**.[3]

Historically, the AICPA was responsible for setting all professional services standards for our profession. This changed with the issuance of the **Sarbanes-Oxley Act of 2002**, which came about following a series of large-scale public company audit failures (e.g., Enron, Worldcom). At the time, the public generally believed that our profession had failed at regulating itself (in other words, prior to 2002 there was no external organization designated to oversee our profession).

The PCAOB is intended to fill this void. As its name implies, the *Public Company Accounting Oversight Board* oversees accountants providing certain services to public companies. Accounting firms providing auditing services to issuers are required to register with the PCAOB, and the PCAOB monitors these **registered public accounting firms'** compliance with its rules and standards, and with applicable securities laws.

> **Now YOU Try 9.1**

1. Considering the preceding discussion, explain in your own words: Does the PCAOB oversee *public companies*, or *accountants* providing services to public companies? Why is this the case? Explain.

   _____

   _____

   _____

2. Assume that you are performing agreed-upon procedures for a public company. Which standard setter's guidance would you follow? Explain.

   _____

   _____

3. Assume that you are performing litigation support services for a public company. Which standard setter's guidance would you follow? Explain.

   _____

   _____

   _____

---

[3] For simplicity, this book uses the terms *public company* and *issuer* interchangeably, and it uses the terms nonpublic company, private company, and nonissuer interchangeably. In practice, slight differences may exist between these definitions.

Why the PCAOB Became Involved in Standard Setting

Does it strike you as redundant that we have two separate standard setters responsible for issuing auditing standards? Although there may be truth to this concern, the PCAOB issues auditing standards for the following reasons:

- First, the PCAOB was *mandated by the Sarbanes-Oxley Act* to issue auditing, quality control, and ethics and independence rules and standards.[4]
- Second, one of the PCAOB's objectives in issuing standards is to *facilitate its own inspection and enforcement activities*.

First, the PCAOB issues auditing standards for registered public accounting firms, because the Sarbanes-Oxley Act mandated that it do so. Within these standards, the PCAOB was required to provide guidance on certain specific matters, including the following:

- Auditors must describe their testing of *internal controls* within the financial statement audit report.
- Firms must subject all audit reports to a *concurring* or second partner review and approval.
- Auditors must *maintain workpapers* for a period of at least 7 years following an audit.[5]

Under Sarbanes-Oxley, the PCAOB was given the option to, at its discretion (1) issue its own original rules and standards or (2) adopt for its own use standards issued by other organizations. Initially (starting in 2003), the PCAOB chose a combination of issuing its own guidance, while adopting *on an interim basis* a great deal of existing AICPA guidance. In the years since that time, the PCAOB has replaced its *interim* use of certain AICPA standards with its own original PCAOB standards.

Second, recall that the PCAOB is designed to oversee the work of public company auditors. To that end, the PCAOB performs annual **inspections** of certain large registered firms and selects other firms for inspection using a risk-based approach. The PCAOB can investigate and impose sanctions on firms and auditors who violate professional standards or securities laws. Issuing auditing rules and standards allows the PCAOB to establish clear expectations for its inspections of and, when necessary, enforcement actions against, registered firms.

To improve your understanding of the preceding discussion, complete the following **Now YOU Try**.

Now YOU Try 9.2

1. Describe the relationship between standards the PCAOB issues versus the standards it has adopted from the AICPA.

_____

_____

_____

2. Contrast accounting standards, in which the standard setter (the FASB) differs from the regulatory body (the SEC), to the standard setting and enforcement of public company auditing standards.

_____

_____

_____

---

[4] Sarbanes-Oxley Act, Sec. 103. "Auditing, Quality Control, and Independence Standards and Rules." Par. (a)(1), and par. (b)(1).

[5] Sarbanes-Oxley Act, SEC. 103. Par. (a)(2)(A)(i–iii).

PCAOB Oversight and Funding

The SEC oversees the PCAOB and has the authority to approve the PCAOB's budget, plus all proposed rules and standards of the PCAOB before they are finalized. Like the FASB, the PCAOB is funded through *accounting support fees* assessed to public companies.

Standards Overlap

For its part, the AICPA also issues auditing standards, ethics standards, plus standards for other professional services engagements (compilations, consulting, tax, and so on). In the years since the PCAOB's formation, the AICPA has continued to revise and update its own standards, creating increasing divergence between the *interim* auditing and attestation standards the PCAOB adopted versus the standards actually in use by the AICPA today.

As a result, our profession must now carefully adhere to two similar, but increasingly divergent, sets of standards. This overlap can be confusing for even experienced researchers. Fortunately, as we'll discuss more in a moment, the PCAOB is in the process of reorganizing and renumbering its standards, so this overlap issue should be resolved soon.

[**TIP**] from the Trenches

> To ensure that you are using an appropriate source of guidance, always start your research by clearly determining which standard setter has authority: the PCAOB or the AICPA. Then conduct your research by focusing primarily on that standard setter's materials. Do not assume that an auditing standard (i.e., "AU-C") you find on the AICPA's website is the same as the corresponding AU you find on the PCAOB's website.

Other Applicable Guidance

Finally, all CPAs are expected to comply with the AICPA's Code of Professional Conduct, even if they are performing services under the authority of the PCAOB. Public company auditors must also comply with certain professional conduct standards issued by the SEC.

Considering this discussion, complete the decision tree in the following **Now YOU Try**.

[Now **YOU** Try 9.3]

Complete the decision tree in Figure 9-3 by identifying the applicable standard setter for each engagement.

Figure 9-3

Decision tree for identifying the applicable standard setter

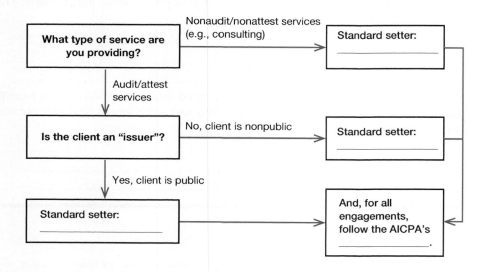

Let's now take a closer look at the auditing standards of the AICPA, followed by discussion of the PCAOB's auditing standards.

RESEARCHING AUDITING STANDARDS

AICPA Auditing Standards

Content and Organization

The AICPA's **auditing standards** provide auditors with guidance on the proper conduct of an audit, from acceptance, to planning, to fieldwork, to preparing documentation and issuing an audit report. The **Auditing Standards Board** (ASB) of the AICPA issues **Statements on Auditing Standards** (or **SAS**), which are then organized into sections of the professional standards referred to as **AU-Cs**. Auditing standards issued by the AICPA comprise the body of guidance referred to as **generally accepted auditing standards** (GAAS).

> **LO2** Navigate and apply auditing standards and interpretive guidance of the AICPA, applicable to nonpublic companies.

In 2014, the ASB completed a project (the "Clarity Project") to improve existing auditing standards and to converge U.S. auditing standards with International Standards on Auditing (ISAs) issued by the International Auditing and Assurance Standards Board (IAASB). As a result of this project, AU-C numbers now generally correspond to ISAs, wherever a comparable ISA is available. This project replaced all pre-Clarity auditing standards, referred to as AUs.

The AICPA's clarified auditing standards have been codified into sections, as follows:

- AU-C 200—299: General Principles and Responsibilities
- AU-C 300—499: Risk Assessment and Response to Assessed Risks
- AU-C 500—599: Audit Evidence
- AU-C 600—699: Using the Work of Others
- AU-C 700—799: Audit Conclusions and Reporting
- AU-C 800—899: Special Considerations
- AU-C 900—999: Special Considerations in the United States

Each section of the auditing standards (i.e., each "AU-C") is further organized as follows:

- Introduction: Describes the purpose, scope, and effective date of the section.
- Objective: Provides context for the requirements, establishes a framework for auditor judgment.
- Definitions: Defines key terms used within the section.
- Requirements: Sets forth the requirements of the standard and expectations for auditors.
- Application and Explanatory Material: Provides examples and other explanatory information necessary for applying guidance requirements. Also includes special considerations, such as applying the guidance to small company audits and government audits.

Let's discuss a few of these areas in more detail: objectives, requirements, and application material.

Having *objectives* in audit standards provides auditors with an overall context for the requirements of the standard. Knowing what's trying to be achieved by the rules can help auditors exercise judgment, as necessary, in applying the requirements of a standard. In some cases, an auditor may conclude that procedures *beyond* those required by a standard are necessary to achieve the standard's objectives.[6]

> As a CPA, you are expected to rely frequently on your own professional judgment. Each auditing standard now includes a section for Objectives; this section is intended to provide auditors with a framework for exercising good professional judgment.

> **TIP** from the Trenches

Within the *requirements* of audit standards, auditors should understand the meaning of two terms, in particular:

---

[6] AICPA, AU-C Section 200, *Overall Objectives of the Independent Auditor and the Conduct of an Audit in Accordance With Generally Accepted Auditing Standards*. Par. .23(a).

■ **Must**: The auditor must follow the guidance without departure.

■ **Should**: Auditor must comply or, in rare circumstances, may depart from the requirement by performing alternate procedures that achieve the intent of the requirement, provided the auditor documents the justification for departure.

These terms are also described within audit standards as "unconditional" and "presumptively mandatory" requirements, respectively.

Finally, remember how we referred to Implementation Guidance (Section 55 in the FASB Codification) as "required reading"? A similar rule holds true for the *application and explanatory material* within auditing standards: auditors should view these sections as required reading. According to AU-C 200 (Overall Objectives of the Independent Auditor):

.21   The auditor should have an understanding of the entire text of an AU-C section, including its application and other explanatory material, to understand its objectives and to apply its requirements properly.

.22   The auditor should not represent compliance with GAAS in the auditor's report unless the auditor has complied with the requirements of this section and all other AU-C sections relevant to the audit.

Considering the preceding guidance, respond to the following **Now YOU Try**.

Now
YOU
Try
9.4

1.   Considering the preceding discussion and the guidance in par. 21–22 of AU-C 200, what sections of an auditing standard do you think an auditor is required to consider, in order to state in the audit report: "We conducted our audit in accordance with auditing standards generally accepted in the United States of America"? Explain.

_____

_____

_____

_____

2.   Next, explain the relationship between an "SAS" and an AU-C.

_____

_____

_____

Interpretive Publications

The AICPA issues a number of **interpretive publications**, which are recommendations on the application of GAAS in specific circumstances, such as for particular industries. Following are the AICPA's four interpretive publications for audits:

■ Auditing interpretations of GAAS (e.g., AU-C 500, *Audit Evidence*, is interpreted by AU-C 9500, *Audit Evidence: Auditing Interpretations of Section 500*)

■ Exhibits to GAAS, generally located at the end of a given AU-C. For example, AU-C Section 580, *Written Representations*, is accompanied by exhibits illustrating sample management rep letters.

■ Auditing guidance included in AICPA Audit and Accounting Guides, (e.g., The Audit Guide, *Analytical Procedures* offers practical guidance for performing analytical procedures during an audit)

■ AICPA Auditing Statements of Position (SOP), included within the AICPA's *Professional Standards* publication [7]

The term "interpretive publications" carries a certain level of authority, as explained by AU-C Section 200 (Overall Objectives of the Independent Auditor):

> Interpretive publications are recommendations on the application of GAAS in specific circumstances, including engagements for entities in specialized industries. An interpretive publication is issued under the authority of the ASB after all ASB members have been provided an opportunity to consider and comment on whether the proposed interpretive publication is consistent with GAAS. (par. .A81)

Furthermore,

> AU-C Section 200 states that an auditor "should consider applicable interpretive publications in planning and performing the audit" (par. 27).

Complete the following **Now YOU Try** to improve your familiarity with the interpretive publications applicable to audits.

Now **YOU** Try **9.5**

1. Let's talk about why interpretive publications carry some level of authority. Considering the preceding excerpts, what body authorizes the issuance of these publications? Why might standards approved by this body have more authority than other publications?

    _____

    _____

2. What term is used to describe the expectation that auditors will consider interpretive publications (e.g., *must, should, may*)? Explain the significance of this term in this context.

    _____

    _____

3. Flip ahead for a moment to Figure 9-7, which shows an excerpted list of AU-Cs from the AICPA's website. What type of interpretive publication is shown next to AU-C 230, *Audit Documentation*? What responsibility would you have with respect to this guidance, if you are applying AU-C 230?

    _____

    _____

    _____

Figure 9-4 illustrates the hierarchy of AICPA auditing guidance, including an auditor's responsibility to consider each type of guidance in the hierarchy.

---

[7] AU-C 200, par. 14 (Definitions). Definition of "interpretive publications."

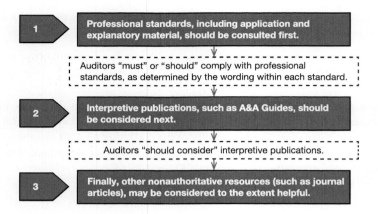

Other Publications

As noted in the preceding hierarchy, other (nonauthoritative) publications may be considered to the extent an auditor finds them helpful. The AICPA issues publications for a wide range of service offerings and industries. Publications that include nonauthoritative auditing discussion include the following:

- The *Journal of Accountancy*;
- The AICPA's *CPA Letter Daily* email newsletter; and
- The AICPA's nonauthoritative *Audit Data Standards*, which offer standard formatting guidance for common audit data needs.

These, along with resources issued by groups outside of the AICPA (such as firm auditing guides, audit programs, or checklists) may be helpful to professionals, but compliance with these publications is not required by the AICPA.

> Clearly, accountants should carefully comply with the hierarchy of professional services guidance described in Figure 9-4. But accountants should also know that their best safeguard against the risk of professional errors is to arm themselves with knowledge. Read the *Journal of Accountancy* regularly, as well as firm publications describing issues relevant to the profession. Awareness of current, or high-risk issues will make you better prepared to identify and manage areas of risk.

Researching AICPA Standards

AICPA standards can be accessed on www.aicpa.org. To begin a search for guidance, browse to the AICPA's *Standards* section, under the *Research* tab. This first step is illustrated in Figure 9-5.

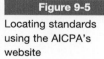

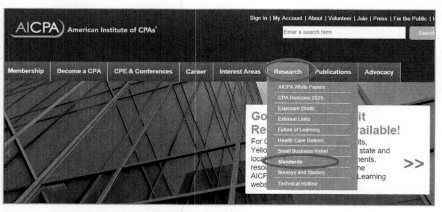

© 2015, American Institute of CPAs. Used by permission.

Once on the Standards page, researchers can browse to the appropriate type of standard (e.g., audit standards, Code of Conduct). The Standards page is illustrated in Figure 9-6.

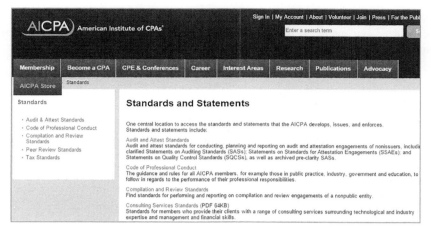

Figure 9-6

The AICPA's "Standards" page, where researchers can browse to various AICPA standards

After selecting a type of standard (e.g., *Auditing Standards*), researchers can search for the appropriate standard by searching the page by keyword. For example, a "ctrl + f" (i.e., "find") search on the page for relevant keywords allows researchers to jump to relevant standards. Figure 9-7 illustrates a keyword search, within audit standards, for the term "documentation." The first search result is SAS No. 122, or AU-C Section 230, *Audit Documentation*.

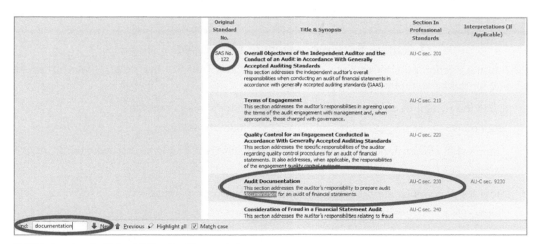

Figure 9-7

Sample keyword ("ctrl + f") search for AICPA audit standards

Now that you have a general understanding of AICPA guidance sources and search methods, let us turn to the rules and standards of the PCAOB.

PCAOB Rules and Auditing Standards

Auditors subject to the PCAOB's authority must comply with the PCAOB's rules, auditing standards, and ethics and independence standards. PCAOB Rule 3100 states:

LO3 Navigate and apply auditing standards and staff guidance of the PCAOB, applicable to public companies.

> A registered public accounting firm and its associated persons shall comply with all applicable auditing and related professional practice standards.

In preparing audit reports of issuers, auditors may not refer to PCAOB guidance as *generally accepted auditing standards*. Instead, audit reports, for engagements performed in accordance with PCAOB guidance, should state:

> We conducted our audits in accordance with the **standards of the Public Company Accounting Oversight Board (United States).**[8]

Let's take a closer look now at the PCAOB's *rules*.

PCAOB Rules of the Board

The PCAOB's **Rules of the Board** both (1) govern the PCAOB's conduct as an organization and (2) establish certain standards for auditor conduct. The Rules are organized as follows:

- Section 1: General Provisions (including definitions, such as "issuer")
- Section 2: Registration and Reporting
- Section 3: Professional Standards
- Section 4: Inspections (conducted by the PCAOB, of registered public accounting firms)
- Section 5: Investigations and Adjudications
- Section 6: International
- Section 7: Funding (of the PCAOB)

Using the titles of Sections 1–7, take a moment to complete the Now YOU Try exercise below, intended to familiarize you with content from the PCAOB rules. These section titles should be sufficiently descriptive to allow you to complete this exercise.

Now YOU Try 9.6

Locating Information within the PCAOB's Rules

Provide the section number and title (from the PCAOB's Rules of the Board) that you would consult for guidance on the following issues.

1. Does the receipt of contingent fees impair an auditor's independence?

   Section No. _____ : _____ (title of section)

2. Under what circumstances is a public accounting firm required to register with the PCAOB?

   Section No. _____ : _____

3. How are *accounting support fees* allocated among public companies?

   Section No. _____ : _____

4. What disciplinary sanctions might a registered firm face, if it is found to be in violation of PCAOB rules?

   Section No. _____ : _____

5. How frequently does the PCAOB conduct inspections of registered public accounting firms?

   Section No. _____ : _____

---

[8] PCAOB Auditing Standard No. 1, *References in Auditors' Reports to the Standards of the Public Company Accounting Oversight Board.* Appendix: Illustrative Reports.

As an auditor, you may find yourself referring most often to Section 3 (Professional Standards) of the PCAOB's rules. Certain content from this section (specifically, rules numbered 35xx) forms the body of the PCAOB's **ethics and independence standards**. Section 3 includes, for example, Rule 3520, "Auditor Independence":

> A registered public accounting firm and its associated persons must be independent of the firm's audit client throughout the audit and professional engagement period.

In addition, Section 3 includes Rule 3101, "Certain Terms Used in Auditing and Related Professional Practice Standards." This rule defines the following terms used within PCAOB standards:

(1) **Unconditional Responsibility**: The words "must," "shall," and "is required" indicate unconditional responsibilities. The auditor must fulfill responsibilities of this type in all cases in which the circumstances exist to which the requirement applies. Failure to discharge an unconditional responsibility is a violation of the relevant standard and Rule 3100.

(2) **Presumptively Mandatory Responsibility**: The word "should" indicates responsibilities that are presumptively mandatory. The auditor must comply with requirements of this type specified in the Board's standards unless the auditor demonstrates that alternative actions he or she followed in the circumstances were sufficient to achieve the objectives of the standard. Failure to discharge a presumptively mandatory responsibility is a violation of the relevant standard and Rule 3100 unless the auditor demonstrates that, in the circumstances, compliance with the specified responsibility was not necessary to achieve the objectives of the standard.

Note: In the rare circumstances in which the auditor believes the objectives of the standard can be met by alternative means, the auditor, as part of documenting the planning and performance of the work, must document the information that demonstrates that the objectives were achieved.

(3) **Responsibility To Consider**: The words "may," "might," "could," and other terms and phrases describe actions and procedures that auditors have a responsibility to consider. Matters described in this fashion require the auditor's attention and understanding. How and whether the auditor implements these matters in the audit will depend on the exercise of professional judgment in the circumstances consistent with the objectives of the standard. [Bold emphasis added]

These terms from Rule 3101 might call to mind the "must" and "should" requirements introduced in AICPA standard AU-C 200. Take a moment now to flip back to those AICPA definitions, then complete the following exercise.

Must and Should Requirements

1. Both the PCAOB and AICPA state that *unconditional* responsibilities can be indicated by the word: _____.

    The PCAOB's definition states that unconditional responsibilities can *also* be indicated by the terms: _____ and _____.

2. Both the PCAOB and AICPA state that *presumptively mandatory* responsibilities can be indicated by the word: _____.

Now
[**YOU**]
Try
9.7

3. Unlike the AICPA definition, the PCAOB definition includes *consequences* for auditors of noncompliance with unconditional and presumptively mandatory responsibilities. Complete the following statement using the definition of "unconditional responsibility":

   Failure to discharge an unconditional responsibility _____

   _____ .

4. Which of the three types of responsibility is unique to the PCAOB? What words indicate this type of responsibility?

   Responsibility unique to PCAOB: _____

   Words that indicate this responsibility: _____

Recall that these terms from Rule 3101 describe an auditor's responsibility to comply with PCAOB auditing standards. We'll discuss these standards next.

PCAOB Auditing Standards, and Interim Use of AICPA Auditing Standards

Auditors subject to the PCAOB's authority currently must use a combination of both

- The PCAOB's own **auditing standards** (abbreviated "AS") and
- Certain AICPA guidance (AU) adopted as interim by the PCAOB.

The presentation of these standards and interim standards is shown in Figure 9-8.

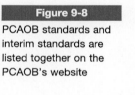

Figure 9-8

PCAOB standards and interim standards are listed together on the PCAOB's website

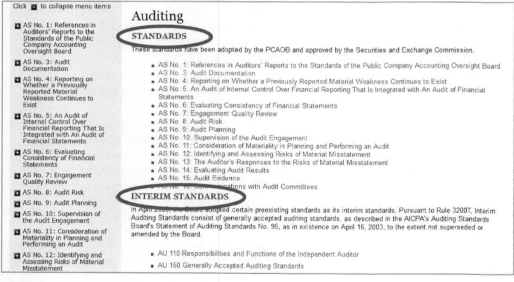

© PCAOB. Used with permission.

As the PCAOB issues its own standards, it generally discontinues its interim use of related AICPA guidance. For example, upon issuing AS 3, *Audit Documentation*, the PCAOB discontinued its interim use of SAS 96, the AICPA's original audit documentation standard. (The AICPA has also since replaced its own use of this guidance.) With the issuance of AS 3, the PCAOB met one of Sarbanes-Oxley's directives—to issue requirements for audit workpaper retention.[9]

PCAOB Standards Reorganization

The PCAOB is in the process of reorganizing its auditing standards. This change will affect the organization, but not the substance, of the PCAOB's standards. The updated organization will be

---

[9] PCAOB Auditing Standard No. 3, *Audit Documentation* (AS 3). Par. 14.

effective, subject to SEC approval, on December 31, 2016, with early adoption permitted. Figure 9-9 illustrates the demonstration version of the standards reorganization.

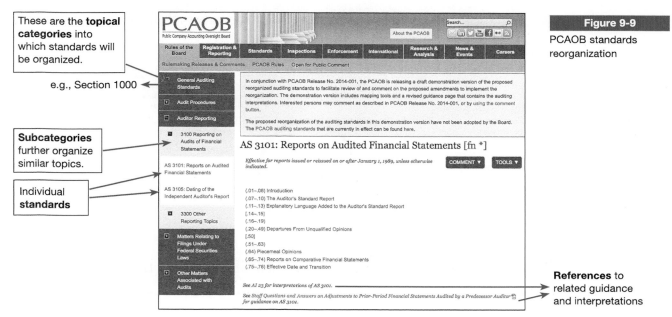

© PCAOB. Used with permission.

Figure 9-9

PCAOB standards reorganization

These are the **topical categories** into which standards will be organized.

e.g., Section 1000

Subcategories further organize similar topics.

Individual standards

References to related guidance and interpretations

As you can see in Figure 9-9, individual **standards** (such as AS 3101) will be organized into **topical categories**, then into **subcategories**. Each standard will be assigned a unique section number. Furthermore, the reorganized standards will be presented in a way that generally follows the flow of the audit process (for example, procedures that take place toward the end of an audit would be near the end of the *Audit Procedures* topical category). Considering this information and the preceding figure, complete the following **Now YOU Try**.

---

1. Within which *topical category* might an auditor expect to find independence standards for auditors? What section number is assigned to standards in this topical category?

2. What two standards can you find within the *subcategory* AS 3100 (Reporting on Audits of Financial Statements)?

3. Referring to Figure 9-9, what two types of interpretive guidance are available related to AS 3101? What acronym (e.g., "AS") is used to describe *Interpretations*?

4. Within which *topical category* might an auditor find guidance for *performing an audit of a client's internal controls*?

Now YOU Try 9.8

References to paragraphs within the reorganized standards would be shown as "AS 3101.01," for example, for the first paragraph in AS 3101.

Researchers can browse to PCAOB rules and standards from a few locations on the homepage (www.pcaobus.org), as illustrated in Figure 9-10.

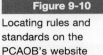

Figure 9-10

Locating rules and standards on the PCAOB's website

© PCAOB. Used with permission.

Considering Figure 9-10, respond to the following **Now YOU Try**.

Now YOU Try 9.9

Refer to Figure 9-10. What are two other types of standards issued (or adopted) by the PCAOB that could apply to public company auditors? Explain.

_____

_____

Certain PCAOB standards are accompanied by appendices, which often contain illustrative examples and the standard setter's basis for conclusions. Appendices can provide researchers with valuable context for understanding the guidance.

PCAOB Staff Releases

The PCAOB's staff issues the following guidance intended to highlight emerging or noteworthy audit practice issues, and to interpret rules and standards of the Board:

- **Staff Audit Practice Alerts**
- **Staff Q&As**

These resources are located under *Standards*, and then *Guidance* on the PCAOB's website, as illustrated in Figure 9-11.

Auditors should carefully consider guidance set forth in Staff Audit Practice Alerts. Often, these alerts highlight areas of concern noted during PCAOB inspections and set expectations for future PCAOB inspections. The following **Now YOU Try** illustrates the application of PCAOB standards and practice alerts.

Now YOU Try 9.10

Recall that the Sarbanes-Oxley Act requires auditors of public companies to express an opinion on both: (1) the financial statements, and (2) management's internal controls over financial reporting. Together, an audit of these two areas is referred to as an *integrated audit*.

Guidance

STAFF AUDIT PRACTICE ALERTS

Staff Audit Practice Alerts highlight new, emerging, or otherwise noteworthy circumstances that may affect how auditors conduct audits under the existing requirements of PCAOB standards and relevant laws. The statements contained in Staff Audit Practice Alerts are not rules of the Board and do not reflect any Board determination or judgment about the conduct of any particular firm, auditor, or any other person.

- Alert No. 13: Matters Related to the Auditor's Consideration of a Company's Ability to Continue as a Going Concern (Sept. 22, 2014) 🗎
- Alert No. 12: Matters Related to Auditing Revenue in an Audit of Financial Statements (Sept. 9, 2014) 🗎
- Alert No. 11: Considerations for Audits of Internal Control over Financial Reporting (Oct. 24, 2013) 🗎
- Alert No. 10: Maintaining and Applying Professional Skepticism in Audits (Dec. 4, 2012) 🗎
- Alert No. 9: Assessing and Responding to Risk in the Current Economic Environment (Dec. 6, 2011) 🗎
- Alert No. 8: Audit Risks in Certain Emerging Markets (Oct. 3, 2011) 🗎
- Alert No. 7: Auditor Considerations of Litigation and Other Contingencies Arising from Mortgage and Other Loan Activities (Dec. 20, 2010) 🗎
- Alert No. 6: Auditor Considerations Regarding Using the Work of Other Auditors and Engaging Assistants from Outside the Firm (July 12, 2010) 🗎
- Alert No. 5: Auditor Considerations Regarding Significant Unusual Transactions (April 7, 2010) 🗎
- Alert No. 4: Auditor Considerations Regarding Fair Value Measurements, Disclosures, and Other-Than-Temporary Impairments (April 21, 2009) 🗎
- Alert No. 3: Audit Considerations in the Current Economic Environment (Dec. 5, 2008) 🗎
- Alert No. 2: Matters Related to Auditing Fair Value Measurements of Financial Instruments and the Use of Specialists (Dec. 10, 2007) 🗎
- Alert No. 1: Matters Related to Timing and Accounting for Option Grants (July 28, 2006) 🗎

STAFF QUESTIONS AND ANSWERS

Staff questions and answers set forth the staff's opinions on issues related to the implementation of the standards of the PCAOB. The PCAOB publishes questions and answers to help auditors implement, and the Board's staff administer, the Board's standards. The statements contained in the staff questions and answers are not rules of the Board, nor have they been approved by the Board.

- Auditing Standard No. 7, Engagement Quality Review (Feb. 19, 2010) 🗎

RELATED INFORMATION

- Current Activities

RULES

- Standard-Setting Rules

Figure 9-11

Within the Guidance page, researchers can access Staff Audit Practice Alerts and Staff Q&As

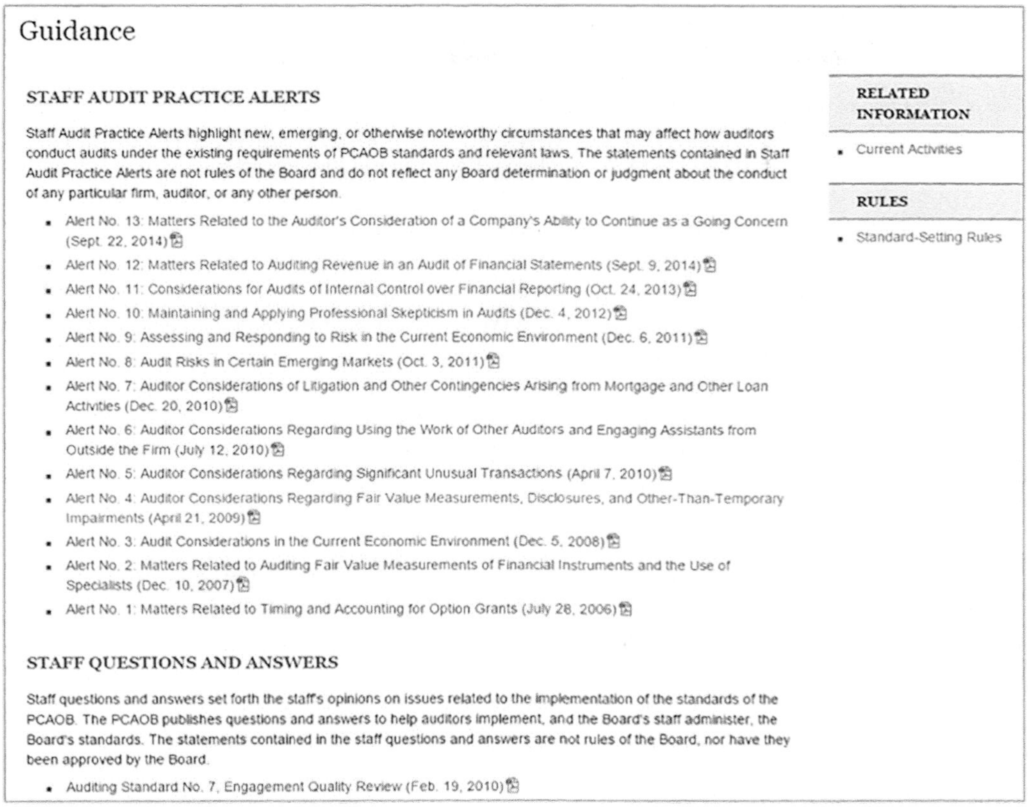

The PCAOB issued AS 5, *An Audit of Internal Control over Financial Reporting That Is Integrated with an Audit of Financial Statements*, to establish expectations regarding integrated audits. (Note: AS 5 will be renamed AS 2201 under the pending standards reorganization.)

Based on significant audit deficiencies noted during its annual inspections process, the PCAOB staff issued (among other guidance) Staff Audit Practice Alert No. 11, *Considerations for Audits of Internal Control over Financial Reporting*.

Auditors must now consider both AS 5 and Alert No. 11 when planning and performing an integrated audit.

AS 5 includes the following requirement:

21. The auditor should use a **top-down approach** to the audit of internal control over financial reporting to select the controls to test. **A top-down approach begins at the financial statement level and with the auditor's understanding of the overall risks to internal control over financial reporting.** The auditor then focuses on entity-level controls and works down to significant accounts and disclosures and their relevant assertions. This approach directs the auditor's attention to accounts, disclosures, and assertions that present a reasonable possibility of material misstatement to the financial statements and related disclosures. The auditor then verifies his or her understanding of the risks in the company's processes and selects for testing those controls that sufficiently address the assessed risk of misstatement to each relevant assertion.

    Note: The top-down approach describes the auditor's sequential thought process in identifying risks and the controls to test, not necessarily the order in which the auditor will perform the auditing procedures. [Bold emphasis added]

Alert No. 11 states:

> One of the potential root causes for the deficiencies in audits of internal control, as cited in the general inspection report, is improper application of the top-down approach set forth in PCAOB standards. For example, the general inspection report notes that, in some instances, it appears that firms, in implementing a top-down approach, placed undue emphasis on testing management review controls and other detective controls without considering whether they adequately addressed the assessed risks of material misstatement of the significant account or disclosure. In some instances, inspections staff observed that firms failed to test controls for all relevant assertions of the significant accounts and disclosures. In other instances, it appeared to the inspections staff that firms did not sufficiently understand the likely sources of potential misstatements related to significant accounts or disclosures as part of selecting controls to test. [Footnotes omitted]

Considering the preceding guidance, respond to the following.

1. Describe the relationship between AS 5 and Alert No. 11. What advice would you give to an auditor performing an integrated audit and in the process of applying AS 5?

2. In your own words, explain the top-down approach.

3. What specific concern does Alert No. 11 raise, with respect to how auditors are performing the top-down approach?

4. Think for a moment: What potential consequences could be associated with an auditor's failure to appropriately apply the top-down approach?

The AICPA and PCAOB's professional standards continually evolve. Chapter 14 of this book describes steps that accountants can take in order to stay current with the changing body of accounting and auditing standards.

SEC Ethics Requirements

Finally, in addition to complying with PCAOB rules and standards, auditors of public companies must comply with certain professional standards of the SEC. Among these, the SEC's Regulation S-X sets forth certain requirements for auditors, including

- ■ Auditor qualifications requirements,
- ■ Requirements related to auditor independence,
- ■ Required elements of the audit report, and
- ■ Requirements for audits performed by multiple firms.[10]

    Regulation S-X is available on the SEC's website, www.sec.gov.

Searching for Auditing Guidance within Firm Research Databases

Arguably the most efficient way to search AICPA and PCAOB guidance is through a **research database**. Individuals with access to firm research databases (such as Deloitte's *Technical Library* or KPMG's *Accounting Research Online*) can perform keyword searches of, or can browse directly to, auditing standards and interpretations. Trial subscriptions are frequently available.

Figure 9-12 illustrates a search for the keyword "documentation" using Deloitte's *Technical Library*. Notice how the researcher has specified the AICPA and/or PCAOB literature sources in which to search for this term.

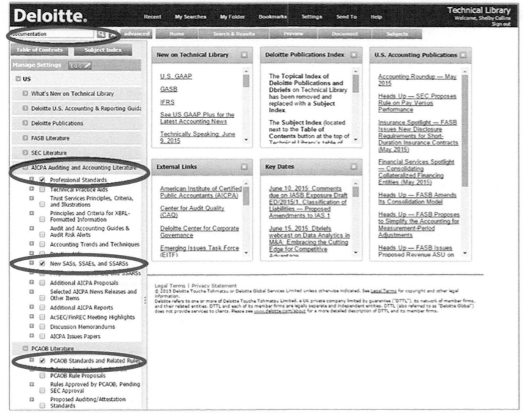

Figure 9-12

Search for auditing guidance using Deloitte's *Technical Library*

---

[10] SEC, Regulation S-X, Reg. § 210.2-01 (parts a and b): "Qualifications of Accountants"; Reg. § 210.2-02: "Accountants' Reports"; Reg. § 210.2-05 "Examination of Financial Statements by More than One Accountant."

[11] See Ch. 5, fn 4.

THE AICPA'S CODE OF CONDUCT

LO4 **Perform** research using the AICPA's revised Code of Conduct, understanding the Conceptual Framework approach set forth in the Code.

Released in June 2014, the AICPA's **revised Code of Professional Conduct** (the "Code of Conduct" or the "Code") establishes mandatory ethics requirements applicable to all CPAs. The revised Code will be fully effective as of December 2015, with early adoption permitted. Individuals who violate provisions of the Code can be sanctioned by the AICPA.

As a professional, you should consult the Code whenever you face a potential ethics or independence issue. You've had enough training in previous accounting and auditing courses to know that CPAs are expected to fulfill their professional responsibilities with the utmost integrity. Trust your instincts and consult the Code if a situation or circumstance seems questionable to you.

[TIP] from the Trenches

> The revised Code is available in .pdf format, and in an online interactive version, at aicpa. org. Go to Research, then Standards, then Code of Conduct. A no-cost login is required to access the online version of the Code.

The Revised Code Is Organized Into Three Parts

Guidance in the Code is organized into three **parts** and a **preface** (plus appendices), as follows:

- Preface (applies to all CPAs)
- Part 1 – Applies to CPAs in public practice
- Part 2 – Applies to CPAs in business
- Part 3 – Others (applies to retired or unemployed CPAs)

Part 1 of the Code applies to *members* (of the AICPA) who are in *public practice*. That is, CPAs engaged in performing professional services for a client must apply this part of the Code.

Part 2 of the Code applies to *members in business*. These are CPAs who work (either through employment, on a contractual basis, or as a volunteer) in areas such as industry, the public sector, education, the not-for-profit sector, or for regulatory or professional bodies.[12] These individuals might work for the business as an executive, a staff member, in governance (such as on the company's Board), or in an advisory or administrative capacity.

Finally, Part 3 of the Code applies to members who are not in public practice, nor in business. Such members include individuals who are retired or unemployed.

In some cases, an accountant may have multiple roles (for example, working with two organizations) and thus would be subject to multiple parts of the Code.

Take a moment to complete the following Now YOU Try, on identifying parts of the Code.

Now **[YOU]** Try **9.11**

Identifying Parts of the Code

John is an auditor who works for a CPA firm. In his spare time, he also serves on the Board of Directors of his community's YMCA. This is an unpaid position.

Which part(s) of the Code apply to John? Explain.

The _____, because _____.

Part _____, because _____.

Part _____, because _____.

---

[12] ET 0.400.32 (Definitions)

TIP from the Trenches

When you see references to the Code of Conduct, you'll notice that the first number signifies what Part of the Code was consulted. ET 1.XXX, for example, refers to a reference from Part 1 of the Code. ET 0.XXX refers to guidance from the Code's Preface.

Next, let's look at what's included in the Code of Conduct.

The Preface—What's Included?

The Code's Preface includes:

- The Principles of Professional Conduct
- Definitions
- A list of recent changes to the Code

The **Principles of Professional Conduct** ("**principles**") acknowledge the CPA profession's responsibility to serve the public and establish a framework for individuals to apply specific rules in the Code. Following are select *principles* from the Code:

Section	Principle
The Public Interest, ET 0.300.030	Members should accept the obligation to act in a way that will serve the public interest, honor the public trust, and demonstrate a commitment to professionalism.
Objectivity and Independence, ET 0.300.050	A member should maintain objectivity and be free of conflicts of interest in discharging professional responsibilities. A member in public practice should be independent in fact and appearance when providing auditing and other attestation services.
Due Care, ET 0.300.060	A member should observe the profession's technical and ethical standards, strive continually to improve competence and the quality of services, and discharge professional responsibility to the best of the member's ability.

The **definitions** in the Preface cover key terms used throughout the Code. Defined terms include, for example, *member, public practice, direct financial interest, client,* and so on. Wherever defined terms are used in the Code, they are presented in italics.

Next, given that the AICPA will continue to periodically update the Code, the Preface includes a list of recent Code **revisions** and additions.[13] This list will be updated as changes are made to the Code.

Finally, the Preface includes the stated requirement that AICPA members must adhere to the *rules* and *interpretations* of the Code.

.02 The AICPA bylaws require that *members* adhere to the rules of the code . . .*Members* must be prepared to justify departures from these rules. (ET 0.100.010)

.01 A *member* who departs from the *interpretations* shall have the burden of justifying such departure in any disciplinary hearing. (ET 0.100.020)[14]

Rules and interpretations are located in parts 1, 2, and 3 of the Code. Let's take a look at these parts of the Code now.

---

[13] ET 0.600 (New, Revised, and Pending Interpretations and Other Guidance)

[14] In these excerpts, the terms *members* and *interpretations* are italicized, indicating that these terms are defined in the Code's definitions section.

Parts 1 and 2 of the Code—What's Included?

Parts 1 and 2 of the Code include:

- Rules and interpretations
- Conceptual Frameworks
- Nonauthoritative guidance

Ethics rules (i.e., the "**rules of conduct**") and **interpretations** build upon the Principles of Conduct from the Preface. *Rules* set forth the Code's requirements. *Interpretations* provide detailed guidance for applying specific rules. As stated in the Preface, CPAs must adhere to *both* rules and interpretations.

In circumstances where specific ethics interpretations are not available, CPAs should look to the Code's conceptual frameworks. The Code's three separate **conceptual frameworks** are as follows:

- Conceptual Framework for Members in Public Practice (ET 1.000.010)
- Conceptual Framework for Independence (ET 1.210.010)
- Conceptual Framework for Members in Business (ET 2.000.010)

It's worth noting that the three frameworks are quite similar in their construct, requiring CPAs to consider *threats* and *safeguards* in evaluating ethics issues. However, they're written in a way that is tailored to members applying that specific *part* of the Code.

Finally, grey shaded boxes in parts 1 and 2 of the Code offer links to **nonauthoritative guidance**. This is guidance that has not been through the AICPA's full due process, and thus should not override or replace use of the Code. However, it can assist researchers in applying the Code. Examples include the standard setter's basis for conclusions and Q&As.

Part 3 of the Code—What's Included?

Part 3 of the Code includes just a single rule (the **acts discreditable** rule: "A *member* shall not commit an act discreditable to the profession") and related interpretations. Again, this part of the Code applies to CPAs who are not in public practice, nor in business.

Take a moment to attempt the following Now YOU Try, on where to locate the Code's conceptual frameworks.

Now YOU Try 9.12

The Three Conceptual Frameworks

Looking at the ET references for the three Conceptual Frameworks, which two frameworks would you expect to find in Part 1 of the Code? State the full name of each framework.

_____

_____

The Conceptual Framework Approach

Recall that in circumstances where a specific ethics interpretation is not available, CPAs should evaluate a situation using one of the Code's three conceptual frameworks. This is referred to as applying a **conceptual framework approach**.

Under this approach, CPAs should:

- First, identify *threats* to compliance with the rules;
- Next, evaluate the *significance* of these threats; and
- If the threats are at an unacceptable level, identify and apply *safeguards* to minimize these threats.
- In the event that safeguards do not reduce threats to an acceptable level, remove yourself from the situation (e.g., by declining an engagement, resigning from your employment, etc.).

Figure 9-13 illustrates the conceptual framework approach.

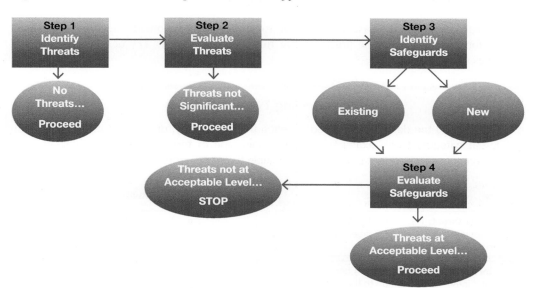

Figure 9-13

The Conceptual
Framework Approach

Source: Ellen Goria, "Revised AICPA Code of Ethics…What's the Fuss?" AICPA *Journal of Accountancy*, Feb. 1, 2014. © 2015, American Institute of CPAs. Used by permission.

Now
YOU
Try
9.13

1. In your own words, explain the four steps in the conceptual framework approach.

    _____

    _____

    _____

    _____

2. In what circumstances should a researcher apply one of the Code's three conceptual frameworks?

    _____

    _____

Each of the Code's three conceptual frameworks provides examples of potential *threats* to compliance with the Code, and *safeguards* that could reduce the risk of these threats. Let's consider now what is meant by the terms *threats* and *safeguards*.

Threats
The Preface defines **threats** as follows:

> In connection with independence, threats are relationships or circumstances that could *impair* independence. In connection with any rule but the "Independence Rule" [1.200.001], threats are relationships or circumstances that could compromise a *member's* compliance with the rules. (Source: ET 0.400.49)

For example, if your close friend asks you to serve as the auditor for his company, this should immediately raise a few red flags in your mind. The Code would describe these red flags as *threats*.

Threats are generally classified into one (or more) of seven broad categories (i.e., threat *types*), for members in public practice. The following **Now YOU Try** defines and provides examples of these categories.

Understanding Types of Threats

1. Considering the definition provided for each threat category, draw a line connecting each threat category to an example illustrating this type of threat. Draw multiple lines if you encounter examples that could involve multiple threat categories.

Threat category	Example situations involving threats
i. Adverse interest threat: The threat that a member will not act with objectivity because the member's interests are opposed to the client's interests.	**a.** The CPA advised management on the proper accounting for judgmental aspects of a merger transaction, and management accepts the CPA's recommendations.
ii. Advocacy threat: The threat that a member will promote a client's interests or position to the point that his or her objectivity or independence is compromised.	**b.** A member's close friend is employed by the client.
iii. Familiarity threat: The threat that, due to a long or close relationship with a client, a member will become too sympathetic to the client's interests or too accepting of the client's work or product.	**c.** The client is involved in a lawsuit against the CPA's firm.
iv. Management participation threat: The threat that a member will take on the role of client management or otherwise assume management responsibilities.	**d.** The CPA performs bookkeeping services for the client.
v. Self-interest threat: The threat that a member could benefit, financially or otherwise, from an interest in, or relationship with, a client or persons associated with the client.	**e.** The client threatens to dismiss the CPA's firm from the engagement.
vi. Self-review threat: The threat that a member will not appropriately evaluate the results of a previous judgment made or service performed or supervised by the member or an individual in the member's firm and that the member will rely on that service in forming a judgment as part of another service.	**f.** A CPA has a financial interest in the client, and the outcome of the engagement could affect the value of that interest.
vii. Undue influence threat: The threat that a member will subordinate his or her judgment to an individual associated with a client or any relevant third party due to that individual's reputation or expertise, aggressive or dominant personality, or attempts to coerce or exercise excessive influence over the member.	**g.** The CPA firm endorses a client's services or products.

Example (line connecting i. to c.)

Source: ET 1.100.010 (Conceptual Framework for Members in Public Practice), par. .10-.16.

2. Identify one example from above that could involve multiple types of threats. Explain.

_____

_____

_____

_____

_____

3. The Conceptual Framework for members in business includes six broad categories of threats, which are the same as those shown above but which exclude one. Which threat from the above list do you think is not included in the list for members in business, and why?

_____

_____

_____

_____

Safeguards

The Preface defines **safeguards** as follows:

> Actions or other measures that may eliminate a *threat* or reduce a *threat* to an *acceptable level*. (Source: ET 0.400.43)

Recall that if identified threats are at an unacceptable level, the next step in the conceptual framework approach is to apply safeguards to minimize these threats. Three broad categories of safeguards exist for members in public practice:

1. Safeguards created by the profession, legislation, or regulation.
2. Safeguards implemented by the client.
3. Safeguards implemented by the firm, including firm policies and procedures.

The following **Now YOU Try** will familiarize you with these categories of safeguards.

Understanding Safeguards

Draw lines matching each category of safeguard to *two* examples illustrating this safeguard.

Now **YOU** Try 9.15

Categories of safeguards		Sample safeguard
i. Safeguards created by profession, legislation or regulation	Example	a. State Board-required continuing education and training on independence and ethics rules.
ii. Safeguards implemented by the client		b. Rotation of senior personnel who are part of the engagement team.
iii. Safeguards implemented by the firm		c. The tone at the top emphasizes the client's commitment to fair financial reporting and compliance with the applicable laws, rules, regulations.
		d. The client has a strong governance structure, including an active audit committee, to ensure appropriate decision making, oversight, and communications regarding a firm's services.
		e. Professional standards and the threat of discipline.
		f. Internal policies and procedures relating to independence and ethics communications with audit committees or others charged with client governance.

Source: ET 1.100.010 (Conceptual Framework for Members in Public Practice), par. .17-.23.

Notably, only two categories of safeguards apply to members in business (ET 2.000.010):

1. Safeguards created by the profession, legislation, or regulation; and
2. Safeguards implemented by the employing organization.

Safeguards implemented by the employing organization could include, for example, the company's:

- Audit committee charter, including independent audit committee members, and its
- Internal policies and procedures related to purchasing controls

The following Now YOU Try walks through each step of the conceptual framework approach.

<table>
<tr><td>

Now
YOU
Try
9.16

</td></tr>
</table>

Applying the Conceptual Framework Approach

Assume that Smith & Dunn, LLP has had a long association with an audit client, and the client is significant to the firm. Jeff Smith, founder and CPA, is concerned that this association could pose threats to the firm's compliance with the AICPA's ethics rule on independence.

Considering the preceding discussion of threats, safeguards, and the conceptual framework approach, respond to the following.

1. Assume that Jeff is unable to locate interpretations that relate to his issue. Next, Jeff should apply the:

   _____

   This framework is located in ET _____.

2. Refer to Figure 9-13. Jeff's first step in applying a conceptual framework approach is to:

   _____

3. Refer now to the types of threats listed in Now YOU Try 9.14. Which of these threats might be present in this situation?

   _____

   _____

4. After identifying threats, Jeff must next evaluate:

   _____

5. If Jeff is not comfortable that the identified threats are at an acceptable level, he must

   _____

6. Safeguards in this case might include (brainstorm):

   _____

   _____

7. Finally, if these safeguards, new or existing, do not reduce the threat of noncompliance to an acceptable level, Jeff's firm should:

   _____

<table>
<tr><td>

TIP from the
Trenches

</td><td>

The best way to improve your comfort with the revised Code, and particularly the conceptual framework approach, is to read it. After reading this chapter, take a few minutes to click around the Code. Be sure to scan ET 1.000.010, which describes the conceptual framework approach.

</td></tr>
</table>

How Is Guidance in the Code Organized?

Within the Code, guidance is organized into topics, subtopics, and sections. References to the Code use the following format:

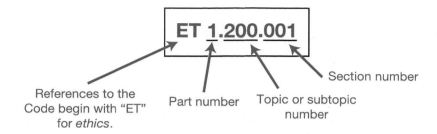

In other words, this reference is to Part 1 of the Code, Topic 200 (Independence), Section 001.

Paragraphs are shown as 2-digit numbers, so ET 1.200.001.**01** means paragraph .01 of the Independence topic, section 001.

The difference between topics and subtopics in the Code's numbering system is subtle. *Topics* are the first level of subject matter you'll see listed after you click the plus sign next to Part 1 in the Code. Figure 9-14 shows the list of topics included in Part 1 of the Code.

© 2015, American Institute of CPAs. Used by permission.

Figure 9-14

Topics included in Part 1 of the Code

Notably, the conceptual frameworks for parts 1 and 2 are included in the *Introduction* topics (ET 1.000.010 and 2.000.010, respectively). Looking at Figure 9-14, the Conceptual Framework for part 1 would be located within the branch 1.000 (Introduction).

Subtopics are accessible by clicking the + symbol, down one level further from topics. Figure 9-15 depicts several of the subtopics available under topic 1.200, Independence. Notably, the conceptual framework for independence is located within ET 1.210.

Several of the subtopics available under Topic 1.200, Independence

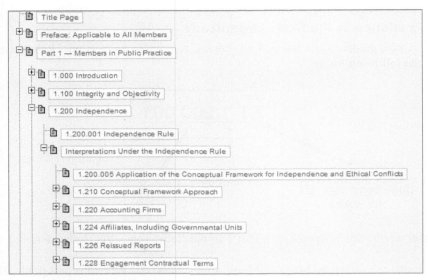

© 2015, American Institute of CPAs. Used by permission.

The third set of numbers in a Code reference denotes the section. Specifically:

- Sections numbered .001 are for *rules*.
- Sections numbered .005 tell you *how to apply the Conceptual Framework* to the rule.
- The Code's conceptual frameworks are located within section .010 of ET 1.000, 1.210, and 2.000.
- Other section numbers generally refer to ethics interpretations.

The following **Now YOU Try** walks through the Code's numbering system, and illustrates the application of an ethics rule, interpretation, and nonauthoritative guidance.

Now YOU Try 9.17

Applying Rules and Interpretations from the Code of Conduct

Assume that you are performing an audit and want to engage an external valuation firm to assist in reviewing the fair values of the client's private equity investments. However, you are concerned about the risk of disclosing confidential client information to the valuation firm. You've decided to consult the Code of Conduct for guidance on *confidential client information*.

- The *Rule* briefly states the ethics requirement. Per ET **1.700.001** (Confidential Client Information):

.01 A *member* in *public practice* shall not disclose any *confidential client information* without the specific consent of the *client*.

- **ET 1.700.005** addresses *how CPAs should apply the Conceptual Framework* to the confidential client information rule:

.01 In the absence of an *interpretation* of the "Confidential Client Information Rule" [1.700.001] that addresses a particular relationship or circumstance, a *member* should apply the "Conceptual Framework for Members in Public Practice" [1.000.010].

◼ *Interpretations* illustrate the application of the rule to a specific scenario. Per **ET 1.700.040** (Disclosing Information to a Third-Party Service Provider):

> .01 When a *member* uses a *third-party service provider* to assist the *member* in providing *professional services*, *threats* to compliance with the "Confidential Client Information Rule" [1.700.001] may exist.
>
> .02 *Clients* may not expect the *member* to use a *third-party service provider* to assist the *member* in providing the *professional services*. Therefore, before disclosing *confidential client information* to a *third-party service provider*, the *member* should do one of the following:
>
>   a. Enter into a contractual agreement with the *third-party service provider* to maintain the confidentiality of the information and provide reasonable assurance that the *third-party service provider* has appropriate procedures in place to prevent the unauthorized release of confidential information to others... [Or:]
>
>   b. Obtain specific consent from the *client* before disclosing *confidential client information* to the *third-party service provider*. [Explanation added]

◼ Finally, *nonauthoritative guidance* can assist researchers in applying and interpreting the Code. The following guidance is located just after **ET 1.700.040** in the Code.

> A nonauthoritative basis-for-conclusions document that summarizes considerations that were deemed significant in the development of this interpretation is available at www.aicpa.org/InterestAreas/ProfessionalEthics/Resources/Tools/ DownloadableDocuments/Basisfor_ConclusionsOutsourcing.pdf.
>
> In addition, nonauthoritative sample client disclosure language that could be used to fulfill the requirement discussed in this interpretation is also available at www.aicpa.org/InterestAreas/ProfessionalEthics/Resources/Tools/ DownloadableDocuments/Sample_Disclosure_Notification.pdf.

Considering the preceding excerpts, respond to the following.

1. What are two actions a member might take before disclosing confidential client information to a third-party service provider?

_____

_____

2. Could a researcher have answered question 1 using only the guidance in ET 1.700.001 (the ethics rule)? What value did interpretive guidance add to your ability to answer this question?

_____

_____

3. Recall that when a specific ethics interpretation is not available, CPAs should evaluate a situation using one of the Code's three conceptual frameworks.

    i. Should a researcher apply a conceptual framework in this case, and which one would apply?

_____

    ii. Explain why a researcher should or should not consult the applicable conceptual framework for this issue.

_____

4. Describe what each number means for the following reference to the Code: ET 1.700.001.01.

    1 indicates that this guidance is from _____ of the Code.

    .700 refers to the _____, Confidential Client Information.

    .001 is the section number, which tells me that this is an ethics _____.

    .01 is the _____ number.

5. What two sources of nonauthoritative guidance are referenced, to assist researchers in applying the authoritative rule and interpretation? How might each be useful to a researcher?

    _____

    _____

How Can I Search for Guidance in the Code?

Researchers can *browse* to guidance within the Code or can perform *keyword searches*. This book advocates the use of user-directed, browse searches when possible, as these searches will improve your familiarity with the content and layout of the Code.

To search the Code using a browse approach, first decide which *part* of the Code applies: Part 1, for accountants in public practice? Part 2, for accountants in business? Or both?

Next, click on the topic and/or subtopic that appears most relevant and read the rule for that topic. Look for interpretations under the rule that relate to your specific issue. If no interpretations are available that are on point, you must then apply the appropriate Conceptual Framework (as identified in section .005 of the topic).

Keyword searches can easily be performed using the search bar (or advanced search option) within the Code.

Figure 9-16 illustrates these steps.

Figure 9-16

Topics included in Part 1 of the Code

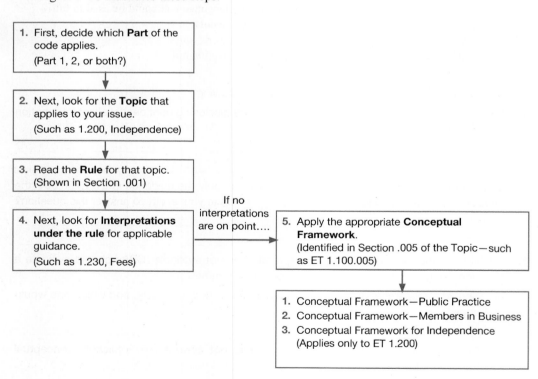

> While keyword searches are often useful when navigating the Code, they can sometimes lead researchers to guidance that doesn't apply, or that doesn't make intuitive sense. One professor said that her students—asked to locate continuing education (CPE) requirements in the Code—who used keyword searches consistently responded with guidance from the wrong "Part" of the Code.
>
> The lesson: If you do perform a keyword search, be sure you understand the context (part, topic, section, and related paragraphs) for the guidance you locate.

[TIP] from the Trenches

The Code Will Continue to Change

The AICPA's Professional Ethics Executive Committee (PEEC) will continue to update the Code as necessary to clarify its provisions or to reflect new ethics interpretations and rulings. As changes are approved and implemented, AICPA members are notified through updates in the *Journal of Accountancy*. Additionally, all recent changes to the Code will be listed in ET 0.600 (Preface – New Guidance). Because the Code will continue to change, beware of saving the pdf version of the Code to your computer, as it could become outdated.

> Here's a topic to round out our discussion of ethics: *personal finance*. Part of ensuring your ability to act ethically is making sure you have a handle on your own finances. At this point in your life, you may be starting to earn your first real income, while at the same time managing some amount of student debt. Do you have a plan for how you will manage your new influx of cash?
>
> My favorite source for personal financial advice is Dave Ramsey, who teaches "seven baby steps" to financial peace (daveramsey.com). Also see his book *The Total Money Makeover*—it's awesome. (His guidance has a religious undertone that I'm not advocating for one way or another.) Or consider Suze Orman's *The Money Book for the Young, Fabulous, and Broke*. The short time my class and I devote to this topic every semester is one of their favorites.

[TIP] from the Trenches

STANDARDS FOR OTHER PROFESSIONAL SERVICES

Next, let's briefly introduce a few other sources of client service guidance issued by the AICPA and PCAOB.

LO5 Identify guidance applicable to other professional services engagements, including attestation, compilation, and review standards.

Attestation Standards

For Nonpublic Companies

The AICPA issues **Statements on Standards for Attestation Engagements** (SSAEs), which are organized into sections referred to as "ATs." These provide guidance on attestation services provided to nonpublic companies. Attestation standards, notably, do not apply to certain attest engagements that are covered by other guidance, such as financial statement audits and reviews.

CPAs performing attest engagements are expected to conduct their engagements in accordance with these standards. Attestation standards include, for example,

- Guidance for performing agreed-upon procedures engagements (AT 201)
- Guidance for performing reviews of pro-forma financial information (AT 401)
- Guidance for performing examinations of internal controls that are integrated with an audit of the financial statements (AT 501)

Interpretive guidance is available for certain of the attestation standards; this interpretive guidance often applies only narrowly, to specified industries or circumstances. For example, AT 501 (Examinations of Internal Controls) is interpreted by AT 9501, which addresses the application of AT 501 to insured depository institutions (e.g., banks). Accountants providing attestation services should always check interpretive guidance, when available, to determine whether it applies to their engagement.

Notably, the Auditing Standards Board of the AICPA has proposed changes to its attestation standards as part of its Clarity project. Among the proposed changes, current attestation standards would be reorganized into a chapter format. Visit www.aicpa.org to learn more about the status of this project.

For Public Companies

The PCAOB relies upon a combination of its own attestation standards (AT No. 1, AT No. 2, and so on) and AICPA attestation standards adopted on an interim basis (AT 101, AT 201, and so on). The attestation standards issued by the PCAOB to date have focused on services provided to *brokers and dealers* of financial securities.

Compilation and Review Standards (SSARS)

Accountants may also provide compilation services to nonpublic clients. In a **compilation**, an accountant prepares financial statements using information obtained from management, but does not provide any assurance over the information compiled. Additionally, the accountant must generally prepare a compilation report, describing the accountant's role in preparing the financial statements. Independence is not required for compilation engagements; however, a lack of independence must be disclosed in the compilation report.

Issued by the AICPA's Accounting and Review Services Committee, **Statements on Standards for Accounting and Review Services (SSARSs)** cover compilation and review services provided to nonissuers. These standards are currently codified in the professional standards as "AR" sections; however, with the completion of a recent Clarity project (effective December 2015), the standards will be codified with the prefix **AR-C**.

Under the Clarity project, accounting and review services guidance will be organized into the following sections:

- Section 60, General Principles for Engagements Performed in Accordance with Statements on Standards for Accounting and Review Services
- Section 70, Preparation of Financial Statements
- Section 80, Compilation Engagements
- Section 90, Review of Financial Statements

In particular, accountants providing compilation and review services should become familiar with the requirements in AR-C Section 60 (*General Principles*). As its name implies, this standard provides overall guidance for accountants performing compilation or review services. For example, AR-C 60 describes differences between compilation and review services and sets forth reporting requirements for accountants performing these engagements.

Like it has for auditing engagements, the AICPA has designated four *interpretive publications* as authoritative for compilation and review engagements. These are (1) compilation and review interpretations of SSARSs, (2) appendixes to SSARSs, (3) compilation and review guidance included in A&A Guides, and (4) AICPA Statements of Position applicable to compilation and review engagements.[15]

Other Professional Standards

In addition to the standards described above, the AICPA's professional standards also include:

---

[15] AICPA, AR Section 60, *Framework for Performing and Reporting on Compilation and Review Engagements.* Par. .18, "Interpretive Publications."

- Consulting services standards—Statement on Standards for Consulting Services (SSCS)
- Quality control standards—Statements on Quality Control Standards (SQCSs)
- Peer review standards—Standards for Performing & Reporting on Peer Reviews (PRP)
- Personal financial planning standards—Statements on Standards in Personal Financial Planning (PFP) Services
- Tax standards—Statements on Standards for Tax Services (SSTSs)
- Valuation services standards—Statements on Standards for Valuation Services (SSVS)

As you can see from the above list, these standards cover client services (such as consulting and tax services) as well as guidance on firms' internal quality control procedures. Tax standards (SSTSs) are described in Chapter 11 of this book.

DOCUMENTATION OF PROFESSIONAL SERVICES RESEARCH

You know from previous chapters that *accounting* positions must be supported with documentation. Now let's take a moment to discuss why documentation is also important from the *service professional's* perspective.

> **LO6** **Understand** the role documentation plays in performing audit and professional services research.

Creating and maintaining sufficient **documentation**, or working papers, is critical to professional service engagements. Particularly for attestation engagements (such as audits), where the accountant must attest to the validity of an assertion, documentation is necessary to demonstrate the basis for the accountant's conclusions, and to demonstrate that the engagement complied with relevant professional standards. Audit documentation includes, for example, memoranda, confirmations, correspondence, schedules, audit programs, and letters of representation.

As noted previously, one of the first audit standards issued by the PCAOB was AS 3, *Audit Documentation*. The PCAOB prioritized the issuance of this standard because it viewed audit documentation as one of the "fundamental building blocks" of the Board's oversight function.[16] Shortly thereafter, the AICPA also updated its own guidance on audit documentation.

Within their audit documentation standards, the PCAOB and AICPA set forth requirements for the

- *Required elements* of audit documentation.
- *Retention period* for audit documentation.
- Process for *making changes* to audit documentation after the audit report is issued.

To comply with AICPA and PCAOB documentation requirements, auditors are required to document the procedures performed, evidence obtained, and conclusions reached with respect to financial statement assertions. Additionally, auditors must document any significant audit findings or issues and how these matters were resolved. Both the PCAOB and AICPA require auditors to place particular emphasis, within their documentation, on areas with the greatest risk of material misstatement.

Recall from our discussion of accounting research that research memoranda should include quotations from authoritative literature as support for conclusions reached. Similarly, auditors should support their choice of audit procedures and conclusions with citations from both professional standards and accounting standards. References to audit research may be included within audit schedules, or within memoranda documenting significant audit issues, depending on the complexity of the issue. Guidance for citing from audit standards is provided within the next section of this chapter.

Whether you are performing services for issuers or for nonissuers, *prepare documentation with the expectation that it will be reviewed by an external party*. Documentation may be reviewed, for example, in the event of

- Quality control reviews (from other partners in the CPA firm),

---

[16] AS 3, Appendix A: Background and Basis for Conclusions. Par. A4.

- Peer reviews (performed by other CPA firms),
- PCAOB inspections,
- SEC inquiries, or
- Litigation involving the audit client or audit firm.

The threat of a review can be disconcerting to some auditors; in recent years, the SEC and PCAOB have sanctioned numerous accountants who have gone back into their workpapers, just before an inspection was to begin, to add key documents or schedules that supported the audit opinion. Such was the case for the auditors described in Case Study 9.3, located at the end of this chapter. Don't jeopardize your career; before the workpapers for an engagement are finalized, think again about whether your documentation is sufficient to support a review.

TIP from the Trenches	An auditor's best defense for supporting his or her professional judgments is sufficient, contemporaneous, and complete documentation. In fact, the process alone of documenting an issue can often shed light upon whether the position is supportable. Identify the areas of greatest risk in the audit, then consider whether your documentation of these issues is sufficient to withstand review.

Citing Professional Standards

Following are examples of appropriate initial and subsequent references to professional standards. After each citation, notice the list of "required elements" included in the citation.

Initial Reference:

AU-C section 700, *Forming an Opinion and Reporting on Financial Statements* (par. 27), states that audit reports "should describe management's responsibility for the preparation and fair presentation of the financial statements."

This initial reference includes the following required elements:

- The type of standard is named: "AU-C section XXX."
- The title of the standard is fully written out, and italicized.
- The paragraph number is provided.
- Excerpts from the guidance are enclosed in quotes.

Subsequent References (once the standard has already been named in your documentation):

Audit reports should be in writing (AU-C 700.22).

This second citation includes the following required elements:

- The type of standard (AU-C) is named.
- The standard number and paragraph are provided (700.22).

When in doubt, err on the side of providing *too much* detail about the source of guidance you are citing. Your objective in clearly citing professional standards is to allow readers to retrace your steps and locate the guidance that you are relying on. Remember that a "reader" of your documentation could be anyone ranging from an audit supervisor to a PCAOB inspector.

CHAPTER SUMMARY

Compliance with professional standards is more than a "nice to know." As a professional, your career depends on it. Accounting professionals are held accountable for compliance with numerous professional services standards and ethics rules. Determining which standards to follow often depends on the type of engagement being performed, and on the type of client being served. The two primary standard setters for professional guidance are the AICPA and the PCAOB.

The two sets of guidance available from the PCAOB and AICPA currently have significant overlap. Accountants should strive to only search for guidance on the website (or related firm research database content) of the rulemaker with authority for each engagement. To fully comply with AICPA standards, auditors should consider standards and interpretive publications. To fully comply with PCAOB requirements, auditors should apply PCAOB auditing standards, rules, and staff releases. In all cases, CPAs are also subject to the ethics guidance detailed in the AICPA's Code of Professional Conduct.

Finally, paying careful attention to documentation requirements may be an accountant's best defense against professional risk. Documentation should focus in particular on key risk areas, and should adequately support the accountant's opinions, as well as the sufficiency of procedures performed.

REVIEW QUESTIONS

1. What are some of the differences between attestation and consulting services?

2. In what circumstances is an accountant subject to the rules and standards of the PCAOB?

3. Fill in the blank: If Jason is a public company auditor, then his firm must be a _____ public accounting firm.

4. What source of guidance applies to all CPAs, and relates to a CPA's own ethical conduct?

5. Explain the AICPA's definitions of "must" and "should." In what section of an audit standard would you expect to find these terms?

6. Explain the relationship between a SAS and an AU-C.

7. Describe the "hierarchy" of auditing guidance sources issued by the AICPA.

8. Identify the sources of AICPA audit guidance that are considered "interpretive publications."

9. Aside from issuing audit and ethics standards, what are some of the PCAOB's other responsibilities?

10. What Act established the PCAOB? What else did this Act require of the PCAOB?

11. How is the PCAOB funded?

12. Are PCAOB standards referred to as "generally accepted auditing standards"?

13. What are two functions of the PCAOB's *rules*?

14. What are the three levels of responsibility defined in PCAOB Rule 3101? What are the words that may be used (such as "must" and "should") within the guidance to indicate these types of responsibility?

15. Explain the differences in the applicability of the Code's preface, versus Part 1, versus Part 2, and Part 3.

16. What are the Principles of Professional Conduct, and where are these located within the Code?

17. Describe the role of rules, interpretive guidance, and nonauthoritative guidance within the AICPA's Code of Conduct.

18. Identify the three Conceptual Frameworks that are included within the Code. In what ET sections are these Frameworks located?

19. What are the four steps in the conceptual framework approach, and when should a researcher use such an approach?

20. Explain the meaning of the terms threats and safeguards and provide two examples of each.

21. Must a CPA always apply safeguards after a threat has been identified? In what circumstance might a researcher not have to identify and apply safeguards?

22. Aside from auditing standards, what are some of the other professional standards issued by the AICPA?

23. Which type of standard should an accountant apply, if he or she is performing a financial statement review for a client? Also, what specific standard number provides a framework for performing review engagements?

24. Explain why documentation is critical to audit research. Then, complete the following sentence: Prepare your auditing documentation with the expectation that _____.

EXERCISES

Code of Conduct Exercises

Instructions: **Answer the following in complete sentences using the AICPA's revised Code of Conduct, providing the ET references for each of your responses. For questions with multiple parts, include multiple ET references as appropriate.**

1. *Using the Code,* provide an example of when a member in public practice might also be considered a member in business. Hint: This is in the introduction to one of the parts of the Code.

2. List three examples of individuals who are considered "covered members" in the Code's definitions section.

3. Provide the Code reference to the rule that governs "acts discreditable" for "members in business."

4. Provide the Code reference to the rule that requires even part time faculty members (who may be teaching this course to you!) to comply with the integrity and objectivity rule. *Hint:* This issue is addressed directly in the Code.

5. Provide two examples of what is meant by the term "affiliate." Next, brainstorm: What terms might equate to this idea of "affiliate" in U.S. GAAP (accounting guidance)? (This is a 2-part question.)

6. Using the definitions section of the Code, describe in your own words what is meant by the term partner equivalent. Outside of the definitions section, describe one instance where this term is used.

7. Scan Part 3 of the Code. To whom is this section applicable, and what is the primary focus of this section?

8. What are the three broad categories of safeguards identified in Part 1 of the Code, in the Conceptual Framework for members in public practice? Which category of safeguard cannot be relied upon, by itself, to reduce threats to an acceptable level?

9. Jim, a retired CPA, neglected to file his tax return this year. What does the Code say about this?

10. According to Appendix A of the Code, which body has the AICPA designated as having the authority to set accounting standards under the Accounting Principles Rule (in ET 1.320 and 2.320 of the Code)? Include relevant excerpts from Appendix A to support your response.

Auditing Standards (and Related Topics) Exercises

11. Consider AICPA guidance. Why should an auditor perform risk assessment procedures? Also, what are three risk assessment procedures an auditor should undertake in order to assess an entity's risks of material misstatement in an audit?

12. Consider AICPA guidance. Can analytical procedures be used as a form of substantive testing? Citing from the applicable AU-C, justify your response.

13. Does accepting contingent fees impair an auditor's independence? Use the PCAOB website to respond.

14. Locate the PCAOB standard (AS) on supervision of an audit engagement.
    a. Who does the guidance say is responsible for the engagement and its performance?
    b. Who else is required to comply with the requirements of this AS?

15. Locate the PCAOB's audit standard on performing integrated audits. When an auditor is reporting on the results of an audit, must the auditor issue separate or combined reports on the company's financial statements and internal controls?

16. Go to the PCAOB's website and list one proposed audit standard named on the site. Where did you navigate within the site to find this?

17. Locate a PCAOB Staff Audit Practice Alert. Briefly, summarize the main issue addressed in this particular alert. Next, describe the role you think these alerts play in establishing auditing requirements for registered public accounting firms.

18. Under "Inspections" on the PCAOB's website, locate the link to Firm Inspection Reports. Review a firm inspection report and describe some of the findings (or deficiencies) cited by the PCAOB. In particular, look for firm inspection reports that say: "QC criticisms are now public."

Exercises Related to Other Professional Services Standards

19. Using the AICPA website, locate AR Section 60, *Framework for Performing and Reporting on Compilation and Review Engagements.*
    a. What is the corresponding Statements on Standards for Accounting and Review Services (SSARSs) number for this guidance? SSARS No. _____
    b. Using guidance from AR 60, briefly summarize how a compilation service differs from a review or an audit of financial statements.

20. a. What performance requirements apply to a financial statement review? Specifically, what are the procedures that will "ordinarily" provide an accountant with a reasonable basis for obtaining limited assurance?
    b. Can an accountant perform a review for a client in an industry for which he or she has no prior experience? Explain.

21. John is performing a compilation engagement and must assemble his documentation. Generally speaking, what should the goal of John's documentation be? What are three items (or pieces of information) that John should include in his documentation?

CASE STUDY QUESTIONS

Navigating the Revised Code Linda is a former big four auditor who chose to stay home with her children once she started a family. She has maintained her CPA license all the while and now performs part-time bookkeeping services for local businesses. Linda is not very familiar with the revised Code. Explain to her what part(s) of the Code she is subject to, if any. Make your case using definitions and concepts from the Preface, as well as the introduction(s) to the applicable part(s) of the Code.   9.1

Auditor Independence Utilize the AICPA website to respond, however to respond to this case, please consult not only auditing standards (AU-C), but also the AICPA's revised Code of Conduct.   9.2
Facts: Tim Smith is an audit partner in a CPA firm, and Tim recently invested in a diversified mutual fund managed by Fidelity Investments. He owns less than 1% of the total shares outstanding of the mutual fund itself. One of the mutual fund's holdings is shares of Lava Corp. Lava Corp is one of Tim's clients and is a nonpublic company.

Required: What guidance tells Tim that he must be independent of Lava Corp, *and* does his investment impair his firm's independence on this audit?

Respond to these questions in the form of an issues memo. Explain your analysis, citing from the guidance to support your response. If the guidance states that a "covered member" must be independent, you will need to define covered member to fully explain your analysis. Make a clear, reasoned argument, using a logical discussion of relevant guidance. You can use the following headers to begin your response.

Issue 1: What guidance requires Tim to be independent of Lava Corp?

Issue 2: Does this investment impair Tim's firm's independence on this audit?

PCAOB Disciplinary Orders Utilize the PCAOB website to respond.   9.3
Facts: On August 1, 2011, the PCAOB issued Orders formally barring two former Ernst & Young auditors from future audits of public companies.[17] Peter C. O'Toole and Darrin G. Estella, as partner and senior manager for a public company audit, respectively, were charged with violating PCAOB rules and auditing standards with the improper creation, addition, and backdating of audit documentation prior to a PCAOB inspection.

Following is part of the PCAOB's summary findings related to this matter. This is from the PCAOB's Order related to Mr. O'Toole.

> Respondent improperly created, added, and backdated a working paper in advance of the Board's inspection of the Audit. Others under his supervision and authorization improperly created, added, and backdated other working papers in advance of the Board's inspection. Respondent, and others supervised and authorized by him, provided misleading documents and information to the Board, in violation of Rule 4006. This conduct also violated AS3 because the documents added to the working papers did not indicate the dates that documents were added to the working papers, the names of the persons preparing the additional documentation, and the reason for adding the documentation months after the documentation completion date.[18]

---

[17] PCAOB Release No. 105-2011-004, August 1, 2011, and Release No. 105-2011-005, August 1, 2011.

[18] PCAOB Release No. 105-2011-005, August 1, 2011. Page 3, par. 3.

The PCAOB's Order goes on to describe the workpaper that was added to the audit files (postaudit, but in advance of the PCAOB inspection), as one that supported audit work related to the client's valuation of a key investment. According to the PCAOB's report, Mr. O'Toole anticipated that the valuation of that investment would be a key focus of the PCAOB inspection.[19]

Required: Evaluate this case in the form of an accounting issues memorandum. In the Facts section of your memo, use the facts presented above, along with any salient points from the PCAOB Order, to describe the issues at hand.
Next, list then analyze the following two issues:

1. How were the auditors' actions in violation of PCAOB Rule 4006? What should the auditors have done differently?
2. How were the auditors' actions in violation of AS 3? What should the auditors have done differently?

In your analysis, present relevant excerpts from the applicable auditing rules and standards alongside your consideration of the case facts and details from the PCAOB Order. Finally, present a brief conclusion which summarizes your analysis.

9.4 Auditor Independence

Facts: Assume that Jim White's recently-deceased grandfather left him an inheritance, which includes a direct investment in shares of WellCorp, his audit client. Jim is the partner on the WellCorp engagement; WellCorp is a privately-held company. Jim anticipates that, if necessary, the shares could be sold immediately.

Required: Determine 1) whether Jim is a covered member with respect to this client, and 2) whether it is appropriate for Jim to keep the inherited shares of WellCorp stock.

9.5 Records Requests Wilson & Smith, LLP has completed its audit procedures related to June 30, 20X1 year-end of CompuSoft, Inc. However, per the terms of its engagement letter with CompuSoft, fees are due and payable to Wilson & Smith before the audit report will be issued to the client. CompuSoft has not yet remitted payment for the audit. Wilson & Smith has refused to release its audit report until fees are paid. Is this refusal by Wilson & Smith appropriate under the Code of Conduct? What defined term would the applicable Code section use to describe the audit report, in this circumstance?

9.6 Processing Payroll for an Audit Client Collins & Harper, LLC serves as the independent auditor for Springfield Spirits, Inc ("Springfield"). Springfield has requested the firm's assistance with its payroll processing function. Springfield is being asked to perform this service while continuing to serve as Springfield's auditor.

Can Collins and Harper perform this nonattest service for Springfield? What considerations should Collins & Harper's management keep in mind when accepting and performing this service?

9.7 Sell Additional Services, or Not? Dan is a partner for a regional CPA firm, which performs the audit for Alpha, Inc., a public company. Through meetings with management, Dan has learned that Alpha is considering acquiring another company in the industry. Dan's firm has a large advisory practice which specializes in helping clients evaluate mergers & acquisitions. Advise Dan: Should he try to sell these additional advisory services to Alpha? Is his firm permitted to perform this nature of engagement for a public audit client?

9.8 VIE Noncompliance with GAAP If the small company you are auditing is the primary beneficiary of a variable interest entity (VIE) but does not want to consolidate, can your firm issue a qualified opinion? Assume that the company you are auditing is nonpublic.

9.9 You Create the Ethics Case

Required: Create a hypothetical ethics case (situation), then describe the guidance that applies to this issue. The simplest way to complete this assignment is:

- By "backing into" a case idea by looking up guidance in the AICPA's revised Code of Conduct then inventing a hypothetical situation based on this guidance.

However, if you want to go the extra mile on this assignment, you can be creative in how you come up with case ideas. For example, you can generate ideas using any one of the following:

- News stories
- AICPA Disciplinary actions—Go to AICPA.org, then *For the Public* (at very top right), then *Disciplinary Actions* to generate ideas of ways individuals have breached AICPA rules and standards.
- Your experiences in practice, etc.

After describing a hypothetical ethics situation, next locate ethics guidance that addresses this issue. Limit your search for guidance to the AICPA's revised Code of Conduct. Limit your response to one page and use the following headers to organize your submission:

- Situation:
- Applicable Guidance (and how it would apply to this issue):
- Inspiration for this case idea (how did you come up with this case idea?):

---

[19] PCAOB Release No. 105-2011-005, August 1, 2011. Pages 5–6, par. 13.

Chapter 10

Governmental and Industry Accounting Research

Jon has just been scheduled to work on the audit of a school district, starting on Monday. He is a staff auditor at a regional public accounting firm, and this is his first governmental audit client. He wonders how this engagement will differ from his private-sector experiences. Jon knows that state and local governments must follow GASB accounting standards but has otherwise forgotten much of what he learned about governmental accounting (let alone governmental audits). Now, Jon is unsure of how to prepare for work on Monday and feels uncomfortable holding himself out as a "government auditor."

As Jon likely knows by now, much of the training that auditors receive takes place on the job. That is, much of his initial audit work will involve reviewing prior year workpapers, then performing specific steps required by the current year audit program.

But Jon also wants to be able to understand the broader context for the audit steps he will perform. That's why he decides to take a few simple steps, this weekend, to educate himself for the week ahead. First, he dusts off his old governmental accounting textbook.

Continued

Learning Objectives

After reading this chapter and performing the exercises herein, you will be able to

1. **Understand** the environment of governmental financial reporting, including circumstances in which state, local, and federal government financial statements may be required.

2. **Research** and **apply** guidance applicable to state and local governments, particularly within the GASB Codification.

3. **Become** familiar with federal government accounting standards issued by the FASAB.

4. **Recognize** and **apply** government auditing standards issued by the GAO.

5. **Become** familiar with several industry accounting resources, including professional organizations and standards.

Flipping through the table of contents provides him with a much-needed refresher on issues that are unique to governmental accounting. Second, Jon looks up the client's comprehensive annual financial report (CAFR) from last year, to get a feel for the final product his audit team will be working toward. Finally, Jon scans the GASB's website to see what's new in the world of state and local government accounting. There, he reads the headlines then accesses a few short video clips on GASB activities, which he enjoys from the comfort of his couch.

A little bit of preparation will go a long way in making Jon feel confident when he reports to the client's site on Monday. This preparation will also allow Jon to better understand each step he performs in the audit program, allowing him to exercise professional care as an auditor.

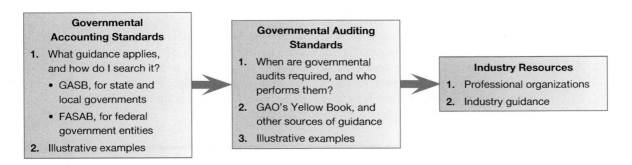

Organization of This Chapter

As you now know, guidance in the FASB Codification only applies to *nongovernmental* entities. So where should preparers of government financial statements go for guidance? And what professional standards apply to governmental auditors?

This chapter introduces sources of governmental accounting and auditing guidance, as well as several resources for accountants in industry. Readers will have the opportunity to apply guidance from each of the governmental accounting and auditing sources covered, from GASB, to FASAB, to GAO guidance.

In addition to describing key authoritative sources of guidance, this chapter describes select nonauthoritative resources used in practice by government accountants and auditors, and by accounting professionals in industry.

The preceding graphic illustrates the organization of topics within this chapter.

Let's begin now with the guidance applicable to governmental accounting.

GOVERNMENTAL ACCOUNTING RESEARCH

LO1 **Understand** the environment of governmental financial reporting, including circumstances in which state, local, and federal government financial statements may be required.

The first thing to understand about governmental accounting research is that the *research process* itself is no different from the process performed for nongovernmental entities. Like the accounting research process described in Chapter 3, governmental research starts with obtaining an understanding of the entity and its industry, then understanding the specific transaction, followed by identifying the researchable question then searching the literature and documenting conclusions.

What is unique about governmental accounting research, however, is the *body of knowledge* required to perform it. Governmental accounting differs fundamentally from private-sector accounting for a number of reasons. These include:

- The purposes of these entities differ. Governments exist for the public good, while private-sector companies exist for the benefit of their owners (shareholders).

- Governments generate revenues through taxation; private-sector companies generate revenues through sales of goods or services.

- Governments offer services for which they do not receive reciprocal value, such as social services; private-sector companies sell their goods and services in arm's-length exchanges to obtain profit.

- The community of government financial statement users, and their motivations, differ from those interested in private-sector financial statements.

Governmental financial statements are based on standards that reflect these unique qualities. These standards come in the form of guidance from the Governmental Accounting Standards Board (GASB) for state and local governments, and the Federal Accounting Standards Advisory Board (FASAB) for federal government reporting entities.

As in our opening scenario, it's important when performing governmental accounting research to refamiliarize yourself (if necessary) with the basics of governmental accounting. Governmental accounting textbooks (or governmental chapters in advanced accounting textbooks) can be a good resource for this. Once you review some of these basics, you will be ready to research more specific issues in governmental accounting and auditing. To help you along in this process, complete the following Now YOU Try.

[Now
YOU
Try
10.1]

Take a moment to brainstorm: What are some issues you can think of that might be unique to governmental accounting?

_____

_____

_____

The next sections of this chapter introduce, first, the standards for state and local government financial statements and, next, standards for federal government financial statements.

State and Local Accounting Standards

LO2 **Research** and **apply** guidance applicable to state and local governments, particularly within the GASB Codification.

Financial statements are an important means by which state and local governments and agencies can demonstrate their accountability to the public. The laws of many individual states, in fact, *require* that audited financial statements be prepared at the state and local government levels. Users of these financial statements range from parties interested in understanding the government's priorities (such as citizens and taxpayer groups) to lawmakers interested in setting future agendas and to parties interested in government bond issuances (such as investors, analysts, rating agencies, and municipal bond insurers).

The **Governmental Accounting Standards Board** (GASB) establishes accounting standards for state and local government entities. The AICPA Audit and Accounting Guide, *State and Local Governments*, par. 1.01, defines **governmental entities** as follows:[1]

> Public corporations and bodies corporate and politic are governmental entities. Other entities are governmental entities if they have one or more of the following characteristics:
>
> ■ Popular election of officers or appointment (or approval) of a controlling majority of the members of the organization's governing body by officials of one or more state or local governments;
>
> ■ The potential for unilateral dissolution by a government with the net assets reverting to a government; or
>
> ■ The power to enact and enforce a tax levy.
>
> Furthermore, entities are presumed to be governmental if they have the ability to issue directly (rather than through a state or municipal authority) debt that pays interest exempt from federal taxation. However, entities possessing only that ability (to issue tax-exempt debt) and none of the other governmental characteristics may rebut the presumption that they are governmental . . . [Footnotes omitted]

Figure 10-1 provides examples of state and local government entities subject to the GASB's guidance.

General purpose state and local governments	• State of California • Los Angeles County
Public benefit corporations and authorities	• The New York City Transit Authority
Public employee retirement systems	• The Teacher Retirement System of Texas
Governmental utilities, public hospitals and other healthcare providers	• El Paso Water Utilities, Texas • Health & Hospital Corp of Marion, Indiana
Public colleges and universities	• The Ohio State University

Figure 10-1

Examples of state and local government entities subject to GASB guidance

Take a moment now to consider the need for financial statements at the state and local government levels, in the following **Now YOU Try**.

Now YOU Try 10.2

1. Why might a state government require that audited financial statements be prepared at its statewide and local levels? Explain.

_____

_____

_____

_____

---

[1] As of press time, the GASB has tentatively decided to move this definition into the GASB Codification but has not yet done so.

2.   What organizations do you interact with or frequent that you expect might apply GASB guidance?

_____

_____

GASB guidance is considered *authoritative* for state and local government entities. In other words, these entities must apply GASB guidance in order for their financial statements to be "in conformity with generally accepted accounting principles," which is necessary for a government to receive an unmodified audit opinion. Although the GASB cannot force compliance with the standards it sets, the audit process and state laws requiring GAAP financial statements compel certain governments to comply.[2] In addition, many state and local governments are required, under borrowing agreements, to provide lenders with audited financial information.

Located just downstairs from the FASB in Norwalk, Connecticut, the GASB is an independent organization focused on creating and improving standards for state and local governments. The objective of these standards is to facilitate governments' public accountability, and to provide information that is useful to financial statement users. Like the FASB, the funding and administration of the GASB are overseen by the **Financial Accounting Foundation** (FAF). The GASB is funded primarily through an **accounting support fee** assessed to broker-dealers and investors in the municipal bond trading market.[3] Additionally, a portion of the GASB's funding comes from sales of its publications.

Considering the GASB's funding sources, respond to the following Now YOU Try.

Now YOU Try 10.3

In your own words, explain why it makes sense that an *accounting support fee*, assessed to participants in the municipal bond trading market, is used to fund the GASB.

_____

_____

_____

Guidance Issued by the GASB

The GASB issues the following guidance:

- Standards (Statements of Governmental Accounting Standards, or GASB Statements)
- Interpretations
- Technical Bulletins
- Implementation Guides (Q&As), issued by GASB staff
- Concepts Statements (Statements of Governmental Accounting Concepts)

The GASB uses the **GAAP hierarchy** depicted in Figure 10-2 to prioritize authoritative sources of state and local government accounting guidance.[4]

---

[2] GASB, *Facts About GASB*. 2015-2016. Page 1.

[3] This fee was established in 2012 through the Dodd-Frank Wall Street Reform and Consumer Protection Act.

[4] GASB Statement No. 76, *The Hierarchy of Generally Accepted Accounting Principles for State and Local Governments*, par. 4-8.

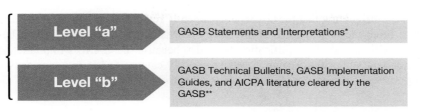

Figure 10-2

GAAP hierarchy for state and local entities

If the accounting treatment for a transaction or other event is not specified within a source of *authoritative GAAP* (level a or b), next a governmental entity should:

Consider guidance for **similar transactions.**

Next, consider nonauthoritative sources, as long as:
- The source doesn't conflict with authoritative guidance, and
- The source is consistent with the GASB Concepts Statements.

Examples:
- GASB Concepts Statements;
- Guidance from other standard setters (e.g., FASB, FASAB, international public- and private-sector standard setters)
- Practices that are widely recognized and prevalent in state and local government

* Includes standards and interpretations of the National Council on Governmental Accounting (NCGA), the GASB's predecessor.
** Authoritative only if specifically made applicable to state and local governmental entities.

Within Figure 10-2, level "a" and "b" sources are considered *authoritative*; however, the degree of their authority varies. Preparers of government financial statements should prioritize the use of level "a" sources; when such guidance is not available, level "b" guidance should be considered.

If authoritative guidance is not available for a transaction, guidance for similar transactions should be considered next, followed by nonauthoritative sources. Considering the GAAP hierarchy, respond to the following **Now YOU Try.**

Now YOU Try 10.4

1. In your own words, describe the order in which sources should be considered in applying the state and local government GAAP hierarchy.

   _____

   _____

   _____

   _____

2. Now, compare this state and local GAAP hierarchy with the FASB's guidance for using authoritative versus nonauthoritative sources.

   _____

   _____

   _____

3. Finally, in a sense, the GASB gives one nonauthoritative source priority over other sources. Name this source, and explain why you believe it is given priority.

   _____

   _____

   _____

It's worth noting that the GASB only recently revised these hierarchy levels (in 2015). Prior to that time, the GASB's GAAP hierarchy consisted of four levels (a–d). The hierarchy was revised with a goal of simplification, and also because the GASB's Implementation Guidance, an important authoritative source, was previously categorized as lower-priority *level d*. Among other changes, the revision elevated this source to *level b*.

Researching GASB Guidance

GASB guidance can generally be accessed (1) using the GASB's *Governmental Accounting Research System* (**GARS Online**) database or (2) using original standards on the GASB website.

GARS Online

The GARS Online database, depicted in Figure 10-3, includes access to the **GASB Codification** plus other related resources.

Much like the FASB Codification, the GASB Codification organizes authoritative guidance by topic and is the preferred method for accessing state and local government accounting guidance. Researchers can purchase a GARS Online subscription directly from the GASB or can obtain low-cost academic access through the American Accounting Association ($250 per school, per year). The GASB Codification can also be accessed within certain accounting research databases, such as CCH's *Accounting Research Manager* and PwC's *Inform* database.

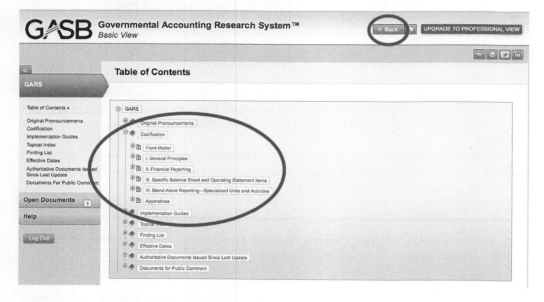

Figure 10-3

Homepage of GARS Online (blue circles added)

Reproduced with permission of the Financial Accounting Foundation.

Notice in Figure 10-3 that authoritative content (namely, the Original Pronouncements, the Codification, and Implementation Guides) has been circled for emphasis. **Unlike the situation for FASB guidance, the GASB's original pronouncements (to the extent not superseded) remain an authoritative source of guidance, despite the existence of the Codification.**

To access guidance in the Codification, click the + signs next to each heading (or else you'll just be directed to the preface of each section, if you click the heading itself). Also circled is the GARS Online "Back" button (use this, rather than your browser's "back" button, which may cause you to be logged off of GARS Online). Figure 10-4 further describes the content included within GARS Online.

GARS Link	Content
Original Pronouncements	Includes all original sources of governmental accounting guidance, such as: GASB Standards and Interpretations, Technical Bulletins, Concepts Statements, certain AICPA guidance, and Standards and Interpretations of the GASB's predecessor (the NCGA).
Codification	Includes the following currently-effective content, organized by topic: • GASB Standards, Interpretations, and Technical Bulletins • References to relevant AICPA Audit & Accounting Guides and Statements of Position • Links to related Implementation Guides
Implementation Guides	Includes: • The current-year *Comprehensive Implementation Guide* (Q&As), which includes all currently-effective implementation guidance organized by topic • Original Implementation Guides by standard, as issued
Finding List	Cross references each original pronouncement, by paragraph, to its location in the GASB Codification. Also identifies those paragraphs considered "background information" and thus not incorporated into the Codification.
Effective Dates	Lists the effective dates for each original pronouncement.
Documents for Public Comment	Links to guidance currently being proposed by the GASB.

Figure 10-4

Content included within GARS Online

Take a moment now to complete the following **Now YOU Try**, intended to improve your familiarity with the contents of GARS Online.

Considering the GARS Online screenshot from Figure 10-3 and the content descriptions in Figure 10-4, identify which resource a researcher would use:

1. For Q&As related to a particular Codification topic? _____

2. To find background information or the basis for conclusions in an original GASB standard?

   _____

3. If a researcher wants to locate the Codification reference for GASB Statement No. 34, par. 2? _____

Also, respond to the following:

4. What key sources of guidance were used to populate the GASB Codification? What level(s) in the GAAP hierarchy are these sources?

   _____

   _____

Now YOU Try

10.5

You may have noticed in Figure 10-3 that the GASB Codification includes four parts (I–IV) plus appendices; let's take a moment now to understand how guidance is organized within these four parts.

The Four Parts of the GASB Codification

Figure 10-5 illustrates the four parts of the GASB Codification, describes how guidance from each part should be referenced, and summarizes types of content located within each part. Take a moment to review Figure 10-5, then respond to the questions that follow.

Figure 10-5

The four parts of the GASB Codification, plus appendices

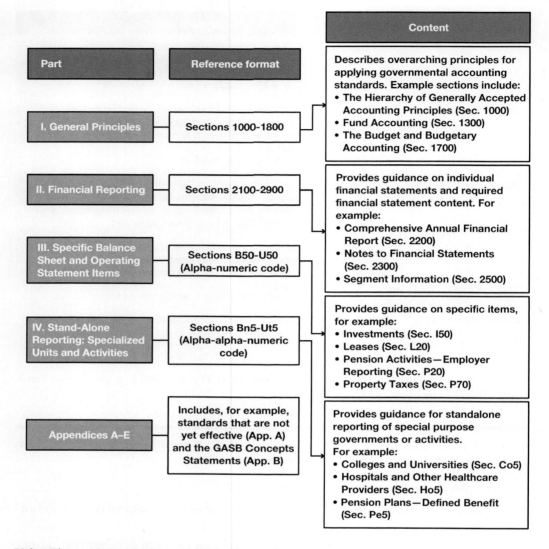

Using Figure 10-5, complete the following Now YOU Try.

In what part (I, II, III, or IV) of the Codification might a researcher find:

1. Sections entitled "Defining the Financial Reporting Entity" and "Cash Flow Statements"? _____

2. Guidance on differences between the cash and accrual bases of accounting? _____

3. Sections entitled "Bankruptcies," "Pension Plans," and "Regulated Operations"? _____

4. Sections entitled "Inventory" and "Nonmonetary Transactions"? _____

Browse Searches within GARS Online

As you know from prior chapters, a *browse search* means little more than attempting to navigate directly to appropriate guidance within a research database. In this case, researchers must first determine which *part* of the GASB Codification to search, then should look for relevant topics within that part. Browse searches are generally preferable to keyword searches in that they allow a researcher to understand how an issue fits into the broader context of the Codification.

Because the GASB Codification contains guidance with varying degrees of authority (recall the hierarchy of authoritative guidance), each paragraph within the Codification indicates its source material. This is also helpful to researchers looking for background information that is included within original standards, but which has not been included within the Codification. Also, where relevant, topics link to separately located content such as Implementation Guides and certain AICPA content. Certain topics also include paragraphs .901–.999, Nonauthoritative Discussion.

To illustrate the format of an individual topic, Figure 10-6 depicts the top-of-page matter for Topic Po50 (Postemployment Benefit Plans Other Than Pension Plans). Notice that the page lists the topic's source material ("Sources") and provides links to related topics (under "See Also"). Also circled in Figure 10-6 is the link to *Implementation Guidance* related to this topic.

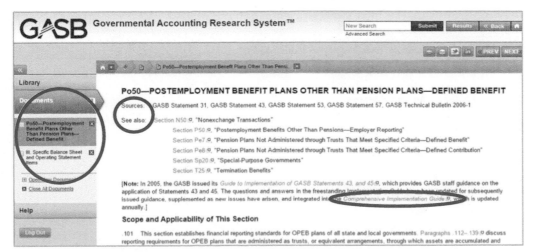

Figure 10-6

Sample GASB Codification section, Po50 (Postemployment Benefit Plans Other Than Pension Plans), blue circles added

Reproduced with permission of the Financial Accounting Foundation.

Considering Figure 10-6, respond to the following.

---

1. What are some sources used to generate this Codification topic Po50? Why might a researcher want to review these source materials?

_____

_____

_____

2. Circled in Figure 10-6 is a link to Implementation Guidance related to this topic. You should treat this information as *required reading*. Why do you think this is the case?

_____

_____

_____

Now
[**YOU**]
Try
10.7

A few additional observations regarding Figure 10-6: Notice that the list of "Open Documents" on the left side of the screen keeps a running list of any documents a researcher views. Click two of the checkboxes, and you'll have the option to view two documents concurrently. Additionally, researchers can use the "See Also" links for additional direction if an initial search proves fruitless.

[**TIP**] from the Trenches

When researching an issue that is new to you, chances are pretty good that you won't always end up in the right place the first time. Take advantage of the "See Also" links within each standard to generate ideas about possible other, or related, areas to search for relevant guidance.

Keyword Searches within GARS Online

Keyword searches within GARS Online are generally most appropriate when a researcher has a search term in mind but is not familiar with how that term fits into the literature.

The keyword search function within GARS Online is fairly straightforward, particularly for researchers familiar with FASB Codification searches. This function is depicted in Figure 10-7.

Figure 10-7

Advanced keyword search of GARS Online, blue circles added

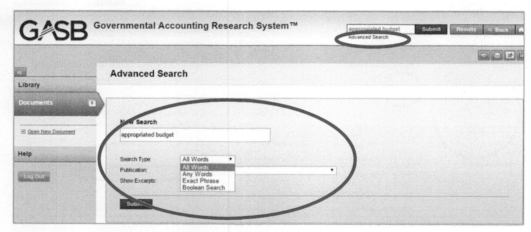

Reproduced with permission of the Financial Accounting Foundation.

As illustrated in Figure 10-7, a researcher can choose to search for all words, any words, an exact phrase, or using a "Boolean operator" search (where the terms "and," "or," or "not" are inserted between two search terms). Additional guidance on conducting Boolean searches is available under the GARS Online help menu (see left-hand link). Also in Figure 10-7, the search field "Publication" allows researchers to specify whether to search just within the Codification or within another area of GARS Online (such as Original Pronouncements only). Your best bet? Stick with the default option, to search the full GARS Online database, and your results will be organized by part anyway (e.g., "2 results in Original Pronouncements," "2 results in GASB Codification").

Keyword Searches within Other Research Databases

For researchers using other databases to access the GASB Codification, the mechanics of performing a keyword search will differ slightly. For example, Figure 10-8 illustrates a sample keyword search of the GASB Codification for the term "infrastructure" using CCH's *Accounting Research Manager* database.

Notice in Figure 10-8 that {Government, GASB, and GASB Codification} have been selected in the fields for {Subject, Author, and Book}, respectively. If, for example, a researcher is interested in interpretive governmental content authored by CCH, he or she could select "Government" as the subject, then "CCH" as the author. Alternatively, suppose a researcher is searching for a keyword within the GASB's original pronouncements; in this case, the researcher could select "GASB" as the author, then "GASB Statements" as the book.

Figure 10-8

Keyword search of the GASB Codification using CCH's *Accounting Research Manager*

Now **YOU** Try

10.8

Notice in Figure 10-8 the fields for Subject and Author in CCH's advanced search feature. If the Subject were changed to "Accounting" (i.e., nongovernmental content), what is one "Author" search option that you might expect to see?

An extended example applying guidance from the GASB Codification to a local government's sales and property tax revenues is provided in the **Appendix** to this chapter. Intended to expose beginning researchers to a range of issues, the example touches upon revenue recognition, application of the accrual/modified accrual bases of accounting, and fund accounting.

Now that you have a basic understanding of GARS Online and the GASB Codification, let's discuss another (albeit less desirable) option for accessing GASB guidance.

Accessing Standards on the GASB Website

A less ideal way to research GASB literature is by accessing full texts of the GASB's original standards free of charge on its website, www.gasb.org, under "Pronouncements." This manner of searching is less than ideal because

- These standards are only available in their original, *as issued* form on the GASB website and do not reflect revisions that may have occurred since their issuance.

- Guidance is not organized by topic. Therefore, in some cases, researchers must navigate through multiple standards and interpretations in order to understand the guidance applicable to a single topic.

- Finally, the GASB website does not include the full population of guidance applicable to government financial statements. For example, certain AICPA literature is considered authoritative for government financial statements but is neither accessible nor clearly referenced on the GASB's website.

Researchers using the GASB website therefore risk using outdated, or incomplete, sources. Recognizing these limitations, the GASB website cautions that its standards page is intended to serve only as a "general reference."[5]

To search for original standards on the GASB website, researchers can navigate to the Pronouncements page (under the Standards & Guidance tab). There, researchers can perform keyword searches on the page (using, for example, ctrl + f). Alternatively, researchers can perform an Advanced Search from the homepage, for any instances of a term on the GASB website. Figure 10-9 illustrates an advanced search for the term "infrastructure."

Figure 10-9

Search of the GASB website. Circled emphasis added.

Reproduced with permission of the Financial Accounting Foundation.

The current **status** of standards listed on the GASB website varies; certain standards are still fully applicable, while others may be fully or partially superseded. Figure 10-10 illustrates the standards list from the GASB website, including links to status information. Notice, for example, that Statement No. 22 has been fully superseded. Notice also the link to the Status page for each standard (such as under Statement No. 24).

Figure 10-10

Status information on the GASB website

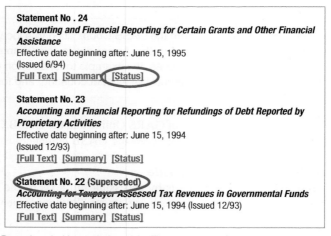

Reproduced with permission of the Financial Accounting Foundation.

When accessing standards on the GASB website, it is essential to review a standard's Status page. On this page, a researcher can determine how a given standard has been *affected by* subsequent guidance issuances, can identify ways this standard *affects* (or has changed) other standards, and can find references to *Other Interpretive Literature* related to the standard. It is critical to understand how current a standard is before relying upon it.

---

[5] www.GASB.org, Pronouncements. Accessed on 5/24/2015.

> The GASB's website can be a useful reference but should not be relied on as a source of authoritative guidance if you are performing governmental accounting in practice. There is just too much risk involved—you could inadvertently apply outdated guidance or miss an important interpretive source.

[**TIP**] from the Trenches

Additional Sources for State and Local Guidance

Numerous nonauthoritative resources are available to assist government accountants in the preparation of financial statements. These resources often include practical explanations of authoritative requirements, illustrations, and checklists. For example,

1. GFOA's "Blue Book," *Governmental Accounting, Auditing, and Financial Reporting (GAAFR)*

First published in 1934, the *Blue Book* of the **Government Finance Officers Association** (GFOA) provides practical guidance, reference materials, such as a model comprehensive annual financial report (CAFR), and chapters devoted to specialized topics (such as capital assets and derivatives). In addition to the Blue Book, the GFOA also offers training programs and program checklists designed to assist preparers.

Notably, the GFOA is also responsible for the Certificate of Achievement for Excellence in Financial Reporting Program, which is awarded to state and local governments for high quality financial reporting. Figure 10-11 illustrates the seal awarded to recipients of this distinction.

Figure 10-11

The GFOA's "Certificate of Achievement" seal for excellence in government reporting

Used with permission from GFOA.

2. PPC's *Guide to Preparing Governmental Financial Statements*

PPC's *Guide to Preparing Government Financial Statements* is a comprehensive government GAAP guide that offers a plain-English discussion of authoritative GAAP and walks users through issues involved with preparing financial statements, as well as offering checklists and additional resources.

3. Resources from the Association of Government Accountants (AGA)

The AGA, a professional organization for government accountants, offers online toolkits, guides, and training materials intended to improve the quality of government financial reporting. AGA publications, including its quarterly magazine, the *Journal of Government Financial Management,* assist government accountants in staying current with important industry news.

4. Interpretive Guidance within Firm Research Databases

Certain research databases offer subscribers access to interpretive guidance and tools for government accounting. CCH's *Accounting Research Manager*, for example, gives subscribers access to CCH's governmental GAAP practice manual, a governmental GAAP guide, audit tools, and checklists.

Next, we will discuss the accounting standards applicable to federal government financial statements.

Federal Accounting Standards

The **Federal Accounting Standards Advisory Board** (FASAB) establishes accounting standards applicable to U.S. government financial statements. Under the CFO Act of 1990, the U.S. government and its **component entities**, or federal reporting entities, are required to prepare annual, audited financial statements.

LO3 Become familiar with federal government accounting standards issued by the FASAB.

Specifically, the **CFO Act** required *executive* branch entities of the U.S. government to prepare audited financial statements; *legislative* and *judicial* branch entities are generally not subject to this requirement and instead report limited cash-basis financial information.[6] Annually, the financial statements of entities from each branch of the U.S. government are aggregated to create the government-wide **consolidated financial report** (CFR). This report is audited by the Government Accountability Office (GAO).

Figure 10-12 illustrates several of the executive branch entities (depicted as *significant reporting entities*) that are required to prepare audited financial statements.[7] Note, however, that not all entities required to comply with the CFO Act are shown in this graphic.

Figure 10-12

Organization of the U.S. government, including "significant" executive branch reporting entities required to prepare audited financial statements

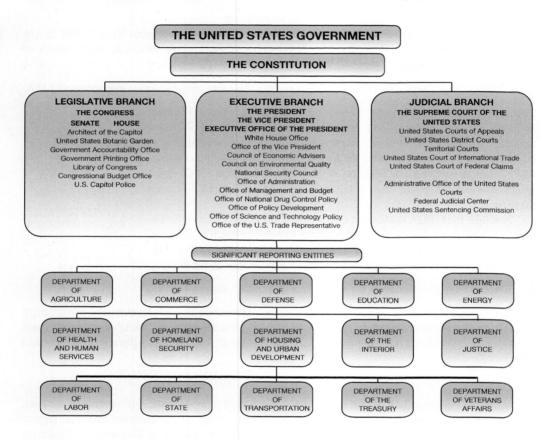

The FASAB was established in 1990 in order to create accounting standards for the financial reports required under the CFO Act. Federal officials representing the Department of the Treasury and the Office of Management and Budget (OMB), both Executive Branch entities, and the Government Accountability Office (GAO), a legislative branch agency—having the authority to set these standards—created the FASAB and delegated to it their standard setting responsibilities.

Collectively, the Department of Treasury, the OMB, and the GAO (i.e., the **sponsor agencies**) fund the FASAB. Of the FASAB's nine-member board, three members are appointed by the sponsor agencies, and six members are selected from the public. Two of the FASAB's sponsor agencies, the GAO and OMB, have the right to review and, at their discretion, object to, FASAB standards before they are issued as final.

---

[6] 2014 *Financial Report of the U.S. Government*, Note 1A: Reporting Entity. Page 55.

[7] This illustration was excerpted from the 2014 Financial Report of the U.S. Government, Management's Discussion and Analysis, Exhibit 1, page 2. The original illustration (not reproduced in full in this chapter) also lists several of the "other significant reporting entities" (such as the Securities and Exchange Commission) required to prepare audited financial statements.

1. Within Figure 10-12, locate the FASAB's three *sponsor agencies* and circle them.

2. Considering the *significant reporting entities* depicted in Figure 10-12, which entities' financial statements would you be most interested in reviewing? Why?

_____

_____

_____

_____

3. What perspectives or priorities might you expect members appointed by the GAO and OMB to bring to the FASAB board? Explain.

_____

_____

_____

_____

Now
YOU
Try
10.9

Notably, proposed legislation has been introduced that would endeavor to make the FASAB more independent by creating a more stable source of funding for the FASAB (such as a fee on the sale of Treasury notes) and by removing the Treasury Department's voting rights on the board. The FASAB has been criticized for failing to require the federal government to provide a complete picture of its liabilities (including Medicare and Social Security). Advocates of the proposed legislation would like the FASAB board to be more independent (some argue that the Treasury Department should not participate in creating the standards that it must implement), and would like the FASAB to have less reliance on its sponsor agencies for funding.

Guidance Issued by the FASAB

Guidance issued by the FASAB is referred to as **GAAP for federal entities**. The FASAB's authoritative sources of guidance are compiled and codified together in the *FASAB Handbook of Federal Accounting Standards and Other Pronouncements* (the "**FASAB Handbook**"), available free of charge at www.fasab.gov, under "Standards." The FASAB Handbook, depicted in Figure 10-13, reflects the current population of FASAB guidance and is generally updated annually. Individual standards issued between updates are also available on the FASAB's website.

FASAB guidance can also be accessed in certain, but not all, firm research databases. PwC's *Inform* database, for example, provides its subscribers access to FASAB's final and proposed guidance.

Figure 10-13

The FASAB Handbook
(cover image)

The FASAB Handbook includes:

- FASAB Standards, also referred to as Statements of Federal Financial Accounting Standards (SFFAS)
- Concepts Statements, also referred to as Statements of Federal Financial Accounting Concepts (SFFAC)
- Interpretations, also referred to as Interpretations of Federal Financial Accounting Standards
- Technical Bulletins (TB)
- Technical Releases (TR), also referred to as Federal Financial Accounting and Auditing Technical Releases
- Staff Implementation Guidance

The hierarchy depicted in Figure 10-14 applies to the use of FASAB guidance.

Figure 10-14

Hierarchy for the use of FASAB guidance[8]

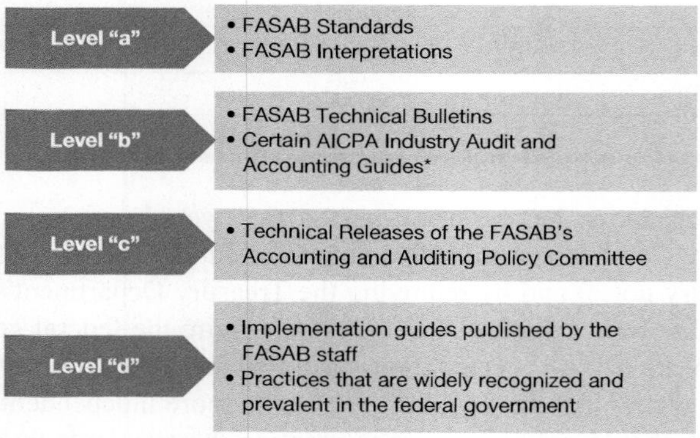

Level "a"	• FASAB Standards • FASAB Interpretations
Level "b"	• FASAB Technical Bulletins • Certain AICPA Industry Audit and Accounting Guides*
Level "c"	• Technical Releases of the FASAB's Accounting and Auditing Policy Committee
Level "d"	• Implementation guides published by the FASAB staff • Practices that are widely recognized and prevalent in the federal government

*If specifically made applicable to federal reporting entities by the AICPA and cleared by the FASAB

Preparers of federal government financial statements should utilize accounting guidance in the order of priority listed. That is, if guidance in level a is unavailable for a transaction, guidance in levels b–d may be applied in descending order. If none of these sources (a–d) offers relevant guidance, entities should consider guidance for similar transactions, then they may consider other sources of guidance such as the FASAB Concepts Statements or FASB, AICPA, GASB, or IASB guidance, articles, or textbooks.

Guidance within the FASAB handbook is organized by standard, and each standard is presented as a separate chapter. The Status page of each standard lists other standards and interpretive guidance that affect, or are affected by, the standard. For example, Figure 10-15 illustrates the Status page of SFFAS 33 (Pensions, Other Retirement Benefits, and Other Postemployment Benefits).

Figure 10-15

Sample "Status" page, showing guidance that affects (or is affected by) SFFAS 33

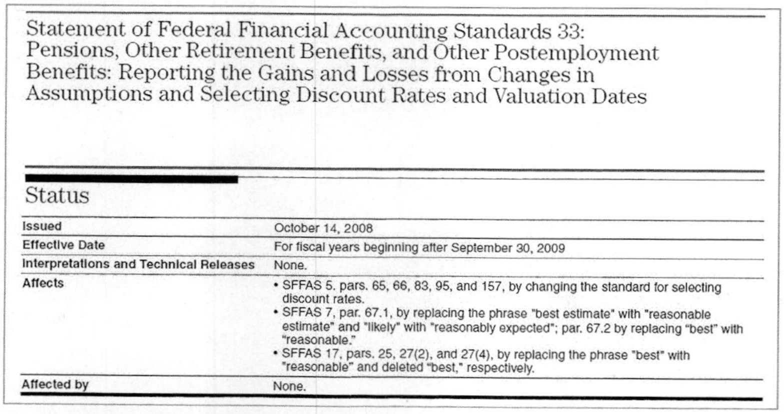

Statement of Federal Financial Accounting Standards 33: Pensions, Other Retirement Benefits, and Other Postemployment Benefits: Reporting the Gains and Losses from Changes in Assumptions and Selecting Discount Rates and Valuation Dates

Status

Issued	October 14, 2008
Effective Date	For fiscal years beginning after September 30, 2009
Interpretations and Technical Releases	None.
Affects	• SFFAS 5, pars. 65, 66, 83, 95, and 157, by changing the standard for selecting discount rates. • SFFAS 7, par. 67.1, by replacing the phrase "best estimate" with "reasonable estimate" and "likely" with "reasonably expected"; par. 67.2 by replacing "best" with "reasonable." • SFFAS 17, pars. 25, 27(2), and 27(4), by replacing the phrase "best" with "reasonable" and deleted "best," respectively.
Affected by	None.

Source: FASAB Handbook, as of June 30, 2014

---

[8] SFFAS 34, *The Hierarchy of Generally Accepted Accounting Principles, Including the Application of Standards Issued by the Financial Accounting Standards Board*, FASAB Handbook 2014 revision, par. 5.

To search for guidance within the FASAB Handbook, researchers can (1) perform "ctrl+f" (find) keyword searches within the Handbook or (2) scan the Handbook's table of contents to locate standards relevant to their searches. Within each individual standard is a table of contents, which can help researchers efficiently navigate to relevant guidance.

Applying FASAB Guidance

The following example illustrates the accounting for government Medicare obligations (a type of "social insurance"). Readers will have the opportunity to review and apply FASAB guidance applicable to this issue.

Accounting for Medicare

Now
[YOU]
Try
10.10

Facts about Medicare: Medicare is a national health insurance program for people ages 65 and older, as well as for certain individuals with disabilities. Generally, U.S. citizens and permanent residents meeting the age requirement are eligible for Medicare if they or their spouse worked for at least 10 years in Medicare-covered employment. Medicare is funded, in part, through a payroll tax levied on employees and employers.

Required: Read the following excerpts from SFFAS 17, *Accounting for Social Insurance*, then respond to the questions that follow.

14. The following programs are designated as social insurance and subject to these standards:
    - Old-Age, Survivors, and Disability Insurance (OASDI or "Social Security");
    - Hospital Insurance (HI) and Supplementary Medical Insurance (SMI), known collectively as "Medicare";
    - Railroad Retirement benefits;
    - Black Lung benefits; and
    - Unemployment Insurance (UI). . . .

Characteristics of Social Insurance Programs

15. These programs were developed to carry out the responsibilities of the government and generally have characteristics that make them unique. . . . This statement identifies the following five characteristics common among social insurance programs:
    (1) Financing from participants or their employers,
    (2) Eligibility from taxes/fees paid and time worked in **covered employment**,
    (3) Benefits not directly related to taxes/fees paid,
    (4) Benefits prescribed in law, and
    (5) Programs intended for the general public.

Questions:

1. First, recall from the reading: Is SFFAS 17 applicable to state and local governments, or to federal government entities? Explain.

_____

2. Read the "Facts about Medicare" above, then explain how you determined (under both par. 14 and 15) that Medicare is within the scope of this guidance:

    Par. 14: _____

    Par. 15: _____

    _____

    _____

    _____

SFFAS 17 states the following regarding the recognition and measurement of social insurance benefits:

22. The expense recognized for the reporting period should be the benefits paid during the reporting period plus any increase (or less any decrease) in the liability from the end of the prior period to the end of the current period. The liability should be social insurance benefits due and payable to or on behalf of beneficiaries at the end of the reporting period, including claims incurred but not reported (IBNR).

3. How does SFFAS 17 require governments to measure the liability for social insurance benefits?

_____

_____

4. Brainstorm, recalling from previous financial accounting courses: Is this recognition model consistent with how nongovernmental entities record employee retirement healthcare obligations? Explain.

_____

_____

_____

_____

5. What level in the FASAB hierarchy is this guidance? Explain.

_____

6. What other resources might you consult for additional interpretation of this SFFAS?

_____

_____

Referencing Governmental Accounting Guidance

Citing Standards

References to governmental accounting standards follow a similar format as references to other, nongovernmental sources. For example, following are sample references to GASB and FASAB standards:

- Per GASB Statement No. 72, *Fair Value Measurement and Application* (Statement 72 or GASBS 72) par. 28, "Valuation techniques should maximize the use of relevant observable inputs and minimize the use of unobservable inputs."
- Per Statement of Federal Financial Accounting Standards No. 1 (SFFAS 1), *Accounting for Selected Assets and Liabilities*, par. 18, "*intragovernmental assets and liabilities* arise from transactions among federal entities."

Both citations include the following required elements:

- The full name of the standard type (e.g., GASB Statement No., or Statement of Federal Financial Accounting Standards No.). This full introduction is necessary whenever guidance is first cited in a memo. Without this, a reader might have difficulty understanding how to locate this guidance.
- Full name of standard is included, in italics.
- Paragraph number is included.
- An indication (in parenthesis) that future references to this source will be abbreviated as "GASBS 72" or "SFFAS 1."

Future references to these standards may simply state: "Per GASBS 72, par. 28" or "Per SFFAS 1, par. 19," for example.

Citing the GASB Codification

References to the GASB Codification can be cited as follows:

> GASB Cod. Sec. 2300, par. 102 (Notes to Financial Statements) states: "The notes to the financial statements should communicate information essential for fair presentation of the basic financial statements that is not displayed on the face of the financial statements."

In this example, identification of the "GASB Cod" is provided initially; future references to the Codification within the same memo can be abbreviated as "Sec. 2300.102."

Next, we'll turn our attention to the standards for performing governmental audits.

GOVERNMENTAL AUDITING STANDARDS

In What Circumstances Are Government Audits Required?

Recall from our discussion of governmental accounting standards that many state, local, and federal government entities are required to prepare audited financial statements. These audits may be required by

LO4 **Recognize** and **apply** government auditing standards issued by the GAO.

- The CFO Act, which requires certain federal entities to prepare annual, audited financial statements;
- The laws of individual states, which may require annual audited state and local government financial statements; or
- Compliance with debt or other covenants, requiring governments (borrowers) to provide audited financial statements.

In addition to financial statement audits, entities may be required to undergo **performance audits** in certain circumstances. The objectives of individual performance audits can vary but might focus on, for example,

- The efficiency and effectiveness of a government program (e.g., Are government resources being expended in the manner intended?);
- An entity's internal controls and governance structure;
- An entity's information security; or
- An entity's compliance with laws and regulations.

Following are two circumstances in which performance audits are currently required.

"Single Audit" Requirement for Recipients of Federal Funding

Entities receiving federal funding in excess of $750,000 are required by the U.S. government's Office of Management and Budget (**OMB**) **Circular A-133** to undergo a **single audit**.[9] Illustrated in Figure 10-16, a single audit is defined as a financial statement audit plus a *program* (aka, performance) audit of programs for which federal funds have been received. Single audits must be conducted in accordance with both Circular A-133 and governmental auditing standards, and these audit requirements apply to both governmental and nongovernmental entities receiving federal funding.

---

[9] OMB Circular No. A-133, "Audits of States, Local Governments, and Non-Profit Organizations." Revised to show changes published in the Federal Register June 27, 2003 and June 26, 2007. Subpart B (Audits), Section .200 (Audit Requirements), par. (a). Also revised to reflect updates to 2CFR Chapter I and Chapter II Parts 200, 215, 220 225 and 230, *Uniform Administrative Requirements, Cost Principles, and Audit Requirements for Federal Awards.*

Figure 10-16

A "single audit" combines required financial statement and performance audits, for recipients of federal funds

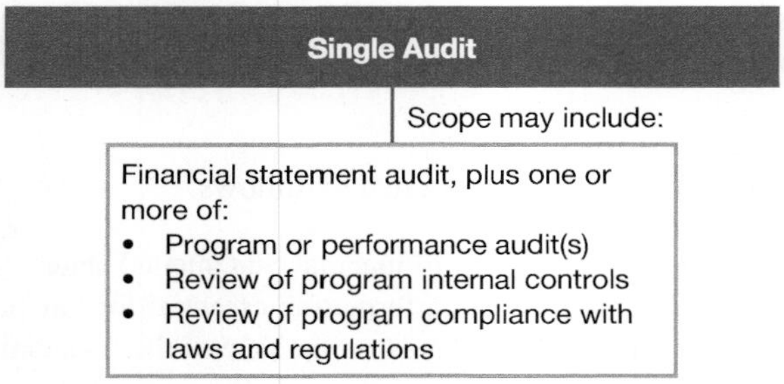

Single Audit
Scope may include:
Financial statement audit, plus one or more of: • Program or performance audit(s) • Review of program internal controls • Review of program compliance with laws and regulations

Annually, the OMB prepares a **Compliance Supplement** document that includes specific guidance to assist auditors in complying with the requirements of Circular A-133. This Compliance Supplement also includes department-specific guidance for auditing federal award programs.

■ For example, auditors reviewing the effectiveness of the Department of Justice "COPS" grants—funds awarded to local governments for the purpose of hiring additional police officers—must consult the Department of Justice chapter within the annual Compliance Supplement. That chapter instructs local government auditors, when conducting performance audits, to ask questions including: "How many active COPS grant position(s) were filled/hired? Full-Time and Part-Time."[10]

Considering the requirements of Circular A-133 and the Compliance Supplement just described, respond to the following.

Now YOU Try 10.11

1. In your own words, explain why a financial statement audit, plus a performance audit, could be beneficial in the case of these local governments that received Department of Justice COPS grants.

_____

_____

_____

2. Generally speaking, in what circumstances is a local government subject to this *single audit* requirement?

_____

_____

_____

State-Required Performance Audits

Certain states require their municipal governments and agencies to submit to periodic performance audits, which can range in their objectives and scope. For example,

■ In New York, the Office of the State Comptroller (OSC) conducts performance audits of state agencies, public authorities, and local governments (including towns, villages, school districts, and fire districts). The focus of these audits can vary, from a review of internal controls, to a review of the entity's governance structure, to reviews of specific programs' efficiency and effectiveness. The type of audit required is determined based on a risk assessment by the OSC.

---

[10] OMB Circular No. A-133, Compliance Supplement 2014. Department of Justice supplement: "Public Safety Partnership and Community Policing Grants." Section L(2), Performance Reporting.

■ The need for regular oversight over school district governance and controls, in particular, was underscored by the $11 million, Roslyn, New York, School District fraud, uncovered in a 2005 audit.[11] Perpetrated primarily by the district's Superintendent and the school district's chief financial officer, this fraud might have been prevented had effective governance and internal controls been in place. In response to this fraud, the New York OSC initiated a 5-year effort to review the internal controls of all New York school districts, in addition to continuing to require annual, independent financial audits of all school districts in the state.[12]

Clearly, government audits can range widely in their objectives and complexity; these examples illustrate just a few of the circumstances in which government audits are required. Next, let's discuss the parties who perform government audits.

Who Performs Government Audits?

You may be wondering: do all *government auditors* work for the government? It's true that many auditors of government financial statements work for federal, state, or local governments; however, individuals in public accounting firms also frequently perform government audits. Therefore, even if your future involves working for a public accounting firm, it is possible that *you* will be assigned to a governmental client.

Often, the governmental entity under audit can engage a firm of its choice; however, in many cases, the federal government may conduct (or assign responsibility to another agency for conducting) an audit of a state or local government that receives federal government funds. Similarly, state auditors may audit municipalities or appoint another auditor of the state's choice.

Many federal agencies have an **Office of the Inspector General** whose mission is, in part, to audit the programs and operations of the agency.[13]

Figure 10-17 illustrates a sample of CFO Act agencies and their auditors, as well as their fiscal year 2014 audit opinion.

CFO Act Agency	Opinion	Auditor
Department of Agriculture	Unmodified	Office of Inspector General (OIG) of the Agriculture Dept.
Department of Commerce	Unmodified	KPMG LLP
Department of Defense	Disclaimer	OIG of the Defense Dept.
Department of Education	Unmodified	CliftonLarsonAllen LLP
Department of Energy	Unmodified	KPMG LLP

Figure 10-17

Sample of fiscal year 2014 CFO Act agencies audited, opinions received, and auditors

Unfortunately, as a profession, our ability to perform quality governmental audits has historically been underwhelming.

EXAMPLE

In a June 2007 project, several federal agencies worked together to test (based on statistical sampling) the audit quality of federal funds recipients. Of the 208 audits sampled,[14]

■ 63 audits were found to be "unacceptable" and could not be relied on.

■ 30 audits had significant deficiencies and were considered to be of "limited reliability."

■ 115 were considered "acceptable" and thus could be relied on.

Continued

[11] Huefner, Ronald J. "Local government fraud: the Roslyn School District case." *Management Research Review,* copyright Emerald Group Publishing Limited. Vol. 33, No. 3, 2010. Page 199.

[12] Division of Local Government and School Accountability, of the Office of the New York State Comptroller. "Making the Grade: Five Years of School District Accountability." 2009 Annual Report. February 2010. Page 2.

[13] Inspector General's Act of 1978, as amended.

[14] President's Council on Integrity and Efficiency, "Report on National Single Audit Sampling Project." June 2007. Page 2.

It's worth noting that the acceptable audits represented an overwhelming majority (92.9%) of the federal awards (in dollars) reviewed. However, based on *numbers of audits*, the results showed significant percentages of unacceptable audits and audits of limited reliability. Per the government report:

> . . . For those audits not in the acceptable group, in our opinion, lack of due professional care was a factor for most deficiencies to some degree. [15]

The report offered the following recommendations to the government and the accounting profession: (1) improve *audit standards* and guidance, particularly related to documentation and audit sampling; (2) require *minimum levels of training* for government auditors; and (3) establish *clear consequences* for unacceptable audits.

Consistent with these recommendations, the next section of this chapter introduces readers to the authoritative guidance applicable to government audits, and describes the minimum training requirements applicable to government auditors.

Standards for Government Audits

The U.S. Government Accountability Office—Standard Setter

The U.S. **Government Accountability Office** (GAO) serves as the primary standard setter for government audits, establishing professional standards for audits of financial statements, attestation engagements, and performance audits. The GAO's standards, codified in the **Yellow Book** of government auditing standards, are collectively referred to as **generally accepted government auditing standards**, or **GAGAS**. In addition, the GAO's **Green Book** sets forth standards for internal control in the federal government.

Despite its important role in setting government auditing standards, to call the GAO simply a standard setter would be an understatement. A legislative-branch, nonpartisan agency, the GAO describes its mission as twofold: (1) to support Congress by providing objective, fact-based information and (2) to help improve the performance and ensure the accountability of the federal government. Also referred to as the *congressional watchdog*, the GAO is the audit and investigative arm of Congress, frequently studying the ways taxpayer dollars are spent.

The GAO is headed by the Comptroller General of the United States, who is appointed by the U.S. president to serve a 15-year term. Having long-term requirements supports the agency's independence and the ability of its leaders to develop institutional knowledge.

In addition to issuing auditing standards, the GAO performs certain audits. Notably, the GAO is responsible for auditing the annual federal government-wide financial statements.

Content and Organization of GAO Guidance

The GAO's *Yellow Book* is the authoritative source for government audit requirements, covering a range of topics including auditor ethics, and engagement planning, performance, and reporting requirements.[16] Using AICPA standards as a base, GAGAS adds to and/or modifies these requirements in order to address government-specific audit issues.

It is important to understand that auditors adhering to the Yellow Book *must also comply, in full, with the audit and attestation standards of the AICPA*. The AICPA's audit and attestation standards are **incorporated by reference** into GAGAS, meaning that although AICPA standards have not been copied into the Yellow Book, the Yellow Book requires auditors to fully comply

---

[15] President's Council on Integrity and Efficiency, "Report on National Single Audit Sampling Project." June 2007. Page 3.

[16] GAO, *Government Auditing Standards* (i.e., the "Yellow Book"). 2011 Revision. Chapter 1, par. 1.04.

with these standards in addition to government-specific Yellow Book standards. Notably, certain of the AICPA's clarified standards include "governmental consideration" paragraphs specific to governmental audits. PCAOB standards are not incorporated into GAGAS.

Per Chapter 4 (Standards for Financial Audits) of the Yellow Book:

> 4.01 . . . GAGAS incorporates by reference the American Institute of Certified Public Accountants (AICPA) Statements on Auditing Standards (SAS) . . . All sections of the SASs are incorporated, including the introduction, objectives, definitions, requirements, and application and other explanatory material. Auditors performing financial audits in accordance with GAGAS should comply with the incorporated SASs and the additional requirements in this chapter. . . .
>
> 4.02 GAGAS establishes requirements for performing financial audits in addition to the requirements contained in the AICPA standards. Auditors should comply with these additional requirements, along with the incorporated SASs, when citing GAGAS in their reports.

In the auditor's (or attestation provider's) report, when stating that an engagement was performed in accordance with GAGAS, it is not necessary to state that the engagement also complied with AICPA standards. Because GAGAS incorporates AICPA standards by reference, it is understood that an engagement performed in accordance with GAGAS also complies with AICPA standards.[17]

Following is a brief **Now YOU Try** exercise intended to reinforce the sources of guidance that must be followed under GAGAS.

Understanding Compliance with GAGAS

Now YOU Try 10.12

Review the excerpt from **par. 4.01** and the preceding discussion, and respond to the following.

1. For an auditor to comply with GAGAS, he or she must also comply with the AICPA's _____ .

2. Specifically, an auditor must comply with all sections of the AICPA's SAS, including the introduction, objectives, _____ .

3. When citing compliance with GAGAS in the auditor's report, it is not necessary to also state that the audit complied with AICPA standards because: _____

The Yellow Book is accessible on the GAO's website, as follows:

- www.gao.gov/yellowbook; or
- www.gao.gov, then "Resources For" then "Auditing and Accountability" then "Government Auditing Standards."

Figure 10-18 illustrates the cover page and the first table of contents page from the Yellow Book.

Within the Yellow Book, guidance is organized by topic. Therefore, when searching for guidance, researchers may find it most efficient to scan the Yellow Book's table of contents. This offers researchers the benefit of getting a feel for available guidance and seeing how it is organized. Alternatively, researchers can perform keyword searches of the entire document, using ctrl + f.

---

[17] GAO, *Government Auditing Standards* (i.e., the "Yellow Book"). 2011 Revision. Chapter 4, par. 4.18; Chapter 5, par. 5.19, 5.51, and 5.61.

Figure 10-18

GAO's *Government Auditing Standards* (Yellow Book) cover page and excerpt from table of contents

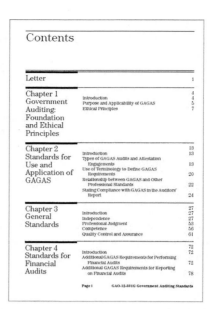

Figure 10-19 lists the chapters and summarizes some of the key content included in the Yellow Book.

Figure 10-19

Yellow Book chapters and content summary

Chapter	Examples of chapter content
Chapter 1, Government Auditing: Foundation and Ethical Principles	• Describes the purpose and applicability of GAGAS (identifies entities subject to) • Role of government auditors • Role of ethics in audits
Chapter 2, Standards for Use and Application of GAGAS	• Defines types of GAGAS engagements (financial/performance audits, attestation engagements) • Defines "unconditional" and "presumptively mandatory" requirements • Describes the relationship between GAGAS and other professional standards (such as AICPA guidance)
Chapter 3, General Standards	• Requires auditors to be independent, to use professional judgment, to possess technical competence • Audit firms must maintain a system of quality control
Chapter 4, Standards for Financial Audits	• Requires auditors to comply with AICPA audit standards in addition to specific GAGAS field work and reporting standards
Chapter 5, Standards for Attestation Engagements	• Requires auditors to comply with AICPA attestation standards in addition to specific GAGAS standards
Chapter 6, Field Work Standards for Performance Audits	• Provides guidance for performance audits, including audit planning, evidence, and documentation
Chapter 7, Reporting Standards for Performance Audits	• Provides guidance on communicating the results of performance audits
Appendixes	• Supplemental guidance • Conceptual Framework for independence

Notably, within Yellow Book Chapter 3 (General Standards), the section on auditor competency includes certain training requirements for government auditors. Specifically, government auditors must earn at least 80 hours of continuing education credits in the fields of audit and attestation every 2 years, and 24 hours of this must pertain specifically to the government environment and government auditing.[18]

---

[18] GAO, *Government Auditing Standards* (i.e., the "Yellow Book"). 2011 Revision. Chapter 3, par. 3.76. Also: GAO, *Guidance on GAGAS Requirements for Continuing Professional Education*, April 2005. Par. 18–19.

Take a moment now to practice your Yellow Book research skills with the following **Now YOU Try** exercise.

Locating Information within the Yellow Book

Now
YOU
Try
10.13

Provide the chapter number that you would consult for guidance on the following questions.

1. Are GAGAS applicable to nonprofit entities?

   Chapter No. _____

2. What audit evidence is required for auditors engaged to perform "performance" audits?

   Chapter No. _____

3. What are the minimum training requirements necessary for a government auditor to demonstrate "competence"?

   Chapter No. _____

4. Like the AICPA, does GAGAS use the word "must" to indicate an unconditional requirement?

   Chapter No. _____

5. What additional documentation (beyond AICPA requirements) is required for financial statement audits performed under GAGAS?

   Chapter No. _____

Citing GAO Guidance

The following example illustrates an appropriate reference to guidance from the Yellow Book.

▪ Per *Government Auditing Standards, December 2011 Revision,* Section 3.02 (Independence):

> **3.02** In all matters relating to the audit work, the audit organization and the individual auditor, whether government or public, must be independent.

Note that the preceding reference contains the title of the source (*Government Auditing Standards*) as well as the date of revision. As a researcher, err on the side of caution and assume your reader does not know what a "yellow book" is—only use this term after introducing the full title of the source.

Because the Yellow Book is revised periodically, it is necessary to include the date of the revision you have consulted. Without this complete information, future readers of your memo may have difficulty locating your original source.

Note also that section and paragraph numbers (e.g., 3.02) should be included any time specific guidance is cited.

Other Governmental Audit Resources

In addition to the GAO's Yellow Book and the OMB's Circular A-133 and supplements, several other sources of authoritative guidance exist for government audits. These include (but are not limited to):

▪ OMB Bulletin No. 14-02, *Audit Requirements for Federal Financial Statements* (as amended), which establishes additional audit requirements for federal government financial statements.

▪ FASAB Technical Releases, located within the *FASAB Handbook*, which set forth certain requirements for audits of federal government entities.

▪ State-specific audit requirements, often included within individual states' audit manuals. States may require governmental auditors to comply with these requirements in addition to complying with GAGAS.

Nonauthoritative Resources

A number of practical, nonauthoritative resources are also available to aid government auditors. These include (but are not limited to) the following.

1. GAO Financial Audit Manual (FAM)

The GAO produces an audit manual (the FAM) intended to improve the consistency, efficiency, and effectiveness of government audits. The FAM includes, for example, practical guidance to auditors for identifying and addressing areas of key risk.[19]

2. AICPA Resources

The AICPA recently issued an audit guide, *Government Auditing Standards and Circular A-133 Audits*, intended to provide auditors with practical resources and tips for performing government audits.

In addition, the AICPA's Governmental Audit Quality Center (GAQC) strives to improve the quality of governmental audits by providing educational resources, community forums, and practice aids (including audit checklists) to its members.

3. PPC Guides

PPC's *Guide to Single Audits* and PPC's *Guide to Audits of Local Governments* offer resources for understanding and performing government audits and include audit programs, checklists, confirmations, auditor's reports, and the like.

Applying Governmental Auditing Standards

Following are two examples illustrating the application of governmental audit guidance. The first example illustrates an audit report for a local government performance audit. The second example illustrates the GAO's audit findings related to its audit of the U.S. federal government.

Now
[YOU]
Try
10.14

Audit of Local Government's Receipt of Grant Funds

Facts: In 2012, the U.S. Department of Justice's Office of the Inspector General (OIG) conducted a program audit of "COPS" grant money received by the City of Newark, New Jersey. The COPS program offers federal grant money to local governments in order to enhance their local policing efforts and to upgrade existing police communication systems.

Following is an excerpt from the Yellow Book describing the reporting requirements for performance (including program) audits:

> **7.08** Auditors should prepare audit reports that contain (1) the objectives, scope, and methodology of the audit; (2) the audit results, including findings, conclusions, and recommendations, as appropriate; (3) a statement about the auditors' compliance with GAGAS; (4) a summary of the views of responsible officials; and (5) if applicable, the nature of any confidential or sensitive information omitted.

Following are excerpts from the OIG's audit report on Newark's use of COPS funds.[20]

> The purpose of this audit was to determine whether reimbursements claimed for costs under the grant were allowable, supported, and in accordance with applicable laws,

Continued

---

[19] GAO/PCIE *Financial Audit Manual*, Volume 1. July 2008. Section 110 (Overview), par. 14–15. The GAO is in the process of updating this manual.

[20] U.S. Department of Justice Office of the Inspector General Audit Division, Audit Report GR-70-12-007. July 2012. Pages i–ii, 17.

regulations, guidelines, and terms and conditions of the grant, and to determine program performance and accomplishments. COPS awarded Newark $2,787,001 to implement the grant program and required Newark to provide $929,000 in local funds for a total project cost of $3,716,001.

We examined Newark's accounting records, financial and progress reports, and operating policies and procedures and found the deficiencies below resulting in net questioned costs totaling $3,539,432.

- Newark significantly changed the scope of the grant project without prior written approval from COPS.
- Newark did not achieve the performance objectives related to voice communications funded by the grant.
- Newark purchased wireless network equipment and services totaling $2,777,569 that were not procured using a competitive process or approved for purchase under the New Jersey State Cooperative Purchasing program, which is in violation of grant regulations requiring competition. . . .

We conducted this performance audit in accordance with generally accepted government auditing standards. Those standards require that we plan and perform the audit to obtain sufficient, appropriate evidence to provide a reasonable basis for our findings and conclusions based on our audit objectives.

Using the excerpted GAGAS requirements and the OIG audit report, respond to the questions that follow.

Questions:

1. What law or standard, discussed within the chapter, requires certain recipients of federal grant funds to be audited?

_____

2. Describe how the OIG's audit report satisfies the GAGAS requirements excerpted in par. 7.08. (Or note any areas not covered in this excerpt).

   i) _____

   ii) _____

   iii) _____

   iv) _____

   v) _____

Audit Report—Federal Government-Wide Financial Statements

Facts: One of the GAO's responsibilities is to audit the consolidated U.S. government-wide financial report on an annual basis. However, fiscal year 2014 marked the eighteenth consecutive year that the GAO expressed a disclaimer of opinion on this report.[21] The following example focuses on the GAO's reported internal control findings which were, in part, responsible for this disclaimer of opinion.

Now
YOU
Try
10.15

[21] 2014 *Financial Report of the U.S. Government*. Management's Discussion & Analysis, page 5.

The following excerpts from the Yellow Book describe auditor reporting requirements related to internal controls:

Reporting on Internal Control and Compliance with Provisions of Laws, Regulations, Contracts, and Grant Agreements

4.19   When providing an opinion or a disclaimer on financial statements, auditors should also report on internal control over financial reporting . . .

Presenting Findings in the Auditors' Report

4.28   When performing a GAGAS financial audit and presenting findings such as deficiencies in internal control . . . auditors should develop the elements of the findings to the extent necessary . . . If auditors sufficiently develop the elements of a finding, they may provide recommendations for corrective action. [Footnotes omitted]

The next excerpt is from the GAO's consolidated federal government audit report:

Basis for Disclaimers of Opinion on the Consolidated Financial Statements

The federal government is not able to demonstrate the reliability of significant portions of [its] financial statements . . . principally resulting from limitations related to certain material weaknesses in internal control over financial reporting and other limitations affecting the reliability of these financial statements and the scope of our work . . . As a result of these limitations, readers are cautioned that amounts reported in the accrual-based consolidated financial statements and related notes may not be reliable.

. . . The underlying material weaknesses in internal control, which have existed for years, contributed to our disclaimer of opinion on the accrual-based consolidated financial statements. [These include] the federal government's inability to

- satisfactorily determine that property, plant, and equipment and inventories and related property, primarily held by the Department of Defense (DOD), were properly reported in the accrual-based consolidated financial statements;
- reasonably estimate or adequately support amounts reported for certain liabilities, such as environmental and disposal liabilities, or determine whether commitments and contingencies were complete and properly reported;
- support significant portions of the reported total net cost of operations, most notably related to DOD, and adequately reconcile disbursement activity at certain federal entities;
- adequately account for and reconcile intragovernmental activity and balances between federal entities;
- reasonably assure that the consolidated financial statements are (1) consistent with the underlying audited entities' financial statements, (2) properly balanced, and (3) in accordance with [GAAP]; . . .

Questions:

1.   According to par. 4.19 of the Yellow Book, when must auditors report on internal controls over financial reporting?

_____

2.   What reasons does the GAO give for its disclaimer of opinion?

_____

_____

3. Describe how the GAO's audit report excerpt satisfies the requirements in par. 4.28 of the Yellow Book—and identify any areas not shown in this particular excerpt that are also required by par. 4.28.

_____

_____

_____

_____

_____

_____

Finally, let us turn our attention to several resources available to management accountants.

INDUSTRY RESOURCES

The last section of this chapter introduces additional professional resources available to management accountants (also known as "industry" accountants). Namely, we will discuss professional organizations, as well as standards available to management accountants, internal auditors, and government contractors. The population of standards and professional resources described below is not all-inclusive; rather, this discussion is intended to introduce just a few of the many resources available to practicing accountants.

> **LO5** **Become** familiar with several industry accounting resources, including professional organizations and standards.

Professional Organizations

Numerous professional groups, or trade organizations, are available for accountants in industry. These organizations offer members the opportunity to network, attend industry-specific training courses, and to exchange best practices. Also, in some cases, these organizations issue standards applicable to professionals in a particular industry. Professional organizations of accountants include, just to name a few:

- The American Institute of CPAs (AICPA)
- The Institute of Management Accountants (IMA)
- Institute of Internal Auditors (IIA)
- The International Federation of Accountants (IFAC)
- Financial Executives International (FEI)
- The Association of Certified Fraud Examiners (ACFE)

As a practitioner, it may be both helpful (or often, necessary) to become familiar with the professional groups applicable to your industry, and the resources they offer.

Next, let's discuss a few sources of industry guidance available to management accountants. Recall that Chapter 3 also discusses resources for getting to know a new industry.

AICPA Accounting and Auditing Guides

See Chapter 3 for a more complete discussion of these guides, which can be indispensable for accountants seeking information on a specific industry.

Library Databases

Business databases—such as **Hoovers**, **Mergent Online**, **IBISWorld**, **S&P NetAdvantage**, and **LexisNexis** (to name a few)—can assist in your understanding of an industry, from learning about industry trends, supply chains, and competitors, as well as key financial ratios applicable to the industry. These databases are frequently accessible through your school, firm, or community library.

Management Accounting Standards

The Institute of Management Accountants (IMA) is a professional organization focused on the development and advancement of management accountants and finance professionals working inside organizations. Its members include, for example, individuals ranging from CFOs, to treasurers, to staff accountants.

As part of its mission to support management accountants, the IMA issues Statements on Management Accounting (SMAs). These standards are intended to provide valuable, in-depth information, best practices, and implementation guidance on a range of management accounting subjects. SMAs cover topics ranging from leadership and ethics, to cost management, to corporate governance. Application of SMAs is not required; rather, these standards are intended to be useful to individuals and corporations.

Internal Audit Resources

The Institute of Internal Auditors (IIA) is a professional association dedicated to supporting and advancing the internal audit profession. The IIA issues guidance, which is primarily divided into two types: (1) mandatory and (2) strongly recommended. Following are the IIA's "mandatory" sources of guidance:

- Definition of Internal Auditing
- IIA's Code of Ethics
- *International Standards for the Professional Practice of Internal Auditing* (Standards)

These sources receive their authority as "mandatory" through internal audit charters maintained within business organizations. Internal audit charters give the internal audit department access to business unit information and records, while simultaneously establishing expectations for the work and conduct of the internal audit department. For reference, the IIA makes a Model Internal Audit Activity Charter available at its website, www.theiia.org.

The IIA's sources of "strongly recommended" guidance consist of: Position Papers, Practice Advisories, and Practice Guides. Internal auditors are encouraged to comply with these sources of interpretive guidance, as applicable.

The IIA's mandatory standards consist of requirements and interpretive guidance governing the planning, performance, and reporting of internal audit engagements. These standards are contained within a single booklet, accessible on the IIA's website.

Cost Accounting Standards (for Government Contractors and Certain Universities)

The **Cost Accounting Standards Board**, created by the Office of Federal Procurement Policy (an executive branch entity), establishes cost accounting standards (CAS) for government contractors and universities receiving government grants. For contractors, these standards apply in full to entities awarded projects in excess of $50 million (individually, or in the aggregate), and in part to certain contracts of lesser amounts. Government contractors (excluding small businesses) must comply with these standards in the measurement, assignment, and allocation of costs to negotiated contracts with the U.S. government. Among these requirements, contractors must disclose their cost accounting practices in writing to the government (the "CAS Disclosure Statement").

Contracts with the U.S. Department of Defense make up the majority of procurement contracts subject to CAS. As defense contractors submit cost-based contract proposals to the Department of Defense, these costs must be determined in accordance with CAS.

Guidance issued by this board includes CAS, as well as rules and regulations. Collectively, these sources of guidance are codified within the "Code of Federal Regulations" (CFR), at Title 48, Chapter 99. Proposed and final rules are published in the *Federal Register*, a daily news publication of the federal government.

In addition to government contractors, colleges and universities receiving government grants in excess of $25 million are also subject to certain CAS requirements. For example, these entities must disclose their cost accounting policies to the federal government and follow certain project costing guidelines.

As you begin to specialize as a professional, take the time to become familiar with the organizations and standards available for your industry.

[**TIP**] from the
Trenches

APPENDIX 10A: APPLYING THE GASB CODIFICATION, AN EXTENDED EXAMPLE

Recognition of Tax Revenues, Using Fund Accounting

The following example illustrates the recognition of sales and property tax revenues by a local government. In doing so, the example touches on the different bases of accounting applicable to governments (accrual and modified accrual), as well as the use of fund accounting. For teaching purposes, this example has been kept very simple; however, in practice, these issues can be much more nuanced and can require professional judgment and as necessary, additional research.

Facts: Assume that the Town of Hampton imposes two taxes on its residents:

1. A 10 cents per-gallon fuel tax, charged on purchases of gasoline from gas stations located in the town.

2. A 2% property tax, charged annually on the assessed value of residential properties. This tax is billed in January of each year; collections generally occur within 15 to 30 days.

Respond to the questions that follow using the guidance provided.

Are the Town of Hampton's two taxes considered "nonexchange transactions"?

GASB Cod. Sec. N50.104 (Nonexchange Transactions) defines a "nonexchange transaction" as one where a government *"either* gives value (benefit) to another party without directly receiving equal value in exchange *or* receives value (benefit) from another party without directly giving equal value in exchange."

Per Section N50, par. 104, nonexchange transactions are divided into *four classes*:

- **Derived tax revenues**, imposed by governments on exchange transactions; examples include taxes on sales of goods or services, and corporate or personal income taxes.

- **Imposed nonexchange revenues**, based on assessments imposed by a government entity on a nongovernmental entity (excluding assessments on exchange transactions); examples include commercial and residential property taxes, and fines and penalties.

- **Government-mandated nonexchange transactions**, when a governmental entity provides resources to a lower-level governmental entity and requires the recipient to use the funds for a specific purpose; examples include federal programs that state/local governments must perform (using federal funding), or state programs performed by local governments (using state funding).

- **Voluntary nonexchange transactions**, resulting from agreements entered into by willing parties; examples include grants and donations.

Questions:

1. First, do the two taxes appear to meet the definition of a "nonexchange transaction"?

    _____

    _____

2. Next, identify which class of nonexchange transaction each Town of Hampton tax falls under. Explain.

    Fuel tax: _____

    Property tax: _____

In What Circumstances Are the Accrual and the Modified Accrual Bases of Accounting Used?

In governmental accounting, revenues may be recognized on an *accrual* basis, or using a *modified accrual* basis. Understanding what basis of accounting applies is an important step in determining how the Town of Hampton should recognize its tax revenues.

Section 1600 (Basis of Accounting) of the GASB Codification describes circumstances in which each basis is most appropriate:

> **Government-wide Financial Statements (Statement of Principle)**
>
> The government-wide statement of net assets and the statement of activities should be prepared using the economic resources measurement focus and the accrual basis of accounting.
>
> **Fund Financial Statements (Statement of Principle)**
>
> In fund financial statements, the modified accrual or accrual basis of accounting, as appropriate, should be used in measuring financial position and operating results.
>
> a. Financial statements for governmental funds should be presented using the current financial resources measurement focus and the <u>modified accrual</u> basis of accounting. Revenues should be recognized in the accounting period in which they become available and measurable . . .
>
> b. Proprietary fund statements of net position and revenues, expenses, and changes in fund net position should be presented using the economic resources measurement focus and the <u>accrual</u> basis of accounting.
>
> c. Financial statements of fiduciary funds should be reported using the economic resources measurement focus and the <u>accrual</u> basis of accounting. [Underlined emphasis added]

3. Based on the guidance above, explain when each basis of accounting (accrual vs. modified accrual) applies.

Accrual: _____

_____

Modified Accrual: _____

_____

What Are Some Common Funds Used in Governmental Accounting, and Should the Property and Sales Tax Revenues be Recorded in a Fund?

Next, in order to determine which basis of accounting is most appropriate for its sales and property tax revenues, the Town of Hampton must determine whether the revenues will be recorded within a fund.

Per Section 1300 (Fund Accounting) of the GASB Codification:

> **Fund Accounting Systems (Statement of Principle)**
>
> Governmental accounting systems should be organized and operated on a fund basis. A fund is defined as a fiscal and accounting entity with a self-balancing set of accounts recording cash and other financial resources, together with all related liabilities and residual equities or balances, and changes therein, which are segregated for the purpose of carrying on specific activities or attaining certain objectives in accordance with special regulations, restrictions, or limitations.

Section 1300 requires governments to report governmental, proprietary, and fiduciary funds to the extent that they have activities meeting the criteria for these funds. Following is a list of the three **fund categories** (shown in bold) from Section 1300, each followed by a description of certain funds that are included within that category.

Governmental Funds

.104   The *general fund* should be used to account for and report all financial resources not accounted for and reported in another fund.

.105   *Special revenue funds* are used to account for and report the proceeds of specific revenue sources that are restricted or committed to expenditure for specified purposes other than debt service or capital projects . . .

.106   *Capital projects funds* are used to account for and report financial resources that are restricted, committed, or assigned to expenditure for capital outlays . . .

.107   *Debt service funds* are used to account for and report financial resources that are restricted, committed, or assigned to expenditure for principal and interest . . .

Proprietary Funds

.109   *Enterprise funds* may be used to report any activity for which a fee is charged to external users for goods or services . . . [Such as where a government utility passes its operating costs on to its customers]

.110   *Internal service funds* may be used to report any activity that provides goods or services to other funds, departments, or agencies of the primary government and its component units, or to other governments, on a cost-reimbursement basis . . .

. . . **Fiduciary Funds** should be used to report assets held in a trustee or agency capacity for others and therefore cannot be used to support the government's own programs. . . . [I]ncludes pension (and other employee benefit) trust funds, investment trust funds, private-purpose trust funds, and agency funds. (Par .102(c)). [Emphasis and comments added]

4.   What are the three fund categories used to organize governmental accounting systems?

_____

5.   Assume that the Town of Hampton plans to use these tax revenues to fund its general government operations. In this case, which *fund* appears to be appropriate? How did you ascertain this?

_____

_____

6.   Considering your response to the previous question and the guidance provided above from Section 1600 of the GASB Codification, what basis of accounting applies to that fund?

_____

Based on This Fund Type and Basis of Accounting, When Can Hampton Recognize Its Sales and Property Tax Revenues?

Broad revenue recognition guidance for non-exchange transactions is provided in GASB Cod. Sec. N50 (Nonexchange Transactions). Additional guidance on the recognition of property tax revenue is also provided in Section P70 (Property Taxes).

Per Section N50:

Revenue Recognition in Governmental Fund Statements

.127   When the modified accrual basis of accounting is used, revenues resulting from non-exchange transactions should be recognized as follows:

a.   *Derived tax revenues.* Recipients should recognize revenues in the period when the underlying exchange transaction has occurred and the resources are available.

b.   *Imposed nonexchange revenues—property taxes.* Recipients should recognize revenues in accordance with Section P70. [Footnotes omitted]

Per Section P70:

> **Application of the Modified Accrual Basis to Property Tax Revenues**
>
> .104   When a property tax assessment is made, it is to finance the budget of a particular period, and the revenue produced from any property tax assessment should be recognized in the fiscal period for which it was levied, provided the "available" criteria are met. *Available* means collected within the current period or expected to be collected soon enough thereafter to be used to pay liabilities of the current period. Such time thereafter shall not exceed 60 days. Governments should disclose in their summary of significant accounting policies the length of time used to define *available* for purposes of revenue recognition in the governmental fund financial statements.

7.   What is the principle applicable to each tax, for determining when the Town of Hampton can recognize revenues? Cite your source for each response.

Fuel tax: _____

_____

Property tax: _____

_____

CHAPTER SUMMARY

Audited financial statements are often required for governmental entities ranging from local governments, to state governments, to individual and consolidated federal agencies. Additionally, certain states require their municipal governments and agencies to undergo periodic compliance audits. While the process for performing governmental accounting and auditing research is no different from the process for performing FASB research, the body of knowledge required to perform governmental engagements is fundamentally different. It is therefore imperative for accountants performing such engagements to educate themselves about how governmental accounting and auditing requirements are unique.

The authoritative sources for governmental accounting standards are the GASB (for state and local governments) and the FASAB (for federal government entities); governmental auditing standards are established by the GAO. In addition to these authoritative sources, practitioners may find value in certain nonauthoritative resources, such as practical guides including interpretive discussion, model financial statements, and checklists.

Finally, extensive industry resources are available to management accountants; this chapter named just a few. Practicing accountants may find significant value in becoming familiar with the professional organizations and resources available for their specific industry or practice area.

REVIEW QUESTIONS

1. Does the FASB Codification apply to governmental entities? Explain.
2. What are a few of the reasons for which governmental accounting differs from private-sector accounting?
3. Describe two circumstances in which state and local governments might be required to issue audited financial statements.
4. What are some steps a beginning accountant might take, when first assigned to a governmental accounting or audit engagement, in order to become more familiar with fundamentals of governmental accounting and auditing?
5. How is the GASB funded? What is the role of the Financial Accounting Foundation (FAF)?
6. Aside from general purpose state and local governments, list three other types of entities that may be subject to GASB's accounting standards.

7. What is meant by the term the GASB "hierarchy"? What are the two authoritative levels in the hierarchy, and what should a researcher do if authoritative guidance is not on point?

8. When searching for GASB guidance, why is it preferable to use the GASB Codification, as opposed to searching for individual standards on the GASB's website?

9. Are the GASB's original pronouncements (used to populate the Codification) authoritative? Explain.

10. Describe the information available on a standard's "Status" page, on the GASB website.

11. Is guidance issued by the FASAB referred to as "GAAP"? Explain.

12. Complete the following sentence. The FASAB's authoritative guidance is compiled and codified in _____.

13. Which entities are required to comply with FASAB guidance? Explain, and name three examples of specific entities that comply with FASAB guidance.

14. Who are the FASAB's three sponsor agencies? What is their role?

15. Who audits government financial statements?

16. What is the role, in part, of the Office of the Inspector General, within a given federal agency?

17. Are auditors subject to the GAO's Yellow Book also required to comply with AICPA audit standards? Explain the relationship between the Yellow Book and AICPA guidance.

18. Describe whether (or in what circumstances) use of the following sources of industry guidance is considered "mandatory":
    - Management accounting standards
    - Internal audit standards
    - Cost accounting standards

19. Assume you have written a memo and included the following citation. How might you abbreviate future references to guidance from this standard, within the same memo?

    > Per Statement of Federal Financial Accounting Standards No. 1, *Accounting for Selected Assets and Liabilities*, par. 18, "***intragovernmental assets and liabilities*** arise from transactions among federal entities."

20. Do the GAO's auditing standards apply solely to audits of financial statements?

EXERCISES

The following exercises require students to access information and guidance using the following websites, as appropriate: GASB standards and GASB Codification (www.gasb.org or www.aaahq.org), FASAB (www.fasab.gov), GAO (www.gao.gov/yellowbook).

1. Complete the following chart, identifying the relevant standard setter and type of standards applicable to each preparer or auditor.

Preparer/Auditor	Standard setter	Name of applicable standards
U.S. Department of Justice's financial statements		
New York City Transit Authority's financial statements		
U.S. federal government-wide financial statements		
The state of Oregon's financial statements		
The City of Beverly Hills' financial statements		
KPMG auditor, auditing the Department of Commerce		
State Auditor's Office, auditing the state of Texas		

Governmental Accounting Research Exercises

2. *a.* Using the GASB Codification, locate and describe the *requirement* that each governmental entity should publish an annual comprehensive annual financial report (CAFR). Name two items that should be included in the financial section of the CAFR.

    b. Next, describe what "Part" (I, II, III, or IV) of the GASB Codification this requirement is included within, and why.

3. Locate the Status page for GASB Statement No. 22, *Accounting for Taxpayer-Assessed Tax Revenues in Governmental Funds*. When did this standard initially become effective? What GASB Statement superseded this standard?

4. *a.* When, and at what value, must a state government record the cost of food stamps in fund financial statements? Explain.

    b. Provide both the GASB Codification reference to this guidance, as well as the original GASB standard number. Describe how you located the original GASB standard number.

5. Assume the Town of Olson is undergoing a bankruptcy, and a bankruptcy plan of adjustment, restructuring the town's debt, has been confirmed by a court. Locate the appropriate accounting guidance, then respond to the following questions.

    a. *When* (i.e., at what date) is it appropriate for the town to recognize gains from adjustments to its prebankruptcy debt? Cite your source.

    b. Locate the summary of the original standard for this issue, and describe the objective of this standard.

6. Using GARS Online, what is one GASB standard that has been issued recently but not yet incorporated in the GASB Codification? Describe how you navigated to this standard within GARS Online.

7. Locate the Foreword to the FASAB Handbook. Summarize the section that describes the *Origins of the Documents*.

8. Locate the FASAB's accounting standard on fiduciary activities.

    a. What are fiduciary activities, and what are examples of these? Cite your sources for these responses.

    b. According to the Introduction of this standard, should fiduciary assets be recorded on government entities' balance sheets? If not, how should they be addressed in the financial statements?

    c. Using the standard's table of contents, determine whether (and if applicable, identify) any Interpretations or Technical Releases relate to this standard.

9. Locate SFFAS 24, *Selected Standards for the Consolidated Financial Report of the United States Government*.

    a. Read, then summarize the discussion in par. 8.

    b. Using SFFAS 24's Basis for Conclusions, describe one reason why the FASAB decided not to require budgetary information (as required by SFFAS 7) to be reported in the CFR (consolidated financial report of the U.S. government).

10. Using FASAB guidance, respond to the following:

    a. What is "general" PP&E? In your response, cite from the actual requirement and not just the summary guidance that describes general PP&E.

    b. How should the cost of general PP&E be initially recorded?

    c. How is depreciation expense calculated for general PP&E?

11. Locate SFFAS 5, *Accounting for Liabilities of the Federal Government*, then respond to the following:

    a. How does the FASAB define a "nonexchange transaction"? Provide an example of a nonexchange transaction. Cite your sources for these responses.

    b. Should a liability be recognized for federal nonexchange transactions? Cite your source.

Governmental Auditing Research Exercises

12. Locate the "Yellow Book," *Government Auditing Standards*, 2011 Revision (or more recent if available). What *types of audits* does the Yellow Book say the requirements and guidance in GAGAS apply to?

13. Locate the guidance within the Yellow Book that states that AICPA auditing standards are incorporated by reference, and which explains what sections of a SAS must be applied in order to comply with these AICPA auditing standards.

14. Locate the 80-hour and 24-hour training requirement (within the Yellow Book) for government auditors. Explain this requirement, citing your source.

15. Locate the Yellow Book appendix that includes information to accompany Chapter 3.

    a. Using that appendix, name one example circumstance of a *self-interest threat* to auditor independence.

    b. Explain how this appendix might help a researcher interpret guidance within the main body of a Yellow Book chapter.

16. Locate the auditor's report included within the 2014 federal government-wide financial statements (Financial Report of the U.S. Government).
    a. Who performed the audit of the federal government-wide financial statements?
    b. Name one management responsibility described in the audit report. To respond, look for the document actually labeled *Independent Auditor's Report*.
    c. In this context, who exactly is *management*? Explain your response.
    d. Identify one of the auditor's summary findings described on the first page of the audit report.

Citing Governmental Accounting Standards

17. Imagine you are writing a memo and including the following excerpt from GASB guidance: "Under the *accrual* basis of accounting, most transactions are recognized when they occur, regardless of when cash is received or disbursed." Locate this quote in GARS Online and write out the full source citation for this quote. Assume this is the first reference to GASB guidance that you are including in your memo.

18. Imagine you are writing a memo and including the following excerpt from FASAB guidance: "Interest accrued on the liability of loan guarantees is recognized as interest expense." Locate this quote in the FASAB Handbook and write out the full source citation for this quote. Assume this is the first reference to FASAB guidance that you are including in your memo.

CASE STUDY QUESTIONS

Outline and Minimum Content of a CAFR Provide an outline for the minimum content of a comprehensive annual financial report (CAFR). Include in your outline only the major content categories—no need to drill down to the i, ii level. Provide the source reference for where (using the GASB Codification) you found this information.   **10.1**

Role of Your State Comptroller's Office Perform a Web search for your state's Comptroller's office (or Treasurer, or other agency responsible for overseeing local government finances within the state). Identify the agency, then describe one oversight function performed by the agency related to state or local government finances. For example, describe any financial audits, compliance audits, or other reporting requirements performed or required by the agency or Comptroller's office. Describe how this oversight function contributes to the state or local government's accountability to the public. Your response should require approximately 1–2 paragraphs.   **10.2**

Federal Financial Statements Locate the most recent audited financial statements of a CFO Act agency (that is, an individual federal reporting entity). Determine who audited the agency. What, if any, audit findings were named? What internal control findings, if any, were described? What other commentary did you identify, in the auditor's report, which was notable to you? Your response should require approximately 1–2 paragraphs.   **10.3**

Reviewing a CAFR Review the most recent CAFR of a state or local government in your area. Using that report, identify: **10.4**

  1. The entity's most significant source of revenues and most significant expense
  2. The entity's most significant asset, and its most significant liability
  3. Two of the individual funds used by the government (look for separate fund financial statements)
  4. Who prepared the report
  5. Who audited the report, and using what auditing standards

Finally, note one other interesting difference between this report and the form or content of financial statements prepared by nongovernmental entities.

Control Environment in Towns and Villages Town and village governments are frequently prone to control deficiencies, due to factors including lack of trained personnel, poor oversight, and small size (in some cases). These control deficiencies can in turn increase the risk of local government fraud.   **10.5**

    In a performance audit of a local government, focused on internal controls, what are the auditor's responsibilities for assessing controls? To respond, consult the GAO's *Yellow Book*, within the chapter for Performance Audits. Also, brainstorm other resources you might consult for guidance on evaluating a government's internal control structure.

Recent Changes to Pension Reporting *Facts:* Issued in June 2012, GASB Statement No. 68, *Accounting and Financial Reporting for Pensions*, requires government entities to record their net pension liability (that is, the difference between pension assets and liabilities) in the financial statements for the first time, in a manner similar to the   **10.6**

calculation required for nongovernmental pensions. This new requirement is expected to dramatically increase the liabilities reported by state and local governments.

Required: Locate a recent news article describing the issuance of GASBS 68, then prepare a few paragraphs in response to the following questions.

1. What are some of the different reactions this guidance has received from the public?
2. For defined benefit pension plans, how do pre-GASBS 68 pension reporting requirements differ from the GASBS 68 requirements? Focus in particular on how the new guidance affects liability and expense recognition and measurement.

10.7   **Government Downsizing** *Facts:* Frustrated by high property tax rates, residents in the Village of Williamsville voted to dissolve their village government, instead agreeing to receive similar services (formerly provided by the Village government) from their county government, Erie County. No consideration must be paid by (or to) the county to effect this transfer. The effects of this transfer/dissolution will be that all village assets and liabilities (cash balances, buildings, infrastructure, and accounts payable) will become property and responsibility of the county, six employees will transfer to the Erie County district offices, and three employees will be involuntarily terminated and given 3 months of severance pay. The three terminated employees were responsible for Williamsville's animal control division, which will be discontinued.

Required: You have been asked to write a brief accounting issues memo to the Erie County government files describing the accounting implications of the Williamsville dissolution. In your memo, address the appropriate accounting for the transaction: merger, acquisition, or transfer of operations? Also, address how Erie County should recognize and measure the additional assets and liabilities, and describe—broadly—the accounting implications of the discontinuation of the animal control operations and the principle for *recognition* of the related employee terminations. In doing so, assume that the Village of Williamsville has prepared financial statements as of the merger date. Feel free to identify other issues that should be considered, as well.

10.8   **Pending Litigation** *Facts:* A lawsuit has been initiated against a federal government agency for alleged discrimination. The plaintiff in the case has requested damages of $4 million, although the government agency's legal counsel estimates that the plaintiff may be willing to settle for as little as $2 million; at this point, it is not clear what amount within the range will be paid. The government's lawyer believes the plaintiff will likely prevail in the lawsuit.

Required: You have been asked to assist in evaluating the accounting by the government agency for this litigation (e.g., should a liability be recorded and, if so, for what amount?). Draft an email evaluating this issue to your accounting supervisor, Molly.

10.9   **Infrastructure Accounting** *Facts:* When GASB Statement No. 34, *Basic Financial Statements*, was issued, it became one of the most critical governmental accounting standards available, covering a wide range of issues on government financial statement preparation. One of the biggest issues that state and local governments faced, in adopting this guidance, was the requirement that infrastructure (such as roads, bridges, sewer systems, and rail lines) be capitalized. This standard has since been codified in the GASB Codification; therefore, any references you make to the authoritative literature should refer to the GASB Codification.

Required: Act as though you are a local government accountant, and your town is adopting this guidance for the first time. Write a brief email (or memo) to your accounting supervisor explaining the requirement from the GASB Codification that requires infrastructure to be capitalized, and explain the options available for subsequently measuring infrastructure (depreciation versus the *modified method*). Emphasize that the town must select between these two options, and include your recommendation. Cite from authoritative literature as support for your email.

Chapter 11

Fundamentals of Tax Research

It is income tax preparation season, and CPA Susan Jones is preparing her client Nora Smith's federal income tax return. Ever since her mother lost her job a year ago, Nora has been paying the real property taxes and mortgage on her mother's house in order to help her avoid foreclosure. Now, Susan needs to determine whether Nora can deduct any part of the payments on her personal federal income tax return. Susan starts her search for the applicable federal tax law by looking at the most fundamental primary source, the Internal Revenue Code. She then turns to other primary sources of tax law, such as regulations, rulings, and cases, as well as explanations in secondary sources, to reach a conclusion.

As a professional performing tax services, it is important to be familiar with the many different sources of tax law and to know how to locate guidance within these sources. This chapter will teach you the fundamentals of tax research and the professional standards applicable to tax services.

After reading this chapter and performing the exercises herein, you will be able to

1. **Understand** the circumstances in which an accountant would perform tax research services.

2. **Understand** and **apply** the tax research process.

3. **Contrast** and **understand** the relative precedential values of the different primary sources of tax law.

4. **Differentiate** between primary and secondary sources of tax law.

5. **Navigate** and **use** an online tax research service (Thomson Reuters Checkpoint).

6. **Identify** the key sources of professional standards for tax services.

Learning Objectives

Organization of This Chapter

Previous chapters in this text have focused on accounting and auditing research related to both governmental and nongovernmental entities. By contrast, this chapter focuses on **tax research**, a type of accounting research specifically focused on determining the proper tax treatment of transactions and events.

After first identifying *who* generally performs tax research, and *when*, this chapter describes the tax research *process*, and notes its similarities and differences with the accounting research process described in Chapter 3.

The chapter then describes key sources of federal tax law and their relative importance as precedent. The sources of federal tax law include primary sources, such as the Internal Revenue Code, Treasury Regulations, Internal Revenue Service rulings, and court decisions; and secondary sources, such as treatises and periodicals.

Next, the chapter demonstrates the use of an online tax research service, followed by a discussion of how and when to update tax research, focusing on the use of a citator.

Finally, this chapter concludes by discussing the professional standards that govern a CPA's own conduct for providing tax services.

The preceding graphic illustrates the organization of content within this chapter.

This chapter focuses solely on research related to U.S. federal tax issues and does not address state tax research. The *process* for researching state tax issues is very similar, but the *sources* involved (e.g., individual state tax statutes, state tax agencies' regulations and rulings, and state court decisions) can be quite different.

WHO PERFORMS TAX RESEARCH, AND WHEN?

LO1 **Understand** the circumstances in which an accountant would perform tax research services.

Tax research is generally performed by in-house corporate accountants and by public accountants for their clients. In addition, because tax research is essentially a type of legal research focused on tax, it is also common for tax research to be performed by tax lawyers on behalf of their clients. For example, a tax lawyer may advise a client on how to structure a transaction or may represent a client in a litigated tax dispute. Finally, individuals working for government tax agencies may also perform tax research, such as in the course of auditing tax returns. This chapter primarily refers to the taxpayer as a "client," but the lessons in the chapter are intended to apply equally to both in-house accountants and public accountants performing tax research.

Tax research is unique in that it focuses on compliance with tax laws. Accordingly, this research may be performed

- For tax and transactional *planning* purposes,
- For purposes of tax *compliance*, and
- During and after tax *audits*.

Tax professionals are often asked to determine the tax treatment of a proposed transaction or event before it occurs. This is called **tax planning**. Accountants who are consulted before a transaction or event occurs may be in a position to not only advise the client as to the tax results of the proposal, but may also be able to suggest other alternative structures that may lower or defer tax.

For example, suppose that a business client has contacted you for advice regarding its plan to sell a warehouse and use the proceeds to purchase a larger warehouse. The client's initial questions might focus on the tax treatment of the sale, such as whether or not the client will have a taxable gain, whether the gain will be ordinary or capital, and ultimately how much tax will be due. Being consulted in advance, however, puts the tax professional in a position of being able to research and suggest an alternative, such as structuring the transaction as a like-kind exchange pursuant to Section 1031 of the Internal Revenue Code, which can produce a better tax result for the client.

Tax research is also performed for **tax compliance** purposes; that is, the preparation and timely filing of accurate tax returns. Sometimes, a tax professional may not learn about a transaction or other event that affects the client's tax return until the return is being prepared. In this context, the primary questions for the tax professional (and which may require research) may be "How is the completed transaction treated for tax purposes?" and "How and where should the transaction be reported on the client's tax return?"

Finally, tax research may be necessary even after tax returns have been filed, such as when a client is being audited by a governmental tax agency. During an audit, the government tax auditor may review whether transactions or other events were properly reported and, ultimately, whether the correct amount of tax was paid. The tax professional may be asked to research these issues in anticipation of, or in response to, a position taken by the government auditor. Tax research may also be used to support a dispute of the results of a tax audit (e.g., through the administrative process or litigation).

THE TAX RESEARCH PROCESS

LO2 **Understand** and **apply** the tax research process.

The tax research process is very similar to the accounting research process introduced in Chapter 3. The major differences are the unique (tax) subject matter and the relevant sources of guidance. The steps in the research process described in Chapter 3 are somewhat abbreviated in this chapter, but that does not mean that steps not included here are irrelevant. For example, the pre-step of understanding the client's business or industry is also relevant to tax research, but has been incorporated within the first step of understanding the relevant facts. Similarly, step 3 in the accounting research process to "stop and think" is also applicable throughout the tax research process. Figure 11-1 depicts the key steps in the tax research process.

| 1. Understand the relevant facts. | 2. Identify the tax issues. | 3. Find, analyze and update applicable sources of tax law. | 4. Document and communicate tax research results. |

Figure 11-1

The tax research process

To some extent, these four steps are intertwined and often cannot be performed in a straight 1-2-3-4 order. For example, a **tax authority** (i.e., a source of tax law that provides guidance) found in step 3 of the research process may require the researcher to go back to step 1 and ask more questions, which may lead to the identification of additional tax issues (step 2). As a result, tax researchers have to be flexible and open to following where their research takes them.

Step 1: Understand the Relevant Facts

First, you must gather and understand both the relevant tax and nontax facts related to the client's tax issue(s). When performing tax research for a new client, this step may include gaining an understanding of the client's tax situation generally, including its general tax treatment and tax issues that are relevant to its business or industry. This is similar to the pre-step of the accounting research process.

Facts may be obtained either directly from the client and/or indirectly from others at the researcher's firm who have directly communicated with the client. Where applicable, facts may also be obtained from, and/or confirmed with, reliable outside sources.

- For example, if the client's records do not indicate how much the client paid for an asset, it may be necessary to request this information from the seller of the asset or from other records (such as county real estate transfer records).

- Similarly, it may be necessary or advisable to obtain an appraisal (prepared by a third-party qualified appraiser) of an asset, such as in the case of a donation to a charity.

Consider the following questions when gathering **tax facts** relevant to an issue:

- **How is the client generally treated for tax purposes?**
  - Is the client an individual, a business entity, or another type of taxpayer (such as a trust or estate)?
  - Is the client a U.S. domestic taxpayer or a foreign person or entity?
  - If the client is a corporation, is it a C corporation, or has it elected to be treated as an S corporation?
  - If the client is a limited liability company (LLC), is it treated as a disregarded entity, as a partnership, or as a corporation for tax purposes?
  - Is the client subject to special income tax rules, such as those applicable to charitable organizations, real estate investment trusts (REITs), banks or insurance companies?

- **What type of tax is involved?** Does the issue involve income tax, estate tax, excise tax, or another type of tax?

- **What are the client's relevant tax attributes?** The client's tax year; the amounts, if any, of the client's taxable income, net operating loss (NOL) and tax credit carryovers; and the adjusted tax bases of the client's relevant assets are examples of **tax attributes**.

- **When will the transaction take place?** Is this research being performed for a proposed transaction, a completed transaction, or for a tax position that is under audit?

- **Are other parties involved?** If so, are any other parties considered "related parties" for which loss recognition may be limited under the Internal Revenue Code?

- **What tax years are involved?** Does the current year, or another year's, tax law apply to this transaction?

- **What are the dollar amounts involved in the transaction?** Dollar amounts may include, for example, the tax basis of an asset sold, the amount of depreciation or other expense claimed, or the amount of payments received.

- **What is the location of the client and/or the transaction?** This question is particularly relevant when researching state, local, and foreign tax issues.

- **What documentation is necessary to evidence the transaction for tax purposes?** Is contemporaneous documentation (such as in the form of a store receipt or an acknowledgment from a charity for a gift of $250 or more) necessary to claim a deductible expense or credit on a tax return?

A researcher should also consider the **nontax facts** related to a transaction; that is, the client's business purpose or other motivations for undertaking the transaction. Such facts are particularly relevant when determining how best to structure a proposed transaction. Researchers should consider, for example,

- **Why is the client undertaking this transaction?** This may explain why the transaction is being structured in a particular way.
  - For example, while it may be desirable for tax purposes for a seller to structure the sale of a corporate business as a stock sale, nontax facts such as environmental liabilities, or a buyer's unwillingness to purchase the corporation's stock, may rule out this option. The tax researcher needs to know these nontax facts to efficiently perform research that is useful to the client.

- **What documentation exists that evidences the transaction?** The tax researcher should review all documentation related to the transaction, including contracts, written correspondence, appraisals, and receipts, to properly research the tax issues and accurately report the transaction on a tax return.

Figure 11-2 lists just a few of the factual questions a researcher might ask in determining the proper income tax treatment of a client's sale of a building.

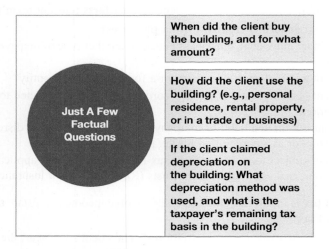

Figure 11-2

A few factual questions related to a client's sale of a building

Step 2: Identify the Tax Issues Involved

Armed with the facts of your client's transaction, your next step is to identify the tax issues related to the transaction. This is another way of saying "define the problem" (step 2 of the accounting research process described in Chapter 3), but is focused on the relevant tax concerns.

As you identify each relevant tax issue, you should also use your substantive tax knowledge to "stop and think," as you would do in step 3 of the accounting research process. Consider what *you* think would be the most appropriate tax treatment for the transaction or event as well as any relevant sources of tax law with which you are familiar.

For beginning researchers, identifying the tax issues applicable to a given fact pattern may require some trial and error, and may even require some preliminary research. To assist with this learning curve, the following are a number of common income tax issues to consider as a starting point.

First, ask yourself what *type of tax* is involved: Is it an income tax issue? An estate or gift tax issue? An excise tax issue? A sales or use tax (or other state tax) issue? An employment (e.g., FICA/Social Security tax) and withholding tax issue?

Once you determine the type of tax involved, more specific tax issues can be identified. For example, assume you are researching issues related to a client's income tax return. Specific tax issues related to the client's cash receipts might involve, for example,

- Is the item included in gross income for tax purposes?
- Is the item considered ordinary income or capital gain income?
- If the item is capital gain income, is it short term or long term?
- Is the item considered active or passive income?

On the other hand, tax issues related to cash payments might include, for example,

- Is the item deductible as an expense?
- Do any limitations (such as the at-risk and passive activity loss limitations) apply?
- What documentation is required to claim the payment as an expense for tax purposes?
- What year (or years) is the item deductible?
- Is a purchased asset depreciable or amortizable for tax purposes?

The tax issues involved can vary considerably depending upon the facts. Figure 11-3 illustrates just a few of the tax issues involved when evaluating a client's sale of a building, assuming that the building was being rented to an unrelated tenant.

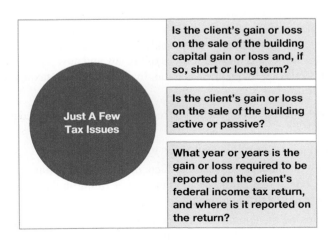

Figure 11-3

A few tax issues involved in a client's sale of a building

Next, list the tax issues that you have identified. Decide which issues require more research and which you are comfortable answering with only minimal, confirming research. With experience, you will become better able to organize and prioritize the tax issues involved.

Take a moment to complete the following **Now YOU Try** exercise, intended to get you thinking about steps 1 and 2 of the research process.

Determining Facts and Identifying Tax Issues

Your client, Heather Stark, loves dogs and volunteers for an organization called People for Dogs Inc. ("PFD"). PFD's mission is to temporarily provide foster homes and, ultimately, to find permanent homes for stray dogs. Heather volunteers for PFD, by temporarily fostering several dogs each year. During 2015, Heather spent a considerable amount of time and money on the dogs that she fostered, including paying for dog food, veterinary services, dog toys, feeding dishes, and other supplies. You have been asked to prepare Heather's 2015 federal income tax return.

1. Referring back to the lists of sample questions for determining the facts relevant to an issue, list two tax or nontax facts questions you might ask Heather:

   _____

   _____

2. Identify a relevant "tax facts" question that you might ask the PFD organization:

   _____

3. List two tax issues that you would need to research in order to prepare Heather's 2015 federal income tax return:

   _____

   _____

4. Take a moment to stop and think. What do you think the answers to the two tax issues you identified will be?

   _____

   _____

Step 3: Analyze Tax Research Findings

The third step in the tax research process involves finding, analyzing, and updating tax law that is relevant to the client's issue. This step is similar to step 4 (search for guidance) of the accounting research process described in Chapter 3, but is focused on using tax law as guidance. Later in this chapter, we will describe the sources of tax law and how to update research results. For now, we will focus on the *process* of identifying and analyzing how tax law applies to a research issue.

Assume that a researcher has located sources of tax law and now must analyze whether each tax authority found is relevant to the client's issue. In analyzing each tax authority, a researcher should consider the following:

- Does the Internal Revenue Code section or regulation being considered apply to the client's situation?
- Are the facts of the case or ruling analogous to the client's situation?
- What are the key differences between the facts of the case or ruling and the client's situation? Does the Code, a regulation, or another case or ruling indicate that these factual differences should lead to a different result?
- What is the reasoning or rationale for the conclusions reached in the case or ruling? Does that reasoning or rationale apply to the client's situation?

Part of analyzing each tax authority found includes considering its relative weight as precedent. You will find, as considered later in the discussion of sources of federal tax law, that not all sources of tax law are equal. At times, the conclusions reached by different sources of tax law may be inconsistent; in these cases, the researcher must take into account the relative **precedential values** of the sources found. The precedential value of a tax authority refers to how strong the authority is for the client's situation. This takes into account both the relative weights of different sources of tax law and the relevance of each authority to the client's situation.

■ For example, as discussed below with respect to court decisions, appellate court decisions (particularly decisions of the U.S. Supreme Court and of the client's applicable Circuit of the U.S. Court of Appeals) have a greater precedential value than trial court decisions.

■ Therefore, if a trial court and an appellate court reach different conclusions on a tax issue in cases involving similar facts, the tax researcher would generally give greater weight to the appellate court's decision in his or her analysis.

■ However, if one authority ruled on a fact pattern that was more closely aligned with the client's situation than another, greater weight might be given to that (closely aligned) authority.

At times, a tax researcher may only be able to find sources of tax law that are of relatively low precedential value. For example, if a tax issue has not been litigated in court, the only authority that may exist is an IRS ruling interpreting an Internal Revenue Code provision. The ruling is of lower precedential value than some other sources of tax law (such as a Code provision or regulation). In some circumstances, the client may wish to pursue a tax treatment that conflicts with a lower precedent source, as described in the following **TIP from the Trenches.**

Not all sources of tax law are irrefutable. If the only relevant tax authority is of limited precedential value, the tax researcher may consider recommending taking a contrary position on a tax return. The recommendation should only be made after careful consideration, disclosing the risks (including that it may be necessary to litigate the issue) to the client, and properly disclosing the position taken on the client's tax return to minimize penalties.

[**TIP**] from the Trenches

The tax professional can make reasoned conclusions for the issues researched only by thoroughly analzying the relevant sources of tax law found. As with identifying tax issues, a researcher's ability to analyze tax research findings should improve as the researcher gains experience.

Step 4: Document and Communicate Tax Research Results

As a general rule of thumb, if you find the need to research a tax issue, you should take the time to document your research, including your conclusions and any alternative ways of structuring the transaction for tax purposes, similar to what you would do in steps 5 and 6 of the accounting research process described in Chapter 3.

In documenting research findings, a tax researcher often prepares

■ A memorandum to the client's file; and

■ A written communication of tax advice to the client.

Part of documenting one's research findings is writing a **memorandum to the client's file.** A file memorandum should be dated and would usually include a statement of the relevant facts (including from whom the facts were obtained), an identification of the tax issue or issues involved, the researcher's conclusion on each identified issue, a discussion of the authority supporting the conclusion(s), and an indication of the next steps to be taken (such as contacting the client or verifying a fact relied on). The discussion of supporting authority should describe and cite the sources of tax law relied on in reaching the conclusion(s), and describe and cite any significant and relevant contrary authority that the researcher ruled out in reaching the conclusion(s).

EXAMPLE

The following is an example of a short memorandum to client Nora Smith's file regarding the tax issue identified in this chapter's opening scenario. The length of a tax memorandum to a client's file may vary from very short, such as this example, which essentially involves one issue for which the tax law is very clear, to several pages if there are multiple issues or the conclusion needs a longer explanation.

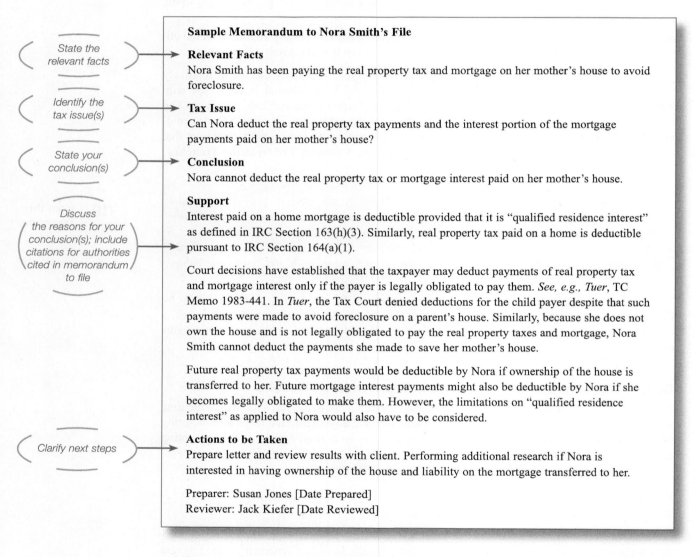

State the relevant facts

Identify the tax issue(s)

State your conclusion(s)

Discuss the reasons for your conclusion(s); include citations for authorities cited in memorandum to file

Clarify next steps

Sample Memorandum to Nora Smith's File

Relevant Facts
Nora Smith has been paying the real property tax and mortgage on her mother's house to avoid foreclosure.

Tax Issue
Can Nora deduct the real property tax payments and the interest portion of the mortgage payments paid on her mother's house?

Conclusion
Nora cannot deduct the real property tax or mortgage interest paid on her mother's house.

Support
Interest paid on a home mortgage is deductible provided that it is "qualified residence interest" as defined in IRC Section 163(h)(3). Similarly, real property tax paid on a home is deductible pursuant to IRC Section 164(a)(1).

Court decisions have established that the taxpayer may deduct payments of real property tax and mortgage interest only if the payer is legally obligated to pay them. *See, e.g., Tuer*, TC Memo 1983-441. In *Tuer*, the Tax Court denied deductions for the child payer despite that such payments were made to avoid foreclosure on a parent's house. Similarly, because she does not own the house and is not legally obligated to pay the real property taxes and mortgage, Nora Smith cannot deduct the payments she made to save her mother's house.

Future real property tax payments would be deductible by Nora if ownership of the house is transferred to her. Future mortgage interest payments might also be deductible by Nora if she becomes legally obligated to make them. However, the limitations on "qualified residence interest" as applied to Nora would also have to be considered.

Actions to be Taken
Prepare letter and review results with client. Performing additional research if Nora is interested in having ownership of the house and liability on the mortgage transferred to her.

Preparer: Susan Jones [Date Prepared]
Reviewer: Jack Kiefer [Date Reviewed]

Documenting tax research results would also usually include printing (or saving digital) copies of relevant sources of tax law relied on, and of any **significant contrary authority** that the researcher has ruled out (such as a source with significantly different facts or of lesser precedential value). The memorandum and related documentation become part of the client file and should be organized so that the original researcher, or another tax professional, can be quickly reacquainted (or acquainted) with the relevant authority at a later date (such as when it's time to prepare the related tax return or defend the conclusion reached during a tax audit).

Communicating tax research results involves providing the client with tax advice that is based on the conclusions reached through research. Tax advice may be provided orally, such as in person or over the telephone. However, it is always suggested (and sometimes required by professional standards) that the tax advisor follow up the oral advice with a written communication to the client. Alternatively, the tax advice may initially be provided in written form.

Tax advice (whether oral or written) should be provided in a way that the client can understand. In communicating tax advice to a client with little or no tax knowledge, for example, the tax professional should usually explain things as simply as possible and should not rely on technical terms that only someone with a sophisticated level of tax knowledge would be expected to understand without explanation. By contrast, when communicating tax advice to a more tax-sophisticated client, the adviser may use technical terms and, depending on the client, may assume a fairly high level of tax knowledge.

Written communication of tax advice to a client may be in the form of a letter or memorandum to the client. In either case, the substance of the communication should include the key elements noted in Figure 11-4.

Figure 11-4

Key elements included in written communication of tax advice to a client

Statement of what the writer was asked to determine

- Identifies the question(s) asked by the client

Summary of the conclusion(s) reached

- This should also include any recommendations made

Statement of the relevant facts

- Indicate any research done to determine the facts
- For client-provided facts: "It is my understanding from you that . . ."
- Indicate sources of facts obtained other than from the client
- Where appropriate, may include statement: "I have relied on the facts as provided by you and have not done any independent investigation regarding them."

Summary of controlling tax law

- Analysis of tax law supporting conclusion(s) reached
- Discussion of alternatives considered and why rejected

Statement of limitations on advice provided

- Indicate assumptions made, including no change in tax law after written advice provided to client

EXAMPLE

The following is an example of a letter to client Nora Smith regarding the tax issue identified in this chapter's opening scenario.

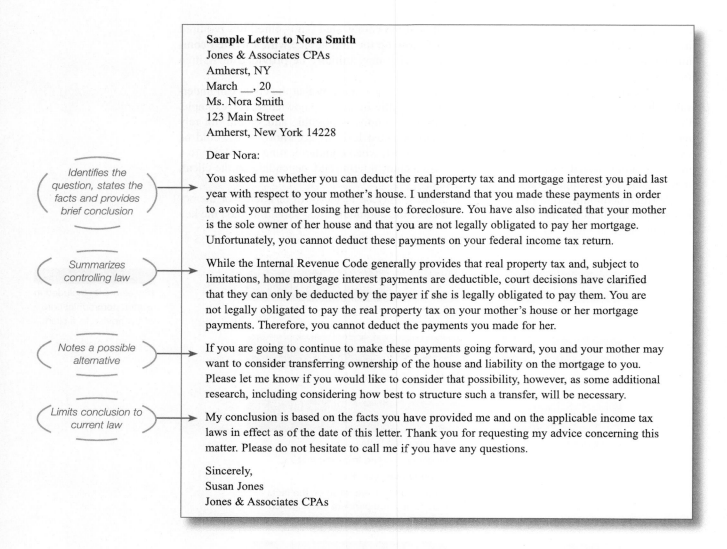

Sample Letter to Nora Smith
Jones & Associates CPAs
Amherst, NY
March __, 20__
Ms. Nora Smith
123 Main Street
Amherst, New York 14228

Dear Nora:

Identifies the question, states the facts and provides brief conclusion

You asked me whether you can deduct the real property tax and mortgage interest you paid last year with respect to your mother's house. I understand that you made these payments in order to avoid your mother losing her house to foreclosure. You have also indicated that your mother is the sole owner of her house and that you are not legally obligated to pay her mortgage. Unfortunately, you cannot deduct these payments on your federal income tax return.

Summarizes controlling law

While the Internal Revenue Code generally provides that real property tax and, subject to limitations, home mortgage interest payments are deductible, court decisions have clarified that they can only be deducted by the payer if she is legally obligated to pay them. You are not legally obligated to pay the real property tax on your mother's house or her mortgage payments. Therefore, you cannot deduct the payments you made for her.

Notes a possible alternative

If you are going to continue to make these payments going forward, you and your mother may want to consider transferring ownership of the house and liability on the mortgage to you. Please let me know if you would like to consider that possibility, however, as some additional research, including considering how best to structure such a transfer, will be necessary.

Limits conclusion to current law

My conclusion is based on the facts you have provided me and on the applicable income tax laws in effect as of the date of this letter. Thank you for requesting my advice concerning this matter. Please do not hesitate to call me if you have any questions.

Sincerely,
Susan Jones
Jones & Associates CPAs

The applicable standards of professional tax practice, briefly described at the end of this chapter, must also be considered in communicating tax advice to the client.

The next section of this chapter introduces the sources of U.S. federal tax law, including primary and secondary sources. Being familiar with these sources, and understanding their relative weights and importance, will help enable researchers to perform the third and fourth steps in the tax research process.

SOURCES OF FEDERAL TAX LAW

Primary Sources of U.S. Federal Tax Law

LO3 Contrast and understand the relative precedential values of the different primary sources of tax law.

The **primary sources** of U.S. federal tax law are issued by the U.S. federal government and generally have precedential value, the level of which varies among the primary sources. By contrast, **secondary sources** of tax law (discussed later in this chapter) are not precedential. In addition, taxpayers may incur a substantial understatement penalty under Section 6662 of the Internal Revenue Code for taking a position on a tax return for which there is neither **substantial authority** nor adequate disclosure. Only some of the primary sources of tax law constitute substantial authority. These are listed in Treasury Regulation Section 1.6662-4(d)(3)(iii).

The primary sources of U.S. federal tax law are depicted in Figure 11-5. The sources discussed in this chapter, and that a beginning researcher is most likely to encounter, are noted with an asterisk.

Figure 11-5

Primary sources of U.S. tax law

The Internal Revenue Code

The **Internal Revenue Code** (the "**IRC**" or the "**Code**") is a federal statute and an important primary source of federal tax law and a substantial authority. The IRC is codified at Title 26 of the United States Code ("U.S.C."). The IRC is often amended, and the current version of the Code is the "Internal Revenue Code of 1986, as amended." The Code is accessible within online tax research services such as Thomson Reuters Checkpoint (discussed later in this chapter), or for free through the IRS's website (www.irs.gov).

Organization of the Internal Revenue Code

The Code is organized in the following order: First into subtitles (lettered A through I), followed by chapters (organized by chapter number), then subchapters (lettered A, B, C, etc.), parts (numbered I, II, III, etc.), and sections (organized by section number).

Each Code section (or §) may be further organized in the following order:

- Subsections lettered (a), (b), (c), and so on;
- Paragraphs numbered (1), (2), (3), and so on;
- Subparagraphs lettered (A), (B), (C), and so on;
- Clauses numbered (i), (ii), (iii), and so on; and
- Subclauses numbered (I), (II), (III), and so on.

Figure 11-6 shows part of IRC § 132, "Certain fringe benefits." To locate Section 132 within the Code, a researcher would browse to this section as follows:

IRC (Title 26 of the U.S. Code)

> Subtitle A (Income Taxes)

>> Chapter 1 (Normal Taxes and Surcharges)

>>>Subchapter B (Computation of Taxable Income)

>>>>Part III (Items Specifically Excluded from Gross Income)

>>>>>Section 132

Within Section 132, a researcher will find subsections, paragraphs, and so on. For example, the last arrow shown in Figure 11-6 points to IRC § 132(e)(2)(B). Alternatively, it can be cited, by reference to the United States Code, as 26 U.S.C. § 132(e)(2)(B).

Reading and Interpreting the Internal Revenue Code

Interpreting an IRC section requires careful and thorough reading and analysis. When reading a section of the Code, keep the following considerations in mind:

- **Definitions.** Terms used within a Code section may be defined in that section or elsewhere in the Code. Definitions may apply only for purposes of a particular portion (such as a subtitle, chapter, or section) of the IRC, so the researcher must always consider to which parts of the Code a definition applies. Definitions are not bold or highlighted in the Code but are often shown in "quotation marks," as you'll notice in the case of the term "de minimis fringe" shown in IRC § 132(e)(1) in Figure 11-6.
  - IRC Section 7701 includes a number of definitions that apply to the entire Code, including the definitions of person, corporation, partnership, foreign, domestic, and taxpayer.

- **General Rules and Exceptions.** Many IRC sections begin by stating a general rule, which is followed by exceptions, definitions or other rules limiting its application. For example, the general rule described in IRC § 132(a) in Figure 11-6 is followed by several definitions and rules that limit its application. A researcher must read the entire Code section to be certain a situation is covered by that Code section and to determine the applicable tax treatment. Reading only part of a Code section can result in missing important (and relevant) information, and can lead to providing erroneous tax advice.

- **Effective Dates.** The IRC is frequently amended, so some provisions of the Code only apply to certain tax periods. The applicable period may be stated in the Code section. If the Code section does not state an effective date (as is the case in Figure 11-6), the researcher may need to refer to amendments to the Code section to determine the effective date of any changes made by the amendment. In this case, a researcher might search for amendments to Section 132 to identify the effective date of applicable amendments.

- **Cross References.** A Code section often refers to one or more other sections of the IRC. It is necessary for the tax researcher to actually look at the provisions of the cross-referenced Code sections to conclusively determine the proper tax treatment.

Figure 11-6

Internal Revenue Code
Section 132

Internal Revenue Code Section 132 – Certain fringe benefits

Subsection ▶ **(a) Exclusion from gross income**

Gross income shall not include any fringe benefit which qualifies as a—

(1) no-additional-cost service,

(2) qualified employee discount,

(3) working condition fringe,

(4) de minimis fringe,

(5) qualified transportation fringe,

(6) qualified moving expense reimbursement,

(7) qualified retirement planning services, or

(8) qualified military base realignment and closure fringe.

(b) No-additional-cost service defined

For purposes of this section, the term "no-additional-cost service" means any service provided by an employer to an employee for use by such employee if—

(1) such service is offered for sale to customers in the ordinary course of the line of business of the employer in which the employee is performing services, and

(2) the employer incurs no substantial additional cost (including forgone revenue) in providing such service to the employee (determined without regard to any amount paid by the employee for such service).

(c) [omitted].

(d) Working condition fringe defined

For purposes of this section, the term "working condition fringe" means any property or services provided to an employee of the employer to the extent that, if the employee paid for such property or services, such payment would be allowable as a deduction under section 162 or 167.

Subsection ▶ **(e) De minimis fringe defined**

For purposes of this section—

(1) In general

The term "de minimis fringe" means any property or service the value of which is (after taking into account the frequency with which similar fringes are provided by the employer to the employer's employees) so small as to make accounting for it unreasonable or administratively impracticable.

Paragraph ▶ **(2) Treatment of certain eating facilities**

The operation by an employer of any eating facility for employees shall be treated as a de minimis fringe if—

(A) such facility is located on or near the business premises of the employer, and

Subparagraph ▶ **(B)** revenue derived from such facility normally equals or exceeds the direct operating costs of such facility.

The preceding sentence shall apply with respect to any highly compensated employee only if access to the facility is available on substantially the same terms to each member of a group of employees which is defined under a reasonable classification set up by the employer which does not discriminate in favor of highly compensated employees. For purposes of subparagraph (B), an employee entitled under section 119 to exclude the value of a meal provided at such facility shall be treated as having paid an amount for such meal equal to the direct operating costs of the facility attributable to such meal.

(f) – (o) [omitted].

Take a moment to complete the following **Now YOU Try** exercise, intended to improve your familiarity with the guidance included within Code sections.

Now
[YOU]
Try
11.2

Code Section 132

Refer to Figure 11-6 to answer the following questions:

1. List three terms that are defined in Section 132:

    _____

    _____

    _____

2. To what part of the Code do these definitions apply?

    _____

3. What other Code sections are referred to in IRC § 132?

    _____

4. Assume that your client is an employer who operates a snow-plowing service. The client would like to provide its employees with the benefit of snow-plowing their home driveways for free during the winter. What is the result or tax consequence if it can be established that the snow-plowing benefit provided to the client's employees is a "no-additional-cost service"?

    _____

    _____

■ **Common Terms.** Some words used in the Code should be interpreted in accordance with their everyday meanings. Such **common terms** include, for example, references to dollar amounts or time periods and words such as "and" and "or."

● For example, the phrase "less than $100" includes amounts of $99.99 or less, but not $100. By contrast, "$100 or less" and "not more than $100" do include $100, as well as lesser amounts.

● If an IRC section provides that a form must be filed "within 30 days" after an event occurs, the tax researcher should know that 30 days is not necessarily the equivalent of one month. The 30-day period would start on the day after the event occurs and would end on the 30th day thereafter.

● When a list of terms is joined by "and," all items in the list are required to be true or correct. When a list of terms is joined by "or," only one of the items in the list is required to be true or correct.

Take a moment to complete the following **Now YOU Try** exercise, which focuses on the everyday meanings of a few common terms used in the Code.

Now
[YOU]
Try
11.3

Common Terms

Answer the first two questions. The common term is highlighted in each question.

1. The phrase "**before** August 1, 2015" refers to the period that ends on what date?

    _____

2. The phrase "**after** August 1, 2015" refers to the period that begins on what date?

    _____

Refer again to Figure 11-6 to answer the next two questions.

3. Choose the correct answer (a, b, or c):

For an employer-provided benefit to be considered a "no-additional-cost service," which of the following is required?

(a) The service must be offered for sale to customers in the ordinary course of the line of business of the employer in which the employee is performing services.

(b) The employer cannot incur a substantial additional cost (including forgone revenue) in providing the service to the employee (determined without regard to any amount paid by the employee for the service).

(c) Both (a) and (b) are required.

---

4. To be excluded from gross income, an employer-provided fringe benefit must be both a working condition fringe and a de minimis fringe. Is the previous sentence true or false? Why?

Understanding Legislative History

Understanding the **legislative history** of tax laws can provide researchers with additional background on, including the intent behind, enacted laws. For federal tax legislation, legislative history comprises

- Reports of the House Ways and Means Committee, and reports of the Senate Finance Committee;

- Reports of the Joint Conference Committee; and

- General Explanations of the Joint Committee on Taxation.

As noted, the IRC is frequently amended by **federal statute**. A legislative bill becomes a federal statute only after it is passed by a majority vote of each house of the U.S. Congress (i.e., the House of Representatives and the Senate) and then signed into law by the President. If the President vetoes a bill, Congress can override the veto by a two-thirds vote of both houses of Congress.

Before being considered by the full House of Representatives or the Senate, proposed tax legislation is generally first considered by committees, who issue reports on their findings:

- The **House Ways and Means Committee** writes and reviews draft tax legislation for the House.

- The **Senate Finance Committee** writes and reviews draft tax legislation for the Senate.

If a tax bill that is passed by the House of Representatives differs from a tax bill passed by the Senate, it is referred to the **Joint Conference Committee** (composed of members of the House Ways and Means and the Senate Finance Committees), which must prepare a compromise version of the proposed legislation for vote by both the House and Senate. The Joint Conference Committee may also issue a committee report that becomes part of the legislative history of the ultimately enacted tax legislation.

In addition, the **Joint Committee on Taxation**, a nonpartisan committee with members from the House Ways and Means and Senate Finance Committees and with a professional staff of economists, attorneys, and accountants,[1] prepares a report that is a general explanation of newly enacted tax legislation.

Collectively, these reports of the House Ways and Means Committee, the Senate Finance Committee, and the Joint Conference Committee become part of the legislative history of a tax law. The legislative history of a statutory change and the Joint Committee on Taxation's general explanation are considered substantial authority, and reviewing them can aid a tax researcher in understanding the reasons for the legislation (i.e., the "legislative intent") as well as the meaning

---

[1] See IRC §8002 and *https://www.jct.gov/about-us/overview.html* for additional information regarding The Joint Committee on Taxation.

of the statutory changes. This can be particularly helpful to a tax researcher when reviewing new tax legislation for which there are no regulations or other guidance. Figure 11-7 reviews the process by which tax legislation is adopted.

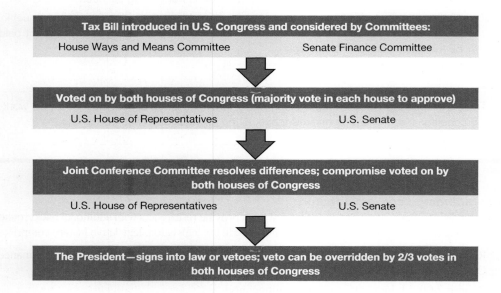

Figure 11-7

The process of adopting tax legislation

Federal statutes are referred to by **Public Law** (or "**P.L.**") number. A Public Law number includes two numbers with a hyphen in the middle (e.g., P.L. 111-92). The first number indicates the 2-year Congressional Session in which it was enacted, and the second number indicates the number of the bill (in sequential order) enacted by that session of Congress. For example, P.L. 111-92 (the "American Recovery and Reinvestment Tax Act of 2009"), was the ninety-second bill enacted into law by the 111th Session of Congress (2009–2011). Committee Reports reference the related tax legislation by Public Law number.

Federal Tax Regulations

The **Internal Revenue Service (IRS)** is the largest of the U.S. Treasury Department's bureaus and "is responsible for determining, assessing, and collecting internal revenue in the United States."[2] As an administrative agency of the U.S. federal government, the IRS issues many different administrative sources of federal tax law. Figure 11-8 lists the sources of federal tax law issued by the IRS that are discussed in this chapter.

Federal tax **regulations** are the Treasury Department's official interpretation of the IRC, are considered substantial authority, and have the greatest precedential value of any of the sources of federal tax law listed in Figure 11-8. While the Treasury Department is the official issuer of tax regulations, it does so with much IRS involvement; accordingly, Figure 11-8 shows lines from both Treasury and the IRS for regulations.

Authority to issue tax regulations is found in IRC § 7805, which provides that the Secretary of the Treasury "shall prescribe all needful rules and regulations for the enforcement of this title, including all rules and regulations as may be necessary by reason of any alteration of law in relation to internal revenue." Tax regulations that are issued to interpret a section of the Code under this general grant of authority to issue regulations are sometimes referred to as "**general regulations**" or "**interpretive regulations.**"

Other Code sections give the Secretary authority to set (rather than merely interpret) the requirements for a specific area of tax law. For example, IRC Section 385(a) authorizes the

---

[2] *http://www.treasury.gov/about/organizational-structure/bureaus/Pages/default.aspx.*

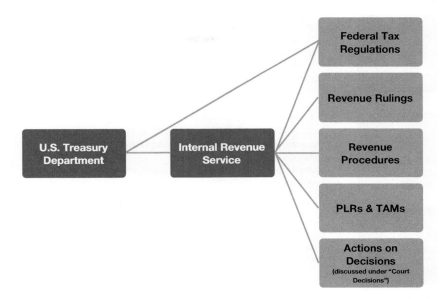

Figure 11-8

Sources of U.S. federal tax law issued by the IRS

Secretary "to prescribe such regulations as may be necessary or appropriate to determine whether an interest in a corporation is to be treated for purposes of this title as stock or indebtedness (or as in part stock and in part indebtedness)." Regulations issued under such a special grant of authority are sometimes referred to as **legislative regulations**.

Courts use a deferential standard when reviewing regulations (meaning, they often "defer" to the Treasury Department) and will generally uphold a regulation provided that it is based on a permissible construction (interpretation) of the statute.[3] If there is clearly a conflict between a Code provision and a regulation, however, the Code provision controls, as its authority as a statute is of greater precedential value than a regulation.

Federal tax regulations are issued in final, proposed, and temporary formats.

- **Final regulations** are the Treasury Department's final, official interpretations of the tax law and are issued by a **Treasury Decision (T.D.)**.

- **Proposed regulations** are not considered official interpretations of the tax law until they have been through a finalization process. When issuing a proposed regulation, the IRS will generally provide a public comment period (of at least 30 days) and may schedule a public hearing to discuss a proposed regulation. Following this public outreach, the Treasury Department may finalize the proposed regulation, revise and repropose it, or withdraw it for further study.

- **Temporary regulations** are official interpretations of the IRC, but are effective for only a temporary period, usually 3 years. A temporary regulation is usually issued with a proposed regulation to provide some immediate, reliable guidance for a temporary period while the IRS requests and receives comments on the proposed regulation and works towards issuing a final regulation.

Final, proposed, and temporary federal tax regulations are published in three places: the **Federal Register,** the **Internal Revenue Bulletin (I.R.B.),** and the **Cumulative Bulletin (C.B.)**. Final and temporary federal tax regulations are also compiled and published in Title 26 of the **Code of Federal Regulations (C.F.R.)**. Figure 11-9 compares the Federal Register, I.R.B., C.B., and C.F.R.

---

[3] *Mayo Foundation for Medical Ed. & Research v. U.S.,* 107 AFTR 2d 2011-341, 131 S.Ct. 704 (2011).

Figure 11-9

Comparison of the Federal Register, I.R.B., C.B., and C.F.R.

Federal Register
- Published every weekday (not including federal holidays) by the U.S. Government Printing Office (GPO)
- Includes rules and regulations issued by all agencies of the federal government
- Can be accessed on the GPO website (www.gpo.gov/fdsys/)

Internal Revenue Bulletin (I.R.B.)
- Published weekly by the IRS
- Includes Federal Tax Regulations (final, proposed, and temporary), IRS Revenue Rulings and Revenue Procedures, and Actions on Decisions
- Recent copies are available on the IRS website (www.irs.gov)

Cumulative Bulletin (C.B.)
- Published annually by the IRS
- Usually published in 2 volumes per calendar year
- Compiles all the items included in the year's I.R.B.s

Code of Federal Regulations (C.F.R.)
- Published annually by the U.S. GPO
- Includes final and temporary rules and regulations of federal government agencies
- Can be accessed on the GPO website (www.gpo.gov/fdsys/)

Federal tax regulations are organized first by a number that designates the type of tax or regulation involved (followed by a period), and then by IRC section number. The numbering system is as follows:

Number	Type of Tax or Regulation
1	Income tax
20	Estate tax
25	Gift tax
31	Employment tax
301	Procedural regulation

For example, the citation to Regulation § 1.132-3 indicates that it

- Is an income tax regulation (1),
- Was issued with respect to IRC § 132 (132), and
- Is the third final regulation that was issued related to IRC Section 132 (-3).

Similar to Code sections, regulations are broken down by paragraphs, subparagraphs, and clauses. For example, "Regulation § 1.132-3(a)(2)" refers to subparagraph (2) of paragraph (a) of Regulation § 1.132-3. Treasury regulations are often cited using the abbreviation "Treas. Reg." or just "Reg." before the section number. A final regulation can also be cited by reference to the Code of Federal Regulations as "26 C.F.R. § 1.132-3." The "26" in this citation refers to Title 26 of the C.F.R., the title within the C.F.R. where federal tax regulations are codified.

Proposed regulations should be cited with either the word "Proposed" or the abbreviation "Prop." at the beginning of the citation. For example, "Prop. Reg. § 1.351-2" informs the reader that the regulation cited has not been finalized. Temporary regulations include a "T" in the citation to clearly indicate that the regulation cited is only temporary. For example, in "Treas. Reg. § 1.162-10T," the "T" indicates that it is a temporary regulation.

Final, proposed, and temporary regulations may be accessed using an online tax research service such as Thomson Reuters Checkpoint (introduced below), or for free through the IRS website (www.irs.gov). Final and temporary regulations are also available on the U.S. Government Printing Office (GPO) website (www.gpo.gov/fdsys/).

Consider the following **TIP from the Trenches** related to finding tax regulations.

> Despite that tax regulations can be accessed for free through the GPO and IRS websites, the search engines on these sites are limited and best used when the researcher already knows the citation for the regulation and just needs to retrieve it. When searching for regulations without a citation, such as by keyword search or by reference only to the related IRC section, it is generally more efficient to use an online tax research service.

[**TIP**] from the Trenches

Revenue Rulings

The IRS issues several primary sources of federal tax guidance. One such source is an IRS **Revenue Ruling**. Revenue Rulings are issued by the IRS National Office and are published in the I.R.B. A Revenue Ruling is "an official interpretation by the IRS of the internal revenue laws and related statutes, treaties, and regulations"[4] and is considered a substantial authority. Revenue Rulings may

- Involve the application of the Code and regulations to a particular factual situation.
  - As a result, a Revenue Ruling can be an important source of guidance for taxpayers in the same or a similar situation, because it can be relied on in determining the tax treatment of a transaction.
  - However, the IRS cautions against reaching the same conclusion reached in a Revenue Ruling in another case unless the facts and circumstances are essentially the same as those described in the Revenue Ruling.
- Contain informational updates, such as inflation-related adjustments to certain provisions of the Code and changes in the applicable federal rates of interest applicable to certain tax calculations.

The IRS sometimes modifies, revokes, or issues guidance that supersedes a Revenue Ruling. Therefore, the researcher must be certain that any Revenue Ruling relied on is still "good law." Revenue Rulings are cited by number and by reference to where they appear in the I.R.B. or the C.B. Figure 11-10 illustrates sample Revenue Ruling citations.

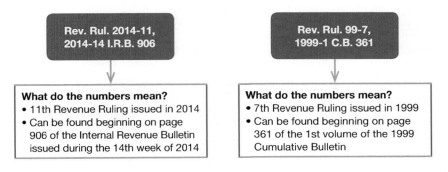

Figure 11-10

Revenue Ruling citations

Take a moment to complete the following **Now YOU Try** exercise, intended to help you practice properly citing Revenue Rulings.

---

[4] Rev. Proc. 89-14, 1989-1 C.B. 814.

Citing Revenue Rulings

Provide the citation to the following Revenue Rulings:

1. The 12th Revenue Ruling issued during 2008 and that can be found beginning on page 520 of the 1st volume of that year's Cumulative Bulletin:

2. The 17th Revenue Ruling issued during 2014 and that can be found beginning on page 1093 of the Internal Revenue Bulletin issued during the 24th week of 2014:

Revenue Procedures

A **Revenue Procedure** is an official statement published in the I.R.B. that affects the rights or duties of taxpayers or others under federal tax law.[5] The topics of Revenue Procedures are varied, but generally they involve guidance in the nature of "how to" do something, such as how to request a private letter ruling (discussed below) from the IRS or how to make certain elections under the Code. Revenue Procedures are also considered substantial authority.

Like Revenue Rulings, Revenue Procedures are cited by number and by reference to where they appear in the I.R.B. or the C.B. For example, Revenue Procedure number 2013-4 would be cited as "Rev. Proc. 2013-4, 2013-1 I.R.B. 126," which indicates that

- It is the 4th Revenue Procedure issued in 2013 (2013-4), and

- It can be found beginning at page 126 of the Internal Revenue Bulletin issued during the 1st week of 2013 (126 and 2013-1).

Private Letter Rulings and Technical Advice Memoranda

The IRS National Office issues **Private Letter Rulings** or **PLRs** to taxpayers seeking guidance regarding, or to confirm the tax consequences of, proposed or not-yet-reported transactions. In some cases, the IRS may refuse to issue a requested PLR; this refusal may lead the taxpayer to reconsider and/or restructure a proposed transaction.

The IRS National Office also issues **Technical Advice Memoranda** or **TAMs**. A TAM may be requested by an IRS agent during a federal tax audit, for which the agent seeks National Office input. The TAM describes the IRS's tax analysis and conclusion regarding the audit issue. In some cases, a taxpayer may choose to litigate this decision in court. Figure 11-11 contrasts a Private Letter Ruling and a Technical Advice Memorandum.

Figure 11-11

Comparison of a PLR and a TAM

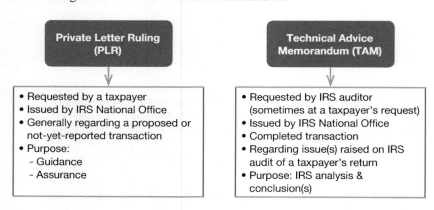

Both PLRs and TAMs provide that they "may not be used or cited as precedent." This means that PLRs and TAMs are not precedent that the IRS is required to follow in other cases. However, a tax adviser should review relevant PLRs and TAMs (involving facts that are similar to the client's)

---

[5] Id.

when researching a tax issue, because they provide guidance as to how the IRS has treated the issue under similar circumstances. PLRs and TAMs are frequently cited when documenting tax research, but with the understanding that they are not binding on the IRS as precedent for the client. For the taxpayer for whom it was requested, however, a PLR or a TAM is substantial authority that can be relied on to avoid certain statutory penalties.[6]

PLRs and TAMs are cited in a similar format, by number. For example, let's "decode" PLR 200601002:

- The first four digits[7] of the PLR refer to the year it was released to the public (2006);

- The next two digits indicate the week it was released ("01" means the PLR was released during the first week of 2006); and

- The final three digits indicate the order in which the ruling was released during the week ("002" means the PLR was the second one released during the week).

Take a moment to complete the following Now YOU Try exercise regarding PLRs and TAMs.

PLRs and TAMs

Answer the following questions based on the information just provided.

1. List two ways in which PLRs and TAMs differ.

   _____

   _____

2. What does the citation "PLR 201415012" tell you about this ruling?

   _____

Now
[**YOU**]
Try
11.5

PLRs and TAMs are not published in the I.R.B. or the C.B. However, they are made available for public inspection by the IRS and, more practically, can be accessed using an online tax research service (discussed later in the chapter).

Court Decisions

When the IRS and a taxpayer disagree about the proper tax treatment of a transaction, their dispute may end up being litigated in court. This litigation may result in the court issuing a written decision interpreting other sources of tax law, including the Code and regulations. Court decisions are another primary source of tax law and can provide important guidance for the tax researcher. A relevant court decision is considered substantial authority provided that it has not been overruled or reversed on appeal.

There are a number of different federal courts that hear and decide federal tax cases, including trial courts (where the case is initiated and tried) and appellate courts (which decide appeals of trial or lower appellate court decisions). Understanding each court's **jurisdiction** (i.e., the types of cases the court has authority to hear and decide) helps the researcher to determine whether a decision is precedent for the client's situation being researched. Court decisions appear in **reporters** (volumes in which a number of court decisions are published) and are also accessible using online tax research services.

Trial Courts

The **trial courts** that can hear and decide federal tax cases are the U.S. Tax Court, the U.S. District Court, and the U.S. Court of Federal Claims. Figure 11-12 contrasts these three federal trial courts.

---

[6] Treatment of a PLR or a TAM as substantial authority is subject to the limitations in Reg. §1.6662-4(d)(3)(iv).

[7] For pre-2000 PLRs and TAMs, only the first two digits refer to the year issued. For example, TAM 9715002 (April 11, 1997) was the second ruling issued during the fifteenth week of 1997.

Figure 11-12

Trial courts that decide
federal tax cases

U.S. Tax Court	U.S. District Court	U.S. Court of Federal Claims
• Decides only federal tax cases • Based in Washington, D.C.; trials in many U.S. cities • Litigate case before paying tax alleged to be due • No jury	• Decides different types of federal cases • 94 Districts located throughout the U.S. • Refund claims only • May be a jury trial if a question of fact	• Decides only cases involving monetary claims against the U.S. Federal Government • Based in Washington, D.C.; trials in many U.S. cities • Refund claims only • No jury

A taxpayer initiates a case in **U.S. Tax Court** ("Tax Court") by filing a petition, which is generally required to be filed within 90 days of receiving a notice of deficiency from the IRS following a tax audit. The Tax Court is the only court at which the taxpayer may litigate a federal tax deficiency without first paying the tax. The U.S. Tax Court issues three types of decisions: regular decisions, memorandum decisions, and summary decisions. Figure 11-13 briefly summarizes the differences between these three types of Tax Court decisions and their relative precedential values.

Figure 11-13

Types of U.S. Tax Court
decisions

Tax Court Regular Decisions

- Often involve issues being decided for the first time by the Tax Court
- Highest precedential value of all Tax Court decisions
- Decisions reported in the Tax Court of the United States Reports (abbreviated "T.C.")
- Can be appealed to an appellate court

Tax Court Memorandum Decisions

- Historically, have involved previously-decided and factual (as opposed to legal) issues
- Have precedential value, but less than Tax Court regular decisions
- Decisions reported in RIA's Tax Court Memorandum Decisions ("RIA T.C. Memo") and CCH's Tax Court Memorandum Decisions ("TCM")
- Can be appealed to an appellate court

Tax Court Summary Decisions

- Applies to small cases; tax and penalties at issue cannot exceed $50,000
- Cannot be used or cited as precedent per IRC §7463(b)
- Decisions not officially published, but available through online tax research services (e.g., RIA's "TC Summary Opinions")
- Cannot be appealed to an appellate court

As shown in Figure 11-13, regular and memorandum Tax Court decisions may be used as precedent, and therefore should be considered when they involve an issue of law relevant to a client's situation. Additionally, despite the prohibition against citing and using summary decisions as precedent for other cases, a researcher should review them to see how the Tax Court has decided cases that are similar to the client's.

As an alternative to filing a petition with the U.S. Tax Court, a taxpayer may choose to pay the tax, penalty, and interest alleged to be due and file a lawsuit seeking a refund of the amount paid either in a **U.S. District Court** or in the **U.S. Court of Federal Claims**.

- The U.S. District Court with jurisdiction over a taxpayer's refund claim is generally the district in which the taxpayer resides. The U.S. District Court has jurisdiction over federal tax cases—like the Tax Court—as well as cases involving any federal statute or the U.S. Constitution, cases in which the U.S. government is a party, and cases in which the parties are of diverse citizenship (e.g., citizens of different states) and more than $75,000 is at issue.

- The jurisdiction of the U.S. Court of Federal Claims is limited to cases involving monetary claims against the U.S. federal government (including claims for tax refunds).

Decisions of the U.S. District Courts are reported in the **Federal Supplement** (**"F. Supp."**) or "F. Supp. 2d" (the second series of the Federal Supplement). Decisions of the U.S. Court of Federal Claims are reported in the **Federal Claims Reporter** (**"Fed. Cl."**).

To locate tax decisions within online tax research services, see RIA's American Federal Tax Reports ("A.F.T.R." or "A.F.T.R.2d") or CCH's U.S. Tax Cases ("U.S.T.C."), for example.

Appellate Courts

The appellate courts that decide appeals of federal tax cases are the U.S. Court of Appeals and the U.S. Supreme Court. Appellate courts do not hold trials of cases. Instead, an appellate court has to decide whether any errors of law (which can include an error in interpreting tax law) were made by the trial court or a lower appellate court. An appellate court is sometimes referred to as a **higher court**, because appellate court decisions are of greater precedential value than trial court decisions, with the U.S. Supreme Court's decisions being of the highest precedential value. Decisions of an appellate court must be followed by trial courts in cases that can be appealed to that appellate court.

A researcher may find court decisions that reach different conclusions on the same issue of tax law. Assuming the facts are similar to the client's situation, the researcher should give more weight or importance to the decision of the court with greater precedential value, and less or no weight to the decision of the court with less precedential value. Figure 11-14 illustrates the hierarchy of the different courts that decide federal tax cases (and the hierarchy of regular and memorandum U.S. Tax Court decisions). The higher the court is on this hierarchy, the greater the precedential value of the court's decisions.

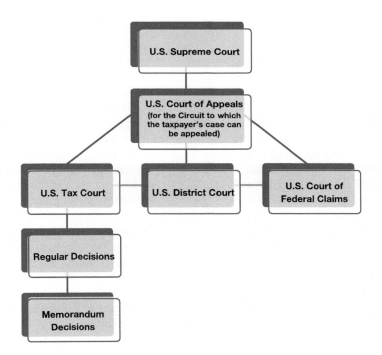

Figure 11-14

Hierarchy of federal courts

<u>U.S. Court of Appeals</u>

The **U.S. Court of Appeals** hears appeals of decisions of the three federal trial courts described previously. There are 13 Circuit Courts of the U.S. Court of Appeals (11 of the Circuits are referred to by number and there are also a D.C. Circuit and a Federal Circuit). An appeal of a Tax Court decision would be to the Circuit that has jurisdiction over the geographic area within which the taxpayer resided when the Tax Court petition was filed. An appeal of a U.S. District Court decision would be to the Circuit that has jurisdiction over the geographic area where the District Court is located. An appeal of a decision of the U.S. Court of Federal Claims is made to the U.S. Court of Appeals for the Federal Circuit. Figure 11-15 depicts the geographic boundaries of the U.S. Court of Appeals.

Figure 11-15

Geographic boundaries of the U.S. Court of Appeals[8]

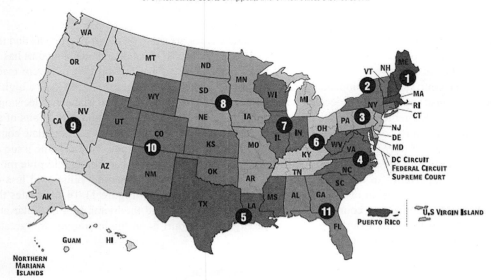

Geographic Boundaries
of United States Courts of Appeals and United States District Courts

For example, considering the map in Figure 11-15, if a taxpayer lived in Jacksonville, Florida, when she filed her petition with the Tax Court, an appeal of the Tax Court's decision would be filed with the U.S. Court of Appeals for the Eleventh Circuit (which includes Alabama, Florida, and Georgia). The Eleventh Circuit also has jurisdiction over appeals of decisions of the U.S. District Courts located in Alabama, Florida, and Georgia.

Decisions of the U.S. Court of Appeals are reported in the **Federal Reporter**, which is abbreviated "**F.**," "F.2d" (for the second series), or "F.3d" (for the third series). Decisions of the U.S. Court of Appeals in tax cases are also available in online tax research services such as RIA's American Federal Tax Reports ("A.F.T.R." or "A.F.T.R.2d") and CCH's U.S. Tax Cases ("U.S.T.C.").

The different Circuit Courts of the U.S. Court of Appeals may interpret tax law differently, as long as the issue has not been decided by the U.S. Supreme Court. A trial court must follow the law as interpreted by the Circuit Court to which the case could be appealed. Because decisions of the Tax Court are appealed to different Circuit Courts, the Tax Court may interpret the law differently in different cases based on the taxpayer's residence, creating conflicting precedents.

U.S. Supreme Court

The highest appellate court in the U.S. federal court system is the **U.S. Supreme Court**. A decision of the U.S. Supreme Court in a federal tax case must be followed by all trial and appellate courts in federal tax cases involving the same issue. The only exception to this is if the Code (or, in some cases, a regulation) is changed in a way that makes the Supreme Court's decision no longer applicable. There are nine justices on the U.S. Supreme Court, which is located in Washington, D.C. The Supreme Court is primarily an appellate court and, with respect to federal tax cases, may decide a case after an appellate decision is issued by the U.S. Court of Appeals.

The U.S. Supreme Court has discretion over which cases it will decide and issues a **writ of certiorari** if it agrees to hear and decide an appeal. More often, however, the Supreme Court decides not to grant certiorari. When the Supreme Court has granted certiorari, but has not yet decided the case, the citation to the case includes "**cert. granted.**" Finding that certiorari has been granted in a relevant case should put the researcher on alert that the U.S. Supreme Court

---

[8] Source of map: *http://www.uscourts.gov/file/document/us-federal-courts-circuit-map.*

will be deciding the issue. If the Supreme Court has refused to grant certiorari in a case, the citation to the case includes "**cert. denied.**" The Supreme Court's denial of certiorari is not an indication that the Court agrees with the Court of Appeals' decision in the case. Instead, it is just an indication that the Supreme Court chose not to decide the case.

U.S. Supreme Court decisions are reported in United States Reports ("U.S.") (its official reporter), as well as in the Supreme Court Reporter ("S.Ct.") and the United States Supreme Court Reports, Lawyers' Edition ("L.Ed."). Tax decisions of the U.S. Supreme Court are also published in, and may be cited by reference to, online tax research services such as RIA's American Federal Tax Reports ("A.F.T.R." or "A.F.T.R.2d") and CCH's U.S. Tax Cases ("U.S.T.C.").

Citing Court Decisions

The citation to a court decision generally includes the following information:

- The names of the parties with a "v." (for versus) in between. Citations of Tax Court decisions generally include only the taxpayer's name and omit "v. Commissioner."

- The volume number of the reporter in which the decision appears, the abbreviation for the reporter, and the first page number on which the decision appears. Alternatively, the paragraph number for the case may be included in lieu of a page number and/or volume number.

- An abbreviation indicating the court that decided the case (if not obvious elsewhere in the citation).

- The year in which the case was decided (if not obvious elsewhere in the citation).

Although citations to court decisions generally refer to volume and page numbers of paper reporters, and some court decisions may also be available on the website of the court that issued the decision, it is generally more efficient and thorough to research court decisions using an online tax research service (discussed later in this chapter).

Take a moment to complete the following **Now YOU Try** exercise, intended to acquaint you with case citation format and determining from the citation which court decided the case.

Case Citations

For each of the cases cited below, indicate whether it is a U.S. Tax Court Regular Decision, U.S. Tax Court Memorandum Decision, U.S. District Court Decision, U.S. Court of Federal Claims Decision, U.S. Court of Appeals Decision, or a U.S. Supreme Court Decision.

Now
YOU
Try
11.6

1. *Langley*, TC Memo 2015-11

2. *Nacchio v. U.S.*, 115 Fed. Cl. 195 (2014) **or** 113 A.F.T.R.2d 2014-1288 (Ct. Fed. Cl.) **or** 2014-1 USTC ¶50,231 (Ct. Fed. Cl.)

3. *Weisman v. Commissioner*, 103 F.Supp.2d 621 (E.D.N.Y. 2000) **or** 87 A.F.T.R.2d 2001-1897 (DC NY 2000)

4. *Commissioner v. Schleier*, 515 U.S. 323 (1995) **or** 115 S.Ct. 2159 (1995) **or** 75 A.F.T.R.2d 95-2675 (S Ct)

5. *Churchill Downs, Inc.*, 115 T.C. 279 (2000)

6. *Mitchell v. Commissioner*, 775 F.3d 1243 (10th Cir. 2015) <u>or</u> 115 A.F.T.R.2d 2015-346 (CA-10)

Actions on Decisions

A federal tax case is generally initiated by a taxpayer who disagrees with an IRS decision regarding the taxpayer's tax liability. If the IRS disagrees with the court's decision in a federal tax case involving a significant issue decided in the taxpayer's favor, the IRS may indicate whether or not it will continue to litigate the tax issue decided in the case. The IRS does this by means of an **Action on Decision** (AOD). An IRS **acquiescence** to a case means that the IRS will no longer litigate the issue decided in the case. An IRS **nonacquiescence** to a case means that the IRS does not agree with the court's interpretation of the tax law in a case and will continue to litigate the issue in other cases. The IRS publishes AODs in the I.R.B. AODs are included in the list of substantial authority that can be relied upon to avoid tax penalties. A full citation to a case in which the IRS has acquiesced includes "Acq.," and the full citation to a case in which the IRS has issued a nonacquiescence includes "Nonacq.," followed by the I.R.B. citation where it appears, for example, *Norris,* TC Memo 2011-161, Nonacq. AOD 2011-005, 2011-52 I.R.B.

Secondary Sources of U.S. Federal Tax Law

LO4 Differentiate between primary and secondary sources of tax law.

Secondary sources of U.S. federal tax law include editorial content provided by tax services, tax treatises, and tax periodicals. Although secondary sources are not binding on the IRS or the courts, and are not substantial authority for purposes of avoiding tax penalties, they can be very helpful to a tax researcher for a number of reasons.

First, consulting a secondary source may be a good first step in your research process. When confronting an issue with which you have little or no experience, you may use a secondary source as background reading to identify and get acquainted with the issue.

Second, a secondary source may help you identify the primary sources of law related to the issue. You can then review the identified primary sources and determine whether they resolve the issue or whether you need to do further research. In either event, you should not rely on the secondary source's discussion of a primary source. It is always necessary to look at the primary source yourself, because the discussion in a secondary source summarizes the primary source. What is left out of the summary may make a difference in the client's case.

Third, you may not be certain of your interpretation of a primary source of tax law. Consulting a secondary source can reinforce your interpretation or may lead you to focus on a different interpretation worth considering.

Tax Services

Tax services generally include a publisher's annotations to and explanations of primary sources of tax law and are periodically updated for new developments. Although these services originated in paper form, they are now generally accessed via an online tax research service that is available by subscription. The primary online services are Thomson Reuters Checkpoint (which includes RIA tax databases) and CCH's IntelliConnect. In addition, online legal research services, such as LexisNexis and Westlaw, include access to primary sources of tax law and may also include some secondary sources.

Tax Treatises

Tax **treatises** are published in book form (although some are also accessible via an online tax research service) and provide an in-depth discussion of tax issues. A few examples of tax treatises include:

- Bittker, *Federal Income Taxation of Individuals*
- Bittker & Eustice, *Federal Income Taxation of Corporations & Shareholders*
- Mertens, *Law of Federal Income Taxation*
- Saltzman, *IRS Practice and Procedure*

See the following **TIP from the Trenches** regarding when to consult a treatise.

When the researcher has little or no background knowledge related to the tax issue being researched, a treatise may be the best first place for the researcher to start. Treatises can be used for in-depth background reading to get acquainted with the tax topic involved. Reading the relevant part of a treatise may also help the researcher to better define the issues to be further researched. The treatise will point the researcher to many primary sources of tax law cited within the treatise.

[TIP] from the Trenches

Tax Periodicals

Tax **periodicals** include scholarly and practitioner journals dealing with tax matters. Examples of tax periodicals include the following:

- *The Tax Adviser* (AICPA)
- *TAXES—The Tax Magazine* (CCH)
- *Journal of Taxation* (WG&L)
- *Tax Notes* (Tax Analysts)
- *Daily Tax Report* (BNA)

Tax periodicals include articles that highlight new developments in tax law. Reading tax periodicals on a timely basis helps the tax professional to stay current. Articles in tax periodicals may also be consulted during the research process and provide the researcher with insight in the form of an author's interpretation of tax law.

Consider the following **TIP from the Trenches** regarding using secondary sources for research.

As a beginning researcher, you may find it useful to *start* your research using a secondary source. When using a secondary source, remember that it is not precedent, but can point you in the right direction (towards primary sources) and is often quite user-friendly. For example, beginning tax researchers using Thomson Reuters Checkpoint (discussed later in the chapter) often find that using the Federal Tax Coordinator is a good starting point, and topics can be searched by table of contents, index, or keyword(s).

[TIP] from the Trenches

Take a moment to complete the following **Now YOU Try** exercise designed to test your knowledge of primary versus secondary sources of tax law.

Primary versus Secondary Sources

For each listed item, indicate what it is a citation for and whether it is a primary source or secondary source of tax law.

1. *Estate of Rosen*, 131 T.C. 75 (2008)

_____

2. Bittker & Eustice, *Federal Income Taxation of Corporations & Shareholders*

_____

3. Ho, R. and Kwock, B., "Tax Strategies for Chinese Nationals Who Invest in U.S. Real Estate," 120 *Journal of Taxation* 304 (WG&L June 2014)

_____

4. IRC §1361(c)(2)(A)(iii)

_____

5. Rev. Rul. 2012-22, 2012-48 I.R.B. 565

_____

[Now **YOU** Try]
11.7

USING AN ONLINE TAX RESEARCH SERVICE TO FIND TAX LAW

LO5 **Navigate** and **use** an online tax research service (Thomson Reuters Checkpoint).

With so many sources of tax law, subscribing to and using an online tax research service is a necessity for the professional tax researcher. These services include Thomson Reuters Checkpoint and CCH IntelliConnect. LexisNexis and Westlaw—two legal research services—also include access to tax law sources. These services are available by paid subscription, and often make arrangements with colleges and universities so that access may be provided free-of-charge to students.

While it may require time and effort to become comfortable using these services, the benefits of doing so are numerous. Researchers can experience efficiency, mobility, and the confidence of knowing you are using a dedicated, professional tax research service designed to help you find accurate and relevant results. The following **TIP from the Trenches** highlights the importance of consulting professional resources in performing tax research.

[TIP] from the Trenches

Researchers should not perform tax research using a general Internet search engine, such as Google or Bing. While some of what the researcher may find will be accurate and authoritative (such as some of the information on the IRS website [www.irs.gov]), other results of the search will be secondary authorities (at best) and incorrect information (at worst). Relying on those results in taking a position on a tax return can lead to the imposition of tax, penalties, and interest.

The remainder of this discussion of online tax research services focuses on Thomson Reuters Checkpoint, which includes access to primary sources of tax law, as well as secondary source material which it classifies as *Editorial Materials* and *News/Current Awareness*. Figure 11-16 shows the Search screen (with the Search button circled) for Thomson Reuters Checkpoint. The Search screen lists the different sources within which the researcher can search on Checkpoint.

Figure 11-16

Thomson Reuters Checkpoint Search screen

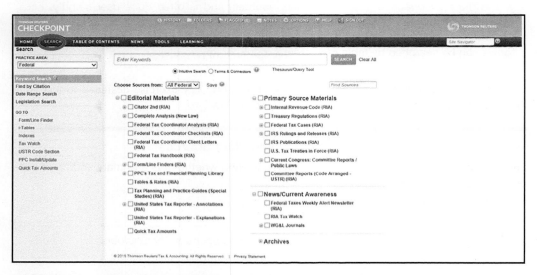

©2015 by Thomson Reuters/Tax & Accounting. Reprinted with permission. All rights reserved. This information or any portion thereof may not be copied or disseminated in any form or by any means or stored in an electronic database or retrieval system without the express written consent of Thomson Reuters/Tax & Accounting.

Sources of tax law can be searched in a variety of ways on Thomson Reuters Checkpoint, as well as on most of the other online tax research services.

Table of Contents and Index Searches on Thomson Reuters Checkpoint

One way to search on Checkpoint is to think of each database in its Editorial Materials as a large book (or multivolume set). Books have tables of contents and indices and so do these databases.

The table of contents of each database may be viewed by clicking on the "Table of Contents" tab followed by clicking on *Federal Library* and then *Federal Editorial Materials*. From there, the researcher can click on a database, such as the "United States Tax Reporter" and see its table of contents by groups of Code sections. The researcher can go further, and ultimately access the material in the United States Tax Reporter, by continuing to click onto more and more specific content headings such as one for a particular Code section or its related annotations and explanations. Figure 11-17 illustrates how a table of contents search through the United States Tax Reporter can ultimately lead to accessing its listings for Code Section 61, including the Code section itself, regulations, explanations and annotations.

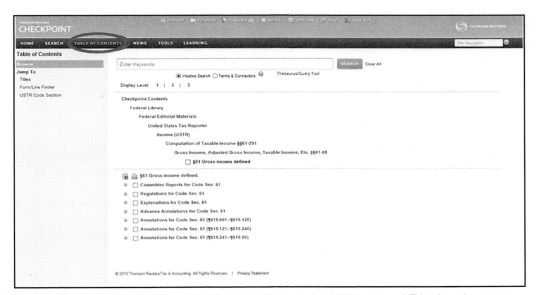

Figure 11-17

Sample table of contents search on Thomson Reuters Checkpoint

Editorial materials may also be accessed by an index search. This is akin to performing a Master Glossary search within the FASB Codification. To begin an index search on Checkpoint, a tax researcher would again click on the *Table of Contents* tab, followed by *Federal Library*, then *Federal Editorial Materials*, and then *Federal Indexes*. From there the researcher can click on a database, such as the *Code Arranged Annotations & Explanations (USTR) Topic Index* or the *Federal Tax Coordinator 2d Topic Index*, to see the alphabetical index for that database.

When searching in Checkpoint's Editorial Materials, it is important to remember that the results of the search (such as in the form of annotations or explanations) are secondary sources. However, they generally provide links to connect to the primary sources that are annotated or explained in the Editorial Material.

Keyword Searching

An important method for accessing the information on an online tax research service is by searching for keywords in one or more selected databases. This can include primary source material databases, such as *Federal Tax Cases*, *Internal Revenue Code*, or *IRS Rulings & Releases*, or the databases in Checkpoint's Editorial Materials, or a combination of both. On Checkpoint, a **keyword search** involves using its Search screen (see Figure 11-16), selecting the databases to be searched and entering words (which can be entered as either an *Intuitive Search* or by using *Terms & Connectors*) that one would expect to find in the expected search result documents.

To perform an **Intuitive Search**, you can enter a sentence, a question, a citation, or terms and connectors. Checkpoint interprets your query using historical usage data and editorial information embedded within the content to determine the most relevant results for the terms entered.[9] In a **Terms & Connectors** search you would enter specific words and phrases (but generally not as a sentence, question, or citation) as well as Checkpoint's relevant search connectors. The connectors filter the results of your search by taking into account things such as the proximity of the searched terms within a document. Whether using an Intuitive Search or Terms & Connectors keyword search, search results will include documents within the selected database(s) that will need to be reviewed for relevance and analyzed.

Keyword search results can be limited by making use of the available connectors or expanded by using the Thesaurus/Query Tool, which can be accessed from the Search screen on Checkpoint. The Search Connectors used in Checkpoint are listed in Figure 11-18.

Figure 11-18

Thomson Reuters Checkpoint search connectors[10]

Search Connectors

To locate documents:	Use:	Example:
containing any of my keywords	OR, I	funding OR deficiency
containing all of my keywords	space, &, AND	funding & deficiency
that contain one keyword but exclude another	^, NOT	funding ^ deficiency
containing my exact phrase	" "	"funding deficiency"
containing variations of my keywords	* (asterisk)	deprecia*
disabling automatic retrieval of plurals and equivalencies	# (pound sign)	#damage (retrieves only damage, not damages)
containing single-character variations	? (question mark)	s????holder (retrieves stockholder, shareholder)
containing compound words	- (hyphen)	e-mail (retrieves e-mail, e mail, email)
containing terms that occur at least # times	atleast#()	atleast5(customer)

Note: The # character does not turn off the automatic retrieval of possessives (for example, customer's).

Using Connectors in Intuitive Search

If the **Terms & Connectors** search method is selected, the AND, SPACE, or & connectors can all be used to require more than one term in each of the documents of your search results. However, if **Intuitive Search** is left as the default search method, Checkpoint will read the word "AND" and any SPACE as it would any other word used in your query. Although the most relevant documents are likely to have all words used, you may get results that have only most of the words.

Also, when using the **Intuitive Search** method, the use of quotations to search for a phrase will find the most relevant documents that include the exact phrase <u>and</u> relevant variations that contain the keywords within 3 words of one another.

To search for a word or phrase:	Use:	Example:
within n words of another (in any order)	/# (where # equals number)	"disclosure exception" /7 negligence
within n words of another (in exact order)	pre/# (where # equals number)	"disclosure exception" pre/7 negligence
within the same sentence (20 words) as another (in any order)	/s	"disclosure exception" /s negligence
within the same sentence (20 words) as another (in exact order)	pre/s	"disclosure exception" pre/s negligence
within one paragraph (50 words) as another (in any order)	/p	"disclosure exception" /p negligence
within one paragraph (50 words) as another (in exact order)	pre/p	"disclosure exception" pre/p negligence

---

[9] Checkpoint User Guide at p. 78 (Thomson Reuters 2015).

[10] Checkpoint User Guide at pp. 91-92 (Thomson Reuters 2015).

Consider the following **TIP from the Trenches** with respect to index/table of contents searches versus keyword searches and Intuitive versus Terms & Connectors keyword searches.

> Researchers with limited tax knowledge should start their use of an online tax research service by index or table of contents searching. Keyword searching is an "art" that improves as one's knowledge of tax law and its key terms increases. Without sufficient tax knowledge, keyword searches can yield far too many or far too few search results. When first performing keyword searches, a novice tax researcher may find it more helpful to use an Intuitive Search, because it allows the researcher to enter a question (such as is a particular item taxable or deductible) in the query box. After becoming more experienced with tax terminology and using the databases on Checkpoint, the tax researcher may find that performing a Terms & Connectors keyword search can be more efficient and produces fewer, but more relevant and specific, results.

[**TIP**] from the Trenches

EXAMPLE

The following is an example of how one might use keyword searches to find guidance regarding the tax issue identified in this chapter's opening scenario.

Sample Keyword Searching Regarding Nora Smith's Issue

Step One: Search in the Internal Revenue Code database for "mortgage interest deduction" and "real property tax deduction" (without quotation marks) to determine that Sections 163 and 164 are the relevant Code sections.

Determine and review applicable Code and regulations sections

Step Two: Review Code Sections 163 and 164 and the related regulations to determine what, if anything, they say about deducting these items when paid for someone else, such as one's parent. You will find that the Code and regulations are not particularly helpful on this issue and will want to research further.

Step Three: Search in the Federal Tax Coordinator Analysis, USTR—Annotations, USTR—Explanations, Federal Tax Cases, and IRS Rulings and Releases databases (at once or seperately) using relevant terms. For example, an Intuitive Search for "interest property tax 163 164 and mother or father" retrieved a number of relevant (and some irrelevant) items, including Ann ¶645.005 Who can deduct—in general (a secondary source) and *Tuer*, TC Memo 1983-441 (a primary source discussed in the Sample Memorandum to Nora Smith's File above). To gain experience keyword searching on Checkpoint, you should modify your search, adding or eliminating terms, and try both the Intuitive Search and the Terms and Connectors search options, to see how your modifications affect the search results.

Search using relevant terms in secondary and primary source databases

---

Citation Searches

Sometimes the tax researcher has the citation for a specific source of tax law, and just needs to retrieve it. The tax researcher can look up the source by using the *Find by Citation* link under the Search tab. For example, if you want to retrieve Revenue Ruling 99-7 by a citation search, click on *Rulings/IRB* under *Find by Citation*. This will bring up a *Find a Ruling by Citation* screen on which the researcher can type 99-7 in the box under *Revenue Rulings*, click the *Search* button and immediately start reading Revenue Ruling 99-7. This search is illustrated in Figure 11-19. Similar **citation searches** can be used to find court decisions (*Find a Case by Citation*) and sections of the Code and regulations (*Find a Code or IRS Reg Section by Citation*).

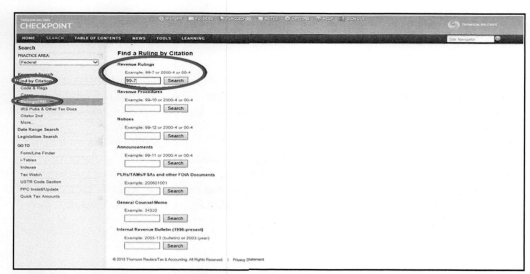

Additional Guidance for Using Thomson Reuters Checkpoint

In addition to the search options described above, online tax research services offer useful links between related sources of tax law. For example, when viewing a Code section on Checkpoint, a number of buttons that link to related material appear above or within the text of the Code section. These buttons link to the following:

- The regulations (*Regs* button) issued with respect to that Code section,
- Legislative history material (*Com Rpts* and *Hist* buttons),
- RIA explanations and annotations (*Expl*, *Annot*, and *Adv/Annot* buttons),
- Related material in RIA's Federal Tax Coordinator (*FTC* button), and
- For recently amended Code sections, the *New Law Analysis* button.

The *Adv/Annot* button refers to the most recently issued annotations that have not yet been added to the more permanent annotations (*Annot*) database. To be current when researching annotations, both *Annot* and *AdvAnnot* should be reviewed. There may also be a *New Law Analysis* button if the Code section has been recently amended.

Figure 11-20 highlights the buttons that appear on Checkpoint above and within Code Section 104.

When viewing a regulation, the researcher will see many of the same buttons that appear when viewing the related Code section. In addition, an *IRC* button gives the researcher quick access to the related Code section.

When viewing a case or ruling, the researcher may see buttons linking to where the case or ruling appears in an annotation (*Annot* button) or in the Federal Tax Coordinator (*FTC*). Cases and rulings also include a *Track It* button, where the researcher can choose to be notified by email when the case or ruling being tracked is cited in subsequent sources of tax law, and a *Citator* button (discussed later under Citators).

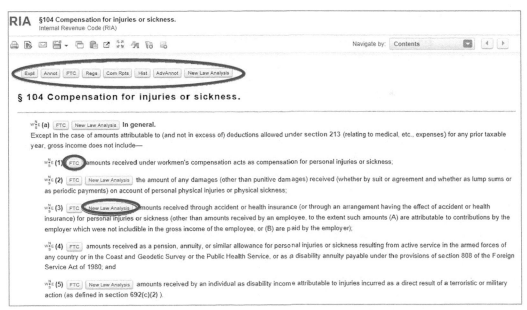

Figure 11-20

Buttons linking to related sources of tax law on Thomson Reuters Checkpoint

UPDATING TAX RESEARCH RESULTS

Tax law changes frequently. The Code can be amended by legislation, the Treasury Department can replace a regulation, a court decision may overrule the decision in a different, prior case or may reverse a lower court's decision in the same case, and the IRS may modify or declare obsolete a Revenue Ruling or Revenue Procedure. For these reasons, it is necessary for you to know that you are relying on sources of tax law that are current and still good law.

For amendments to the Code and new or amended regulations, it is generally necessary to look at the Code or regulations themselves. For amendments to the Code, Checkpoint helpfully includes aids such as the *New Law Analysis* button within Code sections that have been recently amended for easy access to information regarding those amendments. The buttons for access to the related Congressional Committee Reports (*Com Rpts*) and legislative history (*Hist*) are also very helpful.

Checkpoint also provides helpful information when viewing a regulation that has not been amended to reflect relevant amendments to the Code. For example, just above the text of Reg. § 1.162-2 on Checkpoint cautionary information indicates that the regulation has not been amended to reflect changes made by several amendments to Code Section 162. The tax researcher would then look to those Code amendments to determine whether or not IRC § 162 was changed in a way that would make the regulation unreliable in the client's situation.

Updating research findings is part of the third step in the research process (finding, analyzing, and updating applicable sources of tax law). Each time the researcher finds a relevant tax authority, it is necessary to update it to make sure that it is still reliable and authoritative. Tax advice must be current as of the date it is provided to the client. Consider the following **TIP from the Trenches** regarding updating the client on subsequent tax law developments.

[**TIP**] from the Trenches	Absent an agreement to provide updates to a client, once tax advice has been provided to the client, a CPA is generally not required to provide the client with updates for subsequent tax law developments affecting that advice. From a client relations standpoint, however, it may be advisable to at least alert the client if it appears that a new development could put the client in a worse tax position (or could give the client a more positive tax result) than indicated in the predevelopment advice. It is then the client's decision whether to engage the CPA's services for a more thorough analysis of the affects of the new development on the client's situation. By contrast, in-house corporate tax accountants are generally expected to update the tax advice provided to their employers for relevant tax law developments.

Citators

Citators are used to update court decisions and IRS Revenue Rulings and Revenue Procedures. For court decisions, a tax researcher can use a citator to learn whether the decision has been affirmed, reversed, modified, or remanded (sent back to the trial court or a lower appellate court) by an appellate court, whether the U.S. Supreme Court has granted or denied certiorari in the case, and whether the IRS has issued an AOD acquiescing or nonacquiescing in the court's decision. Relying on a case that has already been reversed is relying on a discredited authority and can amount to malpractice. Therefore, the tax researcher must check a citator for the subsequent history of the case. The citator will also indicate the other subsequent cases in which the case being checked has been cited and, if so, whether a subsequent case approved, criticized, or otherwise commented on the decision. This information may indicate how reliable the case is. For example, it may not be advisable to rely too strongly on a case that has been criticized in several subsequent court decisions. Citators can also be used to learn the prior history of the case checked on and to access the lower court's decision in the same case.

Similarly, IRS Revenue Rulings and Revenue Procedures can be updated using a citator. In this case, the citator will indicate whether the ruling or procedure has been cited in a court decision, and whether the IRS has clarified, modified, superseded, revoked, or declared the ruling or procedure obsolete. Again, the tax researcher should use this information to determine whether he or she is relying on current, good law or whether it is necessary to look further, such as at a more recent ruling that may have superseded the prior one found by the researcher.

Online tax research services have citators that make updating the law relatively easy. On Checkpoint, the citator is known as *Citator 2nd* (RIA) and can be accessed in two ways. One way to use the citator is by pushing the *Citator* button when viewing a court decision or ruling. This gives the researcher access to the citator information related to that case or ruling. For example, you might try finding Revenue Ruling 99-7 (hint—the quickest way to do this would be through a Citation Search described above) on Checkpoint and clicking on the *Citator* button. Figure 11-21 shows part of Revenue Ruling 99-7 with the Citator button circled.

Clicking on the Citator button will bring up a reference to the ruling on the right-hand side of the screen. If you click on this reference, you will see the citator results. A portion of the citator results for Rev. Rul. 99-7 is shown in Figure 11-22.

Using the Citator 2nd results, the tax researcher would click on the subsequent rulings and cases listed to review where and how they reference Rev. Rul. 99-7.

The other way to access the Citator 2nd (RIA) is by clicking on the *Search* tab on Checkpoint. This will bring up the option *Find by Citation* on the left side of the screen. Clicking on *Find by Citation* and then *Citator 2nd* will bring up the option of finding citations by a *Case Name, Case Citation,* or *Ruling Citation*. Each of these options has a box where the researcher can type in either a case name or the citation to a court decision or IRS ruling and access the cases and rulings that cite the case or ruling entered, or a list of the cases and rulings cited within the case or ruling entered. At this screen the researcher will also need to indicate whether he or she wants to check the Citator or Advanced Citator. The Advanced Citator would include

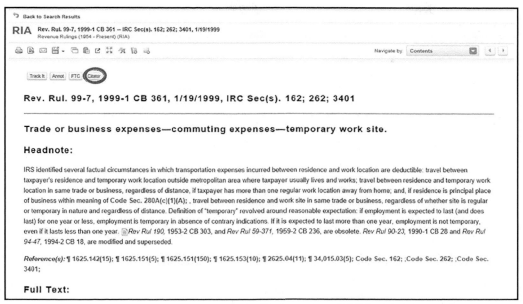

Figure 11-21

Citator button and Revenue Ruling 99-7

Figure 11-22

Citator 2nd (RIA) partial results for Revenue Ruling 99-7

only the most recent rulings and cases in which the item searched for is cited. In addition, the researcher can check the *Cited* box to search for only the cases and rulings in which the searched for item is cited or can check the "Citing" box to also retrieve the cases and rulings cited within the item searched.

Figure 11-23 illustrates a Citator 2nd search for Revenue Ruling Number 99-7. The results of this search will include Revenue Rulings, Revenue Procedures, and other IRS documents numbered 99-7. This is less efficient than finding the ruling and clicking on the Citator button, but may be helpful for finding a document by number when uncertain of its type.

Figure 11-23

Citator 2nd (RIA) search on Thomson Reuters Checkpoint

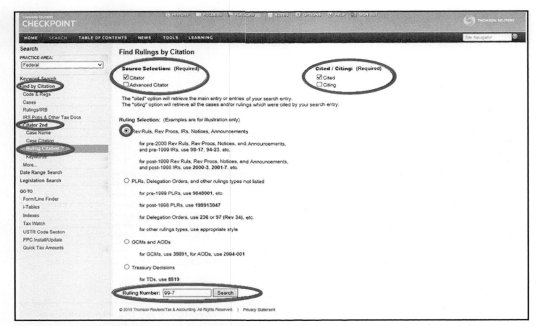

STANDARDS OF PROFESSIONAL TAX PRACTICE

LO6 Identify the key sources of professional standards for tax services.

Accountants who practice before the IRS, including preparing tax returns and representing clients during tax audits, are subject to rules of practice designed to help maintain the integrity of the federal tax system. The standards for professionals who practice before the IRS are set forth in Circular 230. CPAs are also subject to the American Institute of Certified Public Accountants (the AICPA) Statement on Standards for Tax Services (SSTS).[11] These standards reinforce the need for a tax professional to competently follow the steps of the tax research process to arrive at reasonable and supportable conclusions. These standards are briefly discussed below. A tax professional should be fully familiar with their requirements.

Circular 230

Circular 230[12] is a set of regulations issued by the U.S. Treasury Department that provides the rules of conduct for practicing before the IRS, including who may practice before the IRS and the standards for providing tax advice and issuing tax opinions. Circular 230 provides aspirational standards and requirements that should be followed by all professional tax advisers and that are consistent with the tax research process as described in this chapter. As set forth in Section 10.33(a) of Circular 230, the aspirational or "best practices" standards include

- "Communicating clearly with the client regarding the terms of the engagement."
- "Establishing the facts, determining which facts are relevant, evaluating the reasonableness of any assumptions or representations, relating the applicable law (including potentially applicable judicial doctrines) to the relevant facts, and arriving at a conclusion supported by the law and the facts."

---

[11] Attorneys practicing before the IRS are also subject to the rules of professional conduct in effect in the jurisdictions within which they practice.

[12] Circular 230 is part of Title 31 of the Code of Federal Regulations. It may be accessed online at *http://www.irs.gov/pub/irs-pdf/pcir230.pdf.*

■ "Advising the client regarding the import of the conclusions reached, including, for example, whether a taxpayer may avoid accuracy-related penalties under the Internal Revenue Code if a taxpayer acts in reliance on the advice."

■ "Acting fairly and with integrity in practice before the Internal Revenue Service."

With respect to written advice, Circular 230 sets forth requirements that the tax practitioner must follow, including basing written advice on reasonable factual and legal assumptions; reasonably considering all relevant facts and circumstances that the practitioner knows or reasonably should know; using reasonable efforts to identify and ascertain the relevant facts; not unreasonably relying on the taxpayer's or anyone else's representations, statements, findings, or agreements; relating the law and authorities to the facts; and not, in evaluating a federal tax matter, taking into account the possibility that a tax return will not be audited or that a matter will not be raised on audit.[13]

AICPA Statements on Standards for Tax Services

The cover of the AICPA's Statements on Standards for Tax Services is shown in Figure 11-24.[14]

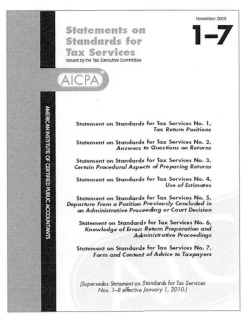

©AICPA, Used with permission.

Figure 11-24

Cover of the AICPA's Statements on Standards for Tax Services

The AICPA's **Statements on Standards for Tax Services** (SSTS) supplement the AICPA's Code of Professional Conduct and Circular 230 and apply to CPAs providing tax services. The SSTS consist of seven Statements, each of which includes an introduction, statement(s), and explanation(s). Many of the statements and explanations are relevant to the tax researcher. For example, paragraph number 4 of SSTS No. 1, regarding taking positions on tax returns, includes the following statement: "A member should determine and comply with the standards, if any, that are imposed by the applicable taxing authority with respect to recommending a tax return position, or preparing or signing a tax return." Determining the applicable standard with which to comply necessarily involves researching the applicable tax law.

---

[13] Circular 230, Section 10.37.

[14] The AICPA's Statements on Standards for Tax Services apply to members of the AICPA and may be accessed online at *http://www.aicpa.org/InterestAreas/Tax/Resources/StandardsEthics/StatementsonStandardsforTaxServices/ DownloadableDocuments/SSTS,%20Effective%20January%201,%202010.pdf.*

SSTS Nos. 2 and 3 primarily relate to obtaining information from the client (the factual investigation portion of tax research). Paragraphs 2 and 3 of SSTS No. 7, regarding the form and content of advice to taxpayers, stresses the need to provide competent tax advice that "compl[ies] with relevant taxing authorities' standards," including "return reporting and disclosure standards" and "the potential penalty consequences of the return position." Explanation paragraph 7 of SSTS No. 7 states that the member should consider a number of factors in deciding the form of advice provided to a taxpayer. The decision as to form includes whether the advice should be provided in writing and, if so, the form and level of detail. These factors include the importance of the transaction, the amount involved, the existence of authority and precedent, the tax sophistication of the taxpayer, and the potential penalty consequences.

Providing competent tax advice to a client involves researching the law and the facts and reaching supportable conclusions that are appropriately communicated to the client. This is necessary both to provide a professional service to the client as well as to comply with the applicable standards imposed on practitioners by the IRS and on its CPA members by the AICPA.

CHAPTER SUMMARY

As a tax professional, you will be expected to provide sound and accurate tax advice to your clients or employer. You will need to ask questions in order to learn the relevant facts, and will need to know how to find and analyze the many sources of tax law to enable you to reach reasoned, supportable conclusions. You will also have to communicate the advice to your client or employer in a way that can be understood. While doing each of these things, you must always remember to comply with the professional standards applicable to providing tax advice as prescribed by the IRS and the applicable professional organization, such as the AICPA.

By following a professional and systematic approach to tax research, exercising good judgment, and following the applicable professional standards, a tax professional can enjoy a successful and rewarding career while establishing and maintaining an ethical reputation.

REVIEW QUESTIONS

1. What types of accountants perform tax research? Who else performs tax research?

2. At what points in the life of a transaction might it be necessary for an accountant to perform tax research?

3. Identify the four key steps in the tax research process.

4. Identify four "tax facts" questions a researcher might ask during step 1 of the tax research process.

5. Identify two "nontax facts" questions a researcher might ask during step 1 of the tax research process.

6. List at least five primary sources of tax law and two secondary sources of tax law. How do primary sources and secondary sources differ?

7. Compare and contrast the Internal Revenue Code and Treasury Regulations with respect to the following questions:
   a. How and by whom are amendments to the Internal Revenue Code adopted? How and by whom are Treasury Regulations promulgated?
   b. Which of these two sources of tax law has greater precedential value?

8. Compare and contrast Revenue Rulings and Revenue Procedures. Where are they published? How do they differ?

9. Compare and contrast Private Letter Rulings and Technical Advice Memoranda. How do they differ?

10. List the trial courts that can hear and decide federal tax cases. For each of these courts, indicate the following:
    a. Is the court's jurisdiction limited to federal tax cases, or can it hear and decide other types of cases? If so, what other types of cases?
    b. Does the taxpayer have to pay the tax alleged to be due before initiating litigation in the court?

11. Which type of U.S. Tax Court decision has the greatest precedential value? Which type of U.S. Tax Court decision cannot be appealed to an appellate court?

12. What is an appellate court? List the appellate courts that may issue decisions in federal tax cases. Which of these courts is the highest judicial authority on issues of U.S. federal tax law?

13. List and briefly describe the three methods of searching using an online tax research service.

14. What is a citator? Why is it important to use a citator when conducting tax research?

15. What professional standards apply to CPAs who represent taxpayers in preparing federal tax returns and providing tax advice to clients? Who sets these standards?

EXERCISES

Except as otherwise noted, answer the following using an online tax research service, such as Thomson Reuters Checkpoint.

1. Find IRC Section 62. How many subsections does it have? What are they?

2. Find the regulations issued pursuant to IRC Section 382. How many regulations are there? How many are (a) final regulations? (b) proposed regulations? (c) temporary regulations? Properly cite one of each of these types of regulations.

3. Use the Federal Tax Coordinator 2d Topic Index to find all the items in the Federal Tax Coordinator 2d that mention the term "vacation homes."
   a. How many items are listed?
   b. Click on the link to ¶M-6006. What is the title of this paragraph?
   c. Which Internal Revenue Code section is discussed in ¶M-6006?
   d. List four other primary sources of tax law discussed in ¶M-6006 and that can be accessed from it (by clicking on the links to those sources).

4. Use the Code Arranged Annotations & Explanations (USTR) Topic Index to find all the items in the United States Tax Reporter (USTR)—Annotations (RIA) and USTR—Explanations (RIA) that mention the term "personal injuries."
   a. How many items are listed?
   b. Click on the link to ¶1044.02. Is this an Annotation or an Explanation paragraph? What is the title of this paragraph? Which Internal Revenue Code sections are discussed in this paragraph? List three other different types of primary sources of tax law that are referred to in this paragraph and that can be accessed from it (by clicking on the links to those sources).
   c. Click on the link to ¶1045.02(35). Is this an Annotation or an Explanation paragraph? What is the title of this paragraph? List two different types of primary sources of tax law that are referred to in this paragraph and that can be accessed from it (by clicking on the links to those sources).

5. Keyword Searches
   a. Using a Keyword Search in the Federal Tax Cases database search for cases using an "Intuitive Search" with the phrase "can an employee deduct the cost of work clothes." How many cases did this search find?
   b. Now change your keyword search to a "Terms & Connectors" search and search for the following set of terms "work clothes employee deduction" (not in quotes and not separated by commas). How many cases did this search find?
   c. Now change your "Terms & Connectors" keyword search to the following set of terms "work /3 clothes employee deduction" (again not in quotes and with no other connectors or commas). How many cases did this search find?

6. Using a Citation Search or a Keyword Search in the IRS Rulings & Releases database, find Revenue Ruling 2003-12.
   a. Provide the citation to this ruling.
   b. What Code sections are discussed in the ruling?
   c. What are the facts of the ruling?
   d. What issue is decided in the ruling?
   e. What did the IRS conclude with respect to this issue?
   f. When viewing the ruling, click on the "FTC" button at the top. What are the paragraph numbers and headings or titles under which this ruling is cited in the Federal Tax Coordinator 2d?
   g. When viewing the ruling check the citator to see in what cases and rulings Revenue Ruling 2003-12 was cited. What did you find? Did Revenue Ruling 2003-12 affect any prior ruling(s)? If so, which one(s) and how?

7. Using a Citation Search or a Keyword Search in the IRS Rulings & Releases database, find Revenue Procedure 2010-13.
   a. Provide the citation to this procedure.
   b. Which Code section is discussed in this procedure?
   c. What does this procedure require taxpayers to report to the Internal Revenue Service?
   d. When viewing the procedure, click on the "Annot" button at the top. What is the paragraph number and heading or title under which this procedure is annotated in the USTR Annotations (RIA)?
   e. When viewing the procedure, check the citator to see its "judicial history" and in what other sources of tax law Revenue Procedure was cited. What did you find?

8. Using a Citation Search or a Keyword Search in the Federal Tax Cases database, find the 2010 Tax Court regular decision in the *Philip A. Driscoll* case.
   a. Provide a proper citation to the Tax Court's decision in the case.
   b. Which Code sections are discussed in the case?
   c. What tax years were involved in the case?
   d. What are the facts of the case?
   e. What issue was decided in the case?
   f. What did the Tax Court conclude with respect to this issue?

9. Now check the citator for the 2010 Tax Court decision in the *Driscoll* case from Exercise 8. (*Hint:* Click on the "Citator" button when viewing the Tax Court's decision in *Driscoll* and then click on the link to the Citator results on the right side of the screen to see the Citator results.)
   a. What is the subsequent judicial history of the *Driscoll* case? (*Hint:* Check both the judicial history of the Tax Court's 2010 decision in *Driscoll* and any subsequent court decisions in the case to determine the final judicial conclusion of the case with respect to the issue identified in your answer to Exercise 8.*e*.)
   b. Review the court's decision in another case in which the Tax Court's 2010 decision in *Driscoll* was "cited favorably."
      i. What was the issue in that other case?
      ii. How do the facts of that case differ from the facts of the *Driscoll* case?

10. Using a Citation Search or a Keyword Search in the Federal Tax Cases database, find the 2011 Tax Court regular decision in the *Ronald A. Mayo* case.
    a. Provide the citation to the case.
    b. What did the IRS decide after the court decided this case?
    c. Indicate how you found this IRS decision and cite it.

11. Using a Citation Search, find IRC Section 130. Using the legislative history material available by clicking on the "Hist," "Com Rpts," and "New Law Analysis" buttons answer the following questions:
    a. What is the name and Public Law number of the statute that most recently amended Section 130?
    b. How did that statute amend Section 130? In other words, what changes were made to Section 130 by the statute referred to in answer to 11.*a*?
    c. What Committee's report is available with respect to the statute identified in your answer to 11.*a*? What does that Committee report say about this amendment?

12. Using the AICPA's Statements on Standards for Tax Services (SSTS) (available online at http://www.aicpa.org/InterestAreas/Tax/Resources/StandardsEthics/StatementsonStandardsforTaxServices/Downloadable Documents/SSTS,%20Effective%20January%201,%202010.pdf), answer the following questions and indicate the Statement number and paragraph number of the SSTS where you found each answer:
    a. May a CPA rely on information provided by third parties in preparing a client's tax return? When should a CPA not rely on information provided by the client or a third party in preparing the client's tax return?
    b. What should a CPA do if he or she discovers an error on a client's previously filed tax return?
    c. What should a CPA do if he or she discovers an error on a client's previously filed tax return during the course of representing the client in an administrative proceeding before the IRS regarding that return?

CASE STUDY QUESTIONS

11.1 **Employee Wages vs. Compensation Paid to an Independent Contractor, Finding and Analyzing the Relevant Code Sections and Regulations and a Relevant Case** *Facts:* Your client, Denver Language School (which will be referred to as "DLS"), is a school that is just starting operating. DLS is located in Denver, Colorado, and will specialize in teaching its students foreign languages. Jack Lundquist is a Spanish professor. Jack has agreed to teach online Spanish courses as an adjunct professor at DLS. DLS and Jack have agreed that Jack will teach approximately 6 to 10 online Spanish courses for DLS each year and that they will enter into a separate contract for each course. Each course will last 10 weeks, and DLS will pay Jack $5,000 for each course. For each course, DLS will provide an outline of the material to be covered, and Jack will use the outline to create his course syllabus. Jack will set his own work hours and will record and upload his online classes for student viewing according to his own schedule, but within certain timing requirements set by DLS (so that students can view the classes by set days and times). DLS will provide the website used for the course and will register and enroll DLS students in the course. Jack will provide DLS with a copy of his course syllabus and the students' grades at the end of each course. DLS's payroll supervisor has asked you for guidance regarding whether Jack will be DLS's employee and whether the amounts DLS will pay to Jack will be considered "wages" for federal employment tax purposes.

Required:
First Step: Identify and properly cite the Code sections and regulations that define the terms "wages" and "employee" for employment tax (i.e., withholding, FICA and FUTA) purposes. Review the definitions. Do they resolve DLS's issue? Why or why not?

Second Step: Find and review a relevant court decision that involves DLS's issue and similar facts. Provide a proper citation for the case. Briefly describe the facts of the case and the court's reasoning and conclusion(s). Indicate whether you think the court would reach the same conclusion(s) in the DLS–Jack situation and why or why not.

Can a Swimming Pool Be a Deductible Medical Expense? Finding and Analyzing the Relevant Code Sections and Regulations and a Relevant Revenue Ruling *Facts:* Your clients, Holly and Greg Orman, are a married couple with two young sons, Blake (age 6) and Jonah (age 4). In late 2014, the Ormans learned that Blake has a medical condition that makes his muscles very weak. In addition to prescribing physical therapy that will include exercises to strengthen Blake's muscles, Blake's doctor suggested that swimming regularly could greatly improve Blake's muscle strength. The Ormans live in a rural area far from any public swimming pool. They are considering installing a swimming pool in the backyard at their house. However, the Ormans would like to know whether the cost of installing a swimming pool may be deductible as a medical expense for federal income tax purposes.

11.2

Required:
First Step: Identify and properly cite the Code sections and regulations that discuss the deductibility of medical expenses. Indicate whether and, if so, where, they indicate whether the cost of a swimming pool may be deductible as a medical expense.

Second Step: Find and review a relevant Revenue Ruling that involves the issue of whether the cost of a swimming pool may be deductible as a medical expense. Provide a proper citation for the Revenue Ruling. Briefly describe the facts of the ruling and the IRS's reasoning and conclusion(s). Indicate whether you think the IRS would reach the same conclusion(s) in the Ormans' situation and why or why not.

Payment of Ex-Spouse's Divorce Attorney's Fees, Writing a Client Letter *Facts:* Your client, Norman Westerly, was formerly married to his ex-wife, Maria Eastman. Although Norman and Maria ultimately reached an agreement regarding the division of their property, their divorce was drawn out and litigious. Each party's attorney spent many hours representing them during the divorce proceeding, which resulted in substantial legal fees being separately incurred by both Norman and Maria. As he was ordered to do by the divorce judge, Norman paid $25,000 of Maria's divorce attorney's fees to Maria's attorney. Norman would like you to determine whether his payment of Maria's divorce attorney's fees is deductible for federal income tax purposes.

11.3

Required:
First Step: Identify the relevant Code sections and regulations and find a court decision that is relevant to Norman's situation. Be sure to check the citator to make sure that the case is current and that subsequent authority has not affected the precedential value of the decision.

Second Step: Based on your findings in the first step, write a brief letter to Norman telling him whether or not he can deduct the $25,000 he paid to Maria's divorce attorney.

Business-Related Education Expense, Writing a Client Letter *Facts:* Your client, Martin, is employed as an Assistant District Attorney ("ADA") by the City of San Francisco. In his position, he prosecutes persons accused of committing crimes. As an ADA, Martin frequently has to interview witnesses and crime victims who speak Chinese, but do not speak English. Martin knows a little Chinese, but is considering taking a conversational Chinese course at a local language school to improve his ability to speak with Chinese-speaking witnesses and victims. Martin has asked his boss whether there is any money in the Office of the District Attorney's budget to pay for him to take the course, but he was told that there is not. Martin has asked you whether the cost of the course is deductible for federal income tax purposes if he pays for it himself.

11.4

Required:

First Step: Identify the relevant Code section and regulations and find a court decision that is relevant to Martin's situation. Be sure to check the citator to make sure that the case is current and that subsequent authority has not affected the precedential value of the decision.

Second Step: Based on your findings in the first step, write a brief letter to Martin telling him whether or not he can deduct the cost of the conversational Chinese course on his federal income tax return.

11.5   **Trust's Payment of Investment Advice Fees, Writing a Memorandum to the Client's File** *Facts:* Your client, Aaron Truman, is employed as an elementary school history teacher. Aaron's mother, Mrs. Susan Truman, recently died and her last will and testament provided for the creation of the "Susan Truman Trust" (the "Trust"). Most of Mrs. Truman's assets were sold and the proceeds (approximately $2 million) were transferred to the Trust. The principal and income of the Trust are payable to Mrs. Truman's six children at set intervals. Mrs. Truman's will named Aaron as the sole trustee of the trust. Aaron wants to invest the assets of the Trust to earn a fair amount of income, but he has very little personal investment experience. As a result, Aaron hired Erin Russert, a well-respected professional investment adviser, to advise Aaron on how to invest the Trust's assets. You will be meeting with Aaron next week and know that he will be asking you whether there are any limitations on the deductibility of the investment advice fees the Trust is paying to Erin.

Required: Is there any authority indicating whether the Trust can deduct the investment advice fees it is paying to Erin? Research this question, considering the relevant Code section(s), regulation(s), cases, and/or rulings, and write a brief memorandum to the client's file that addresses this question.

11.6   **Charitable Gift of Property Subject to a Condition, Writing a Memorandum to the Client's File** *Facts:* Your clients, Justin and Kim Horton, recently purchased oceanfront property in Wilmington, North Carolina. The Hortons paid $2.5 million dollars for the property. There is an existing, modest house on the property that was built in 1948. The Hortons purchased the property for the land (and oceanfront location) as opposed to the existing house. The Hortons would like to demolish the house and build a large, multi-million-dollar house on the property. Rather than paying a contractor $45,000 to demolish the existing house, the Hortons are considering donating the house (but not the land) to the Wilmington Volunteer Fire Department ("WVFD") with the stipulation that the WVFD will quickly burn it down as part of its firefighter training program.

Required: Is there any authority indicating that Justin and Kim cannot claim a deduction for this donation? Research this question considering the relevant Code Section(s), regulation(s), cases and/or rulings and write a brief memorandum to the client's file that addresses this question.

Chapter 12

The International Research Environment

You may be skeptical of whether this chapter will be of much relevance to you. You know that U.S. GAAP is still the predominant reporting framework in the United States, and it is hard to imagine when, or if, that will change.

But the fact is that international accounting and auditing standards are already impacting U.S. accountants. Our economy is becoming increasingly global, and the expectations for professionals and CPA exam candidates have followed suit. For example, as a professional your company may engage in cross-border merger activities, which will require you to understand differences between U.S. GAAP and IFRS. Or perhaps an international subsidiary of your company is required to prepare *statutory* financial statements (for its home country) under IFRS. Or, perhaps you are participating in implementing changes to your firm's ethics code, and these changes are driven largely by recent U.S. convergence with international ethics standards.

Continued

Continued

Learning Objectives

After reading this chapter and its appendix, and performing the exercises herein, you will be able to

1. **Understand** the context in which accounting research is performed internationally, and the role of IFRS in international accounting research.

2. **Understand** the structure and mission of the IFRS Foundation, including its standard-setting bodies the IASB and the IFRS Interpretations Committee.

3. **Navigate, apply,** and **understand** the scope of the two prevailing sets of international accounting guidance: full IFRS, and IFRS for small and medium-sized entities (SMEs).

4. **Review** jurisdiction profiles to understand circumstances in which IFRS applies internationally, and understand circumstances in which IFRS applies to U.S. practitioners.

5. **Become** familiar with the standards and standard setters applicable to international auditing.

In all of these cases, having experience navigating IFRS and international auditing standards, and understanding the global context in which they apply, will be an asset to you as a professional. This chapter aims to provide you with such a foundation.

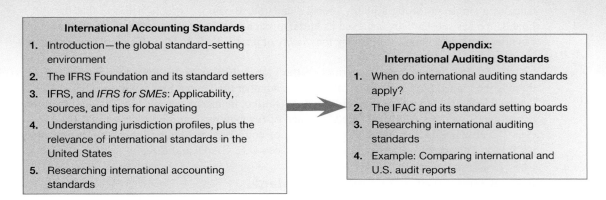

International Accounting Standards
1. Introduction—the global standard-setting environment
2. The IFRS Foundation and its standard setters
3. IFRS, and *IFRS for SMEs*: Applicability, sources, and tips for navigating
4. Understanding jurisdiction profiles, plus the relevance of international standards in the United States
5. Researching international accounting standards

Appendix: International Auditing Standards
1. When do international auditing standards apply?
2. The IFAC and its standard setting boards
3. Researching international auditing standards
4. Example: Comparing international and U.S. audit reports

Organization of This Chapter

This chapter begins with a discussion of the global standard-setting environment, including circumstances in which companies prepare financial statements internationally. Next, the chapter introduces the IFRS Foundation and its standard-setting bodies, the IASB and the IFRS Interpretations Committee.

Next, the chapter differentiates between the applicability of *full IFRS* versus the *IFRS for SMEs* publication, describing the contents of each reporting framework, along with tips for navigating the guidance.

The chapter also describes circumstances in which international accounting standards are relevant to U.S. accountants, and explains how to research *jurisdiction profiles*, which detail the applicability of IFRS to different countries. Finally, the appendix to this chapter covers international auditing and ethics standards, as well as the organizations responsible for setting these standards. An example is provided at the end of this chapter that allows readers to compare excerpts from U.S. versus international audit reports.

The preceding graphic illustrates the organization of content within this chapter and its appendix.

This chapter and its appendix focus primarily on IFRS accounting guidance and IAASB auditing standards, both of which are widely used internationally. It's worth noting that other country- or region-specific sources of international accounting and auditing guidance exist, but are not a primary focus of this chapter.

Acknowledging the duplication inherent in this phrasing, for purposes of easy readability, this chapter occasionally refers to International Financial Reporting Standards (IFRS) as *IFRS standards* or *IFRS guidance*. Also, the terms country, jurisdiction, and region are at times referred to collectively as *country* or *jurisdiction*.

INTRODUCTION

IFRS: The Predominant Global Financial Reporting Framework

LO1	**Understand** the context in which accounting research is performed internationally, and the role of IFRS in international accounting research.

Required for listed companies in over 100 countries, and translated into more than 30 languages, **International Financial Reporting Standards (IFRS)** are considered the predominant global financial reporting framework. Of the countries that have not adopted IFRS, several major economies, such as China and India, have converged or intend to substantially converge their standards with IFRS.[1]

Just a handful of years ago, the IFRS Foundation's mission was to gain global acceptance as a single set of high-quality global standards. Today, it's widely believed that the IFRS Foundation has substantially achieved its initial mission of gaining global acceptance and therefore can now turn its attention to improving the *quality* of its standards and the efficiency of the markets it serves.

There are a few notable exceptions to the global shift toward IFRS adoption; key among these is the United States. It's currently unclear whether the United States will ever adopt IFRS. On the whole, the two sets of standards are very similar, thanks in part to a long-running focus on convergence, which notably included issuance of revenue recognition guidance in 2014. However, it's now a widely held belief that the era of convergence is ending. Later in this chapter, we'll take a closer look at the relationship between U.S. GAAP and IFRS.

A Brief History of International Standards

In the past, the applicable financial reporting framework for each country generally was established by its **national standard setter**, each issuing unique accounting standards. For example, Japanese companies relied primarily on standards of the Accounting Standards Board of Japan, and Canadian companies relied primarily on the Canadian Accounting Standards Board.

The slow shift toward global accounting standards began in 1973, with the formation of the **International Accounting Standards Committee (IASC)**. With a goal of harmonizing global accounting standards, the IASC issued standards that were largely viewed as "voluntary adjuncts" to the use of national standards.[2]

However, the IASC's standards took on a new momentum in June 2000, when the European Commission announced its plans to require listed companies in the European Union (EU) to adopt international accounting standards by 2005. At that time, "no other country or countries in the developed world had yet announced a commitment to the IASC's standards."[3] In 2001, the IASC was replaced by the **International Accounting Standards Board (IASB)**. In the 15 or so years since its formation, the IASB has seen the use of its standards go from "0 to (over) 100," and the key catalyst for this global acceptance was the EU's commitment to adopting these standards.

The growth in acceptance of the IASB has not, however, replaced the need for national standard setters. The IASB continues to collaborate with national standard setters, and, in some cases, countries adopting IFRS require their national standard setter to **endorse** each new IFRS before it is accepted for use in the country. This endorsement process can, at times, result in country-specific variations of IFRS—referred to as **jurisdictional IFRS** (such as "IFRS as adopted by the EU") or in **carve-outs** of guidance that a country chooses not to adopt. Such variations can be minor or can result in significant differences across standards. The endorsement process also can result in delays in a country's implementation of newly issued IFRS guidance. Jurisdictional variations of IFRS run counter to the IASB's prior mission of creating a *single set* of high-quality global accounting standards.

---

[1] Source for "31 translations" and "more than 100 countries" statistics: 2014 Annual Report of the IFRS Foundation. Pages 20 and 26.

[2] Zeff, Stephen A. "The Evolution of the IASC into the IASB, and the Challenges it Faces." Published in *The Accounting Review* of the American Accounting Association. Vol. 87, No. 3, 2012. Page 834.

[3] Zeff, Page 824.

Considering this brief history, complete the following **Now YOU Try**.

YOU
Try
12.1

Fill in the blanks in the following timeline.

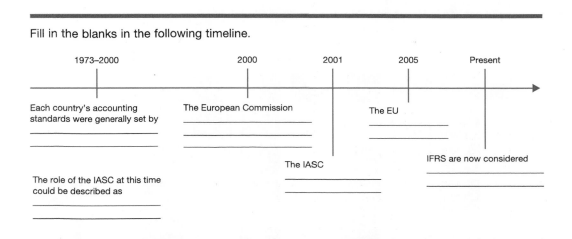

When Are Financial Statements Required Internationally?

For many **listed** (or public) companies around the world, the issuance of audited financial statements is required by securities regulators (such as agencies that are the equivalent of our SEC).

For **nonlisted** (or nonpublic) companies, financial statements are often required by the laws and regulations of individual countries (or **jurisdictions**). Each jurisdiction sets its own criteria for determining which companies must issue such **statutory** (or *government-required*) financial statements, and determines the applicable financial reporting framework. In some cases, these statutory financial statements are also designed to fulfill tax reporting requirements. Companies may also issue financial statements to satisfy the needs of their current or prospective investors and lenders.

These bodies that require financial statements (regulators, governments, and the like) are the same bodies that generally can determine which financial reporting framework should be used to prepare the financial statements. Increasingly, countries have moved to require or permit the use of IFRS in place of their jurisdiction-specific models.

Let's look now at an example of a corporation that has benefited from the move toward global accounting standards.

EXAMPLE

HSBC—A Beneficiary of Global Standards

As one of the world's largest banks, HSBC Holdings plc ("HSBC") has been a vocal supporter of the global move toward IFRS. Based in London, and with subsidiaries located around the globe, HSBC's support not only reflects its responsibility to *prepare* consolidated, global financial statements, but also its role as a major institutional investor (i.e., a *user* of global financial statements). Figure 12-1 illustrates the global nature of HSBC's organization, with locations in 73 countries and territories across the globe.[4]

---

[4] HSBC Holdings plc, *Annual Report and Accounts* 2014, page 1.

Figure 12-1

HSBC's simplified organizational chart[5]

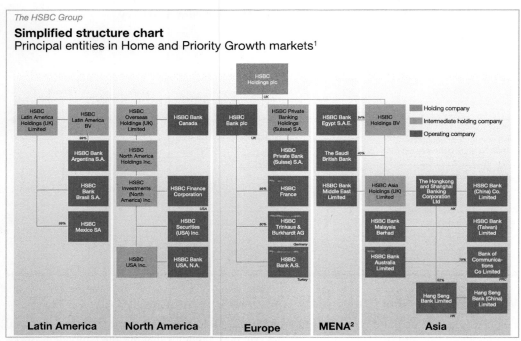

The HSBC Group

Simplified structure chart
Principal entities in Home and Priority Growth markets[1]

1 At December 31, 2014. All entities wholly owned unless shown otherwise (part ownership rounded down to nearest percent). Excludes other associates, insurance companies and special purpose entities.
2 Middle East and North Africa

Image used with permission from HSBC Holdings Plc.

The following figure, Figure 12-2, illustrates several of the international stock exchanges on which shares of the parent company, HSBC Holdings plc are listed. HSBC's shares are held by approximately 216,000 shareholders in 127 countries and territories around the world.[4]

Figure 12-2

Select markets in which HSBC Holdings plc shares are listed

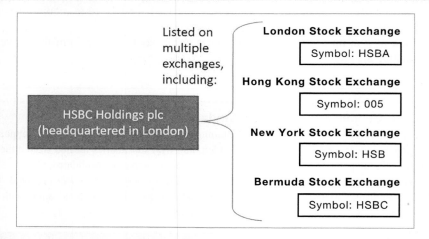

Considering the preceding discussion of HSBC Holdings Plc, complete the following **Now YOU Try**.

---

[5] The HSBC Group, *Simplified Structure Chart: Principal entities in Home and Priority growth markets.* As of December 31, 2014.

1. Describe how HSBC and its subsidiaries might have prepared their individual country finan-
    cial statements before the widespread acceptance/adoption of IFRS.

    _____

    _____

    _____

2. Considering the profile of HSBC provided in the preceding pages, in your own words
    explain why you would expect this company to be an advocate for a single set of global
    financial reporting standards.

    _____

    _____

    _____

    _____

As you might imagine, HSBC has been vocal in its support for a single set of global accounting
standards. In a 2009 letter to the U.S. SEC voicing support for the use of IFRS in the United
States, HSBC stated: "The costs of maintaining separate ledgers and processes for IFRS and
U.S. GAAP are very significant in North America." Allowing U.S. issuers to use IFRS, HSBC
wrote, would "eventually eliminate the need to maintain two complete sets of financial records
and the need to analyze every transaction under both IFRSs and U.S. GAAP."[6]

This example illustrates the clear benefits afforded to HSBC of the global shift toward
IFRS. However, it is important to understand this example in context. As a London-based
corporation, HSBC already reports under IFRS in certain jurisdictions and expects to see
additional benefits from the continued expansion of IFRS globally. Not all multinational
corporations share this view. For example, U.S.-based multinationals Citigroup and Wal-Mart
have expressed concern to the SEC that the benefits of an outright adoption of IFRS would
not exceed its costs, instead expressing a preference for continued convergence between U.S.
GAAP and international standards.[7]

Let's take a closer look now at the IFRS Foundation and its standard-setting bodies.

THE IFRS FOUNDATION AND ITS STANDARD-SETTING BODIES

Headquartered in London, England, and with a regional office in Tokyo, Japan, the **IFRS
Foundation** oversees two independent standard-setting bodies, the IASB and the IFRS
Interpretations Committee (IFRIC).

The IFRS Foundation , both directly and through its standard-setting bodies, has a
challenging mission as illustrated in Figure 12-3.

> **LO2** Understand
> the structure
> and mission of the IFRS
> Foundation, including its stan-
> dard-setting bodies the IASB
> and the IFRS Interpretations
> Committee.

---

[6] Iain Mackay, Senior Executive VP and CFO, HSBC North America Holdings Inc. "Comment letter to the SEC." In
reference to SEC File Number: S7-27-08. April 20, 2009. Page 2.

[7] Per comment letters in response to SEC File Reference No. S7-27-08, authored by: Robert Traficanti, Citigroup Vice
President and Deputy Controller, April 20, 2009. Page 2. Steven P. Whaley, Senior Vice President & Controller, Wal-
Mart Stores, Inc., April 20, 2009. Page 2.

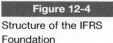
Figure 12-3

The challenging mission of the IFRS Foundation and its standard-setting bodies

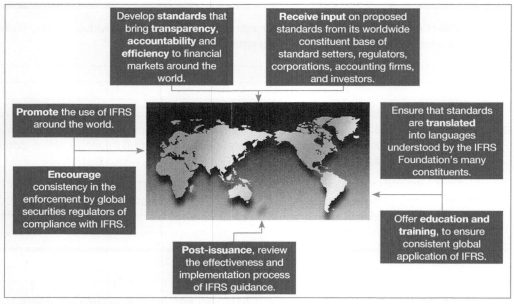

Image of world used with permission from Microsoft.

Let's briefly look at how the IFRS Foundation is organized and funded.

The IFRS Foundation has a three-tier structure, as illustrated in Figure 12-4.

Figure 12-4

Structure of the IFRS Foundation

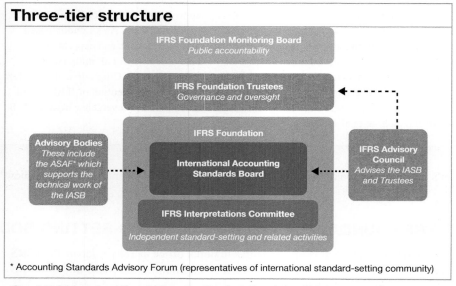

Three-tier structure

* Accounting Standards Advisory Forum (representatives of international standard-setting community)

Source: IFRS Foundation, *Annual Report 2014*. Introduction.

Standard-Setting Bodies of the IFRS Foundation

The International Accounting Standards Board (IASB)

The IASB is an independent standard-setting organization whose current 14 full-time board members represent a diversity of countries and constituencies (including, for example, financial statement users, preparers, auditors, and academics).

---

[8] Reproduced by Cambridge Business Publishers with the permission of the International Financial Reporting Standards Foundation®. Reproduction and use rights are strictly limited®. No permission granted to third parties to reproduce or distribute.

The IASB's responsibilities include

■ Developing *full IFRS*,

■ Issuing guidance for small- and medium-sized entities (*IFRS for SMEs*), and

■ Approving the issuance of IFRS interpretive guidance.

The IASB cannot perform these responsibilities in isolation, however. For the IASB to maintain its authority as global standard setter, it must collaborate extensively with the national and regional standard-setting bodies representing its constituents.

The IASB is hopeful that this collaboration (in particular with the ASAF) will reduce instances of nonendorsement of its final standards.

The IFRS Interpretations Committee (IFRIC)

The **IFRS Interpretations Committee (IFRIC)** issues authoritative guidance on emergent issues that are "likely to receive divergent or unacceptable treatment, in the absence of such guidance."[9] That is, this committee is intended to respond, in a timely manner, to issues that arise regarding the clarity or application of IFRS guidance. The IASB must approve all interpretive guidance before it is issued as final. Take a moment now to read and react to the following Now YOU Try.

The IFRS Interpretations Committee has been criticized for not issuing enough interpretive guidance, and for not responding in a timely manner to areas of diversity in practice. This has recently begun to change, as the IFRS Interpretations Committee has become more active in issuing interpretive guidance in recent years. Yet, IFRS was initially heralded as being a more principles-based reporting framework. Do you think the recent increase in interpretive guidance is a positive development for IFRS? Explain.

Now
[**YOU**
Try]
12.3

_____

_____

_____

_____

Governance and Oversight of the IFRS Foundation

The Monitoring Board

The IFRS Foundation's **Monitoring Board** provides for the formal interaction between the IFRS Foundation and individuals representing the **capital markets authorities** (i.e., securities regulators) it serves. These include

■ The U.S. SEC

■ The European Commission

■ Korea's Financial Services Commission (FSC)

■ The Brazilian Securities Commission (CVM)

■ The Financial Services Agency of Japan (JFSA)

■ The Growth and Emerging Markets Committee of the International Organization of Securities Commissions (IOSCO)

Members of this board represent capital markets authorities responsible for setting the form and content of financial reporting in their respective jurisdictions.

Recall that under the Securities Exchange Act of 1934, the U.S. SEC was given authority to set U.S. accounting standards, but it chose to delegate this authority to the FASB. In a similar fashion, many international capital markets authorities have chosen to entrust standard setting

---

[9] IFRS Foundation, *2015 Blue Book*. Preface to International Financial Reporting Standards, par. 14.

for listed (e.g., public) companies to the IASB, but still desire oversight over the process in which standards are set. Accordingly, members of this board participate in the appointment of IFRS Foundation Trustees, provide input into the IASB's processes, and—as its name implies— generally *monitor* the activities of the IFRS Foundation.

Trustees

The IFRS Foundation's **Trustees** provide governance and oversight over the Foundation. Representing a diversity of geographic and professional backgrounds, the Trustees are responsible for

■ Appointing members to the IASB, the IFRS Interpretations Committee, and the IFRS Advisory Council;

■ Providing governance over the independence, funding, and processes of the IASB; and

■ Promoting and supporting the use of IFRS globally.

In fulfilling these duties, the Trustees are held publicly accountable to the Monitoring Board, to whom the trustees must report at least annually.[10]

Advisory Bodies of the IFRS Foundation

The IASB regularly receives input from various advisory groups, including the **IFRS Advisory Council** and the **Accounting Standards Advisory Forum (ASAF)**. Comprised of individuals representing a diversity of geographic and professional backgrounds, the Advisory Council provides a forum for representatives of constituent organizations to provide input into the IASB's standard setting. The Advisory Council meets with members of the IASB at least three times per year in order to:

■ Advise the IASB on its agenda decisions and priority of projects, and

■ Provide views on existing standard-setting projects or application issues associated with existing standards.

Members of the IFRS Advisory Council are appointed by the Trustees.[11]

The ASAF formalizes the process through which the IASB receives input from regional and national standard setters. Comprised of representatives from member standard setters, the ASAF advises the IASB on its technical projects, which should reduce the risk of nonendorsement by various jurisdictions once a standard has been issued.

Other formal advisory bodies to the IASB include, for example, the Emerging Economies Group and the Capital Markets Advisory Committee.

Considering the preceding discussion, respond to the following Now YOU Try.

Now YOU Try 12.4

1. During 2015, one of the groups just described began a review of the structure and effectiveness of the IFRS Foundation and the IASB. Among the questions being posed was: *What is the optimum size of the IASB?* Which of the groups just described would you expect to take on this question? Explain.

_____

_____

_____

_____

[10] IFRS Foundation Constitution, updated January 2013. Par. 13, 15, 19b, 24.

[11] www.ifrs.org. About Us > IFRS Advisory Council. Accessed on 5/28/2015.

2. Given the IFRS Foundation's mission, explain what value you would expect the Foundation's advisory bodies to bring to its standard-setting activities.

_____

_____

_____

_____

Funding for the IFRS Foundation

The IFRS Foundation is funded through a combination of

- Mandatory levies, imposed by certain countries' governments and regulatory bodies on listed and/or nonlisted companies, similar to the accounting support fee that funds the FASB;

- Contributions from national standard setters and/or governments;

- Voluntary contributions from public accounting firms and certain U.S. companies (such as Bank of America and Citigroup);[12] and

- Sales of IASB publications and subscriptions.

While the IFRS Foundation has established "target contributions" from its member countries (based in part on each country's GDP), it lacks the authority to impose funding requirements and thus must rely on this mixed-attribute funding system. Securing stable sources of funding for the IFRS Foundation remains an ongoing challenge, and one that the SEC has historically cited as a concern in its consideration of whether to adopt IFRS.

Next, let's discuss the sources of guidance issued by the IFRS Foundation.

INTERNATIONAL FINANCIAL REPORTING STANDARDS (IFRS)

Applicability of IFRS

The IASB issues two types of international financial reporting standards: **full IFRS** and **IFRS for SMEs.** Full IFRS applies to profit-oriented entities with **public accountability,** and _IFRS for SMEs_ applies to entities that do not have public accountability, as illustrated in Figure 12-5.

Notably, in 2013, the IASB created a subset of the _IFRS for SMEs_ publication that applies specifically to **micro-sized entities,** such as those with just a few employees.

LO3 Navigate, apply, and **understand** the scope of the two prevailing sets of international accounting guidance: full IFRS, and IFRS for small and medium-sized entities (SMEs).

Figure 12-5

Applicability of full IFRS, versus _IFRS for SMEs_

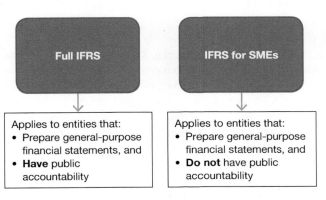

Not-for-profit entities, while not the intended users of IFRS and _IFRS for SMEs,_ are permitted to apply this guidance to the extent they believe application is appropriate.[13]

---

[12] 2014 Annual Report of the IFRS Foundation. Page 48.

[13] IFRS Foundation, _2013 Blue Book._ Preface to International Financial Reporting Standards, par. 9, plus _IFRS for SMEs_ Exposure Draft dated Oct. 2013, Basis for Conclusions par. BC23-BC26.

General-Purpose Financial Reporting

The term "general-purpose financial reporting" encompasses (1) **general-purpose financial statements** plus (2) other financial reporting (i.e., information that assists in the interpretation of the financial statements, such as footnote disclosures).[14] The *IFRS for SMEs* glossary defines "general-purpose financial statements" as

> Financial statements directed to the general financial information needs of a wide range of users who are not in a position to demand reports tailored to meet their particular information needs.[15]

That is, many financial statement users (e.g., shareholders, creditors, and employees) cannot individually request financial information from a reporting entity; rather, they must rely on general-purpose financial statements—either presented separately or within an annual report. Such financial statements differ, for example, from financial statements prepared for a specific purpose, such as for tax reporting.

Take a moment to apply your understanding of the term *general-purpose financial statements* in the following **Now YOU Try** exercise.

General-Purpose Financial Statements

Assume that a company uses *IFRS for SMEs* as the starting point for its financial statements, then adjusts these statements to comply with requirements specific to its national taxing authority. The entity sends the financial statements to the taxing authority only.

Using the definition of *general-purpose financial statements*, consider whether these financial statements would be considered general-purpose or special-purpose financial statements. Explain.

_____

_____

_____

Example based on IFRS Foundation's "Training Material for the *IFRS® for SMEs* (version 2013-1)," Module 1, Page 8, Ex4.

Public Accountability

The *IFRS for SMEs* publication defines *public accountability* as follows:

> 1.3 An entity has public accountability if:
> (a) <u>its debt or equity instruments are traded in a public market</u> or it is in the process of issuing such instruments for trading in a public market (a domestic or foreign stock exchange or an over-the-counter market, including local and regional markets), or
> (b) <u>it holds assets in a fiduciary capacity for a broad group of outsiders</u> as one of its primary businesses. Most banks, credit unions, insurance companies, securities brokers/dealers, mutual funds and investment banks would meet this second criterion.[16] [Emphasis added]

Considering this definition, take a moment to complete the following **Now YOU Try**.

---

[14] *IFRS for SMEs* (2009), par. P5.

[15] *IFRS for SMEs* (2009), Glossary.

[16] *IFRS for SMEs* (2009). Par. 1.3. Reflects updates issued by the IASB on 5/21/2015 that will be incorporated in 2015 *IFRS for SMEs* publication.

Now
YOU
Try
12.6

Considering the preceding definition, but in your own words, describe what it means for an entity to have *public accountability*.

_____

_____

_____

The IASB has concluded that any entity with public accountability, *regardless of its size*, should follow full IFRS.[17] Scope guidance from the *IFRS for SMEs* publication emphasizes this point:

> If a publicly accountable entity uses this IFRS, its financial statements shall not be described as conforming to the *IFRS for SMEs*—even if law or regulation in its jurisdiction permits or requires this IFRS to be used by publicly accountable entities.[18]

That is, even if directed by a government authority to issue financial statements using *IFRS for SMEs*, entities with public accountability cannot assert that their financial statements comply with *IFRS for SMEs*. Rather, these entities should apply full IFRS or other acceptable standards.

Individual Jurisdiction Considerations

So this is all pretty simple, right?

- Not publicly accountable?—Check.
- Issues general-purpose financial statements?—Check.
- Apply *IFRS for SMEs*.

But wait . . . there's just one more consideration. See, this is just the *intended scope* of the *IFRS for SMEs* publication. Ultimately, the determination of which entities may utilize this guidance rests with authorities in individual countries. To that end, many individual jurisdictions have established additional criteria for determining which entities may report using *IFRS for SMEs* including, for example, criteria based on revenue, assets, employees, or other factors. Certain countries may decide, for example, that entities that are economically significant in that country should be required to use full IFRSs rather than the *IFRS for SMEs*.

Take a moment to apply your understanding of SMEs in the following **Now YOU Try** exercise.

Now
YOU
Try
12.7

Understanding the Scope of *IFRS for SMEs*

Respond to the following, referring back to the preceding discussion as necessary.

1. A publicly accountable entity has been required by its national taxing authority to issue financial statements following the guidance in *IFRS for SMEs*.

   Can the entity describe its financial statements as prepared in conformity with *IFRS for SMEs*? Explain.

   _____

   _____

---

[17] *IFRS for SMEs* (2009), Basis for Conclusions. Par. BC76.

[18] *IFRS for SMEs* (2009), Basis for Conclusions. Par. 1.5.

2. An entity meets the IASB's *intended scope* of entities that should apply *IFRS for SMEs*. What other consideration should enter into the entity's decision about whether use of *IFRS for SMEs* is appropriate for its statutorily required financial statements?

_____

_____

TIP from the Trenches

The IASB's issuance of different guidance for entities with and without public accountability differs from U.S. GAAP, where the Codification applies to *all nongovernmental entities*. That said, the number of private company alternatives available within the Codification has increased in recent years as a result of collaboration between the FASB and the Private Company Council.

The next section of this chapter offers a closer look at *full IFRS*.

Understanding "Full IFRS"

To comply with full IFRS, entities must comply with standards, interpretations, and the Conceptual Framework. Following is discussion of each of these sources, followed by discussion of the priority in which these sources should be considered.

Standards

IFRS standards comprise **IFRSs** and **IASs**, as illustrated in Figure 12-6.

Figure 12-6

Standards comprise IFRSs and IASs

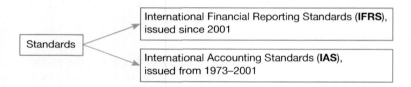

Each standard within IFRS is intended to address a specific accounting topic. For example, observe the following standard titles.

- IFRS 3, *Business Combinations*
- IFRS 15, *Revenue from Contracts with Customers*
- IAS 7, *Statement of Cash Flows*
- IAS 16, *Property, Plant and Equipment*

When changes are required to an existing standard, the IASB's policy is to amend or replace existing IFRS when appropriate, but to not change how the standards are numbered. New standards are created as necessary to address comprehensive emerging issues. Chapter 14 of this book provides further discussion of the IASB's standard-setting process.

Now YOU Try 12.8

Considering the IASB's history discussed earlier in the chapter, explain which standard setter likely issues/issued each type of standard: IFRSs and IASs. Explain.

_____

_____

_____

Content within IFRS standards is generally organized into sections similar to those used in the Codification (e.g., Objective, Scope, Recognition, and so on). That said, section headers are not as standardized as those in the Codification and may be unique to a given topic.

Interpretations

Interpretations offer guidance on narrow-scope issues that could otherwise result in the inconsistent application of IFRS. Interpretations comprise IFRICs and SICs, as illustrated in Figure 12-7.

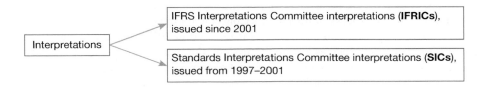

Figure 12-7

Interpretations comprise IFRICs and SICs

When researching an issue, be sure to scan the list of available interpretations to identify any guidance relevant to your research topic. The following **Now YOU Try** illustrates the limited-scope nature of an IFRIC.

Reading and Understanding an IFRIC

Now YOU Try 12.9

IFRIC 10, *Interim Financial Reporting and Impairment*, resolves a conflict between the requirements of IAS 34 (Interim Financial Reporting) and IAS 36 (Impairment of Assets). Specifically, this IFRIC answers the question: Should an entity reverse an impairment charge recorded for goodwill, if the value of the entity's goodwill recovers in a subsequent interim period?

Per IAS 36, par. 124, "An impairment loss recognised for goodwill shall not be reversed in a subsequent period." However, "IAS 34 requires year-to-date measures in interim financial statements. This requirement might suggest that an entity should reverse in a subsequent interim period an impairment loss it recognised in a prior interim period" (IFRIC 10, BC3).

Here's what the IFRIC decided: "An entity shall not reverse an impairment loss recognised in a previous interim period in respect of goodwill." (IFRIC 10, par. 8).

The rationale for this decision is described in IFRIC 10's Basis for Conclusions:

"The IFRIC concluded that the prohibitions on reversals of recognised impairment losses on goodwill in IAS 36 . . . should take precedence over the more general statement in IAS 34 regarding the frequency of an entity's reporting not affecting the measurement of its annual results." (BC9). [Footnotes omitted]

Questions:

1. Explain the conflicting requirements in IAS 36 and IAS 34 that this Interpretation sets out to clarify.

   _____

   _____

2. Explain the conclusion reached in IFRIC 10 and the rationale for this conclusion.

   _____

   _____

3. Why do you suppose the IFRIC addressed this issue, as opposed to the IASB? Explain.

   _____

   _____

   _____

Conceptual Framework

The IASB's *Conceptual Framework for Financial Reporting* (the "Framework") sets forth the conceptual underpinnings for the more specific requirements of IFRS Standards and Interpretations. The purpose of the Framework is generally twofold: first, to assist the IASB in the development of new standards, and second, to assist practitioners in applying judgment in the preparation of financial statements, in the absence of more specific guidance.

As you'll see in the IAS 8 hierarchy in Figure 12-8, the Framework in IFRS *is* considered authoritative, but it has less authority than standards and interpretations of the IASB. Contrast this with U.S. GAAP, where the Conceptual Framework is nonauthoritative.

The IASB is in the process of revising its Conceptual Framework and expects to issue final guidance in 2016. The *proposed* Framework (as released in 2015) would add significant depth to the existing framework, such as adding discussion of measurement bases; refining definitions of assets, liabilities, and other financial statement elements; and prioritizing use of the income statement (for example, over recording items in other comprehensive income).

To improve your familiarity with the *proposed* content of the IASB's Conceptual Framework, complete the following **Now YOU Try**.

Now YOU Try 12.10

1. Match the following concepts from the IASB's proposed Conceptual Framework with its likely chapter in the Framework. The first line has been drawn for you as an example.

Excerpt from Proposed Framework

Financial statements consist of statements, including a statement of financial position and statement(s) of financial performance, and notes to the financial statements. Assets, liabilities and equity are recognized in the statement of financial position. Income and expenses are recognized in the statement(s) of financial performance.
An asset is a present economic resource controlled by the entity as a result of past events.
Because the statement of profit or loss is the primary source of information about an entity's financial performance for the period, there is a presumption that all income and all expenses will be included in the statement of profit or loss . . .
If financial information is to be useful, it must be relevant and faithfully represent what it purports to represent. The usefulness of financial information is enhanced if it is comparable, verifiable, timely and understandable.
Measurement bases can be categorized as: (a) historical cost . . . ; or (b) current value . . . . . . When selecting a measurement basis, it is important to consider what information that measurement basis will produce in both the statement of financial position and statements(s) of financial performance.
The objective of general purpose financial reporting is to provide financial information about the reporting entity that is useful to existing and potential investors, lenders and other creditors in making decisions about providing resources to the entity.
An entity recognizes an asset or liability (and any related income, expenses or changes in equity) if such recognition provides users of financial statements with: (a) relevant information about the asset or the liability and about any income, expenses or changes in equity . . . ; (b) a faithful representation of the asset or the liability and of any income, expenses or changes in equity . . . ; and (c) information that results in benefits exceeding the cost of providing that information. . . .
A financial concept of capital is adopted by most entities in preparing their financial statements. Under a financial concept of capital, such as invested money or invested purchasing power, capital is synonymous with the net assets or equity of the entity. Under a physical concept of capital, such as operating capability, capital is regarded as the productive capacity of the entity based on, for example, units of output per day.

Chapters in Proposed Framework

Chapter 1: The objective of general purpose financial reporting
Chapter 2: Qualitative characteristics of useful financial information
Chapter 3: Financial statements and the reporting entity
Chapter 4: The elements of financial statements
Chapter 5: Recognition and derecognition
Chapter 6: Measurement
Chapter 7: Presentation and disclosure
Chapter 8: Concepts of capital and capital maintenance

*Excerpts, chapter titles, and paragraph references are based on the 2015 exposure draft of the revised IASB Conceptual Framework. Footnotes omitted.
Sources: par 1.2, 2.4, 3.6, 4.5, 5.9, 6.4, 6.53, 7.23.

2. Now, contrast the IASB's proposed Conceptual Framework to the FASB's existing Conceptual Framework. Refer back to Chapter 5, on nonauthoritative sources of U.S. GAAP, as necessary to respond. Comment on any aspects of the Framework that strike you.

_____

_____

_____

_____

The sources of guidance comprising *full IFRS* should be considered in the order of priority set forth in IAS 8, as discussed next.

The IAS 8 Hierarchy

The **IAS 8 hierarchy** prioritizes the sources of guidance that entities should consider when developing accounting policies for items or transactions. This hierarchy is illustrated in Figure 12-8.

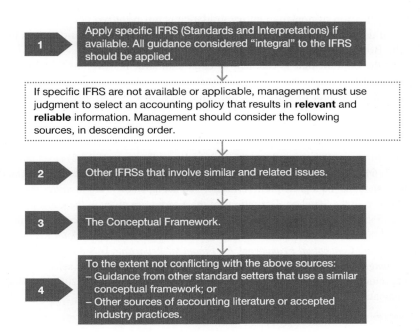

Figure 12-8

The IAS 8 Hierarchy[19]

If a researcher locates a specific IFRS that is *on point*, or directly relevant to a transaction, management should apply that IFRS (source 1 in Figure 12-8). If such guidance is not available, management will have to use its judgment in selecting an appropriate policy; the guidance listed in sources 2–4 should be considered in descending order.

Considering Figure 12-8, complete the following **Now YOU Try**.

In your own words, describe the steps management should take (and sources a researcher should consider) if a specific IFRS is not available for a particular issue.

_____

_____

_____

_____

Now
[**YOU**]
Try
12.11

Differentiating between Integral *versus* Not Integral *Content*

As noted in the first box of the IAS 8 hierarchy, guidance that is considered *integral* to a standard should be given priority. IFRS distinguishes between guidance that is considered **integral** to a standard (i.e., mandatory) and guidance that is **not integral** to the standard (i.e., nonmandatory), as follows:

---

[19] IAS 8, par. 7–12.

IFRSs are accompanied by guidance to assist entities in applying their requirements. All such guidance states whether it is an integral part of IFRSs. <u>Guidance that is an integral part of the IFRSs is mandatory.</u> Guidance that is not an integral part of the IFRSs does not contain requirements for financial statements.[20] [Emphasis added]

That is, researchers are required to apply all guidance that is considered "integral" to a standard. The application of non-mandatory guidance is not *required* per se; however, consideration of this guidance may be useful in helping researchers apply the guidance in the manner intended by the Board.

To identify the content that is integral to each standard, researchers can look to (1) the **authority paragraph** at the bottom of each standard's "Contents" page (see Figure 12-9) and (2) information in the header of each appendix that indicates its authority (see Figure 12-10).

Figure 12-9

Authority paragraph for IFRS 2, located within the standard's "Contents" page

International Financial Reporting Standard 2 *Share-based Payment* (IFRS 2) is set out in paragraphs 1–64 and Appendices A–C. All the paragraphs have equal authority. Paragraphs in **bold type** state the main principles. Terms defined in Appendix A are in *italics* the first time they appear in the Standard. Definitions of other terms are given in the Glossary for International Financial Reporting Standards. IFRS 2 should be read in the context of its objective and the Basis for Conclusions, the *Preface to International Financial Reporting Standards* and the *Conceptual Framework for Financial Reporting*. IAS 8 *Accounting Policies, Changes in Accounting Estimates and Errors* provides a basis for selecting and applying accounting policies in the absence of explicit guidance. (Source: 2015 Red Book, IFRS 2 Contents)

Figure 12-10

Header indicating authority of IFRS 2's Implementation Guidance (circle added for emphasis)

Guidance on implementing

IFRS 2 *Share-based Payment*

This guidance accompanies, but is not part of, IFRS 2.

Definition of grant date

IG1   IFRS 2 defines grant date as the date at which the entity

Considering Figures 12-9 and 12-10, complete the following **Now YOU Try**.

[20] IFRS Foundation, *2015 Blue Book*. IAS 8, *Accounting Policies, Changes in Accounting Estimates and Errors*. Par. 9.

1. Refer to the authority paragraph for IFRS 2. Which appendices to this standard are considered mandatory?

   _____

2. According to the authority paragraph, do all paragraphs in the standard have equal authority? What is the significance of paragraphs that are presented in bold?

   _____

   _____

   _____

3. Both the objective and Basis for Conclusions for IFRS 2 are *not* considered *integral* to the standard. What do you think it means for the standard to be read "in the context of" this guidance?

   _____

   _____

Notice in the authority paragraph for IFRS 2 that the standard's *Introduction* is not identified as an integral part of the standard. Paragraphs within a standard's Introduction (numbered IN1, IN2, etc.) often *summarize* or *highlight* requirements from the standard but are not themselves considered integral.

Don't make the mistake that some of my students have, of quoting "requirements" from the Introduction, rather than quoting from the standard itself.

[**TIP**] from the
Trenches

Performing IFRS Research

Accessing IFRS Guidance

To access IFRS guidance, researchers can (1) subscribe to eIFRS (searchable), or (2) register at www.ifrs.org for free (but limited) access to individual standards (not searchable).

Subscriptions to eIFRS can be purchased

- Directly from the IFRS Foundation, or
- For students and academics, through a discounted (approximately $20–25) annual subscription from IAAER, the International Association for Accounting Education & Research.

Certain research databases (such as Deloitte's *Technical Library*) also include searchable access to IFRS guidance.

Understanding the *Bound Editions*

IFRS guidance is organized into three **bound editions**, each available for purchase in printed form or accessible to e-IFRS subscribers. Before beginning a search of IFRS guidance, researchers are often prompted to select from among these bound editions.

The **Red Book** includes all IFRS standards and interpretations, *including those not yet effective*, and related appendices (such as the standard setter's basis for conclusions).

The **Blue Book** includes *only* the standards, interpretations, and related appendices *that are mandatory for the current financial reporting year*. For example, introductory material within the 2015 Blue Book states:

> This volume does not contain those Standards or changes to Standards with an effective date after January 1, 2015. Readers seeking the consolidated text of IFRS issued at January 1, 2015 (including Standards with an effective date after January 1, 2015) should refer to the 2015 IFRS (Red Book), which is being issued in the first quarter of 2015.[21] [Underlined emphasis added]

The **Green Book**, *A Guide through IFRSs*, presents IFRS guidance as well as extensive cross-references and other annotations intended to serve as *educational material*. For example, notice how the following paragraph from IFRS 3 (Business Combinations) in the Green Book includes extensive cross-referencing to explanatory material, such as links to the glossary [G], appendices, and the IASB's basis for conclusions:

> 3. An entity shall determine whether a transaction or other event is a <u>business combination</u> by applying the definition in this IFRS, which requires that the assets[G] acquired and liabilities[G] assumed constitute a <u>business</u>. [Refer: <u>Appendix A</u>] If the assets acquired are not a business, the reporting entity shall account for the transaction or other event as an asset acquisition. <u>Paragraphs B5–B12</u> provide guidance on identifying a business combination and the definition of a business.
>
>   [Refer: <u>Basis for Conclusions paragraphs BC5–BC21</u>]

To help you remember these bound editions, consider the following TIP.

[**TIP**] from the Trenches

> Think of the Red Book as the book that will help you be **prepaRED** for future transactions. Think of the Green Book like a **green chalkboard**, ready to teach and provide additional explanations.

For your reference, the contents of the 2015 Blue Book are illustrated in Figure 12-11, along with commentary pointing out some of the content included in each bound edition.

---

[21] IFRS Foundation, *2015 Blue Book*. "Changes in this Edition" section.

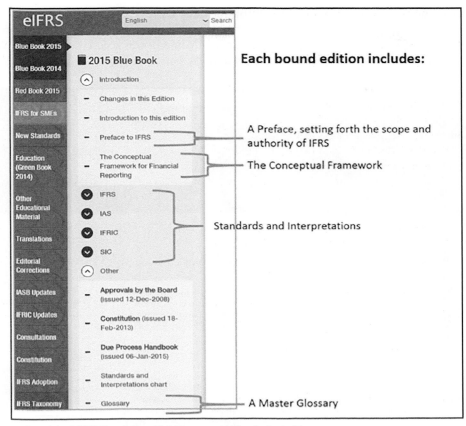

Figure 12-11
Blue Book contents,
shown in eIFRS

Considering the preceding discussion of bound editions, complete the following **Now YOU Try**.

Now
YOU
Try
12.13

1. Which bound edition would be most helpful to a researcher whose company is reviewing the accounting for a proposed transaction, which will likely be executed in 1 year's time? Briefly explain.

2. Which bound edition might a researcher consult if he or she is interested in further explanations or context for interpreting the guidance? Briefly explain.

TIP from the
Trenches

Even if you are just preparing current-year financial statements and are most interested in standards with current applicability (such as the standards included in the current-year Blue Book), do not overlook standards with future applicability.

Per IAS 8 (par. 30), entities must *disclose* any possible impacts that newly issued IFRS guidance will have, when adopted. Additionally, standards with future applicability could impact management's earnings forecasts.

Performing Research within eIFRS ("Subscribers Only")

The eIFRS homepage is shown in Figure 12-12. From this screen, researchers can browse directly to specific guidance (by clicking on a bound edition), can access the *IFRS for SMEs* publication, or can perform keyword searches within the bound editions.

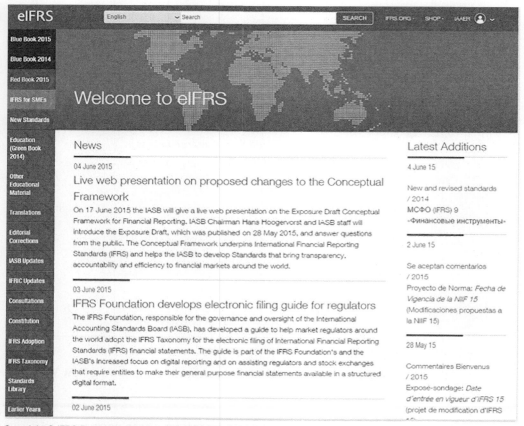

Copyright © IFRS Foundation. All rights reserved. [See footnote 8.]

Considering this screenshot, complete the following **Now YOU Try**, which will familiarize you with the layout of eIFRS.

Now YOU Try 12.14

Respond to the following using Figure 12-12.

1. First, locate and **circle** the keyword search bar.

Next, identify the link you'd click, on the left-hand navigation panel, for information on each of the following.

2. If you are in the process of preparing **2015** financial statements and want guidance that applies to the *current reporting period* only? _____

3. For the IFRS for micro-sized entities publication, a subset of *IFRS for SMEs*?

    _____

4. To access the Spanish-language version of standards? _____

5. For first-time adoption resources? _____

6. For the bound edition of IFRS that includes extensive cross-references to other educational material? _____

7. If it's 2015, and you are researching future-period reporting requirements?

    _____

8. To locate the 2013 version of the Red Book? _____

Next, let's discuss how to perform searches within eIFRS.

Browsing Directly to Standards in eIFRS

If you have a general idea of the topic you are researching, your best bet may be to browse directly to the applicable standard within eIFRS.

First, select the Bound Edition (Red, Blue, or Green Book) most relevant to your situation. Next, scan the list of standards, or search on the page (for example, using ctrl + f) for keywords in the title of standards.

Next, if you are reviewing a standard for the first time, consider reading the standard's **Introduction**. While not considered *integral* content, the Introduction section (paragraphs IN1, IN2, and so on) provides a useful, high-level summary of the standard and can be a perfect starting point for a researcher who is reading a standard for the first time. Once you determine that the standard is relevant, be sure to review all guidance considered "integral" to the standard, and look for any relevant interpretations of the standard.

In the wrong place? Look for references to other related standards. The **Related Documents** link provided for each standard lists other standards that significantly reference, or which are significantly referenced by, a given standard.

Considering this information, complete the following **Now YOU Try**.

Label the arrows in the following screenshot—which shows the contents of IFRS 2—with the number matching each item's description.

Now
YOU
Try
12.15

Figure 12-13

Contents of IFRS 2

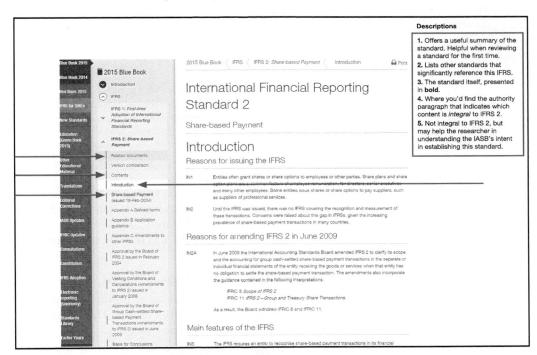

Finally, if you are curious about how the 2014 version of IFRS 2 compares, say, to the 2015 version of this same standard, click the *Version Comparison* link (shown just under the *Related documents* link) to see marked changes.

Performing a Keyword Search in eIFRS

If you are looking for a specific term in the guidance or are unsure where to begin a browse search, try a Keyword search instead.

Let's assume that you are searching for the term "self-constructed" within the Blue Book. This search is illustrated in Figure 12-14.

Figure 12-14

Search for the term "self-constructed" within the Blue Book

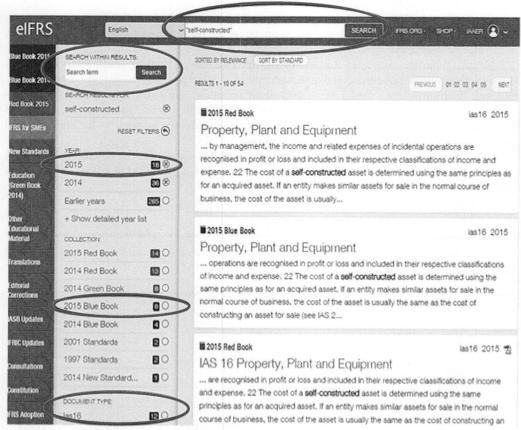

As illustrated in Figure 12-14 you can choose to search for an additional term within your search results ("Search within"). You also have the option to narrow your search results by year, by bound edition, or by standard. These options are circled in Figure 12-14.

Additional *search tips* are available under the **Help** and the **FAQs** links at the bottom of your eIFRS page. I'll summarize a few:

- To search for an exact phrase, enclose the search phrase in "double quotes."

- Interestingly, a search for the term *self-constructed* without quotation marks returned 0 results. A search for this term without the hyphen returned 109 results. The moral of this story? Try performing your search multiple ways if at first you strike out.

- Use of an asterisk* at the end of a search term will include *extensions* of the word. *Self-construct** will yield results including *constructed*, *constructing*, and *construction*.

- Once you click on a search result, you can use ctrl + f to search for specific terms on that page.

In some cases, you may open a document within eIFRS that shows up in **pdf** format on your screen. This is the case in the following image. If this happens, you'll be unable to perform a keyword search (ctrl + f) on the page. For example, notice the keyword search (at top left) for IASC, which appears on the page but was not found as a search result.

$$\left[\text{TIP}\right]\text{ from the Trenches}$$

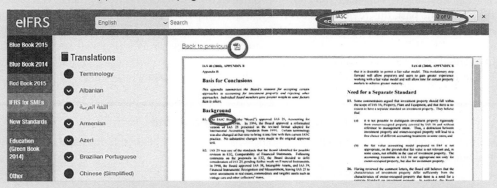

Copyright © IFRS Foundation. All rights reserved. [See footnote 8.]

If this happens to you, simply click on the Acrobat icon (circled in the preceding image) to access a keyword-searchable version of the document.

Accessing Individual Standards on the IFRS Website ("Registered Users Only")

By completing a brief, free online registration, "registered users" of the IFRS website can access current-year **unaccompanied** individual IFRS standards, interpretations, and technical summaries of standards. (This is also known as Basic access.)

Access to unaccompanied guidance means that the standards are not accompanied by implementation guidance or the IASB's basis for conclusions, and prior year (superseded) guidance is not included. Another major downside of this limited access is that you cannot perform keyword searches of the full population of IFRS guidance (such as within bound editions).

Statement of Compliance with IFRS

Now that you understand what it takes to research and apply IFRS, let's discuss the requirements for representing compliance with IFRS.

Per IAS 1 (Presentation of Financial Statements), entities whose financial statements comply fully with IFRS must make an explicit and unreserved **statement of compliance** in the financial statement footnotes.[22] As a researcher, you might find it useful to look for this compliance statement (generally located in note 1 or 2 of companies' financial statement footnotes) when determining whether an entity has prepared its financial statements in accordance with IFRS.

Figure 12-15 illustrates the statement of compliance footnote from an annual report of Anheuser-Busch InBev ("AB InBev"), which is based in Belgium.

2. STATEMENT OF COMPLIANCE

The consolidated financial statements are prepared in accordance with International Financial Reporting Standards as issued by the International Accounting Standards Board ('IASB") and in conformity with IFRS as adopted by the European Union up to 31 December 2014 (collectively "IFRS"). AB InBev did not early apply any new IFRS requirements that were not yet effective in 2014 and did not apply any European carve-outs from IFRS.

Used with permission of AB InBev.

Figure 12-15

Anheuser-Busch InBev, Statement of Compliance (from 2014 Annual Report, p. 26)

---

[22] IFRS Foundation, *2013 Blue Book*. IAS 1, *Presentation of Financial Statements*. Par. 16.

In Figure 12-15, notice not only the "unreserved" statement of compliance with IFRS, but also a statement that the financial statements are in conformity with "IFRS as adopted by the European Union." AB InBev also makes a point of stating that it did not apply any EU-specific exceptions to IFRS. But, why all of this explanation?

As noted previously, certain countries (or regions) require their local authorities to *endorse* IFRS before they are adopted for use in the country. In the EU, the Accounting Regulatory Committee (i.e., representatives from member state governments), as advised by the European Financial Reporting Advisory Group (EFRAG), must endorse new IFRSs before they are approved for use in the EU. In the past, this review process resulted in a temporary carve out of key financial instruments guidance (the "IAS 39 carve out"). However, *at any given time*, if differences exist between IFRS and "EU IFRS," and these differences are relevant to an entity's financial statements, the entity cannot represent compliance with IFRS.

The following Now YOU Try looks at HSBC's IFRS compliance footnote.

The IFRS Compliance Footnote

Read the following excerpt from HSBC Holdings plc's IFRS compliance footnote, then respond to the questions that follow.

1 Basis of preparation

(a) Compliance with International Financial Reporting Standards
The consolidated financial statements of HSBC and the separate financial statements of HSBC Holdings have been prepared in accordance with IFRSs as issued by the IASB and as endorsed by the EU. EU-endorsed IFRSs could differ from IFRSs as issued by the IASB if, at any point in time, new or amended IFRSs were not to be endorsed by the EU.

At 31 December 2014, there were no unendorsed standards effective for the year ended 31 December 2014, affecting these consolidated and separate financial statements, and there was no difference between IFRSs endorsed by the EU and IFRSs issued by the IASB in terms of their application to HSBC. Accordingly, HSBC's financial statements for the year ended 31 December 2014, are prepared in accordance with IFRSs as issued by the IASB. (Source: HSBC Holdings Plc, Annual Report and Accounts 2014, Note 1a, page 345.)

Questions:

1. Does HSBC comply in full with IFRS, and does it also comply with "IFRS as endorsed by the EU"?

2. What is one potential difference, cited by HSBC, that can arise between the EU-IFRS and IFRS as issued by the IASB?

Let's now turn our attention to the *IFRS for SMEs* publication.

IFRS for Small and Medium-Sized Entities

Overview of *IFRS for SMEs*

Recognizing the complexity of applying full IFRS, the IASB created the 230-page *IFRS for SMEs* publication as a simplified set of guidance for entities without public accountability. In doing so, the IASB acknowledged differences (versus listed companies) in the users and uses of SME financial statements, and the more limited resources generally available to SMEs in preparing financial statements. According to the IASB, such entities are estimated to account for over 95% of all companies around the world.[23]

The *IFRS for SMEs* publication is illustrated in Figure 12-16. Increasingly, individual jurisdictions (and particularly taxing authorities) are turning to this guidance in establishing their statutory reporting requirements.

Figure 12-16

The *IFRS for SMEs* publication

To create the *IFRS for SMEs* publication, the IASB started with full IFRS then made certain modifications, including the following:

- Topics not relevant to SMEs were omitted, such as earnings per share, interim financial reporting, and segment reporting.

- Many principles for recognizing and measuring assets, liabilities, income, and expenses have been simplified. For example, goodwill is amortized, rather than tested for impairment; also, all borrowing and research and development costs are expensed, rather than capitalized in certain circumstances.

- Significantly fewer disclosures are required (roughly a 90% reduction versus full IFRS).[24]

Furthermore, revisions to the *IFRS for SMEs* publication will be limited to once every three years. Notably, a group known as the SME Implementation Group (SMEIG) periodically develops nonmandatory Q&As designed to assist practitioners in applying the *IFRS for SMEs*. These Q&As are accessible on www.ifrs.org, under "IFRS for SMEs."

Judgment Hierarchy and Statement of Compliance

The judgment hierarchy shown in Figure 12-17 applies to an entity's selection of accounting policies under *IFRS for SMEs*.

---

[23] Per ifrs.org website, "About the IFRS for SMEs." Accessed June 2015.

[24] Id.

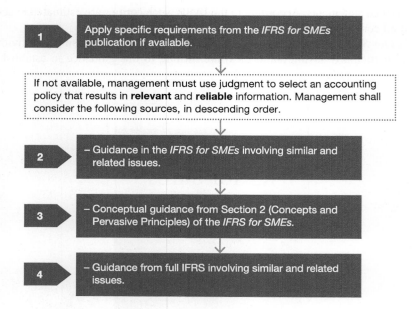

1. Apply specific requirements from the *IFRS for SMEs* publication if available.

If not available, management must use judgment to select an accounting policy that results in **relevant** and **reliable** information. Management shall consider the following sources, in descending order.

2. – Guidance in the *IFRS for SMEs* involving similar and related issues.

3. – Conceptual guidance from Section 2 (Concepts and Pervasive Principles) of the *IFRS for SMEs*.

4. – Guidance from full IFRS involving similar and related issues.

Similar to full IFRS, the authority paragraph in the *IFRS for SMEs* makes clear which parts of the standard and its appendices are mandatory. This guidance is as follows:

> The *International Financial Reporting Standard for Small and Medium-sized Entities (IFRS for SMEs)* is set out in Sections 1–35 and the Glossary. Terms defined in the Glossary are in **bold type** the first time they appear in each section. The *IFRS for SMEs* is accompanied by a preface, implementation guidance, a derivation table, illustrative financial statements and a presentation and disclosure checklist, and a basis for conclusions. (Source: *IFRS for SMEs* 2009, Contents page)

Also similar to full IFRS, entities whose financial statements comply with all requirements of the *IFRS for SMEs* must "make an explicit and unreserved statement of such compliance" in their financial statement footnotes,[26] like this illustrative example from the *IFRS for SMEs* publication:

> *Note 2 Basis of preparation and accounting policies*
> These consolidated financial statements have been prepared in accordance with the *International Financial Reporting Standard for Small and Medium-sized Entities* issued by the International Accounting Standards Board . . .[27]

Considering the preceding discussion, respond to the following.

Now YOU Try 12.17

1. Why did the IASB create the *IFRS for SMEs* guidance?

_____

_____

---

[25] *IFRS for SMEs* (2009). Par. 10.3–10.6.

[26] *IFRS for SMEs* (2009). Par. 3.3.

[27] *IFRS for SMEs* (2009). Illustrative Financial Statements, illustrative note 2, "Basis of Preparation and Accounting Policies."

2. According to the IFRS for SMEs authority paragraph, which sections of the *IFRS for SMEs* are considered "mandatory"?

_____

_____

How Do I Know Whether IFRS Applies to a Particular Country?

The IFRS Foundation provides detailed **jurisdictional profiles** on its website that describe the extent to which countries require or permit the use of IFRS or *IFRS for SMEs*. To view these profiles, go to ifrs.org, then *Use around the World*. Figure 12-18 illustrates the Jurisdictional Profiles page on the IFRS website.

> **LO4** **Review** jurisdiction profiles to understand circumstances in which IFRS applies internationally, and understand circumstances in which IFRS applies to U.S. practitioners.

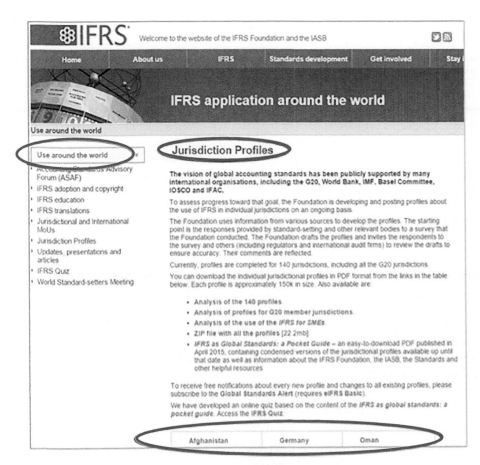

Figure 12-18

Jurisdiction Profiles page on ifrs.org

Deloitte's IAS Plus website (www.iasplus.com) is also a great resource for information about jurisdictions applying IFRS. Under the *Jurisdictions* tab, researchers can select a country, then read about that country's unique financial reporting requirements and access links to more information. For example, Figure 12-19 illustrates a search for the reporting requirements in Nigeria.

Figure 12-19

Financial reporting
requirements in Nigeria,
courtesy of Deloitte's
IAS Plus website (page
excerpted)

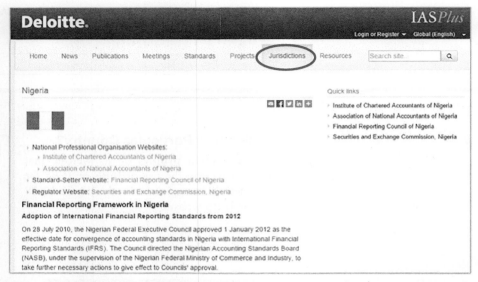

Material on IAS Plus website is © 2015 Deloitte Global Services Limited, or a member firm of Deloitte Touche Tohmatsu
Limited, or one of their related entities.[28]

Now
YOU
Try
12.18

In addition to jurisdictional profiles, Deloitte's IAS Plus site offers additional discussion and historical information for every single IFRS standard. Using the screenshot in Figure 12-19, circle
where on the page you would click to access a detailed discussion of each IFRS standard.

Using these resources as a starting point, researchers should take care to understand whether
IFRS applies as issued by the IASB, and/or whether other jurisdiction-specific requirements
apply.

When Are International Standards Relevant to U.S. Accountants?

Currently, the SEC requires *U.S. public companies* to prepare their financial statements in
accordance with U.S. GAAP. It remains unclear whether the SEC will ever move to broadly
require or permit the use of IFRS in the United States and—if so—how such a change would
be accomplished.

In years past, the SEC gave serious consideration to a possible move to IFRS but noted the
following concerns, including

- Is the IASB's funding mechanism sufficiently developed? Or does the IASB's funding
  expose it to potential independence concerns?

- Are IFRS being applied consistently globally?

- Is the IASB sufficiently involving (and relying on) regional and national standard-setting
  bodies in the development of new standards?

- How much cost and effort would be required (by U.S. companies) to adopt IFRS?

- Is the interpretive and industry-specific guidance in IFRS sufficiently developed?[29]

---

[28] Deloitte refers to one or more of Deloitte Touche Tohmatsu Limited, a UK private company limited by guarantee, and
its network of member firms, each of which is a legally separate and independent entity. Please see www.deloitte.com/
about for a detailed description of the legal structure of Deloitte Touche Tohmatsu Limited and its member firms.

[29] U.S. Securities and Exchange Commission, Final Staff Report: *Work Plan for the Consideration of Incorporating
International Financial Reporting Standards into the Financial Reporting System for U.S. Issuers.* July 13, 2012.
("SEC Staff Report, July 2012"). Pages 4–6.

Some speculate that the SEC's (and the U.S. Congress's) greatest concern is the fear of ceding standard-setting authority to an organization outside of the United States.[30] One possible solution to that concern, raised by the SEC, would be the required endorsement by the FASB of IFRS guidance prior to its adoption in the United States.[31] Others speculate that the move to IFRS could ultimately be like the U.S.'s consideration of the "metric system" (a lot of talk about adopting, but ultimately no decision to change).

For now, the SEC has left open the possibility that it will reach a decision on this matter; however, the timing of this decision is not clear. In recent years, much of the SEC's attention has been focused elsewhere, in particular on rulemaking related to financial reform legislation (e.g., the Dodd-Frank Act of 2010), however the SEC's draft strategic plan for 2014-2018 does indicate that it intends to consider the use of global standards.

This all being said, international standards are already relevant in the United States in certain circumstances. These include

- Foreign private issuers' filings in the United States;
- For U.S. nonpublic companies, who now have the option to apply IFRS; and
- Other areas relevant to U.S. accountants.

Foreign Private Issuers

Foreign private issuers, listed in the United States, have the option to present financial statements in accordance with U.S. GAAP, IFRS, or their home-country accounting standards (with a reconciliation to U.S GAAP). In 2007, the SEC eliminated the requirement that foreign private issuers must reconcile their IFRS financial statements to U.S. GAAP. The U.S. Exchange Act Rule 3b–4(c) defines "foreign private issuer" as follows:

Any foreign issuer other than a foreign government <u>except</u> an issuer that meets the following conditions:

(1) More than 50 percent of the issuer's outstanding voting securities are directly or indirectly held of record by residents of the United States; <u>and</u>
(2) any of the following:
    (i) The majority of the executive officers or directors are United States citizens or residents;
    (ii) more than 50 percent of the assets of the issuer are located in the United States; or
    (iii) the business of the issuer is administered principally in the United States.[32] [Emphasis added]

While U.S. public companies are required to file a Form 10-K annual report with the SEC, foreign private issuers generally file their annual reports in the United States using **Form 20-F**.

Considering this definition of foreign private issuer, take a moment to complete the following **Now YOU Try** exercise.

---

[30] PwC video perspective, *The Quarter Close, Third quarter 2012.* Posted on 9/17/2012 by PwC Assurance Services. From 3:46 to 4:30 (minutes: seconds).

[31] SEC Staff Report, July 2012, page 35. "As it relates to considering the needs of U.S. investors and the U.S. capital markets, the Staff believes that it may be necessary to put in place mechanisms specifically to consider and to protect the U.S. capital markets—for example, maintaining an active FASB to endorse IFRSs."

[32] U.S. Code of Federal Regulations, definition of "foreign private issuer." 17 CFR 240.3b–4(c). Last updated October 6, 2008.

Now
[YOU]
Try
12.19

Foreign Private Issuers

Based on our earlier discussion of HSBC Holdings plc (the HSBC parent company), would you generally expect this company to meet the definition of a "foreign private issuer" in the United States? Explain, identifying any assumptions you made in reaching this conclusion.

U.S. Nonpublic Companies

Technically, U.S. nonpublic companies have the option to apply the simplified *IFRS for SMEs* accounting framework and still receive an unmodified audit opinion. Unlike the AICPA's *FRF for SMEs*, which is a non-GAAP framework, *IFRS for SMEs* is considered generally accepted accounting principles for companies within its scope.

Recall that U.S. nonpublic companies are not required by the SEC to issue financial statements, but often do so to satisfy the needs of their investors and lenders. In order for these financial statements to receive an unmodified audit opinion, they must be prepared in accordance with *generally accepted accounting principles*.

Since 2008, the AICPA has recognized the IASB as a *designated standard setter* with the authority to establish international accounting principles, effectively giving AICPA members the option to use IFRS as an alternative to U.S. GAAP.[33]

However, although no public information is available on this matter, it is believed that very few, if any, entities will choose to exercise this option. Lenders would have to be willing to accept financial statements prepared under IFRS; such a change would likely be market-driven.[34] Furthermore, recent private company simplification efforts by the FASB (in coordination with the Private Company Council) will likely reduce nonpublic companies' interest in using IFRS.

Other Areas Relevant to U.S. Accountants

U.S. accountants may face a variety of situations involving the use of IFRS, as illustrated in Figure 12-20.

Figure 12-20

Example circumstances in which U.S. accountants would use IFRS skills

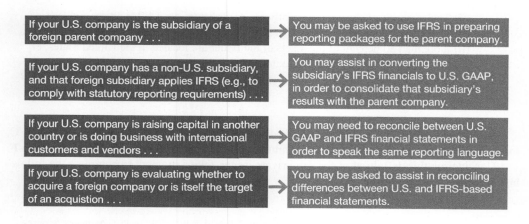

In addition, IFRS skills are relevant to U.S. accountants:

---

[33] AICPA Code of Professional Conduct, Appendix A.

[34] AICPA website: www.ifrs.com, "IFRS FAQs," developed by the American Institute of Certified Public Accountants. Questions No. 14 and 15. Accessed on May 28, 2015.

- *On the CPA exam.* For the "foreseeable future," both IFRS and U.S. GAAP will be tested on the CPA exam.[35] Candidates are expected to demonstrate knowledge of international accounting and auditing requirements, as well as familiarity with the international standard-setting environment.[36]

- *As a nonauthoritative source of guidance.* Recall that U.S. accountants may look to IFRS by analogy as a nonauthoritative source of guidance if GAAP is not responsive to a specific issue.

- *To monitor emerging accounting guidance.* Accountants may be asked to monitor emerging changes in U.S. accounting standards. Decisions reached by the IASB could in some cases influence future U.S. GAAP requirements.

Finally, consider another benefit of IFRS experience, described in this **TIP from the Trenches.**

Another key benefit of having IFRS experience? It enhances your marketability as a professional. While a U.S. adoption of IFRS remains uncertain, employers (ranging from accounting firms to corporations with international business to institutional investors) seek out individuals with IFRS experience in order to be prepared for evolving accounting requirements impacting their business or their clients' businesses.

[**TIP**] from the Trenches

The moral of this story? International standards are already relevant, *today*, to U.S. accountants.

Compare and contrast the reporting frameworks available to nonpublic companies considering the use of *IFRS for SMEs*, the Codification, and the AICPA's *FRF for SMEs*.

Now
[**YOU**]
Try
12.20

_____

_____

_____

_____

Citing International Accounting Standards

Following are examples of acceptable references to IFRS guidance.

- Per International Accounting Standard No. 16, *Property Plant and Equipment* (IAS 16), par. 29:

  An entity shall choose either the cost model in paragraph 30 or the revaluation model in paragraph 31 as its accounting policy and shall apply that policy to an entire class of property, plant and equipment.

- Later references might describe this source as follows: Per IAS 16, par. 29 . . .

---

[35] AICPA.org, Uniform CPA Examination FAQs—International Financial Reporting Standards (IFRS). Accessed May 28, 2015.

[36] AICPA, *Content and Skill Specifications for the Uniform CPA Examination.* Approved May 15, 2009; update approved October 3, 2013. Effective date: January 1, 2015.

Also, following is an acceptable method for citing guidance from the *IFRS for SMEs* publication:

- Per *IFRS for SMEs* (July 2009 revision), Section 1.1 (Scope): "The *IFRS for SMEs* is intended for use by **small and medium-sized entities** (SMEs)."

It is necessary to include the revision date when citing from the *IFRS for SMEs* publication. It is also helpful to show (in parentheses) a description of the section from which guidance is being cited. For example, saying "Section 1.1" by itself is not descriptive, so it is helpful to also describe this section as relating to Scope.

NONAUTHORITATIVE RESOURCES

Extensive nonauthoritative resources are available to assist practitioners in understanding and applying international accounting standards. The following discussion highlights a small sample of available resources.

Deloitte's IAS Plus Website

A great starting point for researchers applying, or looking for additional information on, IFRS, Deloitte's IAS Plus website (www.iasplus.com) includes news, detailed histories and summaries for each IFRS standard, information about each jurisdiction where IFRS is used, and extensive interpretive guidance (such as guide books for individual IFRS standards) and training resources (such as e-learning modules available for each standard).

Comparison Guides

Comparison guides, generally available free of charge from major accounting firms, summarize key provisions of U.S. GAAP and IFRS and highlight areas of difference. As a beginning researcher, if you were to look at two standards (a U.S. GAAP standard and an IFRS standard) side by side, you may not pick up on nuances implied by different choices of words. Or you may struggle to *efficiently* identify differences in requirements. These guides can efficiently point out such differences.

Before you even log on to eIFRS, you might consider consulting a comparison guide. Used as a starting point, the guide will (1) identify the names of applicable IFRS (standards and interpretations) that are relevant to a topic and (2) highlight key areas of difference in IFRS versus U.S. GAAP requirements. Both sets of standards frequently change, so be sure that you are using the most current available guide, and always use these guides *in addition to* authoritative sources.

To locate comparison guides, try a Web search for "IFRS vs GAAP," or some variation of this (such as adding the word "comparison" or "guide").

Other Resources

Extensive resources are available that can assist in a researcher's understanding of IFRS; the following discussion names just a few. Caution: When searching for nonauthoritative guidance, be thoughtful about consulting reputable sources. Avoid unknown websites, and avoid textbooks which could be outdated.

For plain-English *summaries* of IFRS guidance, researchers can consult

- Technical Summaries published by the IASB, available for each standard.
- Pocket Guides to IFRS, published by the major accounting firms, which summarize IFRS requirements by standard (e.g., Deloitte's *IFRSs in your pocket*, 2013).

For *in-depth analysis* of IFRS requirements, researchers can consult

- IFRS accounting manuals, available for purchase from major accounting firms or available through subscriptions to firm research databases. For example, PwC's *Manual of accounting—IFRS* offers in-depth guidance on the preparation of IFRS financial statements, including examples from company reports and model IFRS financial statements.

- IFRS guide books by topic. For example, you can search Google for "IFRS 15 Guide" to be directed to firm guidance on the revised IFRS revenue standard.

  For *"model" IFRS financial statements*, researchers can consult, for example,

- Firm websites, such as BDO International and Grant Thornton, which annually publish illustrative financial statements and notes as a technical reference for accountants.

- The Ernst & Young "Core Tools Library," accessible online, which offers industry-specific illustrative IFRS financial statements (e.g., Oil & Gas, Real Estate).

  Several firms offer IFRS *training modules* by topic, including

- The IFRS Foundation's training modules explaining and illustrating the application of *IFRS for SMEs*.

- Firm-produced IFRS learning modules by topic (Web search: "IFRS e-learning" or "learning modules").

  The above-named resources are generally accessible via Web search, and most are free of charge. Consider now the following TIP from the Trenches.

> Asked what nonauthoritative resources she would recommend to beginning researchers, a former IASB project manager was quick to name the following, which she herself frequently consults: (1) Deloitte's "IAS Plus" website; (2) accounting firm IFRS vs. U.S. GAAP comparison guides; and (3) the IASB's own educational resources.

[**TIP**] from the Trenches

Sustainability Reporting

In 2014, the EU issued a directive requiring disclosure by public-interest entities of environmental, social, employee, human rights, diversity, and other issues. The directive indicated that specific requirements for complying with these disclosure guidelines should be established by, and go into law in, each EU member state by December 2016. Expect the **International Integrated Reporting Council (IIRC)** to play a key role in the establishment of specific guidance for member states.

APPENDIX 12A: INTERNATIONAL AUDITING STANDARDS

When Do International Auditing Standards Apply?

As a private standard-setting organization, the IASB lacks the authority to enforce (i.e., ensure that entities are properly applying) its accounting standards. Rather, enforcement is generally left up to national laws, securities regulators, and the audit process. This section of the text focuses on international auditing standards, focusing in particular on their relevance to U.S. accounting professionals.

LO5 Become familiar with the standards and standard setters applicable to international auditing.

Globally, external audits are frequently required for entities with public accountability, as well as for certain statutory financial statements. Governments and securities regulators in individual countries or regions determine the applicable auditing standards for their jurisdictions. Often, these auditing standards are based on the **International Standards on Auditing (ISAs)** issued by the International Auditing and Assurance Standards Board.

In the United States, recall that two organizations are primarily responsible for establishing auditing standards: the PCAOB for public company audits and the AICPA for nonpublic company audits. Notably, the PCAOB's auditing standards also apply to *foreign private issuers*, as these entities are still considered issuers of securities in the United States—no exception was made under Sarbanes-Oxley for "foreign" issuers.[37] Also notable, the AICPA's auditing standards apply to U.S. nonpublic companies that choose to prepare financial statements in accordance with IFRS.

As U.S. accounting firms increasingly perform multinational audits, U.S. auditors are expected to become familiar with international auditing and ethics standards. For example,

■ When auditing a U.S. subsidiary of a foreign parent, a U.S. auditor may be expected by the parent company to perform the audit in accordance with international standards.

■ The "reverse" is also true—when auditing a U.S. parent with a foreign subsidiary, the audit of the foreign subsidiary may be required by statutory laws to comply with international auditing standards.

The graphic in Figure 12-21 summarizes several scenarios for U.S. auditors, and the applicable auditing standards.

Figure 12-21

Sample audit scenarios and applicable source of standards

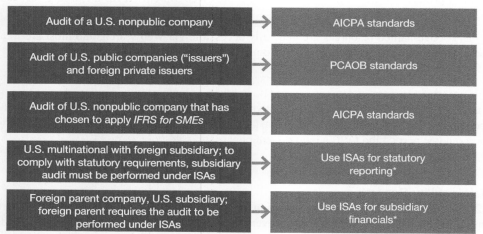

*To the extent the audit is performed by U.S. auditors, the auditors must also adhere to U.S. auditing and ethical standards.

In circumstances where U.S. auditors must comply with international auditing standards, the U.S. auditor is expected to *also* comply with U.S. auditing and ethical standards. Two U.S. auditing standards shed light on the interaction between U.S. auditors and international reporting:

■ AU-C 700, *Forming an Opinion and Reporting on Financial Statements*, permits U.S. auditors to express an opinion on financial statements prepared in accordance with U.S. GAAP, IFRS, or *IFRS for SMEs*.

■ AU-C 910, *Financial Statements Prepared in Accordance with a Financial Reporting Framework Generally Accepted in Another Country*, applies to U.S. auditors engaged to report on financial statements prepared in accordance with *financial reporting frameworks other than U.S. GAAP or IFRS (as issued by the IASB)*, such as audits of financial statements prepared using other national GAAP or jurisdictional variations of IFRS.

● This standard describes how auditors should consider both international and U.S. auditing standards in their performance of the audit, and provides guidance for selecting the appropriate form for the auditor's report.

---

[37] Sarbanes-Oxley Act of 2002, Sections 101(c)(2) and 103(a)(1).

Next, let's look at the organizations responsible for establishing global auditing and ethics standards.

The International Federation of Accountants (IFAC) and Its Standards Boards

Through its four independent standard-setting boards, the **International Federation of Accountants** (IFAC) establishes international standards on ethics, auditing and assurance, accounting education, and governmental (public sector) accounting. The IFAC's mission is, in part, to serve the public interest by "contribut[ing] to the development, adoption, and implementation of high-quality international auditing and assurance standards . . ."[38]

The IFAC and its standard-setting boards are illustrated in Figure 12-22. Like the use of IFRS, standards of the IFAC's various boards are progressively gaining worldwide acceptance; IFAC members represent approximately 130 countries and jurisdictions globally.[39]

Figure 12-22

The IFAC and its standard-setting boards

Take a moment to improve your familiarity with the IFAC's standard-setting bodies by completing the following simple **Now YOU Try** exercise.

Matching Guidance to Standard Setters

The standard setters illustrated in Figure 12-22 issue guidance that is organized into the following handbooks. Match each handbook to the standard setter that issues it.

Handbook of International Quality Control, Auditing, Review, Other Assurance, and Related Services Pronouncements: _____

Handbook of International Education Pronouncements: _____

Handbook of the Code of Ethics for Professional Accountants: _____

Handbook of International Public Sector Accounting Pronouncements: _____

Now YOU Try 12.21

The IFAC's "member bodies," comprised of global professional accountancy organizations, agree as a condition of membership to adopt or substantially converge with certain of the IFAC's standards, including International Standards on Auditing (ISAs) and the international **Code of**

[38] International Auditing and Assurance Standards Board (IAASB), *Handbook of International Quality Control, Auditing Review, Other Assurance, and Related Services Pronouncements,* 2012 Edition, Volume 1. Page 4.

[39] IFAC.org, "Membership." "IFAC is comprised of 173 members and associates in 129 countries and jurisdictions*, representing approximately 2.5 million accountants in public practice, education, government service, industry, and commerce." *As of November 15, 2012. Accessed October 20, 2013.

Ethics.[40] To the extent differences exist between these and national ethics standards, member bodies agree to promote standards that are not less stringent than those of IFAC. The AICPA is a member body of the IFAC and thus has agreed to these requirements. As another example, the Financial Reporting Council (of the U.K. and Ireland) uses ISAs as the basis for its own auditing standards.

Following is further discussion regarding each of these standards boards.

International Auditing and Assurance Standards Board (IAASB)

The **International Auditing and Assurance Standards Board** (IAASB) establishes standards for a range of services, applicable to entities of all sizes, including small and medium-sized entities. The IAASB's "Handbook" includes the following standards:

- International Standards on Auditing (ISAs) for audits
- ISREs for review engagements
- ISAEs for assurance engagements
- ISQCs for quality control
- ISRS for "related services" (e.g., agreed-upon procedures, compilations)

The IAASB Handbook can be downloaded from www.ifac.org. Researchers can search for guidance within the handbook by perusing the table of contents or by performing keyword searches (using ctrl + f).

While not included within the IAASB Handbook, accountants should also consider the **IESBA Code of Ethics**, which applies broadly to all professional accountants, regardless of the service being provided. For audit and assurance engagements, accountants should also consider the IAASB's "International Framework for Assurance Engagements" (the "Framework"), which describes the objectives of assurance engagements and identifies engagements to which the IAASB's auditing and assurance standards apply. While the Framework by itself is not authoritative, accountants are expected to read standards-level guidance for audit and assurance engagements in the context of the Framework.

International Standards on Auditing (ISAs)

For auditors just starting out with international auditing standards, a good starting point is ISA 200 (Objectives of the Independent Auditor, Conduct of an Audit in Accordance with ISAs). ISA 200 sets forth guidance on the proper use and application of ISAs in an audit, for example:

- An auditor should consider all parts of an ISA in order to properly apply it. This includes consideration of the standard's Objectives section, as well as the Requirements and Application and Explanatory Material sections. If necessary to achieve a standard's Objectives, auditors may need to perform procedures beyond those required within a given standard.
- Requirements within ISAs are described using the word *shall*.
- Similar to the notion of the IFRS "compliance statement," accountants cannot represent compliance with ISAs in their audit reports unless they comply fully with all ISA requirements. Therefore, to the extent jurisdictional variations exist of ISAs, entities may not be able to represent compliance with ISAs unless they still comply fully with ISA standards.[41]

The AICPA's recent Clarity initiative has resulted in increased convergence between U.S. non-public company auditing standards and ISAs. Certain differences remain, where deemed necessary by the AICPA, but in all cases the AICPA's requirements meet or exceed ISA requirements. The PCAOB did not participate in this convergence project.

One notable difference between U.S. and international auditing standards is that ISA standards do not require auditors to report on the effectiveness of internal controls. However, this

---

[40] Per IFAC *Statements of Membership Obligations* (2012), Ch. 3 par. 12(a) and Ch. 4 par. 12(a).

[41] ISA 200, *Overall Objectives of the Independent Auditor and the Conduct of an Audit in Accordance with International Standards on Auditing.* Par. 18-20, A55, A58, A70.

requirement may be imposed on a jurisdiction-specific basis (e.g., individual countries may require such reporting).[42]

Reporting of Key Audit Matters and Partner Name

The IAASB recently made significant changes to the audit report, requiring (among other changes) that the engagement partner be named on the audit report and requiring discussion of **key audit matters** (KAMs). These changes apply to audits of listed entities conducted under ISAs.

The requirement to report on KAMs is set forth in ISA 701. Par. 8 of ISA 701 defines KAMs as:

> Key audit matters—Those matters that, in the auditor's professional judgment, were of most significance in the audit of the financial statements of the current period. Key audit matters are selected from matters communicated with those charged with governance.

In identifying KAMs to report on, auditors would consider matters discussed with the audit committee (or others charged with governance) that required significant auditor attention. Within the report, auditors are required to: (1) describe each KAM, (2) explain why it was considered to be of significance to the audit, and (3) describe how the matter was addressed in the audit.

In the United States, the PCAOB is considering a similar requirement to report on *critical audit matters* in auditors' reports.

Interpretive Guidance from the IAASB

The IAASB and its staff have issued several sources of nonauthoritative, interpretive guidance related to certain standards included in the Handbook. These include

- IAASB-published "practice notes," designed to provide practical assistance and application guidance for the IAASB's various standards. Practice notes include, for example, the International Auditing Practice Notes (IAPNs).
- The basis for conclusions to each ISA.
- Staff Q&As on the application of standards.
- Training modules for certain standards, including videos and informational slides.

These resources are generally accessible on the "Publications & Resources" page of www.ifac.org.

International Ethics Standards Board for Accountants

The **International Ethics Standards Board for Accountants** (IESBA) issues and maintains a model Code of Ethics for Professional Accountants to be followed by—or to serve as a minimum standard for jurisdiction-specific ethics codes for—professional accountants throughout the world. As noted previously, this Code of Ethics applies broadly: professional accountants must comply with the Code of Ethics in all circumstances, regardless of the functional role, or type of engagement, being performed by the accountant.

U.S. accountants are generally expected to abide by the IESBA's Code of Ethics when performing an audit in accordance with ISA auditing standards.

The Code of Ethics is organized in a manner similar to the AICPA's revised Code, and includes the following three parts:

- Part A, which establishes fundamental principles of professional ethics applicable to all users of the Code.
- Part B, which applies the framework to public accountants.
- Part C, which applies the framework to accountants in business.

---

[42] ISA 200, Par. A1 (Scope of the Audit)

Other IFAC Standards Boards

The IFAC's International Public Sector Accounting Standards Board (IPSASB) establishes minimum standards (**International Public Sector Accounting Standards**, or **IPSAS**) for governments and other public sector entities and strives to promote the use, globally, of an accrual-based approach for the preparation of government financial statements. IPSAS are formulated using IFRS as a starting point, then are revised as necessary to address issues unique to public sector accounting.[43]

The IFAC's **International Accounting Education Standards Board** (IAESB) develops educational standards applicable to member bodies' accountants. For example, the IAESB has established a guideline educational syllabus, outlining educational standards to be achieved by its members. IFAC member bodies are required to consider these educational standards while formulating their own educational programs for accountants.

Comparing International Audit Reports

Let's now review excerpts from audit reports illustrating the use of different accounting and auditing frameworks. For this, we'll return to our example of HSBC.

Figure 12-24 depicts the relationship among the London-based holding company HSBC Holdings plc and a few of its subsidiaries. The North American holding company (HSBC North America) does not issue public securities and generally does not issue financial statements (except for form FR Y-9C, a required filing with the Federal Reserve for bank holding companies). However, the other entities depicted in Figure 12-23 do issue securities, as noted in the illustration.

Figure 12-23
Partial depiction of HSBC Holdings Plc's organizational structure. This illustration is not a complete depiction of HSBC's subsidiary relationships; not all intermediate subsidiaries and holding companies have been reflected in this illustration.

Comparing International Audit Reports

Now YOU Try 12.22

Using the information in Figure 12-23 and the following audit report excerpts, respond to the questions that follow. The excerpts below are taken from filings with the U.S. SEC and filings in the U.K.

I. Report of Independent Registered Public Accounting Firm
. . . We conducted our audits in accordance with the standards of the Public Company Accounting Oversight Board (United States) . . .

Continued

---

[43] International Public Sector Accounting Standards Board, *Process for Reviewing and Modifying IASB Documents* (October 2008). Page 1.

In our opinion, the consolidated financial statements referred to above present fairly, in all material respects, the financial position of the Company as of December 31, 2014 and 2013, and the results of its operations and its cash flows for each of the years in the three-year period ended December 31, 2014, and the financial position of the Bank as of December 31, 2014 and 2013, in conformity with U.S. generally accepted accounting principles. [From annual report Form 10-K filed with U.S. SEC]

Questions:

1. In audit report excerpt I, which financial reporting (accounting) framework are the auditors opining on?

_____

2. What audit standards did the auditors follow, in conducting the audit? _____

3. Which entity (or possible entities) do you think this opinion relates to? Explain._____

_____

II. Independent Auditor's Report to the Members of [Company]

In our opinion. . . the Group financial statements have been properly prepared in accordance with International Financial Reporting Standards as adopted by the European Union ('IFRSs as adopted by the EU'); . . .

In arriving at our audit opinion above, our strategy was to increase our audit procedures in areas where we identified a higher risk of material misstatement of the financial statements.

. . . the risks of material misstatement that had the greatest effect on our audit were areas where significant judgement was required and were as follows:

[Following is one example risk excerpted from this auditor's report]:

The Risk	Our Response
Impairment of Loans and Advances *Refer to the critical accounting estimates and judgements in Note 1(k) on the Financial Statements...* The impairment of loans and advances is estimated by the directors through the application of judgement and use of highly subjective assumptions. Due to the significance of loans and advances (representing 41% of total assets) and the related estimation uncertainty, this is considered a key audit risk. The portfolios which give rise to the greatest uncertainty are typically those where impairments are derived from collective models, are unsecured or are subject to potential collateral shortfalls. In 2014, we continued to pay particular attention to collective impairment methodologies, focusing specifically on US mortgages, the commercial and global banking portfolios, and Brazilian personal and business loans, either due to their relative size or the potential impact of changing inputs and assumptions. We also focused on portfolios that were potentially more sensitive to developing and emerging global economic trends. In addition, we also focused on individually significant exposures that either continued to be, have become, or were at risk of being individually impaired.	Our audit procedures included the assessment of controls over the approval, recording and monitoring of loans and advances, and evaluating the methodologies, inputs and assumptions used by the Group in calculating collectively assessed impairments, and assessing the adequacy of impairment allowances for individually assessed loans and advances. We compared the Group's assumptions for both collective and individual impairment allowances to externally available industry, financial and economic data and our own assessments in relation to key inputs. As part of this, we critically assessed the Group's revisions to estimates and assumptions, specifically in respect of the inputs to the impairment models in the commercial and global banking portfolios and the consistency of judgement applied in the use of economic factors, loss emergence periods and the observation period for historical default rates. For a sample of exposures that were subject to an individual impairment assessment, and focusing on those with the most significant potential impact on the financial statements, we specifically challenged the Group's assumptions on the expected future cash flows, including the value of realisable collateral based on our own understanding and available market information. We also assessed whether the financial statement disclosures appropriately reflect the Group's exposure to credit risk, specifically considering those portfolios identified in 2014 as presenting the greatest risk.

Continued

Continued from previous page

> Under International Standards on Auditing (UK and Ireland) we are required to report to you if, based on the knowledge we acquired during our audit, we have identified other information in the annual report that contains a material inconsistency with either that knowledge or the financial statements, a material misstatement of fact, or that is otherwise misleading.
>
> . . . As explained in Note l(a) to the Group financial statements, in addition to complying with its legal obligation to apply IFRSs as adopted by the EU, the Group has also applied IFRSs as issued by the IASB. . . .
>
> [From annual report filed in UK]

4. In excerpt II, which <u>two</u> financial reporting (accounting) frameworks are the auditors opining on? _____ and _____

5. What audit standards did the auditors follow, in conducting the audit? _____

6. Explain why the auditor in this case is describing impairment of loans and advances as a risk. What reporting requirement is the auditor following in describing this information? What was the auditor's response to this risk?

    _____

    _____

    _____

    _____

7. Which entity do you think this opinion relates to? Explain. _____

    _____

> **III. Report of Independent Registered Public Accounting Firm to the Board of Directors and Shareholders of [Company]**
>
> . . . We conducted our audits in accordance with the standards of the Public Company Accounting Oversight Board (United States). . . .
>
> In our opinion, the consolidated financial statements referred to above present fairly, in all material respects, the financial position of [Company] . . . and the results of its operations and its cash flows . . . in conformity with International Financial Reporting Standards (IFRSs) as adopted by the European Union (EU) and IFRSs as issued by the International Accounting Standards Board (IASB).
>
> [Form 20-F Annual Report, filed with the U.S. SEC]

8. Recall from earlier in the chapter—when does report Form 20-F apply? _____

9. In excerpt III, what <u>two</u> financial reporting (accounting) frameworks are the auditors opining on? _____ and _____

10. What audit standards did the auditors follow, in conducting the audit? _____

11. Which entity do you think this opinion relates to? Explain. _____

    _____

*Company names have been replaced by bracketed text ("[Company]") for purposes of this exercise.
**References for these excerpts are located immediately following the case studies at the end of this chapter.

CHAPTER SUMMARY

For years, international accounting and auditing standards were established by individual jurisdictions. Today, the IFRS Foundation, through its standard-setting bodies the IASB and the IFRS Interpretations Committee, is considered the predominant global accounting standard setter. Full IFRS is required for many publicly accountable entities internationally, and *IFRS for SMEs* guidance is required or permitted for many entities without public accountability. The increased (although not total) use of a single set of global standards has streamlined what were once diverse reporting requirements for multinational entities. The guidance comprising full IFRS is organized into bound editions, and guidance within these bound editions should be prioritized using the IAS 8 hierarchy.

International auditing, ethics, and public-sector standards are also increasingly being converged with standards of the IFAC and its four standard-setting bodies. As we've discussed in this chapter, several circumstances exist in which U.S. accountants may be called upon to apply these international standards. The global context, as well as the research skills, you've acquired from this chapter, should help prepare you for the challenges ahead.

REVIEW QUESTIONS

1. Describe the global standard-setting environment prior to 2001, and describe what the role of the IASC was in the years prior to 2001.

2. What occurred in 2000 that began the shift toward use of the IASC's guidance? Explain.

3. Describe the relationship between the IASC and the IASB.

4. What is meant by the terms *jurisdictional IFRS* and *carve-outs*?

5. Who establishes the requirement that *listed* companies issue audited financial statements? Who establishes this requirement for *nonlisted* companies?

6. Briefly explain why a large multinational corporation, such as HSBC, might be supportive of increasing the global use of IFRS.

7. Describe the relationship between the IFRS Foundation and the IASB.

8. What is the role of the IFRS Foundation's Monitoring Board? Its Trustees?

9. Does the IASB have the authority to impose funding requirements on its member countries? Contrast the IASB's funding regime with the FASB's funding mechanism.

10. In what circumstances does the IFRS Interpretations Committee handle an issue, and what is the name of the guidance they issue?

11. Are U.S. public companies allowed to issue financial statements in accordance with IFRS? What about U.S. nonpublic companies? Explain.

12. Which U.S. organization has the authority to determine whether IFRS is permitted in the U.S.?

13. In your own words, how is a "foreign private issuer" defined? What is the significance of this designation?

14. Identify the sources of guidance comprising full IFRS.

15. Explain the difference between integral and not integral guidance. What does it mean for a standard to be read *in the context of* other guidance?

16. Name two differences between the content of full IFRS and the guidance in *IFRS for SMEs*.

17. Why was the *IFRS for SMEs* created?

18. Are public (*listed*) companies permitted to apply IFRS for SMEs? Explain.

19. Differentiate between the Red, Blue, and Green Books.

20. Describe the purpose and authority of the IASB's Conceptual Framework.

21. When should a researcher turn to the IAS 8 hierarchy? In other words, what is a situation in which that hierarchy might be relevant?

22. Once you have located relevant IFRS or IAS guidance, what interpretive guidance should you also look for?

23. Where can a researcher find guidance regarding which countries around the world apply IFRS? Name two sources.

24. (From Appendix) What is one implication of the U.S. AICPA being a member body of the IFAC?

25. (From Appendix) Name the four standard-setting bodies of the IFAC.

26. (From Appendix) What is a recent, significant change required to audit reports prepared under ISAs?

EXERCISES

Exercises requiring *basic* (*free*) *access* **to ifrs.org. (Become a registered user for free to access individual standards.)**

These questions involve IFRS, as well as firm resources. Cite the source for each of your responses.

1. Has Tanzania adopted IFRS? Describe your process for locating this information.

2. Locate an IFRS/U.S. GAAP comparison guide. Name one difference between the U.S. GAAP and IFRS requirements related to *lease scope*.

3. Locate IAS 7, and identify the guidance considered integral to this standard. Explain how you located this information.

4. Locate the 2015 Form 20-F of Honda Motor Co.
    a. First, determine whether the financial statements were prepared in accordance with IFRS, and describe where you located this compliance statement.
    b. Also in this note about presentation, what does the company say with respect to its initial application of IFRS? Explain.
    c. Considering what you learned in this chapter, why is Honda permitted to prepare financial statements for the U.S. SEC in accordance with IFRS?
    d. Is Honda permitted to use IFRS to prepare financial statements filed with its home country? Explain, and describe how you found this information.
    e. Finally, identify Honda's auditor and describe the auditing standards applied by the company's auditors.

5. Assume that an entity complied with IFRS guidance in all respects, except that the entity has never included an IFRS compliance statement in its financial statement footnote disclosures. Is the entity subject to the guidance for first-time adopters of IFRS? Use authoritative guidance to respond.

6. Locate the IFRIC related to levies, then respond to the following.
    a. What is a levy?
    b. What is the obligating event that should cause an entity to record a liability for levies on its financial statements?
    c. What are two standard numbers that are described as being related to this Interpretation (under "References")?

7. Navigate to Deloitte's iasplus.com website. Name two specific resources that you might find useful on this website if you are researching the accounting for a client's possible acquisition of another entity.

8. Can a subsidiary—whose parent uses full IFRS—use *IFRS for SMEs* if the subsidiary itself is not publicly accountable?

9. Within the IFRS for SMEs, locate the principle for recognition of assets, liabilities, income, and expenses. That is, what two criteria must be met for recognition to occur?

10. Correct the following source citation, improving it in any way appropriate. IASB standard 2 tells us that "Inventories shall be measured at the lower of cost and net realisable value."

11. (Relates to Appendix topics) Smith Sisters, LLC is in the planning phase for its initial audit of New Client, Inc. It will perform this audit under ISAs. Is Smith Sisters, LLC required to contact New Client's predecessor auditor as part of its engagement planning?

12. (Relates to Appendix topics) Within the handbook of international ethics standards, what are two examples of safeguards (against threats such as client involvement in illegal activities) that an auditor should consider applying during its client acceptance (or "professional appointment") procedures?

Exercises Requiring Access to eIFRS

Note: You may have to log out of your "free" eIFRS Basic access in order to use your more advanced IAAER-sponsored eIFRS access.

13. a. What is the main principle (denoted in bold within a standard) for classifying noncurrent assets as held for sale?
     b. What is the role of the "one year" rule in applying this principle?
     c. An entity plans to sell a property that is currently in use, and the transfer will be accounted for as a sale and finance leaseback. Would the one year rule be met in this case? (*Hint:* Consult application guidance in responding to this issue.)

14. Refer to the Red Book's introductory material. What are two objectives of the IASB? Can this same information be found in the introductory material to the Blue Book and the Green Book, as well?

15. An entity sells inventories at a loss after the reporting period but before financial statements are issued. Must the financial statements be adjusted to reflect this loss?

16. Name two examples of investment properties. When should an investment property be recognized as an asset?

17. Go to par. 10(a) of IAS 1 in the Green Book. What are the educational materials referenced at the end of this paragraph? Brainstorm: In what circumstances might a beginning researcher choose to perform research using the Green Book?

18. A company has an interest rate swap that allows the company to receive a fixed rate and pay a variable rate based on LIBOR. The company is evaluating how to classify this instrument within its fair value hierarchy disclosures. What level in the fair value hierarchy is the LIBOR swap rate input to this measurement?

CASE STUDY QUESTIONS

Navigating the IFRS Bound Editions Using the most recent Red Book, summarize (in 1 paragraph per bullet) the information presented in the following sections of the Red Book: **12.1**

- Changes in this edition
- Introduction to this edition
- Preface to IFRS
- The Conceptual Framework (summarize the chapters included and any current developments noted in the Foreword)

Finally, can you find the IFRS Foundation's *Constitution* within the Red Book? If so, where? What is the purpose of this document?

Definition of Joint Venture, Accounting Implications Research whether the definition of *joint venture* differs between IFRS and U.S. GAAP. Considering the Energy Works sample memo included in Chapter 4, evaluate whether the JV in this fact pattern would still be considered a *joint venture* under IFRS. Explain. Next, describe the accounting implications of this determination.   **12.2**

Building a Warehouse *Facts:* A South African public company constructed a warehouse during 20X1. Costs involved in building the warehouse (or incurred after construction) included, among others: **12.3**

- Payment of wages and benefits to construction workers, who were already employed by the company ($3 million).
- Exterior paint for the building ($80,000).
- A test production run, in which the plant tested its ability to produce its products ($100,000).
- Payment of wages to construction workers for service issues arising after the plant was placed in service ($200,000).

In 20X2, an appraisal by the company's local tax assessor indicated that the building's value had increased by $5 million.

Required:

1. Determine whether the company is subject to the requirements of IFRS (based on the home country). Cite your source for this determination.
2. Locate the relevant guidance, then determine which of the above-listed costs may be included in the initial measurement (i.e., capitalized value) of the plant when the plant is first recognized in 20X1, citing your sources. Certain costs may be addressed directly by the guidance; others may require judgment in applying principles from the guidance.
3. Determine whether the property's value should be adjusted in year 2 (20X2).
4. Using an IFRS/U.S. GAAP comparison guide, state how your response to question 3 would differ if this company had been subject to U.S. GAAP. Cite the source for your response.

IFRS for SMEs Now, assume that the South African company's Controller (from the previous case study) has asked whether your response to item 3 (regarding the year 2 value of the plant) would change if the company applied *IFRS for SMEs* (assuming the company was permitted to apply this guidance). Draft a brief email to the company's Controller explaining the different accounting, and cite your source.   **12.4**

IFRS for SMEs Dissenting Opinion Within the Basis for Conclusions to the *IFRS for SMEs* (2009 revision) a Board member challenged the choice of steps in the *IFRS for SMEs* judgment hierarchy. Recall that this judgment hierarchy is illustrated in Figure 12-17 of this chapter. Locate this Board member's dissenting opinion, and describe the con-   **12.5**

cerns he raised regarding the judgment hierarchy. Additionally, describe one other concern he raised with respect to issuance of the *IFRS for SMEs* publication.

Your response should require approximately two paragraphs and should clearly reference the source of your research.

12.6   **Regulatory Deferral Accounts** Your client, a Ukrainian regulated, public telecommunications company has been applying IFRS for several years. To date, the entity has not applied *regulatory accounting*, in which entities can record as assets costs they expect to recover through rates approved by a regulator, and has chosen not to analogize to the use of U.S. GAAP (which permits this accounting treatment). This is because, until recently, IFRS did not include explicit guidance for regulatory accounting. However, with the issuance of a new standard in 2014, regulatory accounting guidance is now available within IFRS.

The chief accounting officer for your client has asked when this guidance will become effective, and what suggestions you have for adopting this standard. Additionally, he has asked you to explain (in terms his board can understand) what is meant by the term *regulatory deferral account*. Research this issue and prepare a response. You may find the Basis for Conclusions useful in formulating a thoughtful response.

12.7   **(Relates to Appendix)** Harmon Phillips, LLC received a phone call from a prospective client, requesting the firm's assistance in evaluating the accounting treatment for a proposed transaction. The client has laid out a set of hypothetical facts and has asked for Harmon Phillips' general views on the proposed transaction, indicating that its own auditor had a different view from the client's.

What ethical considerations (from the IESBA Handbook) should Harmon Phillips apply in providing their opinion to the potential client? Imagine that you are a staff member of the firm and have been asked to email your findings to Phil, a partner with the firm.

12.8   **(Relates to Appendix) Inappropriate Relationship** Ciao Bella, a listed entity based in Italy, made headlines when it dismissed its long-time auditor, Dietrick & Dietrick. Neither entity offered details beyond this: The company discovered an "inappropriate personal relationship" between the company's Chief Accounting Officer and the engagement partner on the audit. The press speculated that the relationship between the two was likely romantic. For its part, the firm withdrew its audit reports for the two preceding fiscal years. A new auditor has been hired to re-audit the periods in question.

Write a memo to the staff of Dietrick & Dietrick reminding members of the firm of the professional standards that were violated in this situation.

ADDITIONAL REFERENCES

Now YOU Try **12.22**   ** Excerpt No. 1: HSBC USA Inc, 2014 Form 10-K. Page 130; Excerpt No. 2: HSBC Holdings Plc, 2014 Annual Report. Page 329. Excerpt No. 3: HSBC Holdings Plc, 2014 Form 20-F, Page 329.

Chapter 13

Delivering Effective Presentations

Jess is a senior in the accounting advisory practice for a firm. The partner she reports to has asked her to prepare a presentation introducing the revised revenue recognition standard to clients of their practice. The presentation will be offered as a "lunch and learn" for several key clients. The objectives of the presentation will be to generate goodwill (the team plans to give the presentation at no charge), to help their clients understand the new standard and begin formulating an implementation strategy, and—of course—to offer her team's assistance and resources for helping make the client's adoption a success.

Jess has been asked to pull from existing firm resources as a starting point for her slides, but to consider the specific types of transactions, and industries, of the team's clients.

Eventually, Jess will submit her preliminary draft of the slides to the partner, who will review and suggest changes. Come presentation day, Jess will assume a prominent role in presenting to the client.

Now, imagine for a moment that you are Jess. Would *you* be ready to take this project on? How confident are you that your slide deck would be effective, and that you would be engaging as a presenter? Read on; this chapter should help.

After reading this chapter and performing the exercises herein, you will be able to

1. **Understand** circumstances in which you will use presentation skills in practice.

2. **Create** effective content.

3. Know what it takes to **deliver** a high-quality presentation.

4. **Work** effectively in a team to create and deliver presentations.

Learning Objectives

Organization of This Chapter

So far in this book, you've learned to communicate accounting issues in written form. But it's important that you also be prepared to verbally *describe* and *defend* your research. This chapter covers expectations and strategies for creating and delivering effective oral presentations. These skills can be applied to accounting research presentations, as well as broadly to other professional presentations you make. The preceding graphic illustrates the organization of content within this chapter.

Knowing that you have a presentation to prepare, this chapter is kept intentionally brief. It offers broad strategies for preparing and delivering content, with an emphasis on PowerPoint, but that can be applied to a range of presentation formats and visual aids.

WHEN WILL I USE PRESENTATION SKILLS IN PRACTICE, AND WHAT IS THE FORMAT?

> **LO1** **Understand** circumstances in which you will use presentation skills in practice.

In practice, you could be asked to make presentations to your peers, to colleagues in other departments, to your company's management, or to clients. The objectives of these presentations can vary; the goal may be one or more of the following:

- ■ To convey, or *teach* information (such as explaining the requirements of a new accounting standard)

- ■ To *share a judgment you've made* (such as by corporate accountants, in the process of preparing financial statements; or by auditors, describing their positions on key judgments taken by clients)

- ■ To *convince* the audience of your point of view (for example, the need to invest in updated accounting systems infrastructure, or the need to improve a company's existing controls)

- ■ To *sell* services to an existing or potential client

To illustrate the role of presentations in practice, assume for a moment that the FASB has just issued a new accounting standard that has wide-ranging impacts on a corporation with multiple business units. Accountants may make the following presentations related to the new standard, just to name a few:

Prior to issuance of the standard, the company's auditors might offer a training course to corporate and business unit accountants, broadly explaining the expected requirements of the standard and offering the help of their national office and advisory practice to assist with complex issues.

Prior to and following issuance of the standard, the accounting policy group, which manages the project rollout, might arrange conference calls with corporate accountants in each business unit (OpCo) who will: (1) identify specific areas of impact, and (2) assist in implementing changes in these areas.

Next, the controller's group might present and explain the new standard to company management, describe areas of expected impact to the company, and lay out the timeline for adoption and future touchpoints with management.

In addition,

- ■ The company's accounting policy group might present (and discuss) implications of the standard with other potentially affected functions, such as: information technology, risk, strategy, operations, finance, and investor relations.

- ■ Then, as implementation progresses, the project manager, along with corporate accountants managing aspects of the implementation, might present key accounting judgments to company management, including the chief financial officer (CFO).

As you can see, presentations can be given in a range of settings and to a variety of audiences. Given this, it is very likely that *you* will be involved—at some point—in giving or preparing a presentation.

Presentation Formats

By now, I'm sure you're used to the standard classroom format for presentations: A group of three to five students stands in the front of the class, presenting a case with the help of PowerPoint slides.

This format is used for good reason. It helps you become accustomed to *standing and presenting* in front of a group, which is one presentation format that you will likely use in practice. This format can be useful for teaching something to a group, proposing changes to existing practices, or selling a service.

Other formats that you may encounter in practice include presenting in a *boardroom setting*, where the discussion takes place around a table. This format might be used if you are discussing preliminary accounting judgments with management, your auditors, or your peers.

Or, the presentation could occur via *phone or online conference call* (like a WebEx). This format is often used to communicate with team members or clients who work at different locations.

No matter the format, the key ingredients for a great presentation are relatively constant—you must have great content and a great delivery.

In what professional (or, if not, academic) circumstances have you delivered a presentation, or presented the results of your research informally? What was the format, and who was your audience?

Now
YOU
Try
13.1

_____

_____

_____

As a professional, it may feel like you're being punished when you're asked to present in front of others. However, you are actually being given an opportunity. Succeed at this presentation, and you'll create a strong impression on your supervisors and peers that can open doors to future opportunities.

TIP from the Trenches

What Are The Qualities Of A Great Presentation?

Broadly speaking, a great presentation includes the following elements:

1. Content that is well-researched, useful, and presented in a logical order
2. Speakers who engage the audience, and who are well-rehearsed
3. Speakers who have thought beyond the case facts
4. When applicable, team members who challenge and support each other

For purposes of this chapter, we'll bucket these qualities into three main sections: (1) *creating* effective content, (2) *delivering* a high-quality presentation, and (3) considerations for those working in groups.

One other key element, which applies to every item on this list, is *preparation, preparation, preparation*. The more completely you prepare for your presentation, the more successful it will likely be.

CREATING EFFECTIVE CONTENT

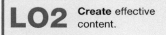

LO2 Create effective content.

Generally speaking, your presentation should be accompanied by materials (visual aids or handouts) that reinforce key points for your audience. The process for creating effective content and for creating visual aids often goes hand in hand. To that end, the following discussion encompasses both how to plan content as well as how to prepare effective visual aids. We'll focus on PowerPoint; however, the concepts described herein can also extend to other presentation media.

The first step in creating effective content is to *picture your audience*. Are you presenting to a class of your peers, who share your base level of accounting knowledge? Or are you communicating accounting systems needs to your company's IT director? Keep this image of your audience in mind as you create your content; these are the people you must reach.

Next, work to fully *understand* the case facts, the questions at hand, available alternatives, and your conclusion. If your presentation involves an accounting issue, one of the best ways to gain this understanding is to first prepare an accounting issues memo. The writing process alone can cause you to consider the issue more carefully. However, if a full memo is not required (such as by your supervisor or instructor) prior to your presentation, you might still create an *outline* of how you would document the issue in order to stimulate this thinking process.

You're now ready to start drafting your slides. Your first lesson: *Don't re-create the wheel*. If you can, start with an existing slide deck used for a past or related presentation in your company, then work from there. In doing so, take note of the level of detail on the slides, how the slides are organized, and any bullet, font, or numbering conventions. (More on bullets and font later.)

Next, create a *title slide* and *agenda slide* for your presentation, which will serve as a rough draft outline for your presentation, then insert *placeholders for individual slides* that follow the order of this outline. The following TIP emphasizes the importance of agenda slides.

> [**TIP**] from the Trenches
>
> Early in my career, I was counseled to *never call a meeting without having an agenda prepared*. Having an agenda shows that your meeting has a valid purpose, and that the meeting is organized. In short, an agenda shows respect for your participants' time.
>
> The same principle holds true for leading a presentation: Always share your agenda with attendees. This brief step shows respect for your colleagues, clearly prepares them for what's to come, and demonstrates to them that you've been thoughtful in organizing the presentation.

As you develop the outline (agenda) for your presentation, don't feel that you must stick absolutely to the research questions you were assigned. Rather, take a step back and ask yourself:

How can I organize this information so that it is most clear to my audience?

Consider for a moment the following TIP regarding organizing your presentation.

> [**TIP**] from the Trenches
>
> A common pitfall I see with my students is organizing their entire case presentation around the set of case study questions they were given. The case study questions aren't, in all cases, the most logical order for a presentation. Perhaps your audience requires additional context, or background understanding, of the case facts or accounting principles to be applied. Or perhaps the steps you took to analyze the issue offer a more logical path than the questions you were given.
>
> Think outside the box. Organize your presentation in a way that will be most understandable to your audience.

Once you've outlined the topics that you plan to cover (that is, you now have a title slide, agenda slide, and placeholder slides that follow the agenda), you can begin drafting content for each slide. This content could be, for example, four bulleted speaking points per slide, or alternatively could be just a single image that you can speak about.

Next, begin writing the speaking notes that will accompany each slide, refining your draft slide content as you go.

There is some debate in practice about how much detail should be included on each slide. Inspirational talks—such as TED Talks videos—often include only a single image or phrase on each slide. Accounting research slides presented to a CFO, on the other hand, might include detailed bullets and key excerpts from the applicable guidance.

Ultimately, the amount of information you include on each slide will likely be driven by your organization (company or accounting firm), and by the setting in which you will deliver the presentation. So it's critical that your first step in laying out your slides is to look for examples of other presentations given by peers or leadership in your organization. More on slide detail in a moment.

If you do include images (pictures) in your presentation, use *high-quality images* (e.g., jpg file types), rather than hokey cartoon clip art. Check out istockphoto.com for ideas. Don't include images if doing so is inconsistent with your firm's style.

Now
YOU
Try
13.2

1. Recap the step-by-step process described for preparing slides and speaking notes, starting with the first lesson: *Don't re-create the wheel.*

   _____

   _____

   _____

2. Now think: Have you ever been in the audience when a presenter is talking, but you're having trouble deciding whether to listen or whether to read what is on the presenter's slides? As an audience member, you might have bounced between listening and reading, concerned that you could miss out on important information. What suggestions would you make to the presenter in this scenario?

   _____

   _____

   _____

Find Ways to Make the Information Resonate

As you create content and speaking notes for your slides, be creative in finding ways to make the information resonate with your audience. Ask yourself:

- Can I draw a **transaction structure picture** (see Chapter 4), or a **timeline**, to enhance the facts/background information that I present in my slides?
- If numbers are being presented, can I include a **graph** or other visual depiction of the numbers?
- When presenting my accounting analysis, would **key excerpts** from the guidance help my audience have a clearer picture of the issues?
- Can I share a **personal anecdote** that will help my audience connect with this information?
- Can I involve my audience by **asking them a question** during the presentation?
- Can I bring in an **example from practice** that illustrates the concepts related to my case?

One of the preceding bullets suggests working in a personal anecdote when possible. Audiences engage with the speaker more, and get emotionally invested, when listening to a story. Ask yourself: Can I tell a personal story that relates to this topic, and that will help deliver my message?

Tell only true stories that come from your own experience or from reliable sources (such as a trusted news source). Don't tell a story that could cause you to lose credibility with your audience!

Another aspect of making content resonate is that it should be *tailored to your audience*. Don't present the broad, boilerplate requirements of a new accounting standard to a client whose adoption of the guidance is already well under way. Rather, perhaps a presentation on "common implementation issues our national office has consulted on" would be more meaningful.

Finally, if you are presenting to a classroom of your peers, a key goal of your presentation should always be to *teach your peers*. Act as though your peers will be tested on the information you are presenting, and make the concepts as understandable as you can. According to one field test, students' test results improved once their peers focused on *teaching* as a key goal of their presentations.[1] With this goal in mind, you should take creative license to present in a way that reaches your peers.

Now
YOU
Try
13.3

1. In what circumstances would you imagine that a picture or timeline could assist in presenting the facts or background of a transaction?

    _____

    _____

2. Where (or how) might you look for examples from practice that illustrate the concepts involved in your case?

    _____

    _____

How Much Detail Should I Include in My Slides?

The amount of detail you include in your slides will be driven primarily by the size of your audience, and by your firm's existing practices.

Picture yourself sitting in an audit committee meeting, around a table. Your audience is somewhere between 6 and 25 people. Each person at the table has a copy of the slide deck, and critical accounting judgments are being discussed. The people at the table need enough detail that they can choose to agree or disagree with the accounting judgments at hand.

In this case, the slides depicted in Figure 13-1 might be appropriate. In the first slide (at left), the presenter has highlighted in bold the indicators of gross reporting that he believes are relevant to the accounting issue, and that he plans to discuss further in the slides that follow. The slide at right presents a key excerpt from the guidance that will help the audit committee members assess the reasonableness of the judgment made for one of these indicators. The presenter has highlighted in bold the words from the excerpt that he believes are critical to the analysis.

Figure 13-1

Sample slides that could be handed out, and presented from, in a small-group setting

INDICATORS OF GROSS REPORTING

1) The Entity is the Primary Obligor in the Arrangement
2) The Entity Has General Inventory Risk—Before Customer Order is Placed or Upon Customer Return
3) **The Entity Has Latitude in Establishing Price**
4) The Entity Changes the Product or Performs Part of the Service
5) **The Entity Has Discretion in Supplier Selection**
6) The Entity is Involved in the Determination of Product or Service Specifications
7) The Entity Has Physical Loss Inventory Risk—After Customer Order or During Shipping
8) **The Entity Has Credit Risk**

Source: ASC 605-45 (Revenue Recognition—Principal Agent Considerations)

CREDIT RISK

The Entity Has Credit Risk
45-13   If an entity assumes credit risk for the amount billed to the customer, that fact may provide weaker evidence that the entity has risks and rewards as a principal in the transaction and, therefore, that it should record revenue gross for that amount. **Credit risk exists if an entity is responsible for collecting the sales price from a customer but must pay the amount owed to a supplier after the supplier performs, regardless of whether the sales price is fully collected.** [Emphasis added]

Analysis: This indicator of gross reporting is met, because the company must pay its supplier regardless of whether it collects from customers.

---

[1] Alford, DiMattia, Hill, & Stevens. 2011. A Series of Revenue Recognition Research Cases Using the Codification. *Issues in Accounting Education* 26 (3): 618.

If you do include this level of detail on your slides (e.g., actual excerpts), be careful to choose only the most relevant excerpts that you think will enhance your audience's understanding of the research issue. If it makes sense to do so, present parts of the quote that you plan to read aloud in bold, to draw attention to this information. Remember that if you add bold emphasis to an excerpt, you should write "[Emphasis Added]" after the quote.

On the other hand, imagine that you are presenting a case to your peers, who do not have a copy of your slide deck. There are 40 students in your class. In this case, your slides will need to include less detail, because your peers will otherwise struggle to read along on your slides while you speak. These students need to learn from your presentation, but they will not be held accountable for the reasonableness of your judgments. Here, you need to focus more on teaching *concepts*, and less on reading *excerpts*. Too much detail in this setting will detract from your presentation.

In this case, the slides shown in Figure 13-2 would be appropriate.

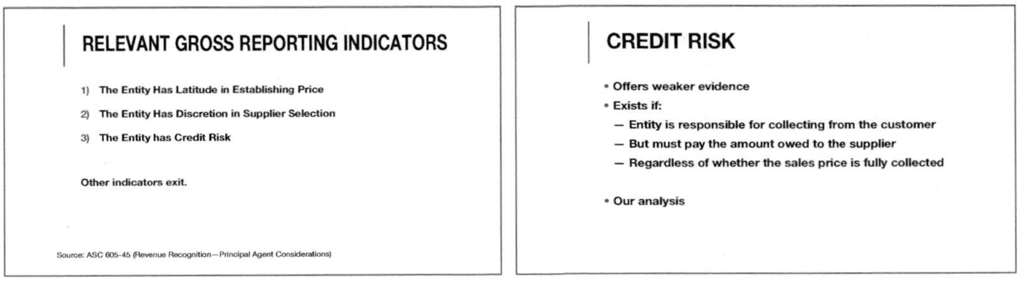

Figure 13-2

Sample slides that could be shown to a larger audience

RELEVANT GROSS REPORTING INDICATORS	CREDIT RISK
1) The Entity Has Latitude in Establishing Price	• Offers weaker evidence
2) The Entity Has Discretion in Supplier Selection	• Exists if:
3) The Entity has Credit Risk	— Entity is responsible for collecting from the customer
	— But must pay the amount owed to the supplier
Other indicators exit.	— Regardless of whether the sales price is fully collected
	• Our analysis
Source: ASC 605-45 (Revenue Recognition—Principal Agent Considerations)	

Considering these examples, take a shot at the following **Now YOU Try**.

Now YOU Try 13.4

1. Take a look at the two preceding figures. Contrast the discussion of credit risk in Figure 13-1 with the discussion in Figure 13-2.

   _____

   _____

2. In your own words, explain why you think a difference in the level of detail is warranted for these slides.

   _____

   _____

   _____

3. Now imagine that you are presenting to 500 people in an auditorium, and your prepared slides will appear on a projection screen. In this case, what level of slide detail do you think is appropriate? Explain.

   _____

   _____

   _____

To the extent that you do incorporate guidance excerpts in your presentation, remember the following tips:

■ Only include Codification excerpts to the extent that they are valuable to the audience's understanding of the accounting analysis you performed.

■ Be highly selective in choosing only the most relevant guidance, and limit the amount of text included in excerpts. (Consider using ellipses . . . to cut out less relevant parts of a paragraph.)

■ Bold key passages to help your audience understand your areas of focus in reviewing the guidance.

All of this being said, never put so much information on the slides that your role as a presenter is moot. No one in the audience wants to hear you read from a slide word for word!

[**TIP**] from the Trenches

> If the slides you've prepared are so detailed that your audience will be tempted to read while you speak, take this as a sign that you should distribute your slide deck to audience members in advance of the meeting. This allows your audience to come to the meeting prepared to listen and offer constructive feedback on or questions about your presentation.

Let's look next at a few style points related to your slides.

Does Font Choice Matter?

The font chosen for your presentation should more or less be consistent across all slides. That said, there are different schools of thought on which font to choose; some argue that slide decks should use only **sans serif** fonts, which have cleaner breaks between letters and thus are more visible to audience members in the back of the room.

Figure 13-3 depicts a **serif** font, Times New Roman (at left). Notice the small lines ("serifs") extending off of each letter. Arial (at right) is a sans serif font, which lacks these small connector lines.

| Figure 13-3 |

Sample serif and sans serif fonts

Sample Serif font

AaBbCc

Sample Sans Serif font

AaBbCc

On the other hand, visiting Big Four professionals often come in and present to our students using standard firm templates that feature serif fonts! The bottom line is to *follow the conventions expected for your classroom or firm*.

It *is*, however, important to consider font size. If your slides will be shown on a projector, aim for a font size large enough that people in the back of the room can read the slide.

Use Consistent Bullet Style

Bullet style should be consistent from slide to slide. Have a rule that you follow across slides, for example:

- Level 1 bullets are black circles. Text at this level is generally 26 pt.
  - Level 2 bullets are open circles. Text at this level is generally 22 pt.
    - Level 3 bullets are dashes. Text at this level is generally 18 pt.

The above is not a strict rule. The point here is that you should utilize a *uniform* style across slides within your presentation. If you've started with an existing slide deck from your firm, stay consistent with the firm's style for presenting bullets.

Additionally, the sentence structure used within bullets should be consistent, as illustrated in the following **Now YOU Try**.

Explain what's wrong with the following set of bullets.

Jack is happy because

      ○ His new car is more fuel efficient than his last car,

      ○ The Red Sox won the World Series, and

      ○ Ice cream sundaes.

_____

_____

_____

Now
YOU
Try
13.5

This example is a bit goofy, but I think you get the point.

Edit Your Presentation

Finally, before delivering your presentation (or sending it off), print and re-read your slides. Check for:

- Spelling and grammar (verbs should flow with nouns)
- Punctuation—consistent within each list; in other words, all bullets should either have periods at the end or not.
- Consistent bullet style within and across slides (e.g., dot, dash, open circle), and consistent sentence structure for same-level bullets
- Consistent font used for all slides
- Type size—consistent (within each slide) for bullets of the same level

Typos are unprofessional. Don't undermine all of your effort and preparation by having noticeable errors or inconsistencies in your slides.

Now that your slides and content are all set, let's talk about how to *deliver* a great presentation.

DELIVERING A HIGH-QUALITY PRESENTATION

Let's assume that a high-quality presentation is characterized by being accurate, informative, and engaging. The previous section of this chapter discussed how to create engaging *content*. Now, let's discuss how you can be an engaging *speaker*.

LO3 Know what it takes to **deliver** a high-quality presentation.

First and foremost, it's important as a presenter that you care about the topic you are presenting. Passionate speakers are more likely to engage the audience than speakers who lack enthusiasm about their topic.

But what if the information you are presenting is not interesting? Chances are, if you think the content is boring, your audience will agree. Find ways to bring the topic alive. Think and think about ways to make the topic resonate—is it through telling related stories? Through visual aids? Through questions to your audience? Your job as the speaker is to make this content meaningful for your audience, so think carefully about how to make this happen. If needed, go back and revise your slides to incorporate content that will engage the audience.

Tips for Powerful Body Language

Let's talk about your body language when presenting. Here are a few do's and don'ts, as illustrated in Figure 13-4.

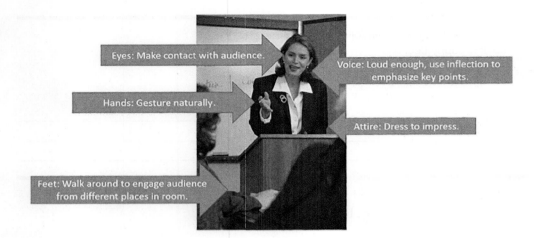

Figure 13-4

Using body language to engage the audience

Do:

- Make **eye contact** with your audience.
- **Speak loudly** enough that people in the back row can hear you.
- **Speak with inflection**, changing your voice and tone to emphasize key points.
- Incorporate **hand gestures**, also to emphasize key points.
- **Move**. Periodically change where you are speaking from.

Don't:

- **Read** your presentation (either from note cards, or from your PowerPoint slides).
- Let the audience see that you are **scared**. Prepare, prepare, prepare, and then if you are still nervous, fake confidence.
- **Lean** on walls or the podium. (*Do:* Stand up tall.)
- **Chew gum** while presenting.

To deliver a great presentation, prepare for the presentation by *practicing*. Practice not only your spoken words, but also your use of eye contact, movement, and tone of voice.

Then, as you present, watch to see how the audience reacts to the information you're sharing. Look for cues from them that they are able to follow along. If the audience appears lost, this may indicate that you should slow down and take more time to explain your topic. If the audience seems disinterested, try to engage them by ramping up your own enthusiasm for the topic. At a minimum, if you've lost your audience, consider stepping out from behind the podium to engage them with your body language.

[**TIP**] from the Trenches

Want to see a speaker really engage his or her audience? Watch a TED Talks video (Google: "best TED Talks"). Notice the subtle ways these speakers connect with the audience: through voice inflection, pauses, hand gestures, and a genuine interest in the topic. Most of all, notice the level of preparation. One highly successful TED speaker (Dr. Bolte-Taylor: "My Stroke of Insight") reportedly rehearsed her talk 200 times before delivering it.

[Now **YOU** Try]

13.6

1. Think of a presentation you've observed that has really impressed you. Describe the presentation, and explain what the speaker did to engage you in the topic.

_____

_____

_____

_____

2. Now, think about a presentation you've given that didn't go so well. What were some of the things you might have done differently, if you could do it over?

_____

_____

_____

_____

3. Finally, think about the best presentation you've ever given. What did you do well?

_____

_____

_____

_____

Are Note Cards Okay to Use? Yes, but don't read from them. When rehearsing your presentation, practice referring quickly to your notes so they are familiar to you when it's show time.

   On the other side of the coin, I've had students attempt to memorize their presentations then freeze in the moment. Sometimes holding note cards gives you confidence, even if you've rehearsed enough that you don't end up using them.

[**TIP**] from the Trenches

What If You Have a Fear of Presenting?

There's a great TED Talk that speaks to this issue, too. Look up Amy Cuddy's talk on body language. She suggests striking a power pose (think: hands on hips) for two minutes before the situation that intimidates you, arguing that this pose can improve your confidence, as well as how you are perceived by the audience.

Think beyond the Case Facts

Like it or not, as a presenter you are holding yourself out as an expert on your particular case or topic. So it's not enough to limit your research to understanding the case questions. Rather, if your issue relates to recognition, as a presenter you should be prepared to speak about measurement, disclosure, SEC reporting, and any other issues that could relate to your topic. Arm yourself with knowledge, so that you are prepared to defend or further elaborate upon your research and conclusions.

   In other words, even if your case focuses on two narrow questions, as a presenter you should be prepared to speak about issues beyond those two questions. Figure 13-5 illustrates this point.

Figure 13-5

Be prepared to discuss issues and concepts beyond your limited-scope research questions

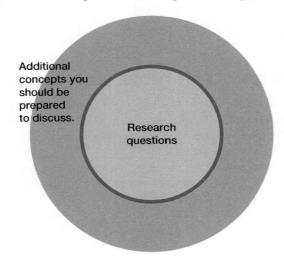

Also, seek to understand the *underlying concepts* related to your issue. Take an accounting example: If your topic relates to nonmonetary exchanges, consider:

- What does *commercial substance* really mean? What are the implications of this concept?
- Do I understand (and am I prepared to explain) the difference between *monetary* and *nonmonetary transactions*?
- Why might an investor care about the disclosures that are required for this topic?
- What additional examples can I share with my peers to further illustrate these concepts?

As an example of the last bullet, I once had a presenting team bring two different candies (Snickers and Skittles) to class to demonstrate that exchanging these candy varieties *has* commercial substance because individuals might value them differently (someone might like one candy more than the other). It was clear that the team thought outside of the box in considering what this term means.

Anticipate questions that might stem from the accounting concepts, or the facts, in your case. Be prepared for "what if" questions, for example:

- *What if* the amount of boot (cash exchanged) was changed slightly?
- *What if* the assets exchanged were different?
- *What if*, instead of swapping assets, one company received equity in the other company?

As you think through possible questions, consider going back to your slide deck to incorporate *basket slides* that could assist in responding to anticipated Q&As. The term *basket slides* refers to slides at the end of your deck that anticipate possible audience questions, but that are not part of the prepared remarks that you deliver.

What Should You Wear?

I know the expectations for attire can vary by presentation, by firm, and by audience. But in all cases, I'd ask you to keep in mind something that my mom always told me: *When in doubt, over-dress.* You generally can't go wrong, when delivering a presentation, by showing up in professional attire.

[**TIP**] from the Trenches

A former supervisor of mine was truly on the fast-track, moving from a corporate manager position, to director, to vice president within only a handful of years. Her work ethic certainly played a major role in this, but I'll focus on another habit for purposes of this discussion: Nearly every day, she wore professional attire to work. She wanted to project herself as a professional, no matter with whom she met that day. (Plus, working in accounting policy is a great way to have face time with management.) With this attire, she was prepared to step into the C-suite at a moment's notice.

CONSIDERATIONS FOR THOSE WORKING IN A GROUP

LO4 Work effectively in a team to create and deliver presentations.

Imagine for a moment that you and four other members from your advisory services practice have 30 minutes on the calendar with a potential client. You're trying to sell them on your firm's mergers and acquisitions support services, and the potential fees from this engagement could be significant.

Would you work together to develop a presentation, or each take one slide and go your separate ways? Would you each focus on your own notes only, or would you help one another develop the strongest presentation possible?

The truth is that, in practice, you have to be sure your entire team is strong before delivering a presentation. If one member of your team is weak, it's your job as a team to help him or her improve. You can't risk turning off the client by having a member of your team be underprepared. Some other firm will come along and offer a more cohesive product that impresses the client more.

The most effective group presentations are ones where *each group member believes that he or she is responsible for the quality of the whole presentation, not just his or her own part.*

Ideally, your team will have the time and resources to follow these steps (or a variation thereof) to create a successful group presentation:

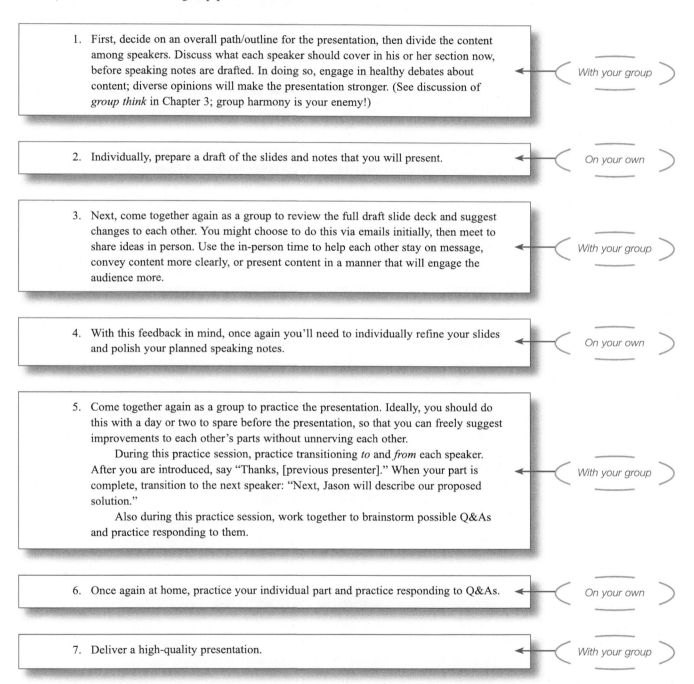

1. First, decide on an overall path/outline for the presentation, then divide the content among speakers. Discuss what each speaker should cover in his or her section now, before speaking notes are drafted. In doing so, engage in healthy debates about content; diverse opinions will make the presentation stronger. (See discussion of *group think* in Chapter 3; group harmony is your enemy!)

   With your group

2. Individually, prepare a draft of the slides and notes that you will present.

   On your own

3. Next, come together again as a group to review the full draft slide deck and suggest changes to each other. You might choose to do this via emails initially, then meet to share ideas in person. Use the in-person time to help each other stay on message, convey content more clearly, or present content in a manner that will engage the audience more.

   With your group

4. With this feedback in mind, once again you'll need to individually refine your slides and polish your planned speaking notes.

   On your own

5. Come together again as a group to practice the presentation. Ideally, you should do this with a day or two to spare before the presentation, so that you can freely suggest improvements to each other's parts without unnerving each other.

   During this practice session, practice transitioning *to* and *from* each speaker. After you are introduced, say "Thanks, [previous presenter]." When your part is complete, transition to the next speaker: "Next, Jason will describe our proposed solution."

   Also during this practice session, work together to brainstorm possible Q&As and practice responding to them.

   With your group

6. Once again at home, practice your individual part and practice responding to Q&As.

   On your own

7. Deliver a high-quality presentation.

   With your group

On presentation day, plan to be "on" at all times while your team is presenting. Nod your head to show agreement with key points that members of your team make. Alternate your gaze between acknowledging your fellow speakers and connecting with the audience. Among other benefits, staying engaged will allow you to jump in as needed to help a team member who stumbles or needs support.

[TIP] from the Trenches

In a group presentation, it's very common for team members to develop an outline then to divvy up slides to the person who will present that section. Doing so is fine, but it's also critical for *every group member to review the full presentation* to improve the presentation's consistency and to add value to each other's parts. Remember: *You are responsible for the quality of the whole presentation, not just your own part.*

What If a Member of My Group Is a Non-native English Speaker?
If a member of your group speaks English as a second language, and if you think he or she could benefit from some coaching (on pronunciation, word choice, or voice projection), ask if he or she is open to some feedback. It could be a win-win.

[Now **YOU** Try 13.7]

Imagine that you have just delivered a group presentation and received constructive criticism from your instructor that your group could have performed better. What specific aspect of your presentation do you think your instructor might have commented on? How could you have improved this?

(In this exercise, you're being asked to think ahead to the potential weaknesses your group is at risk of exhibiting.)

_____

_____

_____

_____

[TIP] from the Trenches

Don't be afraid to create healthy friction within your team. Some of the worst presentations I've observed are those where the teams got along the best. Respectfully challenge each other's ideas, content, and presentation styles, in order to create the best possible presentation. Don't settle for mediocre work just because you're in a group.

CHAPTER SUMMARY

This chapter described strategies for creating and delivering effective oral presentations, including tips for creating effective content, for engaging your audience, for delivering your message, and for working with a team. Practice and refine these skills, and you can add yet another talent to your resume: strong presentation skills.

REVIEW QUESTIONS

1. Describe three possible reasons for which a presentation might be given in practice.
2. What are three possible formats, or settings, for delivery of a presentation?
3. What is the first step involved in creating effective content?
4. Is it necessary to write an accounting memo before delivering a presentation on an accounting issue? Explain.
5. Explain what is meant by the advice: *Don't recreate the wheel.*
6. Why does the author suggest including an agenda slide each time you deliver a presentation?

7. True or false: Your presentation should generally be organized around the case questions as they were given to you.

8. To make your content resonate with the audience, what might you consider including in your slides to enhance your delivery of each of the following:
   a. Background/Facts
   b. Numbers
   c. Dates
   d. Accounting guidance

9. Differentiate between the amount of detail your slides might include if you are presenting to an audit committee (in a boardroom setting with 15 people) versus if you are standing and presenting to a group of 40 of your peers. Why might a difference in detail be appropriate?

10. Complete the following sentence: If your slides are so detailed that your audience will be tempted to read them while you speak, consider _____.

11. Which font style tends to be easier for an audience to read from far away: serif, or sans serif? Explain.

12. What are two things you should check for when reviewing your slides for possible editing errors?

13. Is it acceptable to use notecards when delivering a presentation? Explain.

14. In what circumstances might a *power pose* be useful to strike before a presentation?

15. Name two suggestions described for *thinking beyond the case facts*.

16. Complete the following sentence: The most effective group presentations are ones where each group member believes _____.

EXERCISES

1. Perform a Google search for a big four slide deck focused on the revised revenue standard (e.g., "KPMG powerpoint revenue standard," or something similar). The Google results page often shows the file type first (look for *ppt*). Then, answer the following:
   a. Describe the firm name, date of deck, and purpose/title of the presentation.
   b. Who does it appear the audience for this presentation is?
   c. Does the deck include an agenda slide?
   d. What level of detail is included in the slides? In what presentation settings might this level of detail be most appropriate?
   e. What font style is used (e.g., a serif font? sans serif?)
   f. Are pictures or graphics included, and for what purpose?
   g. What is one strength of these slides? One possible weakness?

2. Describe your personal biggest challenge when delivering presentations. Did this chapter address that challenge, and what tips did it offer?

3. A company is contemplating the acquisition of a peer company in its industry and is performing its initial, internal research to determine the benefits, costs, and potential effects of the merger. Brainstorm four possible presentations that might occur with stakeholders within or outside of the company. Describe the possible setting and purpose of each meeting.

4. Imagine you are presenting an accounting issue to a class of your peers. The issue is whether a company must record a contingent liability for a patent infringement lawsuit filed by a competitor. Prepare a draft agenda (using bullet points) for this hypothetical presentation.

5. Now imagine that you are presenting the same issue to students in an MBA program, who do not have a deep accounting background. Name three ways in which the focus, delivery, or content of your presentation might change in light of this audience.

6. Strike a power pose for two minutes. Describe how you feel after doing this.

7. Brainstorm two ways that you can improve the quality of your *group's* final product and delivery, in circumstances where you are assigned to present with a team.

8. Now brainstorm how (and when) you will communicate these suggested improvements to your group.

9. You are delivering a presentation, and the subject matter concerns whether a company should report revenues on a gross or net basis. *Thinking beyond the case facts*, list four other considerations you should be prepared to address (such as during Q&A) or background understanding you should gain before presenting.

10. You are delivering a presentation, and the subject matter concerns whether a company should report convertible debt simply as a liability, or whether embedded features (like the conversion option) in the debt should be separately accounted for as derivatives. *Thinking beyond the case facts*, list four other considerations you should be prepared to address (such as during Q&A) or background understanding you should gain before presenting.

CASE STUDY QUESTIONS

13.1   **Create a Team Contract** Work with your team to develop a one-page outline (or a contract, of sorts) detailing how you plan to work together on this project. Comment on your expectations for giving each other constructive feedback. Discuss how you will communicate as a group if a team member is not pulling his or her weight.

13.2   **Watching and Learning from Great Presenters** Watch a TED Talks video of your choice—pick any topic that you find interesting. Prepare a half-page written summary describing: (1) The topic (what was the talk about?), and (2) Was the presenter effective? Give specific feedback on what made the presentation engaging.

13.3   **Practice Delivering the Facts** Videotape yourself walking through the facts of the Energy Works scenario introduced in Chapters 3 and 4. Prepare a list of four areas where your delivery could be improved. Then videotape yourself trying it again. Alternatively, work with a peer to practice delivering the facts, and provide each other with written constructive feedback.

Chapter **14**

Staying Current with Emerging Accounting Guidance

Good news: An effort as simple as *staying current* can help to fast-track your career.

Imagine for a moment Jen, a staff auditor, who is sitting at a picnic table in a cramped room at her client's site. Today, for the first time, Jen will meet the engagement partner, who is dropping in to meet with the client. He will be in town for only a few hours, then he's off to meet with another client.

While the partner is there, Jen receives an email alert: "FASB issues long-awaited lease accounting standard."

Jen turns to the partner and says: "Oh, did you see? The FASB's new lease accounting standard was just issued. This will affect our client's accounting for equipment and vehicle leases. Maybe you can mention this during your meeting today."

Suddenly, the partner notices a few things about Jen:

First: Jen is not just any staff auditor. She is a staff auditor who *takes the initiative to stay current*.

Second: Jen has the client's interests in mind, and she is thoughtful in considering how emerging guidance will affect *this* client specifically.

Continued

Continued

Learning Objectives

After reading this chapter and performing the exercises herein, you will be able to

1. **Understand** the professional advantages of staying current.

2. **Describe,** generally, the standard setters' "due process" for issuing new guidance.

3. **Identify**—and subscribe to—useful resources for staying current.

Third: Jen has effective *communication skills*. Rather than spending the partner's time on small talk, she provided him with information that was clear, succinct, and useful to his meeting with the client.

Jen may not realize it yet, but this simple action will have a lasting impact on the partner's impression of her. Before long, he will begin to request her services on other engagements and will trust her with increasing amounts of responsibility. *This* is how successful careers begin.

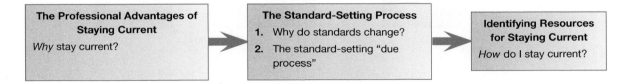

Organization of This Chapter

Accounting research is dynamic. This chapter is designed to teach you the importance of staying informed as the rules for our profession continually change. This chapter will also explain why standards change, standard setters' processes for revising standards, and what you can do to stay current.

The chapter does not provide an exhaustive explanation of standard setting; rather, it is intended to introduce the process and provide you with a general feel for how new guidance is established.

Additionally, this chapter does not present "current events" in standard setting, given how rapidly our profession can change. However, it will provide you with the tools necessary to take on this challenge yourself.

THE PROFESSIONAL ADVANTAGES OF STAYING CURRENT

LO1 **Understand** the professional advantages of staying current.

What does it mean to *stay current*? It means recognizing that accounting standards are continually changing and making a conscious effort to keep up. This phenomenon of changing standards is not limited to just accounting, however; auditing and ethical standards, regulatory requirements, and international requirements are equally dynamic. By the time you enter the workforce, many of the textbooks that you learned from in school will already be outdated. Staying current involves monitoring not only *final* changes to existing rules, but also being aware of *emerging* guidance that is under development.

Professionals in a variety of roles have the responsibility to stay current, as illustrated in Figure 14-1.

Figure 14-1

Examples of professionals who monitor emerging guidance

Why I Monitor Emerging Guidance

- I need to ensure that my clients **comply** with all newly effective guidance.
- It's also important to inform my clients about **emerging** changes in standards.
- Finally, my firm may choose to **comment** on standards being developed.

Auditor

- **I am expected** to inform management about possible effects of emerging guidance, including changes to:
  - **Budgets** and forecasts,
  - **Systems** requirements,
  - Current **transaction accounting**.
- Periodically, my company submits **comment letters** to the FASB.
- We must **disclose impacts** of issued, but not yet effective, guidance.

Corporate Accountant

- I actively **communicate to the FASB** information that is most useful to my analysis of financial statements.
- As new requirements become effective, I may need to **adjust my model** for analyzing financial statements.

Analyst/ Investor

Of course, the professionals depicted in Figure 14-1 are not the only individuals who monitor emerging guidance. Parties ranging from regulators to attorneys to academics—to the extent they are involved in applying or interpreting accounting standards—have an interest in staying current.

At what level of your career should you be expected to monitor emerging guidance? The opening scenario of this chapter says it all. While some view "emerging accounting" as a partner- or director-level matter, the truth is that professionals at all levels will see significant advantages in their careers from staying current.

The flip side is also true: Imagine the loss of trust that could occur if you, an auditor onsite daily with a client, let an important emerging guidance topic (with relevance to that client) slip by without informing your client that it is out there. *As an auditor, there is a professional expectation that you will help the client stay informed about changes in accounting requirements.* Having conversations with your client, early on, about the impacts of emerging guidance can also minimize differences of opinion later regarding the need to apply, or method of applying, new standards.

Of course, financial statement preparers understand that complying with guidance requirements and monitoring changes is *their own responsibility*; however, preparers appreciate when their auditors can leverage firm resources to share news and insights on emerging issues.

You'll have to weigh the advantages of staying current "on work time" versus the advantages of printing articles to read on your train ride home, or while waiting at the dentist's office. Judge this based on your firm's culture; if reading on the clock is acceptable and expected, go for it. If not, invest in this professional development time after hours.

$$\left[\text{TIP} \right] \begin{array}{l} \text{from the} \\ \textbf{Trenches} \end{array}$$

During my career, I was given the advice: "Act like the level you want to be." If a staff accountant starts to perform at a senior level, pretty soon supervisors will notice this, and the individual will be promoted.

Your engagement manager, senior manager, and partner stay informed about emerging issues in the profession; there's no reason you as a first-year associate cannot also be informed. Doing so will actually lighten their load, as they will be able to request your help in monitoring changes to standards and summarizing possible impacts to your clients. Soon, you'll be invited to meetings where these topics are discussed with the client. See? Act like the level you want to be.

$$\begin{array}{c} \text{Now} \\ \left[\textbf{YOU} \right] \\ \text{Try} \\ \textbf{14.1} \end{array}$$

Think for a moment: From your current vantage point (as a student or professional), what advantages might you expect to receive from making an effort to stay current?

_____

_____

_____

THE STANDARD-SETTING PROCESS

Why Do Accounting Standards Change?

An accounting standard setter's decision to revise existing guidance, or to issue new guidance, may be driven by a number of considerations. These include, for example,

LO2 **Describe**, generally, the standard setters' "due process" for issuing new guidance.

- *Practitioners, such as preparers or auditors*, may express concern that existing requirements are unclear, and may request clarification from the standard setter. This can result in changes to, or interpretations of, existing guidance.

- *Simplification* of complex requirements—to reduce the cost and complexity of financial reporting—is a current area of focus for the FASB.

- *Investors and analysts* might drive the request for changes, concerned that existing reporting or disclosure requirements do not provide sufficient, useful information for decision making.

- As *new types of transactions* emerge, standard setters must keep pace, issuing guidance that appropriately reflects the economics of these activities. For example, mortgage securitizations, repurchase financing transactions, and hedge transactions were all—at one point— viewed as "new" transactions that required standard setters' consideration.

- *Standard setters* are also trying to move away from so-called "bright lines" and toward "objectives-based" guidance that places increased emphasis on professional judgment. Certain standards have become infamous for their use of bright lines, such as the "75% and 90%" tests for lease classification, and the now-superseded rules for Qualifying Special Purpose Entity (QSPE) accounting. In both cases, companies have been known to structure transactions around these rules to achieve a desired accounting result.

- *Convergence with international standard setters* has historically been another objective of standard-setting projects. For example, standard setters in India and China are currently working to converge their standards with IFRS. In the United States, however, convergence is no longer a primary focus of current standard-setting projects.

Often, standard-setting projects are intended to achieve several of these objectives at the same time, such as issuing objectives-based guidance that provides useful information to analysts.

As global businesses continually evolve, and as the needs of financial statement users follow suit, expect changing standards to be a constant.

Now
YOU
Try
14.2

Of the preceding reasons described for why standards change, which of these reasons do you think were relevant to the FASB's decision to revise its revenue recognition model? Explain.

_____

_____

_____

_____

The Standard-Setting "Due Process"

Within this book, we have discussed an alphabet soup of standard setters, including the FASB, GASB, IASB, PCAOB, SEC, and so on. Each of these organizations follows an established process when seeking to make changes to its standards. This process is often referred to as the standard setter's **due process**.

While each standard setter's due process may differ slightly, these processes tend to share some common themes, as illustrated in Figure 14-2.

Figure 14-2

Typical standard-setting due process

1. Interested parties **submit agenda topics** to the Board for consideration.

   ↓

2. The Board votes on and **approves items for inclusion on its agenda**, considering pre-agenda research performed by the staff. The Board explains its rationale for topics not added.

   ↓

3. The Board has **initial deliberations** on the issue, in some cases releasing a **Preliminary Views** document or a **Discussion Paper** to solicit constituent feedback on the Board's direction.

   ↓

4. The Board meets with its working groups, advisory bodies, and other constituents through **public roundtables,** as necessary, to gather additional input on the project.

   ↓

5. After reaching tentative decisions on an issue, the Board then issues an **Exposure Draft** (i.e., a proposed standard). This is the formal vehicle for soliciting public comments on proposed guidance.*

   ↓

6. The Board reviews feedback, redeliberates, then issues a **final standard**.

   ↓

7. For major standards, a **transition resource group** of individuals such as preparers, auditors, and users meets to discuss questions related to implementation of the new standard.

   ↓

8. **Post-implementation review** activities are conducted, to understand the _implementation issues_ faced by constituents, to assess whether the standard's _objectives_ were achieved, and to understand _costs and benefits_ associated with adoption and ongoing compliance with the new standard.

* A second, and sometimes even a third, exposure draft may be necessary if significant changes are proposed following the first exposure draft.

As noted, variations of this process exist for individual standard setters. For example, in the IASB's case, after adding an item to its agenda, it must consider whether to conduct the project alone, or jointly with another standard setter.

In contrast to its "standards level" projects, the IASB also has an **annual improvements process** for making narrow-scope amendments to existing standards. Such amendments may include, for example, minor wording changes, clarifications, or the resolution of minor conflicts between standards, which do not introduce new principles or change existing principles. Annually, these collective improvements are exposed for public comment in a single exposure draft, and become effective in the following year.

Now let's consider for a moment the form that final guidance takes at the IASB and FASB. IASB projects generally result in the direct amendment or replacement of existing standards or, as necessary to address new topics, the issuance of a new standard. In contrast, FASB projects culminate in the issuance of a *nonauthoritative* Accounting Standards Update (ASU), a document that explains the reason for the project, the decisions reached, the Board's rationale, and that marks the changes—resulting from this guidance—to be made within the *authoritative* Codification.

For additional discussion of individual standard setters' processes, visit their websites and look for the "standard setting process" page, or a variation of this. This page is located, for example, on www.fasb.org under "About Us," on www.ifrs.org under "Standards Development," or on www.pcaobus.org, under "Standards."

---

1. Why do you suppose that accounting standard setters refer to their process as "due process"?

   _____

   _____

2. Contrast the process required to issue a proposed standard versus a final standard. Explain how these differ.

   _____

   _____

   _____

   _____

[Now
YOU
Try
14.3]

What does the SEC do when the FASB issues a new standard? Consider the case of the revised revenue recognition standard. For this standard, the SEC staff

- Is observing activities of the *Transition Resource Group* as it works through implementation concerns;
- Is reviewing drafts of *industry guidance* being prepared by the AICPA; and
- Has reached out to firms to review draft *firm guidance* related to the revised standard.

The SEC has indicated that its goal in these outreach efforts is to steer practice toward consistent interpretations. The SEC is also evaluating whether it will revise or rescind its own revenue recognition guidance, or issue additional guidance.

IDENTIFYING RESOURCES FOR STAYING CURRENT

Now that you understand why and how standards change, let's discuss the steps you can take to stay current.

LO3 Identify—and subscribe to—useful resources for staying current.

First, Identify the Standard Setters You Want to Monitor

Take a moment to consider which standard setters you will likely need to monitor as a professional. This will greatly depend upon what accounting environment you are working in and what your functional role is, as illustrated in Figure 14-3. The examples in Figure 14-3 are not all-inclusive.

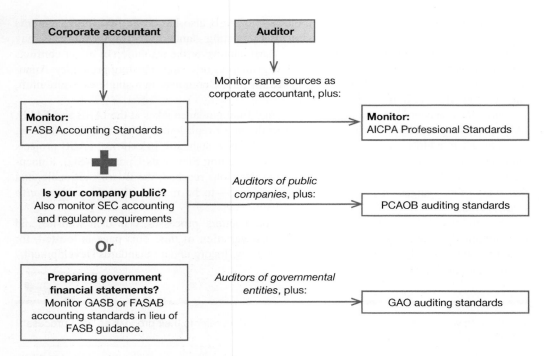

Figure 14-3

Identifying standard setters to monitor

The illustration in Figure 14-3 is meant to serve as a brainstorming tool; in reality, there is no "one size fits all" solution to the set of guidance that each professional should monitor. Also noteworthy:

- All professionals can benefit from monitoring broad business news. Newspapers such as the *Wall Street Journal* can be a useful resource for this.

- *Industry-specific publications* or trade journals are another important reference for both auditors and preparers working in a specific industry.

- Professionals applying *IFRS or international auditing standards (ISAs)* should monitor changes to those standards.

- *Tax professionals* should monitor tax law changes and developments. One way to do this is to sign up for periodic update emails through tax research services, such as RIA Checkpoint or CCH IntelliConnect. Tax professionals can also subscribe to paper or online versions of tax periodicals, such as the AICPA's *The Tax Adviser* or Tax Analysts' *Tax Notes*.

Now that you have an idea of which standards to monitor, let's look at some resources that can assist with this effort.

Next, Identify Resources for Monitoring These Standard Setters

The following discussion introduces just a few of the many resources available for monitoring changes in accounting standards. The key is to find the sources of information that are most interesting, and useful, to your needs as a professional.

Subscribe to Weekly Email Updates

If you're looking for a one-stop shop for standard-setter updates, consider subscribing to weekly emails from a big 4 or other accounting firm, or from a research provider (like CCH). Subscribers can generally choose from a menu of email options (e.g., Interested in international standards? Governmental? Webcast updates?), then will generally receive a once-per-week email summarizing key standard-setting developments. Notably, the AICPA also offers a free, daily email service (**CPA Letter Daily**), which summarizes key business and professional news with relevance to accounting professionals.

Often, these email subscriptions offer updates on a broad range of standard setters, including the FASB, PCAOB, SEC, GAO, IASB, and so on. These emails also generally include links to related publications and invitations to educational webcasts. The PwC and EY email subscriptions illustrated in the following figures, for example, generally include this content.

First, PwC's **CFO Direct** website offers updates and insights on standard-setting activities. The link to subscribe to its newsletter service is circled within Figure 14-4. To locate this page, perform a Web search for "PwC CFO Direct."

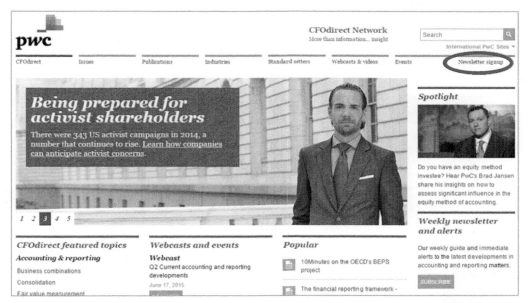

Figure 14-4

PwC's CFO Direct website (circle added)

Similarly, EY's **AccountingLink** website, shown in Figure 14-5, offers standard-setter updates and other educational resources. Subscribers to this website's email alerts (see link circled) can receive EY's weekly *US Week in Review* emails. Locate this page by performing a Web search for "EY Accounting Link."

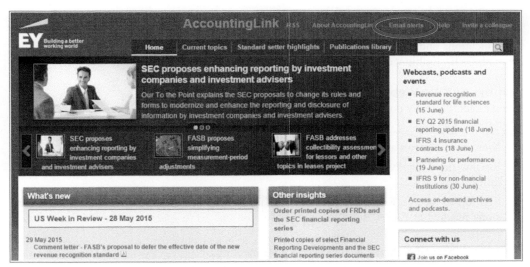

Figure 14-5

EY's AccountingLink website (circle added)

Now
YOU
Try
14.4

EY's AccountingLink Website

Identify one resource from EY's website (Figure 14-5) that might be of interest to an auditor whose client is preparing their Q2 2015 financial statements.

Register for Free Firm Webcasts

Quarterly, the big 4 accounting firms also offer free webcasts on current accounting developments. Locate upcoming webcasts by performing a Web search for: "Deloitte Q1 webcast," for example. These webcasts are often CPE-eligible, meaning that attendees can receive educational credits (necessary to maintain CPA licensure) for participating. Figure 14-6 depicts Deloitte's Quarterly Accounting Roundup webcast.

Figure 14-6

Deloitte's Quarterly Accounting Roundup webcast

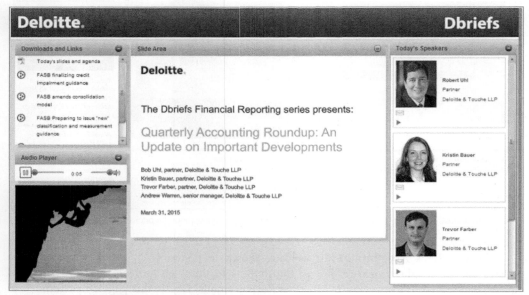

In addition to quarterly updates, the big 4 also offer webcasts as new standards are issued. These webcasts generally provide in-depth discussion of the standard's requirements, as well as implications and implementation issues associated with the new standard. Additionally, on-demand, CPE-eligible webcasts are available anytime on PwC's CFODirect.

Visit the FASB's Website, Subscribe to "Action Alerts"

If you haven't already done so, take a moment to visit the FASB's website now (www.fasb.org). From there, you can

■ View current news and activities of the Board.

■ Review the *Technical Agenda* page, where the FASB lists its current projects and project milestones.

■ Sign up to receive **FASB Action Alert** (aka, *eNewsletter*) emails, which summarize decisions reached at FASB Board meetings. To sign up, go to *Meetings* then *Tentative Board Decisions* on the FASB website.

■ Access live and archived webcasts of FASB meetings.

---

[1] See Ch. 5, fn 4.

In addition, researchers can access final and proposed Accounting Standards Updates on the FASB's website, or can access the Codification (subscription required).

Visit the IFRS Website, Subscribe to Email Alerts

Like the FASB website, the IFRS website offers extensive news and updates on its standard-setting activities, plus extensive educational resources.

Under the tab "Stay Informed" on www.ifrs.org, researchers can select from a menu of email alert options, choosing for example to be notified whenever new standards are issued, or choosing to be notified of changes to specific IASB projects. Figure 14-7 illustrates the process for subscribing to IFRS email alerts.

Figure 14-7

Subscribing to IFRS email alerts

Read the *Journal of Accountancy*

The AICPA's *Journal of Accountancy*, sent monthly to the homes of AICPA members, or available online at www.journalofaccountancy.com, provides updates and practical guidance on a wide range of services including accounting, auditing, taxation, ethics, valuations, and more. Figure 14-8 depicts a *Journal of Accountancy* magazine. If this arrives in your mailbox, take the time to browse it!

Figure 14-8

AICPA *Journal of Accountancy*

© 2015, American Institute of CPAs.
Used by permission.

Finally, consider the following **TIP from the Trenches** regarding next steps in your effort to stay current.

[**TIP**] from the Trenches

Hopefully, this chapter has inspired you to stay informed about changes in our profession. But don't count on always having the enthusiasm to *actively* look up information on your own. Sign up today for **one or two** weekly email updates—these provide a more *passive* way to stay informed on an ongoing basis (the updates will come to you)! Challenge yourself to read *at least one* of these update emails every week.

CHAPTER SUMMARY

Many of the accounting principles that you know today will, over time, evolve and change in favor of new requirements. Expect this change, and resolve to keep pace with it.

This chapter reviewed the reasons for, and the process for, effecting changes to existing standards. Now that you generally understand this process, it's time to focus on the real takeaway of this chapter—*Even if it is not expected of you early in your career, stay current.*

Taking the initiative to monitor emerging guidance—and especially being thoughtful about how proposed changes will affect your company or your client's business—will put you at a tremendous professional advantage versus peers who do not make this effort.

Take a few minutes today to sign up for one or two email subscriptions, or subscribe to a professional journal, or resolve to use other resources—regularly—to stay abreast of changes in our profession.

REVIEW QUESTIONS

1. What are some of the reasons that a financial statement preparer would need to stay current with emerging and recently-issued guidance?

2. What are some reasons that an auditor might need to stay current?

3. At what level should you, as a professional, begin to monitor emerging guidance? Why?

4. List three reasons why accounting standards might require change over time.

5. Describe two ways the SEC has responded to the FASB's issuance of revised revenue guidance.

6. Briefly, describe a typical standard-setting "due process."

7. Name four organizations who regularly engage in standard setting, and who apply some variation of the due process described in this chapter.

8. Differentiate between a *preliminary views* document and an *exposure draft*. What is another name for (or variation of) each?

9. As a public company auditor, describe some of the resources you might monitor to stay current.

10. Name two sources that provide comprehensive weekly updates on standard setters.

11. Contrast the U.S. FASB's process of issuing new guidance (i.e., involving "ASUs" to update the Codification) to the IASB's process for updating its guidance.

12. Name an example of a free firm webcast that you might view in order to receive CPE and stay current.

EXERCISES

1. Describe what steps you currently take to stay current. Include, for example, newspapers you regularly consult, as well as accounting resources.

FASB/EITF

2. Look at the FASB's current technical agenda.
   a. Are any final standards set to be issued this quarter?
   b. Are any exposure drafts ("proposed ASUs") currently out for comment, or expected this quarter?

3. Select one of the FASB's current projects, and describe some of the considerations that led the Board to address this issue.

4. Using the FASB website, locate guidance on the FASB's *standard setting process* (under the About Us tab).
   a. First, briefly describe the significance of due process in standard setting.
   b. Next, identify two ways in which the FASB's standard setting process differs just slightly (or offers more specificity) from the general process description in Figure 14-2 of this chapter.

5. An accountant has been asked by her firm to monitor an upcoming FASB meeting. Walk her through where to find the upcoming meeting materials and what steps she should take to prepare to listen to/view that meeting.

6. What is one of the topics currently being addressed by the EITF? Why do you suppose that the EITF, and not the FASB, is addressing this issue?

7. Locate the most recently issued Accounting Standards Update (ASU). Starting with the ASU's Summary pages, respond to the following:
   a. What was the Board's reason for addressing this issue?
   b. What are some of the key changes this standard will make?
   c. What Codification topics will this "ASU" amend?
   d. Locate the section of the ASU where it shows changes to the Codification. Does this ASU add to, or replace, existing Codification content? Explain.

IASB

8. Select one of the IASB's current projects, and describe some of the considerations which led the Board to address this issue.

9. Locate an agenda from an upcoming IASB meeting and list three or four of the topics they plan to cover. Which of these topics do you think may be the most closely watched by the IASB's constituents? Explain.

PCAOB/AICPA

10. Using the PCAOB's website, locate the most recently issued standard that has been approved by the SEC. Describe the main purpose of this standard.

11. Navigate to the AICPA website. Locate information regarding activities of the Auditing Standards Board (under Standards, Auditing). What is one issue that this Board is currently addressing or plans to address at an upcoming meeting?

12. Using the AICPA website, locate a recent edition of the AICPA's *Journal of Accountancy*, and provide the title and date of a recent article. Summarize (in one or two sentences) what the article is about.

13. Describe the scope and purpose of the AICPA's recently completed Clarity Initiative.

GASB

14. Locate the GASB's technical project agenda and describe two current projects being undertaken. What is the purpose of these projects, and what changes might result from them?

CASE STUDY QUESTIONS

14.1 **Getting up to Speed on a Current FASB Project** *Required:* Choose an emerging guidance topic from the FASB's project page. (Instructor: You may choose to expand this to include current PCAOB, IFRS, AICPA projects, and so on.) In one page, summarize what the project is (how will it change GAAP?), why it's being undertaken, and the timing of completion or next steps in the project. You have only one page, so try to really capture the essence of this project and include information that really gets to the heart of the issues. To be successful in this assignment, you need to really *understand* the project; don't just reiterate the summary from the project page. Firm resources (such as on PwC's CFO Direct page), and "FASB In Focus" summaries can be helpful in explaining projects in plain English. Finally, be prepared to present your summary in class.

14.2 **Selecting and Subscribing to a Resource** This chapter covered numerous resources which offer email subscriptions. Research a few options, then select one subscription for yourself. Actually subscribe to it. In an email to your professor, approximately two paragraphs, explain the resources you considered and why you selected this particular subscription.

14.3 **Quarterly Financial Reporting Update Webcasts** Register to view (or view via PwC CFODirect's on-demand video library) a big 4 quarterly financial reporting update webcast. These webcasts generally run approximately 1.5 hours. (Alternatively, at your instructor's direction, read EY's most recent quarterly *Financial Reporting Briefs* publication.) While watching, assume that you are a corporate accountant for a publicly traded passenger airline that operates in the United States. Assume that your supervisor asked you to view this webcast and to report back on any issues of relevance to your company. Identify two or three issues with potential applicability to your company.

Next, draft an email to your supervisor reiterating his or her request, then summarizing the issues you identified and their potential relevance to your company. Also, be prepared to discuss your findings with the class.

14.4 **Current Events (Newspaper)** Locate a newspaper article describing a current event in the accounting or auditing profession. Topics might include, for example, articles describing recent SEC enforcement actions, articles about new accounting or regulatory rules, state or local government accounting issues, and the like. In one page, summarize the issue addressed, and identify the search term you used to locate this article. As always, clearly cite the source of this article (author, journal, etc.). Be prepared to discuss the article with your peers.

(14.4) **Alternate:** After selecting a newspaper article about a current event in the profession, select a publicly-traded company that might be affected by the current event. In 2–3 paragraphs, discuss why you selected this company and the potential impact of this news on the company.

14.5 **Not for Profit Accounting** Significant changes are on the horizon for not for profit entities. Locate the proposed ASU (or final, if it's available) detailing potential changes to this reporting model, then respond to the following:

    a. What was the Board's reason for addressing this issue?
    b. What are some of the key changes this proposed standard could give rise to?
    c. What Codification topics would this ASU, if issued as final, amend?

Next, locate a news article (such as from the *Journal of Accountancy*) describing the reaction to, and possible impacts of this guidance. Act as though you are an auditor for several not-for-profit entities that have limited resources dedicated to monitoring guidance changes. Summarize the information about this proposed standard that you would communicate to your clients.

INDEX

451

Note: The letter "f" refers to the figure on the stated page. For example, 95f is referring to the figure on page 95.

Note: The letter "*f*" refers to the figure on the stated page. For example, 58*f* is referring to the figure on page 58.

Note: The letter "*f*" refers to the figure on the stated page. For example, 58*f* is referring to the figure on page 58.